The Electronic Communications Code: A Guide for Property Lawyers

The Electronic Communications Code: A Guide for Property Lawyers

Jon Wills

Bloomsbury Professional

LONDON • DUBLIN • EDINBURGH • NEW YORK • NEW DELHI • SYDNEY

BLOOMSBURY PROFESSIONAL

Bloomsbury Publishing Plc
50 Bedford Square, London, WC1B 3DP, UK
1385 Broadway, New York, 10018, USA

Bloomsbury Publishing Ireland Ltd
29 Earlsfort Terrace, Dublin 2, D02 AY28, Ireland

First published in Great Britain 2025

1

British Library Cataloguing-in-Publication Data

A catalogue record for this book is available from the British Library.

ISBN: PB: 978 1 52652 973 2
Epdf: 978 1 52652 975 6
Epub: 978 1 52652 974 9

Typeset by Evolution Design and Digital Ltd (Kent)
Printed and bound by TJ Books Limited, Padstow, Cornwall

FSC www.fsc.org MIX Paper | Supporting responsible forestry FSC® C013056

For product safety related questions contact productsafety@bloomsbury.com

Dedication

This book is dedicated to my late father Tony Wills, who worked for BT (and previously GPO) for some 37 years. He may characteristically have begun reading this book and lost enthusiasm towards the beginning. For that reason Chapter 4 is especially for him.

Foreword

By the Right Honourable Lord Carnwath of Notting Hill CVO

The Electronic Communications Code was created in 1984 and replaced in the Digital Economy Act 2017. The revised Code gave effect with some modifications to the recommendations of a Law Commission report in 2013, which had criticised the current Code as 'complex and confusing… inconsistent with other legislation, and… not up-to-date with modern technology'. Their recommendations were designed to 'set out the legal position in clear terms and provide an efficient forum for dispute resolution'. The government also saw the opportunity for the revised Code to support their strategy to achieve widespread coverage of the country by imposing obligations on operators by way of licence conditions, and by helping operators to extend their networks, to make mast-sharing easier and infrastructure deployment and maintenance cheaper.

The resulting Code sets out the regime that governs the rights of designated electronic communications operators to maintain infrastructure on public and private land. It now applies to the infrastructure forming networks which support broadband, mobile internet and telephone, cable television and landlines. The march of technology cannot be halted, but its positive impacts can be maximised, and its negative effects minimised. This balance between the essential and beneficial aspects of communications technology, and the effects on individuals, is at the heart of the Code.

As a former Chairman of the Law Commission and former Senior President of Tribunals, I am pleased to note the process of law reform conducted in an orderly way, and also the specialist role given to the modernised Tribunal system which I helped to establish. However, the new Code has created its own difficulties, and significant litigation has followed. Happily the Tribunal system has proved an effective home for the litigation generated by the New Code. The Upper Tribunal, and now increasingly the First-tier Tribunal, have the specialist judges and administrative systems that enable cases to be dealt with efficiently and within the statutory time limit that often applies. I understand that their early adoption of online hearings enabled Code litigation to continue unabated during the Covid pandemic.

All this has created the need for a new, comprehensive guide to the Code and the litigation viewed from both a legal and a practical point of view. Jon Wills' new book fills this need. It contains an exposition of the most commonly encountered provisions of the New Code, especially by reference to the large volume of case law which has developed over the past seven years. I congratulate the author and welcome it as an indispensable working-tool for property professionals working in this highly specialist area.

Robert Carnwath

Foreword

Preface

This book is intended as a guide to the most often encountered provisions of the Code, rather than an explanation of each Part or paragraph of the Code. It is predominantly intended for lawyers (including those practising in the property or land law field), who wish to have ready access to a guide to the Code which is relatively comprehensive in its treatment of the case law. Such practitioners have requested that some practical content be included, and **Chapter 21**attempts to satisfy that part of the brief. Other property professionals may also find the book useful, including land agents and surveyors representing those on one or other side of the fence in Code disputes.

Certain abbreviations and stylistic conventions have been adopted for convenience and brevity. These are set out in **Chapter 1**.

This book attempts to set out the law in respect of England and Wales. Occasionally reference is made to case law from Scotland where it might be persuasive or otherwise of assistance in elucidating the law in England and Wales. However, where the law is stated, it is always implied that reference is only being made to England and Wales.

The law is stated as at 17 December 2024.

Jon Wills
January 2025

Contents

Dedication		*v*
Foreword		*vii*
Preface		*ix*
Table of statutes		*xiii*
Table of statutory instruments		*xxvii*
Table of European Legislation		*xxix*
Table of cases		*xxxi*
1	Abbreviations and conventions adopted in the book	1
2	The continuing effect of the Old Code	5
3	Background to the Code	9
4	The Code in 1000 words	13
5	Key definitions and concepts	17
6	Agreements that confer Code rights	31
7	Interpreting the Code	39
8	Applications under para 20	45
9	Para 26 agreements: 'interim' Code rights	57
10	Para 27 agreements: 'temporary' Code rights	73
11	Determination of the terms of an agreement	79
12	Upgrading and sharing	133
13	Consideration	141
14	Compensation	185
15	Third parties: who is bound, registration and assignment	209
16	Termination and renewal of agreements	225
17	Redevelopment	281
18	Part 6 of the Code – removal of ECA	293
19	Obtaining vacant possession: the flow chart	307
20	Notices under the Code	313
21	Procedure and practice	333
22	Settling Code disputes	355
23	Costs	361
Appendix		
	The Electronic Communications Code	371
	The Electronic Communications Code: transitional provisions	459
Index		*467*

Table of Statutes

Communications Act 2003 ... 5.01, 5.43; 7.01
s 23 .... 5.42
32 .... 5.01
106 .... 4.01; 5.02, 5.45, 5.49; 7.01
(3)(a) 5.05
(5) 5.45, 5.46
117 .... 18.18
394 .... 20.62, 20.70, 20.71
(2) 20.74
(3) 20.63, 20.66, 20.69
(4) 20.72
(5), (6) 20.72, 20.74
(7) 20.71, 20.73
(8) 20.73
(11) 20.62
395 .... 20.66, 20.74
405 .... 5.01
Sch 3A (Electronic Communications Code) 1.01, 1.02, 1.03, 1.04, 1.07, 1.08, 1.09; 2.01, 2.08, 2.09, 2.10, 2.11, 2.13, 2.17; 3.02, 3.03, 3.07, 3.10, 3.11, 3.12, 3.14, 3.15, 3.16, 3.17, 3.18, 3.20, 3.21, 3.22; 4.01, 4.02, 4.03, 4.05, 4.06, 4.08, 4.09, 4.10, 4.11, 4.12, 4.13, 4.14; 5.01, 5.02, 5.05, 5.10, 5.11, 5.12, 5.15, 5.17, 5.19, 5.35, 5.52, 5.53, 5.55; 6.04, 6.09, 6.12, 6.28; 7.03, 7.04, 7.05, 7.06, 7.09, 7.10, 7.12, 7.13, 7.14, 7.15, 7.16, 7.19, 7.20, 7.21, 7.22, 7.23, 7.24; 8.06, 8.15; 9.23; 11.16, 11.26, 11.39, 11.40, 11.46, 11.49, 11.70, 11.77, 11.78, 11.118, 11.119, 11.123, 11.137, 11.147, 11.148, 11.150, 11.184, 11.240, 11.241, 11.245, 11.256, 11.257, 11.259, 11.265, 11.266, 11.268, 11.270, 11.276, 11.279; 13.01, 13.03, 13.05, 13.17, 13.19, 13.21, 13.22, 13.23, 13.24, 13.25, 13.27, 13.30, 13.63, 13.65, 13.71, 13.73, 13.83, 13.86, 13.91, 13.125, 13.134, 13.193, 13.202, 13.216, 13.217, 13.218; 14.07, 14.32, 14.41, 14.56, 14.73, 14.76, 14.81, 14.84; 15.01, 15.03, 15.21, 15.32; 16.01, 16.08, 16.10, 16.20, 16.61, 16.75, 16.77, 16.78, 16.79,

Communications Act 2003 – *contd*
16.83, 16.84, 16.85, 16.87, 16.97, 16.100, 16.106, 16.108, 16.110, 16.111, 16.112, 16.113, 16.119, 16.120, 16.125, 16.127, 16.129, 16.130, 16.131, 16.133, 16.138, 16.151, 16.155, 16.158, 16.159, 16.161, 16.162, 16.190, 16.191, 16.192, 16.193, 16.200, 16.205, 16.209, 16.258, 16.260, 16.265; 17.16, 17.17, 17.18, 17.19, 17.21, 17.24, 17.26, 17.27, 17.41, 17.46; 18.04, 18.05; 19.04; 20.01, 20.18, 20.19, 20.26, 20.54, 20.62, 20.66, 20.76; 21.02, 21.06; 23.01, 23.06, 23.15, 23.20, 23.42, 23.44
para 1(4) 5.51
2 .... 5.03, 5.25; 16.93
(2)(c) 16.104
3 .... 4.02; 5.19; 9.10, 9.16; 11.35; 12.01, 12.13; 16.24, 16.93
(1) 5.18, 5.31, 5.44; 12.12, 12.20
(a) 9.12, 9.13, 9.14, 9.55; 18.24
(b) 16.23; 18.24
(c) 11.74; 12.04, 12.05, 12.06, 12.07; 16.24; 18.24
(ca) 5.22; 11.74; 12.09, 12.11, 12.12; 20.35
(d) 9.12, 9.13, 9.15, 9.16, 9.55; 11.64; 18.24
(e) 11.64; 12.05, 12.06; 18.24
(ea) 12.10
(f) 12.05; 16.24, 16.268, 16.269; 18.24
(fa) 12.10
(g) 5.31; 18.24
(h) 18.25
(i) 5.31; 18.24
4 .... 5.24; 11.58
5 .... 5.26, 5.33, 5.35, 5.36
(1) 5.27
(a), (b), (d) 5.30

Communications Act 2003 – *contd*
para 5(3) 5.28, 5.30, 5.38
6 .... 5.45
(a) 5.46
(b) 5.47
7 .... 5.25, 5.48; 18.17
Pt 2 (paras 8–14) 2.05; 5.20, 5.22, 5.23, 5.44; 6.02, 6.05, 6.07, 6.09, 6.10, 6.11, 6.14, 6.20, 6.23, 6.31, 6.39, 6.40, 6.41; 8.01; 9.04; 10.18; 11.11, 11.74, 11.154, 11.211; 12.18, 12.29, 12.31; 13.26; 14.07, 14.96, 14.101; 15.02, 15.04, 15.06, 15.14, 15.15, 15.37, 15.39, 15.60, 15.62, 15.66, 15.67, 15.69, 15.73, 15.75, 15.76, 15.79; 16.03, 16.11, 16.12, 16.13, 16.15, 16.74, 16.98, 16.102, 16.103, 16.119, 16.177, 16.208, 16.250, 16.255, 16.261, 16.265, 16.267; 22.05
para 9 .... 4.03; 5.10, 5.11, 5.23, 5.25; 6.07, 6.09; 8.01; 16.259; 19.04; 20.03
(1) 5.07, 5.32; 6.05; 12.14; 15.04, 15.28; 16.11
(2) 12.14; 15.04
10 .... 4.06; 11.200; 15.05, 15.06, 15.24; 16.158, 16.167; 18.05
(1) 15.06
(2) 15.07, 15.09, 15.11, 15.18
(a) 15.10, 15.22
(b), (c) 15.10
(3) 5.15; 7.18; 15.02, 15.10, 15.24, 15.26, 15.29, 15.31, 15.34; 16.37, 16.221
(4) 15.14, 15.15, 15.17, 15.18, 15.37, 15.39; 16.12
(5) 15.18, 15.19
(a) 15.23
(6) 15.23
11 .... 4.03; 5.23; 6.07, 6.09, 6.11, 6.15, 6.20, 6.21; 15.14; 16.11, 16.91, 16.112, 16.170, 16.195, 16.261; 18.05; 19.04; 23.32

Communications Act 2003 – *contd*
para 11(1) 6.08, 6.09; 15.15; 19.04
(a), (b) 6.16, 6.40, 6.41; 16.170, 16.195
(c) 6.15, 6.40, 6.41; 11.11; 15.15; 16.170, 16.195
(d) 6.15, 6.40, 6.41; 11.12; 16.195
(2) 6.40; 16.195
(3) 16.195
13(1) 18.24
(1ZA) 23.04
14 .... 15.51, 15.52, 15.53; 20.19
Pt 3 (paras 15–18) 6.24, 6.25, 6.26, 6.33, 6.39; 9.17; 11.211; 12.30, 12.33, 12.40; 14.07, 14.96, 14.101, 14.108; 15.79
para 15(a) 15.54
16 .... 2.11; 12.41; 13.57, 13.82, 13.185; 15.35, 15.54, 15.58, 15.74, 15.77, 15.78, 15.79; 16.138, 16.168; 20.18
(1) 5.23; 6.31; 11.154, 11.155; 13.87; 15.54, 15.55, 15.56, 15.57, 15.58, 15.59, 15.64, 15.73, 15.79
(a) 15.74, 15.75
(b) 13.25; 15.74, 15.75
(2) 6.31; 11.155, 11.157; 15.59
(4) 15.54, 15.66, 15.67, 15.69, 15.70, 15.73, 15.74, 15.75, 15.79; 16.138; 20.18
(5) 15.71, 15.72; 20.59
(6) 15.71
(7) 11.156; 15.60, 15.71
(8) 15.61, 15.64, 15.65
(a), (b) 15.62, 15.63, 15.64, 15.65
(9) 15.65
17 .... 4.05; 5.20, 5.22, 5.23; 11.72, 11.78, 11.80, 11.81, 11.82, 11.83, 11.84, 11.87, 11.174, 11.176, 11.199, 11.200, 11.248, 11.269, 11.172, 11.273; 12.18, 12.20, 12.22, 12.28, 12.30, 12.32, 12.33, 12.34, 12.35, 12.37, 12.38, 12.39, 12.40, 12.41, 12.43; 13.57, 13.82, 13.88, 13.89, 13.90, 13.92, 13.185; 16.80

Communications Act 2003 – *contd*
para 17(1) ... 12.19
(a) ... 5.22
(2) ... 6.31; 11.78, 11.81, 11.83, 11.87, 11.269; 12.18, 12.19, 12.22, 12.26, 12.27, 12.28, 12.29, 12.32, 12.34
(3) ... 6.31; 11.78, 11.81, 11.83, 11.87, 11.269; 12.18, 12.19, 12.22, 12.26, 12.27, 12.28, 12.29, 12.32, 12.34, 12.42
(4) ... 12.19, 12.42
(5) ... 4.05; 5.23; 6.31; 12.30, 12.33; 13.87
(a) ... 12.29, 12.32
(b) ... 6.39; 12.31, 12.32; 13.25, 13.90
(6) ... 12.21, 12.42; 20.59
(7), (9), (11) ... 12.42
17A ... 13.57
(6) ... 20.59
Pt 4 (paras 19–27ZA) ... 5.44; 6.02, 6.13, 6.15, 6.24, 6.25, 6.26, 6.29, 6.39; 8.01, 8.39; 9.17; 11.11, 11.69, 11.190, 11.191, 11.192, 11.211, 11.265; 13.26; 14.07, 14.96, 14.101, 14.09, 14.109; 15.02; 16.127, 16.128, 16.202, 16.203, 16.205, 16.207, 16.211, 16.213, 16.259, 16.270. 16.271; 17.22; 18.53, 18.54, 18.55; 20.29; 21.02; 22.21
para 20 ... 2.09; 4.03; 5.08, 5.10, 5.19, 5.23; 6.11, 6.13, 6.15, 6.17, 6.20, 6.36; 8.02, 8.03, 8.07, 8.08, 8.10, 8.20, 8.25, 8.35, 8.39, 8.44, 8.45, 8.50, 8.52; 9.01, 9.02, 9.03, 9.04, 9.07, 9.10, 9.11, 9.22, 9.26, 9.32, 9.35, 9.43, 9.44, 9.57, 9.60, 9.61, 9.65, 9.88; 10.01, 10.02, 10.06, 10.07, 10.09, 10.13, 10.14, 10.18, 10.21; 11.38, 11.41, 11.42, 11.137,

Communications Act 2003 – *contd*
11.138, 11.177, 11.178, 11.192; 13.33, 13.34, 13.35, 13.40, 13.105, 13.183, 13.187, 13.192, 13.194, 13.203; 14.02, 14.03, 14.04, 14.05, 14.09, 14.14, 14.15, 14.21, 14.28, 14.88, 14.94; 15.13, 15.36, 15.43, 15.47; 16.13, 16.15, 16.108, 16.113, 16.116, 16.117, 16.126, 16.174, 16.178, 16.181, 16.182, 16.183, 16.184, 16.205, 16.213, 16.214, 16.250, 16.261, 16.263, 16.267, 16.269; 17.01, 17.08, 17.27, 17.58, 17.59, 17.60, 17.62, 17.68, 17.72; 18.08, 18.48, 18.53; 19.05, 19.13; 20.04, 20.26, 20.27, 20.28, 20.32, 20.33, 20.34, 20.35, 20.57, 20.83, 20.86, 20.88; 21.34
(1) ... 8.03; 9.11; 14.15; 20.57
(2) ... 2.08; 5.23; 8.03; 9.11, 9.32, 9.37; 10.03; 14.15, 14.17; 17.60; 20.02, 20.05, 20.57, 20.59
(a) ... 5.23; 8.04; 11.41; 16.269; 17.60; 20.29, 20.57; 22.03
(b) ... 8.04; 20.57
(2A) ... 8.07; 20.57
(3) ... 13.203; 14.07; 18.54; 20.83, 20.91
(a) ... 8.05; 9.40; 10.09; 14.07; 20.04, 20.80, 20.82, 20.83; 22.10
(b) ... 8.06; 9.40; 10.09; 14.07; 20.04, 20.57, 20.80, 20.81, 20.85
(4) ... 6.18; 8.05; 9.11; 11.17
(b) ... 15.36, 15.43
(5) ... 8.08
(6) ... 8.08, 8.08

Communications Act 2003 – *contd*
para 21 .... 8.10, 8.23, 8.25, 8.35, 8.36, 8.38, 8.39, 8.40; 9.35, 9.44, 9.46, 9.53, 9.59, 9.66, 9.73; 11.25; 16.52, 16.58, 16.200; 17.67, 17.69
(1) 8.10, 8.39; 17.59
(2) 4.03; 8.10, 8.12, 8.18, 8.19, 8.24, 8.51; 11.25, 11.25, 11.214; 16.58; 17.51, 17.52
(3) 3.07; 4.03; 8.10, 8.12, 8.23, 8.25, 8.31, 8.35, 8.51; 11.25, 11.214; 16.58, 16.117; 17.29, 17.51, 17.52, 17.53
(4) 3.07; 8.13, 8.26, 8.29, 8.30, 8.32; 16.56
(5) 4.03; 8.11, 8.17, 8.40, 8.41, 8.42, 8.46, 8.47, 8.49, 8.51; 11.17, 11.21; 16.57, 16.58; 17.01, 17.02, 17.08, 17.12, 17.19, 17.27, 17.50, 17.51, 17.52, 17.53, 17.54, 17.55, 17.56, 17.58, 17.59, 17.61, 17.62, 17.63, 17.64, 17.65, 17.67, 17.72; 21.25
22 .... 4.03; 5.20, 5.22; 6.02, 6.11, 6.12, 6.18; 8.01; 9.04; 10.18; 11.11; 15.04, 15.36, 15.37, 15.75; 16.13, 16.177, 16.184
23 .... 7.14; 9.10, 9.60, 9.61, 9.62; 10.20, 10.20, 10.21, 10.22; 11.06, 11.07, 11.34, 11.36, 11.180, 11.195, 11.198; 13.87, 13.183, 13.187; 16.249
(1) 11.42; 17.60
(2) 4.04; 9.59, 9.62, 9.79; 10.22; 11.34, 11.43, 11.178, 11.180, 11.185, 11.245; 13.190; 15.74; 16.241, 16.249; 17.60
(3) 9.61; 10.21; 11.08, 11.09, 11.36, 11.43, 11.178, 11.180, 11.185, 11.245; 13.25, 13.34, 13.190; 16.241, 16.249; 17.60

Communications Act 2003 – *contd*
para 23(4) 11.36, 11.43, 11.178, 11.185, 11.245, 13.190; 16.241, 16.249; 17.60
(5) 6.38; 9.78; 11.08, 11.32, 11.36, 11.43, 11.45, 11.65, 11.150, 11.157, 11.164, 11.167, 11.168, 11.169, 11.170, 11.171, 11.172, 11.173, 11.175, 11.176, 11.178, 11.180, 11.185, 11.245; 13.190; 16.241, 16.249; 17.60
(6) 11.36, 11.43, 11.178, 11.180, 11.185, 11.245; 13.190; 16.241, 16.249; 17.60
(7) 6.15; 10.19; 11.08, 11.11, 11.36, 11.43, 11.178, 11.180, 11.185, 11.245; 13.190; 16.176, 16.178, 16.241, 16.249; 17.60
(8) 6.15; 11.32, 11.36, 11.43, 11.178, 11.180, 11.185, 11.245; 13.190; 16.241, 16.249; 17.60
(a) 11.12, 11.29, 11.32
(b) 8.50; 11.30, 11.32
24 .... 5.34; 10.21; 11.10, 11.161, 11.185, 11.195, 11.243; 13.03, 13.05, 13.28, 13.29, 13.30, 13.31, 13.32, 13.35, 13.46, 13.71, 13.80, 13.101, 13.112, 13.115, 13.117, 13.120, 13.123, 13.128, 13.129, 13.137, 13.140, 13.143, 13.144, 13.147, 13.153, 13.161, 13.164, 13.179, 13.183, 13.184, 13.185, 13.187, 13.188, 13.189, 13.196, 13.198, 13.199, 13.206, 13.222, 13.227; 14.36; 16.249; 17.63

Communications Act 2003 – *contd*
para 24(1) 13.35, 13.40, 13.44, 13.113, 13.121
(2) 13.36, 13.39, 13.40, 13.43, 13.44, 13.228
(b) 13.56, 13.57, 13.70
(c) 13.23, 13.57, 13.60
(3) 13.36, 13.39, 13.57, 13.59, 13.81, 13.228
(a) 5.34; 13.05, 13.23, 13.39, 13.47, 13.57, 13.61, 13.62, 13.63, 13.64, 13.100, 13.121
(b) 13.61, 13.82, 13.88, 13.89, 13.90, 13.185
(c) 13.23, 13.51, 13.60
(d) 13.61, 13.83, 13.94
(4) 13.37
25 .... 4.06; 6.29, 6.36, 6.37; 9.04; 10.18; 11.31, 11.96, 11.143, 11.159, 11.185, 11.212, 11.213, 11.214, 11.215, 11.251, 11.252, 11.253, 11.254, 11.257; 13.03, 13.183, 13.187, 13.195, 13.1181, 13.203, 13.213, 13.230; 14.01, 14.02, 14.03, 14.04, 14.05, 14.06, 14.07, 14.08, 14.09, 14.12, 14.14, 14.18, 14.19, 14.22, 14.28, 14.30, 14.36, 14.49, 14.51, 14.56, 14.58, 14.102, 14.104, 14.105, 14.110, 14.112, 14.113, 14.115; 16.249, 16.250; 22.02; 23.30, 23.31, 23.34
(1) 6.36, 6.37, 6.39; 11.167, 11.214, 11.251; 13.27, 13.116, 13.203, 13.230; 14.03, 14.05, 14.07, 14.15, 14.16, 14.17, 14.21, 14.23, 14.30, 14.37, 14.49, 14.51; 16.250
(2) 14.23, 14.56
(a) 11.167; 14.24, 14.88
(b) 4.06; 6.36; 11.94, 11.99, 11.137, 11.167, 11.251; 14.27, 14.28, 14.40, 14.111
(3)(a) 14.37
(b) 14.37, 14.43
(4) 14.43, 14.45
(a), (b) 14.43

Communications Act 2003 – *contd*
para 25(6) 11.253; 14.04
26 .... 4.06, 4.07; 5.23; 6.11, 6.15, 6.17, 6.18, 6.32, 6.33, 6.34, 6.36; 8.17, 8.23, 8.25, 8.35, 8.36; 9.01, 9.02, 9.03, 9.04, 9.05, 9.07, 9.08, 9.10, 9.11, 9.18, 9.19, 9.20, 9.22, 9.23, 9.25, 9.27, 9.28, 9.30, 9.32, 9.35, 9.36, 9.38, 9.40, 9.42, 9.48, 9.49, 9.50, 9.51, 9.52, 9.53, 9.55, 9.57, 9.58, 9.59, 9.61, 9.62, 9.63, 9.64, 9.79, 9.84, 9.86, 9.88, 9.89, 9.90; 10.01, 10.11; 11.05, 11.06, 11.11, 11.41, 11.42, 11.137, 11.171, 11.251; 13.183, 13.184, 13.185, 13.187, 13.188, 13.203; 14.14, 14.15, 14.16, 14.24, 14.26; 15.13, 15.36, 15.37, 15.41, 15.44, 15.46; 16.13, 16.15, 16.30, 16.36, 16.175, 16.176, 16.177, 16.178, 16.179, 16.255; 17.67, 17.68, 17.69, 17.70; 18.55; 19.05, 19.13; 20.79, 20.83, 20.86; 22.02; 21.57, 21.67; 23.26, 23.28, 23.30, 23.33, 23.43
(1) 6.32, 6.33; 8.35; 9.05, 9.18, 9.23, 9.61; 14.16, 14.26; 22.02
(a) 15.36
(b) 15.41, 15.43
(2) 6.18, 6.32; 9.06, 9.18, 9.25, 9.32; 15.36; 16.176; 20.05
(a) 9.25, 9.79; 16.176
(b) 9.25, 9.79; 16.176; 18.08
(3) 5.23; 9.11, 9.18, 9.37, 9.73; 10.02; 11.41; 14.16; 20.05, 20.29, 20.57, 20.59, 20.84; 22.02
(a) 9.36, 9.41, 9.42, 9.43
(b) 4.07; 8.23, 8.25, 8.36; 9.36, 9.41, 9.43, 9.53, 9.66, 9.68, 9.73; 17.67; 20.86
(4)(a) 9.40

Communications Act 2003 – *contd*
para 26(4)(b) 6.11, 6.12, 6.18; 9.04; 15.37; 16.177
(c)........... 6.15; 9.59, 9.61, 9.79; 11.06, 11.42; 13.183; 16.176
(d) 13.183
(e)........ 6.36; 9.04; 11.251; 13.203; 14.02, 14.49
(f) 9.04; 14.49
(5).......... 20.80, 20.82, 20.83, 20.84, 20.86, 20.88
(6)(a)......... 9.61, 9.63; 13.183; 14.16, 14.26
(b) 9.61, 9.63; 13.183
(7)..................... 9.08; 16.176, 16.179; 18.08
(8)...................... 9.08; 11.05; 13.185; 16.176, 16.179; 18.08
27................... 4.06, 4.07; 5.23; 6.11, 6.15, 6.17, 6.18, 6.33, 6.34, 6.36; 8.02, 8.25; 9.26, 9.27, 9.32, 9.39; 10.01, 10.02, 10.03, 10.06, 10.07, 10.08, 10.09, 10.14, 10.15, 10.17, 10.18, 10.19, 10.20, 10.21, 10.22; 11.06, 11.11, 11.41, 11.42, 11.137, 11.251; 13.187, 13.189, 13.203; 14.14, 14.15, 14.17, 14.24, 14.26; 15.13, 15.37, 15.41; 16.13, 16.15, 16.30, 16.36, 16.117, 16.175, 16.178, 16.179, 16.180, 16.181, 16.182, 16.183, 16.184, 16.255; 17.67, 17.71, 17.72; 19.05, 19.13; 20.27, 20.79, 20.83, 20.86; 22.02
(1).................... 10.02, 10.03, 10.21; 14.17, 14.26; 20.06, 20.57, 20.59
(a)........ 5.23; 10.03; 11.41; 20.29
(b) 14.17
(c)................ 10.04, 10.05; 15.13; 16.181; 20.27
(2).............. 6.18, 6.34; 10.02, 10.09, 10.12, 10.16, 10.19; 14.17; 15.36, 15.41; 16.178, 16.182; 17.71; 20.06; 22.02

Communications Act 2003 – *contd*
para 27(3).......... 10.07, 10.12, 10.13, 10.16; 14.17
(4)(a)......................... 10.09
(b) 6.11, 6.12, 6.18; 10.18; 15.37; 16.184
(c)......... 6.15; 10.19, 10.21; 11.06, 11.42; 13.187; 16.178
(d) 10.21; 13.187
(e).................. 6.36; 10.18; 11.251; 13.203; 14.02, 14.49
(f) 10.18; 14.49
(5).................... 10.11; 20.80, 20.82, 20.83, 20.84, 20.86
(6)(a).............. 10.21; 13.187; 14.17, 14.26
(b) 10.21; 13.187
(7), (8)....................... 10.01
27ZA.............. 3.20; 8.11, 8.52; 9.47; 10.17
Pt 4A (paras 27A–27I)........ 3.19; 14.49; 15.06, 15.14; 18.08; 21.04, 21.90, 21.92, 21.93
para 27A 21.90
27B 21.90
27C 20.59; 21.90
27D 21.90, 21.92
27E, 27F 21.90
27G 21.90
(1), (4) 18.08
27H............................. 21.90
(2).......................... 14.49
27I............................... 21.90
Pt 5 (paras 28–35) 3.21; 5.23; 6.19, 6.24, 6.25, 6.26, 6.27, 6.39; 7.18; 8.27; 9.17; 11.11, 11.28, 11.177, 11.189, 11.190, 11.191, 11.211, 11.237, 11.238, 11.239, 11.245, 11.252; 13.120, 13.201, 13.203; 14.07, 14.09, 14.10, 14.19, 14.96, 14.101, 14.108, 15.27, 15.28, 15.33, 15.39, 15.40, 15.79; 16.02, 16.03, 16.04, 16.07, 16.13, 16.14, 16.15, 16.16, 16.17, 16.20, 16.21, 16.27, 16.28, 16.31, 16.32, 16.33, 16.46, 16.74,

Communications Act 2003 – *contd*
16.83, 16.100, 16.103, 16.104, 16.105, 16.121, 16.122, 16.124, 16.129, 16.166, 16.177, 16.184, 16.185, 16.198, 16.201, 16.206, 16.207, 16.208, 16.216, 16.218, 16.255, 16.260, 16.261, 16.266, 16.267, 16.273; 17.29; 18.08, 18.09, 18.10, 18.12; 19.05; 20.27, 20.39; 21.02, 21.34; 22.21
para 28 .... 16.216
29(1) 5.23; 15.39, 15.79; 16.02, 16.11, 16.15, 16.177, 16.184
(2) 5.23; 15.39; 16.02, 16.15, 16.16, 16.17, 16.22, 16.27, 16.101; 18.10, 18.11, 18.12
(3) 15.39; 16.15, 16.16, 16.18, 16.27, 16.101; 18.10, 18.12
(4) 15.39; 16.15, 16.16, 16.101; 18.12
(5) 5.50; 11.237, 11.239; 15.39; 16.03, 16.31
30 .... 6.33; 11.19, 11.28, 11.163, 11.285; 16.28, 16.30, 16.40, 16.48, 16.49, 16.124; 19.05
(1) 5.52
(a) 5.53; 14.18; 15.38; 16.104
(b) 16.31
(ii) 16.33, 16.44
(2) 4.06; 5.23; 6.33, 6.34; 9.01, 9.03, 9.07, 9.17, 9.19, 9.25, 9.79; 10.01, 10.19; 11.05, 11.11, 11.29; 15.38, 15.40; 16.04, 16.13, 16.31, 16.32, 16.33, 16.34, 16.36, 16.41, 16.122, 16.175, 16.177, 16.189, 16.193, 16.194, 16.196, 16.252, 16.255; 18.08, 18.11, 18.12, 18.19, 18.20, 18.21; 19.04; 22.02

Communications Act 2003 – *contd*
para 30(3) 4.06, 4.07; 5.23; 6.34; 9.07, 9.18, 9.19, 9.25; 10.01, 10.19; 11.05, 11.11; 13.185, 13.189; 15.41; 16.13, 16.36, 16.175; 18.08; 19.05; 20.86; 22.02
31 .... 4.10; 8.48; 11.28, 11.29; 13.186; 15.20, 15.30, 15.35; 16.04, 16.37, 16.40, 16.42, 16.43, 16.46, 16.47, 16.49, 16.50, 16.57, 16.58, 16.60, 16.63, 16.64, 16.70, 16.104, 16.105, 16.122, 16.123, 16.193, 16.194, 16.230, 16.231, 16.232; 17.07, 17.27, 17.44, 17.49; 18.08, 18.62; 19.06; 20.08, 20.39
(1) 14.20; 15.20; 16.37, 16.59, 16.274; 20.07, 20.53, 20.57, 20.59
(2) 16.38; 20.57
(a), (b) 16.38
(c) 4.10; 16.38, 16.52
(3) 16.04, 16.40; 20.57
(a) 5.23; 16.41, 16.42, 16.43, 16.104, 16.177, 16.184; 19.05
(b) 11.28; 16.33, 16.42, 16.45, 16.46, 16.47, 16.123, 16.230
(4) 4.10; 5.23; 8.41; 11.24; 16.04, 16.52, 16.59, 16.111; 17.07, 17.44; 19.06, 19.07; 20.57
(a), (b) 16.55, 15.56
(c) 8.42, 8.47, 8.51; 11.17, 11.19, 11.21, 11.22, 11.23, 11.29; 16.50, 16.57, 16.58; 17.01, 17.02, 17.07, 17.35, 17.54, 17.55, 17.57, 17.65
(d) 11.25, 11.27; 16.58; 17.29
32 .... 18.08; 20.58
(1) 16.63; 18.08; 19.06
(a) 16.04; 18.08; 20.08, 20.57

Communications Act 2003 – *contd*
para 32(1)(b) 9.88; 11.285; 13.178; 14.20, 14.21; 16.04, 16.67, 16.68, 16.70, 16.72, 16.73, 16.240, 16.253; 17.44; 18.08; 19.07
(2) 16.64; 18.08
(3) 16.65; 18.08; 20.39, 20.57
(3A) 16.66; 20.57
(4) 16.04, 16.55, 16.60, 16.240; 17.45, 17.48; 18.08; 19.07
(5) 16.04, 16.71, 16.240
(6), (7) 16.68
33 .... 4.11; 11.28, 11.195; 15.20, 15.27; 16.04, 16.72, 16.185, 16.216, 16.230, 16.232, 16.237
(1) 14.20; 15.28; 16.220, 16.221, 16.222, 16.223, 16.226, 16.227, 16.232, 16.233, 16.235, 16.238; 20.09, 20.39, 20.53, 20.57, 20.59
(a)–(d) 16.223; 20.09, 20.57
(2) 20.57
(b) 16.227, 16.235
(c) 16.225; 20.39
(3) 16.04, 16.228; 20.57
(a) 16.229
(b) 11.28; 16.230, 16.232
(3A) 20.57
(4) 14.20; 16.235
(5) 9.88; 11.285; 13.178; 14.20, 14.21; 16.04, 16.72, 16.235, 16.238, 16.240, 16.246
(6), (7) 16.238
34 .... 4.11; 6.36; 11.180, 11.194, 11.195, 11.197, 11.251, 11.285; 14.02, 14.14, 14.18, 14.19, 14.20, 14.24; 16.04, 16.63, 16.67, 16.71, 16.72, 16.73, 16.104, 16.105, 16.235, 16.236, 16.240, 16.252; 17.44, 17.49; 18.08; 20.08, 20.40

Communications Act 2003 – *contd*
para 34(1) 14.20; 16.240
(2) 11.196; 16.241, 16.242, 16.243, 16.246, 16.250, 16.255
(3) 11.179, 11.196; 13.190; 14.19; 16.241, 16.242, 16.243, 16.246, 16.249, 16.250, 16.255
(4) 11.179; 13.190; 14.19; 16.241, 16.242, 16.243, 16.246, 16.249, 16.250, 16.255; 18.08; 19.06
(5) 11.179; 13.190; 14.19; 16.241, 16.242, 16.243, 16.246, 16.247, 16.249, 16.250, 16.255
(6) 6.11, 6.19, 6.21; 11.179, 11.194, 11.195, 11.196, 11.197; 13.190; 16.13, 16.170, 16.241, 16.242, 16.243, 16.246, 16.247, 16.250, 16.256; 18.08; 19.06
(7) 6.21
(8) 6.20; 15.79; 16.13, 16.250
(9) 11.179; 13.190; 16.247
(10) 11.179, 11.185, 11.194; 13.190; 14.19; 16.248, 16.249, 16.250
(11) 6.36; 11.178, 11.179, 11.180, 11.185, 11.195, 11.245, 11.251; 13.120, 13.190, 13.191; 14.02, 14.18, 14.19, 14.21, 14.24, 14.26, 14.49; 16.241, 16.249, 16.250
(a), (b) 13.190
(12) 8.27; 11.180, 11.182, 11.185, 11.188, 11.189, 11.194, 11.195, 11.198

Communications Act 2003 – *contd*
para 34(13) ... 16.243
(d) ... 16.104
(14), (15) ... 16.252
35 ... 13.178; 16.73, 16.253
(2)(a), (b) ... 13.80
(2A) ... 3.20; 16.253
(a) ... 13.179
(b) ... 11.285; 13.181
(2B) ... 3.20; 11.286; 13.180
(4) ... 11.285; 13.181
Pt 6 (paras 36–44) ... 2.12; 5.54; 6.24, 6.25, 6.26, 6.39; 9.08, 9.17; 10.04, 10.06, 10.07, 10.08; 11.211; 14.07, 14.85, 14.94, 14.96, 14.101, 14.108; 16.06, 16.113, 16.123, 16.126, 16.172, 16.176, 16.177; 17.47, 17.49; 18.01, 18.48, 18.53, 18.54, 18.55; 19.12; 20.27, 20.88; 21.02
para 37 ... 4.13; 5.54; 10.02, 10.03, 10.19; 14.94; 15.13; 16.169, 16.171, 16.172, 16.173, 16.176, 16.179; 18.02, 18.23, 18.27, 18.28; 19.05; 20.06, 20.13
(1) ... 5.52, 5.54; 9.08; 15.13; 16.170, 16.176; 18.02, 18.04, 18.58, 18.60; 20.10, 20.11, 20.27
(2) ... 16.108, 16.113, 16.170, 16.181, 16.182; 18.03; 19.10, 19.11
(3) ... 18.07, 18.08
(a) ... 9.08; 16.176; 18.08
(aa) ... 18.08
(b) ... 18.08; 19.06
(c) ... 18.08; 19.06, 19.07
(d) ... 18.08, 18.11, 18.12; 19.08; 20.37
(4) ... 18.03, 18.07, 18.13, 18.14
(6) ... 16.170, 16.191; 18.15
(7) ... 18.18, 18.21
(9) ... 18.23
38 ... 18.24, 18.25, 18.27, 18.28; 20.13

Communications Act 2003 – *contd*
para 38(1) ... 18.25
(4) ... 18.26
39 ... 18.57, 18.62, 18.63; 20.15
(1) ... 18.58, 18.64; 20.10, 20.12, 20.53, 20.57, 20.59
(a), (b) ... 18.59
(2) ... 18.60, 18.61, 18.64; 20.11, 20.12, 20.57
(a), (b) ... 18.61
(3) ... 18.60, 18.63; 20.57
(4) ... 18.64; 20.12, 20.57, 20.58
(a)(i) ... 20.57
(5) ... 18.64; 20.12
40 ... 4.13; 9.26; 10.06, 10.07; 14.86, 14.89, 14.90, 14.92, 14.94; 16.172, 16.178; 18.27, 18.30, 18.32, 18.33, 18.46, 18.47, 18.49, 18.62, 18.64; 20.87
(1) ... 10.02; 18.27
(2) ... 10.05; 18.28; 20.13, 20.53, 20.57, 20.59
(3)(a), (b) ... 18.29; 20.57
(4) ... 18.29; 20.57
(5) ... 18.30
(6) ... 18.33
(a) ... 14.89, 14.91
(b) ... 14.89
(7) ... 14.89; 18.33
(8) ... 4.13; 10.06; 14.94; 16.113, 16.126, 16.174, 16.183; 18.48, 18.52, 18.53, 18.54; 20.88
41 ... 18.23; 19.05
(1) ... 18.23
(2) ... 20.14, 20.57, 20.59
(3)(a), (b) ... 20.57
(4) ... 20.57
(5) ... 20.59
43 ... 18.34, 18.37, 18.38
(1) ... 18.34
(2) ... 18.35, 18.36, 18.40
(3) ... 18.36
(5) ... 18.37, 18.38, 18.43; 20.59
(6)(a), (b) ... 18.39
(7) ... 18.39
(8) ... 18.40

Communications Act 2003 – *contd*
para 43(9) ... 18.40, 18.43
(10) ... 18.43
44 ... 17.47; 18.32, 18.42; 19.12
(1) ... 10.05; 18.30, 18.32, 18.33, 18.50; 19.12
(2) ... 18.40, 18.42, 18.43, 18.50
(3) ... 18.30, 18.32, 18.33
(4) ... 18.40, 18.42, 18.43
(5) ... 14.02, 14.49, 14.85, 14.86, 14.87, 14.88, 14.89, 14.90, 14.91, 14.92; 18.42, 18.44
Pt 7 (paras 45–55) ... 11.211; 14.07, 14.96, 14.101; 18.22
para 49(1) ... 20.59
50(2), (3) ... 20.59
51(1), (7) ... 20.59
53 ... 21.02
(1), (2) ... 20.59
54(7) ... 20.59
(9) ... 18.22
Pt 8 (paras 56–59) ... 4.14; 11.211; 14.07, 14.96, 14.101; 18.22, 18.24
Pt 9 (paras 60–64) ... 11.211; 14.07, 14.96, 14.101; 18.24
Pt 10 (paras 65–72) ... 11.211; 14.07, 14.101
para 67(1) ... 20.59
68(2) ... 20.59
71(2) ... 20.59
Pt 11 (paras 73–75) ... 11.211; 14.07, 14.101
para 74 ... 18.24
75(2) ... 20.59
Pt 12 (paras 76–81) ... 11.211; 14.07, 14.101; 21.02
para 78(1) ... 20.59
Pt 13 (para 82) ... 11.211; 14.07, 14.101; 21.02
para 82(3), (4) ... 20.59
Pt 14 (paras 83–86) ... 6.29; 14.07, 14.101, 14.102, 14.109
para 83 ... 14.01
84 ... 4.06; 6.29, 6.36; 9.04; 10.18; 11.185, 11.253; 13.195; 14.01, 14.13, 14.49, 14.73, 14.87, 14.101, 14.109; 16.249, 16.250
(1) ... 14.49

Communications Act 2003 – *contd*
para 84(1)(b) ... 14.87
(2) ... 14.02, 14.50, 14.51, 14.58, 14.75, 14.87
(a) ... 13.27, 13.116, 13.213; 14.52, 14.57, 14.75
(3)(a) ... 14.83
85 ... 14.01, 14.96, 14.97, 14.98, 14.100, 14.101
(1) ... 14.96, 14.98
(2) ... 14.02, 14.97
(7) ... 14.100
(8) ... 14.98
(9) ... 14.99
86 ... 6.29; 11.210, 11.211, 11.213; 14.01, 14.07, 14.101, 14.103, 14.104, 14.106, 14.109, 14.110, 14.113, 14.114, 14.115, 14.116
Pt 15 (paras 87–91) ... 2.07
para 88 ... 6.09; 18.64; 20.21, 20.48, 20.49, 20.50, 20.51, 20.52, 20.58
(1) ... 6.09; 20.41, 20.42, 20.43
(2) ... 6.09; 20.42, 20.45, 20.57
(3) ... 6.09; 18.64; 20.25, 20.47, 20.49, 20.52
(4) ... 20.52
89 ... 16.38; 18.29, 18.39, 18.60, 18.63; 20.21, 20.50, 20.57, 20.58
(1), (2) ... 15.72; 20.53
(3) ... 20.25, 20.54
(4) ... 20.54
(5), (6) ... 20.55
90 ... 20.58
91 ... 20.62
(1) ... 20.67, 20.69, 20.76
(2) ... 20.70
(a) ... 15.72
94 ... 5.02
(1), (2) ... 13.203
(3), (4) ... 20.20, 20.77
(5), (6) ... 20.20, 20.78
95(1) ... 23.12, 23.16
96 ... 4.03
(1) ... 23.12, 23.16, 23.17
(2) ... 23.17, 23.19
(b) ... 8.09; 9.89; 16.69, 16.239; 23.41

Communications Act 2003 – *contd*
para 97 .... 13.31; 21.26, 21.30, 21.33
99 .... 6.25, 6.39; 13.26; 14.108
100 .... 9.17, 9.19; 14.103, 14.105, 14.113, 14.114
(1) 6.22, 6.23, 6.29; 13.26; 14.107, 14.108, 14.109, 14.110, 14.114, 14.115; 16.172
(2) 6.24, 6.26, 6.29, 6.28, 6.33, 6.39; 12.30; 13.26, 14.108, 14.109, 14.110; 22.02
101 .... 5.40
103(2) 11.04, 11.141
105 .... 5.12, 5.14; 18.28; 20.12
(1) 5.06, 5.10; 18.60
(2) 5.14; 18.60
(3), (4) 5.14
(6) 5.13
(7) 5.15
108 .... 5.01; 11.199; 20.10, 20.11
(1) 5.30, 5.33, 5.35; 12.11; 18.04, 18.58, 18.60
(2) 5.56
Compulsory Purchase Act 1965
s 10 .... 14.97, 14.102
Digital Economy Act 2017 .. 5.29; 6.23; 7.24; 9.30; 12.36; 16.265
s 4 .... 3.15, 3.16
(1) 3.14
(2) 3.14; 7.03
5 .... 3.15
Sch 1 .... 3.14, 3.15; 16.265
Sch 2 (Electronic Communications Code: Transitional Provisions) ... 2.06, 2.13; 3.16, 3.17, 3.18, 3.20; 4.09; 5.51; 11.241; 12.40, 12.41; 13.201, 13.226; 14.11; 15.76, 15.77; 16.74, 16.76, 16.77, 16.80, 16.83, 16.84, 16.85, 16.87, 16.90, 16.99, 16.100, 16.103, 16.112, 16.119, 16.158, 16.200, 16.207, 16.243; 18.01, 18.12; 19.05, 19.09
Digital Economy Act 2017 – *contd*
para 1(2) 16.87
(4) 12.40; 16.08, 16.86, 16.119
(a) 16.89, 16.92, 16.94, 16.114; 18.05
2(1) 15.76; 16.98, 16.119
(2) 2.04; 16.102
3 .... 14.11; 16.103
4 .... 16.85
(1) 2.04
(2) 2.12
5 .... 12.41
(1) 15.77; 16.138
(2) 14.77
5A 12.41, 12.42
6 .... 16.101, 16.103, 16.104; 18.09, 18.12
(1) 16.101; 18.12
(2) 11.11; 16.103, 16.124; 19.09
(3) 16.103; 18.12
7 .... 15.27; 16.103, 16.104; 19.05
(1) 4.09; 15.27
(2) 16.104
(3) 16.104, 16.105
(4) 16.104, 16.105, 16.243
11 .... 2.08
12(1)–(3) 2.09
14 .... 2.11
16(1) 2.14, 2.15
(2), (3) 2.15
20(1) 2.17
(2) 2.17; 18.01
(3) 2.17
23 .... 2.07
25 .... 2.13
Sch 3 .... 3.16
Digital Markets, Competition and Consumers Act 2024
s 218 .... 7.03
Heath and Safety at Work etc Act 1974
s 3 .... 11.120
4 .... 11.121
Housing Act 1988 .... 16.164
s 21 .... 16.42
Interpretation Act 1978
s 7 .... 20.70, 20.75
Land Compensation Act 1961
s 5 .... 14.51
r (2)–(4) 14.83
Landlord and Tenant Act 1954 ..... 1.04; 3.05, 3.21; 4.08; 8.27, 8.44, 8.45, 8.46, 8.47; 9.20,

Landlord and Tenant Act 1954 – *contd*
9.21; 11.11, 11.21, 11.28, 11.50, 11.126, 11.134, 11.142, 11.180, 11.181, 11.182, 11.184, 11.185, 11.188, 11.190, 11.198, 11.207, 11.226, 11.231, 11.235, 11.236, 11.237, 11.240, 11.241, 11.243, 11.244, 11.245, 11.252, 11.257, 11.265, 11.269, 11.274, 11.277, 11.283, 11.284; 12.38; 13.39, 13.102, 13.103, 13.104, 13.108, 13.109, 13.110, 13.119, 13.123, 13.177, 13.201, 13.202, 13.203, 13.204, 13.205, 13.206, 13.210, 13.217, 13.224, 13.225, 13.230; 14.06, 14.07, 14.08, 14.09, 14.10, 14.102; 15.27, 15.79; 16.07, 16.27, 16.29, 16.35, 16.41, 16.51, 16.56, 16.60, 16.74, 16.77, 16.78, 16.80, 16.83, 16.103, 16.107, 16.111, 16.119, 16.120, 16.121, 16.124, 16.132, 16.138, 16.164, 16.190, 16.192, 16.198, 16.200, 16.201, 16.202, 16.204, 16.206, 16.207, 16.211, 16.212, 16.213, 16.214, 16.257, 16.274; 17.01, 17.04, 17.10, 17.16, 17.19, 17.20, 17.22, 17.25, 17.26, 17.27, 17.28, 17.30, 17.33, 17.42, 17.46, 17.52, 17.66; 18.11, 18.12; 19.08, 19.09, 19.13; 20.27, 20.28, 20.89; 21.20, 21.21, 21.24, 21.25, 21.41, 21.53, 21.54, 21.55, 21.119; 22.21, 22.24; 23.24
Pt II (ss 23–46) 11.237, 11.238; 14.11; 16.17, 16.18, 16.19, 16.27, 16.77, 16.103, 16.111, 16.118, 16.119, 16.129, 16.198, 16.202, 16.203, 16.210, 16.215, 16.257, 16.272, 16.273, 16.274; 18.10, 18.12; 19.05; 21.41f

Landlord and Tenant Act 1954 – *contd*
s 23(3) 11.227; 17.30
24 ..... 6.27; 9.20; 16.28, 16.34, 16.103, 16.106, 16.118, 16.130, 16.196, 16.274; 19.05
(1) 16.35, 16.119, 16.274
(a) 16.212
(2) 16.35, 16.120, 16.124, 16.190, 16.192; 18.11; 19.08
(3) 19.08
24A 13.177
25 ..... 6.27; 8.45; 9.20; 16.47, 16.60, 16.103, 16.130, 16.192, 16.212, 16.274; 17.27; 19.05, 19.08, 19.09
26 ..... 6.27; 9.20; 16.103, 16.130, 16.212, 16.274; 19.05
(1) 16.212
(6) 16.274
27, 28 ..... 6.27; 9.20; 16.103, 16.130; 19.05
29(2) 16.176
(4)(a) 17.05
30 ..... 16.274
(1) 16.53, 16.60, 16.111, 16.274; 17.14, 17.42; 19.08
(1)(c) 16.57
(d), (e) 17.14
(f) 8.46; 11.21, 11.27; 16.274; 17.02, 17.03, 17.05, 17.06, 17.15, 17.66
(g) 17.14
31(1) 16.274; 17.05
32 ..... 11.227; 16.274
33 ..... 11.228, 11.229, 11.232; 16.274
34 ..... 11.180; 13.205, 13.206, 13.208, 13.216, 13.217, 13.225; 16.274
(1) 13.207
(a), (b) 13.221
(2) 13.207
(3) 11.281
34A 13.225, 13.226, 13.227
(2) 13.227
(3) 13.228

Landlord and Tenant Act 1954 – *contd*
s 34A(4) 13.228
(a) 13.229
(5)(a) 13.226
34B 13.230; 14.11, 14.12, 14.13
(1) 14.11
(2) 13.230
(8)(b) 14.11
34C 13.230; 14.13
35 .... 11.180, 11.183, 11.188, 11.189, 11.229, 11.232, 11.235; 16.274
(1) 11.281
38(4) 9.20
38A 6.27; 16.103, 16.121, 16.130, 16.210, 16.274; 17.04; 18.10, 18.11, 18.12, 18.55; 19.05
(1), (3) 9.21
35(1) 8.27
43(4) 4.08; 11.237, 11.238; 13.103; 16.19, 16.27, 16.83, 16.100, 16.111, 16.129; 18.10; 19.05
64 .... 17.05
(1) 16.45
Landlord and Tenant Act 1988 .... 16.62
s 3(2)(b)(ii) 16.62
Landlord and Tenant (Covenants) Act 1995
s 17 .... 11.90
Land Registration Act 2002 .... 3.05; 23.09
s 27(2)(b)(i) 15.49
111(1), (2) 23.09
Law of Property Act 1925
s 62 .... 11.201
84(1) 23.21, 23.22
146 .... 11.90, 11.94, 11.209; 16.62
147 .... 11.90
Mines (Working Facilities and Support) Act 1966
s 8(2) 13.10
Party Wall etc Act 1996
s 15(1) 20.65
Product Security and Telecommunications Infrastructure Act 2022 .... 3.20, 3.21, 3.22; 4.08; 5.09; 11.234, 11.243; 12.08; 13.204, 13.205, 13.224; 14.10; 15.77; 16.77, 16.80; 21.20, 21.21, 21.24, 21.55
Product Security and Telecommunications Infrastructure Act 2022 – *contd*
s 57 .... 5.22; 11.74; 12.08
(2)(b)(i) 5.22; 11.74; 12.08
(7) 5.22; 11.74; 12.08
58 .... 3.20
(3) 15.77
(a), (b) 12.41
(4) 12.41
61 .... 13.225
63 .... 13.230; 14.08, 14.10, 14.11, 14.13
(2A) 13.230
65 .... 13.230
66 .... 3.20
(2) 8.52; 9.48; 10.17
68 .... 3.20
69 .... 3.20
(2)(a) 8.07; 20.57
(b) 8.08
(3)(a) 20.57
(4)(a) 20.57
(b) 16.238
79(2) 5.22; 11.74; 12.08, 12.41; 15.77
Telecommunications Act 1984 .... 3.14
Sch 2 (Telecommunications Code) 2.01, 2.06, 2.09, 2.11, 2.14, 2.15, 2.16, 2.17; 3.01, 3.02, 3.04, 3.05, 3.06, 3.07, 3.08, 3.09, 3.13, 3.14, 3.15, 3.17; 4.04; 5.05, 5.15; 6.04; 7.01; 11.39, 11.77; 13.05, 13.06, 13.07, 13.12, 13.13, 13.17, 13.30, 13.67, 13.69, 13.71; 14.76; 15.70; 16.75, 16.77, 16.79, 16.80, 16.84, 16.87, 16.88, 16.91, 16.101, 16.103, 16.106, 16.112, 16.119, 16.131, 16.132, 16.134, 16.168, 16.200, 16.205, 16.250; 18.02, 18.05; 19.04
para 2 .... 2.02; 16.74, 16.89, 16.90, 16.92, 16.97, 16.103, 16.112, 16.114, 16.115, 16.119, 16.146; 19.04, 19.05
(1) 5.15; 16.90, 16.91, 16.92, 16.93

Telecommunications Act 1984 – *contd*
para 2(1)(a)–(c) 16.103
(3) 2.03, 2.04, 2.12; 16.138
(4) 2.03, 2.05; 16.92, 16.102, 16.138
(5) 2.03
3 .... 2.02; 16.74, 16.89, 16.94, 16.103, 16.112
(1) 16.95
(2) 16.96
4(4) 2.12
(b) 2.12
(5)–(12) 2.12
5 .... 2.02; 16.88
(1) 2.08, 2.09
6 .... 2.10
7(1) 13.06
17, 18 .... 2.14
20 .... 2.15, 2.16; 16.138
21 .... 2.12, 2.17; 18.01
(2) 2.17; 18.01
(4)(b) 2.17
Telecommunications Infrastructure (Leasehold Property) Act 2021 ...... 3.19; 15.14
s 3(3)(b)(4) 15.14; 20.57
Telecommunications Infrastructure (Leasehold Property) Act 2021 – *contd*
Sch 1
para 4(2)(b) 15.14
Town and Country Planning Act 1990 .... 17.39
s 55(1) 17.39
(1A)(a) 17.39
57 .... 17.39
Tribunals, Courts and Enforcement Act 2007 .... 21.80, 21.81; 23.09
s 3(5) 21.84
11 .... 21.109; 23.09
(1)–(4) 21.95
(5)(d), (e) 21.96
13(1)–(4) 21.106
(6) 21.111
(8)(e) 21.107
(12) 21.106
14A(1)(a), (b) 21.111
(4) 21.111, 21.112, 21.113, 21.114
(a), (b) 21.114
(5) 21.111, 21.112, 21.113, 21.115
(a)–(c) 21.115
14B 21.111, 21.118
(3) 21.118
15(8)(c), (e) 21.107

Table of Statutory Instruments

Appeals from the Upper Tribunal to the Court of Appeal Order 2008, SI 2008/2834
art 2 .... 21.109
Civil Procedure Rules 1998, SI 1998/3132 .... 21.110; 23.18, 23.48
r 3.1(2)(a) 21.120
44.2(2) 23.18
(2)(a), (b) 23.18
Pt 52 (rr 52.1–52.30) 21.111, 21.120
r 52.3(1)(a) 21.120
(2)(a), (b) 21.120
(3)(a) 21.120
52.4(1), (2) 21.120
52.6(1) 21.120
52.7(2) 21.110
52.12(2)(b) 21.120
52.15(1), (2) 21.120
PD 52A 21.119, 21.120
PD 52C 21.111
Pt 55 (rr 55A.1–55.48) 14.94
Digital Economy Act 2017 (Commencement No 3) Regulations 2017, SI 2017/1286
reg 2 .... 3.16; 16.74
Electronic Communications and Wireless Telegraphy Regulations 2011, SI 2011/1210
reg 3 .... 21.26
(2) 13.31; 20.91; 21.27, 21.30, 21.32
Electronic Communications Code (Jurisdiction) (Amendment) Regulations 2023, SI 2023/1220
reg 2(3)(a) 21.05
Electronic Communications Code (Jurisdiction) Regulations 2017, SI 2017/1284
reg 2(1) 21.02
3(1)(aa) 21.01
(2)(a) 21.03
(3) 21.01
4 .... 21.05
(1)(a) 21.02
(2) 21.04
Electronic Communications Code (Transitional Provisions) Regulations 2017, SI 2017/1008
para 3(2) 5.05
First-tier Tribunal and Upper Tribunal (Chambers) (Amendment) Order 2024, SI 2024/376
art 2(2) 21.06
(4) 21.06
First-tier Tribunal and Upper Tribunal (Chambers) Order 2010, SI 2010/2655 .... 21.07
art 5A(j) 21.06
12(a)(v) 21.06
(cc) 21.06
First-tier Tribunal (Property Chamber) Fees Order 2013, SI 2013/1179 .... 21.48
Landlord and Tenant Act 1954, Part 2 (Notices) Regulations 2004, SI 2004/1005
reg 2(2) 20.50
Product Security and Telecommunications Infrastructure Act 2022 (Commencement No 1) Regulations 2023, SI 2023/109
reg 2(a) 5.22; 11.74; 12.08
reg 3(a) 12.41; 15.77
Regulatory Reform (Business Tenancies) (England and Wales) Order 2003, SI 2003/3096 .... 9.21
Telecommunications Infrastructure (Leasehold Property) Act 2021 (Commencement No 1) Regulations 2022, SI 2022/1308
reg 3(c) 15.14
Tribunal Procedure (Amendment) Rules 2024, SI 2024/364 .... 23.03
Tribunal Procedure (First-tier Tribunal) (Property Chamber) Rules 2013, SI 2013/1169
r 3 .... 21.99
6(3)(n)(ii) 21.16
9(2) 21.39
(3) 21.40
(e) 21.40
(4) 21.43
13 .... 23.03
(i)(b) 23.04
(d) 23.03
(1A) 23.05
(7)(a)–(c) 23.48

Tribunal Procedure (First-tier Tribunal) (Property Chamber) Rules 2013, SI 2013/1169
r 13(8) 23.48
(9) 23.49
25... 21.14
(2), (3) 21.14
52(1), (2), (4).. 21.97
(5) 21.98
53(2), (3) 21.100
54(1), (3) 21.101
55... 21.99
(1)(b) 21.99
Tribunal Procedure (Upper Tribunal) (Lands Chamber) Rules 2010, SI 2010/2600
r 8(2) 21.39
(3) 21.40
(c) 9.59; 21.40
Tribunal Procedure (Upper Tribunal) (Lands Chamber) Rules 2010, SI 2010/2600 – *contd*
(4) 21.43
10... 23.09, 23.12
(3) 23.07, 23.08
(a)–(c).. 23.08
(4), (5) 23.07, 23.08, 23.13
(6) 23.07, 23.09, 23.10, 23.13
(d) 23.09
(e) 23.06, 23.09
(g) 23.09
(14) 23.08
21(1) 21.103
(2) 21.104
(3), (4) 21.105
(5), (7) 21.105
55... 21.108
(1) 21.108

Table of European Legislation

Directive 2009/140/EC of the European Parliament and of the Council of 25 November 2009 amending Directives 2002/21/EC on a common regulatory framework for electronic communications networks and services, 2002/19/EC on access to, and interconnection of, electronic communications networks and associated facilities, and 2002/20/EC on the authorisation of electronic communications networks and services 21.30
Directive 2002/19/EC of the European Parliament and of the Council of 7 March 2002 on access to, and interconnection of, electronic communications networks and associated facilities (Access Directive) 3.02
Directive 2002/20/EC of the European Parliament and of the Council of 7 March 2002 on the authorisation of electronic communications networks and services (Authorisation Directive) 3.02
Directive 2002/21/EC of the European Parliament and of the Council of 7 March 2002 on a common regulatory framework for electronic communications networks and services (Framework Directive) 3.02; 21.30
Directive 2002/22/EC of the European Parliament and of the Council of 7 March 2002 on universal service and users' rights relating to electronic communications networks and services (Universal Service Directive) 3.02
Directive 2002/58/EC of the European Parliament and of the Council of 12 July 2002 concerning the processing of personal data and the protection of privacy in the electronic communications sector (Directive on privacy and electronic communications)...... 3.02

Table of Cases

A

A-G v HRH Prince Ernest Augustus of Hanover [1957] AC 436, [1957] 2 WLR 1, [1957] 1 All ER 49 .... 16.188
AP Wireless II (UK) Ltd v On Tower UK Ltd [2024] UKUT 263 (LC), [2024] 9 WLUK 181 .... 2.03; 15.70, 15.79; 16.134, 16.137, 16.140, 16.144, 16.145, 16.146, 16.150, 16.151, 16.160; 20.18
Affinity Water *see* EE Ltd v Affinity Water Ltd [2022] UKUT 8 (LC)
Allison *see* On Tower UK Ltd v Robert Graeme Allison (LC-2022-000322)
Arqiva (Upper Tribunal) *see* Arqiva Services Ltd v AP Wireless II (UK) Ltd [2020] UKUT 195 (LC)
Arqiva (Supreme Court) *see* On Tower UK Ltd (formerly Arqiva Services Ltd) v AP Wireless II (UK) Ltd [2022] UKSC 18
Arqiva Services Ltd v AP Wireless II (UK) Ltd [2020] UKUT 195 (LC), [2020] 6 WLUK 294, [2020] RVR 283 .... 16.91, 16.113, 16.115, 16.208; 18.05; 21.116
Ashloch (Upper Tribunal) *see* Cornerstone Telecommunications Infrastructure Ltd v Ashloch Ltd [2019] UKUT 338 (LC)
Ashloch (Court of Appeal) *see* Cornerstone Telecommunications Infrastructure Ltd v Ashloch Ltd [2021] EWCA Civ 90
Ashloch (Supreme Court) *see* Cornerstone Telecommunications Infrastructure Ltd v Ashloch Ltd [2022] UKSC 18
Audley House *see* On Tower UK Ltd v AP Wireless (UK) Ltd (Audley House) [2022] UKUT 152 (LC)

B

BT (Kenton Road) *see* On Tower UK Ltd v British Telecommunications plc [2024] UKUT 51 (LC)
Betty's Cafes Ltd v Phillips Furnishing Stores Ltd (No 1) [1959] AC 20, [1958] 2 WLR 513, [1958] 1 All ER 607 .... 17.17
Bocardo SA v Star Energy UK Onshore Ltd [2010] UKSC 35, [2011] 1 AC 380, [2010] 3 WLR 654 .... 13.10
Bridgewater Canal Co Ltd v GEO Networks Ltd [2010] EWHC 548 (Ch), [2010] 1 WLR 2576, [2010] 3 WLUK 659 .... 7.01
Burlington Gardens *see* AP Wireless II (UK) Ltd v On Tower UK Ltd [2024] UKUT 263 (LC)

C

Canada Trust Co v Stolzenberg [1998] 1 WLR 547, [1998] 1 ALL ER 318, [1997] 10 WLUK 543 .... 9.45, 9.46; 17.69
Cardtronics Europe Ltd v Sykes (Valuation Officer) [2018] EWCA Civ 2472, [2019] 1 WLR 2281, [2018] 11 WLUK 118 .... 16.128
Central St Giles *see* Cornerstone Telecommunicatons Infrastructure Ltd v Central St Giles General Partner Ltd [2019] UKUT 183 (LC)
Clear Channel UK Ltd v Manchester City Council [2005] EWCA Civ 1304, [2005] 11 WLUK 293, [2006] L & TR 7 .... 16.134, 16.151, 16.153

Compton Beauchamp (Upper Tribunal) *see* Cornerstone Telecommunications Infrastructure Ltd v Compton Beauchamp Estates Ltd [2019] UKUT 107 (LC)
Compton Beauchamp (Court of Appeal) *see* Cornerstone Telecommunications Infrastructure Ltd v Compton Beauchamp Estates Ltd [2019] EWCA Civ 1755
Compton Beauchamp (Supreme Court) *see* Cornerstone Telecommunications Infrastructure Ltd v Compton Beauchamp Estates Ltd [2022] UKSC 18
Cornerstone Telecommnications Infrastructure Ltd v Ashloch Ltd [2019] UKUT 338 (LC), [2019] 11 WLUK 97, [2020] 1 P & CR 16 .... 6.28; 11.180; 13.104; 16.22, 16.202; 18.12; 21.116
Cornerstone Telecommunications Infrastructure Ltd v Ashloch Ltd [2021] EWCA Civ 90, [2021] 1 WLUK 333, [2022] 1 P & CR 8 .... 7.23; 11.180, 11.182; 13.104, 13.201; 16.202; 18.12
Cornerstone Telecommunications Infrastructure Ltd v Ashloch Ltd [2022] UKSC 18, [2022] 1 WLR 3360, [2022] 4 All ER 967 .... 1.04; 4.08; 7.16, 7.23; 11.181, 11.265; 13.104; 16.202, 16.211; 18.12; 21.117; 22.21
Cornerstone Telecommunicatons Infrastructure Ltd v Central St Giles General Partner Ltd [2019] UKUT 183 (LC), [2019] 6 WLUK 259, [2019] RVR 301 .... 20.24; 23.44, 23.45
Cornerstone Telecommunications Infrastructure Ltd v Compton Beauchamp Estates Ltd [2019] UKUT 107 (LC), [2019] 4 WLUK 81, [2019] RVR 247 .... 13.141
Cornerstone Telecommunications Infrastructure Ltd v Compton Beauchamp Estates Ltd [2019] EWCA Civ 1755, [2019] 10 WLUK 293, [2020] 1 P & CR 15 .... 3.03; 11.40, 11.71; 16.265; 18.48
Cornerstone Telecommunications Infrastructure Ltd v Compton Beauchamp Estates Ltd [2022] UKSC 18, [2022] 1 WLR 3360, [2022] 4 All ER 967... 4.12; 5.08, 5.09, 5.10, 5.11, 5.12, 5.23, 5.41; 6.04, 6.28; 7.12, 7.16, 7.18, 7.22; 11.71, 11.241, 11.265; 15.28, 15.32; 16.76, 16.91, 16.113, 16.114, 16.115, 16.116, 16.159, 16.186, 16.207, 16.258; 18.28; 20.03, 20.12, 20.13, 20.26, 20.28; 21.34, 21.41, 21.116, 21.117; 22.01, 22.21
Cornerstone Telecommunications Infrastructure Ltd v Fothringham (LTS/ECC/2019/06) [2020] 2 WLUK 495, [2020] RVR 138, 2020 GWD 11-166...... 11.147
Cornerstone Telecommunications Infrastructure Ltd v Fothringham (LTS/ECC/2020/007) [2020] 8 WLUK 258, [2020] RVR 351, 2020 GWD 31-408....... 11.82, 11.83, 11.145; 12.39; 13.49, 13.124, 13.171, 13.194
Cornerstone Telecommunications Infrastructure Ltd v Gateway Properties Ltd [2023] UKUT 188 (LC), [2023] 7 WLUK 569, [2024] RVR 11 .... 22.21; 23.50
Cornerstone Telecommunications Infrastructure Ltd v Hackney London Borough Council (Tradescant House) [2022] UKUT 210 (LC), [2022] 8 WLUK 22...... 6.38; 9.09, 9.76; 11.45, 11.46, 11.127, 11.172; 13.31; 14.58, 14.71; 22.18
Cornerstone Telecommunications Infrastructure Ltd v Keast [2019] UKUT 116 (LC), [2019] 4 WLUK 100 .... 5.19, 5.20, 5.21, 5.40; 7.06; 11.35, 11.37, 11.38, 11.39; 12.11; 16.147, 16.271; 20.32, 20.35

Cornerstone Telecommunications and Infrastructure Ltd v London & Quadrant Housing Trust [2020] UKUT 282 (LC), [2020] 10 WLUK 209, [2021] L & TR 1 .... 11.39, 11.40, 11.43, 11.44, 11.73, 11.169, 11.173, 11.174; 12.34; 13.51, 13.101, 13.111, 13.112, 13.116, 13.119, 13.120, 13.124, 13.134, 13.142, 13.145, 13.199, 13.200; 14.35, 14.36, 14.52, 14.105; 21.52
Cornerstone Telecommunications Infrastructure Ltd v (1) The Mayor & Burgesses of the London Borough of Merton (2) Centrica Combined Common Investment Fund Ltd (LC-2023-000668) 21.76
Cornerstone Telecommunications Infrastructure Ltd v St Martins Property Investments [2021] UKUT 262 (LC), [2021] 10 WLUK 267 .... 9.54, 9.64, 9.69, 9.71, 9.75. 9.77, 9.78; 11.100, 11.171; 14.58, 14.63, 14.65, 14.66, 14.68, 14.73; 15.43, 15.44, 15.47; 23.36, 23.43, 23.44, 23.47
Cornerstone Telecommunications Infrastructure Ltd v University of London [2018] UKUT 356 (LC), [2018] 10 WLUK 430, [2019] RVR 110; *aff'd* [2019] EWCA Civ 2075, [2020] 1 WLR 2124, [2019] 11 WLUK 405 .... 3.03; 4.07; 5.23; 7.11, 7.20, 7.24; 8.35; 9.10, 9.12, 9.15, 9.16, 9.19, 9.22, 9.28, 9.54, 9.55; 11.05; 16.155
Cornerstone Telecommunications Infrastructure Ltd v University of the Arts London [2020] UKUT 248 (LC), [2020] 8 WLUK 237, [2021] RVR 51 .... 8.16, 8.18, 8.21, 8.23, 8.33, 8.35; 9.48, 9.59, 9.81, 9.87; 11.27, 11.48, 11.53, 11.55, 11.56, 11.57, 11.59, 11.60, 11.63, 11.70, 11.73, 11.75, 11.76, 11.81, 11.87, 11.90, 11.92, 11.104, 11.109, 11.112, 11.113, 11.126, 11.130, 11.131, 11.135, 11.140, 11.146, 11.158, 11.158, 11.170, 11.172, 11.210, 11.214, 11.215, 11.217, 11.221, 11.223, 11.225, 11.259; 14.39; 21.46, 21.52
Crawley *see* Crawley Borough Council v EE Ltd & Hutchinson 3G Ltd [2022] UKUT 158 (LC)
Cunliffe v Goodman [1950] 2 KB 237, [1950] 1 All ER 720, (1950) 66 TLR (Pt 2) 109 .... 17.17
Crawley Borough Council v EE Ltd & Hutchinson 3G Ltd [2022] UKUT 158 (LC), [2022] 6 WLUK 207, [2023] 1 P & CR DG2 .... 14.94; 16.171; 17.47; 18.46, 18.47, 18.48, 18.55

D

Director of Buildings & Lands v Shung Fung Ironworks Ltd (Hong Kong) [1995] 2 AC 111, [1995] 2 WLR 404, [1995] 1 All ER 846 .... 11.150; 14.34, 14.58

E

EE Ltd v Affinity Water Ltd [2022] UKUT 8 (LC), [2022] 1 WLUK 142, [2022] L & TR 14 ... 13.121, 13.123, 13.124, 13.125, 13.127, 13.129, 13.130, 13.133, 13.134, 13.135, 13.136, 13.138, 13.143, 13.144, 13.153, 13.155, 13.171, 13.174, 13.175; 14.58; 21.60
EE Ltd v Aviva Investors (Case No LC-2023-89) ... 20.87
EE Ltd v Hackney London Borough Council (Shoreditch House) [2021] UKUT 142 (LC), [2021] 6 WLUK 243, [2021] RVR 241 ... 1.06; 11.139, 11.148, 11.150, 11.170; 14.35
EE Ltd v Islington London Borough Council [2019] UKUT 53 (LC), [2019] 2 WLUK 262, [2019] 2 P & CR 13 ... 3.08; 6.11, 6.13, 6.14, 6.17, 6.18; 13.13, 13.15, 13.31, 13.42, 13.44, 13.45, 13.46, 13.50, 13.52, 13.54, 13.55, 13.60, 13.62, 13.64, 13.66, 13.69, 13.75, 13.76, 13.82, 13.93, 13.95, 13.97, 13.99, 13.100, 13.101, 13.102, 13.111, 13.138, 13.161; 14.28, 14.29, 14.30, 14.32, 14.34, 14.39, 14.48, 14.51, 14.58, 14.75; 15.44; 16.127; 21.29; 23.21, 23.23, 23.24
EE Ltd v Islington London Borough Council [2018] UKUT 361 (LC), [2018] 10 WLUK 477, [2019] RVR 172 ... 8.15, 8.25; 9.46, 9.49, 9.50, 9.52, 9.56, 9.58, 9.65, 9.66, 9.75, 9.77; 11.53, 11.110, 11.136
EE Ltd v MacDonald (LTS/ECC/2019/0009) [2020] 3 WLUK 511, 2020 GWD 14-210 ... 21.32
EE Ltd v Morriss [2022] EW Misc 1 (CC) ... 6.37; 11.235, 11.248, 11.254, 11.255, 11.258, 11.259, 11.262, 11.275, 11.280, 11.281, 11.282; 13.109, 13.117, 13.119, 13.202, 13.216, 13.220; 14.06, 14.07, 14.09; 21.21, 21.54
EE Ltd v AP Wireless II (UK) Ltd (Vache Farm) [2024] UKUT 216 (LC), [2024] 7 WLUK 510, [2024] RVR 283 ... 11.20, 11.22, 11.25; 13.139, 13.151, 13.154, 13.156, 13.161, 13.163, 13.169, 13.170, 13.171, 13.172, 13.174, 13.175, 13.176
EE Ltd v London Underground Ltd [2021] UKUT 128 (LC), [2021] 5 WLUK 464, [2021] RVR 331 ... 11.101
EE Ltd v Meyrick *see* EE Ltd v Chichester [2019] UKUT 164 (LC)
EE Ltd v Chichester [2019] UKUT 164 (LC), [2019] 7 WLUK 97, [2019] L & TR 21 ... 8.47; 11.20; 17.11, 17.16, 17.18, 17.19, 17.23, 17.30, 17.42

EE Ltd v Edelwind Ltd [2020] UKUT 272 (LC), [2020] 9 WLUK 223, [2021] L & TR 3 .... 15.16, 15.79; 16.138, 16.147, 16.148, 16.150
EE Ltd v HSBC Bank plc [2022] UKUT 174 (LC), [2022] 7 WLUK 6, [2022] RVR 287 .... 14.82; 23.26, 23.27, 23.30, 23.32, 23.33, 23.35
EE Ltd v Stephenson [2021] UKUT 167 (LC), [2021] 4 WLR 116, [2021] 7 WLUK 164 .... 7.13; 8.29; 11.182, 11.184, 11.188; 16.233, 16.236, 16.242, 16.244, 16.246; 20.40
EE Ltd v Stephenson (Pendown Farm) [2022] UKUT 180 (LC), [2022] 7 WLUK 122 .... 11.14, 11.19, 11.20, 11.29, 11.88, 11.107, 11.152, 11.161, 11.162, 11.163, 11.174, 11.194, 11.195, 11.196, 11.198, 11.198, 11.241; 12.38; 13.02, 13.63, 13.79, 13.137, 13.139, 13.140, 13.144, 13.153, 13.155, 13.162, 13.167, 13.170, 13.171, 13.174, 13.198; 14.46
Edelwind *see* EE Ltd v Edelwind Ltd [2020] UKUT 272 (LC)
Elitestone v Morris [1997] 1 WLR 687, [1997] 2 All ER 513, [1997] 4 WLUK 481 ... 5.39
Ewefields Farm *see* On Tower UK Ltd v AP Wireless II Ltd (Ewefields Farm) (LC -2023-321)

F

FR Evans (Leeds) Ltd v English Electric Co Ltd [1977] 7 WLUK 73, (1978) 36 P & CR 185, (1977) 245 EG 657 .... 13.54
First Tower Trustees Ltd v CDS (Superstores International) Ltd [2018] EWCA Civ 1396, [2019] 1 WLR 637, [2018] 6 WLUK 334 .... 6.32
Fothringham *see* Cornerstone Telecommunications Infrastructure Ltd v Fothringham (LTS/ECC/2020/007)
Franses *see* S Franses Ltd v Cavendish Hotel (London) Ltd [2017] EWHC 1670 (QB)

G

Gajapatiraju v Revenue Divisional Officer, Vizagapatam [1939] AC 302, [1939] 2 All ER 317, [1939] 2 WLUK 55 .... 13.54
Gateway Properties *see* Cornerstone Telecommunications Infrastructure Ltd v Gateway Properties Ltd [2023] UKUT 188 (LC)
Gencomp *see* Vodafone Ltd v Gencomp (No 7) Ltd [2022] UKUT 223 (LC)
Gilchrist v R & C Comrs [2014] UKUT 169 (TCC), [2015] Ch 183, [2015] 2 WLR 1 .... 21.85
Goulandris v Knight *see* Knight v Goulandris [2018] EWCA Civ 237
Gravesham *see* Gravesham BC v On Tower UK Ltd (LC-2023-810)
Gravesham BC v On Tower UK Ltd (LC-2023-810) [2024] UKUT 151 (LC), [2024] 6 WLUK 39, [2024] L & TR 26 .... 7.22; 11.31; 14.94; 16.211, 16.213; 18.47, 18.52, 18.53, 18.54, 18.55; 19.13; 20.27, 20.28; 21.17, 21.41, 21.79; 23.11
Gray v IRC [1994] STC 360, [1994] 2 WLUK 137, [1994] 2 EGLR 185 .... 13.45, 13.50

H

HSBC *see* EE Ltd v HSBC Bank plc [2022] UKUT 174 (LC)
Hackney (Shoreditch Hosue) *see* EE Ltd v Hackney London Borough Council (Shoreditch House) [2021] UKUT 142 (LC)
Hackney (Tradescant House) *see* Cornerstone Telecommunications Infrastructure Ltd v Hackney London Borough Council [2022] UKUT 210 (LC)

I

IRC v Gray *see* Gray v IRC [1994] STC 360
IX Ltd *see* On Tower UK Ltd v IX Ltd (LC-2022-000361)
Islington *see* EE Ltd v **Islington** London Borough Council [2019] UKUT 53 (LC)

J

Janes (Gowns) Ltd v Harlow Development Corpn [1979] 1 WLUK 180, (1979) 253 EG 799, [1980] 1 EGLR 52 .... 11.228
Jervis v Harris [1996] Ch 195, [1996] 2 WLR 220, [1996] 1 All ER 303 .... 11.207

K

Keast *see* Cornerstone Telecommunications Infrastructure Ltd v Keast [2019] UKUT 116 (LC)
Kirkham v Information Comr (Record of Proceedings) [2020] UKUT 336 (AAC) 21.85, 21.86
Knight v Goulandris [2018] EWCA Civ 237, [2018] 1 WLR 3345, [2018] 3 All ER 505 .... 20.65

L

London & Quadrant *see* Cornerstone Telecommunications and Infrastructure Ltd v London & Quadrant Housing Trust [2020] UKUT 282 (LC),

M

Mannai Investment Co Ltd v Eagle Star Life Assurance Co Ltd [1997] AC 749, [1997] 2 WLR 945, [1997] 3 All ER 352 .... 20.22, 20.23
Marklands Ltd v Virgin Retail Ltd [2003] EWHC 3428 (Ch), [2003] 11 WLUK 842, [2004] 2 EGLR 43 .... 13.68
Mercury Communications Ltd v London & India Dock Investments Ltd [1993] 6 WLUK 71, (1995) 69 P & CR 135, [1994] 1 EGLR 229 .... 13.08, 13.11

N

New Zealand Farm *see* On Tower Ltd v AP Wireless II (New Zealand Farm) [2022] EW Misc 6 (CC)
No 1 West India Quay (Residential) Ltd v East Tower Apartments Ltd [2018] EWCA Civ 250, [2018] 1 WLR 5682, [2018] 2 WLUK 457 .... 16.62

O

O'May v City of London Real Property Co Ltd [1983] 2 AC 726, [1982] 2 WLR 407, [1982] 1 All ER 660 .... 8.27; 11.180, 11.183, 11.188, 11.190, 11.198, 11.232, 11.235, 11.236, 11.245, 11.283
On Tower UK Ltd v Robert Graeme Allison (LC-2022-000322) 16.145
On Tower Ltd v AP Wirelesss II (UK) Ltd (Patricroft) (LC-2023-000852) 16.115, 16.117, 16.211, 16.213, 16.214, 16.215; 18.01; 20.35, 20.57, 20.91

On Tower UK Ltd v AP Wireless (UK) Ltd (Audley House) [2022] UKUT 152 (LC), [2022] 6 WLUK 256 ... 8.19; 11.19, 11.28, 11.50, 11.103, 11.108, 11.116, 11.117, 11.118, 11.119, 11.123, 11.124, 11.125, 11.126, 11.127, 11.129, 11.134, 11.142, 11.153, 11.162, 11.186, 11.199, 11.201, 11.202, 11.204; 13.80, 13.122, 13.135, 13.136, 13.173; 14.70, 14.113; 15.48
On Tower UK Ltd v British Telecommunications plc [2024] UKUT 51 (LC), [2024] 2 WLUK 380, [2024] L & TR 18 ... 5.33, 5.38; 11.28; 16.33, 16.42, 16.47, 16.48, 16.49, 16.123, 16.231
On Tower UK Ltd v AP Wireless II Ltd (Ewefields Farm) (LC -2023-321) ... 11.20, 11.33, 11.51, 11.206, 11.207, 11.208, 11.287; 13.169, 13.173, 13.180, 13.182
On Tower UK Ltd v IX Ltd (LC-2022-000361) ... 14.07; 23.30, 23.33, 23.34, 23.35, 23.36, 23.47
On Tower UK Ltd v JH & FW Green Ltd (Dale Park) [2020] UKUT 348 (LC), [2020] 12 WLUK 207, [2021] RVR 156; *aff'd* [2021] EWCA Civ 1858, [2022] 4 WLR 27, [2021] 12 WLUK 87 ... 5.22, 5.49; 7.16; 8.27, 8.38, 8.39; 11.68, 11.69, 11.88, 11.186, 11.187, 11.193, 11.198, 11.241, 11.247; 12.34, 12.35, 12.38; 13.71, 13.120, 13.124, 13.137, 13.139, 13.153, 13.156, 13.167, 13.168, 13.170, 13.171, 13.174, 13.193, 13.194; 14.66, 14.72, 14.79; 23.38, 23.39
On Tower Ltd v AP Wireless II (New Zealand Farm) [2022] EW Misc 6 (CC) ... 11.50, 11.51, 11.126, 11.134, 11.142, 11.153, 11.207; 13.202, 13.220; 14.73; 21.21
On Tower (formerly Arqiva Services Ltd) v AP Wireless II (UK) Ltd [2022] UKSC 18, [2022] 1 WLR 3360, [2022] 4 All ER 967 ... 16.113; 21.117

P

Patricroft *see* On Tower Ltd v AP Wirelesss II (UK) Ltd (LC-2023-000852)
Pointe Gourde Quarrying & Transport Co Ltd v Sub-Intendent of Crown Lands [1947] AC 565, 63 TLR 486, [1947] 7 WLUK 99 ... 13.15
Pretoria Energy Company (Chittering) Ltd v Blankney Estates Ltd [2023] EWCA Civ 482, [2023] 5 WLUK 81, [2023] L & TR 28 ... 22.04
Pumperninks of Piccadilly Ltd v Land Securities plc [2002] EWCA Civ 621, [2002] Ch 332, [2002] 3 WLR 898 ... 17.31

R

R v G [2003] UKHL 50, [2004] 1 AC 1034, [2003] 3 WLR 1060 ... 16.188

R (on the application of Spath Holme) v Secretary of State for the Environment, Transport & the Regions [2001] 2 AC 349, [2001] 2 WLR 15, [2001] 1 All ER 195 .... 7.20
R v Soneji (Kamlesh Kumar) [2005] UKHL 49, [2006] 1 AC 340, [2005] 3 WLR 303 20.45, 20.68
R (on the application of Cart) v Upper Tribunal [2011] UKSC 28, [2012] 1 AC 663, [2011] 3 WLR 107 .... 21.84
R (on the application of Sainsbury's Supermarkets Ltd) v Wolverhampton City Council [2010] UKSC 20, [2011] 1 AC 437, [2010] 2 WLR 1173 .... 7.09
Rush & Tomkins Ltd v Greater London Council [1989] AC 1280, [1988] 3 WLR 939, [1988] 3 All ER 737 .... 22.06

S

St Martins *see* Cornerstone Telecommunications Infrastructure Ltd v St Martins Property Investments [2021] UKUT 262 (LC)
S Franses Ltd v Cavendish Hotel (London) Ltd [2017] EWHC 1670 (QB), [2017] Bus LR 1941, [2017] 7 WLUK 7; *revs'd* [2018] UKSC 62, [2019] AC 249, [2018] 3 WLR 1952 .... 11.20; 17.17, 17.20
Shung Fung Ironworks *see* Director of Buildings & Lands v Shung Fung Ironworks Ltd (Hong Kong) [1995] 2 AC 111
Street v Mountford [1985] AC 809, [1985] 2 WLR 877, [1985] 2 All ER 289 .... 16.133, 16.134, 16.152

T

Telefonica UK Ltd v Knowsley Metropolitan Borough Council (LC-2023-715)... 21.20, 21.31
Trocette Property Co Ltd v Greater London Council & Southward London Borough Council [1974] RVR 306 .... 13.50

U

UAL *see* Cornerstone Telecommunications Infrastructure Ltd v University of the Arts London [2020] UKUT 248 (LC)
University of London *see* Cornerstone Telecommunications Infrastructure Ltd v University of London [2018] UKUT 356 (LC)
University of London v Cornerstone Telecommunications Infrastructure Ltd *see* Cornerstone Telecommunications Infrastructure Ltd v University of London [2018] UKUT 356 (LC)
University of the Arts *see* Cornerstone Telecommunications Infrastructure Ltd v University of the Arts London [2020] UKUT 248 (LC)

V

Vache Farm *see* EE Ltd v AP Wireless II (UK) Ltd (Vache Farm) [2024] UKUT 216 (LC)
Vodafone Ltd v Gravesham BC (Claim No K00BS429) 21.54
Vodafone v Hanover Capital Ltd [2020] 8 WLUK 180, [2021] 2 P & CR 3, [2020] EW Misc 18 (CC) 11.230, 11.233, 11.245, 11.257, 11.263, 11.268, 11.269, 11.275, 11.278, 11.279, 11.280; 13.102, 13.103, 13.105, 13.110, 13.111, 13.112, 13.116, 13.117, 13.118, 13.119, 13.120, 13.122, 13.133, 13.134, 13.137, 13.142, 13.146, 13.202, 13.209, 13.210, 13.216, 13.219, 13.220; 21.21

Vodafone Ltd v Gencomp (No 7) Ltd [2022] UKUT 223 (LC), [2022] 8 WLUK 78, [2023] L & TR 10; *rev'sd* Vodafone Ltd v Potting Shed Bar & Gardens Ltd (formerly Gencomp (No 7) Ltd) [2023] EWCA Civ 825, [2024] 1 WLR 141, [2023] 7 WLUK 201 .... 5.15, 5.16; 7.03, 7.18, 7.22; 15.02, 15.03, 15.12, 15.16, 15.24, 15.25, 15.26, 15.30, 15.31, 15.33, 15.69; 16.37, 16.74, 16.134, 16.157, 16.162, 16.187, 16.188, 16.221
Vodafone Ltd v Potting Shed Bar & Gardens Ltd *see* Vodafone Ltd v Gencomp (No 7) Ltd [2022] UKUT 223 (LC)

1

Abbreviations and conventions adopted in this book

Abbreviations

1954 Act:	Landlord and Tenant Act 1954
2003 Act:	Communications Act 2003
2007 Act:	Tribunals, Courts and Enforcement Act 2007
2017 Act:	Digital Economy Act 2017
ECA:	Electronic Communications Apparatus (for the purposes of the Code, this term is defined at para 5(1) of the Code)
(The) Code:	The Electronic Communications Code, as set out at Schedule 3A to the Communications Act 2003
CPR:	Civil Procedure Rules 1998
Deputy President:	The Deputy President of the Upper Tribunal (Lands Chamber)
FTT:	First-tier Tribunal (or specifically the First-tier Tribunal (Property Chamber) where appropriate)
FTT Rules:	Tribunal Procedure (First-tier Tribunal) (Property Chamber) Rules 2013
MSV:	Multi-skilled visit. This is a term introduced by operators in respect of a preliminary survey typically carried out in order to consider the suitability of a site which is thought to have potential as a site for the installation of ECA. As its name suggests, such a visit can involve numerous different types of survey. The term 'MSV' has been used variously to refer to anything from simple non-intrusive surveys to those at which intrusive works may take place over a number of months
(The) New Code:	The Electronic Communications Code, as set out at Schedule 3A to the Communications Act 2003
(The) Old Code:	The Telecommunications Code, as set out at Schedule 2 to the Telecommunications Act 1984, and as amended by the Communications Act 2003. The Old Code is sometimes referred to as 'the 2003 Code'.
TCPA 1990:	The Town and Country Planning Act 1990
Transitional Provisions:	The provisions of Schedule 2 to the Digital Economy Act 2017, which is headed 'The Electronic Communications Code: Transitional Provision'

UT:	Upper Tribunal (or specifically the Upper Tribunal (Lands Chamber) where appropriate)
UTLC:	Upper Tribunal (Lands Chamber)
UTLC Rules	Tribunal Procedure (Upper Tribunal) (Lands Chamber) Rules 2010

Stylistic conventions

References to paragraphs within the Code

1.01 The most important stylistic choice to mention is that where a paragraph number is mentioned, without square brackets, and without express reference to the document within which that paragraph is contained, this is a reference to a paragraph of the Code. Most often, the abbreviation 'para' is used in this context. In this book, the word 'Code' is typically rendered with an initial capital 'C', save where directly quoting sources. By contrast, the Code itself typically uses a lower case 'c' when referring to itself.

Quotation of legislation

1.02 As the Code (and the Transitional Provisions) are reproduced in full at the back of this book, an effort has been made not to quote too much of the legislation within the body of the book. However, where there are key provisions that are being discussed, the most important parts of these are sometimes set out towards the beginning of a chapter for convenience.

Citation of cases

1.03 As the Code is relatively young and as certain fundamental points have benefitted from (needed) clarification in certain cases, references to cases in explaining the Code are frequent. That being the case, it has been thought preferable to abbreviate the name of cases to as few words as possible within the main body of a page in order that sentences are not cluttered with parties, neutral citations, or law report references. Footnotes have been used liberally, both to assist with this and also in relation to legislation.

1.04 In Code cases and in 1954 Act telecoms lease cases, a relatively small number of litigants, crop up in a substantial number of cases. This is, of course, not surprising. The names that appear most frequently in full case names are those of well-known operators. Because of the frequency with which these names appear in cases, it is often convenient to abbreviate the names of cases by reference to the site provider/landowner/respondent party which is not the operator. Where there are two or more non-operator parties, it is often the case that one of these entities is a familiar entity, which similarly crops up frequently in Code cases. In such cases, it is often most convenient to refer to the case by reference to one of the other respondents, often the first respondent, even where that party has not taken (or has ceased to take) an active part in the proceedings. A good example of such a case is *Ashloch*.

1.05 In the Table of Cases, these abbreviations are set out together with the full names and citations of the cases.

1.06 Reference to cases by utilising the names of the respective litigants is of course standard practice and familiar to lawyers. Surveyors very often favour building or property names (Maple House, Pendown Farm, etc). However, as this is principally a legal textbook, and out of habit, this approach has not generally been taken here. However, where the respondent party has appeared in a number of cases, the approach taken has been to refer to the case in that party's name, with the property mentioned in parentheses thereafter (for example '*Hackney* (Shoreditch House)').

The terms 'court' and 'tribunal'

1.07 In cases under the Code, there has always been, and continues to be, a concurrent jurisdiction on the part of the county court, the Upper Tribunal (Lands Chamber) and the First-tier Tribunal (Property Chamber), and this is discussed in more detail in Chapters 5 and 21. The former requirement that proceedings under the Code be commenced in the Upper Tribunal is no longer in force, and at time of writing the expectation of the tribunals is that Code cases will be commenced in the FTT.

1.08 The form of drafting deployed in the Code operates by using the term 'court' to refer to any of the Courts and Tribunals which have jurisdiction. Although it has been technically possible for a New Code case to be heard in the county court, it does not appear that this has thus far happened. Thus, when applications and judicial decisions are being discussed in this book on a general level, the word "Tribunal" tends to be used, to reflect reality.

1.09 Thus, where it is said of a provision that a tribunal can only grant a particular remedy in certain circumstances, it is implied that the same is also true of any court to which the same provision applies. The use of the word 'court' could instead have been deployed for consistency with the Code, but consistency with real-world practice is considered preferable. Further, referring to a court when those who have thus far been procedural custodians of procedure within Code litigation are expecting and encouraging all future cases to be commenced in the FTT may be at best confusing to readers, and at worst may cause them adverse costs consequences or delay.

2

The continuing effect of the Old Code

2.01 The Old Code has been repealed, and a detailed explanation of its provisions is beyond the scope of this work. However, there are two main reasons why it is necessary to have some understanding of the Old Code:

(i) the provisions of the Old Code are relevant to whether an agreement is a subsisting agreement under the New Code, and if so, who is bound by its terms; and

(ii) some of the provisions of the Old Code continue to apply, in respect of agreements entered into, or things done, before the New Code came into force.

Subsisting agreements and who is bound

2.02 In order for an agreement to constitute a 'subsisting agreement' it must have been an agreement for the purposes of paras 2 or 3 of the Old Code or an Order under para 5 of the Old Code. Subsisting agreements are considered in more detail in Chapter 16.

2.03 The effect of paras 2(3) and (4) of the Old Code was that a successor in title of a landowning grantor of Code rights would be bound by the grantor's obligations in the relevant Code agreement. By para 2(5), such a successor would have the benefit of the grantor's rights under the agreement regardless of any assignment of the benefit.[1] However, it is important to note that under the Old Code it was not possible for an operator to assign the burden of a Code agreement, where that Code agreement was not a lease.[2]

2.04 A person who is bound by a right by virtue of para 2(3) of the Old Code continues to be bound by it for as long as they would if para 2(3) of the Old Code continued to have effect.[3]

2.05 A person who is bound by a right by virtue of para 2(4) of the Old Code in consequence of a subsisting agreement is treated as bound pursuant to Part 2 of the New Code.[4]

1 See the *Burlington Gardens* case [2024] UKUT 263 (LC) at [201].
2 Ibid at [221].
3 Para 4(1) of the Transitional Provisions.
4 Para 2(2) of the Transitional Provisions.

What parts of the Old Code continue to apply, and when?

2.06 Below is a summary of the more important ways in which the Transitional Provisions apply, modify or substitute certain provisions of the Old Code.

Notices

2.07 Part 15 of the New Code applies in relation to notices under the Transitional Provisions as it applies in relation to notices under the New Code.[5] Part 15 of the Code makes provision as to certain content and service requirements for notices. These are discussed further at Chapter 20.

Pending notices served under the Old Code

2.08 If a notice was given under para 5(1)[6] of the Old Code before the New Code came into force, but no application to court was made by that time, the notice has effect as a New Code para 20(2) notice.[7]

Pending applications made under the Old Code

2.09 If a notice was given under para 5(1) of the Old Code before the New Code came into force and an application has been made to court in relation to the notice, the Old Code continues to apply in relation to the application.[8] However, an Order made under the Old Code in such a case has effect as an order under para 20 of the New Code.[9]

2.10 The coming into force of the New Code does not affect any application or Order made under para 6[10] of the Old Code.

Compensation

2.11 The repeal of the Old Code does not affect para 16 of the Old Code, or any other right to compensation, as it applies in relation to the exercise of a right before the New Code came into force.[11]

2.12 In relation to a person bound by a Code right by virtue of para 2(3) of the Old Code, paras 4(4) to (12) of the Old Code continue to have effect, but as if in para 4(4)(b), the reference to para 21 of the Old Code were a reference to Part

5 Para 23 of the Transitional Provisions.
6 This was the provision by which an operator gave notice seeking Code rights, or requiring a person to be bound.
7 Para 11 of the Transitional Provisions.
8 Para 12(1) and (2) of the Transitional Provisions.
9 Para 12(3) of the Transitional Provisions.
10 Para 6 of the Old Code related to temporary rights for apparatus which was already installed.
11 Para 14 of the Transitional Provisions.

6 of the New Code. Thus, in such a case, compensation is payable by an operator where depreciation is caused by the fact that *Part 6* is to apply to the removal of apparatus.[12]

2.13 A person entitled to compensation by virtue of the Transitional Provisions is not entitled to compensation in respect of the same matter under any provision of the New Code.[13] Thus, double recovery is avoided.

Overhead apparatus

2.14 The repeal of the Old Code does not affect paras 17 and 18 of the Old Code[14] as they apply in relation to anything whose installation was completed before the repeal.

Power to require alteration of apparatus

2.15 Para 20 of the Old Code related to the right of a person with an interest in land to give notice to require the alteration of apparatus in order to allow the carrying out of a proposed improvement to the land. The repeal of the Old Code does not affect para 20 of the Old Code as it applies in relation to anything whose installation was completed before the repeal.[15] However, this rule does not allow a right under para 20 of the Old Code to be exercised by a person who is a party to, or is bound by, an agreement under the New Code (as distinct from a subsisting agreement) in relation to the apparatus.[16]

2.16 It is thus important to note that, in a case where there is a subsisting agreement under which apparatus was installed before the New Code came into force, the landowner appears to have the option of serving an Old Code para 20 notice in order to seek alteration of the apparatus to carry out improvement works. Where an operator serves a counter-notice rather than agreeing to carry out the alteration, the landowner may apply to court for an Order requiring the alteration. However, such an Order will require the landowner to reimburse the operator's costs of complying with the Order ('unless the court otherwise thinks fit'). Given that such costs can be significant, it is not surprising that the right to serve an Old Code para 20 notice is not one that is regularly taken up by landowners following the coming into force of the Code.

Right to require removal of apparatus

2.17 If a notice was given under para 21(2) of the Old Code before the New Code came into force, requiring the removal of apparatus, the repeal of the Old Code

12 Para 4(2) of the Transitional Provisions.

13 Para 25 of the Transitional Provisions.

14 Para 16(1) of the Transitional Provisions. Paras 17 and 18 of the Old Code related to objections to overhead apparatus, and the operator's obligation to affixed notices to overhead apparatus.

15 Para 16(1) of the Transitional Provisions.

16 Paras 16(2) and (3) of the Transitional Provisions.

does not affect the operation of Old Code para 21 in relation to anything done or that may be done under that provision following the giving of the notice.[17] In such a case, the steps specified in a counter-notice under Old Code para 21(4)(b) (as steps which the operator proposed to take in order to secure a right) are to be read as including any corresponding steps that the operator could take under the New Code or by virtue of the Transitional Provisions.[18]

17 Para 20(1) and (2) of the Transitional Provisions.
18 Para 20(3) of the Transitional Provisions.

3

Background to the Code

3.01 The Old Code came into force as Schedule 2 to the Telecommunications Act 1984. The context of that Act was the privatisation of British Telecom, and the consequential advent of a much more competitive marketplace involving a plurality of network operators. However, this was still a time when phone calls were overwhelmingly made on handsets using fixed-line technology, and the World Wide Web was still some way from its inception.

3.02 At the beginning of the new millennium, following much technological change, a number of European Directives[1] were made. Consequently, a number of amendments were made to the Old Code by the Communications Act 2003. For this reason, the Old Code is sometimes referred to as the '2003 Code'.

3.03 In describing the background to the New Code in the Court of Appeal in *Compton Beauchamp*,[2] Lewison LJ referred to the Old Code, noting the 'wide dissatisfaction with that code for a number of reasons'.

3.04 A review of the operation of the Old Code was commissioned by the government in 2011, leading to a Law Commission Consultation Paper,[3] and then to a Law Commission Report in February 2013.[4]

3.05 The Law Commission cited three main reasons for which the Code needed reform, which might be summarised as follows:

(i) It was complex, difficult to understand, and had been subject to strong judicial criticism. Some of its lack of clarity related to its relationship with other statutory regimes.[5]

(ii) Its approach was outdated and based on much older legislation at a time when other technologies were widespread. One resultant problem was the failure to envisage that a leasehold estate might be necessary or desirable for operators.

(iii) It appeared to be making the rollout of networks more difficult. This may partly have been due to the lack of clarity over important matters. These

1 Namely Directive 2002/19/EC, Directive 2002/20/EC, Directive 2002/21/EC, Directive 2002/22/EC and Directive 2002/58/EC.

2 *Cornerstone Telecommunications Infrastructure Ltd v Compton Beauchamp Estates Ltd* [2019] EWCA Civ 1755. This decision was appealed to the Supreme Court, but no doubt was cast on this summary of the background to the Code, which was also cited in the above form by the Court of Appeal in *The University of London v Cornerstone Telecommunications Infrastructure Limited* [2019] EWCA Civ 2075.

3 No. 205, June 2012.

4 Law Commission Report No. 336: 'The Electronic Communications Code', 27 February 2013.

5 The Law Commission at Law Com 336, para 1.9, cites the Land Registration Act 2002, but one could cite others including the Landlord and Tenant Act 1954.

included who was bound by rights, how to assess the level of payments for rights, and how termination of rights was enforced.

3.06 In diagnosing the problems, the Law Commission commented that it was not clear that the Old Code struck the right balance between operators and landowners. It further envisaged that reform of the law would involve striking a balance in the light of the contrasting interests of those two categories of parties, but also in the interests of the public, who have increasing and evolving reliance on and expectations of communications services.

3.07 The test[6] for the imposition of Code rights puts public interest at its centre. Given that compulsory powers of acquisition are in play and given that the policy imperative behind the Code is the provision of services for the public, this naturally makes a good deal of sense.

3.08 However, as shall be seen, the balance between operators and landowners has not been calibrated by the legislation in the way recommended by the Law Commission in one key area, namely 'consideration'. The Law Commission recommended that consideration should be set by reference to a market value with ransom value stripped out. However, the government instead attempted to enact what it referred to as a 'no scheme"[7] valuation, radically reducing Code rents when compared with the Old Code. The justification was to incentivise and thereby bring about the rollout of sites by operators.

3.09 It was clearly sub-optimal that the Old Code was not a model of clarity. But the fact that it was essentially regarded as providing for something akin to a market rent meant that landowners were relatively content to have ECA on their sites. There was a stark difference between the apparent need for litigation to render the words of the Old Code tolerably clear and the striking paucity of litigation that transpired. This can largely be explained by the parties essentially being sanguine about their lot. A landowner would not be so exercised about giving away favourable terms to an operator if it was to get a decent rent. One might also point to a nervous truce between blocs of parties that did not want to establish any precedent which might markedly and negatively change their position. But that explanation is essentially a negative way of saying a similar thing. The parties were not sufficiently unhappy to fight.

3.10 That equilibrium was shattered by the valuation mechanism in the New Code. Now that landowners are receiving a fraction of what they used to receive (and the figures in the eyes of many have been lower than had been anticipated by government), there is a greater desire on the part of many landowners not to be encumbered by operators whose removal is difficult, expensive and time-consuming. Further, where a landowner realistically accepts that Code rights will be imposed, it is not so willing to allow the operator to have its favoured terms now that it is receiving a lot less for them.

6 See paras 21(3) and (4) of the New Code.

7 The tribunals have generally preferred the term "no-network' (a term coined by the Deputy President in *Islington*) to "no scheme'. Consideration under the New Code is discussed in detail in Chapter 13.

3.11 The result is that the anticipated impetus of the New Code for network rollout has not been as strong as had been desired by policy-makers. This was a possibility that the Law Commission had considered to be a real possibility in recommending that something akin to a market rent be maintained.

3.12 The government's Impact Assessment in advance of the New Code did recognise the risk of increased litigiousness. It included the following assessment of 'Key assumptions/sensitivities/risks":

> 'The impact on the wayleave market has been estimated by an independent consultancy using industry data from across sectors. However, as the move to compulsory purchase principles is a major departure from current practice in the telecommunications market there is uncertainty as to how negotiations between operators and landowners will develop. This is also associated with the risk of an increase in legal disputes, although the staggered nature of contract renewals minimises the impact of this.'

3.13 Plainly there has been not merely an increase in legal disputes, but an explosion in their number.[8]

Machinery by which the Code was brought into force

3.14 Section 4(1) of the Digital Economy Act 2017 repealed the Old Code by providing that it be omitted from the Telecommunications Act 1984, of which it was then a part.[9] Section 4(2) of the 2017 Act inserts Schedule 3A (ie, the New Code) into the Communications Act 2003. The provisions which were to be inserted as Schedule 3A to the Communications Act 2003 were set out as Schedule 1 to the 2017 Act.

3.15 Section 5 of the 2017 Act gave the Secretary of State power to make transitional, transitory or saving provision in connection with the coming into force of section 4 and Schedule 1, ie, in relation to the coming into force of the New Code, and the section which repeals the Old Code and inserts the New Code.

3.16 By regulation 2 of the Digital Economy Act 2017 (Commencement No 3) Regulations 2017, the following legislation was brought into force with effect from 28 December 2017:

(a) Section 4 of the 2017 Act (insofar as it was not already in force).

(b) The Code (insofar as it was not already in force).

(c) The Transitional Provisions (ie, Schedule 2 to the Digital Economy Act 2017).

(d) Schedule 3 to the 2017 Act (insofar as it was not already in force), which made consequential amendments to other legislation.

---

8 For precise numbers, see **21.23**. As Old Code litigation was not conducted in a single specialist tribunal, data is harder to come by, but cases that fought all the way were few and far between.

9 The Old Code was Sch 2 to the Telecommunications Act 1984.

3.17 It is worth noting that certain paragraphs of the Transitional Provisions provide that the coming into force of the New Code, or the repeal of the Old Code, do not affect certain matters. The continuing effect of the Old Code in limited ways is considered in Chapter 2.

Amendments to the Code

3.18 Amendments have been made to the Code (and the Transitional Provisions) since it was first enacted.

3.19 The Telecommunications Infrastructure (Leasehold Property) Act 2021 inserted Part 4A of the Code, which deals with unresponsive occupiers in the leasehold context. It is fair to say that these provisions have not seen a lot of use.

3.20 The Product Security and Telecommunications Infrastructure 2022 ('PSTIA 2022') made more substantial changes to the Code, following a consultation process. These changes are referred to throughout the body of this book as they arise. Since this book was first published after the coming into force of the PSTIA 2022, it does not seem necessary to detail each of the changes made by that Act individually. However, some of the changes made were as follows:

(i) Section 58 amends the Transitional Provisions so as to allow operators under subsisting agreements to upgrade and share the use of apparatus in some circumstances.

(ii) Section 66 inserts a new para 27ZA into the Code, which allows Code rights to be refused on the ground of national security in certain instances.

(iii) Section 68 inserts paras 35(2A) and (2B), which allow the tribunal to award interim consideration, and to amend the terms of an agreement pending determination of a renewal application.

(iv) Section 69 makes various amendments which are intended to encourage the use of ADR.

3.21 The changes that the PSTIA 2022 would make to the law relating to agreements conferring Code rights have not yet all been brought into force. These include some of the most significant, namely the changes to the Landlord and Tenant Act 1954. Renewals of certain leases (namely subsisting agreements whose primary purpose was to grant Code rights) will be brought into line with renewals of Code agreements under Part 5. This will remove the 'no-network' assumption, provide for compensation, and allow for renewals to be carried out within the tribunal system.

3.22 One of the issues initially intended to be addressed by this Act was the problem of whether an operator *in situ* could apply for Code rights. However, this was clarified in a similar way by the Supreme Court, and hence the Act did not need to provide any solution for that matter. Thus the relevant proposed clauses of the original Bill were removed.

4

The Code in 1000 words

4.01 The Code is about rights over land. It regulates the relationship between: (i) occupiers of land; and (ii) operators.[1] Operators provide either a network with electronic communications apparatus ('ECA'), or an infrastructure system to be made available to the providers of such networks.

4.02 In order for operators to assemble and maintain a network or infrastructure system, they need to acquire rights over land. The Code refers to a menu of rights as 'Code rights'.[2] These include installing and keeping ECA on land, doing various things to ECA once it is there (inspecting, maintaining, repairing, upgrading etc), carrying out works in connection with the above or in connection with sharing the use of the ECA with another operator, entering the land for the above purposes, connecting a power supply, interfering with a means of access, and lopping trees.

4.03 Code rights can only be conferred by an agreement between an operator and an occupier of land.[3] Such an agreement must comply with certain formalities[4] and include certain terms. If an agreement is not reached consensually, an operator can serve a notice and ask the tribunal to impose an agreement that confers Code rights (or which renders a person bound by Code rights).[5] To succeed, an operator must show that the prejudice caused to the respondent is capable of being compensated for by money and outweighed by the public benefit likely to result.[6] This is typically not easy for a landowner to resist. If a landowner can show that it intends to redevelop the land and cannot reasonably do so if the Order sought is made, that is a standalone defence.[7] An agreement imposed by the tribunal takes effect as a consensual agreement.[8] Code litigation involves a 'costs' regime.[9]

4.04 Most terms in an imposed agreement are those considered 'appropriate'[10] by the tribunal. Consideration (rent) is determined by a statutory formula that involves disregarding that the right entails use for a network ('the no-network assumption'). This typically depresses consideration to less than would be agreed in the open market or under the Old Code. Much litigation has resulted.

1 Persons designated as such under s 106 of the Communications Act 2003.
2 Para 3.
3 Para 9.
4 Para 11.
5 Para 20.
6 Para 21(2) and (3).
7 Para 21(5).
8 Para 22.
9 Para 96.
10 Para 23(2).

4.05 The Code grants basic rights[11] to share the use of ECA with other operators and upgrade ECA, subject to certain safeguards, but tribunals can enlarge these rights. Terms that make upgrading or sharing rights subject to paying money are void.[12]

4.06 Where an agreement is imposed, the landowner is entitled to compensation for loss and damage sustained as a result of the exercise of Code rights.[13] Such an application can be made later if there is loss not already taken into account.[14] There are provisions detailing who is bound by a Code agreement.[15] An 'ordinary' Code agreement statutorily continues at the end of its contractual term.[16]

4.07 Two types of agreement can only be created by the tribunal (subject to a notice procedure) and do not statutorily continue after their stated term.[17] First, interim agreements,[18] which need not be interim 'to' anything. These sometimes grant rights to undertake preliminary surveys.[19] To obtain such an agreement, an operator must merely show a 'good arguable case'[20] that the ordinary test for imposition is met, but in any event are discretionary. Second, there are temporary agreements,[21] which can be sought only where ECA is already present on land and the landowner has the right to require its removal.

4.08 How one terminates or renews an agreement will depend on what kind of agreement it is and when it was entered into. Where an agreement is a lease granted before the Code came into force, its primary purpose was to grant Code rights, and it was not 'contracted out' of the 1954 Act, it must be terminated or renewed under the Landlord and Tenant Act 1954.[22] The provisions as to valuation of rent and imposition of terms are familiar ones under the 1954 Act, but subject to imminent amendments. New provisions[23] of the 1954 Act will bring these matters into line with the Code (including by applying the no-network assumption). Where a new tenancy is ordered whose primary purpose is to grant Code rights, the 1954 Act will not thereafter apply to it[24] and it will be a Code agreement.

4.09 Where an agreement was entered into before the Code came into force but is not a lease, it will be terminated or renewed under the Code.[25]

---

11 Para 17.
12 Para 17(5).
13 Paras 25 and 84.
14 Para 25(2)(b).
15 Para 10.
16 Para 30(2). This continuation does not apply to interim agreements or temporary agreements imposed under paras 26 and 27 respectively, by virtue of para 30(3).
17 Para 30(3).
18 Para 26.
19 See the Court of Appeal's judgment in *The University of London v Cornerstone Telecommunications Infrastructure Limited* [2019] EWCA Civ 2075.
20 Para 26(3)(b).
21 Para 27.
22 See the Supreme Court's judgment in *Ashloch* [2022] UKSC 18.
23 See the Product Security and Telecommunications Infrastructure Act 2022.
24 By s 43(4) of the Landlord and Tenant Act 1954.
25 See the Transitional Provisions at Sch 2 to the Digital Economy Act 2017, para 7(1).

4.10 Under the Code a landowner generally needs to give 18 months' notice in order to seek to terminate a Code agreement.[26] It must specify and satisfy a ground[27] for termination: (a) substantial breaches by the operator, (b) persistent delay in payments by the operator, (c) an intention to redevelop, or (d) that the test for the imposition of the agreement is no longer met.

4.11 Either party may seek to modify or renew the current agreement by serving six months' notice, which expires after the contractual end of the Code agreement.[28] The tribunal then has a broad range of options, including terminating the agreement, imposing a wholly new one, merely extending the original agreement, and amending its terms.[29]

4.12 The fact that an operator is already in occupation does not stop it from seeking Code rights where it has none, or from seeking additional Code rights. However, it cannot seek to modify its current bargain as to terms outside of the above procedure.[30]

4.13 Where a landowner has the right to require removal[31] of ECA (for example because it has terminated an agreement or the operator has no Code rights), it can serve a notice requiring removal,[32] and seek to enforce its rights by applying for a removal Order, which it is entitled to as of right, subject to the tribunal having discretion over timescales. However, the operator may be able to serve a notice and seek Code rights. If it does so, its application must be determined before any Order requiring removal can be made.[33]

4.14 The Code also confers certain rights to install ECA in particular places such as highways.34

26 Para 31.
27 Paras 31(2)(c) and 31(4).
28 Para 33.
29 Para 34.
30 See the Supreme Court's judgment in *Compton Beauchamp* [2022] UKSC 18.
31 Para 37.
32 Para 40.
33 Para 40(8).
34 Part 8 of the Code.

5

Key definitions and concepts

5.01 This chapter discusses some of the key terms that are used in the Code. Some terms are defined throughout the Code, and in addition there is an interpretation provision at para 108. Other terms are defined within the body of the Communications Act 2003 itself. Section 32 defines electronic communications networks and services, and section 405 is a general interpretation section.

'The court' (para 94)

5.02 The Code makes frequent reference to 'the court'. This is the entity to which applications are made, for example, by operators for the imposition of Code rights or by landowners for Orders that ECA be removed. Although para 94 includes a definition of 'the court', this definition on its own may prove misleading. In practice, the entity exercising the powers of 'the court' under the Code will increasingly be the First-tier Tribunal. The meaning of 'the court' and the different forums that have jurisdiction to hear Code disputes are discussed in more detail in Chapter 21.

'Operator' (para 2)

5.03 By para 2 of the Code, an 'operator' is a person in whose case the Code is applied, by a direction under section 106 of the Communications Act 2003.

5.04 Additionally, where the Secretary of State is providing or proposing to provide an electronic communications network, the Secretary of State is an operator.

5.05 Where, immediately before the New Code came into force, the Old Code applied to an entity by virtue of a direction made by OFCOM under section 106(3)(a), such direction shall be treated as having been made in relation to the New Code.[1]

'Occupier' (para 105(1))

5.06 This is a term that caused much interest, debate, and dispute in the first years of the New Code. In a typical case, para 105(1) helps only by indicating that references to an occupier of land 'are to the occupier of the land for the time being'.

1 By virtue of para 3(2) of the Electronic Communications Code (Transitional Provisions) Regulations 2017.

5.07 The principal reason for which it is important to identify the 'occupier' of land is that Code rights can only be conferred on an operator by an agreement between an occupier and an operator (see para 9(1)).

5.08 Before the Supreme Court judgment in *Compton Beauchamp*,[2] a problem had arisen in that an operator who was already in occupation of land was considered unable to acquire Code rights by serving a para 20 notice, as it was itself the occupier.

5.09 Clause 57 of the PSTI Bill[3] as first introduced to Parliament would have solved this problem by deeming a different person to be the occupier in cases where land was occupied by an operator. The occupier was to be considered to be a person who exercises powers of management or control over the land, or if there was no such person, persons whose interest in the land would be prejudicially affected by the exercise of a Code right. In this sense, the *Compton Beauchamp* judgment would not have made a great deal of difference on the main issue in the case one way or another. In the event, the Supreme Court overturned the previous understanding of the law, clause 57 of the PSTI Bill was not needed, and the PSTIA[4] as enacted did not need to address the issue.

5.10 As to who is the occupier, Lady Rose (with whom the remainder of the court agreed) concluded as follows:

(i) The starting point is that the word 'occupier' in different statutory provisions has no fixed meaning. Rather, its meaning is taken from its statutory context and the purpose of the provisions in which it is used [102].

(ii) It is inherent in para 9, read in context, that the 'operator' who seeks a Code right is different from the 'occupier of the land', who has the power to confer Code rights [116], and the fundamental premise of para 9 is that the operator and occupier are different persons [117].

(iii) Where an operator seeks Code rights under para 20 of the Code, it is not to be regarded as the occupier for para 9 purposes merely because it has ECA installed on that site under previous Code rights. To hold otherwise would frustrate the way the Code should operate [137].

(iv) Accordingly, it is necessary to disregard the actual occupation of the operator, which seeks Code rights, when ascertaining what person is the 'occupier' for para 9 purposes. However, it is only the occupation of *that* operator that is ignored. If another person who happens to be an operator is 'the occupier of the land for the time being'[5] (para 105(1)), that latter operator's occupation is not to be ignored. That latter operator is the occupier who must be approached by the operator who is now seeking Code rights [140].

(v) Where an operator is in occupation through its ECA, and it seeks Code rights, the occupier for para 9 purposes 'will usually be the person who has

2 *Cornerstone Telecommunications Infrastructure Ltd v Compton Beauchamp Estates Ltd* [2022] UKSC 18.
3 Product Security and Telecommunications Infrastructure Bill, introduced to Parliament on 24 November 2021.
4 Product Security and Telecommunications Infrastructure Act 2022.
5 This was the unusual factual situation in *Compton Beauchamp*, and was the reason why the operator lost its appeal despite reversing the Court of Appeal's conclusion that an operator in situ could never use para 20 to seek Code rights.

conferred the rights which led to the installation of the ECA on the site, but may be its successor in title' [138].

Who is the 'occupier' where there is no operator in occupation?

5.11 The problem in *Compton Beauchamp* was a particular one relating to whether, and in what circumstances, an operator who is already in situ is to be considered the occupier of land for para 9 purposes. This gave rise to a wholesale consideration of the structure of the Code in order to reveal the answer to this legal question.

5.12 However, *Compton Beauchamp* does not shed an awful lot of light on how one determines the identity of the occupier where no operator is in situ. In the Court of Appeal, it had been held that the Upper Tribunal was 'correct to hold at [71] that whether a person is an occupier for the purposes of the Code is 'a question of fact rather than legal status; it means physical presence on and control of the land." In a typical situation where there is no operator occupying the relevant land, this would appear to be a test that would be applied when considering who is the 'occupier of the land for the time being' under para 105 and hence the occupier for para 9 purposes.

'Occupier' where the land is unoccupied

5.13 In respect of land that is unoccupied (and which is not a street), para 105(6) provides that the occupier is considered to be:

'(a) the person (if any) who for the time being exercises powers of management or control over the land, or

(b) if there is no person within paragraph (a), to every person whose interest in the land would be prejudicially affected by the exercise of a code right in relation to the land.'

Occupiers in relation to streets

5.14 Section 105 also makes provision as to who is to be considered the occupier in relation to:

(i) a footpath or bridleway that crosses and forms part of agricultural land;[6]

(ii) a street not falling within the above description.[7]

The 'Occupier' under the Old Code – identity and evidence

5.15 Just as under the New Code, it was an 'occupier' who conferred Code rights on an operator under the Old Code (as can be seen from para 2(1) of the Old Code).

6 Para 105(2) and (7).
7 Para 105(3) and (4).

In *Gencomp*,[8] the Deputy President agreed with the parties that the 'person whose agreement was required to confer an old Code right should be understood to have been the person who would have been the occupier if occupation by the operator seeking the right was ignored'.

5.16 Also in that case,[9] the Deputy President gave useful guidance as to any evidential difficulties in establishing whether the purported grantor of historical rights was indeed the occupier:

> 'In most cases it is likely that the proper inference from a formal agreement conferring code rights (especially if it is a lease) will be that the grantor and not a third party was in occupation. An operator wishing to obtain an order from the Tribunal for termination of an existing agreement and the grant of a new agreement will not be required to plead or prove that nobody else was in occupation (which, as Mr Read submitted, may be very difficult). The burden of establishing that the original grantor was not in occupation at the relevant time, and that the existing agreement was therefore not a subsisting agreement, will fall on the site provider trying to defeat the claim for new rights. The circumstances in which proof of those unusual facts is available are likely to be wholly exceptional….'

5.17 These comments would appear to be of similar application in respect of agreements entered into under the New Code.

'Code rights' (para 3)

5.18 Paragraph 3(1) of the Code sets out an exhaustive list of 'code rights' to which the Code makes frequent reference:

> '3(1) For the purposes of this code a 'code right', in relation to an operator and any land, is a right for the statutory purposes—
>
> (a) to install electronic communications apparatus on, under or over the land,
>
> (b) to keep installed electronic communications apparatus which is on, under or over the land,
>
> (c) to inspect, maintain, adjust, alter, repair, upgrade or operate electronic communications apparatus which is on, under or over the land,
>
> (ca) to share with another operator the use of electronic communications apparatus which the first operator keeps installed on, under or over the land,
>
> (d) to carry out any works on the land for or in connection with the installation of electronic communications apparatus on, under or over the land or elsewhere,

8 [2022] UKUT 223 (LC) at [46]. Although the UT's decision was overturned by the Court of Appeal on appeal, one would think that this conclusion as to the effect of the Old Code remains undisturbed, as it was supported by both parties, and the appeal related to the effect of para 10(3) specifically.

9 [2022] UKUT 223 (LC) at [52].

(e) to carry out any works on the land for or in connection with the maintenance, adjustment, alteration, repair, upgrading or operation of electronic communications apparatus which is on, under or over the land or elsewhere,

(ea) to carry out any works on the land for the purposes of, or in connection with, sharing with another operator the use of electronic communications apparatus which the first operator keeps installed on, under or over the land or elsewhere,

(f) to enter the land to inspect, maintain, adjust, alter, repair, upgrade or operate any electronic communications apparatus which is on, under or over the land or elsewhere,

(fa) to enter the land for the purposes of, or in connection with, sharing with another operator the use of electronic communications apparatus which the first operator keeps installed on, under or over the land or elsewhere,

(g) to connect to a power supply,

(h) to interfere with or obstruct a means of access to or from the land (whether or not any electronic communications apparatus is on, under or over the land), or

(i) to lop or cut back, or require another person to lop or cut back, any tree or other vegetation that interferes or will or may interfere with electronic communications apparatus.'

Requirement to specify Code rights in a notice

5.19 A notice seeking Code rights must specify which of those rights set out in the menu of Code rights at para 3 of the Code are sought in a particular case. Failure to specify a particular Code right in a notice will mean that the Tribunal lacks jurisdiction to impose such a Code right upon a Reference being made to it. As Judge Cooke said in *Keast*:[10]

> 'Obviously the Tribunal cannot impose upon the occupier of land any Code right that has not been sought in the paragraph 20 notice; that is perfectly clear from the terms of paragraph 20.'

5.20 The one potential caveat to the above statement is that by para 17, certain limited rights to upgrade ECA and share its use with another operator are conferred automatically to an operator that has entered into an agreement under Part 2. By para 22, an agreement imposed by the Tribunal is treated as an agreement under Part 2. It may well be that the statement in *Keast*, above, insofar as it relates to sharing and upgrading rights means that the Tribunal cannot impose any such Code rights in excess of those granted automatically by para 17. Sharing and upgrading are dealt with in Chapter 12.

10 [2019] UKUT 116 (LC) at [29].

Effects of a right being a 'code right'

5.21 Although it will often make no practical difference which rights in a proposed agreement are 'Code rights' and which are not. This is particularly the case given the breadth of the types of term that the Tribunal is empowered to impose.[11]

5.22 However, the distinction was clearly considered sufficiently important to necessitate the addition of the right to share the use of ECA to the menu of para 3 Code rights by legislation,[12] notwithstanding that sharing rights were already conferred by para 17(1)(a) of the Code. This followed the Tribunal's judgment in *Green* in which a distinction was made between sharing (which was not at that time a Code right) and upgrading (which was indeed a Code right, and remains so).

5.23 In some cases there are certain basic consequences following from a right being categorised as a Code right or not, as follows.

(i) A notice will be invalid if it contains no Code rights

A notice under para 20, 26 or 27 must[13] specify at least one Code right. The Tribunal will lack jurisdiction to impose any agreement which contains the conferral of no Code rights (or which asks for a person to be bound by a right which contain no Code rights). Accordingly, it is necessary to understand what the true scope of a particular Code right is.

The obvious example in the case law thus far is the dispute in *University of London*[14] as to whether the right to carry out non-intrusive surveys (often referred to as MSVs) in order to confirm the potential suitability for land for the future installation of ECA was itself a Code right. The Court of Appeal held that it was. That issue is discussed in Chapter 9, which deals with para 26 agreements.

(ii) An agreement conferring Code rights must satisfy paras 9 and 11

As discussed in Chapter 6, which relates to agreements, in order for an agreement to confer a Code right in respect of land, such conferral must be *by* the occupier of that land and *on* an operator. The formalities and content requirements of para 11 must also be observed.

(iii) A valid agreement containing Code rights will be an agreement under Part 2

If an agreement confers rights, which are Code rights, it will be an agreement under Part 2 of the Code. Hence, by para 29(1), Part 5 of the Code will apply

---

11 See *Keast*, where it is accepted that there may be a limit to the Tribunal's discretion (at [60]), but the arguments seeking to restrict the rights that a Tribunal may impose were rejected in that case.

12 The insertion of the new Code right at para 3(1)(ca) was made by ss 57(2)(b)(i) of the Product Security and Telecommunications Infrastructure Act 2022 ('PSTI 2022'). This came into force on 7 February 2023 by s 79(2) of the PSTI 2022 and reg 2(a) of the Product Security and Telecommunications Infrastructure Act 2022 (Commencement No. 1) Regulations 2023. Note that by s 57(7) of the PSTI, the amendment does not affect any rights conferred under Part 2 of the Code before the coming into force of s 57 (on 7 February 2023).

13 Para 20(2)(a) creates this requirement in respect of a para 20 notice. In the case of rights to be imposed on an interim basis under para 26, para 26(3) requires a notice to be served that complies with para 20(2). In the case of temporary rights under para 27, para 27(1)(a) requires the service of a para 20 notice, such that para 20(2)(a) will apply.

14 *The University of London v Cornerstone Telecommunications Infrastructure Limited* [2019] EWCA Civ 2075.

to it.[15] A number of consequences will flow. These include: that it will be capable of statutory continuation at the end of its contractual term;[16] that in order to terminate it, a site provider will need to give notice[17] under para 31 in reliance on a statutory ground; that automatic sharing and upgrading rights apply;[18] and that certain provisions may be void.[19]

(iv) Some rights may not be sought by an operator with an extant agreement

Following the Supreme Court's decision in *Compton Beauchamp*, an operator is not entitled to seek to modify the terms on which it currently exercises Code rights under an extant agreement. However, it *is* entitled to seek additional Code rights that it does not currently have under its extant agreement. The distinction between a modification of terms and an additional Code right is therefore of some potential importance to an operator occupying under an agreement. It remains to be seen how and where the Tribunals will draw the line between the two.

'The statutory purposes' (para 4)

5.24 It is important to note that no right to do anything can ever be a 'Code right' unless it is a right 'for the statutory purposes'. The statutory purposes are defined at para 4, and are:

- 'providing the operator's network'; and/or
- 'providing an infrastructure system'.

5.25 These definitions bring into play the definition of 'operator' (para 2), 'network' (para 6), and 'infrastructure system' (para 7). Paragraph 9 is also relevant: A Code right may only be conferred on an operator.

'Electronic communications apparatus' (para 5); and 'Land' (para 108(1))

5.26 It is worth considering these two concepts together, for reasons that will become evident.

5.27 Paragraph 5(1) defines 'electronic communications apparatus' for the purposes of the Code as:

'(a) apparatus designed or adapted for use in connection with the provision of an electronic communications network,

15 Save in the case of the very limited exception at para 29(2) concerning particular leases whose primary purpose is not to grant Code rights.

16 By para 30(2). However, this does not apply in the case of an agreement imposed under para 26 or para 27 (see para 30(3)).

17 Such notice is ordinarily required to be of at least 18 months' duration (by para 31(3)(a)), and the permitted statutory grounds are at para 31(4).

18 Under para 17.

19 Paras 16(1) and 17(5) render void certain provisions which purport to restrict assignment, sharing and upgrading.

(b) apparatus designed or adapted for a use which consists of or includes the sending or receiving of communications or other signals that are transmitted by means of an electronic communications network,

(c) lines, and

(d) other structures or things designed or adapted for use in connection with the provision of an electronic communications network.'

5.28 The Code definitions of 'line' and 'structure' are at para 5(3):

> "line' means any wire, cable, tube, pipe or similar thing (including its casing or coating) which is designed or adapted for use in connection with the provision of any electronic communications network or electronic communications service;
>
> 'structure' includes a building only if the sole purpose of that building is to enclose other electronic communications apparatus.'

5.29 Thus the scope of the physical type of equipment or material that is capable of constituting electronic communications apparatus ('ECA') is defined 'in broad terms, which reflect its diversity'.[20] Some structures or pieces of 'kit' that would not otherwise be recognisable as ECA nonetheless fall within that definition where they are designed or adapted for a use that has the requisite relationship with an electronic communications network or service. Whether a particular structure or thing has been adapted such that it is ECA is a question of fact, which will depend on all the circumstances.[21]

5.30 A building is capable of constituting ECA only[22] where its 'sole purpose'[23] is to enclose other ECA. This is an important qualification. By para 108(1), 'land' does not include electronic communications apparatus.

5.31 Paragraph 3(1) provides that for the purposes of the Code, 'a 'code right', in relation to an operator and any *land*, is a right for the statutory purposes…' to carry out certain specified activities [emphasis added]. There is no other definition of Code right in the Code. Furthermore, each of the Code rights expressly mentions land, save for the relatively ancillary rights at para 3(g) ('to connect to a power supply') and para 3(i) (which relates to lopping trees and other vegetation). Thus, it is clear that a Code right can only exist if it relates to land.

5.32 This evident conclusion fits with para 9(1), which makes provision for the manner in which a Code right can come into being:

> 'A code right in respect of land may only be conferred on an operator by an agreement between the occupier of the land and the operator.'

---

20 Per the Explanatory Notes to the Digital Economy Act 2017 at para 403.

21 The Explanatory Notes at para 403 express the view that these circumstances will include 'what the parties have agreed, the nature of the installation and the extent of the adaptation'.

22 This is assuming that a building was not intended to constitute 'apparatus' within paras 5(1)(a) or (b) or a 'thing' within para 5(1)(d). Not only are those words less than obvious descriptors of a building, but if a building could fall within the meanings of those words, it would render the qualification of 'structure' at para 5(3) pointless, and allow a building to constitute ECA without satisfying that qualificatory description.

23 See para 5(3).

5.33 The definition of ECA at para 5 and the provisions relating to land at para 108(1) interact with important consequences. Two such consequences were identified in the *BT (Kenton Road)*[24] case as follows:

> '20. The consequence of the interaction of those provisions is that where the claimant[25] gives a mobile operator the right to mount antennae on one of its masts, the agreement between them is not a Code agreement, because the operator's right is to install apparatus on other apparatus and not on land.
>
> 21. A further consequence is that the right to install equipment on a building is not a Code right if "the sole purpose of that building is to enclose other electronic communications apparatus"….'

5.34 The exclusion of ECA from the definition of 'land' was not something recommended by the Law Commission. Rather, the exclusion became necessary because of the decision to deviate from the Law Commission's recommendation as to the consideration payable in respect of Code rights. The Law Commission recommended that consideration under the Code should be at a market rate. Instead, the Code was enacted with a provision for assessing consideration that contains the 'no-network' assumption,[26] thus substantially reducing what is paid under a Code agreement (see Chapter 13 regarding consideration). Mobile operators need infrastructure providers to stay in business to provide costly infrastructure such as masts. If infrastructure providers could only charge consideration at Code rates, they would not be able to make their profit from charging mobile operators to install ECA on their infrastructure. For this reason, ECA was excluded from the definition of 'land', so that where rights are granted over ECA, those rights cannot be Code rights and will not attract the protection of the Code, or the favourable valuation assumptions at para 24.

5.35 The Explanatory Notes relating to the Code said as follows at 403:

> '*Paragraph 5* defines *electronic communications apparatus* i.e. the apparatus which can be installed on, under or over land. This definition is important for two reasons. Firstly, it defines the scope of what can be installed and kept on land under the provisions of the code. Secondly, because paragraph 108(1) specifically provides that land does not include electronic communications apparatus, anything that falls within the definition of 'electronic communications apparatus' (as it is set out in paragraph 5) cannot have code rights imposed against it. This has the practical effect of ensuring that one code operator cannot seek to exercise code rights against the apparatus of another (or indeed against the apparatus of a person who is not a code operator).'

5.36 The last words above are worth noting: it is true that an operator cannot exercise Code rights against the ECA of another, but that is not because of the fact that the ECA belongs to an operator. It is because it is ECA. Thus, where a site provider has ECA, as defined by para 5, Code rights seemingly cannot be conferred over that ECA in favour of an operator. Code rights can only be conferred which relate to land, and ECA is not land.

---

24 [2024] UKUT 51 (LC).

25 The Claimant was an infrastructure provider which is an operator.

26 Para 24(3)(a).

5.37 A number of Code rights consist of things being done 'on, under or over' land. It is true that where an operator is granted the right to install ECA on a mast, that ECA will be over land in the most literal sense. But the orthodoxy is that where an operator grants another operator the right to install ECA on a mast, that is not to be considered a Code right, as the ECA is installed on ECA. Any other conclusion would arguably render nugatory the intentional carve-out of ECA from the definition of land, as explained in the Explanatory Notes. Is an operator that is an infrastructure provider and has a lease of the land underneath the mast in any different position from a non-operator who owns the freehold and the mast if each were to grant rights to a mobile operator to install antennae on the mast? It is difficult to see why, based on the wording of the legislation.

5.38 In *BT (Kenton Road)*[27] the issue was whether a BT telephone exchange constituted ECA. If it was ECA, it could not be land, and the Claimant operator's lease of land including the roof did not confer Code rights. This question mattered in relation to how the lease was to be terminated. It was held that the sole purpose of the exchange was not to enclose other ECA, and hence under para 5(3) of the Code, the exchange was not ECA and hence Code rights could be conferred over it.

Further points relating to the meaning of 'land'

5.39 At common law, the ordinary position is that chattels that have become attached to land with a sufficient degree of permanence becomes part of the land.[28]

5.40 In *Keast*, the Upper Tribunal held that ECA installed pursuant to Code rights, however firmly it is attached, does not, by virtue of that attachment, become land in accordance with ordinary common law principles. This followed from para 101, which provides that ownership of property does not change merely because the property is installed on or under, or affixed to, any land by a person in exercise of a right conferred by or in accordance with the Code. Judge Cooke held that the effect of para 101 went further than merely ownership and had the effect of indicating that Parliament's intention was to prevent ECA from becoming land. If it were otherwise, ECA could not be sold except by deed, which cannot have been intended.

5.41 Furthermore, the prohibition on acquiring Code rights over ECA does not mean that it is impossible to acquire Code rights over land where ECA is present. In this respect, ECA is in principle just like any other chattel. However, it is important to remember that where the presence of ECA means that an operator is already in occupation of land, any third-party operator that wishes to seek Code rights over that land must seek those rights against the occupying operator.[29]

'Electronic communications network' (s 32)

5.42 By section 32 of the Communications Act 2003, the term 'electronic communications network' means:

27 [2024] UKUT 51 (LC).

28 See *Elitestone v Morris* [1997] 1 WLR 687, including at p 691 where Lord Lloyd approved a threefold classification of items brought onto land.

29 Per Lady Rose in *Compton Beauchamp* at [140].

'(a) a transmission system for the conveyance, by the use of electrical, magnetic or electro-magnetic energy, of signals of any description; and

(b) such of the following as are used, by the person providing the system and in association with it, for the conveyance of the signals—

(i) apparatus comprised in the system;

(ii) apparatus used for the switching or routing of the signals;

(iii) software and stored data; and

(iv) (except for the purposes of sections 125 to 127) other resources, including network elements which are not active.'

5.43 In Code litigation, one rarely needs to have recourse to the main body of the Communications Act 2003, and this provision is not one that has troubled the Tribunals. However, it is included here for completeness, as the term 'electronic communications network' forms part of the definition of 'network', which in turn forms part of the definition of 'statutory purposes', and a right can only be a Code right if it is 'for' the statutory purposes.

5.44 As long as at least one Code right is sought in a Code notice, the jurisdiction of the Tribunal is engaged, and its discretion to grant terms relating to all sorts of ancillary matters is broad. Thus, as long as one of the menu of para 3(1) rights is sought for the statutory purposes, an operator can enter into an agreement under Part 2 or seek an agreement under Part 4. The operators in most Code cases are either mobile network operators or those providing infrastructure systems for mobile network operators. In that context, it is most unlikely to be a fruitful avenue for a respondent to a Part 4 application to dispute whether the rights sought are for the purposes of providing the operator's network or an infrastructure system.

'Network' (para 6)

5.45 Section 106(5) of the Communications Act 2003 allows a section 106 direction to exclude places or parts of an operator's electronic communications network or infrastructure system from the effect of the Code.

5.46 The term 'network' is defined at para 6(a) 'in relation to an operator' to mean the electronic communications network or infrastructure system provided by the operator, save for any parts of the electronic communications network or infrastructure system that are excluded from the effect of the Code by section 106(5).

5.47 By para 6(b) however, where the operator is the Secretary of State, the term 'network' means the electronic communications network which the Secretary of State is providing or proposing to provide.

'Infrastructure system' (para 7)

5.48 Paragraph 7 provides that:

'(1) In this code 'infrastructure system' means a system of infrastructure provided so as to be available for use by providers of electronic communications networks for the purposes of the provision by them of their networks.

(2) References in this code to provision of an infrastructure system include references to establishing or maintaining such a system.'

5.49 In *Green*,[30] the Upper Tribunal observed that:

> 'One of the innovations of the Code was that it enabled infrastructure providers, as well as network operators, to acquire Code rights provided that they have been designated as 'Code operators' by Ofcom under section 106 of the Communications Act 2003.'

'Code agreement' (para 29(5))

5.50 By para 29(5), a 'code agreement' is an agreement to which Part 5 of the Code applies. It is not uncommon for that expression to be used in practice as a shorthand for any agreement that confers Code rights, but it is worth noting the more restrictive meaning that the Code gives it.

'Subsisting agreement' (Transitional Provisions, para 1(4))

5.51 This term is important for understanding the law in respect of agreements that were entered into before the Code came into force. The Transitional Provisions[31] make special provision as to the extent to which the Code applies to 'subsisting agreements' and the extent to which the Code is modified in relation to them. The definition of a 'subsisting agreement' is found at para 1(4) of the Transitional Provisions. That definition, and the effect of an agreement falling within it, is discussed in Chapter 16.

'Site provider' (para 30(1)); and 'Landowner' (para 37(1))

5.52 'Site provider' is not a term that has any general legal meaning outside of the Code. It is sometimes used by those who act regularly under the Code, often as a shorthand to refer to parties acting against operators in Code litigation.

5.53 However, strictly, 'site provider' is the term used at para 30(1)(a) to refer to a person who confers a Code right, or on whom a Code right is binding, as the result of a 'Code agreement',[32] properly so-called. In this regard, it is important to bear in mind the technical definition of a 'Code agreement' (as to which see above).

5.54 Paragraph 37(1) defines 'landowner' as a person with an interest in land. This is in the context of seeking to achieve the removal of ECA or the restoration of land

30 *On Tower UK Ltd v JH & FW Green Ltd* [2020] UKUT 348 (LC) at [5]. This case was appealed to the Court of Appeal but the dictum here was unaffected and is uncontroversial.

31 Ie, Sch 2 to the Digital Economy Act 2017.

32 Nice distinctions of this kind can matter a great deal in Code litigation, as a number of early cases have focussed on precisely what party is entitled to seek what rights and against whom.

under Part 6, as it is only a person with an interest in land who has the right to require removal under para 37.

5.55 In this book, a comment might be made as to what 'landowners' might generally wish to achieve under various provisions of the Code, or what they have generally been successful or unsuccessful in achieving in the past. In this wider context, that term is intended as a generic term referring to those acting against operators in Code litigation. Such parties typically do have an interest in the land to which the litigation relates. However, it is possible for a person to be a party to some types of Code litigation without having an interest in land.

'Alteration' (para 108(2))

5.56 By para 108(2), references to the alteration of any apparatus include references to the moving, removal or replacement of the apparatus.

6

Agreements that confer Code rights

6.01 This chapter considers agreements that *confer* Code rights. Agreements that render a person *bound* by Code rights are considered in Chapter 15.

6.02 Code rights can be conferred on an operator either through a consensual agreement with the occupier of land under Part 2 of the Code, or by the tribunal imposing an agreement under Part 4. Where the latter occurs, the resulting agreement is treated[1] as an agreement under Part 2 of the Code.

6.03 Where practicable,[2] a consensual agreement should be considered to be the default setting rather than an imposed agreement.

6.04 As Lady Rose said in the Supreme Court in *Compton Beauchamp*:[3]

> 'Both the old code and the new Code indicate that the negotiation of voluntary agreements between the parties for the conferral of code rights is the optimal way for the regime to operate.'

Agreements under Part 2

6.05 Paragraph 9(1), within Part 2 of the Code, provides as follows:

> 'A code right in respect of land may only be conferred on an operator by an agreement between the occupier of the land and the operator.'

6.06 The terms 'code right', 'operator' and 'occupier' are therefore of crucial importance in understanding the nature of a Code agreement. These terms are discussed in Chapter 5.

Formalities and content requirements of agreements

6.07 Paragraph 11 sets out certain requirements as to the form and contents of an 'agreement under this Part', ie, under Part 2. As para 9 and para 11 are both within Part 2, the 'agreement' mentioned in para 9 is clearly agreement 'under this Part'. Thus, para 11 creates certain requirements for the agreements referred to in para 9.

6.08 Paragraph 11(1) states as follows:

> 'An agreement under this Part—

1 See para 22.
2 One disadvantage of consensual agreements is considered at **6.35** below.
3 [2022] UKSC 18 at [117].

(a) must be in writing,

(b) must be signed by or on behalf of the parties to it,

(c) must state for how long the code right is exercisable, and

(d) must state the period of notice (if any) required to terminate the agreement.'

6.09 The Code does not spell out[4] the consequences of an agreement not complying with the para 11(1) requirements for an agreement, but as each of those requirements is expressed in mandatory terms ('must…'), one would think that the starting point is that a failure to satisfy any one of those formalities/content requirements would prevent an agreement from being an agreement under Part 2 of the Code. The word 'agreement' at para 9 must be read subject to para 11, and therefore, *prima facie*, a new[5] agreement that does not satisfy para 11 cannot confer Code rights.

6.10 Subject to any arguments as to mistake vitiating the contract, the fact that an agreement does not constitute an agreement for Part 2 purposes does not in principle prevent it from taking effect as a contract between the parties.

6.11 It is worth noting that agreements imposed by the tribunal under paras 20, 26, or 27 are not required to comply with para 11. Such agreements take effect *as* agreements under Part 2 in any event,[6] and there is no need for the parties to execute or sign a further copy of that which has been imposed by Order.[7]

The effect of an agreement imposed by a tribunal

6.12 One of the key features of the Code is, of course, that it allows an operator to apply to have Code rights imposed. By para 22, an agreement imposed under para 20 takes effect for all purposes of the Code as an agreement under Part 2. This is also the case for agreements imposed under para 26 or under para 27, by virtue of paras 26(4)(b) and 27(4)(b) respectively, each of which applies para 22 to the respective case.

The Order is the operative instrument under para 20

6.13 An agreement which is imposed by the tribunal under para 20 has been held to take effect pursuant to the Order which imposes it. As the tribunal said in *Islington*:

> 'the operative instrument in imposing an agreement under Part 4 of the Code is the order under paragraph 20 itself'.[8]

4 This is in contrast to, eg, para 88 of the Code. Para 88(1) creates requirements as to the contents of a notice given by an operator, and para 88(2) requires a notice given by an operator to be in the form published by OFCOM, if any. Para 88(3) then spells out that a notice which does not comply with para 88 is not a valid notice.

5 Ie, one entered into once the Code came into force on 28 December 2017.

6 By virtue of para 22, and paras 26(4)(b) and 27(4)(b). See the discussion from **6.12** onwards. Query whether the different wording used elsewhere, eg, at para 34(6) ('order… to enter into') compels a different conclusion in respect of agreements arising out of different provisions of the Code.

7 See *Islington*: [2019] UKUT 53 (LC) at [148].

8 See *Islington*: [2019] UKUT 53 (LC) at [148].

6.14 It follows that there is no need for the parties to execute or sign any copy of the document which has been imposed by Order. As the tribunal said in *Islington*:[9]

> 'The Tribunal's order... has the same effect as an agreement under Part 2. In those circumstances we can see no purpose in the parties entering in to a parallel agreement conferring the same rights, and there is no reason for them to do so.'

6.15 The fact that para 11 does not apply to an agreement imposed under Part 4 does not pose any practical problems as regards the content of such an agreement. Given that para 23(7) requires[10] the tribunal to include a term specifying duration and para 23(8) requires it to consider imposing a term as to termination, the functions of paras 11(1)(c) and 11(1)(d) are mirrored in Part 4 imposition cases.

6.16 This merely leaves the writing and signature requirements (at para 11(1)(a) and 11(1)(b), respectively). The tribunal will have imposed an agreement (with or without modifications) that started out in written form attached to (or at least described in) a Code notice. Naturally, the act by which the tribunal imposes the agreement will also be embodied in writing. Where the formal proceedings of a Code reference have been undertaken, the justification for the formal requirement of a signature can easily be seen to be negated.

Presumably the same applies under paras 26 and 27

6.17 *Islington* was a para 20 case, but presumably the same conclusion applies in interim rights cases (under para 26) and temporary rights cases (under para 27).

6.18 Under para 26(2), an Order 'imposes' an agreement, and under para 27(2), the tribunal may 'impose' an agreement. This is the same verb as used in para 20(4), under which an Order 'imposes' an agreement. Furthermore, para 22 is applied to para 26 and para 27 cases by para 26(4)(b) and para 27(4)(b), respectively. The logic in *Islington* must surely apply in the same way.

Query whether the same applies under para 34(6)

6.19 It is conceivable that the language of para 34(6) leads to a different outcome in a Part 5 renewal case where a new agreement results. Under para 34(6) the tribunal 'may order the operator and the site provider to enter into a new agreement'. On the face of it, this provision does appear to envisage that the parties will be ordered to carry out a positive act, but it is not immediately obvious why the language of 'imposition' was not used.

6.20 Assuming the parties do indeed need to execute an agreement in these circumstances, do the para 11 formalities requirements apply? By para 34(8), the Code applies to this new agreement 'as if it were an agreement under Part 2'. Thus, it could be argued that para 11 does not strictly apply, as the Code only applies 'as if' the agreement were an agreement under Part 2. In fact, it is not an agreement made under

9 See *Islington*: [2019] UKUT 53 (LC) at [150].

10 Paras 23(7) and (8) apply to para 20 cases. Paras 23(7) and (8) are applied in interim rights cases under para 26 (by para 26(4)(c)) and in temporary rights cases under para 27 (by para 27(4)(c)).

Part 2; rather, it results from the Part 5 process, just as an agreement imposed under para 20 results from the Part 4 process.

6.21 However, even though the formalities requirements of para 11 might not apply, this does not in itself necessarily mean that the new agreement takes effect without the parties needing to do something to 'enter into' it, as seemingly envisaged by the wording of para 34(6). Given that para 34(7) causes the pre-existing Code agreement to continue until the new agreement 'takes effect', the parties would be well-advised to ensure clarity in terms of what they are being required to do by the tribunal's Order under para 34(6) in order to put beyond doubt that the new agreement will take effect, having alerted the tribunal to the fact that the pre-existing agreement will continue until the new agreement will take effect.

Conflict between an agreement and the Code

Starting point: contractual obligations are effective

6.22 The starting point when considering the interaction between the Code and a contractual agreement is the statement at para 100(1) that:

> 'This code does not affect any rights or liabilities arising under an agreement to which an operator is a party.'

6.23 This provision is explained at para 497 of the Explanatory Notes to the Digital Economy Act 2017, as follows:

> 'Paragraph 100(1) concerns the binding quality of agreements made under the code, and whether it is possible to 'contract out' out of provisions of the code. Agreements for code rights are final so that once agreed (see Part 2), it is not possible for either party to re-open the agreement. For example if an operator agrees to pay £5,000 for a (consensual) code agreement, the operator (or landowner) cannot then apply to the court to get a better price or improve the accompanying terms that relate to the code right that has been agreed.'

6.24 However, that general proposition is subject to the immediate and very important qualification at para 100(2) that:

> '(2) Sub-paragraph (1) does not apply in relation to paragraph 99 or Parts 3 to 6 of this code.'

6.25 Thus para 99 and each of the provisions of Parts 3 to 6 of the Code *are* presumably capable of affecting 'any rights or liabilities arising under an agreement to which an operator is a party'.

6.26 Or, as explained at para 498 of the Explanatory Notes to the Digital Economy Act 2017:

> 'Paragraph 100(2) ensures that an operator cannot be required by a landowner to agree to exclude the effect of paragraph 99 and Parts 3 to 6 of the code. This is commonly known as a 'no contracting out' rule.'

6.27 Thus, for example, the parties cannot 'contract out' of the security of tenure, renewal and termination provisions of Part 5 in the same way as a landlord and tenant can do under section 38A of the 1954 Act in respect of sections 24 to 28 of that Act.

6.28 However, the argument that one cannot contract out of certain Parts of the Code has no bearing on the question of whether as a matter of construction, those Parts apply to any given factual situation in the first place.[11]

6.29 In most cases, the effect of paras 100(1) and (2) will be tolerably clear. However, there may be some corners of the Code where things are not so clear-cut. For example, paras 25 and 84 contain the principal provisions relating to compensation. One of these is in Part 4 (no contracting out), whereas the other is in Part 14 (no prevention of contracting out). Para 86 (also in Part 14) then creates an exclusion of any compensation that is not provided for in specified portions of the Code. It is hard to be certain of which of these provisions one can expressly contract out of and which one can supplement (and therefore arguably impliedly contradict) by providing for additional compensation. This particular issue is discussed in Chapter 14 relating to compensation.

Voiding provisions

6.30 There are certain paragraphs of the Code which expressly render an agreement void insofar as it attempts to achieve some impermissible end.

6.31 For example:

(i) Paragraph 16(1) renders an agreement under Part 2 void to the extent that it prevents or limits assignment of the agreement to another operator, or makes assignment subject to conditions, including a condition requiring the payment of money.[12]

(ii) Paragraph 17(5) renders an agreement under Part 2 void to the extent that it prevents or limits the upgrading or sharing of the ECA to which the agreement relates, where the conditions in paras 17(2) and (3) are met, or makes upgrading or sharing of such apparatus subject to conditions, including a condition requiring the payment of money.

'Contracting in'

6.32 Under English law, parties have considerable freedom of contract and can generally even agree that black is white.[13] However, they cannot agree that the Code means Y when it means X, and they cannot agree that it applies when it does not. So, for example, parties can seek to negotiate the terms of a para 26 agreement, and

11 See the discussion of para 100(2) by the Deputy President in *Ashloch* at first instance [2019] UKUT 338 (LC) ([55]–[57] and elsewhere). The case proceeded up to the Supreme Court as part of the *Compton Beauchamp* hearing, with the same result as to the main issue, and casting no doubt on the discussion of para 100(2).

12 Para 16(2) provides that para 16(1) does not prevent a term requiring the assignor to enter into a guarantee agreement. NB para 16 does not apply to subsiting agreements, as explained in Chapter 15.

13 See *First Tower Trustees Ltd v CDS (Superstores International) Limited* [2018] EWCA Civ 1396 at [47].

there is nothing problematic with the draft agreement stating on its face that it is a para 26 agreement or an 'interim rights' agreement. However, if the parties were to purport to enter into such an agreement consuensually, it would not, as a matter of law, constitute a para 26 agreement and the parties would not have validly created rights 'on an interim basis',[14] as a para 26 agreement can only come into existence by being judicially imposed. It is conceivable that the contract would be voided if it is clear that both parties shared a fundamental mistake as to the nature and effect of the agreement.

When a consensual agreement cannot be used

6.33 As discussed in Chapter 9 (concerning para 26 interim rights cases), an agreement of the kind described in para 26 cannot be entered into by the parties without judicial involvement. Paragraph 26(1) begins 'An operator may apply…', and this is a necessary pre-requisite for an Order under para 26. Parties should avoid entering into an agreement consensually, without judicial involvement, where they are attempting to enter into a purported para 26 or interim Code rights agreement. No consensual agreement can be 'contracted out'[15] of the security of tenure provision at para 30(2), and accordingly parties might unwittingly create an agreement with security of tenure, even in an attempted MSV case. Parties need to ensure that where they have in principle agreed an interm rights agreement, that agreement is imposed by the tribunal on the application of the operator under para 26, having followed the correct para 26 notice procedure.

6.34 In the same way, parties cannot consensually enter into an agreement that has the same effect as a temporary Code rights agreement imposed under para 27. 'Temporary' Code rights are those resulting from an Order under para 27(2) only, and when such rights are conferred, para 30(3) operates so as to disapply the security of tenure that would otherwise arise under para 30(2). For the reasons given above in relation to para 26, there can be no contracting out of para 30(3). Accordingly, parties need to ensure that where they have in principle agreed to a temporary rights agreement, that agreement is imposed by the tribunal on the application of the operator under para 27(2), having complied with the notice procedure described in para 27.

One disadvantage of a consensual agreement for site providers

6.35 Given that a consensual agreement is considered to be the 'optimal' means of conferring Code rights under the statutory regime (as it prevents the need for legal costs and tribunal time to be expended), it is perhaps not ideal that there are any disincentives at all in the statutory scheme for such an arrangement.

6.36 However, it is vital for those advising landowners (or any person who is to confer or be bound by Code rights) to be aware that there is one important trap

14 An expression used and defined at para 26(1) and (2).

15 Para 30(2) continues an agreement after its contractual term has expired, and para 30(3) disapplies that provision in the cases of agreements imposed under paras 26 and 27. The effect of para 100(2) is that Part 3 of the Code (*inter alia*) does affect contractual rights of the parties. Para 30 is within Part 3 and hence notwithstanding any attempted provision to the contrary in an agreement, one cannot 'contract out' of para 30(2).

for the unwary. Paragraph 25 gives rise to compensation arising from the exercise of Code rights. Para 84 makes related provision as to such compensation. However, the right to such compensation only arises where an Order is made under para 20[16] (imposing an agreement) or under a different provision of the Code such as para 26[17] (in respect of interim rights), para 27[18] (in respect of temporary rights), or para 34 (in respect of certain renewals or modifications of Code agreements).[19] Under para 25, compensation can be awarded at the time of making the order in respect of Code rights, or at any time afterwards, on an application being made.[20]

6.37 Thus, as has been recognised judicially,[21] where an agreement is agreed consensually, without any judicial involvement, there is no right to apply under para 25 for compensation. The only ways of ensuring a future right to seek compensation are either: (i) asking the tribunal to 'rubber stamp' an agreement which the parties have negotiated in order to engage para 25(1), or (ii) seeking to agree to a bespoke contractual compensation provision, which is difficult to achieve and may end up being uncertain in effect. This issue is discussed in Chapter 14 (relating to compensation).

Can a consensual agreement cause prejudice for later Code References?

6.38 In the *Hackney* (Tradescant House)[22] case, the tribunal made the point that terms in consensual agreements are included or rejected for all sorts of reasons, and thus terms that have been previously agreed consensually do not have an impact on the determination of terms where the tribunal is asked to impose an agreement. This removes a potential disincentive to the parties coming to a consensual agreement. Judge Cooke said as follows:

> '47. … Terms in consensual agreements are included or rejected for all sorts of reasons; concessions may be made for speed, terms may be horse-traded, experience between particular parties may mean that one or the other insists on particular terms that it would not otherwise seek. None of that is relevant to the Tribunal's decision about the terms that are appropriate, and that are required to minimise loss and damage[23] to the respondent.
>
> 48. That means that operators and site providers can reach agreements on whatever basis is convenient to them, without fear that they have then compromised their position when terms are in dispute before the Tribunal.'[24]

16 This is what para 25(1) says in plain terms.
17 Para 26(4)(e) applies para 25 to para 26 cases.
18 Para 27(4)(e) applies para 25 to para 27 cases.
19 Para 34(11) applies para 25 to particular cases under para 34.
20 See para 25(2)(b).
21 For example, by the Deputy President, sitting as a county court judge, in *EE v Morriss* [2022] EW Misc 1 (CC) at [30].
22 [2022] UKUT 210 (LC) at [43]–[49].
23 The reference to minimising loss and damage is clearly a reference to para 23(5) of the Code.
24 [2022] UKUT 210 (LC) at [47] and [48].

The later consensual amendment of agreements

6.39 An agreement under Part 2 is a consensual contractual agreement between the parties. Certain provisions of the Code render certain purported terms void or impermissible,[25] but in principle there is nothing in the Code that prevents such an agreement from being amended by agreement between the parties. Its amendment would be governed by the general law as to formalities and by its own contractual terms.

6.40 Paragraph 11(1)(a) and (b) also apply to to 'the variation of an agreement'[26] under Part 2, such that any amendment must, in any event, be in writing and be signed on behalf of the parties to it. Further, the 'agreement as varied must still comply'[27] with paras 11(1)(c) and (d), such that it must still state for how long the Code right is exercisable and the period of notice required for termination (if any).

6.41 As an imposed agreement takes effect as an agreement under Part 2, there appears to be nothing to prevent it from being amended by later agreements of the parties, but again, each of the formalities at paras 11(1)(a) to (b) will apply to the variation, and the requirements of paras 11(1)(c) and (d) apply to the agreement as varied.

25 For example, a term requiring a payment in return for sharing or upgrading rights is void by para 17(5)(b). Further, para 100(2) in effect means that parties cannot 'contract out' of Parts 3 to 6 or para 99 of the Code. Thus it seems that it would not be permissible to deprive a person of a right to apply for compensation under para 25(1) by amending an imposed agreement to that purported effect.

26 By para 11(2).

27 By para 11(2).

7

Interpreting the Code

Introduction

7.01 In the *Bridgewater Canal*[1] case, Lewison J delivered a powerful and indeed now notorious critique of the drafting of the Old Code. As no book or article on any iteration of the Code would be complete without reproducing that critique, I do so here:

> 'The Code is not one of Parliament's better drafting efforts. In my view it must rank as one of the least coherent and thought-through pieces of legislation on the statute book. Even its name is open to doubt. Although section 106 of the Communications Act 2003 says that the code set out in Schedule 2 to the Telecommunications Act 1984 is referred to as 'the electronic communications code' in 'this Chapter', the amendments made by the 2003 Act did not include changing the title to Schedule 2, so that in Schedule 2 itself it is still called 'The Telecommunications Code'. I have simply called it the Code.'[2]

7.02 He went on at [26] to opine that it was 'lamentable' that the drafting did not make a particular question clear.

7.03 Although the name of the New Code is clear and well-established as the Electronic Communications Code,[3] it too is referred to by those with familiarity simply as 'the Code'. It has been described as 'a lengthy and highly complex set of provisions' by Nugee LJ in *Gencomp*[4] but has certainly not garnered the degree of opprobrium heaped upon the Old Code.

7.04 The relative proliferation of litigation under the New Code when compared with its predecessor may have been caused by a number of factors. However, chief amongst them is surely the different level of consideration payable under the New Code, rather than a further slide in standards of drafting when compared with the Old Code.

---

1 *Bridgewater Canal Company Ltd v Geo Networks Ltd* [2010] EWHC 548 (Ch).

2 Para [7] of the judgment.

3 Albeit with a variety of official approaches to capitalisation. Within Sch 3A of the Communications Act 2003 itself, 'THE ELECTRONIC COMMUNICATIONS CODE' is included as a heading with a confident 'all caps' rendering. Section 4(2) of the Digital Economy Act 2017, which inserts the Code into the Communications Act 2003, is headed 'The electronic communications code'. Numerous statutes including s 218 of the Digital Markets, Competition and Consumers Act 2024 refer to 'the electronic communications code'. Most judicial decisions refer to the 'Electronic Communications Code', and this book takes that latter approach. I also pause to note the official Welsh name for the Code: 'gweithredwr cod cyfathrebu electronig'. One would hope that it has garnered the familiar epithet 'y cod'.

4 *Vodafone Ltd v Potting Shed Bar and Gardens Ltd & Anor* [2023] EWCA Civ 825 at [15], a case in which Lewison LJ, as he then had become, was also sitting.

7.05 Having said that, the lack of clarity at the outset in respect of basic questions (such as: Who can apply for such rights? Against whom? In what circumstances?) created the need for the tribunals and indeed courts to step in and interpret how the Code works. This process has ultimately largely been conducted by reference to how it is was intended to function, rather than necessarily by adhering too closely to the words used.

A strict approach in appropriation statutes?

7.06 Towards the outset of Code litigation, in *Keast*, the landowner sought to emphasise that as the Code effectively allows the compulsory acquisition of rights over land, it should be very strictly construed.

7.07 The importance of the actual words used in legislation was highlighted in relying on the pronouncement in *Bennion on Statutory Interpretation* that:[5]

> 'Context and mischief do not constitute a licence to judges to ignore the plain meaning of the words that Parliament has used.'

7.08 The tribunal referred to this proposition in its judgment, although it did not accede to the interpretation of the disputed provisions which was urged upon it by the landowner.

7.09 The tribunal went on to endorse the relevance of a Supreme Court dictum in respect of the strictness of the proper approach to the construction of statutes that expropriate:

> '13. The courts take a particularly strict approach to the construction of statutes that expropriate private property: *R (Sainsbury's) v Wolverhampton City Council* [2011] 1 AC 437. Where there is any ambiguity, the construction chosen will be the one that interferes least with private property rights. It seems to me that that principle is relevant both to the construction of the Code and to the exercise of the Tribunal's discretion under the Code, for example in its judgment as to what are the 'appropriate' terms to be imposed alongside Code rights. I bear this closely in mind in assessing the preliminary issues, all of which challenge the Claimant's application on the basis that it is out of line with the requirements of the Code – whether as to the form of the notice, the nature of the rights sought, or the OFCOM direction that authorises the Claimant to seek them.'

An overwhelmingly purposive approach

7.10 However, since these observations, judges have very much favoured a purposive approach in order to ensure that the Code constitutes a coherent scheme, rather than either excessive literalism or strictness in favour of a party whose land rights are being expropriated.

5 7th edn at para 9.1.

7.11 In the *University of London* case, the Court of Appeal noted that 'Where the legislation uses an imprecise word, a court is entitled to place strong reliance on the legislative purpose underpinning the legislation.'[6]

7.12 So what is that purpose? At its most basic, the Code is, of course, the 'current regime for sorting out when, where and on what terms, telecoms operators can acquire the right to install their ECA on a particular piece of land…'.[7]

7.13 But in terms of what this particular Code is trying to achieve, Mr Justice Fancourt summed it up neatly in *Stephenson*,[8] saying:

> 'The purpose underlying the Code is to ensure that operators can use and exploit sites more flexibly, quickly and cheaply than had previously been the case, at lower than open market rents, in furtherance of the public interest of providing access to a choice of high quality electronic communications networks, while providing a degree of protection to site owners' legitimate interests.'

7.14 The legislative purpose expressed in this sort of way has often guided tribunals' understanding of the tests contained within the Code. For example, in deciding what terms should be considered 'appropriate' under para 23 of the Code, or what weight is required to be given to the terms of an old agreement that is being renewed, when the Code requires the tribunal to 'have regard to' those terms.

7.15 It is perhaps notable that on the relatively rare occasions when the tribunals have been overturned in the higher courts, it has largely been in circumstances where the tribunals have stuck to a more literal analysis, whereas the higher courts have prioritised an approach that concentrates on the manner in which the Code is supposed to function.

7.16 The Supreme Court's judgment in *Compton*[9] and the related *Ashloch* and *On Tower* cases constitutes the most authoritative statement on the proper approach to the interpretation of the Code. The Court endorsed[10] the proposition that in interpreting the Code, one should seek to ascertain how the Code is intended to function rather than embark on an overly intricate analysis of individual words used. In that case, the question of who is to be considered an 'occupier' under para 9 of the Code was the key question.

7.17 At [106] it was said that:

> '…the starting point here is not to try to define the word 'occupier' and then allow that definition to mandate how the regime established by the code works. The correct approach is to work out how the regime is intended to work and then consider what meaning should be given to the word 'occupier' so as best to achieve that goal.'

---

6 *The University of London v Cornerstone Telecommunications Infrastructure Limited* [2019] EWCA Civ 2075 at [47].

7 Per Lady Rose in *Compton Beauchamp*, at [1].

8 *EE Ltd and Hutchison 3G UK Ltd v Stephenson and AP Wireless II (UK) Ltd* [2021] UKUT 167 (LC) at [53]. This summary was offered in the context of a comparison between the legislative purposes behind the 1954 Act and the New Code.

9 *Cornerstone Telecommunications Infrastructure Ltd v Compton Beauchamp Estates Ltd* [2022] UKSC 18.

10 At [102]–[107], including by reference to authority.

7.18 The Court of Appeal's judgment in *Gencomp*[11] constituted another example of this approach. The Court had to consider whether a set of provisions that was intended to specify what persons are to be treated as parties to a Code agreement was intended to be exhaustive. It described the proper approach to construction as follows:

> '74. The question whether paragraph 10(3) is exhaustive or not therefore seems to me unclear as a matter of language. But interpretation of a legal text is never simply a matter of language. It is always relevant to seek to understand how the instrument is intended to work and why. And in the particular context of the Code, we have the benefit of guidance on this from the Supreme Court in *Compton Beauchamp*...
>
> 75. Applying that approach, it seems to me that the regime is intended to work in such a way that the person currently entitled to the benefit and burden of the agreement as operator, and the person currently entitled to the benefit and burden of the agreement as site provider, are parties to the agreement and can exercise the rights conferred by Part 5 of the Code. That can in my judgement be achieved by construing paragraph 10(3) as not intended to define exhaustively who is to be treated as a party to the agreement.'

External aids to construction

7.19 Given the imperative of ensuring a coherent Code, it is perhaps unsurprising that the genesis of the structure and content of the Code have often featured in judicial analysis of the meaning of Code provisions. That being the case, it is equally unsurprising that certain external aids to construction have readily been taken into account.

7.20 A source of considerable assistance in respect of the interpretation of the Code has been the Law Commission's report.[12] In the *University of London* case,[13] Martin Rodger QC, Deputy Chamber President, concluded that the report was a legitimate aid to construction but that there was reason for at least some degree of caution:

> '49. Law Commission papers and reports (with or without a draft bill) are a legitimate external aid to statutory interpretation if they form part of the relevant background and legislative history. Their utility, and the use of other external aids (i.e. material not contained within the statute itself) was discussed by Lord Nicholls of Birkenhead in *R v Secretary of State for the Environment, Transport and the Regions ex p Spath Holme Ltd* [2001] 2 AC 439 at 397C to 398F. He described them as 'a useful tool' in identifying the purpose of the legislation but warned that a balance must be struck and that courts should be 'slow to permit external aids to displace meanings which are otherwise clear and unambiguous and not productive of absurdity'.

11 Known in the Court of Appeal formally as *Vodafone Ltd v Potting Shed Bar and Gardens Ltd & Anor* [2023] EWCA Civ 825 due to a change of name of Gencomp (No.7) Ltd.

12 Law Commission Report No.336: 'The Electronic Communications Code', 27 February 2013.

13 *Cornerstone Telecommunications Infrastructure Ltd v The University Of London* [2018] UKUT 356 (LC). This case was appealed, unsuccessfully, to the Court of Appeal. Nothing was said in the judgment of the Court of Appeal which cast doubt on the judgment of the Upper Tribunal in relation to the issue of using Law Commission reports as an aid to construction, and indeed the Court of Appeal itself referred to the Law Commission a dozen times in its judgment.

50. There may be an additional reason for caution in the use of Law Commission material as an aid to the interpretation of the Code. The Law Commission anticipated that the owners of suitable sites would willingly confer Code rights on operators (and would compete for opportunities to host apparatus) in return for consideration measured by the true market value of the rights. As enacted however the Code does not provide for the economic value of Code rights to be shared in the way originally intended; site owners are to be compensated only for the value of the rooftop or field margin in a 'no scheme' or 'no network' world, a value which is expected to be nominal. It may therefore be unsafe to place weight on statements made by the Law Commission about the thinking underlying its proposals, because those proposals differed in at least this fundamental respect from the principles on which the Code as enacted is based.'

7.21 In interpreting the Code, neither the tribunals nor the higher courts have been overly restrictive in their use of extraneous sources. The legislative purpose or function of the Code has most often been paramount, and any paper trail that elucidates that purpose and how different provisions might be connected to that purpose has largely been considered to be of assistance.

7.22 More recently in *Gencomp*[14] the Court of Appeal also made repeated reference to the Law Commission's report. In *Compton*, the Supreme Court referred to the Law Commission report,[15] and the government's response[16] to the consultation prompted by the Law Commission's report and the policy reflected in those documents in interpreting the Code. The Upper Tribunal did similar on appeal in *Gravesham*.[17]

7.23 Regard has also been paid to the Explanatory Notes to the Code. For example, in *Ashloch* in both the Court of Appeal[18] and Supreme Court.[19]

7.24 The *University of London*[20] case illustrates that there are limits to the extent to which statements of government policy and explanatory notes to legislation can influence the interpretation of legislation, including the Code. The Court of Appeal in that case referred to the Law Commission report in noting that the Law Commission envisaged that interim rights should be allowed to be granted, in order to govern the relationship between the parties pending resolution of payment terms at a later full hearing. Reference was also made both to a government policy document[21] and also para 422 of the explanatory notes to the Digital Economy Act 2017 in concluding that the government appears to have taken a similar view. However, there are limits to the extent to which such documents can mandate the answer to a question of interpretation, and the Court went on to caution that:

> 'The question for us, however, is whether the Code as actually drafted goes further. Neither statements of policy nor explanatory notes can dictate the proper interpretation of legislation.'

---

14 *Vodafone Ltd v Potting Shed Bar and Gardens Ltd & Anor* [2023] EWCA Civ 825.
15 Law Com 336.
16 *A New Electronic Communications Code*, published in May 2016 by DCMS.
17 *Gravesham BC v On Tower UK Ltd* [2024] UKUT 151 (LC).
18 *Cornerstone Telecommunications Infrastructure Ltd v Ashloch Ltd and AP Wireless II (UK) Ltd* [2021] EWCA Civ 90 at [70]–[71].
19 [2022] UKSC 18 at [133].
20 [2019] EWCA Civ 2075.
21 Namely the Executive Summary in the policy document published by the Department of Culture, Media and Sport in May 2016.

8

Applications under para 20

Part 4 of the Code

8.01 Part 4 (paras 19 to 27) deals with the powers of tribunals to impose agreements. A Code right may only be conferred on an operator by an agreement between the occupier and the operator.[1] That, of course, may be done consensually under Part 2. However, when a consensual agreement cannot be reached, an operator may turn to the tribunal to seek to have an agreement imposed on the parties that confers Code rights (or renders a person bound by Code rights). Such an imposed agreement is then treated as an agreement under Part 2.[2]

8.02 This chapter considers the principal route by which a Code agreement is imposed: para 20. Agreements imposed on an 'interim' basis under para 26 and on a temporary basis under para 27 are considered at Chapters 9 and 10 respectively.

The para 20 notice

8.03 Where an operator requires a person to confer a Code right on it, or to be otherwise bound by a Code right which is exercisable by the operator, it may serve a notice on that person.[3] The person on whom such a notice is served is referred to in the Code as a 'relevant person'.[4]

8.04 The notice must set out the Code right, the land to which it relates, and all of the other terms of the agreement that the operator seeks.[5] It must also state that the operator seeks the person's agreement to those terms.[6] For additional requirements as to the form, content, and service of notices, see Chapter 20.

The application to the tribunal

8.05 If the relevant person does not agree to confer or be otherwise bound by the Code right within 28 days of service, the operator may then apply to the tribunal for an Order imposing an agreement between them that confers the Code right on the operator or provides for the Code right to bind the relevant person.[7]

1 Para 9.
2 See para 22.
3 Para 20(2).
4 Para 20(1).
5 Para20(2)(a).
6 Para 20(2)(b).
7 Para 20(3)(a) and (4).

8.06 The operator may equally apply for such an Order at any time after the notice is given if the relevant person gives notice in writing that it does not agree to confer or be otherwise bound by the Code right.[8]

Para 20 applications: obligations in respect of ADR

8.07 The para 20 notice must[9] also contain information about the availability of alternative dispute resolution in the event that the operator and the relevant person are unable to reach agreement and explain the possible consequences of refusing to engage in alternative dispute resolution.

8.08 Before an operator makes an application under para 20 it must, if it is reasonably practicable to do so, 'consider the use of one or more alternative dispute resolution procedures to reach agreement with the relevant person' (Para 20(5)[10]). By para 20(6), either party may at any time give the other a notice in writing stating that it wishes to engage in alternative dispute resolution in relation to the agreement sought.

8.09 There are potential cost consequences if a party unreasonably refuses to engage in alternative dispute resolution (under para 96(2)(b), discussed in Chapter 23).

The test for making a para 20 Order

8.10 The tribunal may[11] make an Order under para 20 'if (and only if)' both of the conditions at para 21(2) and (3) are satisfied.

8.11 However, this is subject to two absolute bars to the making of an Order, namely where the Respondent succeeds in the redevelopment defence at para 21(5), or where para 27ZA prevents an Order on national security grounds. Each of those absolute bars is considered later in this chapter, at **8.40** and **8.52** respectively.

The para 21(2) and (3) conditions

8.12 The two conditions which an applicant for an Order must satisfy are as follows:

> '(2) The first condition is that the prejudice caused to the relevant person by the order is capable of being adequately compensated by money.
>
> (3) The second condition is that the public benefit likely to result from the making of the order outweighs the prejudice to the relevant person.'

---

8 Para 20(3)(b).

9 By para 20(2A). This provision was inserted on 7 November 2023 by s 69(2)(a) of the Product Security and Telecommunications Infrastructure Act 2022. Accordingly, the requirement for a notice to contain these details did not exist prior to 7 November 2023.

10 This provision, together with para 20(6), was inserted on 7 November 2023 by s 69(2)(b) of the Product Security and Telecommunications Infrastructure Act 2022. Accordingly, the para 20(5) obligation imposed on an operator to consider ADR did not apply to applications made before 7 November 2023.

11 Para 21(1). As to whether there is a discretion under para 21, see the section below at **8.36**..

8.13 In deciding whether the second condition is met, the tribunal must have regard to the public interest in access to a choice of high-quality electronic communications services.[12]

The first condition

8.14 This condition has been the subject of judicial consideration in only a handful of cases.

8.15 In the first (interim) decision in *EE v Islington*,[13] a very early case under the Code, the Deputy President said as follows:

> 'It may be better not to speculate on what type of prejudice would be incapable of adequate compensation by money and to leave it to individual cases to provide examples, but there may be cases in which aesthetic or personal considerations meant that compensation for any diminution in financial value did not provide adequate recompense for the prejudice that the building owner might suffer.'

8.16 This statement might lead one to conclude that an operator will fail to satisfy the first condition only in very rare circumstances. Indeed, an operator's case that this condition is met is seldom actively opposed by landowners. However, in *University of the Arts ('UAL')*[14] the Upper Tribunal accepted the respondent's submission that the condition was not satisfied.

8.17 In that case, the respondent university opposed the installation of ECA in the context of a proposed substantial redevelopment in the Elephant and Castle area, which the tribunal accepted was very likely to go ahead. However, as the respondent was not the party with the intention of carrying out the redevelopment, it could not rely on para 21(5). Instead, it was concerned at the risk that its obligations to give vacant possession of its building to the developer would be compromised by the presence of the operator's ECA. Although it was content in principle to enter into a para 26 agreement (with no security of tenure), it was not open to the tribunal to impose such an agreement without the operator having sought it.

8.18 The tribunal said that what stood out in this case was risk, and specifically the risk of litigation. As *UAL* is the only case thus far in which the tribunal refused to impose an agreement because the para 21(2) 'first condition' test was not met, the full reasoning of the tribunal is perhaps instructive:

> '55 …there is a very high risk that it will take litigation to remove the claimant, so as to enable the respondent to give vacant possession of its building, and the outcome of that litigation, as of very nearly all litigation, cannot be predicted.
>
> 56. The consequence of risk is stress; the risk of litigation will cause stress and uncertainty to the respondent's employees, at a time when they are preparing for a move of the entire institution to a new building (itself a stressful process). If litigation becomes a reality there will be further stress, with its associated operational consequences. Whether or not the respondent is the successful

12 Para 21(4).

13 [2018] UKUT 361 (LC) at [34].

14 *Cornerstone Telecommunications Infrastructure Ltd v University Of The Arts London* [2020] UKUT 248 (LC).

party in any litigation there will be reputational damage in terms of how the respondent is regarded by the public, and difficulties in its relationship with the developer and with its students and prospective students. We regard all these as prejudices that cannot be compensated in money.

57. There is a further risk, albeit a lower risk, that the respondent will be unsuccessful in that litigation and will be unable to meet its obligations to the developer. Injunction proceedings might then be taken against it. Again this involves prejudice, in terms of stress, damage to the relationship with the developer, and reputational damage, that cannot be compensated in money.'

8.19 The case of *Audley House*[15] did not involve consideration of the para 21(2) test, as that was a renewal case, and in any event there was no dispute that there would be renewed Code rights. However, the tribunal noted that 'if criminal liability is a possibility, that is something for which money cannot compensate the site provider'. Following the decision in that case, it will be a rare case in which the tribunal considers that there is a risk that the site provider, rather than the operator, will be criminally liable for health and safety breaches. It will be rarer still that the tribunal would be unable to impose suitable provisions to protect the site provider and would therefore have to refuse to confer Code rights. However, it is useful to have another example of the kinds of situations in which the 'first condition' at para 21(2) might be engaged.

The second condition

8.20 In practice, it is usually the second condition that constitutes the principal balancing exercise in determining a para 20 application. Balancing private prejudice against public benefit might be thought not to be a straightforward task.

8.21 Indeed, in *UAL*, the UT said as follows at [62]:

'The weighing of private prejudice against public benefit is difficult; the two are not obviously commensurable.'

8.22 However, the tribunal clearly considered the test to throw a high hurdle in the way of a landowner seeking to avoid the imposition of an agreement, which would not be surmounted in the typical case. It went on to opine that:

'Public benefit will generally outweigh inconvenience and annoyance and readily calculable losses…'

8.23 As *UAL* is the only fully contested[16] case thus far in which the tribunal has refused to impose an agreement on para 21(3) grounds, it is perhaps instructive to set out its thoughts on the nature of the test:

'It is clear that Parliament in enacting the Code intended private landowners to participate in the provision of telecommunications sites for the public good by suffering the use of their land for that purpose, being compensated for any damage caused but for consideration calculated on a basis that prevents them

15 [2022] UKUT 152 (LC) at [52].

16 That is, where the full para 21 test is in issue, rather than the 'good arguable case' version of it which applies in para 26 cases by virtue of para 26(3)(b).

from making a profit out of the deal as they could under the Code's statutory predecessor. The test for the imposition of such rights is quite a stiff one; for the respondent to escape this public duty, unless it is itself going to redevelop the site, it must show either that it will suffer loss that cannot be compensated in money, or that the prejudice it will suffer is so great that it outweighs the public benefit derived from the use of the site. *The level of prejudice must be very high indeed to outweigh the public benefit*, in the light of the public demand for, and dependence upon, the availability of electronic communications. The benefit is perhaps even higher today than it was when the Code was enacted and certainly in the current circumstances[17] we are all keenly aware of it.' [emphasis added]

8.24 Applying the test, it was held on the facts that the case 'crosses the boundary between prejudice that has to be suffered for the public good and prejudice that is too much to ask'. The tribunal had in mind the non-monetary prejudice which it had identified at the para 21(2) stage and also the risk of substantial monetary penalties and/or damages in the event that the respondent was unable to give vacant possession to the developer. It acknowledged that the respondent would seek to recover any such losses from the operator but considered that 'the process of doing so is hardly likely to be easy.'

8.25 The fact that the second condition is a freestanding condition to be satisfied separately from the first condition indicates that it is logically possible for prejudice to outweigh the public benefit resulting from the grant of Code rights even where it is capable of being adequately compensated by money. Thus, the fact that there is adequate compensation cannot mean that the resulting prejudice is *necessarily* reduced to zero in the para 21(3) balance. Nonetheless, the tribunal has treated itself as entitled to reduce the weight to be given to prejudice on the ground that it will be compensated in money. In *Islington*[18] the Deputy President said as follows:

> 'I bear in mind that that prejudice will be compensated in money which has to some extent to be set off against the weight to be given to it.'[19]

Factors to be taken into account

The para 21(4) factor: high quality communications services

8.26 As stated above, in deciding whether the second condition is met, the tribunal must have regard to 'the public interest in access to a choice of high-quality electronic communications services'.[20]

17 The hearing and decision in *UAL* fell in between the first national 'lockdown' in respect of the COVID-19 pandemic (which became legally effective on 26 March 2020), and the second 'lockdown' in respect of England which commenced on 5 November 2020. The hearing was conducted by remote video platform, and the Upper Tribunal was one branch of the judicial system which reacted particularly nimbly to allow hearings to continue relatively unaffected by the pandemic, by conducting them remotely where appropriate.

18 The interim rights decision at [2018] UKUT 361 (LC).

19 [2018] UKUT 361 (LC) at [44]. Although this was an interim decision, and hence only a 'good arguable case' had to be shown under para 26(3)(b) in respect of the para 21 test, the legal question as to whether the Tribunal is permitted to reduce the weight to be given to certain factors in the para 21(3) balance pursuant to the existence and adequacy of compensation is surely one which is common to para 20, 26 and 27 cases.

20 Para 21(4).

8.27 Where legislation mandates a decision-maker to 'have regard to' a factor, one might expect the legislative purpose and the context of that mandate to have a considerable bearing on the weight that the factor is given. To use an example from the Code itself, para 34(12) provides that a tribunal must 'have regard to' the terms of the existing Code agreement where the terms of a renewal agreement are being determined. This language is very similar to the mandate in the analogous renewal mechanism under the 1954 Act: section 35(1) of that Act tells a court to 'have regard to the terms of the current tenancy and to all relevant circumstances'. However, the Court of Appeal in *Green* held that the two pieces of legislation had different legislative purposes, which caused the similar phrases to have differing impacts in the two legislative contexts (and consequently the case law under the 1954 Act (the *O'May* case[21]) is not of similar application under Part 5 of the Code). The obligation to have regard to the terms of the existing agreement under para 34(12) does not elevate the existing terms to any special status.

8.28 By contrast, tribunals do appear to consider the express inclusion of a requirement to have regard to 'the public interest in access to a choice of high quality electronic communications services' to be highly significant.

8.29 Fancourt J in *Stephenson*[22] clearly considered para 21(4) to be so significant that it constituted a key element of the Code's overall legislative purpose:

> 'The purpose underlying the Code is to ensure that operators can use and exploit sites more flexibly, quickly and cheaply than had previously been the case, at lower than open market rents, in furtherance of *the public interest of providing access to a choice of high quality electronic communications networks*, while providing a degree of protection to site owners' legitimate interests.' [emphasis added]

8.30 In this context, it will be a rare case in which the para 21(4) factor is not given very considerable weight.

8.31 Landowners are rarely, if ever, in a position to challenge operators in respect of the radio planning merits of a site in order to diminish the 'public benefit' element of the para 21(3) test. The tribunal's starting point is surely that an operator has done its own homework and would be unlikely to want to occupy a building that does not serve its purposes. One would think that evidence to the contrary would therefore have to be compelling. Landowners typically do not wish to spend money speculatively on expert advice on the off chance that there might be an argument that the operator has got it wrong. Furthermore, as set out below, even showing that there is a better site elsewhere is most unlikely to help a landowner's cause. Showing that there is no public benefit at all from a radio planning point of view is surely difficult to achieve, and in that context, landowners generally think that there is little to be achieved under the para 21(3) test other than by demonstrating the prejudice that is likely to result.

Other factors to be taken into account

8.32 In addition to the para 21(4) factor, which is a mandatory consideration, the tribunal will take into account all other relevant factors. Given the not readily

21 *O'May v City of London Real Property Co Ltd* [1983] 2 AC 726.

22 [2021] UKUT 167 (LC) at [53]. This was the preliminary issue judgment in the case.

'commensurable' nature of public benefit and private prejudice, the precise number of users who are likely to benefit from a new communications site may not be a factor that will often come into play. However, one would think that any factor that affects the extent to which the public will benefit from new Code rights is, in principle, capable of being relevant.

8.33 On the other side of the ledger, any type of prejudice that will be suffered by the relevant person is in principle capable of being relevant. However, there is a distinction between 'inconvenience and annoyance' (an expression used in *UAL* as mentioned above), which is likely to exist to some extent in most cases, and prejudice which is likely to be given substantial weight.

8.34 The tribunal has rejected the relevance of a number of factors, which are addressed below.

Factors not to be taken into account

8.35

(i) Alternative sites

There are a number of features of the Code that frustrate landowners. One potential response from a layperson to the idea that ECA might be installed on their land is to say that there is a much better building next door.

However, it seems that it will not be a fruitful avenue for a landowner to argue that there is an alternative site that is more suitable than their own.

In *University of London*, the Upper Tribunal rejected the notion that the comparative suitability of alternative sites had any direct relevance to the para 21(3) test. The Deputy President said:

> 'There was a certain amount of cross examination and submission about the availability of alternative sites which might be used by the claimant instead of the University's Building. I do not regard that evidence as directly relevant to the paragraph 21 test to be applied by the tribunal. The focus of paragraph 21(3) (the second condition) is the public benefit likely to result from the making of the order sought by the operator. No comparison is required (or permitted at this stage) between that public benefit and the public benefit which might result from the making of a different order conferring rights over different land.'[23]

The Deputy President relied on the fact that the Law Commission had considered, and rejected, a possible test under which an operator would have to show that there was no reasonable alternative to the proposed site. The Law Commission concluded that such a test would be impractical, stringent, and could result in a stalemate where several sites were suggested as possible and none could be shown to be unique. However, he did just about leave open the door to a potential argument relating to alternative sites when it came to the stage of the tribunal's discretion:

---

23 [2018] UKUT 356 (LC) at [131]. The decision was upheld by the Court of Appeal, and in any event no question in respect of the relevance of alternative sites to the para 21(3) test was in issue in that appeal.

> 'It might possibly be argued that the availability of an alternative site was relevant to the exercise of the Tribunal's discretion (as to which I express no concluded view) but, generally, a comparison between sites is not required to demonstrate satisfaction of the second paragraph 21 condition.'

However, in *UAL*, the tribunal saw that door as closed when considering it 'well-established that it is no part of the tribunal's task to consider whether alternative sites would do just as well', on the strength of the *University of London* decision.

Even if such an argument could in theory be made, there may be any number of reasons, of which the landowner is unaware, why the operator may have discounted those other sites. In addition to radio planning considerations, there may be planning or listed buildings reasons why a site might be inappropriate, there may be structural concerns, or the roof may be difficult to access or covered with an inconvenient material. It will be a rare case indeed in which the tribunal is willing to condescend into such matters.

(ii) Alternative agreements at the proposed site?

A variation on the above theme is the relevance of an alternative type of agreement in respect of the subject site. In *UAL*, the landowner sought to avoid an agreement being imposed that conferred security of tenure on the operator because it had an obligation to transfer its land to a developer with vacant possession, and an operator with security would jeopardise that. It therefore sought to rely on its willingness to enter into a para 26 agreement without security of tenure on the same roof as that over which para 20 rights were sought, arguing that this was relevant to the exercise of the tribunal's discretion. Indeed, it had recently agreed just such an agreement with rival operators. It was common ground that the tribunal could not actually *impose* a para 26 under the instant Reference, as the tribunal's jurisdiction to grant one is reliant on an application for such an agreement having been made by an operator.[24]

The tribunal held that whether any public benefit arising from the making of a para 26 agreement was a relevant factor in a para 20 case 'will depend upon the circumstances in an individual reference'.[25] However, it approached the para 20 application by comparing the public benefits that would be conferred by the para 20 agreement with the absence of such an agreement, without assuming that a para 26 agreement would be imposed instead. Its reasoning was that: (i) the operator had not sought a para 26 agreement, and it was not known whether it would do so if it failed to obtain a para 20 Order, and (ii) the benefits of a para 20 agreement are not diminished by the fact that the same benefits could be achieved for a certain period by a para 26 agreement. This reasoning would seem to preclude a landowner from raising the possibility of a para 26 agreement as an argument in any case where the operator does not seek one. In such cases, it will be 'all or nothing' for the operator. In *UAL*, it was the latter.

Where an operator seeks Code rights in respect of a site where it only needs rights for a very short period, such as for a weekend music festival,

24 See para 26(1).
25 *UAL* at [48].

it would be expected to be better off seeking rights under para 26, because of the lower burden of proof. However, if it did seek para 20 rights, with the consequence of (presumably quite unnecessary) security of tenure, a landowner would have to fashion its arguments quite carefully. One would hope that the inherent prejudice of having an operator with secure rights over its land would be given some weight, although the public benefit of the para 20 agreement may be considered to be considerable if tens of thousands of people are to descend on the land for a festival. Under the reasoning in *UAL*, the willingness of a landowner to grant a para 26 agreement would not be held to diminish the public benefit achieved by the para 20 agreement sought. There seems no doubt that a para 26 agreement would be far more appropriate, but it is not certain that a tribunal would allow that to feature in its decision-making. It may be that a landowner would have to argue that the tribunal could reasonably infer that the operator would seek a para 26 agreement if its para 20 application failed, and that that possibility should have some weight. If time did not allow for such an application to be made, following service of the relevant notice, it would be hard to see how the tribunal could reach that conclusion on the facts. The tribunal may instead rely on a general discretion to refuse relief, which has been posited to exist even in para 20 cases.[26] It may be that this putative case would be a paradigm example of a situation in which para 20 relief would be refused as a matter of inherent discretion.

(iii) Public 'disbenefit'

The second condition entails a balancing of public benefit against private prejudice. In *UAL*, the argument was made that the grant of the Code rights sought would jeopardise or at least delay a considerable redevelopment project, which itself brought major public benefits. Thus, an element of public 'disbenefit' was argued to be the result of the grant of the Order sought, which should be considered in the balance.

The UT found the assertion of disbenefit to be too speculative to consider on the facts. Furthermore, it rejected the principle that was being advanced, concluding that 'we do not think that the Code requires a net assessment of the public benefit in this way'.[27]

Does the tribunal have a discretion?

8.36 In the para 26 context,[28] the tribunal has made clear that it considers itself to have discretion as to whether to impose an agreement, even if the 'good arguable case'[29] version of the para 21 test is satisfied.

8.37 However, in the context of an application for an agreement with security of tenure, the tribunal has also given an indication that it considers that it has discretion, even where the relevant test is met.

26 See the section below under **8.36**].
27 *UAL* at [59].
28 See Chapter 9.
29 See para 26(3)(b).

8.38 In *Green*, the tribunal said:

> 'Our understanding of the Code is that the Tribunal may (not 'must', so there is a discretion) confer a Code right on the claimant provided that the conditions set out in paragraph 21 are met.'[30]

8.39 It is right to note that *Green* was a renewal case under Part 5, and the Court of Appeal[31] pointed out that para 21 is not applicable in such a case. Thus, the meaning and effect of para 21 did not really arise in *Green*. However, it is nonetheless at least of note that the Upper Tribunal appears to have considered that the use of the word 'may' in para 21(1) confers a discretion.[32]

Para 21(5) – the redevelopment defence

8.40 Paragraph 21(5) creates a 'redevelopment' proviso or defence on which a respondent to an application for Code rights can rely. If the respondent is successful, no order under para 21 can be made, regardless of the public benefit that may have resulted.

8.41 The para 21(5) redevelopment defence is in very similar terms to the para 31(4) redevelopment ground for terminating an extant agreement. A more detailed discussion of redevelopment as a ground to resist or terminate a Code agreement can be found at Chapter 17.

8.42 However, there are two points of difference between a para 21(5) case and a para 31(4)(c) case that are worthy of consideration:

(i) in the para 21(5) case, the operator is not yet in situ on the respondent's land; and

(ii) the precise contents of the agreement which the respondent asserts would thwart its redevelopment are arguably not yet precisely known.

8.43 These two points are briefly considered below.

Operator not yet on the land

8.44 As to the first of these points, it is worth remembering that an application under para 20 can come out of the blue, from a landowner's point of view. This is of considerable importance, given that it is the landowner that will have the burden of proof in respect of any redevelopment argument and hence will have to produce and/or collate substantial evidence. Yes, 28 days' notice must be given before an operator can make an application to the tribunal, and yes, it is expected that an operator will engage

30 [2020] UKUT 0348 (LC) at [49].

31 *On Tower UK Ltd v JH & FW Green Ltd* [2021] EWCA Civ 1858. See [32], [36] and [39] of the judgment. The Court of Appeal cast no doubt on the proposition that there is a discretion under Part 4 even when the para 21 test is met by an operator, despite quoting that part of the judgment below more than once. However, that was not a question that was in issue on appeal, and so one cannot safely derive any approval of that proposition from the Court of Appeal's decision.

32 One would imagine that the Tribunal here was quoting para 21(1) ('the court may make an order under paragraph 20 if (and only if) the court thinks that both of the following conditions are met').

positively with a landowner before serving such a notice or at least before making the tribunal application. However, the time available to a landowner to produce a redevelopment case is minimal compared with the time it would have in equivalent cases under the 1954 Act.

8.45 In the 1954 Act context:

(i) the parties will already have been in a landlord and tenant relationship, with knowledge of when the contractual term of the tenancy is coming to an end;

(ii) often it is the landlord itself which prompts the ground (f) litigation with a section 25 notice under the 1954 Act;

(iii) the notices that prompt 1954 Act termination litigation are between 6 and 12 months in duration; and

(iv) the litigation process does not have to be concluded within 6 months (unlike para 20 applications). Indeed, ordinarily it will take very considerably longer than that, and it is the landlord's intention at the date of trial which must be evidenced.

8.46 The redevelopment ground under the 1954 Act (ground (f) of section 30(1)) is well-known to property lawyers. There are obvious, and intentional, similarities between that ground and the para 31(4)(c) redevelopment ground for termination under the Code. However, there is no exact equivalent for the para 21(5) defence under the 1954 Act, because under the 1954 Act a landlord is never having to prove its redevelopment intentions in advance of a tenant being present on its land.

Terms of the agreement not yet known

8.47 Under both para 21(5) and para 31(4)(c), a landowner has to show the requisite intention[33] to carry out redevelopment. However, in addition, it has to show that it could not reasonably do so on a particular factual premise. The wording of this factual premise is different under para 21(5) than under para 31(4)(c), as follows:

(i) under para 21(5) a landowner has to prove that it could not reasonably redevelop 'if the order were made';

(ii) by contrast, under para 31(4)(c) a landowner has to prove that it could not reasonably redevelop 'unless the code agreement comes to an end'.

8.48 Thus, in the para 31 termination context, the landowner has to prove that the *existing* Code agreement would not reasonably allow the redevelopment. The goal posts are very clearly fixed. The terms of the existing agreement are known.

8.49 However, in the para 21(5) context, one must consider the compatibility of the proposed redevelopment with 'the order'. Does 'the order' mean the Order that is sought by the applicant operator with no amendments, or does it mean the Order that the tribunal would make but for the redevelopment argument? If it means the

33 In both its subjective and objective forms, as per the relevant 1954 Act case law, as applied in the UT in the context of the Code in *EE Ltd and Hutchison 3G UK Ltd v Meyrick 1968 Combined Trust Of Meyrick Estate Management* [2019] UKUT 164 (LC)..

latter, then that requires a landowner to satisfy the burden of proof as regards the incompatibility of its redevelopment plans with an agreement whose terms are not yet certain.

8.50 Given that the tribunal is obliged to consider whether to impose a 'lift and shift' provision,[34] and given that the tribunal may have jurisdiction to make an Order in respect of a lesser area of land than that specified in the operator's para 20 notice, the ultimate terms of an agreement may have a very considerable effect on that agreement's compatibility with a landowner's redevelopment plans. It may be that a landowner's rock solid case against the Order originally sought may be totally thwarted by the goal posts moving.

8.51 Paragraph 21(2) and 21(3) both refer to 'the order'. If the tribunal is never going to impose the agreement precisely as sought, why should it be required to consider the prejudice caused by an Order imposing the agreement in that precise form? It might be argued that when considering those tests, the tribunal has to consider the prejudice and public benefit that would be caused not by an Order for the precise agreement originally sought but by an Order for an agreement with 'appropriate' terms. That being the case, it could easily be argued that the expression 'the order' in para 21(5) has a like meaning. Whether such an interpretation would be consistent with the legislative intention is arguably a different matter. It would seem strange for para 21(5) to be robbed of its force by the introduction of a 'lift and shift' provision when the para 31(4)(c) redevelopment ground is not affected by such a possibility.

The national security bar

8.52 By para 27ZA,[35] the tribunal must refuse a para 20 application if the Secretary of State certifies that the Order sought would be likely to prejudice national security, defence, or 'law enforcement'. The latter term means 'the prevention, investigation, detection or prosecution of criminal offences including the safeguarding against and the prevention of threats to public security'.

34 See para 23(8)(b).

35 Inserted by s 66(2) of the Product Security and Telecommunications Infrastructure Act 2022.

9

Para 26 agreements: 'interim' Code rights

9.01 Paragraph 26 is headed 'Interim code rights'. It provides a procedure for having an agreement that confers Code rights (or provides for a person to be bound by a Code right) imposed for a fixed period, that is not continued by para 30(2). As will be seen, this lack of statutory continuation is the central difference between the effect of a para 26 agreement and that of an agreement imposed under para 20. As discussed further below, para 26 agreements need not be interim 'to' anything, and can be entirely freestanding.

9.02 As for the procedure by which a para 26 agreement comes into being, there are two main differences from the procedure that follows from an 'ordinary' para 20 notice. Those differences are:

(i) a para 26 agreement cannot be entered into consensually – it requires an Order to be made by the tribunal; and

(ii) when an application is made in respect of a para 26 agreement, the test that an operator must surmount is less onerous than for the imposition of an agreement under para 20.

9.03 Paragraph 26 agreements are imposed in a variety of circumstances, for example:

- to allow 'MSVs' (multi-skilled visits), which are a type of survey typically intended to ascertain or confirm the suitability of a site for the installation of ECA;
- to allow ECA to be installed on a genuinely interim basis, pending the determination of a concurrent application for a para 20 agreement, which (if granted) would then have statutory continuation under para 30(2);
- to allow the temporary installation and operation of ECA to provide for a short-term event such as a music festival;
- to provide for communications services to be continued following the decommissioning of a nearby site (for whatever reason), before a new site can be identified and Code rights sought over it pursuant to para 20; or
- to provide certainty in the settlement of a dispute as to what rights an operator continues to hold in respect of a property which it is already occupying but which it accepts that it will have to vacate at some point in the future (for example, because its Code rights are likely to have lapsed before the Code came into force or because the landowner has an intention to redevelop the site).

9.04 If an agreement is imposed under para 26, it takes effect as an agreement under Part 2 of the Code.[1] The provisions of paras 25 and 84 (as regards compensation) apply[2] to an agreement under para 26 just as they do to an agreement under para 20.

1 By para 22, applied to a para 26 case by para 26(4)(b).
2 By virtue of para 26(4)(e) and (f).

The nature of para 26 agreements: lack of statutory continuation

9.05 Although para 26 agreements are said by para 26(1) to be imposed 'on an interim basis', this phrase is not used in the sense that would be expected by lawyers practising in most fields.

9.06 Paragraph 26(2) provides that an Order under para 26 imposes an agreement 'on an interim basis' if it provides for a person to be bound either:

(a) for the period specified in the Order; or

(b) until the occurrence of an event specified in the Order.

9.07 Once the period specified has lapsed, or once the specified occurrence has occurred, the para 26 agreement comes to an end. It is not subject to the statutory continuation of para 30(2) that affects 'ordinary' Code agreements imposed under para 20 or agreed consensually. This is because of para 30(3), which expressly disapplies para 30(2) in respect of Code rights that arise by virtue of an Order under para 26.

9.08 The consequence of this is that once the para 26 agreement has come to an end, the person on whom it had been binding then has a right to require the removal of any ECA that has been placed on land in accordance with that agreement,[3] unless an agreement has been imposed under para 20 relating to the Code right imposed under the para 26 agreement. That right to require removal is subject to, and must be exercised in accordance with, Part 6 of the Code (which is discussed in detail at Chapter 18).

MSVs

9.09 In the *Hackney* (Tradescant House)[4] case, Judge Cooke noted that interim rights are often sought as the basis for an operator 'to carry out the investigation that is needed before deciding whether or not to seek the right to place equipment on the site.'[5] She continued:

> 'Such an investigation is known as a 'multi-skilled visit' or MSV. It may be a simple visual inspection, or it may involve intrusive works that penetrate the fabric of a building.' [6]

9.10 In the *University of London* case, the rights that were sought were non-intrusive survey rights. The question arose as to whether such rights were capable of being Code rights under para 3 at all, and hence whether an operator is permitted to seek them in isolation (whether under para 20 or para 26). If the Code right to install ECA is being sought under para 3(a), then one might think that there would be jurisdiction to allow survey rights as part of the appropriate 'other terms' of the agreement under para 23.

9.11 However, where no ECA installation rights are sought, a right to survey would only be able to be requested under the para 20 process or para 26 process if it is

3 See para 26(7) and (8), and para 37(1) and (3)(a).
4 [2022] UKUT 210 (LC).
5 At [7].
6 At [8].

itself a Code right. Paragraph 20 only applies at all where an operator requires a Code right to be conferred (or someone to be bound by a Code right),[7] para 20(2) requires that a Code right be set out in the notice; and the only agreements that a tribunal can impose under para 20(4) are those that confer a Code right or render someone bound by a Code right. Similarly, under para 26(3), a para 26 notice must comply with para 20(2), and the only agreements that a tribunal can impose under para 26(1) are those that confer a Code right or render someone bound by a Code right (on an 'interim basis').

9.12 At first instance, the UT[8] had held that the right on the part of an operator for the statutory purposes to carry out non-intrusive survey works constituted a Code right because it fell within the rights mentioned at para 3(a), or 3(d), or alternatively was an implied Code right. Paras 3(a) and (d) contain these rights:

> '(a) to install electronic communications apparatus on, under or over the land,
>
> …
>
> (d) to carry out any works on the land for or in connection with the installation of electronic communications apparatus on, under or over the land or elsewhere'

9.13 The site provider appealed. The Court of Appeal doubted that the right to install ECA under para 3(a) carried with it a right to assess the suitability of a site. However, it held that non-intrusive surveys did indeed fall within para 3(d) of the Code.

9.14 As has frequently been the case when the higher courts have had to interpret disputed provisions of the Code, the Court of Appeal relied on the perceived legislative purpose in reaching its conclusion.

9.15 The court said as follows:

> 'The context in the present case is a Code designed to facilitate the provision of electronic communications apparatus in the public interest. It is not necessary for the "works" in paragraph 3(d) to amount to the installation of electronic communications equipment, because that right is already encompassed within paragraph 3 (a). So the right under paragraph 3 (d) must be wider. Nor is it necessary that the works be 'for' the installation of such equipment, because the Code uses the phrase 'for or in connection with'. It is enough that they are 'in connection' with that installation. The width of the definition is emphasised by the phrase 'any works'. Where the legislation uses an imprecise word, a court is entitled to place strong reliance on the legislative purpose underpinning the legislation. That purpose is undoubtedly to facilitate the improvement of electronic communications throughout the country. That purpose cannot be sensibly achieved unless operators can acquire (compulsorily if need be) the right to assess the suitability of potential sites.'[9]

7 See para 20(1).

8 *Cornerstone Telecommunications Infrastructure Ltd v The University Of London* [2018] UKUT 356 (LC).

9 *The University of London v Cornerstone Telecommunications Infrastructure Limited* [2019] EWCA Civ 2075 at [47].

9.16 Although the *University of London* case related to an MSV permitting only non-intrusive works, it is clearly the case that intrusive works undertaken as part of a survey for the requisite purpose would *a fortiori* constitute 'any works on the land…' under para 3(d).[10]

Can only be imposed by tribunal

9.17 Where a person confers Code rights on an operator by consensual agreement under para 9, the agreement is statutorily continued beyond its contractual term by para 30(2). Paragraph 100 of the Code makes clear that parties are not intended to be able to 'contract out' of the provisions of Parts 3 to 6 of the Code, including the security of tenure provision at para 30(2). In order for parties to be able to avoid the consequences of para 30(2) in a consensual agreement, there would need to be an express provision or procedure that allowed that to happen. There is none.

9.18 Paragraph 26 does not create a species of agreement that parties can decide to create consensually. Rather, it creates a procedure by which an Order can be sought from the tribunal that confers Code rights or makes a party bound by Code rights on a basis that has no statutory continuation:[11] 'An operator may apply to the court for an order…' (para 26(1)), 'An order under this paragraph imposes an agreement…' (para 26(2)), and 'The court may make an order under this paragraph if (and only if)…' (para 26(3)).

9.19 Why should this be so? In *University of London*,[12] the Court of Appeal set out a likely explanation at [76]:

> '76. There are two features of paragraph 26 which, at first sight, might be puzzling. The first is that an order of the UT is required under paragraph 26 even if the parties agree on the terms of interim code rights. We consider that the probable explanation is that the policy underlying the Code is that agreements to confer code rights cannot exclude the security of tenure for which paragraph 30 (2) provides: see paragraph 100. Paragraph 30 (3) disapplies paragraph 30 (2); but only where the interim or temporary code right is conferred by order of the UT. We consider that the probable explanation is that the legislative intention was that, since interim code rights should not attract security of tenure, the oversight of the UT was required for their conferral.'

9.20 Those who practise in the field of commercial landlord and tenant law may observe that this structure is not dissimilar from the position under the 1954 Act prior to the 2004 reforms. Prior to 1 June 2004, in order to 'contract out' of the security of tenure provisions of sections 24 to 28 of the 1954 Act, it was necessary for a joint application to be made to court for an Order under section 38(4) of the 1954 Act (now repealed).

9.21 It might seem curious for the oversight of the tribunal to be considered necessary in order to achieve what 'contracting out' does under the 1954 Act. After

10 And indeed, it had been accepted by the site provider that such intrusive works would amount to 'works' as that term is used in para 3 of the Code – see at [48] of the Court of Appeal's judgment.

11 By virtue of para 30(3).

12 *The University of London v Cornerstone Telecommunications Infrastructure Limited* [2019] EWCA Civ 2075.

all: (a) such oversight is surely in place in order to protect the operator, (b) para 26 is only engaged upon the application of an operator, so an operator must already be 'on board' with the idea of an agreement conferring no security of tenure, (c) it is no longer considered necessary[13] in the wide variety of commercial lease cases to which the 1954 Act rather than the Code applies, and (d) operators are specialist commercial entities who understand their interests and the regulatory landscape within which they operate to a far greater degree than, for example, the average tenant of a family business. Nonetheless, the Court of Appeal's explanation appears the most likely.

Can be sought on a freestanding basis

9.22 The second point which the Court of Appeal had to consider in *University of London* was whether a para 26 agreement could be sought as a freestanding agreement or whether it was necessary to be seeking a 'full' Code agreement under para 20 in order to be permitted to seek a para 26 agreement. It was concluded that a freestanding application is indeed permissible in principle.

9.23 The Code refers to the rights sought under para 26 as 'Interim code rights' (at least in the heading to para 26), and then talks of rights being imposed 'on an interim basis' at para 26(1). One could be forgiven for thinking that para 26 is dealing with rights that are necessarily interim and which are imposed on a genuinely interim basis. However, that need not be the case at all, as a matter of ordinary language or even as a matter of conventional 'legalese'.

9.24 The word 'interim' comes directly from the Latin adverb meaning something like 'in the meantime'. At least in British English, and used adjectivally, it surely connotes both: (i) that something is temporary; and (ii) that it is intended to exist and have effect until something more permanent exists (or until a decision is made not to bring into being the permanent equivalent).

9.25 An agreement imposed on an interim basis under para 26, however, may in a given case only satisfy the first of those strands of meaning. This is essentially because para 26(2) defines 'on an interim basis' as only having this first essential strand of meaning – the rights are temporary in that they will last for the period specified in the para 26 Order (see para 26(2)(a)) or until the occurrence of an event specified in the Order (see para 26(2)(b)). This definition, coupled with the effect of para 30(3), means that para 26 rights will come to an end in accordance with the para 26 Order and the contractual terms of the imposed agreement, and are not continued by para 30(2).

9.26 Paragraph 27 agreements, by contrast, are genuinely interim. They can only be sought where an operator serves a para 20 notice 'and also' requires agreement in respect of Code rights on a temporary basis. Further, they can only be granted for securing the objective of maintaining the network (etc) 'until' the proceedings under para 20 (and any proceedings under para 40) are determined.

13 Having been replaced by the procedure set out in s 38A(1) and (3) of the 1954 Act, which involves a notice being given to a tenant in accordance with the Regulatory Reform (Business Tenancies) (England and Wales) Order 2003 before an effective contracting out can take place, with no court supervision of such an arrangement being required.

9.27 These features of the Code have led some to comment that para 26 rights should perhaps have been called temporary rights (because they are), and para 27 rights should perhaps have been called interim rights (because they are). But so long as one understands the species of rights available and the tests for the conferral thereof, the nomenclature perhaps does not much matter.

9.28 One can now indeed understand what is available and in what circumstances in respect of para 26, thanks to the Court of Appeal's judgment in *University of London*.

9.29 The Court of Appeal referred to the Law Commission's report[14] in observing that:

> 'The Law Commission's intention, in recommending the power to grant interim rights, was to enable early access for the purpose of exercising code rights while any dispute about the compensation payable for or other terms of a full-blown agreement was resolved.'

9.30 The court concluded that the government appears to have taken a similar view, citing a government policy document[15] and also para 422 of the explanatory notes to the Digital Economy Act 2017, the latter of which said:

> 'Paragraph 26 provides that an operator may apply for 'interim code rights'. This enables code rights to be granted on an interim basis pending the parties reaching, or the court imposing, a final agreement.'

9.31 However, the court considered that its task was to consider whether the Code as actually drafted goes further than what had apparently been intended.

9.32 In undertaking this task, it noted the following features of para 26:

- Paragraph 26(2) in effect defines what is meant by 'interim', with no reference to any gap between the application under para 20 and its final determination.
- There is no reference in para 26 to the discontinuance of the application before a final hearing, in contrast to the Law Commission's report at para 9.67.
- Paragraph 26 requires a notice which 'complies with' para 20(2). In para 27, where rights are imposed pending a final hearing of a para 20 application, what is required is a notice given 'under' para 20(2). Further, under para 27 the notice under para 20 must 'also' require agreement on a temporary basis.
- The stated objective of para 27 is the provision of the operator's service 'until the proceedings under paragraph 20 … are determined'. The language refers to 'the' proceedings under para 20 and not 'any' proceedings. Thus, in a para 27 case, there are always proceedings under para 20 pending which are distinct from those under para 27. There is no equivalent wording in para 26.
- Paragraph 27 applies only where there is apparatus on the land. Para 26 does not.

14 Law Com 336 at paras 9.50, 9.51, 9.63 and 9.67.

15 Namely the Executive Summary in the policy document published by the Department of Culture, Media and Sport in May 2016.

- There is no security of tenure under para 26, enabling a landowner to require removal as soon as the para 26 agreement expires, whereas para 27 operates in the context of an application for continuing rights under para 20.

9.33 The Court of Appeal did not consider that the lower 'good arguable case' threshold necessarily meant that at a later date the test would be revisited on a 'balance of probabilities' basis. It observed, on the basis of the Law Commission report, that the lower test appears to derive from cases about service of proceedings outside the jurisdiction, where a good arguable case has to be established that one or more gateways apply without that question ever needing to be revisited at trial.

9.34 The court further considered that there would be cases where there is no practical need for a final determination at a later hearing. For example, where the right is by its nature only needed for a particular period of time, such as in the case of an MSV. Also, a one-off event like a music festival was referred to. Although the court did not put it in such terms, it would be absurd if security of tenure attached to Code rights conferred for an MSV or for a music festival, and accordingly, it makes sense that there is a species of application that can be made to secure rights with no such security.

9.35 Landowners will be concerned that as any Code right can in theory be sought under para 26, an operator can obtain the benefit of the lower 'good arguable case', thus circumventing the ordinary application of the test under para 21. However, the tribunals have established that the power to impose a para 26 agreement is indeed a discretionary one. That being the case, there is the power to show disapproval of any attempt to utilise para 26 as a freestanding vehicle to a Code right, where a conventional para 20 application should properly have been made, by exercising its discretion to refuse the application.

Procedure for obtaining a para 26 Order

9.36 There are a number of pre-requisites in order for the tribunal to have power to make an Order under para 26. The first two requirements relate to the service of a valid notice. The final requirement is that either para 26(3)(a) or 26(3)(b) be satisfied.

The notice

9.37 By para 26(3), such a notice must:

(i) Comply with para 20(2). In short this means that it must set out the Code right and all of the other terms of the agreement that the operator seeks, and state that the operator seeks the recipient's agreement to those terms; and

(ii) State that an agreement is sought on an interim basis.

9.38 See also Chapter 20 in respect of the form, content and service requirements of a para 26 notice.

9.39 The question of effectively abridging time under para 26(5) (and the equivalent provision in the para 27 context) is also considered at Chapter 20.

The application

9.40 The operator may apply to the tribunal for an Order under para 26 if:

(a) the recipient does not agree within 28 days of service of the para 26 notice to confer or otherwise be bound by the Code right;[16] or

(b) at any time after the notice is given, the recipient gives notice in writing to the operator that it does not agree to confer or otherwise be bound by the Code right.[17]

The circumstances in which an Order can be made: para 26(3)(a) and (b)

9.41 In order for an agreement to be imposed under para 26, either para 26(3)(a) or 26(3)(b) must be satisfied.

9.42 Paragraph 26(3)(a) is satisfied where the operator, the person on whom the Order would impose the para 26 agreement, has agreed both to the making of the Order and to the terms of the agreement to be imposed by it.

9.43 In default of such agreement under para 26(3)(a), the only way of a para 26 agreement being imposed is if, under para 26(3)(b):

> 'the court thinks that there is a good arguable case that the test in paragraph 21 for the making of an order under paragraph 20 is met'.

9.44 Accordingly, the same para 21 matters must be considered as under a para 20 application. However, rather than being satisfied that the para 21 test is met on the balance of probabilities, the tribunal need only be satisfied that there is a 'good arguable case' that that test is met.

9.45 In *Canada Trust v Stolzenberg* ,[18] the concept of a good arguable case was said to reflect 'that one side has a much better argument on the material available'.

9.46 That dictum was referred to in the interim rights decision in the *Islington*[19] case, in which the Deputy President noted that Parliament adopted the Law Commission's recommendation that the *Canada Trust* standard be applied, and hence that an operator did not need to establish its para 21 case on the balance of probabilities. He went on to state that an operator's case:

> 'need not be free of all doubt or uncertainty at this stage but it must be a case which is more than simply arguable. It must have a certain amount of strength and persuasiveness about it'. [20]

16 Para 20(3)(a), applied to a para 26 case by para 26(4)(a).

17 Para 20(3)(b), applied to a para 26 case by para 26(4)(a).

18 [1998] 1 WLR 547.

19 *EE Ltd & Hutchison 3G UK Ltd v London Borough Of Islington* [2018] UKUT 0361 (LC) at [15].

20 *EE Ltd & Hutchison 3G UK Ltd v London Borough Of Islington* [2018] UKUT 0361 (LC) at [16].

The national security bar

9.47 By para 27ZA,[21] the tribunal must refuse a para 26 application if the Secretary of State certifies that the Order sought would be likely to prejudice national security, defence or 'law enforcement'. The latter term means 'the prevention, investigation, detection or prosecution of criminal offences including the safeguarding against and the prevention of threats to public security'.

Need for a notice – no freestanding jurisdiction to award as 'second prize'

9.48 It is important to note that a notice under para 26 is a pre-condition for the tribunal to have jurisdiction to impose an agreement under that paragraph. The tribunal can therefore not impose an agreement without security of tenure as a 'second prize' where an operator does not manage to tip the balance in a para 20 case in favour of the imposition of an agreement.[22]

When is a para 26 application determined?

9.49 In *Islington*, the Deputy President held that it was the intention of the Code that para 26 applications should be 'determined without delay and by a summary procedure'.[23]

9.50 For that reason, the tribunal gave directions that the para 26 application element of the Reference should be determined at the case management hearing 'if it was possible to do so fairly'.[24] The tribunal has typically adopted that procedural approach in the majority of References which involve a para 26 application.

9.51 Those advising landowners should therefore be aware that they are generally not likely to have a great deal of time to prepare for a hearing at which para 26 Code rights are imposed, once an application is made to the tribunal.

The approach to evidence

9.52 A para 26 application tends to be conducted as a relatively summary procedure. The approach to evidence is therefore different than in many other Code cases. As explained in the interim decision in the *Islington* case, one would not ordinarily expect there to be cross-examination in para 26 cases. Further, disclosure is in the hands of the operator seeking the Order. However, the tribunal will not generally make assumptions in favour of an operator that is in a position to provide evidence.

---

21 Inserted by s 66(2) of the Product Security and Telecommunications Infrastructure Act 2022.

22 For example, in *UAL* where the site provider stated that it was content for a para 26 agreement to be imposed, but none was sought, and so none could be considered by the Tribunal.

23 *Islington* (interim rights judgment) at [2018] UKUT 361 (LC), at [5].

24 *Islington* (interim rights judgment) at [2018] UKUT 361 (LC), at [5].

A discretionary remedy

9.53 It appears well-established that the tribunal has discretion as to whether to make an Order under para 26, even where it has concluded that there is a 'good arguable case' under para 26(3)(b) that the para 21 test is met.

9.54 The UT has stated in numerous cases[25] that its jurisdiction to make any Order conferring interim rights is discretionary. For example, in *University of London,*[26] the Deputy President held at [93] that:

> 'The Tribunal is not obliged to make the order sought, but it must exercise its discretion judicially and on a proper consideration of the relevant facts.'

9.55 The *University of London*[27] case went on appeal to the Court of Appeal. The decision was upheld on both grounds of appeal, neither of which related to the question whether the Upper Tribunal had a discretion as to whether to make a para 26 Order. Although it is true that the Court of Appeal's reasoning on some matters differed from that of the Upper Tribunal,[28] the Court of Appeal expressly agreed that the tribunal has a discretion as to whether to make an Order under para 26. At [80] of its judgment, the Court of Appeal said:

> 'In an extreme case the UT might exercise the discretion which it has under paragraph 26 to refuse to impose the agreement at all.'

Relevance of previous negotiations

9.56 In *Islington,*[29] the Deputy President rejected the proposition that the position taken by parties in negotiations was necessarily irrelevant to the exercise of the tribunal's discretion. It was observed that each case would turn on its own facts, but that 'the tribunal will have greater confidence in imposing an agreement where it is apparent that the rights sought are not objectionable to the site owner in principle, subject to appropriate financial terms'.

Urgency

9.57 Although an operator benefits from a lower threshold test in the context of para 26 than it would under para 20, and although a para 26 Order is often sought as a prelude to a longer agreement under para 20, there is no requirement for any particular urgency to be shown.

9.58 However, urgency is capable of being relevant to the determination of a para 26 application. As the Deputy President said in *Islington*:

---

25 See, eg, *St Martins* at [19].

26 *Cornerstone Telecommunications Infrastructure Ltd v The University Of London* [2018] UKUT 356 (LC).

27 *The University of London v Cornerstone Telecommunications Infrastructure Limited* [2019] EWCA Civ 2075.

28 It held that the right to undertake a non-intrusive 'MSV' was a Code right under para 3(d), whereas the UT had held that it was an express Code right under para 3(a) or in the alternative under para 3(d), or should be taken to be implied as a Code right.

29 In the interim rights judgment at [2018] UKUT 361 (LC), at [21].

'Clearly if an operator has a pressing need for access to the only site capable of meeting an immediate demand the Tribunal will bear that in mind and give it greater weight than where the public's requirements for communication services are adequately satisfied by existing facilities. In an appropriate case urgency might go both to the question of public benefit and how it weighs in the balance and to the exercise of the Tribunal's discretion.'[30]

Limit on duration

9.59 There is no limit on the potential duration of a para 26 agreement as a matter of jurisdiction.[31] However, as the imposition of a para 26 agreement is discretionary, and as an operator does not have to satisfy the full para 21 test to the normal civil standard, a tribunal might be expected to take some persuading before granting such an agreement with a very substantial term. Indeed, if it appears to a tribunal that an operator is using the para 26 procedure to achieve fairly long-term rights in order to avoid having to satisfy the para 21 test on the full basis, it would be open to a tribunal to reject such an application on a summary basis,[32] or to impose an agreement with a shorter duration, if it were considered appropriate to do so under para 23(2) (which applies by virtue of para 26(4)(c)).

Terms

Relevant provisions

9.60 Para 23 of the Code makes provision as to the terms of an agreement which is imposed by the tribunal under para 20.

9.61 The provisions of para 23 are also applied[33] to cases under para 26. The only two modifications to the ordinary operation of para 23 in para 26 cases are as follows:

(a) references in para 23 to the 'relevant person' are to be construed as references to the respondent on whom the para 26 agreement is to be imposed;[34] and

(b) the *duty* in para 23 to include terms as to the payment of consideration is instead a *power* to do so.[35]

9.62 Accordingly, when considering what terms should be imposed in a para 26 agreement, the tribunal is principally considering what is 'appropriate'.[36] There is a fuller discussion of the various provisions of para 23, as well as examples of tribunal decisions on particular terms, in Chapter 11.

30 In the interim rights judgment at [2018] UKUT 361 (LC), at [22].

31 See *UAL* at [43] and [47].

32 The Upper Tribunal has the express power to strike out on the basis that a party's case has no reasonable prospect of succeeding (r 8(3)(c) of The Tribunal Procedure (Upper Tribunal) (Lands Chamber) Rules 2010), having first given the opportunity for submissions under r 8(4). The Tribunal might decide either that such an application was an abuse of process, or simply that as a matter of discretion there would be no reasonable prospect of the Tribunal being convinced to make the Order sought.

33 Expressly, by para 26(4)(c).

34 See para 26(6)(a), and para 26(1) which is referred to therein.

35 See para 26(6)(b). The duty referred to, which applies in the case of an ordinary para 20 application, is contained in para 23(3).

36 By para 23(2).

Judicial guidance as to content of interim agreements

9.63 It is fair to note that although the same[37] set of statutory tests and instructions applies in para 26 cases, the different factual circumstances present in para 26 cases will naturally come to bear on decisions made by the tribunal. Below are some judicial observations that may assist in understanding the approach that the tribunal is likely to take in a para 26 case.

Length and complexity of the document

9.64 The tribunal has been keen to see para 26 agreements which are not overly long or complicated. This is consonant with the tribunal's even greater keenness that 'interim' matters be conducted at a cost that is at least not grossly disproportionate.[38]

9.65 As the Deputy President said in *Islington*:

> 'As to the terms of the agreement, the claimant seeks the imposition on an interim basis of an agreement in the same terms as it seeks under paragraph 20. In principle I do not think that is the right way to go about it. The claimants' proposed agreement under paragraph 20 is an elaborate document, but it need not be if it is only going to be of 3 or 4 months duration.'[39]

Burdens and risks on landowners

9.66 In *Islington*, in the very first judgment in which the para 21 test was substantively considered in the 'interim' context, the tribunal indicated that at the interim stage a landowner should be protected against obligations, undertakings, and risks. This statement of principle is perhaps justified by the fact that an operator only has to satisfy a reduced burden under para 26(3)(b) in this species of application. The Deputy President said as follows in respect of the drafting of the interim agreement:

> 'I consider that in principle it ought to impose no obligations on the site owner other than an obligation not to derogate from the rights which have been granted. It should require no covenants or undertakings from the site owner. It should put the full risk of the operation which the operator wishes to embark on on the operator and none of the risk on the site provider.'[40]

Terms of MSV agreements

9.67 As MSV agreements are of a quite different nature from, and typically have a shorter term than, most other forms of Code agreements, certain particular considerations arise as to their terms.

37 Save for the two modifications already mentioned above, and contained within para 26(6)(a) and (b).

38 The Tribunal referred in *Cornerstone Telecommunications Infrastructure v St Martins Property Investments & Anor* [2021] UKUT 262 (LC) at [20] to its 'repeated insistence that references seeking access rights under paragraph 26 should be conducted as economically as possible'.

39 In the interim rights judgment at *EE Ltd & Hutchison 3G UK Ltd v London Borough Of Islington* [2018] UKUT 0361 (LC), at [48].

40 In the interim rights judgment at *EE Ltd & Hutchison 3G UK Ltd v London Borough Of Islington* [2018] UKUT 0361 (LC), at [48].

Intrusive works in MSV cases

9.68 In an MSV case, not only is the usual para 26(3)(b) 'good arguable case' threshold applicable, but also it has by definition not yet been established even to the operator's satisfaction that the relevant site is an appropriate location for its ECA. Accordingly, the tribunal has been slow to allow any physically intrusive works to buildings in cases where there is a genuine dispute over whether suvh works should be allowed.

9.69 In *St Martins*, the Deputy President said as follows:

> 'There certainly have been occasions when terms permitting intrusive works in the form of section 7 of the claimant's draft agreement have been imposed by the Tribunal. But I am not aware of a case in which terms authorising interference with the structure of the building have been granted where these have been opposed by the site provider.'[41]

9.70 An additional reason for the reticence to allow intrusive works is surely that the content of such works is seldom spelt out in detail in the proposed draft agreement.. It is extremely common for an operator to serve a standard form MSV agreement on a landowner. Standard MSV agreements are generally not overly long in form, but frequently set out what works are intended as part of the MSV on a non-exhaustive basis. Indeed, one such form includes the expression 'without limitation' at the top of the list of rights granted, and then again within the reference to the types of surveys that might be carried out. A landowner may have a particular reason why allowing such free rein would be problematic, beyond the understandable desire to retain control of its own premises.

9.71 In *St Martins*, the building in question was of considerable value, and there was evidence that the roof covering at the building was of a particular type that would cause problems if intrusive works were carried out on it. As in all cases, the facts of this case doubtless influenced the disposition of the tribunal, but one can nonetheless discern principles that will be of wider application in the comments of the Deputy President. He said as follows:

> '16. The claimant's standard form of draft agreement has been seen by the Tribunal before. It includes a schedule of small print terms and conditions section 7 of which deals with what are euphemistically referred to as 'investigative works'. The original draft of the agreement put forward in this case has been modified and amended but in its first form it defined investigative works simply as works to be undertaken pursuant to section 7. The best that could be said of that drafting is that it was circular because section 7 did not explain what works could be undertaken as investigative works at all; it was entirely open ended. That gave rise to a legitimate concern on the part of the building owner and its advisers that the claimant was asking for unrestricted rights to do undefined works, constrained only by the purpose for which they were to be undertaken.'

9.72 The operator then responded with what the tribunal described as a 'more informative definition of investigative works', which would be such as were specified

41 At [20].

in a notice and which were permitted to include certain works that would be listed in the proposed agreement term. These works were noted to be described 'without limitation', however.

9.73 The tribunal confirmed that the tribunal does of course have power to impose rights authorising an operator to investigate the structure of a building, before opining that 'The question in all of these cases is whether and at what stage the tribunal should do so.' The discretionary nature of the tribunal's para 26(3) power to impose an agreement was noted. Two factors referred to in exercising the discretion not to allow intrusive works were the para 23(5) duty to include terms for ensuring the least possible loss and damage pursuant to the exercise of the rights and the low evidential hurdle which an operator has to satisfy under para 26(3)(b).[42]

9.74 The tribunal noted the understandable reluctance of the owner of any valuable, high-quality building 'to allow contractors over whom it has no authority or control to interfere with the structure of its building', before referring to particular sensitivities that existed in the present case to the operator being given *carte blanche* to undertake intrusive works.

9.75 The Deputy President went on to refer back to the earlier *Islington* case, in which the site provider objected to destructive works being undertaken when it had not yet been established that the site was suitable from a radio planning perspective. The solution that had been adopted on that occasion was as follows:

> 'The Tribunal permitted the operator to go onto the roof of a building to carry out non-intrusive works and gave it permission to come back within the same reference to seek the right to carry out intrusive works.'[43]

9.76 In the *Hackney* (Tradescant House)[44] case, a differently constituted tribunal indicated its lack of enthusiasm for an application to carry out 'entirely unspecified intrusive works' in an MSV, and the application for any intrusive element of the proposed works was ultimately dropped.

9.77 Thus, while the particular sensitivities on the facts of the *St Martins* case were relevant, one can see from both *Islington* and *St Martins* a clear reticence on the part of the tribunal to allow unparticularised intrusive works to high-value buildings when landowners object to such works, at a time when the radio planning suitability of the site has not yet been finally confirmed to the operator's satisfaction.

9.78 It remains to be seen what degree of particularisation of works the tribunal would require once radio planning suitability has been confirmed by a survey. One would imagine that it may very much depend on the nature of the building and the facts of the case. But as a general proposition, one would expect a reasonable degree of particularisation to be required. It may be thought that in any case involving a functionally sound and economically viable building, total *carte blanche* is difficult to square with para 23(5). Given that some degree of particularisation was possible for the operator in *St Martins* once pressed, it seems unlikely in a typical case that it is an unreasonable ask of an operator.

---

42 Ie a 'good arguable case' that the para 21 test is met.
43 *St Martins* at [20].
44 [2022] UKUT 210 (LC) at [22].

Term

9.79 As indicated above, there is no jurisdictional bar on any particular term-length. The tribunal will take into account all relevant factors and decide on what term is 'appropriate'.[45] Doubtless the relevant circumstances will include the fact that para 30(2) does not apply to the agreement in question, and hence it will come to an end in accordance with its contractual terms.[46]

9.80 As indicated elsewhere, if an overly long term is sought, this may in an extreme case result in the tribunal considering that the use of the para 26 process is inappropriate and even an abuse of process.

9.81 However, where an unusually long term has been agreed between the parties, and there is a reasonable justification for it on the particular facts of the case, the tribunal has shown[47] itself not to be obstructive to the solution that has been agreed, especially where the parties are represented commercial parties.

9.82 In the case of an MSV, it is not uncommon for an operator to seek the ability to carry out multiple visits during a specified period, often several months. The tribunal does not typically baulk at the imposition of a six-month term in such cases, but naturally if the landowner would be unduly prejudiced by such a long term, it may have a good argument that the term should be shorter. Practical realities of operators' businesses will generally be appreciated. It is far better for a tribunal to allow multiple visits within a liberal timeframe, than attempt to specify the dates of visits at the outset, with the potential for wasted costs or intractable disputes if those dates become inconvenient.

9.83 What is less likely to be appropriate is a term which is open to theoretically open-ended extensions by an operator serving repeated notices indicating that it wishes to carry out particular works on particular occasions.

Agreeing terms

9.84 The tribunal will not entirely unthinkingly 'rubber stamp' an agreement that it perceives to be contrary to the legislation, or inappropriate in some way. This is surely the case in respect of any agreement, but particularly so under para 26, where the tribunal has a special gatekeeper function (a para 26 agreement cannot be agreed between the parties consensually under any circumstances and must receive the approval of the tribunal in the form of an Order).

9.85 However, where the parties have agreed particular terms, and especially where the tribunal is aware that they are two represented commercial parties, any

45 under para 23(2), applied to para 26 cases by para 26(4)(c).

46 Strictly the Order specifies under para 26(2)(a) or (b) the period for which the agreement will be binding, or the event by reference to which the agreement will cease to be binding. However, it is commonplace for the Order to impose the agreement, and for the agreement itself to state its term, or the period during which the relevant rights may be exercised.

47 In the matter between EE/H3G and the University of the Arts referred to in the *CTIL v University of the Arts* matter at [2020] UKUT 248 (LC), at [24], of the latter decision.

agreement between the parties as to the substance[48] of a term is likely to be persuasive, or at the very least material, even in respect of an unusual term or set of terms.

9.86 Thus, even where an unusually long term has been agreed in a para 26 context, the tribunal has been content to approve such an agreed solution. Parties agreeing unusual terms, especially in the Part 26 context, should explain to the tribunal concisely but clearly, why the particular provision has been agreed on the particular facts of the case. Parties should think twice if they are aware that the tribunal has previously shown resistance to a particular agreed term,

9.87 Thus, in the matter between EE/H3G and University of the Arts referred to in the *CTIL v University of the Arts* matter at [24] of the latter decision, the parties had arrived at a solution whereby the landowner would consent to an application by the operators for interim rights for the unusually lengthy period of five years. The parties had explained the circumstances of the case in seeking approval of a Consent Order, and the tribunal made the requested Order, reciting both that it was satisfied that it had the jurisdiction to do so, and that it was a proper exercise of the tribunal's discretion to do so on the facts of the case.

Para 26: lack of obligation in respect of ADR

9.88 The new provisions which apply in respect of applications under paras 20, 32(1)(b) and 33(5) in relation to considering alternative dispute resolution have not been inserted into para 26.

9.89 Thus, it would seem that no similar obligation applies to an operator that is considering a para 26 application. However, on the question of costs, one of the factors to which the tribunal is required to have regard 'in particular' is 'any unreasonable refusal by a party to engage in alternative dispute resolution'.[49] This provision technically applies in all cases regardless of whether there was a Code-imposed obligation to consider ADR.

9.90 However, the reason for not imposing the same obligation to consider ADR in para 26 cases may well have been that such cases can involve urgency. ADR in that context may not be practicable. Accordingly, in such cases of urgency, the tribunal may well be less ready to find that a refusal of ADR was unreasonable.

48 The Tribunal has been more exacting when it comes to the structure or form of an Order settling a matter, not generally favouring Tomlin Orders, but in principle being content with Consent Orders that do *not*: (i) stay matters generally. and (ii) allow enforcement of the agreed terms under the same proceedings.

49 See para 96(2)(b).

10

Para 27 agreements: 'temporary' Code rights

10.01 Paragraph 27 is headed 'Temporary code rights'. It provides a procedure for having an agreement that confers Code rights (or provides for a person to be bound by a Code right) imposed in circumstances where a person has the right to require the removal of apparatus that is already installed. The objective in summary is to allow the operator's network services to be maintained on a temporary basis, pending final proceedings[1] under para 20. As with para 26 agreements, para 27 agreements cannot be entered into without an Order of the Tribunal, and are not statutorily continued by para 30(2).[2]

The pre-conditions for a para 27 Order

10.02 By para 27(1), para 27 only applies where the following three pre-conditions are met:

'(a) an operator gives a notice under paragraph 20(2) to a person in respect of any land,

(b) the notice also requires that person's agreement on a temporary basis in respect of a right which is to be exercisable (in whole or in part) in relation to electronic communications apparatus which is already installed on, under or over the land, and

(c) the person has the right to require the removal of the apparatus in accordance with paragraph 37 or as mentioned in paragraph 40(1) but the operator is not for the time being required to remove the apparatus.'

10.03 These three pre-conditions are discussed below.

(a) The notice under para 20(2)

It is worth noting that the requirement under para 27(1)(a) is to serve a notice 'under' para 20(2). This is in contrast with the requirement in a para 26 case to serve a notice 'which complies with'[3] para 20(2).

Consequently, the OFCOM prescribed form of notice is the same form as is used for a para 20 case. It contains a number of square bracketed references

1 As to the proceedings under para 20, para 27(7) and (8) provide that where it is shown that a landowner was entitled to require removal of the ECA immediately after it was installed, that fact must be disregarded for the purposes of the decision as to whether the ECA should be allowed to remain.

2 By virtue of para 30(3).

3 Para 26(3).

to para 27(1) and to matters that are relevant to para 27 cases, which can be deleted when they are not relevant.

(b) *Requiring agreement on a temporary basis*

The notice must require the recipient's agreement on a temporary basis in respect of a Code right relating to ECA, which is already installed. Paragraph 27 cannot apply to a case where ECA is not already installed. Clause 3 of the OFCOM prescribed form contains a form of words that is targeted at satisfying this requirement.

(c) *The right to require removal*

Paragraph 27 can only apply in a case where a person (the recipient of the notice mentioned above) 'has the right to require the removal' of the ECA. There are a number of reasons for which the person may have the right to require removal, which are set out in para 37 (and para 38 as regards neighbouring land). These are discussed in Chapter 18.

10.04 The second limb of para 27(1)(c) is that the 'operator is not for the time being required to remove the apparatus'. In a case where no notice has been served on the operator under Part 6, this criterion will be satisfied. However, it is perhaps not crystal clear what is meant by 'not … being required'. As the passive voice is used, the person who would theoretically be doing the requiringis not identified. Does the criterion mean that there is no Part 6 notice requiring the operator to remove ECA, or does it mean that there is no Order stating that the operator must remove the ECA?

10.05 Paragraph 27(1)(c) does not refer to the service of a notice, which it could easily have done. On the other hand, the phrase chosen is 'being required', which chimes with what a para 40(2) notice does: it is a notice 'requiring' the operator to remove ECA and restore the land. An Order under para 44 does, of course, require the operator to remove and restore, but para 44(1) does not use that language and instead describes such an Order as one 'that the operator must … remove …' the ECA.

10.06 However, if this linguistic clue is considered conclusive, the result would be that the service of a para 40 notice would preclude para 27 from applying (and hence would preclude an effective para 27 notice from being served). That would be peculiar, because we know from para 40(8) that the tribunal is not permitted to make a removal Order under Part 6 until it has determined any extant para 20 application. Thus it is clear that a para 20 application, even if made after a Part 6 application for a removal Order, may be capable of being valid and effective, and as a matter of policy, takes priority.

10.07 In accordance with that policy, it would seem to follow that a para 20 notice can in principle be served after a Part 6 application has been made. If a para 20 notice can be served in order to seek a 'full' para 20 Code agreement, it would be strange if a para 20 notice could not be served, which also sought temporary rights under para 27. For policy reasons, there is a procedure that generates an agreement regulating the parties' relationship until a para 20 application is determined. There can surely be no policy benefit from the parties in one particular para 20 situation (namely where a para 40 notice has been served) not being able to have their relationship regulated before that application is determined. Further, it is clear from para 27(3) that at the stage where a para 27 Order is being considered by the tribunal, para 40 proceedings may also be on foot. Why should it matter which came first if they can properly both be before the tribunal at once?

10.08 As noted elsewhere in this book (see Chapter 7), the courts will generally interpret the Code by reference to how it is supposed to function in accordance with its underlying purpose rather than by means of a close textual analysis. One might think that para 27 should be capable of applying where a Part 6 notice has been served on an operator but where there is not yet any Order that it must remove ECA.

The operator's application and its timing

10.09 A para 27 Order can only be made on the application of an operator.[4] An operator may make such an application if:

(a) the recipient does not agree within 28 days of service of the para 20/27 notice to confer or otherwise be bound by the Code right;[5] or

(b) at any time after the notice is given, the recipient gives notice in writing to the operator that it does not agree to confer or otherwise be bound by the Code right.[6]

10.10 The tribunal does have the power to make an Order where these time limits have not expired if it 'thinks that the order should be made as a matter of urgency'. It therefore follows that these time limits are not absolute bars preventing the service of a notice before their expiry. If the tribunal considers that the 'urgency' requirement is not met, it could adjourn the matter such that the recipient of the notice will have had sufficient time to consider it in accordance with the statutory scheme. If it is considered that the application was clearly premature, one would imagine that the tribunal would consider that it retains the option of dismissing the application on this basis.

10.11 The question of effectively abridging time under para 27(5) (and the equivalent provision in the para 26 context) is considered in Chapter 20.

The para 27 Order

10.12 By para 27(2), the tribunal may (on the application of the operator) impose an agreement[7] for such temporary Code rights as appear 'reasonably necessary for securing the objective in sub-paragraph (3)'.

10.13 The para 27(3) 'objective' is that:

> '...until the proceedings under paragraph 20 and any proceedings under paragraph 40 are determined, the service provided by the operator's network is maintained and the apparatus is properly adjusted and kept in repair'.

---

4 By para 27(2).

5 Para 20(3)(a), applied to a para 27 case by para 27(4)(a).

6 Para 20(3)(b), applied to a para 27 case by para 27(4)(a).

7 Either an agreement which confers rights, or renders a person bound by rights, as appropriate.

10.14 Thus, it is quite clear that a para 27 Order will only be made where a para 20 application is on foot, and a para 27 Order is a remedy that regulates the parties' relationship until a final decision is made as to whether a 'full' para 20 agreement is to be imposed (and in some cases, the further decision of whether an Order for removal is to be made).

10.15 A para 27 Order can therefore be seen as something that is always genuinely 'interim' in the sense in which lawyers would ordinarily understand the term. As discussed in Chapter 9, the same cannot be said of 'Interim code rights' under para 26.

10.16 The test under paras 27(2) and (3) is one of reasonable necessity for securing the para 27(3) objective. Thus the tribunal has a broad discretion as to whether to make an Order.

The national security bar

10.17 By para 27ZA,[8] the tribunal must refuse a para 27 application if the Secretary of State certifies that the Order sought would be likely to prejudice national security, defence, or 'law enforcement'. The latter term means 'the prevention, investigation, detection, or prosecution of criminal offences, including the safeguarding against and the prevention of threats to public security'.

The nature and effect of a para 27 agreement

10.18 An agreement imposed under para 27 takes effect for all purposes of the Code as an agreement under Part 2 of the Code.[9] The provisions of paras 25 and 84 (as regards compensation) apply[10] to an agreement under para 27 just as they do to an agreement under para 20.

10.19 As is made clear by para 27(2), an agreement imposed under para 27 can be one that confers Code rights or renders a person bound by them. Further, by para 30(3), the statutory continuation of Code agreements under para 30(2) does not apply. Accordingly, a para 27 agreement will come to an end in accordance with its own terms, as is the case for para 26 agreements. It would seem that para 23(7) requires that a term be included in a para 27 agreement specifying how long Code rights are exercisable thereunder.[11] However, despite para 30(3) expressly disapplying para 30(2) (indicating a policy imperative that para 27 agreements should drop dead at the end of their express term), para 37 does not include an express right to require removal where a para 27 agreement has come to an end. This issue is addressed in Chapter 16 on Termination.

The terms of a para 27 agreement

10.20 Para 23 of the Code makes provision as to the terms of an agreement which is imposed by the tribunal under para 20.

8 Inserted by s 66(2) of the Product Security and Telecommunications Infrastructure Act 2022.
9 By para 22, as applied by para 27(4)(b).
10 By virtue of paras 27(4)(e) and (f).
11 Para 23(7) is applied to a para 27 case by para 27(4)(c).

10.21 The provisions of para 23 are also applied[12] to cases under para 27. The only two modifications to the ordinary operation of para 23 in para 27 cases are as follows:

(a) references in para 23 to the 'relevant person' are to be construed as references to the non-operator party on whom the para 27 agreement is to be imposed;[13] and

(b) the *duty* in para 23 to include terms as to the payment of consideration is instead a *power* to do so.[14] Otherwise, consideration is dealt with in the familiar way under para 24.[15]

10.22 Accordingly, when considering what terms should be imposed in a para 27 agreement, the tribunal is principally considering what is 'appropriate'.[16] There is a fuller discussion of the various provisions of para 23, as well as examples of tribunal decisions on particular terms, in Chapter 11.

---

12 Expressly, by para 27(4)(c).
13 See para 27(6)(a), and para 27(1) which is referred to therein.
14 See para 27(6)(b). The duty referred to, which applies in the case of an ordinary para 20 application, is contained in para 23(3).
15 Para 24 being applied to cases under para 27 by para 27(4)(d).
16 By para 23(2).

11

Determination of the terms of an agreement

Introduction

11.01 This chapter concerns the determination of the terms of an agreement that confers Code rights. It is principally concerned with terms other than those that specify the rent/consideration and compensation payable, which are dealt with in Chapters 13 and 14 respectively.

11.02 The terms of an agreement granting Code rights are often of great importance to both operator and site provider. Site providers can be concerned about who has access to their land, how it is obtained, and when. They are also keen to ensure that there is adequate protection in relation to health and safety matters, indemnities, and the extent to which the terms of a Code agreement may facilitate or prevent a potential future redevelopment.

11.03 For their part, operators are often keen to obtain terms that facilitate unfettered sharing and upgrading rights and which do not place too great an administrative or financial burden on them when they are seeking to gain access to sites.

11.04 OFCOM is obliged under para 103(2) of the Code to prepare and publish standard terms that may, but need not, be used in agreements under the Code. It duly published such a document on 15 December 2017, shortly before the coming into force of the Code.[1] It issued an updated set of terms on 8 November 2024.[2]

11.05 Operators will typically have their own standard terms, which they seek to agree to or have imposed, both because of the substantive beneficial content of those terms for the operators concerned and for the sake of consistency and harmonisation. Naturally, such terms will look different depending on what type of agreement is involved. For example, where an agreement for an MSV[3] is sought, the terms will

1 https://www.ofcom.org.uk/__data/assets/pdf_file/0026/108791/ECC-Standard-Terms.pdf.

2 https://www.ofcom.org.uk/siteassets/resources/documents/consultations/category-1-10-weeks/99140-electronics-communications-code/associated-documents/ecc-standard-terms.pdf?v=384632

3 Multi-skilled visit. Many operators' preferred name for a survey or a series of surveys at which information is gathered in order to reach a final decision as to the suitability of a site for the installation of ECA. Such agreements are established as granting Code rights by the Court of Appeal's decision in the *University of London* case.

normally be simpler and less wide-ranging because there is typically no ECA being installed, and the agreement is for a shorter duration with no security of tenure.[4]

Imposed terms in new agreements

Relevant provisions of the Code

11.06 Paragraph 23 of the Code contains a number of provisions that tell the tribunal how it must determine the terms of an agreement that is imposed under para 20. Para 23 also applies in respect of the imposition of para 26 interim agreements[5] and para 27 temporary agreements.[6]

11.07 Some sub-paragraphs of para 23 require certain mandatory terms to be included, while others require the tribunal to consider and determine whether to include terms dealing with certain matters. In relation to the remainder of the terms of the agreement, the tribunal has broad discretion, which must be exercised in accordance with para 23.

(1) Terms which must be included

11.08 Paragraph 23(3) and (7) require terms to be included as to consideration and duration, respectively. In addition, para 23(5) requires the tribunal to impose terms thought appropriate for minimising loss and damage to certain persons, including landowners. This is therefore a consideration that has the potential to affect any discretionary term. Para 23(5) is considered further below.

11.09 *Consideration payable*: Para 23(3) provides that terms must be included as to the consideration payable by the operator to the relevant person in respect of the conferral of the Code rights (or in respect of that person's agreement to be bound).

11.10 The calculation of such consideration is carried out under the provisions of para 24 (dealt with in Chapter 13).

11.11 *Duration of the agreement*: para 23(7) provides that terms must[7] be included specifying for how long the Code right conferred by the agreement is exercisable. Essentially this will be the term or duration of the agreement. Note however, that where para 30(2) applies,[8] it continues an agreement beyond its contractual term.

---

4 Such agreements are normally imposed under para 26 of the Code, and hence by paras 26(8) and 30(3) of the Code, the agreement comes to an end in accordance with its terms and is not continued by para 30(2).

5 By para 26(4)(c).

6 By para 27(4)(c).

7 This is consistent with para 11(1)(c), which provides that a consensual agreement under Part 2 must state for how long the Code right is exercisable. Para 22 provides that an agreement imposed under Part 4 takes effect as an agreement under Part 2.

8 As a generality, para 30(2) applies to Code agreements, ie, agreements conferring Code rights to which Part 5 applies. Hence it does not apply to subsisting agreements which are leases requiring renewal under the 1954 Act – see para 6(2) of the Transitional Provisions. However, it is also worth noting that para 30(2) does *not* apply to para 26 interim agreements or para 27 temporary agreements (by virtue of para 30(3)).

(2) Terms which must be considered

(a) Termination of the agreement

11.12 Para 23(8)(a) provides that the tribunal must[9] determine whether the agreement should include a term permitting the termination of the agreement, and if so, in what circumstances. It would seem likely that this is a requirement that the tribunal must merely consider whether a termination provision should be included, rather than a requirement that the tribunal's written decision must include a passage including a formal determination on the point.

11.13 This provision essentially requires the tribunal to consider the imposition of break clauses. Such clauses may allow any particular person to terminate the agreement and would typically specify the event that would give rise to the right to terminate, the period of notice required, and the conditions that must be satisfied by the particular person in order to terminate the agreement.

Landlord's break clause

(i) For redevelopment purposes

11.14 A landlord's redevelopment break clause was sought in *Stephenson*.[10] The site provider wanted a right to terminate the lease after five years in the event that it had an intention to redevelop all or part of the site or certain associated land. The operators sought to resist the term on the ground that it would prejudice their ability to recover their investment in the site if their occupation might only last five years. The Deputy President agreed to grant the redevelopment break right.

11.15 There was no suggestion that there were any current proposals for redeveloping the land, and whether any suggested potential redevelopment was even a 'realistic possibility' was considered 'rather doubtful' by the tribunal. However, this was not a sufficient reason for refusing the break right.

11.16 The tribunal held that the 10-year term was a relatively long one in the context of a sector that is fast-moving in commercial and technological terms. Further, if the site were to be capable of being developed for a more profitable use by the site provider, 'it is not the policy of the Code to stand in the way of such a redevelopment'.

11.17 The site provider has an associated company, which is a wholesale infrastructure provider, and thus the future development may have been network-related. However, this was not the reason for which it was held that the landlord's potential future redevelopment was not to be thwarted. Rather, the tribunal relied on the fact that a landowner who can demonstrate an intention to redevelop may resist a Code agreement altogether under para 21(5),[11] and an existing site provider can similarly oppose a renewal under para 31(4)(c) on similar grounds.

9 The mandatory requirement to consider whether to include a termination provision fits with the position in respect of consensual agreements, which are required by para 11(1)(d) to state the period of notice (if any) required to terminate the agreement.

10 *EE Ltd & Anor v Stephenson & Anor* [2022] UKUT 180 (LC).

11 The Tribunal referred to para 20(4) but it seems clear that a reference to para 21(5) was intended.

11.18 The Deputy President stated the principle thus:[12]

> 'In circumstances where the site provider is not entitled to share in the economic benefits realised by the use of its land for telecommunications purposes, it would be unfair and inappropriate for it to be prevented from making an alternative use of its land by the imposition of long-term Code rights which cannot be terminated. The fact that the inclusion of a redevelopment break clause may introduce a degree of uncertainty in the investment decisions made by an operator does not seem to me to be a reason for refusing such a clause.'

11.19 Similarly, a landlord's break clause was allowed in *Audley House*.[13] The operator sought to resist the break right by arguing that: (i) there was no evidence that the site provider might want to redevelop, and (ii) such a break would be contrary to the aims of the Code and would discourage investment in communications sites. The tribunal allowed the landlord redevelopment break, concluding that there was no indication in the Code that landowners were to be prevented from developing their land or from terminating agreements where they wished to redevelop. Further, as the Code prevented Code rights from coming to an end upon mere contractual termination, the landlord would still need to terminate those Code rights by satisfying the redevelopment ground at para 31(4)(c) of the Code. The combination of the contractual break right and para 31(4)(c)[14] ensured that both parties' interests were protected.

11.20 In the *Vache Farm*[15] case, a question arose as to whether the site provider should have a redevelopment break clause open to it in circumstances where it wished to redevelop the site in connection with an electronic communications use. The tribunal restated the point from *Stephenson* that it is not the policy of the Code to stand in the way of development. Provided the intention is genuine,[16] it could see no reason why a different approach should be taken where the intended redevelopment is for a telecommunications use, even if that would mean that a particular operator may in the future enjoy less favourable terms at the site. As the operator's proposal was also for a five-year break clause, the tribunal inferred that a minimum term of that duration would satisfy its business needs. The landlord's redevelopment break was included and did not exclude the possibility of telecommunications development. A similar break was included by the FTT in *Ewefields Farm*,[17] and it appears that the FTT considers this issue to be relatively well settled.

12 At [47].

13 See [2022] UKUT 152 (LC) at [205]–[210]. This was a case involving the same site provider as in *Stephenson*, and decided only weeks before *Stephenson*. *Audley House* was not referred to in *Stephenson*, and so it appears that differently constituted Tribunals arrived at a similar conclusion independently.

14 Operating in tandem with para 30 of the Code which continues Code rights and agreements beyond their contractual termination.

15 *EE Limited v AP Wireless II (UK) Limited* [2024] UKUT 216 (LC) at [26].

16 In *EE Limited v Meyrick* [2019] UKUT 164 (LC), for example, the Tribunal held that the landowner's professed intention to carry out redevelopment for the purposes of providing its own network was not a serious intention, but if they were wrong on that, was in any event motivated by a desire to prevent the operator from acquiring Code rights, and thus it would have fallen foul of the principle enunciated by the Supreme Court in the 1954 Act case of *S Franses Ltd v Cavendish Hotel (London) Ltd* [2018] UKSC 62.

17 *On Tower UK Limited v AP Wireless II (UK) Limited and others* LC – 2023 – 000321 and 13 others (*Ewefields Farm*) at [80]–[89].

Wording of landlord's redevelopment break clause

11.21 Where a redevelopment break clause is drafted by a landowner, care should be taken as to the wording of the provision. Where a landowner seeks to resist an agreement under para 21(5) or to terminate it in reliance on para 31(4)(c) because of redevelopment intentions, it must prove the component subjective and objective elements of the intention at the date of trial.[18] It is not necessary to demonstrate that the intended redevelopment was possible, likely, or even intended in its final form as at the date of the notice or statement of case, which first relies on the redevelopment ground. Where there is a *contractual* right to break, a landowner would do well to ensure that its term makes clear when the relevant intention must exist and must be proven, and also that to prove that the requisite intention exists or existed at the relevant date would be feasible.

11.22 Indeed, an issue of this kind arose in the recent *Vache Farm* case. There was a dispute as to whether the relevant landlord break clause should require a 'settled intention' or rather a 'desire' to redevelop. The tribunal considered that there was no reason why the landlord should have to demonstrate the appropriate resolve by reference to more than one date, and as the relevant date for para 31(4)(c) purposes would be the date of the final hearing, that was the date that should be selected. That being established, the wording of the contractual break clause should mirror the language of the Code by referring to 'intention' rather than 'desire'.

11.23 The wording of the break right further mirrored the termination ground at para 31(4)(c), which the site provider would in any event need to satisfy in order to terminate the agreement. It was a necessary element of the condition giving rise to the break right that the site provider could not reasonably carry out its redevelopment if the lease were to continue.

(ii) Upon conditions other than redevelopment

11.24 It is perfectly permissible for a landlord break clause to be agreed or imposed, which can be triggered in circumstances other than redevelopment. However, as the landlord would always need to satisfy a para 31(4) ground to be able to terminate the Code agreement, it perhaps does not make sense for the tribunal to impose a break right that arises in circumstances other than those that constitute a ground under para 31(4).

11.25 In the *Vache Farm*[19] case, the site provider sought a break clause which could be triggered if 'the test under para 21 of the Code for the imposition of the agreement on the Landlord is no longer met.' This criterion mirrors the termination ground at para 31(4)(d) of the Code, and would entail the site provider successfully arguing that one[20] of the issues arising from para 21(2) and 21(3) would be determined in its favour, such that either:

---

18 This follows the law under the 'redevelopment' ground at s 30(1)(f) of the 1954 Act, and the case law thereunder. A wider discussion of these issues is included in Chapter 17.

19 *EE Limited v AP Wireless II (UK) Limited* [2024] UKUT 216 (LC) at [27].

20 The operator would need to satisfy both para 21(2) and 21(3) to have an agreement imposed, so it follows that a site provider would only need to succeed on one of those two issues in order to terminate an agreement.

- the prejudice caused to it by the Order imposing the agreement is not capable of being adequately compensated by money; or
- the public benefit likely to result from the making of the Order does not outweigh the prejudice to it.

11.26 The tribunal declined to grant such a break right. It acknowledged that this would be a ground to terminate the agreement at or after its contractual end date, but noted that there was an absence of evidence as to how the site provider might successfully trigger this break right during the term. One might observe that a similar absence of evidence was not thought fatal to the inclusion of a redevelopment break clause. However, in addition, the tribunal commented that opportunities for dispute should not be made available without good reason. That sentiment has been a common theme in the determination of all sorts of terms under the Code.

11.27 In preferring to limit the site provider's break right to redevelopment, the tribunal called that ground 'familiar', and that seems to have been a quality that recommended that ground to the tribunal. It is a similar (though not identical) ground for termination to that which exists under section 30(1)(f) of the 1954 Act, and as such, its operation is relatively well-known and predictable. A break ground that mirrors the para 31(4)(d) termination ground would be substantially less certain, as it entails the site provider coming to a view as to the manner in which a tribunal might weigh private prejudice against public benefit, two matters that are 'not obviously commensurable'.[21] Conversely, a site provider is well placed to know whether it has an intention of carrying out redevelopment and to what extent it can collate the necessary evidence thereof.

Tenant's break clause

11.28 In *Audley House*,[22] the leases were to be granted for a 15-year term, with an agreed tenant's break right able to be triggered at any time after 7 years. A number of issues arose as to the detail of the tenant's break rights:

(i) The tenant was also entitled to break the lease where damage to its equipment made the exercise of its Code rights impossible. The site provider wanted the operator to have to use reasonable endeavours to reinstate the equipment first. The tribunal considered that this would be an unreasonable limitation on the operator's right to make decisions about its own business.

(ii) The tribunal similarly upheld the tenant's right to break the lease where the exercise of Code rights was impossible because of damage or destruction to the access. The site provider's request that the break right would fall away if the access had been restored by the end of the 12-month break notice period was rejected.

(iii) The tribunal followed the logic in previous 1954 Act cases in refusing to make vacant possession a condition of the tenant breaking the lease. It was 'perfectly legitimate' for the tenant to use the break clause not to leave the

21 This was an observation of the Tribunal in *Cornerstone Telecommunications Infrastructure Ltd v University Of The Arts London* [2020] UKUT 248 (LC) at [62].

22 At [205]–[210].

site but to seek a fresh agreement[23] under Part 5 of the Code, and this would not be possible if vacant possession had to be given.

Effect of para 23(8)(a) in the cases

11.29 There is generally no special mention in the cases of the obligation to consider a break clause under para 23(8)(a). It is right that that obligation connotes no presumption of including or excluding a break clause in favour of either party, whether for redevelopment or otherwise. However, para 23(8)(a) gives termination rights a special status that most other types of term do not enjoy, in that the tribunal must consider them. The Code does not, of course, impose a universal right to break an agreement for redevelopment during its term in the same way as it imposes a universal right[24] to terminate an agreement for redevelopment where the agreement is statutorily continuing under para 30(2). But given that redevelopment is the obvious circumstance in which a landowner may wish to terminate an agreement, it may be thought that the inclusion of 23(8)(a) is at least consistent with the Deputy President's conclusion in *Stephenson* that the policy of the Code is not to stand in the way of redevelopment.

(b) Repositioning and removal

11.30 Paragraph 23(8)(b) provides that the tribunal must determine whether the agreement should include a term:

> 'enabling the relevant person to require the operator to reposition or temporarily to remove the electronic communications equipment to which the agreement relates (and, if so, in what circumstances)'.

11.31 The sort of clause envisaged by this provision is often referred to as a 'lift and shift' clause. Operators are sometimes able to erect temporary masts or to position ECA on alternative parts of a roof or scaffolding. However, being compelled to do so is potentially expensive and risks causing a gap in service. Operators are therefore understandably not keen on such clauses, but a Code agreement that does not include such a provision risks a standoff such as that which occurred in *Gravesham*, where a landowner who needs or wishes to carry out repair or development works cannot do so, potentially causing loss. In a modern imposed agreement, one would then expect a compensation claim under para 25, which an operator would similarly not relish. Perhaps for these reasons, many agreements that are well negotiated (or part-

---

23 This appears to remain perfectly good logic. In the more recent case of *On Tower UK Ltd v British Telecommunication PLC* [2024] UKUT 51 (LC) in which it was held that the service of a break notice by a site provider was not necessary in order to serve an effective para 31 notice which satisfies the last limb of para 31(3)(b). Thus a site provider could serve a para 31 notice without actually satisfying pre-conditions that it would have had to satisfy under a contractual break right. However, that provision only relates to a site provider bringing an agreement to an end, and not an operator. An operator can only serve a Part 5 renewal notice under para 33. Under para 33(3)(b), there is no opportunity for an operator to serve a notice relying on the fact that it 'could' have brought the agreement to an end, as the last limb of that provision again refers only to site providers. Rather, an operator would need to satisfy the first limb of para 33(3)(b), ie, that the notice expires after the date on which the Code right 'would' have ceased to be exercisable but for para 30.

24 Under para 31 in reliance on the ground at para 31(4)(c).

negotiated, leaving only limited terms to be determined by the tribunal) will include a tightly drawn 'lift and shift' right.

11.32 Although paras 23(8)(a) and (b) do not expressly mention redevelopment, it would seem likely that a frequent cause for a landowner to invoke clauses imposed pursuant to either of the para 23(8) duties would be its desire to carry out redevelopment. If a landowner has no redevelopment break clause nor 'lift and shift' provision, it may cause substantial loss by being prevented or substantially delayed in carrying out its redevelopment. These specific duties are therefore consonant with the general duty at para 23(5) requiring the tribunal to include terms that minimise loss and damage to certain persons, including landowners.

11.33 There may be cases where a landlord's redevelopment break clause ensures the least possible loss and damage, such that it would be excessively onerous on an operator to impose a 'lift and shift' clause in addition. *Ewefields Farm*[25] was considered to be such a case. However, in cases where a landlord retains neighbouring land or buildings, different factual considerations may apply.

(3) Discretionary terms

11.34 Under para 23(2), the tribunal must require a Code agreement to contain 'such terms as it thinks appropriate'. Accordingly, save for those terms which must be included and those which must at least be considered (dealt with above), the tribunal has a broad discretion which it must exercise in accordance with the relevant provisions of para 23, and in respect of which the scheme of a Code as a whole will play a significant part.

The breadth of the tribunal's discretion

11.35 In *Keast*[26] the landowner made a number of arguments as to the terms that the tribunal was entitled to impose. It was argued that such terms cannot include free-standing obligations, including positive obligations on the part of the occupier of the land, and nor can they restrict the occupier's activities elsewhere on his or her property. It was argued that if the rights that could be imposed under the Code were totally unrestricted as a matter of jurisdiction, there would be no real sense in taking the trouble to set out an exhaustive list of what could constitute a "code right' at para 3 of the Code. These arguments were rejected by the Upper Tribunal.

11.36 It was held that there is a broad discretion as to terms. Paragraph 23 contains no particular restriction upon the terms that may be imposed, although sub-paragraphs (3) to (8) set out what they must include.

11.37 The tribunal considered that although imposing a positive obligation on a landowner might be a 'rare occurrence', it was not outside the tribunal's jurisdiction.[27] The conclusion of the tribunal was that all of the terms sought were within the

25 *On Tower UK Limited v AP Wireless II (UK) Limited and others* LC – 2023 – 000321 and 13 others (*Ewefields Farm*) at [93]–[96].

26 *CTIL v Keast* [2019] UKUT 116 (LC).

27 *Keast* at [58].

tribunal's jurisdiction, although they would be a matter of discretion and it may be that they would not all be granted at trial. It was, however, accepted that, as a matter of logic, in a given case it is not impossible that a term of a proposed agreement would be outside the scope of the tribunal's discretion.[28]

11.38 One restriction that the tribunal did acknowledge was that it could not impose upon the occupier of land any Code right that has not been sought in the para 20 notice. This was said to be 'perfectly clear from the terms of paragraph 20'.[29]

The exercise of the tribunal's discretion

11.39 In deciding what terms to impose, it was observed in *Keast*[30] that the tribunal will have 'very careful regard to the overall scheme of the Code', which provides for 'a rate of consideration far lower than was payable under the old Code'. In view of the need to be fair to both parties, the terms that will be considered 'appropriate' are likely to be influenced by the basis of consideration. It may be considered inappropriate to impose on a site provider certain obligations intended to facilitate the provision of the operator's network when the consideration receivable by the site provider is to be unrelated to the value of that network.[31] Whether this factor has greatly influenced the determination of terms since the *Keast* case is perhaps debatable.

11.40 In *London & Quadrant* the tribunal noted that the tribunal's 'wide discretion over terms' would be exercised with the statutory purpose of the Code well in mind. The Code was said to be 'part of a government strategy to help operators to extend their networks, to make mast-sharing easier, and infrastructure deployment and maintenance cheaper'.[32]

Starting point and burden

11.41 Where an operator seeks Code rights under para 20 of the Code, the statutory scheme requires an operator to serve a notice setting out the Code right sought 'and all of the other terms of the agreement that the operator seeks'.[33]

11.42 Paragraph 23(1) then provides that 'an order under paragraph 20 may impose an agreement which gives effect to the code right sought by the operator with such modifications as the court thinks appropriate'.[34]

28 *Keast* at [60].

29 *Keast* at [29].

30 *CTIL v Keast* [2019] UKUT 116 (LC).

31 This observation in *Keast* was cited with approval in *London & Quadrant.*

32 This observation drew from Lewison LJ's comments in *Cornerstone v Compton Beauchamp* [2019] EWCA Civ 1755 at [3]. Although the Supreme Court overturned the Court of Appeal's decision on a key issue in that case (whether an operator in situ is barred by its occupation from seeking new Code rights that it does not currently have), there is nothing to suggest any disapproval of comments made at any earlier stage as to the overarching legislative purposes of the Code.

33 Para 20(2)(a) of the Code. The requirement under para 20(2)(a) also applies where interim rights are sought under para 26 (see para 26(3)), and also where temporary rights are sought under para 27 (see para 27(1)(a)).

34 This provision within para 23(1) also applies to an interim rights case under para 26 (see para 26(4)(c)), and to a temporary rights case under para 27 (see para 27(4)(c)).

11.43 These provisions gave rise to a submission in *London & Quadrant*[35] that the terms proposed by the operator are the starting point and that it is for the site provider to justify any departure from those terms. This was rejected by the tribunal. The Code right sought is the starting point for formulating the agreement to be imposed. The mandate at para 23(2) to impose 'such terms as the court thinks appropriate, subject to sub-paragraphs (3) to (8)' involved no presumption in favour of the operator's preferred terms.[36]

11.44 Having said that, the tribunal recognised that from a practical point of view, the operator's standard terms were likely to provide a template for negotiation. Further, the tribunal would normally be concerned only with terms which the parties cannot agree.[37]

Relevance of previously negotiated terms

11.45 In the *Hackney* (Tradescant House)[38] case, the tribunal called into question the relevance of the fact that certain terms had previously been agreed between parties. Judge Cooke said as follows:

> 'Terms in consensual agreements are included or rejected for all sorts of reasons; concessions may be made for speed, terms may be horse-traded, experience between particular parties may mean that one or the other insists on particular terms that it would not otherwise seek. None of that is relevant to the Tribunal's decision about the terms that are appropriate, and that are required to minimise loss and damage[39] to the respondent.'

11.46 The tribunal confirmed that the same applied where a tribunal had previously approved a Consent Order that contained particular terms. The tribunal's hands would not be tied in respect of any of those terms in a future Reference. Rather, in respect of a term that has previously been approved within a Consent Order:

> 'Where the term is in dispute the decision will be taken on the basis of what the Code provides, without regard to what these parties or other parties have agreed on previous occasions.'[40]

Impact of previous terms determined by the tribunals

11.47 The tribunals have now determined a considerable number of disputes in respect of various types of Code agreement terms. The determinations of the tribunals are summarised below by reference to different kinds of terms.

11.48 It is important to remember that decisions on terms will be fact-specific, and hence it will rarely be the case that there is an entirely binding authority on what

35 *Cornerstone Telecommunications Infrastructure Ltd v London & Quadrant Housing Trust* [2020] UKUT 282 (LC).
36 [2020] UKUT 282 (LC) at [43].
37 [2020] UKUT 282 (LC) at [45].
38 [2022] UKUT 210 (LC) at [43]–[49].
39 The reference to minimising loss and damage is clearly a reference to para 23(5) of the Code.
40 [2022] UKUT 210 (LC) at [49].

discretionary term must be imposed (as distinct from what terms a tribunal has the power to impose or what test must be applied in deciding whether to impose it). As the tribunal said in *UAL*:

> 'decisions about terms will depend upon the site, the factual background, and the parties' circumstances. For all those reasons we would caution against any attempt to derive general principles from what we say about the terms of the agreement'.[41]

11.49 However, as the vast majority of Code cases are now likely to be determined in the First-tier Tribunal, considerable respect is likely to be given to the reasoning contained in prior decisions of the Upper Tribunal as regards particular terms. There have now been a number of such decisions, covering a wide variety of types of term.

11.50 The benefits of standardisation have started to be mentioned judicially, at least in cases involving similar parties. In the *New Zealand Farm*[42] case, Judge Rodger QC[43] referred to the 'additional benefit' of standardisation that would be brought by refusing to include a term requiring the operator to give notice before gaining access to a site. Although that was a County Court Act 1954 lease renewal case, the reason for the observation was that a similar conclusion had been arrived at in the *Audley House* case between the same parties under the Code. However, the decision on the substance of the term had been reached on its merits, and for the same reasons in each case. Thus this is not a case in which a choice has been made between two evenly-balanced rival possibilities purely on the basis that standardisation is preferable.

11.51 The FTT in *Ewefields Farm*[44] referred to the mention of standardisation in the *New Zealand Farm* case, before warning future parties as to the wisdom of relitigating past battles:

> 'We would put the parties on notice that in any future references the FTT is likely to exercise its case management powers robustly should parties seek to relitigate agreements and clauses that have already been the subject of judicial determination.'

11.52 Different categories of previous judicial determinations are considered below.

Compensation and Site Payment

11.53 It is the tribunal's preference to assess a global figure for those items of compensation which are contemplated at the outset and found to be compensatable, rather than requiring repeated calculations and potentially applications on a piecemeal basis (see *Islington* at [121] and *UAL* at [81]).

11.54 This preference has the capacity to affect the definition of terms such as 'Compensation' or 'Site Payment' within an agreement, as it will be commonplace

---

41 At [64]. It is also fair to note that as no agreement was imposed in *UAL*, the Tribunal's observations were technically obiter. However, it addressed a considerable number of terms at a time when there had been little judicial guidance, and its conclusions are of course worthy of respect.

42 *On Tower Ltd v AP Wireless (II) (New Zealand Farm)* [2022] EW Misc 6 (CC) at [30].

43 Sitting as a Judge of the county court rather than as Deputy Chamber President of the Lands Chamber.

44 *On Tower UK Limited v AP Wireless II (UK) Limited and others* LC – 2023 – 000321 and 13 others (*Ewefields Farm*) at [55].

for a lump sum to be payable upfront in respect of certain periodical and/or ad hoc running costs.

Set Down Area

11.55 Even though the use of a crane within a car park area might cause inconvenience to a site provider, if there are adequate safeguards, a tribunal may well allow it. In *UAL*, there were adequate notice requirements and a need to comply with the respondent's reasonable health and safety and security requirements. There were likely to be only very few occasions on which the set-down area was needed other than for the installation and removal of ECA. In this context, the tribunal considered that the relevant officers of the parties would be capable of acting reasonably in finding a practical solution ([102]).

Access requirements

11.56 In the context of an urban building in *UAL*, the tribunal did not think it was appropriate for the respondent to retain an unqualified right to specify a particular access route ([106]). Again, there were checks in place on the operator's use of the access route, in that it had to comply with the 'Access Requirements', as to which see more below. The tribunal did accept that there were some rooms in the building that could not be justifiably retained within the potential scope of the access route.

11.57 In *UAL* there was an agreed three-day notice requirement in respect of the operator gaining access to the site through the respondent's university building. The tribunal held that notice by email should be permissible ([109]). Where an emergency access notice was given by telephone, it should be confirmed by email as soon as reasonably practicable, but for the agreement to specify the heading was 'unnecessary micro-management'.

11.58 The tribunal did not consider that the term 'emergency' needed to be defined at all, holding that in the context of the statutory purposes set out in para 4 of the Code such a term extended to 'any matters which require expedited access to the ECA' ([114]). To prescribe the circumstances that constitute certain types of emergencies would risk further disputes ([115]).

11.59 Again in *UAL*, the operator agreed to comply with 'the respondent's reasonable health and safety and security requirements as notified to it in writing', but opposed the imposition of an Access Protocol that it considered unreasonably restrictive and duplicative. The tribunal held that the Access Protocol was not necessary or useful, as it duplicated or contradicted existing provisions in the agreement ([120]).

11.60 It is fair to say that there will be cases in which there is unusual sensitivity or some other circumstance which justifies tighter or more detailed access requirements as part of the agreement. However, in *UAL*, appropriate Access Requirements were considered to be as follows ([121]):

'(a) providing reasonable prior written notice to the Access Contact (either by letter or email) of not less than three days, save in case of emergency where such notice as is reasonable in the circumstances may be given by telephone or email (but if given by telephone shall be confirmed by email as soon as reasonably practicable): and

(b) complying with the Grantor's reasonable health and safety and security requirements notified to the Operator in writing;

(c) providing always that, the Grantor will provide to the Operator an up to date contact telephone number and email address for the Access Contact. Such information will be provided by the Grantor to the Operator in accordance with the notice provisions in paragraph 10.1.2 of this Agreement.'

11.61 The term 'Access Contact' was then defined as being constituted by specified individuals with specified contact details, or such other individuals as shall be notified from time to time ([122]).

11.62 Finally, access was permitted on any day of the week, as weekend working appeared to the tribunal to interfere less with the respondent's use of the building for educational purposes ([124]).

11.63 It should be noted that a proposed additional access right was sought in *UAL* 'to access any other parts of the Grantor's Property as may be reasonably required in order to exercise any right granted in this Agreement … with or without vehicles'.[45]

11.64 It was readily accepted by the tribunal that where rights to carry out works on land were Code rights under para 3(d) and (e) of the Code, rights of access to carry out such works are also Code rights. However, this did not mean that an operator had unlimited rights to carry out work or have access. The extent of any such access was for the tribunal to decide in each case, absent agreement between the parties.

11.65 The tribunal found the extensive proposed right to be unnecessary for the protection of the operator's Code rights, constituting 'an unwarranted freedom to go wherever it wants within the Grantor's Property', notwithstanding proposed safeguards concerning giving reasons and due notice. The tribunal referred to the duty under para 23(5) of the Code for the tribunal to include the terms it thinks appropriate for ensuring that the least possible loss or damage is caused by the exercise of the Code right to occupiers and landowners. It was held that the proposed term would expose the respondent to an unnecessary risk of disruption to its activities, and hence para 23(5) would not permit the proposed term to be imposed.

Apparatus: definition and caps

11.66 This is one area in which operators are typically especially keen for their preferred terms to be included. The generalised desire to ensure flexibility for the entirety of the term is rendered substantially less nebulous when considering the practical reality of being stuck with an equipment cap, or even one specific equipment specification, for the entire duration of a Code agreement which may have a decade to run. It is obvious to any user of mobile phones over the first part of this century that technology in this area moves with some pace. Most will also be familiar with the

45 This issue was considered in *UAL* at [171]–[176].

rollout of 5G services, and this requires real infrastructure in the real world. The need to add equipment, and/or to upgrade equipment, is therefore apparent.

11.67 Where the line is drawn between the installation of new equipment and the upgrading of existing equipment is perhaps not obvious. However, this theoretical distinction and the potential for disputes in respect of it are not lost on the tribunal. The tribunal will therefore sometimes consider the two conceptually distinct sets of rights in tandem.

11.68 In relation to that point, the tribunal said as follows in *Green*[46] (the Dale Park case) at [32]:

> 'unless the parties are to indulge in a pointless dispute about what is an upgrade and what is an extra piece of kit, there is little point in having any limitation on the right to upgrade if there is no limitation on the right to add or change the equipment, and vice versa'.

11.69 Although *Green* was a renewal case, the particular point made above is of equal force in cases relating to the determination of the terms of agreements imposed under Part 4. Accordingly, this section relating to the definition and limitation of apparatus may usefully be read together with the following section which deals with upgrading of apparatus.

11.70 In *UAL*, the tribunal noted that there was no requirement in the Code to specify what apparatus is to be installed and that some agreements do so while others do not. On the facts of the case, it held that the operator would face difficulty if the apparatus were defined at the outset, as it would invite a dispute as to whether an installation constituted an upgrade or an addition. Given the propensity of these parties to disagree on matters, this was to be discouraged. It had sympathy for the point that technological changes may mean that equipment has to be changed or added, and did not wish to see the operator's ability to provide a service being hampered. It also made the practical point that the amount of apparatus would be limited by the strength of the supporting structure and the limited size of the 'Communications Site' over which the equipment could be installed. Again, then, ultimately the tribunal felt justified in granting broader rights as sought by the operator because other features of the agreement were considered to afford adequate protection to the site provider in respect of concerns that it had raised.

11.71 It was noted that the need for a specific list may be greater on open land, for example, to specify mast heights or types. Also, part of the justification for the tribunal's decision was the fact that under the Court of Appeal's decision in *Compton Beauchamp*, operators would be prevented from applying for additional rights in respect of additional ECA. However, given the decision on appeal in the Supreme Court in *Compton Beauchamp*, it is fair to say that an operator has an opportunity always to seek additional rights, albeit not modified terms, in respect of rights already enjoyed.

11.72 It must be appreciated, however, that in the absence of a provision allowing upgrading on a more liberal basis, an operator benefits only from the limited upgrading rights granted by para 17 of the Code.

46 *On Tower UK Ltd v JH and FW Green Ltd* [2021] EWCA Civ 1858.

11.73 In *London & Quadrant*[47] the tribunal referred to its decision in *UAL* and followed it. It rejected the notion that unlimited equipment might be installed as 'fanciful'. There was already to be a term prohibiting the operator from overloading any part of the building and a requirement to provide a construction phase plan, risk assessments, method statements, and any structural calculations on reasonable request. Furthermore, an equipment cap would 'invite dispute' and jeopardise the operator's ability to provide a service to network providers for the duration of the agreement.

The right to upgrade and the right to share

11.74 The right to upgrade ECA is a Code right within para 3(1)(c) of the Code. Since an amendment[48] to the Code made by the PSTI 2022, the right to share the use of ECA with another operator is also a Code right (as set out at para 3(1)(ca) of the Code), but this was not the case when a number of the cases were decided in the UT.

11.75 In *UAL*, the right for an operator to upgrade equipment was described as 'immensely important in view of the constantly advancing nature of technology'.[49]

11.76 It was also said that 'the practice of sharing infrastructure is prevalent in the telecommunications industry and achieves a number of economies'.[50]

11.77 The tribunal referred to the Law Commission's recommendation that Code operators must have the right to upgrade and share equipment without being charged extra for doing so, as was prevalent under the old Code, subject to safeguards for site providers.

11.78 It was noted that that recommendation was accepted and was expressed by the Code in para 17. The safeguards referred to above are those at paras 17(2) and (3) of the Code, namely as to physical appearance and causing no additional burden.

11.79 The tribunal observed that it was open to the parties to agree, or for the tribunal to confer, upgrading and sharing rights without those safeguards. Additional consideration may be payable where broader rights are conferred or agreed.

11.80 The Upper tribunal considered the question of whether it is for the operator to justify rights that are broader than those in para 17, or whether it is for the site provider to justify its insistence on the para 17 safeguards.

11.81 It held that the starting point was para 17 itself:

> 'which was drafted to express policy framed in full knowledge of the importance of sharing and upgrading. If the claimant wants more than the minimum it should

47 At [57]–[58].

48 The insertion of the new Code right was made by ss 57(2)(b)(i) of the Product Security and Telecommunications Infrastructure Act 2022 ('PSTI 2022'). This came into force on 7 February 2023 by s 79(2) of the PSTI 2022 and reg 2(a) of the Product Security and Telecommunications Infrastructure Act 2022 (Commencement No. 1) Regulations 2023. Note that by s 57(7) of the PSTI, the amendment does not affect any rights conferred under Part 2 of the Code before the coming into force of s 57 (on 7 February 2023).

49 *UAL* at [178].

50 *UAL* at [178].

justify that. However if the claimant can show that in this particular case there is little or no reason why the safeguards of paragraphs 17(2) and (3) should be included then that may be a reason to exclude them.'[51]

11.82 It derived support from a similar sentiment expressed in *Cornerstone Telecommunications Infrastructure Limited v Fothringham* LTS/ECC/2020/007, The Lands Tribunal for Scotland said as follows at [18] (in a decision under Code para 20):

'[The importance of sharing and upgrading] is known to and understood by the Tribunal. It was also known to and understood by Parliament when it enacted para 17, so we were considerably surprised to find it said … that the restriction of sharing rights to the extent provided for by para 17 of the Code 'would have devastating consequences for operators under the Code, infrastructure providers in particular, and this for the public interest too."

11.83 In *Fothringham* the para 17 safeguards were indeed included in the agreement. The Lands Tribunal for Scotland considered that it would require 'pretty compelling evidence'[52] to justify imposing rights which went beyond the para 17(2) and (3) limitations. It was considered that in enacting para 17:

'Parliament was striking a balance between the interests of the operators and the public, on one hand, and site providers, on the other. The Tribunal would therefore need to be persuaded that there was some justification for removing the level of protection for site providers which Parliament has provided.'[53]

11.84 One theme running through decisions on terms is that a term is more likely to find favour if it can show a high degree of compatibility or conformity with the Code, and the Code's legislative purpose. That being the case, one can understand that in these earlier decisions, the safeguards expressly included in para 17 were given weight.

11.85 It is true that there is in principle a public interest in facilitating operators to share the use of ECA rather than allowing a proliferation of masts with fewer operators present on each, as referred to above. This is also supported by high level planning guidance. The NPPF[54] at [119] says the following:

'The number of radio and electronic communications masts, and the sites for such installations, should be kept to a minimum consistent with the needs of consumers, the efficient operation of the network and providing reasonable capacity for future expansion. Use of existing masts, buildings and other structures for new electronic communications capability (including wireless) should be encouraged.'

11.86 Further, it is consistent at a general level with the legislative purpose of the Code and with government policy for agreements to facilitate upgrading, as referred to above. Again, this is supported by high level planning guidance. The NPPF[55] at [118] says this:

---

51 *UAL* at [188].
52 *Fothringham* at [20].
53 *Fothringham* at [21].
54 National Planning Policy Framework.
55 National Planning Policy Framework.

'Planning policies and decisions should support the expansion of electronic communications networks, including next generation mobile technology (such as 5G) and full fibre broadband connections. Policies should set out how high quality digital infrastructure, providing access to services from a range of providers, is expected to be delivered and upgraded over time....'

11.87 It was stressed in *UAL* that the decision whether to grant rights that go beyond those in para 17 would depend on the facts of an individual case. Although it was concluded on the facts of that case that the para 17(2) safeguard should not be included because no sufficient aesthetic considerations arose, the para 17(3) safeguard was imposed because it was of possible benefit to the site provider.

11.88 The tribunals have seemingly become more generous to operators in the more recent cases of *Green* and *Stephenson*, imposing unrestricted sharing and upgrading rights. These cases were both renewal cases, and at least in theory there is a slightly different set of considerations that apply to such cases when determining terms.

Reimbursement of costs and expenses

11.89 Site providers are typically anxious to include whatever contractual provisions it can in order to negate the risk of being out of pocket due to circumstances which that arise during the term of the agreement.

11.90 In *UAL*,[56] the site provider sought a number of provisions of the kind that one might find in commercial leases, which would have required the operator to pay costs and expenses incurred in the following situations:

(i) the enforcement of the Operator's covenants in the agreement, the service of a schedule of dilapidations after the end of the term, and the service of any notice or any proceedings under sections 146 or 147 of the Law of Property Act 1925;

(ii) serving a notice under section 17 of the Landlord and Tenant (Covenants) Act 1995;

(iii) a fair proportion of the grantor's costs of maintaining its property and providing services for the benefit of tenants and occupiers of its property;

(iv) the use of any utilities by the operator;

(v) facilitating access and egress; and

(vi) supervising any works to make good being undertaken by the Operator.

11.91 Each of these was rejected.

11.92 The tribunal was well aware that terms of this kind are found in commercial leases. However, it did not consider it appropriate to impose terms of this kind where

56 See [136] et seq.

the provisions of the agreement already provided adequate protection to the site provider. That was the case whether the agreement to be imposed was a lease or not.[57]

11.93 The operator's case was that the site provider can bring a claim to enforce covenants in the agreement and recover its costs if successful. It also argued that the provision of a schedule of dilapidations was unnecessary because there was already a covenant requiring the operator to make good damage. These submissions appeared to find favour.

11.94 The costs of the service of statutory notices were also not to be recoverable contractually, presumably because it was thought adequate that such costs might be recovered in future proceedings. The site provider's stance was criticised as pedantic, but it is fair to note that if proceedings are never commenced in reliance on a section 146 notice, for example, there would be no proceedings within which to recover the costs of that notice. Perhaps the answer is that a claim for compensation can be made at a later date under para 25(2)(b), and the threat of the same should cause the parties to reach agreement on the payment of sums.

11.95 The costs of maintenance were not allowable on the basis that a share of the running costs of the building was already included within an agreed global compensation figure of £9,600. The tribunal is always extremely keen to avoid double counting, and any claim for compensation should pay careful attention to this.

11.96 The tribunal did go on to note that 'of course [the site provider] is entitled to claim under paragraph 25 of the Code if that [ie, the £9,600 figure] proves eventually to have been inadequate'.

11.97 This raises a question as to the circumstances in which a future compensation claim may be made in respect of heads of loss or expense that have already been assessed, in such a way arguably as to reopen the original assessment of such loss.

11.98 As regards the costs of utilities, there was already a specific provision for electricity usage in the agreement, and no other utilities had been evidenced as likely to be used.

11.99 The costs of facilitating access and egress and of supervising works to make good were not to be the subject of a term. It should be remembered that there is nothing stopping a site provider from returning with an application for compensation under para 25(2)(b) if it reasonably incurred costs in facilitating access or supervising works. However, in circumstances where the tribunal was sceptical at the outset that facilitating access or supervising the operator's works was necessary, a site provider should expect some scepticism should it return later with a para 25(2)(b) application.

Costs of access/supervision

11.100 In *St Martins*, in the context of an MSV, the tribunal held that it was not necessary or appropriate for a site provider to be reimbursed for the costs of arranging professional supervision of other professionals. Although a building owner is entitled

57 *UAL* at [144].

to observe surveys and investigations, the operator in general should not pay for this to be done by a professional person. In contrast, it was noted that the tribunal had generally permitted the recovery of the reasonable expense of a security guard to accompany contractors around a building, or of a building manager providing a briefing, or unlocking secure areas where that was necessary.

11.101 There will be limited and exceptional cases in which an operator may be required to pay for a professional instructed by the site provider, where a building is of a sensitive nature or has a restricted access policy. An example of this was *EE and another v London Underground*[58] , where the tribunal considered that supervision at the operator's expense was appropriate.

The right to install an electricity supply

11.102 It was not necessary or appropriate to include a requirement that a supply be installed 'in compliance with any reasonable requirement of the Grantor', as: (i) the grantor lacks technical knowledge, (ii) parties must agree on a route, acting reasonably in any event, and (iii) the operator is already obliged to cause 'as little disruption as reasonably practicable'.

Electricity generator

11.103 As was stated in *Audley House*:[59]

> 'It is usual in telecommunications leases to provide for the operator to be able to use a generator on site if the mains electricity fails.'

11.104 In *UAL*, the Upper Tribunal rejected a number of the restrictions or controls that the respondent sought to place on the operator's right to utilise a power generator on the respondent's land. It was considered inappropriate for the operator to have to wait until a power outage had lasted for more than 24 hours before a generator could be deployed. Nor was it appropriate for the site provider to have a prior right of approval of the precise siting of the generator given the urgency with which it would need to be installed.

11.105 Further, it was not considered practicable to specify operating noise limits for the generator or a vague requirement such as the generator being 'suitably quiet'. However, the respondent's final suggestion that the operator should have to use reasonable endeavours to reduce any noise and disruption when operating a generator did find favour. Such a condition was considered an appropriate condition to impose both in respect of the location of the generator and its operation.

11.106 It was considered appropriate to limit the use of a generator to occasions when there is a power outage, and to require its removal forthwith upon reinstatement of the electricity supply.

58 [2021] UKUT 128 (LC).
59 [2022] UKUT 152 (LC) at [156]

11.107 In *Stephenson*, the site provider was similarly unsuccessful in seeking the right to specify the location of any generator within what was already a small area. Further, a noise restriction was refused, as noise was inevitable and the restriction proposed lacked clarity. Given that the site was a remote rural location, it was unconvincing that anyone would be disturbed.

11.108 In *Audley House*,[60] it was considered that the risk of disturbance from noise was minimal given that the sites were not near residential property. Further, there was no justification for requiring a generator to be placed in a 'suitable location' or for the site provider to be able to specify its location. The operator would be liable for any loss or damage if the generator was placed in an unsuitable location, and it would be in at least as good a position to assess where a generator should go.

Works (method statement)

11.109 In *UAL*, there was a requirement for the operator to provide a method statement for the proposed works. The landowner wanted the ability to make representations as to the method statement, with the operator having an obligation to have due regard to those representations.

11.110 The operator is responsible for site safety, as the tribunal found in *Islington* at [141] in circumstances in which the operator is given exclusive possession.

11.111 It was held that the landowner's proposed wording was not necessary or appropriate, given that there was already adequate protection in the agreement to ensure that the operator undertook works in a safe manner. The tribunal also considered a requirement to 'have due regard' to a landowner's representations was vague as to both meaning and timing and was likely to provoke more dispute.

The need for future structural surveys

11.112 In *UAL*, the landowner sought a requirement that a structural survey be obtained before any additional equipment is added to that installed at the outset. The landowner had already obtained a structural survey, and the tribunal was not persuaded that further surveys would be needed in that context. It further held that the landowner was adequately protected by the other provisions of the agreement (the operator had relied on the operator's liability for the safety of the site, its general civil liability in the event that its future calculations were wrong, its obligations as to carrying out works under the agreement, and the indemnity under the agreement). Finally, the tribunal pointed out that goodwill between the parties should ensure the safe installation and operation of the equipment.

Use of the site: prohibition on damage

11.113 In *UAL*, the tribunal rejected a blanket prohibition on the operator using the site in such a way as to damage the landowner's land. This was rejected, given the

60 At [156] to [166].

obligation to make good any damage caused by installing cables, carrying out the permitted works, and removing the equipment, or to compensate in lieu.

Health and Safety matters

11.114 As indicated above, there have been cases in which the tribunal has imposed terms requiring an operator to comply with the reasonable health and safety requirements of the site provider. There may be cases in which detailed access protocols are approved, such as where the use of land in the vicinity of the Communications Site is particularly dangerous or subject to significant security concerns.

11.115 Below are examples of specific health and safety issues that have arisen in particular cases, rather than disputes restricted to the content of a protocol document or procedure which is to govern access by the operator.

11.116 In the *Audley House*[61] case, the site provider was concerned that it could be held liable for any health and safety breaches, and so sought to include a number of terms in the agreement in order to protect it. These terms included the provision of method statements and risk assessments for every visit, and the identity and qualification of everyone who is to attend.

11.117 The tribunal set out a general principle that:

> 'Landowners are obliged to suffer the presence of equipment and conduits on their land for the benefit of us all, but the safety of that equipment and the management of any risk that it poses for the public remains the responsibility of those who operate it.'[62]

11.118 It added that it was:

> 'no part of the policy of the Code that such a site provider be responsible, let alone criminally liable, for the safety of a telecommunications site on its land'.[63]

11.119 The fear as to the civil liability of site providers was considered most unrealistic in cases where the Code agreement is to be a lease which grants exclusive possession to the operator. The tribunal said as follows:

> 'The fear of civil liability for site providers is wholly unrealistic where the Code agreement requires them to give up exclusive possession of the site and gives them no control over what goes on there. In those circumstances liability in negligence or under the Occupier's Liability legislation is not possible. Nor can there be liability for what happens on the way to the site, where the landowner retains possession of the access way, if the Code agreement gives the landowner no say in what the operator does on the land that gives access to the site. If the operator's employee digs up the farm track, the operator and not the landowner is vicariously liable.'[64]

---

61 *On Tower UK Ltd v AP Wireless (UK) Ltd (Audley House)* [2022] UKUT 152 (LC).
62 *Audley House* at [2].
63 *Audley House* at [57].
64 *Audley House* at [58].

11.120 The site provider's concerns had come from non-delegable statutory health and safety legislation. Section 3 of the Health and Safety at Work Act 1974 created a duty, the breach of which is a criminal offence, to conduct one's 'undertaking' in such a way as to 'ensure, so far as is reasonably practicable' that persons are not exposed to health and safety risks. The tribunal held that 'for the vast majority of site providers what goes on at a telecommunication site on their land is not part of their undertaking'.

11.121 Section 4 of that Act imposed a duty (again subject to a criminal sanction) to take reasonable measures to ensure that 'means of access [to the premises] or egress therefrom' is safe so far as is reasonably practicable. That duty applied to persons with 'control' of premises. The tribunal accepted that a site provider will often remain in possession of an access route and would therefore be subject to this duty. However, it held that 'where a site provider is not entitled to any say in what the operator does while it is using the access to approach the site it will not be reasonably practicable for it to prevent the operator from doing something that makes the access unsafe.'

11.122 Thus, in a typical case, it would seem that a site provider is actually in a better position as regards avoiding any liability for health and safety if it does not seek an array of terms relating to such matters. Such terms may have the unintended effect of involving the site provider in matters for which it would otherwise have no liability due to its lack of control. It would also seem that a site provider would be in a clearer and safer position where a Code agreement is imposed as a lease rather than a licence, which does not grant exclusive possession.

11.123 The tribunal's approach to terms sought by site providers in relation to health and safety matters is perhaps best summed up by the following passage:

> 'There may or may not be reasons for a site provider to have an involvement in the management of a site. In the absence of any such reasons the site provider will not be required or enabled by the Tribunal to manage or control operations on the site, because that duplicates the operator's work, causing it delay and expense and thereby going against the objectives of the Code, and also because it potentially exposes the site provider to liability. It is not the case that the site provider has to be given an involvement or a degree of control in order to protect it from liability; that is the wrong way around.'[65]

11.124 In relation to *Audley House* in particular, part of the site provider's concern was that as its business (its undertaking) includes the management of some telecoms sites, it ran the risk that the operation of the present site by the operator may constitute part of its undertaking. The tribunal held that this did not follow. Its only involvement in the present site would be as site provider, and it would be in no different position as regards health and safety liability than if its business elsewhere did not involve managing telecoms sites. Accordingly, the tribunal was unpersuaded of the need for the giving of any notice to the site provider, the use of an access portal, or adherence to an access protocol.

11.125 The tribunal did acknowledge that in a case where a site provider was an intermediate lessee which had access restrictions in its own lease, the tribunal would have to consider the extent to which these should be replicated in the terms of the Code agreement.[66]

65 *Audley House* at [78].
66 *Audley House* at [84].

11.126 In the *New Zealand Farm*[67] case, a 1954 Act lease renewal, the landlord sought a term requiring the tenant operator to provide copies of method statements and similar documents before work was undertaken. The court accepted the operator's submission that no sufficient reason had been given to introduce these new obligations. Reliance was placed on the observation in *UAL* that it was important 'not to generate requirements for the transmission of information where that would be of little or no practical benefit to either party'.[68] Reference was also made to the *Audley House* decision[69] and it was noted that the landlord was not responsible for health and safety at the site.

11.127 However, in *Hackney* (Tradescant House)[70] the tribunal considered that the situation was very different from that which had presented itself in *Audley House*. The goings on on the roof of Tradescant House were 'very much part of the respondent's undertaking as a landlord, and it retains full control of the access to the roof. It is of course liable for unsafe practice that it could prevent.'

11.128 The site provider accepted, and the tribunal clearly agreed, that it could not be civilly or criminally liable for allowing contractors on to the site without having given final approval to the RAMS in a case where the terms imposed by the tribunal prevented it from doing so. Thus, if the tribunal had imposed a term that allowed the site provider to comment on the RAMS, but not have the last word, that would not operate so as to confer liability on the site provider for health and safety breaches.

11.129 Nonetheless, the tribunal agreed to impose the 'approval condition' for two reasons that it described as 'practical':[71]

(i) If one party has to have the last word about the RAMS, then that should be the one that knows more about the risks. In sharp contrast to the position in *Audley House*, the site provider was considered to be in a much better position to assess the risks on the site than was the operator. This was an MSV case, two features of which were relevant:

 (a) the operator's contractors had not been on site before. The position would be different in the case of an established site such that the operator was familiar with the building and site-specific hazards; and

 (b) the operator was not installing apparatus. The position would be different if it were:

 > 'it is clearly important that telecommunications operators be in control of their own undertaking, and the operator is better placed than the site provider to assess the risks arising from work that involves electronic communications apparatus'.

(ii) In the unlikely event of a real disagreement about safety, an MSV agreement with the 'approval condition' was considered likely to cause less loss and

67 *On Tower Ltd v AP Wireless (II) (New Zealand Farm)* [2022] EW Misc 6 (CC) at [31]–[40].
68 [2020] UKUT 248 (LC) at [70].
69 Between the same parties.
70 [2022] UKUT 210 (LC) at [22].
71 [2022] UKUT 210 (LC) at [60].

damage[72] to the respondent than the same agreement without that condition. If the operator were faced with a demand from the site provider that it regards as creating a risk, it could opt not to carry out the site visit pending resolution of the dispute. By contrast, if the site provider is unable to refuse access where it perceives the actions of the operator to entail a risk, either people will be put at risk or it will have to incur 'the expense and stress of litigation.'

ICNIRP exclusion zones

11.130 The International Commission on Non-Ionising Radiation Protection ('ICNIRP'[73]) is an advisory body. It publishes guidance on exclusion zones that should be observed around equipment that emits non-ionising radiation, both for the public and for those whose occupations give rise to exposure to such radiation. This type of radiation is emitted by dishes and antennae used in electronic communications networks. As noted in *UAL*, prolonged exposure to such radiation can give rise to health risks, and domestic legislation has translated some of the ICNIRP guidance into legal requirements.[74] Real and perceived health risks are matters in which members of the lay public are increasingly interested, especially in the context of 5G rollout.

11.131 A dispute arose in *UAL* as to whether the operator should be obliged to provide plans showing the ICNIRP exclusion zones relating to the general public rather than merely the zones pertaining to those individuals who may come into contact with the radiation in the context of their occupations.

11.132 The landowner wished to ensure that both it and users of the roof were aware of the extent of the relevant exclusion zones. The operator relied on the lack of any statutory obligation to provide details of exclusion zones. The tribunal noted this in rejecting the landowner's request. It observed that the request was late, it did not appear to have come from technical advisers, and was in any event a step too far given that the antennae would be confined to the edge of the building.

11.133 However, it made clear that this was not to be taken as a general principle and that the tribunal's conclusion about terms relating to exclusion zones would depend upon the type of site, the position of the relevant zones, and other practical considerations in individual cases.

11.134 In ***Audley House***, the tribunal accepted that exclusion zones 'are of potential concern to the superior landlord and to any other neighbours whose buildings or activities may in the future fall within them'. However, it added that that was the operator's responsibility and that it was unnecessary to make it also the responsibility of the site provider. It was considered that the operator's responsibilities to abide by legislation (including ICNIRP requirements) were sufficient and therefore did not impose terms that would require the provision of ICNIRP exclusion zone drawings, or oblige or entitle the site provider to check or manage compliance. Again, it was

---

72 See [2022] UKUT 210 (LC) at [61]–[68]. Para [61] of the decision says 'less likely to cause less loss and damage', but presumably one or other 'less' should have been omitted, given that the decision was to include the 'approval condition'.

73 Occasionally abbreviated as 'ICNRP'.

74 *UAL* at [212].

observed that the site provider had no potential criminal liability unless the tribunal put it in a position to control what the operator does. This decision was followed in the *New Zealand Farm*[75] case, a 1954 Act lease renewal involving the same parties.

Drop zone warranty

11.135 In *UAL*, the tribunal agreed to impose a term whereby the operator warranted that no drop zone would be required at ground floor level. It was accepted by the operator that some of the antennae would partially extend beyond the edge of the building and that if the antennae were to become loose, they would present a drop risk. However, it contended that there were ample mechanisms in place to prevent them from becoming detached. The tribunal imposed the warranty as sought by the landowner on the basis that, as the operator was so confident that there was no realistic prospect of the antennae dropping to the ground, there was no reason not to give the warranty requested.

Indemnities

11.136 In its interim rights decision in *Islington*[76] the tribunal observed that when it is considering the terms of an agreement imposing interim Code rights:

> 'It should put the full risk of the operation on which the operator wishes to embark on the operator and none of the risk on the site provider.'

11.137 However, it should always be borne in mind that para 25 applies to all agreements imposed under paras 20, 26, or 27, and hence there is an opportunity to apply for compensation at a later date under para 25(2)(b) in the event that a later loss is caused. Similarly, there will be numerous provisions in most agreements requiring an operator to use reasonable care in undertaking works, to cause as little damage as possible, to comply with statutory requirements, and/or to reinstate any physical damage. There are therefore numerous potential contractual avenues by which losses might be recovered. Indemnities are therefore clearly not the only route of recovery of loss by a landowner against an operator.

11.138 It may be thought that whether an agreement is an interim agreement or a more fulsome para 20 agreement might be at least a factor in deciding what term is imposed by way of indemnity.

11.139 However, in the later case of *Hackney (Shoreditch House)*[77] the Deputy Chamber President cast doubt on how much impact that difference would have, holding:

> '…what is appropriate in any particular case is obviously influenced by its own circumstances but I do not think that the mere fact that one claim is for permanent rights and another only for interim rights necessarily justifies imposing a different form of obligation'.

---

75 *On Tower Ltd v AP Wireless (II) (New Zealand Farm)* [2022] EW Misc 6 (CC) at [41], Judge Rodger QC, sitting as a judge of the county court.

76 *EE Ltd v Islington LBC* [2018] UKUT 361 (LC) at [48].

77 *EE Ltd & Anor v London Borough Of Hackney* [2021] UKUT 142 (LC).

11.140 In *UAL*, there was a dispute as to the form and scope of an indemnity provision under which the operator proposed to indemnify the landowner in respect of losses incurred through third party claims arising out of acts or omissions of the operator.

11.141 The operator proposed an indemnity in the form of that contained in OFCOM's Draft Standard Terms[78] (at clause 8 thereof), headed 'Indemnity for Third Party Claims'. The operator's case was that the sole purpose of such an indemnity is to regulate and manage a third party claim against the landowner resulting from an unlawful act or omission by the operator. The indemnity was not meant to protect the landowner against all loss or damage it may suffer. It was argued that protection against loss or damage caused by the operator was already provided for in the draft agreement.

11.142 The tribunal said as follows at [233] and [235]:

> '233. Two important points of principle shape our conclusions on this clause. The first is that the purpose of the indemnity is to regulate and manage third party claims against the respondent arising from the unlawful acts or omissions of the claimant. It is not a catch all protective provision for the benefit of the respondent covering every conceivable loss or damage, whatever the cause and regardless of the other provisions of the agreement. That being so it is plainly inappropriate for the respondent to seek an indemnity in respect of 'all losses damages costs and expenses and all claims and proceedings brought against the grantor arising from any unlawful act of the operator.
>
> ...
>
> 235. The second point of principle is that the clause is drafted so as to protect both parties; it indemnifies the respondent against third party claims but it also, as drafted, gives the claimant control of those proceedings if it wishes to take control. The respondent of course objects to that. We do not think it is appropriate for the respondent to have the sole right to defend or settle proceedings where the claimant is giving a substantial indemnity.[79] The entitlement of the claimant to conduct those proceedings, subject to the respondent's prior written consent, is a reasonable provision.'

11.143 The tribunal accepted the operator's submission that the indemnity clause is a matter of procedural management and that the landowner was not dependent on the clause for the means to recover compensation (including in respect of third party claims against it), as that is covered by para 25.

11.144 However, as regards more detailed points of drafting, some of the landowner's arguments succeeded. The tribunal did not accept the qualification that third party claims must arise 'directly' from an unlawful act and also rejected the qualification that any claim brought against the landowner must be 'in its capacity as Grantor'. The exclusion of claims in respect of 'consequential losses' was also rejected.

---

78 Produced by OFCOM in accordance with para 103(2) of the Code.

79 This conclusion was repeated in *Audley House* at [204], with neither party being able to settle a claim without the other's consent, not to be unreasonably withheld, and in *New Zealand Farm* at [50]. Thus, the same conclusion has been reached in cases involving a new site, a Code renewal and a 1954 Act renewal.

11.145 As regards an indemnity cap, the tribunal held that it 'was quite difficult to find any obvious rationale for a limit upon it', given the purpose of an indemnity. Having said that, it then accepted the operator's proposed cap of £35 million, noting the observation of the Lands Tribunal for Scotland in *Fothringham*[80] that there was no obligation under the Code to offer an indemnity at all.

11.146 Finally, it was underlined that the imposition of an indemnity cap 'does not in any way limit the claimant's liability to the respondent for loss or damage caused by the claimant, whether directly or as a result of an action brought by a third party.'[81]

11.147 In *Fothringham*,[82] an interim rights case, the Lands Tribunal for Scotland was keen to note the distinction between the following two discrete concepts:

> 'compensation for lawful things done by the applicants under the Code, for which the Code provided redress, and indemnity for the consequences of illegal acts or omissions, which was the point of the proffered indemnity. …
>
> … The distinction between rights under the Code and rights under the indemnity clause is clear enough…'

11.148 In *Hackney (Shoreditch House)*,[83] the Deputy Chamber President took the above as a 'recognition that any contractual right to an indemnity which a site provider is given is in addition to the statutory right to compensation enjoyed under the Code'. The extent for which there is a need an indemnity must be seen in that context.

11.149 In this case, there was a dispute in principle as to whether an indemnity should indeed be restricted to recovery in respect of claims against landowners by third parties.

11.150 The tribunal rejected the submission that limiting the indemnity to third party claims would infringe the requirement in para 23(5) of the Code to impose terms appropriate for ensuring the least possible causation of loss and damage by the exercise of Code rights. It was held that the contractual agreement has to be seen in the context of the other protections offered by the Code, in particular the para 25 right to compensation. It was held that it was clear from Parliament's design of the Code that a full indemnity was not intended, and that a third-party indemnity was consistent with the 'basic structure and expectations of the Code'. The Deputy Chamber President said as follows:

> 'Any statutory right of compensation is controlled or restricted by the overarching legal principles of causation, remoteness of damage and the requirement of mitigation of loss[84]… The proposed indemnity, if applied to the site provider's own losses, would side step those legal limitations. Yet when Parliament designed the Code it saw fit to confer on site providers a right of compensation and not a statutory indemnity against all losses free of those restrictions. It cannot have considered that statutory compensation provided inadequate protection or have

80 *Cornerstone Telecommunications Infrastructure Limited v Fothringham* LTS/ECC/2019/06.

81 *UAL* at [241].

82 *Cornerstone Telecommunications Infrastructure Limited v Fothringham* LTS/ECC/2019/06 at [11]–[13].

83 *EE Ltd & Anor v London Borough Of Hackney* [2021] UKUT 142 (LC).

84 Citing Lord Nicholls' discussion of the three conditions or prerequisites of fair compensation in *Director of Buildings and Lands v Shung Fung Ironworks Ltd and Cross-Appeal Co* (Hong Kong) [1995] UKPC 7.

intended that paragraph 23(5) should oblige the Tribunal to impose an even more comprehensive contractual indemnity.'[85]

11.151 The tribunal also placed reliance on the fact that OFCOM saw fit only to include an indemnity clause limited to third party claims in its published model form of Code agreement.

11.152 In *Stephenson*,[86] there was a dispute as to the wording of an indemnity clause. The operator wanted the indemnity only to cover claims arising from a negligent act or omission by the tenant, whereas the site provider argued that it should extend to claims 'arising by reason of any act, negligence, breach or omission of the Tenant…'. The tribunal favoured the broader clause, saying:

> 'The underlying principle is that the site provider, which is to receive none of the economic benefits of the use of the site for the exercise of the Code rights (because of the no-network assumption), should not be expected to share to any extent in the risks created by the exercise of those rights. If the exercise of the rights causes damage to a third party which results in a claim being brought against the site provider it is appropriate, in my judgment, that the site provider should be indemnified against that claim by the operator whether the operator has acted negligently or not.'

Dispute resolution clauses

11.153 In *Audley House*, the tribunal refused to impose a compulsory dispute resolution clause because it was subject to so many exceptions that it was toothless. The same result occurred in *New Zealand Farm*[87] for different reasons, namely that it was overly prescriptive, the parties were commercial entities who were well capable of devising a sensible route to resolving a dispute, a party seeking early resolution should have access to the courts, and the other party should not be able to use the clause as an obstacle.

Authorised guarantee agreements

11.154 Paragraph 16(1) of the Code renders void any agreement under Part 2 to the extent that it prevents or limits assignment of the agreement to another operator or makes assignment of the agreement to another operator subject to conditions (including a condition requiring the payment of money).

11.155 However, para 16(2) makes clear that the voiding provision in para 16(1) does not apply to a term that requires the assignor to enter into a guarantee agreement.

11.156 Paragraph 16(7) then defines a 'guarantee agreement' as:

---

85 *Hackney (Shoreditch House)* at [17].

86 *EE Ltd & Anor v Stephenson & Anor* [2022] UKUT 180 (LC) at [39] and [40]. This was the second published Tribunal decision in the case, and covered the details of the resulting agreement, following the determination of preliminary issues at [2021] UKUT 167 (LC).

87 *On Tower Ltd v AP Wireless (II) (New Zealand Farm)* [2022] EW Misc 6 (CC) at [51]–[53].

'an agreement, in connection with the assignment of an agreement under Part 2 of this code, under which the assignor guarantees to any extent the performance by the assignee of the obligations that become binding on the assignee under sub-paragraph (4) (the 'relevant obligations').'

11.157 In *UAL*, the landowner sought a provision requiring, consistently with para 16(2) of the Code, a guarantee agreement to be provided as a condition of assignment to another operator. The operator instead offered a clause that allowed the landowner to request a guarantee agreement where 'it is reasonable on an objective assessment of the assignee's ability to pay the sums due under this Agreement'. The obligation to give a guarantee agreement would only have been triggered after the assignment had taken place. The landowner argued that its proposed clause was necessary in order to minimise potential loss and damage, consistently with para 23(5) of the Code.

11.158 The tribunal held that it was reasonable for the operator to give a guarantee agreement at the time of any assignment, as the giving of such a guarantee agreement is expressly allowed for in the Code even where the assignment is to another operator. It was further observed that: 'It is not to be assumed that another operator will have the ability to meet all the relevant obligations under the agreement merely because it is regulated by Ofcom.'[88]

Rent review clauses

11.159 Rent review clauses are not a big issue in litigation over terms. Agreements are typically imposed for a term of 10 years or shorter, network value is stripped out, and compensation is available under para 25 in the case of imposed agreements, such that if something unexpected causes loss or damage, a site provider can seek to recover that loss separately.

11.160 However, what about a situation where the operator loses its operator status, or it assigns the agreement to a non-operator? Should the telecoms company occupier in those events be able to benefit from the Code rent, which is likely far lower than a true open market value?

11.161 This question arose in *Stephenson*. The Deputy President considered it appropriate to impose a provision for a rent review to true open market value in the event that either: (i) the current operator lost its status as an operator, or (ii) the agreement was assigned to a non-operator. This was because of the highly restrictive nature of the valuation formula at para 24, and because 'the Code's policy of promoting improvements in telecommunications for the public benefit does not require that the site provider should be kept out of its fair share' in the event that the agreement ended up in the hands of a non-operator, to whom the beneficial valuation terms of para 24 would never apply.

---

88 *UAL* at [253].

11.162 Similarly, in *Audley House*,[89] the tribunal agreed to an open market rent review in the event that the tenant ceased to be a Code operator. However, it imposed an upwards only RPI-based rent review provision if the tenant remained an operator, refusing an open market review. This was because the latter exercise would be time-consuming and not worth the trouble in the context of Code rents (ie, given the no-network assumption).

Obligation to give vacant possession

11.163 In *Stephenson*, the Deputy President described the inclusion of an obligation on an operator to give vacant possession at the end of the term (which would also require that third-party sharers of the site should remove their apparatus) as 'clearly appropriate'. He similarly endorsed a proposed qualification that that obligation would not apply 'for so long as the lease was continued after the end of the term by paragraph 30 of the Code'.[90]

The impact of para 23(5)

11.164 Paragraph 23(5) provides as follows:

> '(5) The terms of the agreement must include the terms the court thinks appropriate for ensuring that the least possible loss and damage is caused by the exercise of the code right to persons who—
>
> (a) occupy the land in question,
>
> (b) own interests in that land, or
>
> (c) are from time to time on that land.'

11.165 This provision is most likely to be considered in a contested Reference. Accordingly, the focus is likely to be minimising loss and damage to the party or parties to the Reference who are not the operator. However, it is worth noting that the provisions of sub-paras (a) to (c) above are drawn so as to include persons who may not be parties to the Reference.

11.166 It is true that the tribunal does not have a duty to ensure the minimisation of loss and damage. But the terms that it must select are those that it thinks appropriate for *ensuring* that the *least possible* loss and damage is caused to the defined persons. On the face of it, the words chosen appear forceful.

11.167 Further, they appear broad. As the resulting agreement will have been imposed by a tribunal, it will be subject to para 25(1), meaning that the site provider can apply for compensation for 'loss or damage', either at the outset or at any time after the agreement's imposition.[91] Para 23(5) does not refer to the minimisation of

---

89 A case involving the same site provider as in *Stephenson*, and decided only weeks before *Stephenson*. *Audley House* was not referred to in *Stephenson*, and so it appears that differently constituted Tribunals arrived at a similar conclusion independently.

90 *EE Ltd v Stephenson* [2022] UKUT 180 (LC) at [50].

91 under para 25(2)(a) and/or (b).

non-compensatable loss and damage, and thus one might think that it is referring to any and all loss and damage, including that for which compensation may be payable.

11.168 In the above context, in Code decisions thus far, para 23(5) has perhaps not had the impact in assisting site providers that they might have anticipated.

11.169 In *London & Quadrant*[92] the UT commented that para 23(5) 'has an important part to play in resolving disputes over terms'. However, it emphasised that this provision should not be 'viewed in isolation', and was not a prohibition on the imposition of Code rights that may cause loss and damage. The tribunal noted that the agreement would include terms as to consideration and compensation, each of which would take into account any loss and damage caused.

11.170 Submissions that a tribunal should or must include or reject a particular term because of para 23(5) have enjoyed mixed success. In *UAL*,[93] the tribunal expressly held that its chosen set down area term may not satisfy the site provider's desire to minimise any adverse impact on its use of a building on certain days. In *Hackney (Shoreditch House)* the tribunal rejected the notion that para 23(5) meant that it was appropriate for an indemnity to cover more than merely third party claims.

11.171 In the para 26 case of *St Martins*,[94] para 23(5) was referred to in the tribunal's reasoning for exercising restraint in permitting intrusive works to be carried out as part of an MSV. However, given the other reasons given, including the low evidential hurdle under para 26 it is perhaps unlikely that para 23(5) made the crucial difference.

11.172 However, in *UAL*, the tribunal did expressly reject the operator's preferred extensive access right on the basis of para 23(5). Similarly, in the *Hackney (Tradescant House)*[95] case, para 23(5) was expressly given as a reason for imposing a term that allowed the site provider to have the last word as to the approval of method statements in order to allow the operator to carry out an MSV.

11.173 Similarly, in *London & Quadrant*[96] in restricting sharing rights the UT went as far as to say that 'We do not consider that unrestricted sharing of electronic communications apparatus on the roof of a large residential building is compatible with the direction in paragraph 23(5).' However, in a growing number of cases, the tribunals appear willing to grant unrestricted sharing rights without concerns as to para 23(5).

11.174 One example of this is *Stephenson*, a renewal case concerning a rural site at Pendown Farm in Cornwall. The site provider sought to restrict the right to share, such that it applied only to equipment (and not the site), and such that it in all other respects complied with the limitations set out at para 17. The Deputy President[97] rejected the site provider's proposed term, saying as follows:

92 *Cornerstone Telecommunications Infrastructure Ltd v London & Quadrant Housing Trust* [2020] UKUT 282 (LC) at [46]–[47].

93 UT decision at [102].

94 At [19].

95 [2022] UKUT 210 (LC) at [67].

96 *Cornerstone Telecommunications Infrastructure Ltd v London & Quadrant Housing Trust* [2020] UKUT 282 (LC) at [88].

97 who had also sat as part of the Tribunal in *London & Quadrant* some two years earlier.

'It seems to me that it would impose a significant limitation on the opportunity to share with other operators and is, in general terms, inconsistent with the achievement of the objects of the Code and liable to bring the parties into conflict. It is not necessary to introduce the condition to ensure that the least possible loss and damage is caused by the exercise of the code rights, because it has not been suggested that sharing in itself is liable to cause any loss or damage.' [98]

11.175 Similarly, as the possibility of loss and damage being caused to the site provider as a result of upgrading equipment on the mast was theoretical only and could not be substantiated on the evidence, para 23(5) did not make it appropriate to impose any additional restriction.[99]

11.176 It would therefore seem that in respect of issues such as sharing and upgrading, if a landowner wishes to seek to restrict rights along para 17 lines based on a para 23(5) argument, it will need to identify (and successfully evidence) the loss or damage that is argued to result from the enlarged rights that are sought, by reference to the particular facts of the case.

Imposed terms in Code agreement renewal cases

11.177 Where a tribunal is considering what terms to impose in a renewal case under Part 5 of the Code, there are various matters to which it must have regard. In theory at least, the test as to what terms to impose is not precisely the same as in the para 20 context.

11.178 Paragraph 34(11) provides that para 23(2) to (8) apply in such cases, just as they do to cases under para 20. These provisions are those that govern what terms are to be imposed in para 20 cases and commence with the broad discretion at para 23(2) that the tribunal must require a Code agreement to include the terms that it considers 'appropriate'.

11.179 Further, in a case where the parties cannot agree on the terms of the renewal agreement such that the tribunal is to determine them pursuant to para 34(10),[100] para 34(12) has effect. This sub-paragraph provides that the tribunal must also have regard to the terms of the existing agreement. Naturally this is not a consideration that applies in the para 20 context, as there is no existing agreement.

Renewal agreement vs. new agreement: theoretical differences in approach

11.180 The Upper Tribunal in *Ashloch*[101] had sought to distinguish between the approach to terms to be taken in a para 34 Code agreement renewal case, and one

98 [2022] UKUT 180 (LC) at [42].
99 [2022] UKUT 180 (LC) at [34].
100 It is perhaps not entirely clear which categories of cases are referred to in para 34(10). On the face of it, that sub-para follows on from para 34(9), which provides that the terms in para 34(5) or (6) cases are to be such as are agreed between the parties. It therefore appears that para 34(10) is making provision for the Tribunal to determine those terms in para 34(5) and (6) cases, where the parties cannot agree. However, para 34(11) appears to draw a contradistinction between para 34(3), (4) and (5) cases on the one hand, and para 34(10) cases on the other, which might seem to indicate that a para 34(5) case is not a para 34(10) case.
101 [2019] UKUT 338 (LC): at [96] of the judgment.

in which a *new* agreement was being sought. This difference was said to be founded on the fact that under both para 34(12) of the Code, and under the 1954 Act,[102] the starting point was 'the terms of the existing tenancy or Code agreement'. It was said that this approach differed from that under para 23 of the Code.[103] The Upper Tribunal clearly considered that the correct approach under para 34 had similarities with the approach under the 1954 Act, and the well-known 1954 Act case of *O'May v City of London Real Property Co Ltd*[104] was cited as a byword for the starting point from which all fact-specific determinations of terms should commence. Lewison LJ[105] in the Court of Appeal in *Ashloch* cited this passage from the Upper Tribunal's judgment with agreement.

11.181 The Supreme Court had the last word in *Ashloch*, essentially upholding the principal conclusion of both the Upper Tribunal and Court of Appeal that the Code was not open to a sitting tenant operator as a means of renewing a subsisting agreement telecoms lease and that the 1954 Act renewal process must be followed in such circumstances. The Supreme Court did not criticise anything said in the lower courts as regards terms. However, it should be remembered that *Ashloch* was concerned with how the Code and the 1954 Act should function and interact, and specifically the circumstances in which a sitting tenant operator was entitled to utilise the Code rather than renewing its 'subsisting agreement' lease through the 1954 Act process. It was not primarily concerned with what terms should be imposed in Code agreements, or what the test should be for determining that question.

11.182 Thus, in *EE v Stephenson*,[106] Fancourt J (sitting in the Upper Tribunal) pointed out that there were other considerations in play in determinations of terms under the Code as compared with the 1954 Act. He concluded that neither the tribunal nor the Court of Appeal in *Ashloch* decided how para 34(12) operated in the context of Part 5 of the Code as a whole. He thus expressly rejected[107] the argument that it was part of the *ratio* of *Ashloch* that para 34(12) of the Code has the same meaning and effect as section 35 of the 1954 Act.

11.183 In that context, he observed that section 35 of the 1954 Act operates to limit changes in the terms of the tenancy (other than rent and duration), against the will of either party, which is an 'aspect of the provision of business continuity for the tenant… A heavy onus lies on the party seeking a change to justify it, in terms of overall fairness: *O'May*'.[108]

102 The Upper Tribunal referred to s 34 of the 1954 Act, but it is reasonably clear that a reference to s 35 was intended, as it is stated that the terms of the new agreement were the starting point under that section. Section 34 deals with the valuation of rent according to the statutory valuation hypothesis, whereas s 35 makes provision as to the 'other terms' of the new lease. Section 35 says that 'in determining those terms the court shall have regard to the terms of the current tenancy and to all relevant circumstances'.

103 Presumably this meant the approach under para 23 where a *new* agreement is sought, as there is no existing agreement to which to have regard. It should be noted that para 34(11) applies para 23(2) to (8) to renewal cases.

104 [1983] 2 AC 726.

105 At [101] and [102] of his Lordship's judgment, as agreed with at [107] and [112] by the Court's other members.

106 [2021] UKUT 167 (LC).

107 At [58] of the judgment.

108 See judgment in *EE v Stephenson* at [54].

11.184 He then sought to distinguish a Code renewal from a 1954 Act renewal, noting as follows:

> '55. However, one objective of the Code was to change the terms that apply under code agreements, where these restrict operators from doing or having the flexibility to do what they reasonably need to do, or where they operate against the public interest. In the Code there is therefore not the same generally applied presumption against change that has been read into the language of section 35 of the 1954 Act . Rather, site providers are required to put up with a degree of change in the public interest of facilitating the provision of a choice of high quality networks.'

11.185 The conclusion reached on this point was as follows:

> '56. Nevertheless, the words of paragraph 34(12) of the Code must have been intended to reflect the effect that the words have been held to have under the 1954 Act . The terms of the existing agreement are intended to be of some materiality, subject to the other considerations. The words of paragraph 34(12) are that the court shall *also* have regard to those terms. Read in context, this means that, in specifying the terms of the new code rights or the new agreement, regard is to be had to those terms as well as terms that the parties have agreed, if any, and the requirements of paragraphs 23(2) to (8), 24, 25 and 84 of the Code: paragraph 34(10), (11).'

11.186 In *Green*,[109] the tribunal said that in making decisions about the terms of a renewed agreement:

> '... it may be helpful to think in terms of a balancing process between the claimant's requirements and the respondent's concerns, but the Code does not put it like that. Perhaps a better way to look at it is as follows.
>
> 62. First, the Tribunal should consider the term the operator seeks and the reason why it needs the term in question in order to pursue the business for whose purposes it received its Ofcom direction and in light of the public interest in a choice of high quality telecommunications services.
>
> 63. Second, the Tribunal will consider the concerns or objections raised by the respondent and whether in order to minimise loss or damage in accordance with paragraph 23(5) the term should not be imposed, or should be imposed to a limited or qualified extent.
>
> 64. If those concerns do not prevent the imposition of the term and do not require its qualification, then the Tribunal will consider whether, in imposing that term, it should also impose further terms to minimise loss or damage.'[110]

11.187 The Court of Appeal in *Green*[111] approved the comments made by Fancourt J in *EE v Stephenson*.

11.188 Newey LJ (with whom the remainder of the court agreed) said as follows:

109 [2020] UKUT 348 (LC) at [61]–[64].

110 This passage was referred to with approval in *On Tower UK Ltd v AP Wireless (UK) Ltd (Audley House)* [2022] UKUT 152 (LC), which post-dated the Court of Appeal's decision in *Green*.

111 *On Tower UK Ltd v JH and FW Green Ltd* [2021] EWCA Civ 1858.

'47. … I agree with Fancourt J that, despite the similarity in language between paragraph 34(12) of the Code and section 35 of the 1954 Act, things said about the latter will not necessarily apply to the former. As Fancourt J said, the 1954 Act and the Code have very different purposes. When considering whether the terms of a new business tenancy should differ from those of its predecessor, the 'comparatively weak negotiating position of a sitting tenant' and the purpose of protecting the business interests of the tenant may, as Lord Hailsham indicated in *O'May*, be of significant weight. The Code cannot be said to be aiming to protect site providers in a similar way. To the contrary, as Fancourt J pointed out, the Code seeks to enable operators to 'use and exploit sites more flexibly, quickly and cheaply than had previously been the case'.

48. That is by no means to say that the terms of an existing code agreement can be ignored. To the contrary, paragraph 34(12) of the Code specifically directs the Court to have regard to the terms of the existing code agreement, albeit that the Tribunal is also required to have regard to a variety of other factors. As Fancourt J said in para 57, paragraph 34(12) 'cannot be read as imposing an overarching restriction on change', but in an appropriate case the terms of the existing agreement may still be significant. In particular, where a party wishes the new agreement to contain a term found in the existing agreement, that will be a factor to considered and there will be an onus on the party contending for a change to justify it.

49. The weight to be attached to the fact that a term was included in the existing code agreement will in part turn on its consistency with the aims of the Code. If the relevant term cannot be thought to be in conflict with those aims, the case for replicating it in the new agreement may be compelling. Plainly, the position will be different if the term is at variance with the objectives of the Code. In practice, the terms of a code agreement entered into since the introduction of the Code are more likely to accord with its purposes than those of an agreement which pre-dates the Code.'

11.189 Thus, the current state of the law in respect of the terms to be imposed in Part 5 Code agreement renewal cases is as follows:

(i) The tribunal has a duty to have regard to the existing code agreement, but this does not mean that the new agreement has to be the same as the old one;

(ii) Although the wording of para 34(12) is similar to the wording in s. 35 of the 1954 Act, those pieces of legislation have very different purposes;

(iii) The Code seeks to allow operators to 'use and exploit sites more flexibly, quickly and cheaply than had previously been the case';

(iv) The burden is on the party arguing for a change to justify that change;

(v) The weight to be given to the fact that a term was in an existing agreement would be affected by the extent to which it was consistent with the aims of the Code.

11.190 The burden on the party proposing the change is a feature that is not present in the case of a new Code agreement, in respect of which there is no burden on either party (see above). However, given that the duty to have regard to the existing agreement does not connote such a strong presumption in favour of the existing agreement as under the 1954 Act (and as explained in *O'May*), and given that consistency with the Code is a key touchstone, an operator seeking more favourable terms in a Part 5 renewal is in a reasonably strong position. There is no absolute guarantee that it would achieve terms that would be as favourable as those obtained under a new agreement under Part 4. However, one can be sure that in many cases they will do so and that in most cases they will try.

11.191 Cases under Part 4 may be of relevance when considering what terms a tribunal is likely to impose in a Part 5 case. This is, of course, subject to recognising the slightly different tests that are applicable and the general caveat that each case turns on its own facts. Similarly, and probably to a greater extent, where a tribunal is convinced to include a particular new term in a Part 5 case, that may well be of relevance when considering what a tribunal might do in a Part 4 case. This is because: (a) where a term is introduced into a renewed agreement under Part 5, one would expect it to be considered to be consistent with the Code, and (b) under Part 4 a tribunal is likely to consider itself to have a freer rein to include the terms that it thinks appropriate, given the lack of an existing agreement to which it must have regard.

Particular terms in renewal cases

Sharing and upgrading

11.192 As indicated above in respect of Part 4 cases, the tribunal will frequently consider upgrading rights and new equipment rights at the same time.

11.193 As the tribunal said in *Green*[112] (the Dale Park case) at [32]: 'unless the parties are to indulge in a pointless dispute about what is an upgrade and what is an extra piece of kit, there is little point in having any limitation on the right to upgrade if there is no limitation on the right to add or change the equipment, and vice versa'.

11.194 In *Stephenson*,[113] no reference was made to the para 34(12) duty to have regard to the terms of the existing Code agreement, which applies where the tribunal is determining terms under para 34(10). Orders made under para 34(10) include those made in order to determine the terms of the new agreement that results from an Order under para 34(6). Para 34(6) is the provision that allows the tribunal to make an Order for terminating a Code agreement and requiring the parties to enter into a new agreement. It was not made clear in *Stephenson* under which sub-para of para 34 the tribunal was making its Order.

11.195 Reference was made to the tribunal being required by para 34(11) to determine the terms of the new lease in accordance with provisions including para 23 and para 24. However, para 34(11) merely applies various provisions of the Code to different types of para 34 determinations. It was said in *Stephenson* that the parties agreed that having served the necessary notices, the operator was 'entitled to seek renewal of the lease under paragraph 33 of the Code'. Following a successful application under para 33, a para 34 Order will result. Given that there was a reference to a 'renewal' in

---

112 *On Tower UK Ltd v JH and FW Green Ltd* [2021] EWCA Civ 1858.

113 [2022] UKUT 180 (LC). This was the final hearing relating to terms, rather than the preliminary issue hearing which was the subject of a separate decision.

Stephenson, it would appear that the tribunal was proceeding on the basis that the pre-existing agreement would be terminated, and a new agreement ordered. That would mean proceeding under para 34(6), and the determination of terms would then be subject to para 34(12).

11.196 In the preliminary issue hearing in *Stephenson*,[114] the President of the Upper Tribunal (Lands Chamber) had previously stated that:

> 'Whether an order under para 34(6) is the appropriate order to make will be the subject of a trial in due course, when the Tribunal will consider the reasons why the Claimants seek a new agreement and APW's case that extension or modification of the existing agreement under para 34(2) or (3) is more appropriate. At the same trial, the Tribunal will specify the terms of any new agreement, if an order is to be made under para 34(6).'

11.197 Accordingly, it is clear that the operator had been seeking a para 34(6) Order, and that the respondent was suggesting a different type of Order under para 34. When the matter did come before the Deputy President for the final hearing to determine terms, it appears that the parties were agreed on a 'renewal'. One would imagine that that means a para 34(6) Order.

11.198 It is true that, as per *Green*, the terms of the existing agreement are not set in stone and are not subject to quite the same near-presumption against change as exists under *O'May* in the 1954 Act context. Nonetheless, it was said by the Court of Appeal in *Green*[115] that para 34(12) of the Code specifically directs the court to have regard to the terms of the existing agreement, and that there will be an onus on the party contending for a change to justify it. It is not clear from the final decision in *Stephenson* what the existing agreement had to say about sharing and upgrading, and thus it does not appear that this was taken into account or the relevant onus imposed on whichever party was seeking to depart from it. The only paragraph of the Code referred to that governs the determination of terms (other than consideration and compensation) was para 23 (referred to in the decision at [6]).

11.199 In *Audley House*, the tribunal expressed the view that sharing and upgrading rights that are wider than those in para 17, or even unlimited, 'should not be regarded as unusual'. The tribunal granted rights that were not limited by para 17. The operator was a wholesale infrastructure provider, and the tribunal clearly gave great weight to the fact that its 'need for unlimited sharing and upgrading rights is obvious and integral to its business'.[116] The site provider's concerns were not regarded as realistic. Further, the operator's right to share was not restricted to sharing with Code operators. The tribunal considered that the operator's obligation to give vacant possession adequately protected the site provider in relation to the possibility of sub-tenants not vacating. It did not consider that the operator's ability to charge non-Code rents from non-operator sharers was any concern of the site provider's, and in any event, it is something which the statutory scheme does not prevent.[117]

---

114 [2021] UKUT 167 (LC) at [71].
115 *On Tower UK Ltd v JH and FW Green Ltd* [2021] EWCA Civ 1858 at [48].
116 [2022] UKUT 152 (LC) at [128].
117 This is because 'land' under para 108 of the Code does not include ECA. See *Audley House* at [133].

11.200 Finally, the tribunal allowed sharing rights to apply not merely to ECA (as per para 17 of the Code) but to land itself. The site provider's concern that a sharer might acquire Code rights as against it was rejected as incorrect in law by the tribunal. As the site provider's interest is not derived from the operator's, para 10 of the Code will not operate so as to render the site provider bound by any Code rights created by the operator.

Exclusion of LPA 1925, s 62

11.201 In *Audley House*,[118] the tribunal agreed to exclude section 62 of the Law of Property Act 1925, summarising that that statutory provision 'relates to the implication of easements on the grant of a new lease as a result of the parties' practice before the grant of the lease'. It was considered reasonable to protect the site provider and the superior landlord from unforeseen rights arising in the future. There was no reason why the operator should be entitled to rights that are not expressed in the terms of the lease when they had been 'negotiated and litigated in such exhaustive detail'.

Right to lay conduits on superior landlord's land

11.202 In *Audley House*[119], the existing agreement allowed the operator to lay conduits on the superior landlord's land, subject to prior approval, not to be unreasonably withheld. The intermediate lease gave the site provider a similar right. The parties agreed that the operator's right to install conduits should continue to be subject to a qualified consent requirement. The tribunal held that the right to re-route and upgrade such conduits should also be subject to a qualified consent requirement.

11.203 However, the involvement of the site provider and superior landlord in the maintenance of conduits was considered unnecessary and hence no requirement for consent would apply to those operations.

Notification of planning applications

11.204 In *Audley House*,[120] the site provider sought to introduce into the new agreement a requirement that the operator notify the site provider if it makes a planning application in respect of the relevant sites. The site provider had an obligation to its superior landlord not to make a planning application without consent, which obligation included a duty not to 'agree or suffer' that an application would be made by consent.

11.205 The tribunal rejected the proposed term, as planning applications are publicly available, and local planning authorities will publicise planning applications where they are required to do so. It further considered that the site provider would not be in breach of its obligation to its landlord merely by virtue of the operator making a planning application without the site provider's knowledge.

118 [2022] UKUT 152 (LC) at [148] and [149].
119 [2022] UKUT 152 (LC) at [167]–[170].
120 [2022] UKUT 152 (LC) at [167] to [170].

Objections to planning applications

11.206 In *Ewefields Farm*,[121] the FTT refused to include a term preventing the operator from objecting to planning applications. It held that such a term was insufficiently related to the exercise of Code rights.

Right of landlord to enter and carry out repairs

11.207 This type of clause is typically referred to as a *Jervis v Harris*[122] clause. In the *New Zealand Farm* case,[123] such a provision was described as 'giving the landlord the right to serve notice on the tenant requiring repairs to be carried out which, if not complied with, would entitle the landlord to go on to the site and undertake the works itself, recouping the cost from the tenant'. The county court refused to impose such a clause on a 1954 Act lease renewal, considering it pointless in light of the fact that the site provider had no adjacent land. The FTT followed this decision in *Ewefields Farm*[124] for the same reason.

Non-interference by operator

11.208 In *Ewefields Farm*[125] the FTT declined to include a term that would have required the operator to switch off ECA where the site provider considered that interference was being caused to other equipment. It was held that interference was a rare occurrence that is managed by MNOs[126] themselves, and more widely by OFCOM, to whose supervision non-MNOs are also subject.

Payment of compensation as a contractual debt

11.209 Leases very frequently contain provisions requiring a tenant to make particular payments to landlords as a reimbursement for costs incurred by landlords. For example, the costs of producing and serving a section 146 notice (under section 146 Law of Property Act 1925).

11.210 Under the Code, the tribunal (in *UAL*) has concluded that the imposition of a term requiring the payment of compensation by an operator as a contractual debt upon written demand would be contrary to para 86.

11.211 Paragraph 86 provides that:

> 'Except as provided by any provision of Parts 2 to 13 of this code or this Part, an operator is not liable to compensate any person for, and is not subject to any other liability in respect of, any loss or damage caused by the lawful exercise of any right conferred by or in accordance with any provision of those Parts.'

121 *On Tower UK Limited v AP Wireless II (UK) Limited and others* LC – 2023 – 000321 and 13 others (*Ewefields Farm*) at [69].

122 [1996] Ch 195.

123 *On Tower Ltd v AP Wireless (II) (New Zealand Farm)* [2022] EW Misc 6 (CC) at [44].

124 *On Tower UK Limited v AP Wireless II (UK) Limited and others* LC – 2023 – 000321 and 13 others (*Ewefields Farm*) at [72].

125 *On Tower UK Limited v AP Wireless II (UK) Limited and others* LC – 2023 – 000321 and 13 others (*Ewefields Farm*) at [72].

126 Mobile network operators.

11.212 The tribunal described the respondent as 'not content to rely upon the claimant's obligations under paragraph 25'.

11.213 It might not be immediately apparent why a term imposed by the tribunal, requiring costs to be repaid as a contractual debt upon certain events occurring, would be contrary to para 86. The requirement to pay sums under such a clause might be thought to be one of the operator's 'obligations under paragraph 25'.

11.214 After all, in *UAL*, the tribunal thought it appropriate to provide for compensation (under para 25) to be paid up front through contractual provisions requiring the payment of such sums. Hence, there would appear to be no necessary dichotomy between a contractual obligation to make a payment and an obligation under para 25. It is certainly true that the language of para 25(1) allows the tribunal to make an Order for compensation that is wholly separate from the Code agreement and which orders payment of compensation, but that is not how it would have been done in *UAL*.[127]

11.215 If the tribunal's underlying logic in *UAL* was that payment within 14 days of a written demand meant that there was a contractual requirement to make a payment of a sum which had not yet been assessed under para 25 as reasonable or properly incurred, then one can certainly see the objection.

Conduct in negotiating terms

11.216 There have been numerous warnings and criticisms by the tribunals in respect of the conduct of parties, and such statements have by no means been limited to disputes relating to the terms of Code agreements. However, as there are so many different potential terms in Code agreements, the non-financial terms have the capacity to generate wide-ranging disputes that then cause parties to become entrenched in their disagreements and not feel able to settle References. Accordingly, at least in the first few years of the Code, the thorny issues raised by terms have been amongst those in respect of which the tribunal has felt most need to speak out about conduct and to encourage conciliatory behaviour.

11.217 In *UAL*, the tribunal made comment as to the conduct of the parties in negotiating terms. The following was in the context of a discussion on the use of a Set Down Area, but was clearly intended as an observation of much more general application:

> '101. This issue illustrates the gulf that exists in this case (and many others) between those drafting the Code agreement and those who will be called upon to implement it. The former are the lawyers who are concerned with what *could* happen under the terms of the agreement while the latter (engineers, access managers, estate managers and the like) are more concerned with what *should* happen and in so doing are generally desirous of working pragmatically and sensibly towards finding a solution that will work without adversely affecting either party's reasonable requirements.'[128]

127 It is to be noted that there never was a Code agreement in *UAL* because the respondent succeeded on the para 21(2) and (3) tests.

128 [2020] UKUT 248 (LC) at [101].

11.218 The tribunal clearly considers that the parties should be less mistrustful of each other. It may also be inferred from the above that there should be involvement in the negotiation of terms from those professionals whose involvement is more practical rather than theoretical. This might be seen to encourage more involvement from agents/surveyors at the negotiation stage.

11.219 One potential difficulty for site providers is that if they wish to recover the costs of their instructed professionals' time in negotiating the agreement, the involvement of two sets of professionals is unlikely to be conducive. It is unlikely that many site providers will wish to remove lawyers from this process, especially where operators are involving lawyers who are referring to case law to support their position and especially where litigation appears likely or has already commenced.

11.220 It may be that the most potent imperative for a site provider to give ground in respect of terms is a potential adverse decision of the tribunal, with the cost consequences that are likely to follow. Previous conclusions of the tribunals, such as those set out in this chapter, are likely to be considered instructive in this respect.

Evidence relating to the terms of an agreement

11.221 In *UAL* (at [72]), the tribunal gave useful guidance as to how evidence should be assembled and adduced in cases relating to terms. The following points emerge:

(i) Where possible the parties should seek to limit themselves to one witness of fact each in respect of issues relating to terms;

(ii) That witness should be familiar with the requirements and concerns of their organisation;

(iii) The tribunal is likely to be pragmatic when it comes to considering evidence of fact from professional people. It will not be particularly receptive to arguments that evidence constitutes hearsay, given that witnesses will to some extent depend on information provided by colleagues;

(iv) Factual knowledge of professional persons may come from the fact that they have expertise. The tribunal is likely to be pragmatic in accepting such evidence rather than unduly technical in excluding it as expert opinion;

(v) Where there is real dispute about technical matters, a party must seek permission to adduce any expert evidence. The strong indication given is that such cases are expected to be rare;

(vi) Operational issues should be straightforward matters of fact. Examples given of such issues are 'access, electricity supplies, and health and safety'.

11.222 Although most terms can be determined by the tribunal on the basis of straightforward evidence, it is worth bearing in mind that any argument that relies on facts that are not obvious will need to be properly evidenced. In negotiations, the parties will sometimes be arguing on the basis of facts that might be known or assumed as between the parties. However, if negotiations do not conclude in agreement on a particular term, the parties will need to ensure not to overlook the need for evidence regarding such facts.

11.223 In *UAL*[129] the tribunal had to consider an argument by the Respondent that the Claimant should be responsible for acquiring third party consents in respect of access over third party land. However, there was no evidence at the hearing that part of the access route was over third party land, and thus, as the Respondent's concern rested on asserted facts that were unproven, the requested term was not included.

Duplication

11.224 One of the risks in a respondent seeking to amend the proposed agreement of an operator is that they may create duplicative or even contradictory requirements in seeking a specific requirement in one part of an agreement when there is already a generalised requirement in another.

11.225 In *UAL*,[130] a proposed amendment requiring notice to be given in advance of crane access was rejected on the basis that there was already a general notification provision for access. In the same case, the general point was made that 'We deprecate the use of duplicated terms in an agreement 'for the avoidance of doubt' or otherwise.'[131]

Imposed terms in 1954 Act cases

11.226 As this book is a specialist work relating to telecoms interests, the general position under the 1954 Act will be dealt with as a very brief overview.

Property comprised in the tenancy

11.227 The property comprised in the new tenancy is usually 'the holding'.[132] That term means the property comprised in the current tenancy, less any area which is not being occupied by the tenant for the purposes of its business.[133]

Duration of the tenancy

11.228 The court has discretion as to the length of the new tenancy. It may be a periodic tenancy or a fixed term tenancy of not more than 15 years, but in any event it starts from the coming to an end of the current tenancy.[134] The court's task is to determine what length of termis 'reasonable in all the circumstances'.[135]

11.229 In exercising its discretion, the court is not expressly mandated by section 33 to take into account the duration of the current tenancy, as it is in respect of other terms by section 35, though this is not an irrelevant consideration.

129 [2020] UKUT 248 (LC) at [131]–[134].
130 See [93] of the judgment.
131 See [166] of the judgment.
132 Section 32 of the 1954 Act.
133 Section 23(3) of the 1954 Act.
134 Section 33 of the 1954 Act. The Court does have power to order a longer term but only by the consent of the parties: *Janes (Gowns) Ltd v Harlow Development Corporation* [1980] 1 EGLR 52.
135 Section 33 of the 1954 Act.

11.230 As the Deputy President of the Upper Tribunal (Lands Chamber) (sitting as a county court judge) said in the telecoms context in *Vodafone v Hanover Capital Ltd*:[136]

> '…although the duration of the current tenancy may be a relevant consideration, there is no presumption in favour of repeating it, nor any onus of justification on a party seeking a longer or shorter term'.

11.231 The Deputy President went on to cite commentary on the law in this area, concluding that 'each case depends on its own facts'. He then set out some factors that would be relevant, and how the court should approach its task:

> 'The length of the current tenancy, and the length of its continuation by the 1954 Act are relevant considerations, as is the nature of the tenant's business. The primary purpose of the legislation is to protect the tenant so the Court will seek to confer on the tenant a term sufficient to protect it in carrying on its business. The length of term likely to be granted in the open market is of only limited assistance in determining what is reasonable. The Court will seek to balance the degree of protection to which the tenant is entitled in the interests of its business and the need to ensure that the decision is neither unfair on nor oppressive to the landlord.'[137]

11.232 The content of any break clause to be included in the new tenancy is to be determined under section 35 of the 1954 Act, which requires the court to have regard to the terms of the current tenancy and to all relevant circumstances.[138] Its determination is not strictly therefore part of the exercise of ascertaining the reasonable duration of the tenancy under section 33. However, in reality, a court may well have regard to the duration of tenancy in deciding the need for, or form of, any break clause. Similarly, a court may be more relaxed about granting a longer term against one party's case if that party is to benefit from a favourable break clause.

11.233 In *Hanover*,[139] the landlord had wanted a ten-year team, but the operator tenant wanted a three-year term to give it flexibility and sought a rolling break clause for the same reason. Given that the same argument underpinned the operator's argument for a short-term and/or a rolling break, the Deputy President said that 'it is convenient to consider both the duration of the term and the form of break clause together'.[140] He then went on to set out the factors considered and his reasoning for coming to the conclusion that he had reached:

> '39. The conclusion I have reached is that the term of the new tenancy should be one of ten years, with a break clause exercisable on 6 months' notice expiring on the fifth or subsequent anniversary of the term…
>
> 40. …In the circumstances of this case I consider that the operator's wish for flexibility must be balanced against the landlord's understandable desire for a respite from uncertainty and expense. That balance is satisfied by a minimum commitment of 5 years, with the operator being entitled to greater flexibility at fixed intervals after that period has expired…

136 [2020] EW Misc 18 (CC) at [29].
137 [2020] EW Misc 18 (CC) at [30]
138 *O'May v City of London Real Property Co. Ltd.* [1983] 2 AC 726. See p 747, per Lord Wilberforce.
139 [2020] EW Misc 18 (CC).
140 [2020] EW Misc 18 (CC) at [28].

45. I have preferred ten years with breaks exercisable fairly freely after 5 years, rather than a simple 5 year term…'[141]

All other terms

11.234 Thus far,[142] lease renewals in respect of subsisting agreements that grant Code rights have been carried out in the county court. Perhaps for this reason, there are not a great number of reported cases in which terms have been decided upon in the county court context.

11.235 *EE v Morriss*[143] was a case in which an agreement that granted Code rights was agreed to be a lease, and its renewal took place under the 1954 Act. As it was an early example of such a case, the matter came before the Deputy President of the Lands Chamber, sitting as a judge of the county court. He said as follows at [18]:

> 'The dispute over the terms of the new tenancy falls within section 35 of the 1954 Act. In determining those terms, the Court is required to have regard to the terms of the current tenancy and to all relevant circumstances. The burden of persuading the Court to depart from the terms originally agreed falls on the party proposing the change (*O'May v City of London Real Property Company Ltd* [1983] AC 726).'

11.236 The House of Lords decision in *O'May*, referred to in the above passage, is well-known as the leading case regarding the ascertainment of the 'other' terms of a tenancy upon a 1954 Act lease renewal. In addition to the point made above as to burden,[144] it was emphasised in *O'May* that any proposed change must be fair and reasonable and should take into account, amongst other things, the comparatively weak negotiating position of a sitting tenant requiring renewal and the general purpose of the 1954 Act, which is to protect the business interests of the tenant so far as they are affected by the approaching termination of the current lease.

11.237 It is to be remembered that by section 43(4) of the 1954 Act, Part II of the 1954 Act does not apply to any tenancy granted after the coming into force of the Code, where the primary purpose of that tenancy is to grant Code rights. One consequence of the statutory scheme, including this provision, is that a renewal tenancy that is ordered by a court pursuant to the 1954 Act lease renewal process will not itself be subject to any renewal rights under the 1954 Act. Rather, it will immediately be a 'Code agreement' in the full technical sense defined by para 29(5) of the Code, in that Part 5 of the Code will apply in respect of the termination, modification, or renewal of such a tenancy.

141 [2020] EW Misc 18 (CC) at [39], [40] and [45].

142 This is expected to change once the relevant provisions of the PSTIA 2022 come into force and such lease renewals are able to take place within the Tribunal system.

143 [2022] EW Misc 1 (CC). The name of the Respondent in this case is sometimes rendered as 'Morrisss' (sic) in reports. The correct name is 'Morriss', but it may be found with a variety of spellings, which knowledge might prove useful for finding copies of the judgment in that case, which can be found online. At time of writing, the BAILII URL for the judgment is as follows: https://www.bailii.org/ew/cases/Misc/2022/1.html.

144 Which derives from Lord Hailsham's conclusions in *O'May v City of London Real Property Company Ltd* [1983] AC 726 at p 740.

11.238 This was explained in the Court of Appeal judgment in *Ashloch*,[145] and despite the discussion in the Supreme Court judgment[146] at [157], was surely confirmed at [168] of the Supreme Court's judgment, where it is said:

> 'Cornerstone must therefore use its rights under Part 2 of the 1954 Act to renew its lease; that lease will then be caught by section 43(4) of the 1954 Act so that when that lease expires, Part 5 will be available.'

11.239 If Part 5 'will be available', that means that Part 5 'applies' to the renewed tenancy for the purposes of para 29(5) during its term, which in turn means that it is proper to refer to that renewed agreement as a 'Code agreement'.

11.240 What consequences might this status cause for the terms of such a new Code agreement that is imposed pursuant to the 1954 Act?

11.241 There is a potential tension here. On the one hand, the tribunal held in *EE v Stephenson* (see above) that the policy of the 1954 Act and that of the Code are quite different. The Court of Appeal in *Green* (the Dale Park case) agreed (again see above). It is clear that in enacting the Transitional Provisions in their original form, Parliament intended a renewal under the 1954 Act to be just that. An operator would not gain the benefits of the different tests under the Code. No retrospectivity was intended as regards telecoms leases, which parties had already entered into on the basis that any renewal rights were to be those under the 1954 Act. This was as recommended by the Law Commission and as referred to by the Supreme Court in *CTIL v Compton Beauchamp*,[147] where it was said that:

> 'The intention of the Government, following the recommendation of the Law Commission, was that such an operator should not get the retrospective benefit of the new Code, in particular the substantial benefit of the no-scheme valuation of the rights.'[148]

11.242 The Supreme Court in that case had found the Court of Appeal's reasoning to be persuasive. In the Court of Appeal Davis LJ had said of the Transitional Provisions that:

> 'As I read them, they give a degree of primacy, as it were, to subsisting rights. There was a clear concern about retrospective effect. That has an obvious policy purpose.'

11.243 One obvious example of the lack of retrospective effect of the Code on the renewal of a 1954 Act lease, which is a subsisting agreement, is that rent is to be valued[149] in accordance with the 1954 Act methodology, which contains no 'no-network assumption', in clear contrast to the methodology for valuing consideration under para 24 of the Code.

---

145 *Cornerstone Telecommunications Infrastructure v Ashloch Ltd & Anor* [2021] EWCA Civ 90. See the judgment of Lewison LJ at [98], with whom the remainder of the Court agreed.

146 [2022] UKSC 18.

147 [2022] UKSC 18 at [166] and [167] of the judgment.

148 [2022] UKSC 18 at [167] of the judgment.

149 Until the relevant provisions of the PSTIA 2022 are brought into force and amend the valuation basis to include the 'no-network' assumption.

11.244 However, on the other hand, as the Code agreement that results from the 1954 Act lease renewal process will be a Code agreement, it will not be governed by the 1954 Act at all. That fact, coupled with the policy imperative behind the Code is not something that a court can ignore.

11.245 The test that will be applied is that elucidated in *O'May*, and not the provisions of paras 23(2) to (8) of the Code.[150] But this does not mean that in the application of the guidance in *O'May*, the court should totally ignore the position in the real world, including: (i) the existence of other legislation, (ii) the sorts of terms that are being agreed or imposed in the marketplace in Code agreements, and (iii) the needs and expectations of operators providing a service in the modern economy and in the public interest. These latter points very much come across in the small number of cases that have thus far been decided under the 1954 Act in respect of operators' telecoms leases. For example, in deciding on a break clause in *Hanover*,[151] the court said that it had given weight to 'the needs of Vodafone's business, and to the rights which Parliament intended operators to enjoy under the Code'.

The various terms determined by the county court

11.246 There follows a discussion of some of the decisions of the county court in respect of the determination of the terms of a new tenancy which would come into effect as a Code agreement, under various headings pertaining to the various categories of terms discussed.

Equipment rights (including upgrading)

11.247 This right relates to: (i) upgrading ECA, but also (ii) installing new and/or additional ECA. As observed above in respect of renewal agreements, these two types of rights go hand in hand and are often considered together.[152]

11.248 In *EE v Morriss*,[153] the rights under the existing tenancy were unclear. As a result, 'the statutory direction to have regard to the terms of the current tenancy does not provide much assistance'. In this context, the court held that the new tenancy should include unrestricted equipment rights, subject only to the qualified restriction on increasing the height of the mast, which was argued to be necessary due to the particular military training use to which the site provider's neighbouring land was put, including the use of helicopters. This conclusion was consonant with decisions under the Code that have been increasingly relaxed about granting upgrading rights that go beyond those granted by para 17 of the Code.

11.249 The judge held that:

> '...the claimants' need periodically to upgrade its (and any sharers') apparatus should not be allowed to create opportunities for dispute or ransom'.[154]

150 These are applied to Part 5 Code renewals by para 34(11) of the Code.
151 [2020] EW Misc 18 (CC) at [40].
152 See *On Tower UK Ltd v JH and FW Green Ltd* [2021] EWCA Civ 1858 (the Dale Park case) at [32].
153 See [25]–[28] of the judgment.
154 [2022] EW Misc 1 (CC) at [28].

11.250 It may be that a more clearly restrictive existing lease might cause a court to restrict upgrading and new equipment rights to a greater extent. However, the reasoning in the judgment does not appear to be site-specific, and so in the absence of a clear restriction, one might expect the court to have sympathy for an argument along similar lines.

Contractual compensation provisions

11.251 Where it applies, para 25 of the Code gives the tribunal wide powers to order the payment of compensation for loss or damage sustained as a result of the exercise of Code rights. However, para 25 only applies 'If the court makes an order under paragraph 20'[155] for the imposition of a Code agreement, or if it makes an Order resulting in an agreement granting Code rights under certain other provisions of the Code.[156] In a case where para 25 so applies, an Order for compensation can be made when the relevant agreement is imposed or ordered, or at any time afterwards,[157] upon an application being made.

11.252 Where a 1954 Act lease renewal process results in the court making an Order for a new tenancy, even though that new tenancy will be a Code agreement to which Part 5 of the Code applies, there will not have been any Order under para 20 of the Code, nor under any of the other provisions of the Code that apply para 25. Thus, the orthodox assumption[158] thus far has been that in such a case, no application can be made under para 25 by a person bound by a Code right.

11.253 As is mentioned elsewhere in this book, it is open to the parties to a consensual Code agreement to agree a contractual compensation provision. Such a provision might mirror the wording of para 25 (and para 84, which makes further provision as to compensation, and to which para 25(6) refers).

11.254 In *Morriss,*[159] the landowner asked the court to impose a term that allowed for a later compensation claim in a similar manner to para 25 of the Code. As the resulting tenancy was to be a Code agreement, it was argued that it would be fair and in accordance with public policy for such a compensation provision to be imposed.

11.255 The court did not agree to impose such a provision. It observed that:

- Parliament has not seen fit to provide a right to compensation for site providers who voluntarily enter into new Code agreements;
- there was no evidence before the court that consensual Code agreements negotiated in the market include contractual compensation provisions;
- as 'almost all' new Code agreements are consensual, 'site providers entitled to statutory compensation are a tiny minority';[160]

155 See para 25(1).

156 For example, orders for interim Code rights under para 26 by virtue of para 26(4)(e), orders for temporary Code rights under para 27 by virtue of para 27(4)(e), and certain renewals or modifications of Code agreements under para 34 by virtue of para 34(11).

157 See para 25(2)(b).

158 This assumption was confirmed in *EE v Morriss* at [30]–[32], although it was a proposition of law that was not in dispute.

159 See [29]–[34] of the judgment.

160 *Morriss* at [30].

- there was nothing in the current tenancy which would entitle the landlord to claim compensation during the term for loss attributable to the exercise of the rights conferred; and
- at least in theory the consideration agreed in the market for consensual Code agreements will include the monetary value of the risks associated with the grant of the rights.

11.256 The judge said that he could see no unfairness in this conclusion and that any suggested unfairness is the consequence of decisions made by Parliament when it enacted the Code. However, it was said that if in the future there is evidence that contractual compensation provisions are being included in the market, it may be necessary to revisit the issue.

11.257 It is certainly the case that far more landowners, certainly those that are well-advised, now seek to achieve a contractual compensation provision in a consensual Code agreement. It was surely not obvious in the early days of the new Code that a para 25 compensation application would not be available to those site providers who had agreed the consensual imposition of Code rights, and indeed in *Hanover Capital*[161] the court itself had assumed to the contrary. If the evidence exists in a later case that recent consensual agreements are including compensation provisions on a more regular basis, doubtless this will be at least relevant evidence for any court considering whether to impose such a term on a 1954 Act lease renewal of a telecoms lease.

Access

11.258 *Morriss* was an unusual case as regards access,[162] because of the military training use of the land, which sometimes involved explosives, and immersive training scenarios such as mock hijackings. Furthermore, the Judge accepted evidence that there had been problems with contractors arriving without having given notice as required. The parties had agreed that the operator's rights of access should be subject to a formalised access policy. The terms imposed by the court included requiring five days' notice of a request for access (rather than the seven sought by the landlord), and a requirement that the landlord give an alternative date within seven days allowing access where the initial date had been refused for reasons specified in the policy. The landlord was not required to deal with access requests made by third parties like contractors, as opposed to the tenant itself. Details of the company requiring access were required to be given, as was a named contact person, but there was no requirement to give the name of each individual who would be attending. No payment was required in respect of the making of the request.

Indemnity

11.259 In *Morriss*,[163] the uncapped indemnity provision included in the existing tenancy was retained in the new tenancy. The operator had sought a clause based on the indemnity provision imposed in the *UAL* case under the Code, with a cap of £10

161 *Vodafone Limited v Hanover Capital Limited* [2020] EW Misc 18 (CC).
162 See [35] to [38] of the judgment.
163 At [39] and [40].

million. The court held that the level of the landowner's current business insurance was not relevant and that the *UAL* clause carried with it statutory rights to compensation, which would not exist in the case before him. No sufficient justification had been shown for departing from the lease as previously drafted.

Non-interference by landlord

11.260 Another term that was retained from the existing tenancy was a covenant by the landlord that it will not knowingly interfere with the tenant's telecommunications equipment or knowingly allow any other person to interfere or tamper with it.

11.261 The landowner attempted to remove the provision, and the operator sought to augment it with a prohibition on obstructing the site or doing anything that may cause interference with the operation of the equipment.

11.262 The court noted the distinction between interfering with the equipment itself and interfering with the operation of the equipment, which transmitted signals over a large area of retained land. The court was content to rely on the obligation implied by the general law on a landlord not to use its retained land in a way that makes demised premises materially less fit for the purpose for which they were demised. The operator's clause would have prohibited any use of the retained land that interfered with the equipment's operation to any extent. Given the variety of uses of the retained land, this was considered 'an inappropriate extension of the terms originally agreed'.[164]

Break clause

11.263 In *Hanover*[165] the court decided upon a term of ten years, with a break clause exercisable on 6 months' notice expiring on the fifth or subsequent anniversary of the term. The break clause would not be conditional on the tenant giving vacant possession.

11.264 The landlord had proposed a tenant's right to break on 12 months' notice, exercisable on the 5th anniversary of the term, assuming a ten-year term, subject to compliance with covenants, and giving vacant possession at the expiry of the break notice.

11.265 The operator wanted a rolling break clause exercisable on six months' notice in order to allow it flexibility in the future. It also cited the then ongoing appeals in the *Compton Beauchamp* and *Ashloch* cases and the uncertainty created by those. Most importantly, if the operators' view of the law prevailed[166] in those appeals, and an operator in situ is not barred from seeking Code rights, it would wish to be able to

164 *EE v Morriss* at [42].

165 *Vodafone Limited v Hanover Capital Limited* [2020] EW Misc 18 (CC) at [26]–[46].

166 The main issue in those appeals was indeed ultimately determined in the operators' favour, namely that an operator in situ is not barred by the fact of its occupation from seeking Code rights under Part 4 of the Code which it does not currently enjoy. However, the specific question whether an operator can intentionally terminate a Code agreement which has been imposed under the 1954 Act machinery in order then to seek an agreement under Part 4 of the Code on more favourable financial terms, is not a question which has yet directly arisen.

terminate its tenancy early and seek new Code rights under a Code agreement whose terms were to be determined under the Code, it would achieve a lower consideration payment than the rent likely to be payable under the tenancy arising from the present proceedings.

11.266 The judge gave weight to the needs of the operator's business, 'and to the rights which Parliament intended operators to enjoy under the Code'.[167] He also highlighted the costs of the litigation (the operator's had exceeded £300,000 plus VAT), noting that for a landowner who did not have the numerous telecoms sites that the operator does, the proceedings 'represent an expensive and unwanted distraction, hugely disproportionate to the very modest income it will receive whatever view I take of the valuation issues'.[168]

11.267 A balance between the operator's wish for flexibility against the landlord's desire to avoid uncertainty and expense was satisfied by a minimum commitment of five years, with the operator entitled to greater flexibility at fixed intervals (rather than on a rolling basis) after that period has expired.

11.268 The judge did not give much weight to the prospect that appeal decisions may bring a change in understanding of how the Code is intended to work. The proposed break clause would not in any event be contingent on any appeal succeeding. It would not be fair to impose on the landowner the prospect of the operator being able to terminate the new tenancy immediately, on six months' notice, if it was dissatisfied by the rent imposed under it.[169]

11.269 As to the operator's argument for flexibility, the judge noted that para 17 of the Code would already guarantee the right to upgrade, albeit limited by the restrictions in paras 17(2) and (3). The operator's 'desire to avoid the limitations which Parliament has thought it appropriate to impose by giving it the flexibility to seek an entirely new agreement covering additional apparatus at relatively short notice is not a particularly weighty consideration'.[170]

11.270 The judge went on to note that the evidence indicated that operators, including those in the present case, had regularly entered into new Code agreements with break clauses exercisable only after five years. The operators were therefore held not to need the short term or rolling break right sought for operational reasons.

11.271 As to the conditions required to be satisfied in order to exercise a break right, the judge accepted that a condition requiring compliance with covenants, including as to the payment of rent, was 'standard and reasonable'.

11.272 However, he rejected the suggestion of a requirement that vacant possession should be given in order to exercise the break right. It was held that to include such a provision would:

167 [2020] EW Misc 18 (CC) at [40].
168 [2020] EW Misc 18 (CC) at [40].
169 [2020] EW Misc 18 (CC) at [42].
170 [2020] EW Misc 18 (CC) at [43]. Although it is fair to remember that this was a decision under the 1954 Act, the tone of this analysis appears to be less operator-friendly than some of the more recent decisions on upgrading rights which have been content to allow operators greater upgrading rights than para 17 automatically allows.

'...make a break clause much less useful to Vodafone and I do not think it is reasonable to introduce it. It is likely that the introduction of 5G technology will require significant upgrading which may not be possible under the constraints of paragraph 17 of the Code, and an opportunity for renegotiation at annual intervals after 5 years will allow Vodafone to modernise both the agreement and its apparatus.'

11.273 One can see why a landlord would wish to include such a clause in a typical case. Giving vacant possession when an operator wished to remain on the site in the longer term would cause expense to the operator (often out of proportion to the rent payable) and would create a material and uncertain gap in its service to customers. The landlord, knowing this, would be in a much better position when it came to negotiating any changes to the agreement. If the operator is anxious to upgrade in a manner that exceeds the standard para 17 upgrading rights but cannot because it is realistically unable to break its lease, the landlord enjoys something approaching a ransom situation. It is a relatively common theme in decisions relating to Code rights that a ransom situation is undesirable and not in accordance with public policy or the legislative purpose of the Code.

11.274 Finally, the judge said that he granted a ten-year term with breaks rather than a mere five-year term because of the valuation evidence before him in respect of the effect on rent of a ten-year term with no rent review clause, and commented that doing so would provide a possibility that further recourse to lawyers would not be necessary if the operator found the new lease continued to meet its needs beyond the five-year point. The theme of avoiding unnecessary costs and disputes in the middle of a term is one that crops up in the telecoms context both under the 1954 Act and under the Code. Given the relatively low rents payable under a single agreement, one can understand the desire to avoid costs that would be disproportionate.

11.275 In *Morriss*,[171] it was agreed that the new tenancy should have a term of 10 years, with a break clause allowing the tenant to break the lease after five years. In addition, the tenant wanted to have the right to break the term at any time after the 5th anniversary, on giving three months' notice, without having to give vacant possession. Much like in *Hanover* (see above) the landlord objected to such a 'rolling break', and also wished for any tenant's break right to be conditional on giving vacant possession at the expiry of the notice period.

11.276 Again, the operator wished to have flexibility as to its future operational needs as technology changes. In particular, the introduction of 5G might require the installation of stronger or taller masts, which may not be possible in the instant location, which has certain restrictions in planning terms. As to vacant possession, the operator's principal objection was that it would in practice prevent it from remaining on the site having terminated the new tenancy, in order to claim a new Code agreement with more favourable terms, including a lower consideration (rent), and potentially more extensive upgrading rights.

11.277 The landlord submitted that it would not be fair or reasonable to allow the tenant to break the agreement which it had sought under the 1954 Act regime purely in order to avoid the consequences of claiming such a tenancy and instead seek a more

171 *EE v Morriss* at [44]–[52].

favourable package of rights under different legislation. No such provision existed in the existing lease, and the landlord would be left with uncertainty as to its future income prospects.

11.278 The judge noted the similarities with the *Hanover* case, and despite evidence of recent transactions in the market in which unconditional rolling breaks had been agreed, decided upon a similar break right. That is, a break right exercisable after five years and on each subsequent anniversary of the term.

11.279 The judge gave weight to the operator's desire for operational flexibility and to the landlord's interest in certainty and the avoidance of disproportionate expense in legal proceedings. He gave little weight to the notion that the operator would terminate the new tenancy in order to achieve a lower rent under the Code, as he considered that the administrative inconvenience and costs of doing so would likely outweigh any such advantage. The requirement for vacant possession as a pre-condition of the break was rejected, as in *Hanover*. Part of the reason for this was that the landlord's desire to discourage the operator from using the break right to achieve a lower consideration under the Code was misplaced, given the lack of likelihood that the operator would try to do so.

11.280 He was keen to avoid a ransom situation, as in *Hanover*, and expressly used that word in concluding:

> 'I am more influenced by the possibility that technological changes may render the site unsuitable or that upgrades may not be capable of being accommodated within the terms of the new lease without giving rise to a significant dispute or a ransom situation.'[172]

Rent review

11.281 In *Morriss*,[173] it was common ground that section 35(1) of the 1954 Act did not apply to the question of changing any terms relating to rent review, and that therefore there was no specific statutory requirement to have regard to the terms of the current tenancy in that regard. Rather, section 34(3) applies to such a situation, which states the court may, if it thinks fit, include 'such provision for varying the rent as may be specified in the determination'.

11.282 The dispute in *Morriss* was very narrow. The parties had agreed to three-yearly rent reviews. The landlord contended for the use of RPI, which had been the basis for review included in the existing tenancy, whereas the operator contended for CPI, which was thought by the court to be likely to produce lower increases. The court held that neither measure was intended to measure variations in the value of land. In the absence of a persuasive reason for changing the pre-existing basis for review, the RPI measure was to remain.

172 *EE v Morriss* at [50].
173 *EE v Morriss* at [53]–[55].

Rent

11.283 Under the 1954 Act, rent is the final matter to be determined by the court. This is because the rights that are being valued are those that are circumscribed by the terms of the tenancy. Those terms other than rent must therefore be determined first.[174]

11.284 The approach which the court has taken thus far in respect of valuing rent under the 1954 Act is addressed in Chapter 13.

Interim terms in Code renewal cases

11.285 Where an agreement is continuing under para 30, and one of the parties has made an application under paras 32(1)(b) or 33(5) for one of the para 34 modification/renewal orders, either party may apply for an Order for modifying the terms of the existing agreement until the renewal application is finally determined.[175] In deciding whether to make an Order of this kind, the tribunal must have regard to all the circumstances of the case, and in particular to those factors set out at para 35(4), namely:

'(a) the terms of the agreement relating to the existing code right,

(b) the operator's business and technical needs,

(c) the use that the site provider is making of the land to which the agreement relates,

(d) any duties imposed on the site provider by an enactment, and

(e) the amount of consideration payable by the operator to the site provider under the agreement.'

11.286 Whereas the tribunal may decide that an Order for interim consideration has effect from the date of the application for it,[176] there is no similar power in relation to Orders for the interim modification of other terms.

11.287 In *Ewefields Farm*[177] the FTT held that a term in an existing Code agreement requiring the payment of a 'payaway' was not a term in respect of consideration, and as a result its removal from the agreement could not be effected retrospectively to have effect from the date of the application.

174 As Lord Wilberforce said in *O'May v City of London Real Property Co. Ltd.* [1983] 2 AC 726 at p 748A: 'the appropriate rent follows from determination of the terms'.

175 Para 35(2A)(b).

176 Para 35(2B).

177 *On Tower UK Limited v AP Wireless II (UK) Limited and others* LC – 2023 – 000321 and 13 others (*Ewefields Farm*).

12

Upgrading and sharing

12.01 The rights of 'upgrading' and 'sharing' are now both Code rights in their own right, within the menu of Code rights set out at para 3 of the Code.

12.02 However, although the above terms are used as useful shorthand, it is important to understand what the precise definitions of those rights are.

12.03 It is also important to note that no right to do anything can ever be a 'Code right' unless it is a right 'for the statutory purposes'.[1]

The right to upgrade

12.04 The right to upgrade is listed as a Code right at para 3(1)(c) of the Code:

> 'For the purposes of this code a 'code right', in relation to an operator and any land, is a right for the statutory purposes—
>
> ...
>
> (c) to inspect, maintain, adjust, alter, repair, *upgrade* or operate *electronic communications apparatus* which is on, under or over the land'. [emphasis added]

Code rights ancillary to upgrading

12.05 Rights of entry and rights to carry out works related to upgrading are also separately defined as Code rights, in summary as follows:

- Entry (para 3(1)(f)): The right to enter land to do those things mentioned in the para 3(1)(c) Code right (whether or not the ECA in question is on the land which is to be entered); and
- Works (para 3(1)(e)): The right to carry out works on land 'for or in connection with' those things mentioned in the para 3(1)(c) Code right (whether or not the ECA in question is on the land on which the works take place).

The right relates to ECA only

12.06 It can be seen from the above that the para 3(1)(c) right is to upgrade ECA. Thus, a right to upgrade something that is not ECA would seem not to fall within

1 Para 3. See the discussions of 'Code rights' and 'The statutory purposes' at Chapter 5.

the para 3(1)(c) Code right, although it may fall within para 3(1)(e) if it is 'for or in connection with' the maintenance, upgrading, etc of ECA.

12.07 The definition of ECA, set out at para 5, is however fairly broad (see Chapter 5), concerning definitions of certain terms used in the Code). The right on the part of a non-operator to upgrade apparatus is also not capable of being a 'Code right' within para 3(1)(c). Clearly, an operator may carry out upgrading works through its contractors, servants, agents, and employees. However, there may be cases where, on a proper legal analysis, what is being done is not being done by or on behalf of an operator but by or on behalf of some other entity, whether related or otherwise. Whether that is a breach of some contractual prohibition, or whether it is a tort, is not likely to turn on whether it is strictly a Code right, however.

The right to share

12.08 Since an amendment[2] to the Code made by the PSTIA 2022, the right to share the use of ECA with another operator is now also a Code right. It is worth noting that by section 57(7) of the PSTIA 2022, the amendment does not affect any rights conferred before the coming into force of section 57 (on 7 February 2023).

12.09 The right to share is now listed as a Code right at para 3(1)(ca) of the Code:

> 'For the purposes of this code a 'code right', in relation to an operator and any land, is a right for the statutory purposes—
>
> ...
>
> (ca) to share with another operator the use of electronic communications apparatus which the first operator keeps installed on, under or over the land,'.

Code rights ancillary to sharing

12.10 Rights of entry and rights to carry out works related to sharing are also separately defined as Code rights, in summary as follows:

- Entry (para 3(1)(fa)): The right to enter land for the purposes of, or in connection with, sharing the use of ECA (whether or not the ECA is on the land which is to be entered); and
- Works (para 3(1)(ea)): The right to carry out works on land for the purposes of, or in connection with, sharing the use of ECA (whether or not the ECA in question is on the land on which the works take place).

The right relates to the use of ECA only

12.11 It can be seen from the above that the para 3(1)(ca) right is to share the 'use' of ECA. It is not a right to share the land or the use of land. This is a clean distinction,

2 The insertion of the new Code right was made by ss 57(2)(b)(i) of the Product Security and Telecommunications Infrastructure Act 2022. This came into force on 7 February 2023 by s 79(2) of the PSTIA 2022 and reg. 2(a) of the Telecommunications Infrastructure Act 2022 (Commencement No. 1) Regulations 2023.

since by para 108(1) 'land' does not include ECA. Nor does ECA become part of the land under the general law as a result of being annexed to it.[3]

The right is to share with another operator only

12.12 The para 3(1)(ca) right is only to share the 'use' of ECA with another operator. Whilst the right to share the use of ECA with a non-operator can be included in an agreement, that particular right will not constitute a Code right under para 3(1).

How does an operator obtain these rights?

12.13 It must be remembered that para 3 merely sets out those matters that are defined as Code rights. It does not grant those rights.

12.14 As per para 9(1), a Code right may only be conferred on an operator by an agreement between the operator and the occupier. Such agreements can be consensual or imposed by the tribunal. The para 9(1) general rule is subject to only one caveat, which relates specifically to sharing. This is set out at para 9(2) as follows:

> 'But in a case where an operator ('the first operator') has the right to share the use of electronic communications apparatus with another operator ('the second operator') under or by virtue of an agreement under this Part, sub-paragraph (1) does not prevent the agreement from providing for the first operator to permit the second operator to exercise, in connection with the sharing, a code right conferred on the first operator by the agreement.'

12.15 Thus, in those particular circumstances, the 'second operator' can exercise a Code right despite not having been a party to the agreement by which that Code right was conferred.

12.16 An operator can obtain a right to share or upgrade from two different sources:

(i) *The provisions of para 17*: these automatically grant certain sharing and upgrading rights where an agreement is entered into or imposed; and

(ii) *The express terms of an agreement*: such an agreement can be consensual or imposed by a tribunal.

12.17 These two sources are now considered in turn.

Para 17: the source of automatic sharing and upgrading rights

12.18 Paragraph 17 grants automatic upgrading and sharing rights in favour of an operator who has entered into an agreement under Part 2 of the Code. This has been the case since the Code came into force, ie, even before the right to share was not listed as a Code right. However, these rights are subject to important restrictions contained

3 See *Cornerstone Telecommunications Infrastructure Ltd v Keast* [2019] UKUT 116 (LC) at [45].

in the conditions set out at paras 17(2) and (3). It is important to note that para 17 does not apply in the same way to 'subsisting agreements', as to which see below.

12.19 Paragraph 17(1) to (4) provide that:

> '(1) An operator ('the main operator') who has entered into an agreement under Part 2 of this code may, if the conditions in sub-paragraphs (2) and (3) are met—
>
> (a) upgrade the electronic communications apparatus to which the agreement relates, or
>
> (b) share the use of such electronic communications apparatus with another operator.
>
> (2) The first condition is that any changes as a result of the upgrading or sharing to the electronic communications apparatus to which the agreement relates have no adverse impact, or no more than a minimal adverse impact, on its appearance.
>
> (3) The second condition is that the upgrading or sharing imposes no additional burden on the other party to the agreement.
>
> (4) For the purposes of sub-paragraph (3) an additional burden includes anything that—
>
> (a) has an additional adverse effect on the other party's enjoyment of the land, or
>
> (b) causes additional loss, damage or expense to that party.'

12.20 As is consistent with the definitions of the relevant Code rights at para 3(1), the upgrading right at para 17 only relates to upgrading ECA, and the sharing right only allows the sharing of the 'use' of ECA. There is no automatic right to share land. Neither is there any general right to 'share' another operator's Code rights (ie, exercise all of the Code rights that benefit the main operator). However, as set out above, para 9(2) does allow an agreement to *provide* for one operator to permit a second operator to exercise its Code rights 'in connection with the sharing'. Paragraph 17 does not grant any right to share the use of ECA with a non-operator.

12.21 By para 17(6), any right conferred by para 17 to share ECA includes the right to carry out works to the ECA in order to enable the sharing to take place.

The conditions limiting rights under para 17

12.22 The two conditions limiting the rights granted under para 17 are those at paras 17(2) and (3) above (ie, no more than a minimal adverse impact on appearance and no additional burden).

12.23 The origin of these limitations is the Law Commission's report.[4] The Law Commission ruled out a blanket right to share and upgrade without limitation. Its report noted that upgrading usually involved physical change and that the 'possibilities

4 Law Com 336.

are so complex that no general provision can make an automatic right to upgrade either feasible or safe'.[5] Similarly, it was considered that 'sharing may have implications not merely for the Site Provider but also for the other Code Operators already using the mast'.[6]

12.24 It therefore concluded as follows:

> 'So in general, it is not possible for Code Operators to have an automatic right to share or to upgrade equipment. Such rights must be negotiated for, or granted by the tribunal; it may be right for there to be additional consideration payable, depending upon the market itself. The same goes for rights to maintain and repair equipment, which cannot be conferred automatically; the range of technical implications, from access to safety to structural integrity, is such that automatic rights cannot be given and it is for the parties to negotiate them or for the tribunal to confer them.'[7]

12.25 However, the Law Commission thought that it was safe for automatic sharing and upgrading rights to be granted subject to careful limitations, concluding as follows:

> 'We think that the situation where sharing or upgrading take place within the confines of a duct, or even of a cabinet on land, without physical or visual impact on the Site Provider, without requiring a power supply or the addition of an antenna for example, and without conferring Code Rights on additional Code Operators, ought to be permitted. These are cases where there is no possible additional burden on the Site Provider and no technical or safety issues.'[8]

12.26 The references to a lack of visual impact, and no possible additional burden clearly found their way into paras 17(2) and (3) of the Code.

12.27 There have not been reported cases in which a breach of the para 17(2) or (3) limitations has been alleged so as to give rise to a judicial determination on the extent of those limitations.

12.28 However, it is open to an operator to seek broader rights from the tribunal than those granted under para 17, and there have been a number of cases in which the tribunal has had to consider whether to allow such rights on an unrestricted basis or whether to limit the operator's rights as per paras 17(2) and/or (3) (see Chapter 11).

The voiding of certain restrictions on sharing and upgrading

12.29 By para 17(5)(a), an agreement under Part 2 is void to the extent that it prevents or limits the upgrading or sharing of the ECA to which the agreement relates, in a case where the para 17(2) and (3) conditions are met.

5 Law Com 336 at para 3.40.
6 Law Com 336 at para 3.41.
7 Law Com 336 at para 3.42.
8 Law Com 336 at para 3.48.

12.30 Thus neither the parties nor the tribunal can deprive[9] an operator of its limited para 17 rights to share and upgrade.

12.31 Further, by para 17(5)(b), an agreement under Part 2 is void to the extent that it makes upgrading or sharing of 'such apparatus' subject to conditions to be met by the operator (including a condition requiring the payment of money).

12.32 This gives rise to the question of the meaning of 'such apparatus'. Reading the provisions literally, that expression might appear to mean 'the electronic communications apparatus to which the agreement relates'. The potential difficulty with that meaning is that it would appear to prevent the parties granting *more extensive rights* than para 17 rights where those more extensive rights are subject to a condition. This is because para 17(5)(b), unlike para 17(5)(a), does not mention the para 17(2) and (3) conditions. One could imagine the parties agreeing that unrestricted sharing or upgrading rights are to apply, subject to a condition that the operator first informs the site provider of the intention to exercise such rights. It is hard to see how this violates the policy behind the Code. It would appear arguable that para 17(5)(b) should be read as applying only to cases where the para 17(2) and (3) conditions are met.

Express terms regarding sharing and upgrading

(i) Consensual agreements

12.33 In the case of consensual agreements, the parties can agree whatever terms they wish in respect of sharing and upgrading, subject to the voiding provisions at para 17(5), and the inability to 'contract out' of the provisions of Part 3, which includes para 17. Thus the parties can agree that additional or enlarged rights are conferred on an operator, but they cannot cut down those that are automatically conferred by para 17.

(ii) Agreements imposed by the tribunal

12.34 The limited rights granted by para 17 have been described in the tribunal as an 'irreducible minimum'[10] and a 'floor rather than a ceiling'.[11] The tribunal cannot cut those rights down but is empowered to grant more extensive sharing and/or upgrading rights that are not limited by the conditions at paras 17(2) and (3), where appropriate. This conclusion was endorsed by the Court of Appeal in *Green*.[12]

12.35 Having referred to the Law Commission's conclusion that unrestricted sharing and upgrading rights should not be conferred in all cases by the Code, the Court of Appeal in *Green*[13] said as follows:

9 Para 100(2) also makes it clear that one cannot contract out of the provisions of Part 3, which includes para 17(5).
10 *Cornerstone Telecommunications Infrastructure Ltd v London & Quadrant Housing Trust* [2020] UKUT 282 (LC) at [77].
11 *Cornerstone Telecommunications Infrastructure Ltd v London & Quadrant Housing Trust* [2020] UKUT 282 (LC) at [69].
12 *On Tower UK Ltd v JH & FW Green Ltd* [2021] EWCA Civ 1858 at [54]–[69].
13 At [61].

'The Law Commission considered that, exceptionally, an operator could automatically be given rights to share and upgrade where there could be no adverse impact on the site provider, but that the operator would otherwise need to negotiate for or apply for such rights. Nothing in the Commission's report indicates any intention that operators should normally be limited to the rights now given by paragraph 17 of the Code; it merely shows that the Commission thought that the grant of additional rights should be the subject of specific agreement or decision rather than being automatic.'

12.36 It considered that no 'different picture' emerged from either the Department for Culture Media and Sport's 'A New Electronic Communications Code' or the explanatory notes to the Digital Economy Act 2017. The former document stated that the Government agreed with the Law Commission that 'there are some circumstances where it is appropriate for Code operators to upgrade and share apparatus in a way that is unlimited by contractual agreements', and the Court of Appeal noted that 'it nowhere said that there was to be any particular limitation on operators seeking wider rights'.

12.37 It cited the ministerial foreword's reference to a desire to support the rollout of digital communications infrastructure, paving the way for future technological evolution in the coming decades. It then went on to refer to the explanatory notes, which stated that the Government 'intends infrastructure sharing to assist future deployment of technology such as 5G'. It concluded that these objectives 'would be harder to achieve if, for example, operators' sharing rights were usually to be limited to those granted by paragraph 17'.

12.38 Accordingly, there is no presumption in favour of only allowing sharing and upgrading rights to those granted by para 17. In a renewal case where a site provider is contending for the retention of restrictions contained in the current agreement, there will be an onus on the party contending for a change to justify it.[14] However, the weight to be attached to an existing term will in part depend on its consistency with the aims of the Code,[15] and the duty to have regard to existing terms does not mean that a tribunal should treat them with the same deference as is the case in a 1954 Act renewal.[16]

12.39 The Court of Appeal's conclusion as regards the proper approach where an operator seeks greater rights than those conferred by para 17 was as follows:

'While paragraph 17 provides a starting point and it is incumbent on an operator seeking more extensive rights to explain why, it need not establish 'pretty striking circumstances' or 'pretty compelling circumstances'.[17] Nor is it the case that an application for wider rights is to be approached on the basis that it is inherently improbable that such rights are appropriate. Each application must be assessed on its particular merits.'[18]

14 [2021] EWCA Civ 1858 at [48].

15 [2021] EWCA Civ 1858 at [49].

16 The Court of Appeal agreed with Fancourt J's decision in *Stephenson* in this respect: see *Green* at [2021] EWCA Civ 1858, at [47].

17 The Lands Tribunal for Scotland had spoken in *Fothringham* of the need for 'pretty compelling evidence' to justify rights in excess of those conferred by para 17.

18 [2021] EWCA Civ 1858 at [62].

Sharing and upgrading rights and subsisting agreements

12.40 As originally enacted, the Transitional Provisions[19] (at para 5 thereof) disapplied the whole of Part 3 from subsisting agreements.[20] Accordingly, para 17 did not confer any sharing or upgrading rights on an operator whose ECA was kept installed under a subsisting agreement.

12.41 However, with effect from 17 April 2023, para 5 of the Transitional Provisions has been amended[21] such that it only disapplies para 16 (relating to assignment) rather than the whole of Part 3 in the case of subsisting agreements. Further, a new para 5A has been inserted into the Transitional Provisions[22] with effect from the same date, so as to apply a different set of sub-paragraphs rather than those at para 17 of the Code in respect of subsisting agreements.

12.42 In summary, the substituted provisions of para 17 (within para 5A of the Transitional Provisions) allow an operator who is keeping ECA installed on land under a subsisting agreement to upgrade the ECA or share[23] the use of it with another operator where it 'has no adverse impact on the land',[24] 'imposes no burden on any person with an interest in the land',[25] and where a specified notice procedure is followed.[26] As with the para 17 rights in non-subsisting agreement cases, any provision which seeks to prevent, limit, or make subject to conditions, the sharing that is permitted by the substituted provisions of para 17 is void.27

19 Sch 2 to the Digital Economy Act 2017.

20 That term being defined by para 1(4) of the Transitional Provisions.

21 By section 58(3)(a) and (b) of the Product Security and Telecommunications Infrastructure 2022. This change had effect from 17 April 2023 by virtue of 79(2) of that Act and reg 3(a) ofThe Product Security and Telecommunications Infrastructure Act 2022 (Commencement No. 1) Regulations 2023.

22 Which was inserted into the Transitional Provisions by s 58(4) of the Product Security and Telecommunications Infrastructure 2022 and which came into force on 17 April 2023 by virtue of 79(2) of that Act and reg 3(a) ofThe Product Security and Telecommunications Infrastructure Act 2022 (Commencement No. 1) Regulations 2023.

23 This right to share includes the right to carry out works to the ECA to enable such sharing to take place (the substituted para 17(11), found in para 5A of the Transitional Provisions).

24 The substituted para 17(3), found in para 5A of the Transitional Provisions.

25 The substituted para 17(4), found in para 5A of the Transitional Provisions.

26 The substituted paras 17(6) and (7), found in para 5A of the Transitional Provisions.

27 By the substituted para 17(9), found in para 5A of the Transitional Provisions.

13

Consideration

13.01 In contemplating the imposition of a Code agreement by a tribunal, the Code refers to the payments that will be payable by the operator in return for their rights as 'consideration'.

13.02 As discussed elsewhere in this book, an agreement conferring Code rights may be in the form of a lease or something more akin to a licence.[1] Where the agreement is a lease, the consideration will ordinarily be the rent[2] under that lease. Where Code agreements are not drafted as leases, they may use a variety of terms to refer to consideration payments, such as 'Site Payment'.

13.03 Although the Code deals with consideration and compensation separately (at paras 24 and 25 respectively), there is nothing objectionable about a defined term including elements of consideration and compensation, so long as each of those elements, where imposed by the tribunal, have been calculated in accordance with the provisions of the Code.

13.04 As with other categories of terms that are imposed by a tribunal, terms as to consideration are of course contained in consensual agreements that are agreed outside of the tribunal process. Consideration that is agreed consensually is highly likely to be influenced by the parties' assessments of the figure that the tribunal might set in the absence of agreement.

13.05 The test that the tribunal must follow in assessing compensation under the New Code is very different from that under the Old Code. In short, New Code rents are likely in most cases to be substantially lower than Old Code rents because of the statutory formula set out at para 24. This includes the 'no-network' assumption at para 24(3)(a), that has the effect of stripping out any value which is derived from the actual intended use of the land for the purposes of an electronic communications network. In order to understand how the valuation mechanism under the New Code came to be formulated, and the dynamics that are at play in negotiations under the New Code, it is perhaps helpful to have an understanding of the position under the Old Code.

1 A licence in the sense that it constitutes a permission to occupy land without conferring any proprietary interest in that land, and which is governed by the scope of its contractual provisions. This particular form of licence is of course subject to a complex statutory overlay, which includes provisions by which third parties who were not contracting parties, are bound. Such persons would otherwise not be capable of being bound by a licence..

2 The Deputy President noted in *EE Ltd v Stephenson* [2022] UKUT 180 (LC) at [51] that as the proposed Code agreement in that case would be a lease, the consideration 'will therefore be a rent'.

Consideration under the Old Code

13.06 The Old Code states that consideration is to be assessed as a figure that 'would have been fair and reasonable if the agreement had been given willingly'.[3]

13.07 There is debate about how this form of word relates to 'market value'. The word 'if' connotes a hypothetical exercise, and the word 'willingly' is immediately redolent of familiar statutory forms of words where a 'market value' is required to be ascertained. However, the Old Code does not expressly state that rent is to be set at market value, and of course it could have done so.

13.08 In *Mercury Communications Ltd v London and India Dock Investments Ltd*,[4] HHJ Hague QC held that the proper approach was to consider comparable transactions, considering the bargaining strengths of the parties. The judge considered that what was 'fair and reasonable' would go beyond mere diminution in the value of the landowner's land, but would not include a ransom element. He said this, as regards market value:

> '…what I have to determine is not the same as what the result in the market would have been if the grant had been given willingly. That is, however, far from saying that the market result is irrelevant or can afford no guidance. Indeed, in my view the market result is the obvious starting point; and in most cases it will come to the same thing as what is "fair and reasonable".'[5]

13.09 He considered that the words 'fair and reasonable' connoted a degree of subjective judicial opinion rather than merely an objective valuation.

13.10 In *Bocardo SA v Star Energy UK Onshore Ltd*,[6] the Supreme Court considered similar wording[7] in the context of legislation relating to rights to extract oil. The right to pass pipelines under land was assessed according to compulsory purchase principles, even though these principles were not expressly incorporated. Accordingly, the use of the pipes as a means to extract oil was to be disregarded, and the rights were to be valued by reference to their value to the owner of the land rather than the value to the purchaser.

13.11 It has been said that this conclusion might be used to cast doubt on the conclusion in *Mercury Communications*. However, the statutory words were not identical, the legislative purpose of statutes concerning different industries may have a bearing, and the factual circumstances were of course different.

---

3 Para 7(1) of the Old Code.

4 (1995) 69 P & CR 135 at pp 161 to 164. This was a decision of the county court.

5 Pp 144–145.

6 [2010] UKSC 35. This case was referred to in the Law Commission's discussion of this topic (see Law Com 336 at 5.19).

7 Section 8(2) of the Mines (Working Facilities and Support) Act 1966 provided that: 'The compensation or consideration in respect of any right, including a right to enforce restrictions, shall be assessed by the court on the basis of what would be fair and reasonable between a willing grantor and a willing grantee, having regard to the conditions subject to which the right is or is to be granted.'

13.12 The Law Commission report[8] probably puts it best when it says that consideration under the Old Code 'has been regarded as meaning something other than precisely market value'.

13.13 As regards what happened in practice whilst the Old Code was in force, the Deputy President commented in the *Islington*[9] case, that:

> 'In practice consideration was rarely determined by the court but was agreed at levels which reflected the value to the operator of the use of the land for its apparatus.'

13.14 Accordingly, in practice, the values that emerged in most cases were not dissimilar to those that might have been achieved in an open market, *not* disregarding the value generated by the communications use, which would only be present in a world where the operator wished to use the site for its purposes. Given what was generally understood by the 'fair and reasonable' formulation, including in the limited case law, it is doubtful that the rents agreed in most cases included any true ransom element.

The Law Commission recommendations for the New Code

13.15 Prior to the publication of its 2013 report into a proposed revised Code, the Law Commission had made a provisional proposal for tribunal valuations to proceed on a 'no-scheme' basis where agreements were imposed. The basic principle behind such a basis is to strip out the value that is attributable to the existence of the demand for the purpose for which the actual operator would be using the land. This idea bears some relation to the position in the compulsory purchase context, where the 'scheme' for which land is acquired is not taken into account for the purposes of assessing the price to be paid.[10]

13.16 However, the Law Commission concluded in its final report that 'our consultation has not produced evidence that could justify our recommending a "no-scheme" pricing basis in the public interest'.[11]

13.17 The concerns raised in that consultation had included the following:

(i) 'One major concern raised by consultees was that landowners' willingness to reach agreement with Code Operators would be substantially affected.';[12] and

(ii) 'The implication of the change in landowners' attitudes would, it is argued, mean that many more installations would have to proceed by compulsion:

8 Law Com 336 at 5.20.

9 [2019] UKUT 53 (LC) at [55]. This was a case under the New Code.

10 The compulsory purchase principle that requires the value attributable solely to the 'scheme' of the acquiring authority is often referred to as the '*Pointe Gourde* principle', deriving from the case of *Pointe Gourde Quarrying and Transport Co Ltd v Sub-Intendent of Crown Lands* [1947] AC 565, as referred to by the Deputy President in *Islington* [2019] UKUT 53 (LC) at [62].

11 Law Com 336 at 5.76.

12 Law Com 336 at 5.56. This concern has surely been borne out in practice following the enactment of legislation which rejected the Law Commission's recommendation.

and that that will greatly overload the court or tribunal system and indeed the resources of Code Operators themselves.'[13]

13.18 On the other side of the ledger, what was the evidence that lower Code rents would bring benefits for consumers? The Law Commission said this:

> 'It is notable that no Code Operator told us that lower prices would be passed on to the consumer or would be ploughed back into research and development.'[14]

13.19 The recommendation of the Law Commission was therefore that the New Code 'should clarify the definition of consideration by using a familiar definition of market value'.[15] It went on to recommend two assumptions that should be included within the statutory valuation hypothesis. These were:[16]

(i) 'that there is more than one suitable property available to the Code Operator'. The objective of this assumption is to strip out any element of monopoly or 'ransom value' that the landowner could otherwise seek to extract; and

(ii) 'that the Code Operator does not have the entitlement to upgrade or share apparatus, or to assign the Code Rights, conferred by the revised Code'. This was as a result of a policy conclusion by the Law Commission that these additional rights should not raise prices.

13.20 However, the Government did not accept that a true market value approach should be followed, instead deciding that the use of the land for the purposes of a network should be disregarded within the statutory valuation formula. The type of valuation basis that the Law Commission had rejected on the basis of its consultation responses was thus chosen.

The ministerial statement regarding the New Code

13.21 In a ministerial statement[17] responding to a consultation on the new Code and published by the Department for Culture, Media, and Sport in May 2016, the Government explained that the new Code 'will make major changes to the way land is valued'. Under the heading 'Government response: How consideration is to be determined' the statement stated that the Law Commission had recommended only limited changes to the valuation provisions of the Old Code to eliminate any ransom element. But the Government favoured further reform, as it explained in the following passage:[18]

> 'It is quite clear that the cost for "rents" in the telecommunications industry are[19] significantly higher than those enjoyed by utilities and providers of essential services. Government is also clear that site providers should get fair value for

13 Law Com 336 at 5.50. Whilst it would be a stretch to conclude that the Tribunal system has been overloaded, it is clear that there has been an enormous increase in litigation under the New Code when compared with the Old Code, and many would attribute this to the change in the based of valuing consideration, which departed from the reasoned recommendation of the Law Commission.

14 Law Com 336 at 5.63.

15 Law Com 336 at 1.38.

16 Law Com 336 at 5.83.

17 This statement was headed 'A New Electronic Communications Code'.

18 At pp 14–15 of the Ministerial Statement.

19 Sic.

the use of their land, but considers that this should not, as a matter of principle, include a share of the economic value created by very high public demand for services that the operator provides.

The Government is therefore proposing that the revised code should limit the value of consideration by changing the basis of valuation to a "no scheme" rule that reflects the underlying value of the land. This is a rate that is more relevant to the nature of modern digital communications infrastructure rollout, and will work to encourage greater investment and improved network coverage.'

13.22 Whether it is conceptually accurate to refer to the valuation methodology under the Code as a 'no scheme' approach is debatable. The Government's Impact Assessment[20] of the proposed New Code spoke of a 'move to compulsory purchase principles', and the 'no scheme' approach is of course a key concept under such principles.

13.23 Although the Code requires the value attributable to the use of the land for network purposes to be stripped out (the 'no-network' assumption[21]), it does not require the tenant/licensee's activities to be disregarded altogether. Indeed, the statutory scheme requires certain elements of the 'scheme' to be taken into account, in the sense that many of the terms of the actual Code agreement[22] *do* fall to be considered when assessing value. For example, the extent of any access rights and the reasonable expectations of the hypothetical negotiating parties in relation to how frequently such rights will be exercised in practice will be relevant to valuation.

13.24 The Government's Impact Assessment[23] in advance of the New Code included a 'best estimate' based on advice from its consultants that 'wayleave values' would 'reach an equilibrium at up to 40% lower than current rates.' Surveyors advising landowners would generally consider that that figure represented a very substantial underestimate of the reduction in rents or licence fees caused by the implementation of the New Code.

Consensual consideration under the New Code

13.25 It is open to the parties to a consensual agreement that confers Code rights to agree whatever rent, licence fee, or consideration they wish.[24] Indeed, in the case of a consensual deal, there is no requirement under the Code that any financial consideration be payable at all.[25]

20 This was dated 12 May 2016. The words referred to are on p 2 thereof.

21 See para 24(3)(a) of the Code.

22 See paras 24(2)(c) and 24(3)(c) of the Code.

23 Incidentally, the Impact Assessment also stated in unambiguous terms that the 'policy' of the New Code 'will be reviewed' and set a target date of June 2022. Despite pressure from landowners, the Government refused to carry out a review of the Code.

24 Although it is fair to note that requiring an operator to pay an additional sum as a condition of a right to upgade ECA or to share the use would be void by virtue of para 17(5)(b), and requiring an operator to pay an additional sum as a condition of a right to assign the agreement to another operator would be void by virtue of para 16(1)(b).

25 This is in contrast to the position where an agreement is imposed by the Tribunal, in which case the terms of the agreement must include terms as to the payment of consideration (see para 23(3)).

13.26 Paragraph 100(1) provides that the Code 'does not affect any rights or liabilities arising under an agreement to which an operator is a party'.[26] Accordingly the Code does not interfere with the right of a site provider to receive occupational payments as specified in the agreement, or the liability of the operator to pay them.

13.27 Naturally, where a Code agreement is negotiated consensually, well-advised negotiating parties will be aware of the provisions of the Code. When an operator makes contact with a landowner and asks for Code rights to be conferred, it typically refers to the relevant legislation and makes proposals as to annual consideration payments. A landowner can then seek legal and valuation advice if it chooses to do so.[27]

13.28 In the case of a renewal of an agreement entered into under the Old Code, the landowner may be surprised that the level of consideration being offered is much lower than the existing passing rent. In the case of an agreement on a new site, the landowner may similarly be surprised that the level of consideration being offered is much lower than it had understood was the 'going rate' under the Old Code. In either of these circumstances, doubtless, the operator will indicate to the landowner from its point of view why the proper new consideration is so much lower, by reference to the manner in which consideration would be assessed by the tribunal under para 24 of the Code in the event of deadlock.

13.29 Thus, where consensual agreements are reached, in the absence of exceptional features (such as extreme urgency or a particular desire on the part of an operator to avoid the tribunal in a particular case), one would expect consensual consideration to be agreed at rates that at least take account of the methodology by which consideration is valued under para 24 of the Code.

13.30 In any negotiation, an important imperative is the question, 'What is going to happen if I do not agree?' The answer in most cases under the Code is twofold:

(a) the tribunal will[28] order a level of consideration which is much lower than under the Old Code; and

(b) it is likely to cost a lot of money[29] to find that out.

13.31 So, the parties may agree on whatever figure they like. Neither party is likely to recover every penny of its costs in the event of a comprehensive success in the

---

26 It is true that para 100(2) disapplies this provision from certain parts of the Code, namely para 99 and Parts 3 to 6. Thus, para 100(2) disapplies para 100(1) from Part 4, which includes the provisions under which consideration must be set by the Tribunal. Parties therefore cannot enter into an agreement that the statutory valuation mechanism under para 24 will not apply to renewals of agreements, for example. However, Part 4 is not of relevance to a consensual agreement, and para 100(1) is not disapplied from Part 2, which describes agreements conferring Code rights and entered into between occupier and operator.

27 Where an agreement is imposed, a landowner can in theory recover the reasonable costs of legal and valuation advice as to the consideration and other terms of the agreement by virtue of paras 25(1) and 84(2)(a). More is said in relation to this in Chapter 14 relating to Compensation.

28 Assuming that the operator does not give up and walk away, it will apply to the Tribunal for the imposition of an agreement. Assuming an agreement is imposed and not successfully resisted, consideration will be imposed at a rate which follows the para 24 methodology.

29 The legal costs in a typical Code case will typically be disproportionate to the amount of consideration ordered over the term of the resulting agreement. If a landowner unrealistically argues for a figure which is clearly too high, especially without evidence, it may very well find itself paying the costs of both parties to the proceedings.

tribunal, and an operator cannot be confident of obtaining a fulsome Order for costs if a site provider is successful in respect of some of the terms of the agreement or if the tribunal's valuation is a little higher than what the operator had offered. Furthermore, if an operator is looking to get onto land swiftly, tribunal proceedings will not greatly speed this up, despite the six-month time limit[30] for the determination of References relating to new sites. Thus, it may be that operators would be willing to pay a little more in some cases than they think they might be ordered to pay in the tribunal. Doing so is unlikely to have a negative impact as evidence in future tribunal determinations.[31]

13.32 However, it stands to reason that sums agreed in consensual transactions typically will not look unlike a tribunal-imposed para 24 valuation. Such valuations are considered below.

Consideration imposed under the New Code

13.33 Paragraph 20 cases will be considered first.

13.34 Where a tribunal imposes an agreement under para 20, para 23(3) requires it to include a term as to 'the payment of consideration by the operator to the relevant person for the relevant person's agreement to confer or be bound by the code right'.

13.35 Paragraph 24 sets out the relevant provisions as to how consideration is determined. By para 24(1), the amount of consideration payable in an agreement imposed under para 20 must be:

> 'an amount or amounts representing the market value of the relevant person's agreement to confer or be bound by the code right'.

13.36 It is therefore clear from the word 'go' that what is being assessed is a market value, albeit, as we shall see, a value that is subject to some very powerful mandated counterfactual assumptions. The basis for the assessment of this market value and the assumptions that must be applied are set out at paras 24(2) and 24(3). These are considered further below.

Form and timing of consideration payments

13.37 Paragraph 24(4) provides that the terms may provide for consideration to be payable:

> '(a) as a lump sum or periodically,

30 This arises under reg 3(2) of the Electronic Communications and Wireless Telegraphy Regulations 2011, to which para 97 refers. Although there is perhaps not certainty as to the precise range of cases to which the stipulation applies, (para 97 refers to 'certain applications') it has been held to apply to applications for Code rights over a new site. See *EE v Islington* [2019] UKUT 53 (LC) at [18].

31 See, for example, the comments of Judge Cooke in the *Hackney (Tradescant House)* case ([2022] UKUT 210 (LC) at [47]), in which it was recognised that parties make concessions in agreeing terms for a variety of reasons. Although these comments related to non-financial terms, where a concession as to consideration has been made for a particular reason in a particular case, that is surely capable of weakening its evidential value as a comparable. In any event, as is discussed later in this chapter (see **13.147**) the tribunal does not consider that telecoms-related comparables are of assistance in assessing consideration under para 24, as the 'no-network' assumption applies.

(b) on the occurrence of a specified event or events, or

(c) in such other form or at such other time or times as the court may direct.'

13.38 In practice, consideration payments are calculated by reference to an annual timeframe, and the figure is invariably stated in tribunal judgments on that basis.

The valuation hypothesis

13.39 Paras 24(2) and 24(3) describe a hypothetical transaction which must be considered in order to yield the statutory consideration figure. Much of the valuation hypothesis is relatively familiar to those with experience of statutes which mandate a market valuation of property rights, for example the 1954 Act. However, the crucial difference is what has become known as the 'no-network' assumption, at para 24(3)(a), which shall be considered further below.

The para 24(2) description of the hypothetical transaction

13.40 Paragraph 24(2) sets out how one is to calculate consideration for the purpose of para 24(1):

'(2) For this purpose the market value of a person's agreement to confer or be bound by a code right is, subject to sub-paragraph (3), the amount that, at the date the market value is assessed, a willing buyer would pay a willing seller for the agreement—

(a) in a transaction at arm's length,

(b) on the basis that the buyer and seller were acting prudently and with full knowledge of the transaction, and

(c) on the basis that the transaction was subject to the other provisions of the agreement imposed by the order under paragraph 20.'

13.41 The reference to a market value, a willing buyer, and a willing seller demonstrate that we are here dealing with a hypothetical transaction. The transaction that the tribunal must imagine is one that is conducted at arm's length, in which the parties are acting prudently and with full knowledge of the transaction.

The unusual statutory wording

13.42 The expression 'the market value of a person's agreement' is unusual. There was a discussion in *Islington*[32] as to whether this perhaps signalled an intention to borrow the 'value to the owner' or 'no-scheme' principle from the compulsory purchase world. However, the tribunal does not reach a firm conclusion on this point, and the expression 'no-scheme' is rejected in favour of 'no-network' because of the differences between the compulsory purchase legislation and this statutory scheme.

32 [2019] UKUT 53 (LC) at [63].

13.43 It is perhaps notable that the expression at para 24(2) is not 'the value to the person', it is the 'market value' (ie, the value to the market) of the 'person's agreement'. What would be sold in the hypothetical market, regardless of what disregards apply? The person's agreement. Accordingly, it does not seem that a great deal can be read into this choice of words as regards the valuation methodology.

The conventional hypothetical exercise

13.44 Indeed, in *Islington*, the tribunal went straight on to emphasise that the shape of the hypothetical exercise is entirely in keeping with the usual conventions within the field of valuation of property rights, saying:

> 'Whatever the true purpose of expressing the measure of consideration in this unusual way, any suggestion that paragraph 24(1) requires some unconventional approach to determining market value is immediately negated by paragraph 24(2).'[33]

and

> 'The introduction into the Code valuation criteria of the willing buyer and of a specific transaction on a particular date and terms gives an entirely conventional shape to the exercise which must be undertaken.'[34]

13.45 Other than where the statute expressly mandates the tribunal to make a particular assumption or disregard a certain fact, the transaction 'is to be assumed to take place in the open market with all the features present in that market in reality' .[35] The tribunal in *Islington* referred to Hoffmann LJ's explanation of this hypothetical market with real-world characteristics in the tax case of *IRC v Gray*:[36]

> 'It cannot be too strongly emphasised that although the sale is hypothetical, there is nothing hypothetical about the open market in which it is supposed to have taken place. The concept of the open market involves assuming that the whole world was free to bid, and then forming a view about what in those circumstances would in real life have been the best price reasonably obtainable ....'

13.46 As we shall see below, the way in which the tribunal 'shows its workings' and the type of evidence it encourages has undergone a shift from the earliest case of *Islington* to the more recent decisions. This appears to have been due to the effect of the 'no-network' assumption in practice, the relatively low values that are being generated, the extent to which the tribunal has considered expert evidence to have been helpful in Code cases, and concerns as to costs and proportionality. However, the above conclusions in *Islington* as to what para 24 *requires* in the context of the statutory scheme are in categorical terms and have neither been overturned nor expressly doubted. What is *required* by para 24 is surely unaffected by the tribunal's experience of seeking to carry out what is required.

13.47 However, a landowner thinking that it will receive what it considers to be a market value for its land is likely to be disappointed. The 'no-network' assumption

33 [2019] UKUT 53 (LC) at [63].
34 [2019] UKUT 53 (LC) at [64].
35 [2019] UKUT 53 (LC) at [64].
36 [1994] STC 360.

in para 24(3)(a) has a very substantial downwards effect on consideration in almost all cases. This is considered further at **13.63** onwards.

Presumption of reality

13.48 The 'presumption of reality' is a general principle where a statutory formula requires the valuation of some right on certain assumptions. It holds that, unless the statutory scheme expressly or by necessary implication requires some assumption to be made that is contrary to the real-world position, all of the true facts in the real-world are to be assumed.

13.49 In *Fothringham*, the Lands Tribunal for Scotland set out a number of propositions that it regarded as 'uncontroversial' in respect of Code valuations, of which this was the first:

> 'although the transaction we have to envisage is hypothetical, there is nothing hypothetical about the market in which it takes place and we must stick as closely as possible to the reality of that market.'

13.50 In support of this proposition, reliance was placed[37] on the passage in *Trocette Property Co Ltd v Greater London Council and Southwark London Borough Council*[38] at which Lawton LJ said that the 'statutory world of make believe should be kept as near as possible to reality'.

13.51 For example, in *London & Quadrant*, the tribunal made clear that taking into account the real-life practical burdens which a site provider will face in determining consideration does not offend the 'no network' assumption:

> 'Although the rights conferred by the agreement and which will bind the hypothetical parties must be assumed not to relate to the provision or use of a network, they must be assumed in all other respects to correspond to the code rights which the operator will enjoy (paragraph 24(3)(c)). The burdens which the hypothetical parties would expect to fall on the landlord will therefore be the same burdens as will fall on the actual site provider. The retention of the site as simply an area of rooftop, or car park, or field, would entail little or no expense for the hypothetical landlord, especially if none of the other occupants of the building or land had any rights or reason to go there. Its use for the erection, retention and maintenance of steel structures which will be visited regularly by a variety of contractors is likely to involve the landlord in expense which would otherwise have been avoided. That expense would also be taken into account in the hypothetical negotiation.'[39]

Characteristics of the seller

13.52 There is room to take account of the real-world characteristics of the seller. Thus, in *Islington*,[40] the site provider was assumed to be the landlord of the other occupants

37 Reliance was also placed on *EE Ltd v Islington* [2019] UKUT 53 (LC) at [64] and [83], and on *IRC v Gray*, to which reference was made in *Islington*.

38 [1974] RVR 306 at p 311.

39 *London & Quadrant* at [97].

40 [2019] UKUT 53 (LC) at [93].

of the building and to owe contractual and statutory obligations to them. The respondent local authority's real-world duty to obtain best value when disposing of property was not a matter that would affect the valuation, however, since it was incapable of overriding the statutory assumption that the seller is willing to deal at market value.

Consequence of lack of bidders

13.53 As the open market to be assumed is the real one, there is no justification for an assumption that the market is competitive. There is only a statutory mandate to assume one buyer (a willing one), and not any additional bidders that would not exist in the real market. However, even if there is only one bidder, this does not compel the conclusion that the price agreed will be nominal.

13.54 In this regard, the tribunal in *Islington* referred to the rent review case of *F. R. Evans (Leeds) Ltd*,[41] in which it was held that the fact that there was only one potential lessee was not decisive because the single potential lessee was to be assumed to be a willing lessee. Reliance was also placed on the Privy Council decision in *Raja Vyricherla Narayana Gajapatiraju v The Revenue Divisional Officer, Vizagapatam*[42] citing Lord Romer in that case as follows:

> 'But if the potentiality is of value to the vendor if there happen to be two or more possible purchasers of it, it is difficult to see why he should be willing to part with it for nothing merely because there is only one purchaser. To compel him to do so is to treat him as a vendor parting with his land under compulsion and not as a willing vendor. The fact is that the only possible purchaser of a potentiality is usually quite willing to pay for it.'

13.55 However, if the nature of the premises is such that, in reality, nobody would pay anything for them, the correct conclusion may be that their market value is nominal.[43]

Prudent and informed parties

13.56 Insofar as comparables are of assistance,[44] any transaction in which the site provider was ill-informed about the Code and did not understand the nature of the rights that were being conferred, such that it simply agreed to the operator's opening offer, would offend[45] against the valuation hypothesis.

What agreement terms are being valued?

13.57 Paragraph 24(2)(c) is express in requiring the *actual* provisions of the agreement to be valued. This is clearly subject to the assumptions at para 24(3), which

41 (1977) 245 EG 657.

42 [1939] AC 302, 316.

43 *Islington*, [2019] UKUT 53 (LC) at [87].

44 As to which, see further below, including at **13.67**, **13.123** and **13.140** onwards.

45 Para 24(2)(b) requires it to be assumed that the buyer and seller are acting prudently and with full knowledge of the transaction. Naturally the process of valuation by comparable entails adjustments being made for factual differences, but such a difference is likely to be impossible to adjust for.

include the crucial 'no-network' assumption at para 24(3)(a), which is considered below. Thus the actual terms of the agreement are to be valued,[46] but on the basis that neither the right being sold nor any of the terms of the agreement being sold relate to a network.

13.58 Where a statutory formula requires the absence of a real-world fact to be assumed, when it is in fact present, one difficulty that emerges is: what facts are assumed to swarm into that vacuum? This question is not easy, but is considered below in the context of the 'no-network' assumption.

The para 24(3) assumptions

13.59 Paragraph 24(3) provides as follows:

> '(3) The market value must be assessed on these assumptions—
>
> (a) that the right that the transaction relates to does not relate to the provision or use of an electronic communications network;
>
> (b) that paragraphs 16, 17 and 17A (assignment, and upgrading and sharing) do not apply to the right or any apparatus to which it could apply;
>
> (c) that the right in all other respects corresponds to the code right;
>
> (d) that there is more than one site which the buyer could use for the purpose for which the buyer seeks the right.'

13.60 As discussed above, para 24(2)(c) requires the valuation to proceed on the basis that the terms of the notional agreement to be valued are to be the same as those in the actual agreement, subject to any express statutory assumptions to the contrary. Paragraph 24(3)(c) essentially repeats[47] this idea by mandating that the Code right is in all respects the same as the real Code rights, subject to any express statutory assumptions to the contrary.

13.61 It is the three assumptions at sub-paras (a), (b) and (d) that may require the tribunal to proceed on the basis of hypothetical facts that differ from reality.

13.62 As discussed in *Islington*, the making of assumptions that are contrary to the true facts is a 'familiar technique in valuations of all sorts'.[48] In the case of the Code, the matters that must be assumed are 'absolutely critical to the outcome'.[49] This is principally the case because of sub-para (a), the 'no-network' assumption.

---

46 Subject to the caveat that para 24(3)(b) requires an assumption to be made that paras 16, 17 and 17A do not apply to the right granted, or the relevant apparatus. Thus, in cases where the rights to share, upgrade and assign are not set out expressly in the agreement, but are conferred solely by paras 16, 17 and 17A, it appears that the valuation has to proceed on the basis that those rights are to be ignored for valuation purposes.

47 The Tribunal noted in *Islington* that para 24(3)(c) may add nothing of substance to para 24(2)(c): [2019] UKUT 53 (LC) at [70].

48 *Islington* at [65].

49 *Islington* at [65].

The 'no-network' assumption (para 24(3)(a))

13.63 The 'no-network' assumption is perhaps the most significant change made by the enactment of the New Code. In *EE Ltd v Stephenson*[50] Fancourt J said that:

> 'The change from open market value, taking account of demand from telecommunications operators, to market value on a 'no network' assumption is a very significant change introduced by the Code.'

13.64 The phrase 'no-network assumption' to described the mandate at para 24(3)(a) comes from the *Islington* case. The tribunal described its purpose as follows:[51]

> 'The obvious purpose of the no-network assumption is to exclude from the assessment of consideration any element of value attributable to the intention of the operator to use the site as part of its network. The assumption gives effect to the policy expressed in the ministerial statement that the fair return to the site provider 'should not, as a matter of principle, include a share of the economic value created by very high public demand for services that the operator provides'.'

13.65 The phrase 'no-network assumption' was preferred by the tribunal over the expression 'no-scheme' which had been used in the Ministerial Statement but which is not found in the Code itself. The tribunal considered that there was a clear analogy between those two concepts, but that the latter phrase carried baggage with it from the world of compulsory purchase such that its use would 'risk importing with it features which cannot be assumed to have any place in the assessment of consideration under the Code'.

13.66 The tribunal in *Islington* also emphasised the difference between a typical compulsory purchase situation (where a freehold sale divests the seller of its entire interest) and a Code situation (where there is an ongoing agreement under which both parties have ongoing obligations). As the tribunal said at [99]:

> 'The parties will be in this continuing relationship for ten years and (subject to the no-network assumption) the risks and obligations which the relationship creates for the site provider must be taken into account.'

Rejection of the use of 'Old Code' comparables

13.67 One considerable consequence of the no-network assumption has been the sidelining of Old Code comparables.

13.68 In *Marklands Ltd v Virgin Retail Ltd*,[52] Lewison J explained the conventional approach to valuation, especially in the context of property rights:

> 'Valuation essentially proceeds by analogy. The valuer looks for an analogue which is as close as possible to that which he has to value, and which has been the subject matter of a real transaction. He then works on the premise that if the subject matter of his valuation were to be the subject of a similar transaction, it would command

50 [2021] UKUT 167 (LC) at [46].
51 [2019] UKUT 53 (LC) at [68].
52 [2003] EWHC 3428 (Ch) at [9].

the same value as the analogue. Since the analogue will never be identical to the subject matter of the valuation, the valuer will have to make adjustments to the value revealed by the analogue in order to reflect the differences between the analogue and the subject matter of his own valuation. In the case of a property valuation the analogues are usually called 'comparables'. In the case of a property valuation typical adjustments will reflect differences between the comparables in location, terms of letting and so on.'

13.69 In *Islington*, the tribunal rejected the use of transactions which were agreed under the Old Code as transactional evidence of any real worth. The reasons for this included the following:[53]

(i) it would be contrary to the no-network assumption, since they evidence the value of rights 'to provide and use an electronic communications network';

(ii) they were based on a different statutory valuation hypothesis;

(iii) they are historic values, and the use of indexation over a long period is unreliable.

13.70 The landowner's expert had selected comparables where the site provider had not been represented, on the basis that it would therefore be expected to be ignorant of the true value of the rights being granted. This was not an accurate way of stripping out the value attributable to the network, and in any event was contrary to the mandated hypothesis at para 24(2)(b) that the buyer and seller act prudently and with full knowledge of the transaction.

13.71 In *Green*, the tribunal referred to comparables in transactions where rent had been negotiated under the Old Code, but where the parties had entered into the negotiated agreement after the New Code had come into force. In a number of these cases, a 'caveat' had been included to this effect, making clear that the elevated rent that had been agreed (and which would doubtless be unlikely to be the result of a para 24 valuation) was not intended by the parties to reflect a para 24 valuation or set any precedent in respect of such valuations. The tribunal considered that such transactions were 'useless'[54] as comparables for the purposes of valuing under para 24.

13.72 The tribunal has more recently had to grapple with what kind of comparables might be of assistance, and this is discussed further below.

Impact of no-network assumption on assumed agreement terms

13.73 There is perhaps an open question as to exactly how the tribunal must modify the terms of the agreement in order to give effect to the 'no-network' assumption. For example, if one is to assume that the Code *right* does not relate to a network, what is one to assume as to the user clause of the notional agreement and indeed as to the use of the land that the parties would have in mind when negotiating in the hypothetical world?

53 See *Islington* at [95].

54 [2020] UKUT 348 (LC) at [109].

13.74 In *Islington*,[55] the tribunal considered whether terms of the notional agreement, including most obviously the user clause, would have to be modified within the hypothetical exercise. Although it said that it reached no concluded view on that question, the parties had in fact made this assumption in adducing evidence that had regard to alternative use values. The tribunal agreed that this approach was permissible, saying as follows:

> 'we agree with the parties' implicit acknowledgement that the no-network assumption must permit some notional relaxation of contractual terms which would otherwise limit the permitted use to statutory Code purposes only. In principle, therefore, we do not think it is impermissible to have regard to rental values achieved for other uses even where the only permitted use under the imposed agreement is a Code use.'

13.75 The question that arises is: what, if any, use should be assumed in its place? The tribunal's answer to this question in *Islington*[56] was that it would be a question of fact in each case what use may be made of the site on the terms imposed, having regard to the no-network assumption. This approach would be subject to whatever relaxation of those actual terms may be necessary in order to give effect to the no-network assumption, as mentioned above.

13.76 The tribunal summarised the right which it was seeking to value as 'the right to keep installations unconnected to a telecommunications network on the roof of a ten-storey residential building'.[57] Given that the site was on the top of a building, it concluded that values of parking spaces or basement storage were of no real value in determining what would be agreed in the market for the true right.

13.77 It has not yet been conclusively determined how far the concept of 'some notional relaxation' goes. If there were not any 'no-network' assumption, the tribunal would be valuing on the basis of a network-related use, typically by a commercial operator, in a site which it has determined as commercially useful and technically viable and which either benefits from planning permission or presumably is likely to benefit from such permission.

13.78 It might be thought that *with* the 'no-network' assumption, the tribunal would be valuing on the basis of 'the right to keep installations' unconnected to a network, which either benefits from planning permission or presumably is likely to benefit from such permission. For it could be argued that stripping away the network element does not necessarily entail stripping away the planning permission that exists for the activity to which the right relates.

13.79 However, there is no justification for assuming any additional planning permission for any specific use unless the evidence justifies it. There are many activities that would be commercially valuable on many sites if planning permission is to be assumed to exist. But the presumption of reality requires that the real-world chances of acquiring planning permission for various uses are respected. If planning permission

55 [2019] UKUT 53 (LC) at [70].
56 [2019] UKUT 53 (LC) at [70].
57 [2019] UKUT 53 (LC) at [98].

does not exist for a particular use,[58] that in itself does not mean that rents for such a use would not feature in the hypothetical negotiation, but the weight to be given to such rents would surely be diminished. If planning permission exists, or if it can be shown that planning permission would be granted for some alternative use (such as using a roof as a rooftop bar or building another storey on a roof for use as flats or offices), then this fact is relevant to the value that the hypothetical seller would be able to realise in negotiations. If a bar operator or housebuilder would take a lease of the rooftop at a commercial rent, then that is relevant to how much the notional lessee or grantee would be likely to have to pay in the notional world in order to secure the rights, despite the fact that the landlord/grantor is willing.

13.80 In *Audley House*,[59] the tribunal held that it was an 'inevitable consequence of the exercise prescribed by paragraph 24' that the complete prohibition of sub-letting by the site provider for uses other than as a telecommunications site should be ignored for the purposes of determining consideration. Thus, it was considered appropriate to depart from the presumption of reality in order to assess a value for the conferred rights whilst respecting the no-network assumption. However, the tribunal did consider that there would not have been a difficulty in taking account of a real-world use restriction that prevented only some but not all other uses. In the event, as the site could be used for parking in the absence of that prohibition, the valuers agreed a figure for consideration on that basis. It was noted[60] that where the site provider is itself a leaseholder, the user restriction in its lease is relevant to assessing alternative use value. For example, where the only permitted user is agricultural use, a Code valuation could not proceed on the assumption that the site could be let as an industrial unit or for storage or parking.

13.81 The best way to consider the real-life impact of the no-network assumption is to look at how tribunals have approached the task of assessing consideration over the first few years of doing so. Such a potted history is attempted below, from **13.97** onwards. The remaining assumptions mandated by para 24(3) will now be considered.

Disapplication of paras 16 and 17 (para 24(3)(b))

13.82 Paragraph 24(3)(b) requires it to be assumed that paras 16 and 17 do not apply to the Code right or ECA to which the Code right could relate. There has not been a great deal of judicial commentary on this provision. In *Islington*,[61] the tribunal preferred to leave consideration of it for another occasion, and it has not featured heavily in decisions since.

13.83 The background is that the Law Commission[62] recommended a market valuation of consideration under the New Code, but subject to two assumptions. The first of those proposed assumptions was that there is more than one suitable property

58 In *Stephenson* at [68], the Deputy President considered that the lack of planning permission for advertising uses (and a number of other problems) would not mean that likely rents for such a use would not feature in negotiations, but concluded that 'great weight' could not be given to this factor.
59 [2022] UKUT 152 (LC) at [233].
60 At [229].
61 [2019] UKUT 53 (LC) at [69].
62 Law Com 336, para 5.83.

available to the operator. This assumption has found its way into the Code at para 24(3)(d) and sought to remove any ransom element. It is considered below.

13.84 The second proposed assumption was that the operator does not have the entitlements to: (i) upgrade or share apparatus, or (ii) to assign the Code rights. Those two 'entitlements' were expressly said by the Law Commission to be those recommended at their paras 3.24 and 3.51. The para 3.24 proposal was that an operator 'shall be entitled to assign all the benefit of the agreement'. The para 3.51 proposal was that an operator should have a right to upgrade and share ECA if it cannot be seen from outside and imposes no burden on the site provider. It was proposed that any contractual term requiring payment for (or preventing) such upgrading or sharing should be void.

13.85 Accordingly, this second proposed assumption was that the operator did *not* have the rights that were in fact conferred by the Code as regards upgrading, sharing, and assigning. The Law Commission's rationale was that the operator should not have to pay extra for those rights.[63]

13.86 However, the Code as drafted does not expressly require all assignment, sharing, and upgrading rights to be disregarded. It requires it to be assumed that paras 16 and 17 do not apply in the case of the hypothetical agreement.

13.87 For valuation purposes, one can probably ignore the fact that this disapplies the voiding provisions of paras 16(1) and 17(5). The fact that paras 16(1) and 17(5) exist will mean that a tribunal will surely not impose a term under para 23, which would fall foul of those provisions in any event. And it is the actual imposed terms that are being valued. So the fact that the valuation requires one to ignore that those voiding provisions exist is probably of no real effect.

13.88 But para 17 contains further rights. Where nothing is mentioned in the agreement about sharing and upgrading, para 17 would grant limited sharing and upgrading rights in a similar manner to that which was intended by the Law Commission. The disregard at para 24(3)(b) would then require para 17 to be ignored, which would be expected to have the effect that the operator is not paying any additional sum for its sharing or upgrading right, as the Law Commission intended.

13.89 However, if the agreement confers unlimited sharing and upgrading rights that go well beyond those in para 17, or even if rights similar to those in para 17 are expressly set out in the agreement, what is there to stop such rights from being taken into account when consideration is valued? One might say that the no-network assumption requires one to pretend that the rights do not relate to a network and that as sharing and upgrading ECA are network-related concepts, they are similarly to be ignored. However, Parliament has clearly thought it necessary to provide separately in para 24(3)(b) for matters relating to sharing and upgrading . If the no-network assumption required sharing and upgrading to be ignored totally for valuation purposes, why do such matters need to be further addressed by para 24(3)(b)? Further, if the right to gain access to apparatus across the site provider's land attracts a value (albeit one that ignores the fact that the apparatus is used for a network), it could be argued that so too should the right to upgrade it and share it.

63 Law Com 336, paras 3.28 and 3.50.

13.90 If an agreement grants a right for the grantee to share with others, from whom it may extract payment, there is an argument that the valuation does not have to ignore this fact if it does not require considering the substantive (network) use to which the grantee or its sharer will make of the site. If it were not for para 24(3)(b), the obvious answer would be that para 17(5)(b) bans a term which requires payment for sharing. But para 24(3)(b) expressly and intentionally requires the fact that the agreement shall be subject to para 17 be disregarded. If para 17 must be disregarded, does that not require that para 17(5)(b) is to be disregarded?

13.91 Support for this idea might be gained from the fact that the Law Commission considered that although unlimited sharing rights should not be subject to a blanket conferral by the Code, in a given case an operator might obtain such rights from a tribunal and pay extra for them:

> 'So in general, it is not possible for Code Operators to have an automatic right to share or to upgrade equipment. Such rights must be negotiated for, or granted by the tribunal; it may be right for there to be additional consideration payable, depending upon the market itself.'[64]

13.92 Yes, the Law Commission's version of market value was not adopted, but: (i) Parliament did choose a species of market value when it need not have done, and (ii) Parliament chose to require para 17 to be disregarded. It did not select wording requiring all sharing rights or the value of all sharing rights to be disregarded. It has to be said, though, that an argument that consideration is to be increased greatly due to an enlarged right to share is not something that has thus far found favour with the tribunal.

13.93 In *Islington*, the tribunal held that it was incorrect to value a right to install further pieces of ECA by reference to the value of those rights to the operator, as to do that would not respect the 'no-network' assumption. Where an operator derives known income from another operator which is enabled by its rights to share, it seems that the tribunal would conclude that that particular value is contingent on the use of the land for network purposes, as absent such use there would be no possibility of deriving that income.

Plurality of sites (no ransom) (para 24(3)(d))

13.94 Finally, para 24(3)(d) requires the valuer to assume that there is more than one site that the buyer could use. This provision follows the Law Commission's proposal that there should be an assumption of this nature in order to negate any possible ransom that a landowner may otherwise have within the hypothetical transaction.

13.95 In *Islington*, the tribunal described the effect of this provision at [71] as follows:

> 'The effect of the assumption is to neutralise any monopoly of sites which may exist in reality and to eliminate any impact on value attributable to scarcity or undersupply of land suitable for the purpose for which the buyer wishes to take it.'

---

64 Law Com 336 at para 3.42.

13.96 It should be remembered that there is no equivalent requirement for it to be assumed that there is more than one *bidder* in the market (as discussed above).

The development of the tribunal's approach to consideration over time

The two components of the Islington valuation

13.97 The value of some other possible use being made of the relevant land – might be considered to be 'alternative use value'. In *Islington*, it was not demonstrated that there was anything more than a nominal alternative use value, and accordingly, the vast majority of the value in the consideration came from the cost of the burdens on the site provider.

13.98 In having regard to the inconvenience, or burdens, on the site provider, the tribunal agreed that the operator should pay towards the expenses of running the building. Although the parties analysed this issue in terms of compensation, the tribunal concluded that the notional parties would take account of such costs in negotiating consideration. Having considered the service charge payments made annually by flat owners within the building (which averaged some £1,300) the tribunal assessed the overall consideration at £1,000 per annum, of which only a nominal £50 was referable to 'the rights themselves' as distinct from the value of the burdens of running the building placed on the site provider.

13.99 Thus, as early as *Islington*, we can see: (i) alternative use value, and (ii) burdens on the site provider, emerging as two possible elements of the overall valuation.

13.100 *Islington* was the very first Code valuation by a tribunal. Although the likely impact of the assumption at para 24(3)(a) was predictable in broad terms, it was not until *Islington* that that assumption even had its now familiar name (the 'no network' assumption). The judgment in that case was eagerly anticipated by professionals who were interested in the way in which Code valuations should work; the hearing room in the Royal Courts of Justice was so full of such interested persons that some had to be turned away. It is fair to say that nobody at that time quite knew the answers to all of the questions that the new statutory scheme posed.

13.101 Today one has the benefit of a number of further decisions that have since been handed down in a variety of circumstances and with the benefit of different evidence bases. That being the case, it would perhaps not be surprising if the consideration figure in *Islington* were to be assessed in a different sum today.[65] But the careful description in *Islington* as to the principles embodied by the statutory wording and of what para 24 requires of a tribunal, remain instructive and important, especially in the absence of any valuation case yet having made it to the Court of Appeal.

---

65 In *Cornerstone Telecommunications Infrastructure Ltd v London & Quadrant Housing Trust* [2020] UKUT 282 (LC) at [91]–[92] the Tribunal referred to the valuation evidence in *Islington* as 'rudimentary', and commented that it was 'in a stronger position to provide guidance on appropriate levels of consideration for sites of this type than was the Tribunal in *Islington*'.

Beyond *Islington*: the staged approach

13.102 Following the decision in *Islington*, a different approach began to emerge as to the valuation of consideration in Code agreements. This was a staged approach that has ultimately come to be known as the 'three-stage' approach. However, this approach began life as a submission in *Hanover*,[66] a 1954 Act case in the county court as to factors that were said to influence parties who negotiated for a new letting under the Code.

13.103 The *Hanover* case involved a renewal of a 1954 Act lease that granted rights to keep ECA installed. As such, the resulting tenancy could not be a tenancy to which the 1954 Act would apply.[67] Rather, it would be a Code agreement.

13.104 However, the rent was to be determined under the 1954 Act, and hence the 'no-network' assumption was not directly applicable. As discussed in cases such as *Ashloch*,[68] this is conventionally considered to be an advantage to a landowner under the 1954 Act regime when compared with the Code. Given that the difference in valuation mechanism under the 1954 Act and under the Code has been commented upon in the Upper Tribunal, Court of Appeal and Supreme Court,[69] it is perhaps surprising that decisions in the county court have been so influenced by submissions as to Code valuations, and then in turn how valuations under the Code have been influenced by suggestions made in a county court matter.

13.105 The parties in *Hanover* agreed that any negotiation as to rent on a new site would be influenced by the consideration that would be imposed within a Reference under para 20 of the Code. Counsel for the operator in *Hanover* suggested what the judge described as 'a helpful framework which sought to replicate the factors which would influence the hypothetical parties negotiating a rent for a new letting under the Code', which involved consideration of six topics.

13.106 In summary, those six topics were as follows:[70]

1. *Alternative use value*: this would be equal to the rental value of the holding for the most valuable non-operator use and would be a matter of evidence on the facts.
2. *Additional benefits*: if any additional benefits were to be conferred on the tenant, an allowance would have to be made to reflect it. The example was given of an operator being prepared to pay £1,000 in one case for the benefit of a manned security gate.
3. *Adverse effects on lessor*: if the letting would have a greater adverse effect on the willing lessor than the alternative use on which the alternative use value was based, this should be reflected by an adjustment.

66 *Vodafone Ltd v Hanover Capital Ltd* [2020] EW Misc 18 (CC).

67 By s 43(4) of the 1954 Act, because its primary purpose was to grant Code rights, and it was granted after the Code came into force.

68 See [96] of the Upper Tribunal's decision ([2019] UKUT 338 (LC)), as cited by the Court of Appeal at [101] of its judgment ([2021] EWCA Civ 90), and by the Supreme Court at [166] of its judgment (and approved at [167] of the same judgment) ([2022] UKSC 18).

69 In *Ashloch* – ibid.

70 See [89] of the judgment ([2020] EW Misc 18 (CC)).

4. *Fees payable for negotiating the rent*: the evidence demonstrated that operators routinely make a contribution to such fees on new Code lettings and renewals.
5. *Legal fees for conveyancing*: again, the evidence showed that operators usually make a contribution towards these.
6. *Inducement*: the hypothetical tenant may pay an additional amount by way of an inducement to secure the letting.

13.107 The operator went on to submit that on the facts there were no relevant 'additional benefits' or 'adverse effects', such that nothing should be added to the alternative use value under stages 2 or 3 above. The court agreed.

13.108 It was further submitted that the lessor should not get anything in respect of fees under stages 4 or 5 because the lessor was assumed to be willing. The court rejected this on the basis that where a new Code agreement is imposed by a tribunal a site provider is awarded its reasonable legal and valuation expenses as a matter of course as compensation. As no separate fees are to be paid by way of compensation under the 1954 Act, the parties would include a sum[71] to compensate for those fees within the rent.

13.109 The operator further argued that because the hypothetical transaction involved a willing seller, the seller would require no inducement in order to contract. The court accepted this proposition. Thus, where any comparables contained an element of inducement, the value attributable to that inducement needed to be stripped out in order to respect the 'willing seller' principle.[72]

13.110 In *Hanover*, the judge considered that if the only factors to be taken into account were those identified in the submissions and evidence of the operator, the parties would likely agree on some £2,160[73] which they would round up to £2,200 or £2,250. The figure awarded, however, was £5,750 to take into account both competition and the lack of a rent review clause. Further detail is given below when considering *Hanover* in the 1954 Act context.

13.111 In *London & Quadrant*, the tribunal described the evidence in *Islington* as 'rudimentary', noting that the evidence and analysis presented in *Hanover* was more detailed, 'and for the first time it included evidence of the behaviour of professionally advised parties negotiating in the real market for telecommunications sites, and of the value they attribute to the obligations assumed by the site provider and the benefits received by the operator'.[74] The tribunal therefore considered that it was in a 'stronger position to provide guidance on appropriate levels of consideration' than had been the case in *Islington*.

71 The court considered that £4,000 by way of fees was reasonable, and then annualised that capital figure to £445 per annum.

72 Query, in the 1954 Act context, the extent to which this conclusion is affected by the detailed consideration of the same issue in *Morriss*.

73 This was based on an existing use value of £1,715 (based on the value for a car parking use), plus the £445 representing an annualised sum for professional fees.

74 *London & Quadrant* [2020] UKUT 282 (LC) at [92].

13.112 The tribunal in *London & Quadrant* addressed the six stages proposed in *Hanover*, concluding that:

> 'We consider the first three stages of this framework are likely to be necessary components of most valuations by the tribunal under paragraph 24. There may be cases in which the first stage provides a complete answer, because the site has some substantial alternative use value, but even then the exercise of working through each stage is likely to be a useful check.'[75]

13.113 As to the first stage of this process the tribunal said as follows:

> 'Any assessment of the market value of the site provider's agreement to confer and to be bound by Code rights, as required by paragraph 24(1), must begin with the value to the site provider of the land over which the rights will be exercised and which will no longer be available for its current use. But there may be a more valuable alternative use. The no-network assumption dictates that the value of the site as part of an operator's network is to be disregarded, but not its value to any other prospective tenant in the market; if the evidence shows that the site could realistically be turned to some alternative use, its value for that use must also be taken into account. Consideration of the current or alternative (non-network) use value is therefore the first stage of the assessment.'[76]

13.114 In relation to the second stage, it was observed that the hypothetical landlord would assume obligations such as insurance and maintenance. The benefit to the tenant of those obligations would be a factor in the negotiations, unless they were taken into account by a different term of the agreement, such as a service charge mechanism. 'Consideration of the value to the tenant of those benefits is therefore the second stage of the assessment.'[77]

13.115 As to the third stage, it was held that an assessment of any additional adverse effect the Code agreement may have on the site provider, when compared with the use assumed at the first stage, should form the third and final step in the determination under para 24. The tribunal acknowledged that there was no hard dividing line between consideration and compensation, and a reflection of the adverse effect on the site provider could be achieved either by an additional sum by way of consideration, an award of compensation payable at the time of the agreement, or the acknowledgement of a prospect of compensation in the future.

13.116 As a site provider under a Code agreement imposed by the tribunal has a right to compensation for reasonable legal and valuation expenses under paras 25(1) and 84(2)(a), stages four and five of the *Hanover* framework, which deal with the same matters, have no part to play in the tribunal's assessment of consideration under paragraph 24.[78]

13.117 The tribunal held that in a determination of consideration under the Code 'no addition to reflect an inducement is permissible, so the sixth *Hanover* step is never reached'. It was said that when considering comparables, it may be necessary to eliminate any element of an agreed rent that is attributable to inducements to enable

75 At [94].
76 At [95].
77 At [96].
78 *London & Quadrant* at [104].

a proper comparison to be made with the para 24 hypothesis. However, it might be instructive to consider that point in the light of what was said in the county court in *Morriss.*[79]

13.1198 In *Morriss*, which was heard more than a year after both *Hanover* and *London & Quadrant*,[80] the judge said as follows:

> '108. On the evidence before me, capital payments are an established feature of the market, available irrespective of the level of enthusiasm of the particular site provider or the significance of the particular site. They cannot be dismissed as payments for willingness but represent instead a core component of the financial package which willing landlords and tenants agree for the lettings of new sites.
>
> 109. There is a further point. Even if in practice substantial capital payments are paid because site providers are unwilling to transact at a true open market level (which I do not believe to be the case), they nevertheless reflect the real world in which our notional transaction is assumed to take place. Our site provider is willing and does not need to be induced, but his approach is not un-commercial, let alone charitable. There is no reason why, knowing that operators are prepared to make capital payments to secure sites, he would be willing to accept any less than other site providers are known to be receiving. As Mr Sladdin put it, 'as soon as people know about it everyone else will want it'.'

13.119 Although *Morriss* was a 1954 Act case, the above evidence relates to the practice in the real-world market under the Code. If these capital payments are typically not 'payments for willingness' but represent instead a 'core component' of the financial package received by a landowner, it is hard to see why any deduction should be made for them if (and it is a fairly big 'if') one is considering comparable transactions.

13.120 In *Green*,[81] the tribunal observed that the first three stages of the *Hanover* framework had been adopted in *London & Quadrant*, and the use of those stages was agreed by the parties. *Green* was a renewal under Part 5 of the Code, but para 34(11) of the Code applies para 24 to the types of renewal cases referred to in that sub-paragraph. Once the terms had been decided upon in *Green*, the process for assessing the consideration under para 24 was the same[82] as if it had been a para 20 application for fresh Code rights.

13.121 The tribunal explained stages 2 and 3 in *Affinity Water* at [39] in the following terms:

> 'The heart of the dispute lay in stages 2 and 3 of the assessment which are intended to reflect the additional benefits over and above the right of occupation, which will be conferred on the tenant by the agreement and which it would otherwise

79 [2022] EW Misc 1 (CC).

80 *Hanover* was heard in August 2020, *London & Quadrant* the following month, and *Morriss* in late 2021. The Deputy President sat as a judge in each of these cases, in different capacities.

81 In the Upper Tribunal ([2020] UKUT 348 (LC) at [80]). The appeal to the Court of Appeal did not concern consideration.

82 Certain assumptions may be different in respect of a renewal, but these are simply reflections of the real-world differences on the facts. See the discussion below, at **13.190** onwards in relation to the differences in application of para 24 on a renewal.

have to provide for itself, and any adverse effect on the site provider, over and above any effects which would be a consequence of the use of the site for the purpose reflected at stage one. The theory underlying these stages is that they reflect all of the matters which would be in the minds of parties negotiating a rent which did not take account of the economic value to the tenant of the activity it intended to conduct on the site. They attempt to measure what paragraph 24(1) of the Code calls 'the market value of the relevant person's agreement to confer … the Code right' while respecting the statutory no-network assumption in paragraph 24(3)(a).'

13.122 In the *Audley House*[83] case, the tribunal confirmed that even in a case where the alternative use value is high, assessments under stages 2 and 3 are appropriate, and should be considered cumulatively:

> 'There was some discussion at the hearing, in answer to a question posed by the tribunal, as to whether the assessment of benefits and burdens in stages 2 and 3 is appropriate where the site has a valuable alternative use, and we confirm – as is clear from the words just quoted – that the three stages are indeed cumulative and should all be undertaken even where (as is the case for Audley House, as we shall see) the value of the alternative use is considerably higher than that seen in other decisions where the *Hanover* approach has been used. The idea is that the site provider gets the current or higher alternative use value and also a sum to reflect the benefits to the tenant (over and above those conferred by the existing or alternative use) and the burdens undertaken by the landlord (beyond those involved in the existing or alternative use) as a result of the activity envisaged under the lease, such as the installation of a very tall structure and the likelihood of frequent visits, insofar as those benefits and burdens would not be caused by the alternative use.'

Affinity Water and its table

13.123 When the question of consideration came before the tribunal in *Affinity Water*[84] in November 2021, it was in the following context:

- There had by this point been a number of decisions on consideration, both by tribunals in the pure Code context, and by courts in respect of rent imposed under the 1954 Act in agreements which were to be Code agreements. These decisions had not been subject to any intervention on appeal.
- Experts had given evidence that had not always been found helpful by the tribunal, sometimes because of its length, sometimes because of its methodology, and sometimes both.
- The tribunal had shown scepticism as to the helpfulness of the use of comparables in cases involving the assessment of consideration under para 24.
- It had become obvious that at the likely levels of consideration in any mainstream case, the costs of litigation would be disproportionate to the sums involved.

83 *On Tower UK Ltd v AP Wireless (UK) Ltd (Audley House)* [2022] UKUT 152 (LC) at [222].
84 [2022] UKUT 8 (LC).

- The UT was soon to be sending more and more cases to the FTT, culminating in 2024 in the removal of the requirement that References be commenced in the UT, and the concomitant expectation that References would be commenced, and almost always dealt with, in the FTT at first instance.

13.124 Against this backdrop, the UT summarised 'the position which has been reached in other cases', which might serve as guidance as to the approximate levels at which Code consideration might be expected to be set, by reference to different types of properties. This has become known as the '*Affinity Water* table', and was set out at [31] of the tribunal's decision as follows:

Decision	Type of property	Annual consideration
CTIL v Fothringham (Lands Tribunal for Scotland)	Rural, estate location	£600 (£1,500 in year of installation)
On Tower v Green	Rural, adjacent to housing	£1,200
Marks & Spencer	City, department store/offices	£3,850
London & Quadrant	City, residential rooftop	£5,000

13.125 Much to the disappointment on the part of some commentators who come to questions under the Code from a landowner perspective, the '*Affinity Water* table' has been accorded a special place in discourse about valuations under the Code. What is it? It is a list of decisions arrived at in four prior cases. The decisions in those cases were necessarily guided by the evidence available and the arguments made in those cases. Further, valuation methodologies had been deployed in those cases that differed from each other and, in the case of some, utilised what was called in *Affinity Water* itself 'the rather cumbersome and artificial three-stage approach'.

13.126 Finally, in categorising the relevant property in each of the four cases (as 'Rural, estate location', 'City, residential rooftop' etc), the impression has been given (or at least taken) that each of the four cases is an 'ideal type' of valuation, or a model answer, in respect of each of the four types of property.

13.127 In *Affinity Water* itself, the table was not accorded any special or magical status and certainly was not said to constitute a table that would give the correct answer to any particular case or even necessarily provide a mandated starting point in assessing such an answer.

13.128 So what was the intention of the table? The tribunal tells us at [34] of the decision:

> 'These decisions provide guidance not only on an approach to valuing sites on the artificial assumptions required by paragraph 24, but more broadly on the levels of consideration which parties can expect the Tribunal to determine in other cases. Without taking account of any special features or particular sensitivities which a particular location may exhibit, we would be surprised if the value of Code rights fell significantly outside the ranges indicated by previous decisions concerning sites with similar characteristics.'

13.129 Critics of too close an adherence to the *Affinity Water* table would point out that a para 24 valuation is expressly aimed at ascertaining a market value. It is a market value with certain mandated disregards (and the no-network assumption might be described as the mother of all disregards), but a market value nonetheless. A market value is quite impossible to ascertain without taking into account 'any special features or particular sensitivities which a particular location may exhibit', to use the words at [34] in *Affinity Water.*

13.130 In *Affinity Water* itself, the tribunal aggregated figures from the stages of a 'three-stage' approach, and then added an uplift of around 10% to yield a total rent of £3,300 per annum. It considered that it then needed to:

> 'stand back and consider whether this make sense in the light of other evidence, and in particular whether it is consistent with the pattern of value which is emerging from the other Tribunal decisions which we have tabulated…'.

13.131 Doing so, it commented that the consideration likely to be agreed for a water tower under the statutory hypothesis should fall somewhere between that of a greenfield site and an office or commercial building. It thought that it would be closer to the upper end of that range than the lower, for two reasons:

(i) the tenant is being provided with a ready-made structure on which to install its apparatus (for whatever purpose it wishes to use it); and

(ii) the site provider has greater involvement in providing access and maintaining the site.

13.132 It would seem from the above reasoning that it is permissible for the tribunal to consider the operator's need or preference for a structure on which to position its apparatus and to accord value where such a structure is present. This accords with the presumption of reality.

13.133 Despite undertaking the three-stage approach in *Affinity Water* itself, the tribunal said that:

> 'We would suggest that the pattern, or tone, is now becoming clear enough that it should rarely be necessary when presenting evidence to the Tribunal in future for parties to adopt the much more detailed *Hanover Capital* approach to valuation.'

13.134 Given that stages 4 to 6 of the *Hanover* approach had already been analysed in *London & Quadrant* to be inapplicable to a valuation under the Code, it appears that the above conclusion from the tribunal in *Affinity Water* constitutes a reference to the three-stage test that had been utilised in *Affinity Water* itself.

Post-*Affinity Water*

The initial primacy of the figures in the table

13.135 In *Audley House*,[85] the tribunal re-published the *Affinity Water* table, adding to it the £3,300 water tower figure from *Affinity Water* itself. The valuers in *Audley House* had both produced their initial reports before the *Affinity Water* decision was published and had 'relied upon the type of material – extensive analysis of comparables and

85 [2022] UKUT 152 (LC).

exhaustive costings of benefits and burdens – that the tribunal has now explained are unnecessary and unhelpful.'[86] The valuers were thousands of pounds apart. The *Audley House* judgment discloses that the valuers were 'reminded of the tribunal's comments in *Affinity Water*'. Following that doubtless robust reminder, the valuers agreed the consideration in the case.

13.136 It is clear that alternative use value of the subject land remains relevant, and this is not displaced by the *Affinity Water* table. As the tribunal stated in *Audley House*:[87]

> 'Whether high or low, alternative use value is always going to be relevant. This is the use for which the site provider could let the site.'

13.137 In *Stephenson*, the tribunal noted that the valuers had utilised a *Hanover*-style staged approach, taking the decision in *Green* (as it was also a rural mast site) as a reference point. It was noted that in *Green*, the tribunal suggested that in the absence of special features, a rural site that was not close to housing might yield an annual para 24 consideration figure of £750. The Deputy President saw no reason to depart from that figure as the letting value of 'an unexceptional rural site remote from any housing' and imposed that figure accordingly. There was no analysis or adjustment in respect of the fact that nearly two years had elapsed since the tribunal had given its opinion in respect of the £750 figure in *Green*.

Vache Farm: a reconsideration of consideration

13.138 The journey from the 'entirely conventional shape' of the exercise described in *Islington*, through the invention of the three-stage approach, to finding that approach 'cumbersome and artificial',[88] and finally to the application of something that arguably resembles a rate card, had appeared complete. It appeared that for those who disliked the *Affinity Water* table, the only hope of any substantial departure from it was to seek to persuade the Court of Appeal.

13.139 However, in the recent *Vache Farm* case, the tribunal agreed to revisit the approach that had previously been taken in the case of rural sites. The result was a more than doubling of the £750 figure, which had found favour in *Green* and then in *Stephenson* in respect of what the latter case called 'an unexceptional rural site remote from any housing'. This reassessment was the result of a careful consideration of non-telecoms comparables by the tribunal. It surely illustrates the danger in making assumptions about the utility of comparables and also that no individual decision on consideration is safer or more reliable than the evidence on which it is based. The role of comparables will now be considered, culminating in a look at the *Vache Farm* case itself.

The role of comparables in para 24 valuations

13.140 In *Stephenson*, the Deputy President complained that unnecessary time and expense had been incurred in that Reference 'in attempting to value the Site by reference to real-world telecommunications transactions'. He noted that:

86 [2022] UKUT 152 (LC) at [227].
87 [2022] UKUT 152 (LC) at [229].
88 *Affinity Water* at [35].

'The Tribunal has on at least three previous occasions commented on the difficulties which the no-network assumption creates for a valuer wishing to make use of the comparative method.'

13.141 The first of those three occasions was in *Compton Beauchamp*.[89] The Upper Tribunal at [114] had suggested that market evidence of rents agreed for the grant of Code rights might be of value if it could be shown that the parties had had regard to the statutory assumptions when negotiating those rents, or if a coherent basis for adjustment could be suggested in order to ensure that the value referable to the network use was excluded.

13.142 Second in *London & Quadrant*,[90] the Upper Tribunal adopted the three-stage approach (derived from *Hanover*) and did not value by the comparable method, although it did refer to certain comparable transactions that had been provided in evidence.

13.143 Third, in *Affinity Water*,[91] the tribunal explained at [35] why there are dangers in the use of comparable transactions in determining consideration:

> 'The adoption by the Tribunal of the rather cumbersome and artificial three-stage approach to valuation under paragraph 24 of the Code, rather than the more familiar comparative method based on market evidence, is driven by the requirement to make the 'no-network' assumption. It would be attractive to be able to by-pass the artificiality of this approach and to refer directly to market transactions, but there are obvious dangers in doing so. Lettings on Code terms in which the rights being conferred on the tenant do not relate to the provision or use of an electronic communications network are unknown in reality. Consensual Code agreements are invariably entered into so that a site can be used in connection with an operator's network; there are routinely accompanied by capital payments which are often concealed from view, protected by confidentiality agreements and, when they are disclosed, are difficult to analyse; they do not carry statutory compensation rights and rarely include a comprehensive contractual alternative. It therefore remains to be seen whether credible adjustments are possible to account for the many differences between consensual and imposed transactions to enable the total sums agreed as rents to be used as direct comparables when the Tribunal determines consideration under paragraph 24. Where a three-stage assessment has been undertaken and both parties have attributed a specific value to a particular type of burden or benefit, their agreement on that component may nevertheless provide a useful reference point.'

13.144 Having referred to these three cases in *Stephenson*, the Deputy President endorsed what had been said in *Affinity Water*, saying as follows:

> 'Evidence of real-world transactions for telecommunications sites is not promising material on which to base a valuation under paragraph 24. The real market is not the same as, or even similar to, the hypothetical open market which paragraph 24 requires us to assume. The unwillingness of site providers to enter into transactions is an important feature of the real world but is not a feature of the market which

89 [2019] UKUT 107 (LC).
90 [2020] UKUT 282 (LC).
91 [2022] UKUT 8 (LC).

paragraph 24 assumes. The commercial purpose which underlies real-world transactions is specifically to be ignored in identifying the factors which will influence the hypothetical transaction.'

13.145 He referred back to the possibility floated in *London & Quadrant* of using Code comparables with adjustments, but indicated that experience had indicated that this was not justifiable:

> 'But as the Tribunal sees more and more of these valuations, it is increasingly apparent that reliance on evidence of negotiated Code transactions cannot be justified.' (at [59])

13.146 The difficulty of stripping out network value was the intractable problem. The staged approach represented a possible means of solving this issue:

> 'The *Hanover Capital* structured approach addresses that problem by placing very little reliance on real-world transactions (the only exception so far allowed has been where parties to a comparable letting attributed a specific value to the security arrangements at a site).' (at [59])

13.147 The Upper Tribunal's position as regards the use of telecoms comparables can best be seen in the Deputy President's clear instruction at [61] that such comparables should not be used and that the only place for comparables in Code valuations is now in respect of assessing alternative use value:

> 'In future, therefore, parties should avoid the expense of preparing evidence of real-world telecommunications transactions and analysis on the comparative method where the relevant assessment is being undertaken under paragraph 24 of the Code. Where it is said that a particular site has an alternative use value which is more than nominal then a comparable assessment based on transactions for that alternative use will of course be valuable. Thus, for example, where a Code agreement is sought in respect of land which is currently used as a commercial carpark, comparative evidence about the value of parking spaces will be highly relevant but evidence of what other parties have agreed for sites with no alternative use value for lettings on Code terms are of no assistance.'

13.148 It must be remembered that alternative use value is an intrinsic part of the valuation of consideration under the Code. Whilst the 'no network assumption' requires the value attributable to an electronic communications network to be stripped out, there is no similar assumption or disregard in respect of any other alternative use of the land. It is logical that the hypothetical landowner, entering into negotiations as to consideration, will have in mind what value the land has to other prospective users.

13.149 The concept of 'market value' plainly requires the value of the land in the marketplace to be taken into account in respect of any possible uses that are sufficiently plausible and sufficiently valuable to have a bearing on the price and which are not required to be disregarded by the statutory rubric.

13.150 Once it is established that alternative use value is relevant, one then must assess what such value might be. The conventional method of the valuation of rights in land proceeds by reference to comparables, and adjustments thereto. Although the use of *telecoms* comparables has been disparaged by the tribunal for falling foul of the 'no network assumption', there is nothing in the statutory scheme that casts doubt on the appropriateness of the use of the conventional valuation method in respect of existing or alternative use value.

Reassessment under Vache Farm

13.151 In the recent case of *Vache Farm*, the Upper Tribunal were invited to revisit the question of rents for rural sites, resulting in a very substantial departure from the previous position.

13.152 The tribunal explained that the no-network assumption has given rise to difficulties because the parties had been unable to produce much relevant evidence and that consequently the tribunal has had to do its best with a more theoretical valuation model.

13.153 The tribunal then went on to explain the history of how consideration had been determined. It referred to the £750 figure for an unexceptional remote rural site in *Green*, the adoption of that figure in *Stephenson*, and the exhortation of the tribunal in *Affinity Water* that the staged approach to evidence should no longer be necessary in light of the 'tone' of para 24 consideration becoming clear.

13.154 The effect of this history has been that operators have adopted £750 as their 'invariable offer' for rural sites.[92] The tribunal noted that predictability in negotiations was no bad thing, provided that the tribunal's mind was not closed if evidence of a higher figure were to be presented.

13.155 It was common ground that the site had no alternative use value. It will be remembered that the tribunal in *Stephenson* appeared to discourage the use of comparables for purposes other than to ascertain alternative use value. Nonetheless, the site provider asserted that the rural figure in the *Affinity Water* table was not correct and that the hypothetical landlord would not agree to the kinds of figures awarded by the tribunal. It sought to demonstrate this by reference to the orthodox valuation method: by referring to comparables.

13.156 The operator's expert contended for a rent of £1,000, being the £750 figure from *Green*, increased by reference to RPI, and then rounded up.[93] The site provider's expert argued for a value of £2,850 by using a base rent of £1,500, 'derived from the tone of rents agreed for a variety of non-telecommunication lettings of small compounds in rural locations',[94] and applying a £1,350 uplift to take account of burdens arising from this lease.

13.157 He had yet to encounter, since 2018, any letting of a small compound for non-telecoms use for less than £1,000, and therefore suggested that this figure be a minimum value in stage 1 of any staged approach before assessing benefits and burdens.

92 *Vache Farm* at [40].

93 From £977 to £1,000.

94 *Vache Farm* at [45].

13.158 Aside from this general observation of the tone of lettings for non-telecoms purposes, a number of specific non-telecoms comparables were referred to. These included sites such as an airport noise monitoring compound, small Network Rail sites, a meteorological station, and a drilling borehole compound. The expert accepted that a discount would have to be made in respect of these to account for any special value derived from the particular industries to which they related.

13.159 The burdens which the expert asserted would arise from the lease in this case, which were not all present in relation to all of the comparables relating to 'passive' uses, were as follows:

(i) security of tenure and the difficulty of obtaining vacant possession;

(ii) regular access for maintenance;

(iii) rights over adjacent land (eg installation of cables, temporary set down areas, tree lopping); and

(iv) loss of control and management.

13.160 The tribunal acknowledged that in reality, the adverse consequences of letting a small parcel of land for a modest return will often be sufficient to dissuade a landowner from letting at all. It referred to a letter of 5 October 2018 from CAAV[95] to the relevant government department:[96]

> '...If asked, many landowners would prefer to have no third parties on their land at all; it inevitably disrupts their own use and quiet enjoyment of the property for their own purposes, whether that is business, recreation or residential use. If a third party is to be given access, the terms agreed need to be sufficient to make it worth the hassle of dealing with them.'

13.161 The submission was made on behalf of the site provider that landlords would bid against each other until the rent reached a point below which no landlord would consider it worthwhile letting. Despite a site having only nominal alternative use value, a minimum acceptable rent is still required to overcome the landlord's reluctance to take on the burdens of a letting, it was submitted. This was a similar submission to that which had been made in *Islington*, in which the tribunal had rejected it as not consistent with the valuation assumption of a willing party. In *Vache Farm*, however, this idea faired rather better. The tribunal concluded:

> 'Paragraph 24 requires that the landlord must be assumed to be willing, but that does not mean that they will be immune to the practical concerns which cause others to be unwilling, and their willingness is to let the land at its market value. In negotiating to arrive at that market value both parties would be aware of the lettings of other small rural sites for a whole range of different uses and, we consider, would take them into account.'[97]

13.162 The tribunal noted that in *Stephenson*, it was said that such other lettings would not be given 'great weight', but in fairness, in *Stephenson*, the comparable relied on was an advertising hoarding. There is clearly no blanket dismissal of comparables

95 The Central Association of Agricultural Valuers.

96 Department for Digital, Culture, Media & Sport.

97 *Vache Farm* at [77].

from a range of uses where they usefully indicate a 'tone' of what landowners will accept in return for the burdens caused to them by an agreement.

13.163 Evidently the tribunal in *Vache Farm* was content to give such comparables sufficient weight to discredit what had been thought to be the previous orthodox figure. It did note, however, that:

> 'In making the no-network assumption care must be taken not to fill the gap which has been left in the assumed purpose of the hypothetical transaction by assuming an alternative use which has no basis in reality. There is no justification for having regard to the economic value capable of being created by some alternative use of the Site unless that use is one for which the Site could in fact be used.'[98]

13.164 The tribunal considered that the challenge in using non-telecoms comparables (relating to uses to which the subject site could not be put), is to strip out the financial benefit accruing to the tenant from such a use. However, if that could be done successfully, what is left is likely to provide a better measure for a para 24 valuation than a figure comprised of aggregated benefits and burdens in the abstract.

13.165 It was considered credible that at the lower end of the non-telecoms transactions, the agreed rents were getting close to a level at which no letting would take place. The tribunal accepted the four burdens listed above, as more onerous burdens than on a site with a relatively 'passive' use.

13.166 This was an important point for landowners. One of the principal reasons why landowners in the real world are not attracted to operators on their land or building is that the statutory regime giving security of tenure is a substantial inconvenience when it comes to securing vacant possession.

13.167 The tribunal concluded that the *Green/Stephenson* figure of £750 should not stand, concluding:

> 'We are persuaded that the Tribunal's earlier figure of £750 was too low and should be reconsidered, not only because of inflation but in the light of the evidence of non-telecommunications transactions for unexceptional rural sites.'

13.168 Having adjusted the non-telecoms comparables downwards to strip out the tenants' financial benefit from the various uses and having then added value to take into account the four extra categories of burden mentioned above, the tribunal settled on a figure of £1,750 as 'the appropriate annual consideration for a rural mast site[99]'.

13.169 The FTT has recently followed the *Vache Farm* decision in the case of *Ewefields Farm*,[100] in adopting consideration of £1,750pa as its starting point for an 'unexceptional rural site'. Sitting as a three-person panel including two valuer members, the FTT assessed consideration at that level for 10 of 14 sites being dealt with together. The other four sites were not wholly unexceptional rural sites, and

98 *Vache Farm* at [78].

99 It should be noted that insofar as this conclusion was intended to be of broader application than merely the subject site, it was a re-rating of the £750 figure in *Green*, rather than a re-rating of the £1,250 figure in *Green* in respect of a site nearer to residential properties.

100 *On Tower UK Limited v AP Wireless II (UK) Limited and others* LC – 2023 – 000321 and 13 others (*Ewefields Farm*).

values of £2,000pa and £2,500pa were assessed. This was because of their proximity to other land uses, and hence there was considered to be a sufficient prospect of alternative use being possible at the subject sites in the future to justify a degree of hope value.[101] Of the two sites valued at £2,500pa, one of these was considered to be a 'remote rural site', and the other a 'semi rural site adjoining commercial uses'. None of the sites was considered to be an 'urban fringe' location.

13.170 Thus, whilst in *Green* and *Stephenson*, we saw rural sites ranging in value from a floor of £750 up to £1,200, we have already seen rural sites post-*Vache Farm* ranging in value from a floor of £1,750 up to £2,500.

Where next for the Affinity Water table?

13.171 If the £750 figure in *Green* was 'too low', such that an unremarkable remote rural site is now worth £1,750, it surely follows that the £1,250 figure awarded in *Green* for a rural site near houses, is also 'too low', the consideration in *Fothringham* likewise, and so too the sum imposed in *Stephenson* in reliance on *Green*. Thus, half of the figures in the original *Affinity Water* table are unreliable.

13.172 The tribunal in *Vache Farm* declined to update the table, not considering it 'necessary'.[102] This surely cannot be because the rural figures in the table were considered now more reliable than the figure in *Vache Farm* itself. Whether or not that decision was intended as a rowing back from the primacy of the table or not, there is surely scope for parties with sufficient evidence to question the near 'rent card' approach, which has been encouraged by reference to the table.

13.173 In *Ewefields Farm*,[103] the FTT referred to the 'apogee' of the table as having been reached in *Audley House*. This may be a sign that the degree of adherence to it in the future may not be what was once envisaged.

13.174 In any event, as a minimum, the effect of inflation must be contemplated. In *Vache Farm*, the tribunal said that because of evidence that operators adopt the *Affinity Water* guideline figures in negotiations, 'we assume that we need to spell out here the relevance of inflation to those operating in the market'.[104] Given that no inflationary uplift was applied by the tribunal itself in *Stephenson*, when awarding the £750 figure that was a relic of *Green*, it does seem welcome that the tribunal has now spelt this out.

Impact of Vache Farm on urban cases

13.175 Clearly nothing was said in *Vache Farm* in relation to the substance of valuing urban sites. However, there have not been a large number of trials involving the valuation of urban sites, the figures have varied materially between these cases, and *Vache Farm* shows the danger of applying figures from a small number of cases, rather

101 Defined in the Glossary of the RICS Professional Standard 1st edn. 2019 as 'An element of market value in excess of the existing use value, reflecting the prospect of some more valuable use.'

102 *Vache Farm* at [85].

103 *On Tower UK Limited v AP Wireless II (UK) Limited and others* LC – 2023 – 000321 and 13 others (*Ewefields Farm*).

104 *Vache Farm* at [69].

than having regard to expert evidence in a given case before the tribunal. There is no reason why a party should be prevented from adducing relevant expert evidence in an urban case, if it considers that the *Affinity Water* table has been holed below the water line.

13.176 One point that was acknowledged in *Vache Farm* that has not been given a lot of 'air time' in urban cases thus far is the impact of operators' security of tenure on landowners, especially in relation to obtaining vacant possession for redevelopment. Now that it is confirmed that this is a factor that is relevant to consideration, one might expect urban landowners to argue that this should inflate rents in urban settings, where, after all, development occurs more frequently. The relationship between any such uplift in consideration, and the potential for compensation for lost development at a later date may prove a difficult one to negotiate.

Interim consideration: para 35

13.177 Just as the 1954 Act allows an application for the determination of interim rent under business tenancies,[105] the Code makes provision for an interim consideration to be determined.

13.178 Paragraph 35 applies where an agreement is continuing under para 30, and one of the parties has made an application under 32(1)(b) or 33(5) for one of the para 34 modification/renewal orders.

13.179 The parties are free to agree either that, until the application is determined, the old consideration shall continue to be payable or that some other amount shall be payable.[106] However, either party may apply to the tribunal for an Order specifying the consideration that is payable until the application is finally determined.[107] Such consideration must be assessed on the basis set out in para 24. As the new consideration is likely to be lower than the old, it will most frequently be an operator that makes such an application.

13.180 The tribunal may decide that such an Order in respect of such interim consideration has effect from the date of the application for it.[108] This is considered to be a discretionary power.[109]

13.181 Similarly, either party may apply for 'an order otherwise modifying the terms of' the existing agreement until the renewal application is finally determined.[110] In deciding whether to make an Order of this kind, the tribunal must have regard to all the circumstances of the case, and in particular to those factors set out at para 35(4).

13.182 In *Ewefields Farm*[111] it was submitted that the power to backdate interim consideration to the date of the application did not allow the tribunal to disturb

105 At s 24A thereof.
106 Para 35(2)(a) and (b).
107 Para 35(2A)(a).
108 Para 35(2B).
109 See, for example, the FTT's clear statement to this effect in *Ewefields Farm* at [188].
110 Para 35(2A)(b).
111 *On Tower UK Limited v AP Wireless II (UK) Limited and others* LC – 2023 – 000321 and 13 others (*Ewefields Farm*).

rent payable in advance, which fell due before the application, even where some of that rent was referable to time following the application. The FTT rejected this submission, concluding that the Code displaced the common law position, in giving the tribunal the power to determine 'the payments of consideration to be made', without qualifying this power by reference to rental periods that were underway as at the date of the application. It exercised its discretion such that the new consideration was payable from the date of the application.

Consideration imposed by the tribunal: para 26 cases

13.183 Paragraphs 26(4)(c) and 26(4)(d) apply the provisions of paras 23 and 24 to para 26 cases in the same way as those provisions apply in a para 20 case, save for the following differences:

(i) by para 26(6)(a), references to the 'relevant person' are instead references to the person on whom the para 26 agreement would be imposed; and

(ii) by para 26(6)(b), the duty in para 23 to include terms as to the payment of consideration is instead a power.

13.184 Thus, there is no absolute obligation on the tribunal to provide for consideration to be payable. If it is considered that the rights conferred on the operator are so minimal and the impact on a landowner so negligible, it may conclude that no consideration should be payable. However, there has not yet been a contested case in which the tribunal has decided to order no consideration at all. The expectation must therefore be that consideration will be assessed as per para 24 in all but the most exceptional cases.

13.185 Paragraph 24(3)(b) requires it to be assumed that paras 16 and 17 (assignment, sharing and upgrading) do not apply to the right or any apparatus. However, no other part of para 24 requires any particular provisions of the Code to be disregarded. One might therefore think that the tribunal should have regard to the applicability of paras 26(8) and 30(3) (which have the effect of removing security of tenure for para 26 agreements) when assessing consideration.

13.186 Thus the right to be valued will come to an end in accordance with the contractual terms of the para 26 agreement (or in accordance with the Order imposing it). Given that para 26 agreements are not normally granted for long periods, a landowner will typically have certainty that the agreement will come to an end without it having to give long periods of notice, such as the 18-month notice period in para 31. What effect this has on what are normally small consideration values under para 26 agreements is not something that has been the subject of a great deal of analysis.

Consideration imposed by the tribunal: para 27 cases

13.187 Paragraph 27(4)(c) and 27(4)(d) apply the provisions of paras 23 and 24 to para 27 cases in the same way as those provisions apply in a para 20 case, save for the following differences:

(i) by para 27(6)(a), references to the 'relevant person' are instead references to the person on whom the para 27 agreement would be imposed; and

(ii) by para 27(6)(b), the duty in para 23 to include terms as to the payment of consideration is instead a power.

13.188 Thus, as with para 26 cases, there is no absolute obligation on the tribunal to provide for consideration to be payable. However, in most cases, one would expect consideration to be assessed as per para 24.

13.189 Again, in a para 27 case, para 24 does not require para 30(3) to be disregarded. Thus, as observed above in respect of para 26 agreements, one would think that the removal of security of tenure by para 30(3) is to be taken into account in respect of valuation of consideration.

Consideration imposed by the tribunal: 'renewal' cases

13.190 Paragraph 34(11) applies the provisions of paras 23(2) to (8) and 24 to the cases mentioned in para 34(11). These are essentially 'renewal' cases, and include:

(i) modifications of agreement terms under para 34(3);

(ii) modifications to remove an existing Code right under para 34(4);

(iii) modifications to add a Code right under para 34(5);

(iv) cases where an existing agreement is terminated and a new agreement is to be entered into, and the terms of that new agreement are to be decided under para 34(10).[112]

13.191 As para 34(11) simply applies para 24 and does not mandate any alteration to the statutory valuation hypothesis, at first glance one might think that there is no difference in the valuation approach in a renewal case when compared with a para 20 case.

13.192 However, one must remember that in a renewal case there are certain real-world factual circumstances that differ from a para 20 'new site' case. Are these circumstances to be taken into account or disregarded?

13.193 In *Green*,[113] the tribunal considered that:[114]

(i) the Code does not require an assumption of vacant possession and one should not be made;

(ii) the tribunal is not required to depart from reality in respect of the issues of planning permission, any pre-existing supplies of electricity and fibre, foundations and secure perimeter fencing; and

112 Para 34(11)(b) refers to para 34(10) determinations. Where para 34(10) refers to 'the terms', presumably it is referring back to para 34(9), which references both para 34(5) and 34(6) cases. Thus, on the face of it, it would seem that para 34(5) cases are referred to in both para 34(11)(a) and (b), for reasons that perhaps are not clear.

113 [2020] UKUT 348 (LC).

114 The matters in sub-paragraphs (i) and (ii) were said to be common ground (see [83] of the decision), but no doubt was cast on them by the Tribunal. The points made in sub-paragraph (iii) were approved by the Tribunal (see [84]).

(iii) the hypothetical site provider for a renewal is in the same position as the real site provider as regards what structures are already installed. Thus, in a typical renewal case, there is no place for any uplift in consideration to allow for the inconvenience of the initial installation, as no installation will in fact be occurring.

13.194 As regards the last of the above three points, the tribunal contrasted this case with the para 20 case of *Fothringham*,[115] where the Lands Tribunal for Scotland ordered consideration of £600 per annum, save for the first year when £1,500 was payable in order to reflect the additional inconvenience and risk to the site provider of the installation of the mast at the outset of the term. It was acknowledged in *Green*[116] however, that as the renewed agreement terms would allow the operator to install a new mast for 5G purposes, the likely impact of that mast installation on the site provider would indeed have to be considered. The tribunal deployed the three-stage test and assessed the stage 3 burdens on the site provider at £500, including the loss of amenity arising from the new mast.[117]

13.195 The site provider was concerned that the future ECA might be bigger, more powerful, noisier, more unsightly, and involve a taller mast and disruptive installation activity. There was no evidence before the tribunal that these developments, should they transpire, would have an impact on rental levels of the site provider's two nearby residential properties. The tribunal noted that:

> 'Should the impact of future upgrading of the ECA have an impact on rental levels, temporarily or permanently, there is an opportunity for a future compensation claim, in the absence of agreement, under paragraphs 25 and 84.'

Market value rent review: ensuring non-operators pay market value

13.196 Where a Code agreement is imposed or agreed with a consideration payment that follows or reflects para 24, any lawful assignee of that agreement will *prima facie* benefit from the obligation to pay consideration, which is highly likely to be lower than true open market value. If the assignee is a non-operator, it could never have achieved para 24 consideration through the tribunal itself, as it would not have had the right to seek an imposed agreement. Similarly, a landowner is unlikely to agree a consensual rent with a non-operator tenant, which followed para 24, as the non-operator would not have an operator's negotiating position.

13.197 So how can a site provider ensure that an imposed agreement would not allow a non-operator assignee to benefit from the lower Code rent? In a lease that allows assignment to non-operators, the way to deal with the point is to insert a contractual provision to account for it, most obviously a rent review clause, which is triggered upon an assignment to a non-operator. A similar approach can be taken to encompass the possibility of a tenant operator losing its own operator status.

115 *Cornerstone Telecommunications Infrastructure Limited v Fothringham* LTS-ECC-2020-07. See [79] and [82] thereof.

116 See [31], [54] and [84].

117 See [139].

13.198 A clause triggering a rent review to open market level in the event that either the tenant lost its status as an operator or the lease was assigned to a non-operator was approved by the tribunal in *Stephenson*.[118] This was appropriate given the way in which para 24 requires rent to be determined, and that a lease that is no longer in the hands of a Code operator is not contributing towards the objectives of the Code. It might be said that a non-operator might just as effectively contribute towards the roll-out of new technologies and the provision of essential networks, but 'the Code's policy of promoting improvements in telecommunications for the public benefit does not require that the site provider should be kept out of its fair share'.

Interaction between consideration and compensation

13.199 There is a potential overlap between consideration and compensation. In *London & Quadrant*, in the context of assessing the burdens on the site provider, as a component of the aggregate consideration under the staged approach, the tribunal very realistically accepted that 'some of the financial consequences of a Code agreement may be equally well accommodated by additional consideration under paragraph 24 or an award of compensation under paragraph 25',[119] calling this territory the 'border country' between consideration and compensation.

13.200 The tribunal noted that in a real-world negotiation, the rent agreed between the parties would reflect 'any adverse financial consequences for the landlord which were not separately accounted for.' The coexistence of an entitlement to consideration and a right to claim compensation was described as a 'peculiarity' of imposed Code agreements that 'requires care by the tribunal to avoid double counting when making the original order or in the event of a claim for compensation at a later date.' [120]

Rent in 1954 Act cases

13.201 The consequence of the Transitional Provisions, as explained by the Court of Appeal in *Ashloch*, is that certain 1954 Act tenancies entered into before the New Code, and which confer Code rights, must be renewed under the 1954 Act and not within the Part 5 Code procedure.

13.202 Where that procedure is followed, in the absence of agreement as to rent, the correct rent under the resulting new tenancy is ascertained by reference to the provisions of the 1954 Act and not those of the Code. This has occurred in cases such as *Hanover*, *Morriss* and the *New Zealand Farm* case.

13.203 There are a number of differences between the 1954 Act regime and the Part 5 Code regime. Some of the key differences that remain are as follows:

118 [2022] UKUT 180 (LC) at [22] and [23].
119 *London & Quadrant* at [98].
120 *London & Quadrant* at [99].

(i) 1954 Act proceedings still occur in the county court, whereas Code assessments of rent, whether in the case of a new agreement or renewed agreement, typically[121] occur within the tribunal system;

(ii) the 1954 Act does not currently contain any 'no-network' assumption; and

(iii) although a tenancy resulting from the 1954 Act process is a Code agreement, as things stand, it does not enable the landlord to make any later application under para 25(1) of the Code for compensation, because it is not imposed under para 20 of the Code.[122]

13.204 However it is important to note that statutory amendments have been passed by Parliament within the Product Security and Telecommunications Infrastructure Act 2022, but at present have not yet been brought into force. These amendments will have an important impact on all three of the above-mentioned differences between the 1954 Act regime as it stands, and the Code regime. The amendments are considered below, from **13.224** onwards.

Valuation under the 1954 Act (pre-PSTIA 2022 amendments)

13.205 This book is principally about the Code, and there are other works that consider in helpful detail the meaning and consequences of section 34 in 1954 Act lease renewal cases. Further, once the relevant provisions of the PSTIA 2022 have come into force, the current rules for assessing the rent under a renewal tenancy which is to be a Code agreement, will be no more than a historical curiosity. Accordingly, the relevant provisions of the 1954 Act will only be considered here in brief.

13.206 Once the terms of a new 1954 Act tenancy have been determined or agreed, the court must value the rent under the tenancy by reference to the provisions of section 34 of the 1954 Act. The most significant difference between the section 34 valuation methodology and that which applies under para 24 of the Code is that the no-network assumption does not (currently) apply.

13.207 Section 34(1) provides as follows:

'(1) The rent payable under a tenancy granted by order of the court under this Part of this Act shall be such as may be agreed between the landlord and the tenant or as, in default of such agreement, may be determined by the court to be that at which, having regard to the terms of the tenancy (other than those relating to rent), the holding might reasonably be expected to be let in the open market by a willing lessor, there being disregarded—

(a) any effect on rent of the fact that the tenant has or his predecessors in title have been in occupation of the holding,

121 The county court does have jurisdiction in respect of Code matters, and the Code itself refers to the 'court' as imposing an agreement (para 19), operators applying to the 'court' (para 20(3)) etc, rather than the 'tribunal'. In relation to England and Wales this means the 'county court' (para 94(1)), and this definition is only supplemented by the inclusion of Tribunals by virtue of regulations made under para 94(2).

122 Or under any other provisions of the Code to which para 25(1) is applied. For example, para 26(4)(e) applies para 25 to para 26 cases, and para 27(4)(e) applies para 25 to para 27 cases.

(b) any goodwill attached to the holding by reason of the carrying on thereat of the business of the tenant (whether by him or by a predecessor of his in that business),

(c) any effect on rent of an improvement to which this paragraph applies,[123]

(d) in the case of a holding comprising licensed premises, any addition to its value attributable to the licence, if it appears to the court that having regard to the terms of the current tenancy and any other relevant circumstances the benefit of the licence belongs to the tenant.'

13.208 It will immediately be seen that section 34 requires a market value assessment by reference to a hypothetical transaction, with certain specified disregards.

13.209 These provisions must of course be applied to the many different types of land and buildings in respect of which business tenancies are granted. In *Hanover*,[124] the task in respect of a communications site occupied by ECA was described in the following terms:

> 'In order to be faithful to the s.34 valuation hypothesis, it is necessary to envisage what would be likely to happen if the Site, in its assumed undeveloped condition, was offered by the landlord to the open market for use as a mast site on the agreed terms'

13.210 However, as indicated above, the operator in *Hanover* contended that hypothetical parties negotiating a market rent under the 1954 Act would conduct their negotiation with a view to mirroring the basis of valuation under the Code, and that the agreed rent would therefore reflect the 'no network' assumption.

13.211 The tribunal accepted the relevance of the existence of the Code to the hypothetical parties, stating:

> '51. In this imagined negotiation the hypothetical tenant is a Code operator (because the terms of the new tenancy say so and the only permitted use of the Site under those terms is for Code purposes)…
>
> 52. Being prudent and knowledgeable, the parties in the negotiation are aware that the hypothetical tenant (or any other operator in the market) has the right to give notice under paragraphs 20 or 26 of the Code requesting that the hypothetical landlord enter into a tenancy on terms proposed in the notice…'

13.212 The staged approach was contended for, as described earlier in this chapter.[125] An alternative use value of £1,715 was assessed based on the value for an alternative car parking use. On the evidence, it was held that there were 'no relevant additional benefits or adverse effects' to be considered under stages 2 or 3, which would elevate the proper rent above that represented by the existing use value.

13.213 A figure of £445 was then added to represent an annualised sum for professional fees. This was because where a new letting is imposed by the tribunal

123 Section 34(2) circumscribes what improvements this encompasses.

124 *Vodafone Limited v Hanover Capital Limited* [2021] 2 P. & C.R. 3 at [101].

125 See **13.102** onwards.

under the Code, the landlord is entitled to its reasonable legal and valuation expenses as compensation under paras 25 and 84(2)(a). The expectation of receiving these fees is 'the basis of a universal practice concerning contributions to fees on new lettings and renewals', and the negotiating parties would be aware of this.

13.214 Thus the judge considered that if the only factors to be taken into account were those identified in the submissions and evidence of the operator, the parties would likely agree on some £2,160, which they would round up to £2,200 or £2,250.

13.215 However, despite having proceeded through the staged process, the judge then concluded that he was 'quite sure that the hypothetical parties would not agree a rent of £2,200 or thereabouts for a letting of the Site on the agreed terms', because the hypothetical negotiation must be assumed to take place in the open market. The judge noted that the site met the needs of four operators, each of whose apparatus it already hosted. This element of competition was held to be likely to push up rental values above existing use value. Although the evidence of the effect of competition was limited and the court had to use comparables that ordinarily would be considered too historic, the court considered that £5,500 would be the rent achieved in a true open market setting. This figure was then adjusted up to £5,750 to reflect the lack of a rent review clause.

13.216 In *Morriss*, the court noted that in *Hanover*, 'the absence of evidence of rents agreed in the market for new telecommunications sites led the court to consider a structured approach', but that this approach was only necessary where reliable transactional evidence was missing.[126] It decided that it was now in a position to base its conclusion on transactional evidence, saying as follows:

> 'Fortunately, lettings of sites for the provision of electronic communications networks on terms which will be subject to the Code are now quite common, and the Court has evidence of the rents at which transactions take place. In principle, because of the absence of artificial valuation assumptions, evidence of rents agreed in the market is the best evidence on which to base a rent determined under section 34. There may be reason to make adjustments to the evidence, but it provides a reliable starting point.'[127]

13.217 The judge again confirmed the relevance of the Code to a valuation under the 1954 Act. Section 34 does not require the existence of the Code to be ignored, nor does it require an assumption that the parties would be ignorant of it. The parties' contemplation of the valuation approach under the Code does not entail a threat by the hypothetical operator of an application under the Code, merely that the parties would make full use of their bargaining positions. However, the protracted and expensive process under the Code would not be attractive to a hypothetical party, and as such, it would be unlikely to feature significantly in their negotiation.

13.218 The court thus considered the comparable evidence. It was concluded that a capital incentive or inducement paid by an operator under the Code is part of the package agreed between the parties, is an established feature of the market, and cannot be dismissed as a 'payment for willingness'. Taking into account an annualised sum to represent such commonplace inducements, the judge considered that the parties

126 *Morriss* at [88].
127 *Morriss* at [58].

would settle on £3,000, and then added £500 to represent an annualised figure for professional fees, yielding a total of £3,500 per annum.

13.219 Unlike in *Hanover*, no additional sum was added to represent the impact of competition, even though in reality other operators were similarly in occupation at the site. The expert evidence was that if the site were exposed to the open market in accordance with the valuation hypothesis (which is not the way that lettings come about in reality) there would not be an increase to the rent caused by competition.

13.220 In the *New Zealand Farm*[128] case, the Deputy President, again sitting as a county court judge, reiterated the conclusion in *Morriss* as regards capital payments, saying that 'the evidence establishes beyond doubt that capital payments are very widely available and that there is a relationship between rents and premiums such that if no premium were to be offered the transaction would be likely to be completed at a higher rent.'[129] They were therefore not to be disregarded. Similarly, it was confirmed that an 'artificial' *Hanover*-style structured approach was no longer necessary given the availability of real market evidence.[130]

13.221 It was argued that all of the operators who were currently on the site would be very keen to return because of the creation of a 'not-spot' in their network coverage if they did not, thus generating competition. Because of the statutory disregards at section 34(1)(a) and (b), this was held to be an impermissible factor to consider.

13.222 The court's conclusion as to how a landlord and tenant would behave in the hypothetical negotiation was as follows:

> 'A properly advised landlord offering a site to the market at large and looking to receive an annual rent which was not supplemented by a premium would expect to better a rent restricted by the artificial assumptions dictated by paragraph 24 of the Code. They would look around at the transactions taking place and would see that Code consideration is routinely enhanced by annual 'commercial payments' and capital sums. They would recognise the substantial saving in time and money which an operator would achieve by doing a consensual deal rather than by using the Code. So too would the operators to whom the site would be likely to be attractive.'[131]

13.223 Modelling this approach with the transactional evidence, the court concluded that the appropriate rental figure was £3,200 (being £2,750 plus an annualised allowance representing professional fees).

Valuation under the 1954 Act (post-PSTI 2022 amendments)

13.224 The legislative changes of the Product Security and Telecommunications Infrastructure Act 2022 will ultimately bring 1954 Act telecoms[132] lease renewals into line with Code renewals in relation to consideration and compensation. However,

---

128 *On Tower Ltd v AP Wireless (II) (New Zealand Farm)* [2022] EW Misc 6 (CC).
129 At [88].
130 At [91].
131 At [101].
132 Where the primary purpose of the lease is to grant Code rights.

these amendments to the statutory scheme are not yet in force at the time of writing. Further, it is not yet known what, if any, transitional provisions might apply in respect of their operation once they are in force

13.225 Section 61 PSTI 2022 will introduce a new section 34A into the 1954 Act. This new section 34A will disapply section 34 as the basis for assessing the rent under a new 1954 Act tenancy, in favour of the valuation framework set out in section 34A.

13.226 Section 34A will apply where the current tenancy is a subsisting agreement[133] whose primary purpose is to confer Code rights.[134]

13.227 The valuation framework in section 34A mirrors that at para 24 of the Code. The rent payable 'shall be such amount or amounts determined by the court as represent the market value of the landlord's agreement to confer the code rights conferred by the new tenancy' (section 34A(2)).

13.228 For the purposes of assessing that 'market value', the instructions at para 24(2) of the Code are reproduced at section 34A(3). Further, the assumptions at para 24(3) of the Code are reproduced at section 34A(4).

13.229 Thus, the full force of the no-network assumption (at section 34A(4)(a)) will be brought to bear on 1954 Act renewal tenancy rents.

13.230 It should be noted that alongside the shift to Code-style rents in 1954 Act renewal cases, the position as regards compensation will also be homogenised with the position under the Code. Section 63 of the PSTI 2022 will introduce a new section 34B and section 34C into the 1954 Act. Section 34B will create a Code para 25-style power to order the operator tenant to pay compensation to the landlord for loss and damage.[135] As with para 25 of the Code, this power may be exercised when the court[136] grants a new tenancy or at any time afterwards, on the application of the landlord.

133 As per the meaning within the Transitional Provisions at Sch 2 to the Digital Economy Act 2017.

134 For the purposes of s 34A, in respect of the current tenancy, 'code rights' is to be read as per its meaning at para 3 of the Transitional Provisions at Sch 2 to the Digital Economy Act 2017 (see s 34A(5)(a)).

135 The words of s 34B(2) closely follow the language of para 25(1) of the Code.

136 The powers of the 'court' may ultimately be exercised by the FTT or the UT, as s 65 of the PSTI 2022 inserts a new s 63(2A) into the 1954 Act which gives power to the Secretary of State to make regulations providing for those tribunals to have jurisdiction in 1954 Act lease renewals where the primary purpose of the subsisting agreement current tenancy is to confer Code rights. Clearly there are advantages in having the FTT or UT determining matters relating to agreements that will become Code agreements, both in terms of having specialist judiciary and in relation to procedural matters.

14

Compensation

14.01 Compensation is available under the Code in a number of different scenarios and contexts, and to a number of different persons. The relevant provisions which govern the award of compensation are para 25 and paras 83 to 86 of the Code.

14.02 In brief:

- Paragraph 25 creates a right to compensation for a 'relevant person' where an agreement has been imposed under para 20 by which that person confers Code rights, or is rendered bound by Code rights, in respect of loss or damage sustained as a result of the exercise of Code rights. Compensation can be awarded when the agreement is imposed, or upon a later application.
- Where agreements are imposed under certain other provisions of the Code, para 25 is also applied in the same way (see para 26(4)(e) in respect of interim agreements, para 27(4)(e) in respect of temporary agreements, and para 34(11) in respect of certain renewals or modifications of Code agreements under para 34).
- Para 44(5) allows compensation to be ordered when an Order for removal of ECA is made.
- Para 84(2) contains examples of heads of compensation that may be available.
- Paragraph 85(2) creates a right to compensation in respect of injurious affection to neighbouring land in relation to injury caused by the exercise of a Code right.

Compensation under para 25

14.03 Paragraph 25(1) provides that:

> 'If the court makes an order under paragraph 20 the court may also order the operator to pay compensation to the relevant person for any loss or damage that has been sustained or will be sustained by that person as a result of the exercise of the code right to which the order relates.'

14.04 Paragraph 25(6) points out that para 84 makes further provision about compensation in the case of an order under para 20. The remaining provisions of para 25 and those of para 84 will be discussed below.

Necessary pre-requisite: an Order imposing an agreement

14.05 The plain words of para 25(1) indicate that no compensation may be ordered under para 25 unless 'the court makes an order under paragraph 20'.

14.06 Thus, there can be no compensation *under this paragraph* where a Code agreement has been entered into consensually with no judicial involvement. This was acknowledged by the Deputy President, sitting as a county court judge, in *Morriss*.[1] Although that was a case under the 1954 Act, the court was considering whether to impose a contractual compensation provision. The clause was rejected, but part of the court's reasoning was that there was a lack of evidence at that time that in consensual cases, where no para 25 right to compensation arose, parties were commonly agreeing compensation clauses.

14.07 This feature of the Code creates a trap for the unwary. Parties are encouraged to resolve potential disputes without recourse to the tribunal, but doing so may cause a landowner to forgo the possibility of future compensation which the Code would automatically grant if the tribunal imposed the agreement. A potential site provider would be well-advised to ensure a future right to seek compensation. There are only two ways of doing this:

(i) *Attempt to have an express contractual right to compensation written into the agreement.* There has been no real doubt cast on this possibility in the case law. For example, it was not given as a reason for not imposing a contractual term in the 1954 Act case of *Morriss*.[2] It remains to be seen whether an argument might ever be attempted by an operator that para 86 prevents such terms from having effect.[3] Initially there was a wariness on the part of operators to agree such a bespoke clause, but they have become less unusual over time; or

(ii) *Negotiate an agreement and have it imposed by the tribunal.* Even where the parties are completely agreed as to all other terms of an agreement, it is often necessary (where a landowner is properly advised) to seek the 'rubber stamp' of the tribunal in respect of the agreed agreement, in order to give rise to para 25 consequences. From a landowner's perspective, this unfortunately means declining to enter into an agreement consensually unless this course is adopted. Only an operator can apply to the tribunal under para 20(3), so a landowner cannot take matters into its own hands and unilaterally ask the tribunal to rubber stamp the agreement. However, in practice, the parties make what might be colloquially referred to as a 'joint' application, which is in fact an operator's application which the landowner confirms it is content to have imposed. If the parties wish to do this more speedily than the 28-day notice requirement at para 20(3)(a) would allow, it would be necessary for the landowner to give notice under para 20(3)(b) that it 'does not agree' to confer or be bound. This is perhaps a little absurd given that it does agree to a tribunal rubber stamping the agreement. Nonetheless, the correct procedure must be followed.

The latter of the above options is unquestionably the more conventional route to take. The fact that it consumes the time and resources of the tribunal is an unfortunate (and one would imagine unforeseen) consequence of the drafting of para 25(1).

1 *EE v Morriss* [2022] EW Misc 1 (CC) at [30].

2 *EE v Morriss* [2022] EW Misc 1 (CC).

3 Para 86 of the Code limits the extent to which compensation is payable. Except as provided by Parts 2 to 14 of the Code, an operator is not liable to compensate a person for loss and damage suffered as a result of the lawful exercise of any right conferred by or in accordance with any provision of those Parts. See the section on para 86 later in this chapter, from **14.101** onwards.

One can understand a landowner being reticent to take any course that entails tribunal proceedings being initiated, not least because Orders for costs can be made. However, someone in this position may draw some comfort from the words of Judge Jackson in the FTT case of *IX Limited*.[4] The judge recognised that the site provider was 'fully entitled to insist on the imposition of a new agreement by the tribunal' in order to protect their position as to compensation under para 25, describing that stance as a 'thoroughly principled position to take'.[5] In that context, it is unlikely that a tribunal might instead think that such a course was unreasonable in a typical case.

Renewals of subsisting agreements under the 1954 Act

14.08 The position under a renewed 1954 Act tenancy as to para 25 compensation will depend upon whether section 63 of the Product Security and Telecommunications Infrastructure Act 2022 ('PSTIA 2022') has yet come into force.

(i) Before the coming into force of PSTIA 2022 s 63

14.09 Where a 1954 Act lease renewal process results in the court making an Order for a new tenancy, that new tenancy will be a Code agreement to which Part 5 of the Code applies. However, in such a case there will not have been any Order under para 20 of the Code (nor under any of the other provisions of the Code to which para 25 is applied). Thus, the orthodox assumption[6] thus far has been that in such a case, no application can be made under para 25 by a person bound by a Code right pursuant to such an imposed renewal tenancy.

(ii) After the coming into force of PSTIA 2022 s 63

14.10

Once they are brought into force, a number of the provisions of the PSTIA 2022 will affect 1954 Act lease renewals, so as to bring them more closely into line with renewals under Part 5 of the Code in certain important respects. These respects include the assessment of rent (and the no-network assumption), the venue in which the renewal proceedings are tried, and the prospect of compensation for loss resulting from the exercise of Code rights.

14.11 At time of writing, section 63 of the PSTIA 2022 is not yet in force. However, it will insert a new section 34B into the 1954 Act, headed 'Compensation for the exercise of code rights'. That new provision will apply[7] where the court grants a new tenancy under Part 2 of the 1954 Act whose primary purpose is to confer Code

4 *On Tower UK Limited v IX Limited* Case No LC-2022-000361.
5 *IX Limited* at [15].
6 This assumption was confirmed in *EE v Morriss* at [30]–[32], although it was a proposition of law that was not in dispute.
7 See the wording of s 34B(1) within s 63 PSTIA 2022.

rights,[8] in circumstances where the existing tenancy is a subsisting agreement under the Transitional Provisions,[9] and its primary purpose was to confer Code rights.[10]

14.12 Where section 34B applies, it will have a similar effect to para 25 of the Code. It will empower the court to order the tenant to pay compensation to the landlord for any damage or loss that has been sustained or will be sustained by the landlord as a result of the exercise of any of the Code rights conferred by the new tenancy. Such an Order will be able to be made either when the new tenancy is ordered, or at anytime afterwards on the application of the landlord.

14.13 Section 63 of the PSTIA 2022 will also insert a new section 34C into the 1954 Act, which will apply to the court's power to award compensation under the new section 34B. It will be of similar effect to para 84 of the Code.

To whom may compensation under para 25 be payable?

14.14 In short, the answer to this question is as follows:

- n a para 20, 26 or 27 case, it is the person who is conferring or being bound by a Code right;
- in a para 34 case, it is the person who has conferred or been bound, and will continue following the para 34 Order to confer or be bound by a Code right.

Para 20, 26 and 27 cases

14.15 Where an agreement is imposed under para 20, para 25(1) creates the power on the part of the tribunal to pay compensation to 'the relevant person'. This is the person who is required by the operator to confer a Code right or be bound by a Code right (para 20(1)), and on whom a notice is served under para 20(2) seeking that person's agreement to the same.

14.16 Where an agreement is imposed under para 26, the term 'relevant person' at para 25(1) is to be read as if it were a reference to the 'person' mentioned at para 26(1).[11] This person is the person on whom the operator has sought the imposition of an agreement conferring Code rights, or rendering that person bound by Code rights, under para 26(1), and on whom a para 26(3) notice[12] has been served by the operator.

14.17 Where an agreement is imposed under para 27, the term 'relevant person' at para 25(1) is to be read as if it were a reference to the 'person' mentioned at para 27(1).[13] This person is the person on whom the operator has sought the imposition of an agreement conferring temporary Code rights,[14] or rendering that person bound by

8 NB: Code rights as defined by para 3 of the Code. See the wording of s 34B(8)(a) within s 63 PSTIA 2022.
9 Ie, Sch 2 to the Digital Economy Act 2017.
10 NB: Code rights as defined by para 3 of the Transitional Provisions at Sch 2 to the Digital Economy Act 2017. See the wording of s 34B(8)(b) within s 63 PSTIA 2022.
11 This is by virtue of para 26(6)(a).
12 This notice must comply with para 20(2) by virtue of para 26(3).
13 This is by virtue of para 27(6)(a).
14 See in particular paras 27(2) and (3).

temporary Code rights, under para 27, and on whom the operator has served a notice under para 20(2) which also requires that person's agreement on a temporary basis under para 27(1)(b).

Para 34 cases

14.18 By para 34(11), para 25 applies to certain renewal or modification cases where an Order is to be made under para 34. In such cases, the reference in para 25 to the 'relevant person' is surely a reference to the 'site provider', in the sense in which that term is used at para 30(1)(a). That is, a person who has conferred a right (which is to be continued or re-conferred by the renewed or modified agreement), or on whom a Code right is binding (and continues to bind, following the renewal or modification).

14.19 This seems to follow from the structure of para 34 and the various provisions of Part 5 of the Code to which it refers. Paragraph 34(11) applies para 25 to cases where an Order is made under paras 34(3), (4), (5), or (10). These are, of course, all Orders under para 34.

14.20 The function[15] of para 34 is to set out the Orders that can be made on an application under paras 32(1)(b) or 33(5):

- Paragraph 32(1)(b) allows an operator to make an application for an Order under para 34, in order to prevent an existing Code agreement from coming to an end. This provision only applies where a 'site provider' has given a para 31 notice. Para 31(1) allows such a notice to be given by a 'site provider who is a party to a code agreement'.
- Paragraph 33(5) allows an operator or a site provider to make an application for an Order under para 34, in order to prevent an existing Code agreement from coming to an end. This provision only applies where an operator or a 'site provider who is a party to a code agreement' has given a para 33(1) notice (proposing, essentially, a modification or renewal agreement), and the operator and site provider have not 'reached agreement on the proposals in the notice'.[16]

14.21 As stated above, in a para 20 case, para 25(1) allows compensation to be paid to a 'relevant person'. That is the person on whom an operator seeks to have imposed a Code agreement. By contrast, it has been explained above that under paras 32(1)(b) and 33(5), the person who is either to serve the notice that 'kicks off' the renewal procedure or to receive such a notice is the 'site provider who is a party to a code agreement'. That is surely the person who may in an appropriate case be eligible to a payment of compensation under para 25 from an operator, where a modification or renewal Order referred to in para 34(11) is made following a para 32(1)(b) application or a para 33(5) application.

14.22 The position as regards successors in title to site providers is not something which has yet troubled the tribunals. One would think that in principle a successor is entitled to seek compensation for its own losses.

15 See para 34(1).
16 See para 33(4).

In what procedural circumstances can compensation be awarded under para 25?

14.23 Paragraph 25(2) specifies the two situations in which compensation may be ordered under para 25(1).

(i) At the time the agreement is imposed

14.24 By para 25(2)(a), the first of these is 'at the time' the para 20 Order is made. This provision surely applies to Orders made under paras 26, 27, and 34[17] in exactly the same way: when the Order under any of those paragraphs is made, an Order that compensation be paid can also be made. This provision does not specify that the power to award compensation is contingent on any application being made for compensation.

14.25 Clearly, the tribunal must operate fairly and must allow the parties a reasonable opportunity to make submissions before unilaterally imposing a compensation Order. But strictly, an application does not appear to be a necessity in order to confer jurisdiction to award compensation. In some cases, the operator will propose an agreement whose terms provide for an element of compensation (transactional legal fees, for example). In other cases, a respondent landowner will raise the question of compensation in its Statement of Case and indicate the heads of loss for which recovery is sought, including the quantum if it is known. There may also be cases in which a sum is addressed by one or other party as if it were an element of consideration, but the tribunal may consider that it is more properly analysed as compensation.

(ii) Pursuant to an application at a later date

14.26 The second situation in which compensation may be ordered is that under para 25(2)(b), namely:

> 'at any time afterwards, on the application of the relevant person[18]'.

14.27 Under para 25(2)(b), it seems clear that where compensation is to be ordered at a time after the Order imposing the agreement, an application by the receiving party is necessary in order to confer jurisdiction for an Order for compensation to be made.

14.28 In *Islington,*[19] it was confirmed that an application for compensation can be made at any time after the making of the Order imposing the relevant agreement. In that case, the operator had sought to argue that a compensation claim at a later date after the Order imposing the agreement was made was impermissible. In rejecting the operator's proposed restriction, the tribunal said:

> 'The making of an order under paragraph 20 is a condition precedent of any order under paragraph 25, but in our judgment once that condition has been

17 Ie, those para 34 Orders mentioned at para 34(11).

18 'Relevant person' as regards para 26 and 27 cases must be read as the person referred to in paras 26(1) and 27(1) respectively – see paras 26(6)(a) and 27(6)(a). As regards those renewal/modification cases mentioned at para 34(11), the relevant person is surely the person who is to confer or be bound under any renewed or modified agreement – see discussion above.

19 *EE v Islington* [2019] UKUT 53 (LC) at [111].

satisfied there is nothing to restrict the time when an order for compensation may be made. That is the obvious intent of paragraph 25(2)(b) which allows an order to be made 'at any time afterwards' i.e. at any time after the imposition of an agreement under paragraph 20.'

14.29 In rejecting the operator's argument that the risk of 'unanticipated loss'[20] would fall on the site provider, the tribunal was surely indicating that not only could an *Order* for compensation be made by the tribunal at any time after the Order imposing the agreement, but that an *application* for such compensation could similarly in principle be made at any time. This may very well be subject to any arguments about limitation periods and also as to whether the loss in respect of which an applicant seeks compensation has already been contemplated in the original agreement and hence would constitute 'double recovery' if such an application were to succeed.

Is para 25 compensation discretionary?

14.30 The power to award compensation under para 25 is not discretionary. The use of the word 'may' in para 25(1) gave rise to a submission on the part of the operator in *Islington*[21] that the tribunal had a discretion as to whether to award compensation. The tribunal rejected that submission in the following terms:

> 'The power to award compensation is expressed in that way because there are likely to be some cases where there is no need for compensation because no loss or damage will be sustained as a result of the exercise of the code rights imposed. Where loss or damage is sustained we do not consider that the Tribunal could properly refuse compensation (or refuse to give directions for the amount of compensation to be ascertained by agreement, by arbitration, or by the Tribunal itself).'

14.31 It is right to say that a tribunal might decide that a loss is not sufficiently pleaded or evidenced, or that an argument of the site provider is not well-founded, but that the claim that is being advanced may succeed on a given set of facts in the future. In such an event, the tribunal may exercise its discretion to make no Order on such a claim and note the possibility of a future claim, rather than dismissing the claim formally. However, that procedural discretion is quite different from a discretion to refuse to award compensation where the relevant tests are met, which the tribunal does not have.

Requirements to be satisfied

14.32 In *Islington*, the tribunal noted that the no-network assumption, within the Code's consideration provisions, gives effect to the policy that site providers should not share in the economic value created by the very high demand for those services. However, it went on to say that this policy does not have an impact on a site provider's right to compensation:

20 *EE v Islington* [2019] UKUT 53 (LC) at [110].
21 *EE v Islington* [2019] UKUT 53 (LC) at [109].

'...we do not agree that the same policy has any influence in the assessment of compensation. There is nothing in the Code (or the material admissible in its interpretation) to suggest the existence of a policy requiring the owners of suitable sites to bear part of the cost of providing networks through being deprived of fair compensation for any loss or damage which they suffer as a result of the exercise of Code rights.'[22]

14.33 In assessing what constitutes 'fair compensation', the tribunal accepted that it was appropriate to borrow from the well-established case law in the field of compulsory purchase. Thus, in order for a claiming party to claim a loss, it must demonstrate:

- causation;
- that the claimed loss is not too remote;
- that the loss claimed does not exceed that which would have been sustained by a party which behaved reasonably in order to mitigate the loss and avoided unreasonable expenditure.

14.34 The well-known source of these requirements is the *Shun Fung Ironworks*[23] case, which has been referred to with approval by the tribunal in a number of Code cases. In *Islington*,[24] the tribunal said as follows:

'118. The parties agreed that, in assessing compensation under the Code it would be appropriate for the Tribunal to borrow the three general conditions which must be established in support of a claim for fair and adequate compensation in cases of compulsory purchase, as explained by Lord Nicholls in giving the decision of the Privy Council in *Director of Buildings and Lands v Shun Fung Ironworks Ltd* [1995] 2 A.C. 111, 126: first, it is a prerequisite of compensation that there must be a causal connection between the acquisition and the loss in question; secondly, to qualify for compensation that loss must not be too remote; and thirdly, the law expects those who claim compensation to behave reasonably, to take the steps a reasonable person would to eliminate or reduce the loss, and to avoid incurring unreasonable expenditure.'

14.35 The tribunal has similarly referred to these three criteria with approval in the Code context in *Hackney (Shoreditch House)* at [17], and in *London & Quadrant* at [139].

Interaction between consideration and compensation

14.36 As observed above in Chapter 13, in *London & Quadrant* the tribunal accepted that 'some of the financial consequences of a Code agreement may be equally well accommodated by additional consideration under paragraph 24 or an award of compensation under paragraph 25',[25] calling this territory the 'border country' between consideration and compensation. The coexistence of an entitlement to consideration and a right to claim compensation 'requires care by the tribunal to

22 [2019] UKUT 53 (LC) at [130].

23 *Director of Buildings and Lands v Shun Fung Ironworks Ltd* [1995] 2 AC 111 (Privy Council).

24 [2019] UKUT 53 (LC) at [118].

25 *London & Quadrant* at [98].

avoid double counting when making the original order or in the event of a claim for compensation at a later date'.[26]

The procedural options open to the tribunal

14.37 Where the tribunal makes an Order under para 25(1), it may specify the amount of compensation payable (under para 25(3)(a)), or it may give directions for the determination of such an amount (under para 25(3)(b)).

Determining compensation at the outset

14.38 An operator will often prefer a single payment at the outset of the agreement rather than paying fees piecemeal at points throughout the term as they arise. Site providers, however, are typically concerned that such an approach may underestimate those costs that it will ultimately incur.

14.39 The tribunal expressed a preference in *Islington*,[27] which was then referred to in *UAL*[28] as 'the tribunal's practice', as follows:

> 'Our preference is to determine (in principle at least) those claims which can be determined, to dismiss those which are speculative or unfounded, and to leave the respondent to bring a further claim in the event that additional loss or damage (not already taken into account) can be proven to have been sustained in future.'[29]

14.40 The 'not already taken into account' element of the above may give rise to dispute and difficulty. For example, an operator may in theory be ordered to pay compensation of £2,500 on the basis that there should be a £250 payment to reimburse a landlord for each site visit, where it is estimated that there will be one site visit per annum during a 10-year term. In principle, a later compensation claim may be made under para 25(2)(b). If the operator actually visited the site twice as often as anticipated, can a site provider make a subsequent claim for the additional £2,500, or is it prevented from doing so, on the ground that the tribunal has already made a binding determination of compensation under this precise head, albeit by making a rough and ready estimate? Similarly, if the landlord's reasonable costs of these visits increases in an unforeseen manner, can the incremental cost later be claimed?

14.41 These types of questions relating to the adequacy of compensation under an imposed New Code agreement have not yet troubled the tribunal. Partly this is because the Code remains in its relative infancy. However, one does wonder whether a landowner would take the trouble to initiate a compensation claim over a claim of, say, £2,500, and if it did, what the attitude of the tribunal would be to the disproportionate costs involved. But then, if an operator knows that a landowner is never going to claim the £2,500, there is little incentive to agree to pay it consensually.

26 *London & Quadrant* at [99].
27 [2019] UKUT 53 (LC) at [121].
28 *CTIL v UAL* [2020] UKUT 248 (LC) at [81].
29 *EE v Islington* [2019] UKUT 53 (LC) at [121].

14.42 Nonetheless, one can see the merit in the tribunal's established practice as set out above. Where an attempt is made to assess a global figure for likely expenses at the outset, this constitutes the tribunal endeavouring to avoid the need for future determinations of relatively modest sums rather than to create such a need.

Giving directions under para 25(3)(b)

14.43 If the tribunal decides to give directions for the determination of compensation, para 25(4)(a) allows such directions to provide for the parties to agree the amount, and para 25(4)(b) allows such directions to provide for a determination by arbitration. There is no 'and' between these two alternatives. It would seem clear that the tribunal can send the matter straight to arbitration, but that if the para 25(4) course is taken, a more obvious Order would be to direct the parties to agree by a certain date, with arbitration to follow in default of any agreement.

14.44 The tribunal does not habitually send matters of quantum for arbitration. The tribunal itself is particularly well-versed in the Code and the sorts of issues that it can generate. Especially where the likely quantum is relatively modest, it is probably fair to say that the tribunal itself is typically best placed not only to decide the matter but to ensure that costs are not duplicated or rendered unacceptably disproportionate.

14.45 Paragraph 25(4) does not purport to be exhaustive of the types of directions which the tribunal can give, and a much more common scenario is for the tribunal to determine the quantum of compensation itself. If such determination would require further evidence, argument, or tribunal time, and especially where the likely quantum is not large, directions may well be given for the parties to seek to agree compensation, and in default of which revert to the tribunal for a determination.

14.46 By way of a run-of-the-mill example, in *Stephenson*,[30] the Deputy President noted that there was a compensation claim for reasonable legal and valuation expenses. As these were not 'quantified in evidence', the parties were to have further discussions on quantum and revert to the tribunal.

14.47 As is clear from the passage below in relation to transactional costs, the tribunal does not typically require a great deal of evidence on the quantum of such costs and has been content to accept a relatively summary costs schedule verified by a statement of truth. Naturally, what evidence is acceptable in any given case will depend on all the circumstances, including the amounts involved.

14.48 In *Islington*,[31] the tribunal noted that the site provider was 'entitled to its reasonable legal and surveying costs of the agreement and to compensation for loss or damage caused by the installation of the claimants' apparatus', and gave permission to apply to quantify both heads of compensation if they could not be agreed.

30 This is the '*Pendown Farm*' case. The relevant passage of the decision, following the final decision of the tribunal, is at [2022] UKUT 180 (LC) at [80].
31 See [2019] UKUT 53 (LC) at [153].

Heads of loss that can be claimed as compensation

14.49 Paragraph 84(1) makes clear that para 84 applies[32] in relation to the powers of the tribunal to award compensation under paras 25(1) and 44(5), as well as the Part 4A compensation power in para 27H(2).

14.50 Paragraph 84(2) sets out certain types of losses which are in principle able to be awarded:

> '(2) Depending on the circumstances, the power of the court to order the payment of compensation for loss or damage includes power to order payment for—
>
> (a) expenses (including reasonable legal and valuation expenses, subject to the provisions of any enactment about the powers of the court by whom the order for compensation is made to award costs or, in Scotland, expenses),
>
> (b) diminution in the value of the land, and
>
> (c) costs of reinstatement.'

14.51 In *Islington*, the tribunal indicated that it was apparent that the above list is not intended to be exhaustive, as para 84(2) says that the power to order compensation 'includes power' to order payment for the matters identified. It therefore expressed a provisional view that this was the position, although, as it was not necessary to decide the point, left it for an occasion on which it would be fully argued. Nonetheless, the tribunal set out a list of indicators that pointed towards para 84(2) being non-exhaustive:

> 'In this case the relevant power is under paragraph 25(1), which, in apparently unrestricted terms, confers jurisdiction to 'order the operator to pay compensation to the relevant person for any loss or damage that has been sustained or will be sustained by that person as a result of the exercise of the code right'. The reference in paragraph 25 to '*any* loss or damage', the inclusive list of examples in paragraph 84(2), and the incorporation of only some of the heads of compensation available under section 5 of the Land Compensation Act 1961, all suggest that other types of loss or damage may be capable of being the subject of compensation under paragraph 25.'[33]

Expenses

14.52 The first stated permissible head of loss is 'expenses', 'including reasonable legal and valuation expenses'. The fact that the permissible expenses merely 'include' reasonable legal and valuation expenses must surely indicate that in principle other expenses may fall within para 84(2)(a), otherwise, the initial word 'expenses' would

32 Para 84(1) states that para 84 applies to the para 25(1) power to award compensation itself, and para 25(6) states that para 84 makes further provision about compensation in the case of an Order under para 20. The application of para 25 by paras 26(4)(e), 27(4)(e) and 34(11) are surely therefore enough to render para 84 applicable to interim rights, temporary rights and the para 34(11) renewal/modification cases. However, to put the matter beyond doubt, paras 26(4)(f), 27(4)(f) and 34(11) also make it express that para 84 applies to such cases.

33 [2019] UKUT 53 (LC) at [117].

be entirely otiose. Indeed, in *London & Quadrant*,[34] when discussing the interplay between consideration and compensation in respect of the burdens of an agreement, one aspect referred to as being taken into account in a real-world negotiation was the costs of an administration burden. The impression given is that the Code does intend to compensate for administrative burdens that result in expense, whether through consideration or compensation, and without such costs having to constitute 'legal and valuation expenses'.

14.53 In practice, if a surveyor advises a site provider client on valuation and negotiates the terms of an agreement in return for a fee that is modest and reasonable, it would seem absurd for an operator to be able to make a successful defence of a para 25 claim for the negotiation fees on the ground that they are neither legal expenses nor valuation expenses. If a solicitor and surveyor are both instructed, their fees may, in an appropriate case, both be reasonable and claimable. However, any duplication of work is likely to cause the tribunal to disallow some of the fees, either on the grounds of double-counting, or overall reasonableness of quantum.

14.54 In the cases, the costs incurred by a site provider in respect of lawyers and/ or surveyors have often been referred to as 'transactional costs' in order to distinguish them from litigation costs. These 'transactional costs' are dealt with below.

14.55 Litigation costs are not awarded as compensation but are dealt with under the tribunal's powers to award costs, which are set out in the Code, as well as other legislation and procedural rules. They are dealt with in Chapter 23 of this book.

Transactional costs

14.56 Paragraph 25 of the Code allows a site provider to claim, either when an agreement is imposed or at any later date[35] compensation for 'any loss or damage that has been sustained or will be sustained by that person as a result of the exercise of the code right'. It is well-established that in principle such loss includes costs expended in negotiating and advising on the proposed Code agreement.

14.57 Paragraph 84(2)(a) of the Code provides that the power of the tribunal to order the payment of compensation 'includes' the power to order payment for 'expenses (including reasonable legal and valuation expenses…'.

14.58 The authorities demonstrate the following principles as to the professional costs that can be recovered by site providers as compensation under paras 25 and 84(2):

(i) Paragraph 84(2) entitles a site provider to receive as compensation its reasonable legal and valuation expenses (in addition to the wording of para 84(2) itself, see *CTIL v St Martins Property Investments Ltd*[36]). Indeed, 'The MSV, and the process of negotiation leading up to it, should not leave the respondent out of pocket' (*Hackney (Tradescant House)*).[37]

34 [2020] UKUT 341 (LC).

35 Para 25(2).

36 [2021] UKUT 262 (LC) ('*St Martins*') at [33].

37 *Cornerstone Telecommunications Infrastructure Limited v The Mayor and Burgesses of the London Borough of Hackney* [2022] UKUT 210 (LC) at [94].

(ii) In terms of scope, the reasonable costs of negotiation are clearly recoverable in principle. Such costs have been described in the following ways by the tribunal:

(a) 'those incurred in seeking to agree terms for a code agreement' (see *Islington* at [122]); and

(b) 'legal and professional fees that it has occurred in the negotiation of the agreement' (see (*Hackney (Tradescant House)*)[38].

(iii) The costs of seeking advice are also in principle recoverable, and not solely the costs of negotiation:

(a) The Deputy President held that the recoverable costs were those of 'advising on and negotiating the agreement (not the costs of litigation)' in *St Martins* at [32]; and

(b) In *Affinity Water*[39] at [88] the Deputy President held that: 'A site provider is entitled to seek advice on the lease and to recover the reasonable cost of doing so'.

(iv) 'The MSV, and the process of negotiation leading up to it, should not leave the respondent out of pocket'.[40] Although this statement concerned an MSV, because that was what was being sought in the relevant case, it could be said that there is no special reason for distinguishing MSV agreements from other agreements in this respect. Clearly this does not generate a full indemnity in favour of a respondent in respect of costs incurred, not least because any person claiming compensation of any kind will only be able to recover costs insofar as they are reasonably incurred. This is clear from the *Shun Fung* principles mentioned above.

(v) Fees which are *not* recoverable as compensation are those expended in seeking to oppose the principle of a code agreement, and those incurred in attempting to compromise the Reference itself, both of which would fall to be considered as litigation costs (see *Islington* at [122]).

14.59 The tribunal is alive to the need to police the distinction between what might be referred to as transactional costs and those that are properly considered litigation costs to ensure that the latter is not claimed as the former.

14.60 However, the convenient label 'transactional costs' does not necessarily make obvious the scope of professional expenses, which may be recovered as compensation. As indicated above, we are not here dealing solely with solicitors' fees for carrying out the transaction, or even of carrying out a negotiation of the terms of the agreement. In principle a site provider may also recover the costs of reasonable advice on the agreement and its terms.

14.61 The costs in respect of advice that are properly recoverable as compensation will be limited in order to ensure that the transactional/litigation cost distinction is policed. A party is not entitled to oppose a Code agreement, fail in that opposition,

38 [2022] UKUT 210 (LC) at [94].

39 *EE Limited and Hutchison 3G UK Limited v Affinity Water Limited* [2022] UKUT 08 (LC).

40 *Cornerstone Telecommunications Infrastructure Limited v The Mayor and Burgesses of the London Borough of Hackney* [2022] UKUT 210 (LC) at [94].

and then claim as compensation the costs of legal advice as to a desirable strategy for mounting the failed opposition. The costs of such advice would properly be considered litigation costs.

Quantum of 'transactional costs'

14.62 It is commonplace for operators to write to potential site providers seeking an agreement conferring Code rights and to offer to provide an undertaking for legal fees up to a particular amount. The sort of figure typically offered in the first few years of the Code rarely exceeds £1,500. Indeed, potential site providers have been led to believe by letters of this kind that such a figure is a standard figure to which a site provider might be entitled in respect of their legal costs of negotiating and entering into an agreement.

14.63 However, the tribunal in *St Martins* made clear that a site provider is entitled to *all* of its reasonable transactional costs, dispelling the notion that an operator merely has to make a contribution towards the costs incurred by a site provider. It was noted at [31] that the claimant operator had a standard form of agreement that made provision for a contribution towards legal and valuation fees, but that its practice was to seek to limit those to a sum agreed at the start of the process.[41]

14.64 At para [34] of the decision in that case, the Deputy President said as follows:

> 'The notion that an operator should be required only to make a contribution towards the legal expenses incurred by a site provider, and that the site provider should thereby be left out of pocket, is flawed. The site provider is entitled to recoup its reasonable legal expenses – all of them – and in this case, on the material before the Tribunal, those reasonable legal expenses are £11,000.'

14.65 In *St Martins*, the full amount of £11,000 claimed was awarded on the basis that there was no reason to doubt that such a sum had been incurred, and 'no reason to doubt that the efforts made by the respondent's solicitors have been reasonable'.[42]

14.66 The sum of £11,000 awarded in *St Martins* was described by the Deputy President as not being significantly different from that awarded in other cases, citing the 'Dale Park' case,[43] in which 'the tribunal awarded £8,000 for negotiating the agreement'.[44]

14.67 However, the Deputy President made clear that these particular decisions do not set a norm, describing them as 'simply the figures produced by the application of the proper principle to the circumstances of a particular case'.

14.68 It may be frustrating for operators to have to reimburse landowners for the costs of arguing a point that was ultimately conceded in the operator's favour. However, the fact that solicitors 'eventually agreed some matters which they initially

41 See [31] of the judgment in *St Martins*.
42 *St Martins* at [33]
43 *On Tower UK Ltd v JH & FW Green Ltd* [2020] UKUT 348 (LC).
44 *St Martins* at [35].

resisted does not mean their work was undertaken unreasonably.'[45] Thus, if the costs were incurred reasonably on the facts of a given case, the fact that some points were conceded is not likely on its own to diminish the sums claimed.

14.69 It would be quite wrong to assume that a tribunal would consider the sorts of sums mentioned above to be reasonable in every single case. However, where they have been satisfied that a party has in fact spent a particular amount, tribunals have shown a greater willingness to award the entirety of what is claimed, or a substantial proportion thereof, than they have in the context of litigation costs.

14.70 The complexity of the negotiations and the number of terms in dispute are factors that unsurprisingly have influenced the assessment of transactional costs.[46]

14.71 Further, the 'fraught and indeed hostile' nature of a negotiation can seemingly be a factor that justifies an elevated level of recoverable costs.[47] Although the tribunal has often expressed a desire for cordial and constructive relations between operators and site providers, it does not seem that negotiating with hostility will in and of itself be considered so unreasonable as to render the increased costs of negotiating in that manner irrecoverable.

Non-lawyer costs

14.72 In *Green* (the Dale Park case), £4,000 plus VAT was claimed in respect of valuation advice. It is important to underline that far from disallowing that sum in principle, the tribunal sought a breakdown to show how it was calculated. It was noted that there was no entitlement to reimbursement for an expert report or any other 'tribunal facing document'[48] as compensation. These latter costs would be litigation costs and would need to be dealt with as such. The tribunal awarded £3,000 plus VAT. It accepted that it was reasonable for a valuer to carry out a site visit, but it was considered that the site was not so unusual as to justify a greater figure than this. The tribunal referred to the fact that the operator had cited examples of figures agreed for agents' fees where consensual agreements were reached, and on the facts, there was no justification taking this case 'far outside' the range of those agreed fees.

14.73 The tribunal is well-placed to consider what level of fees is reasonable in each case. However, it will doubtless recall the warning of the Deputy President in *St Martins* that the operator's obligation is not merely to offer a contribution to costs falling within para 84, but all of those costs insofar as they are reasonable.[49] It is certainly the case that in the earlier days of the Code, operators would offer relatively low sums as a contribution to costs,[50] and where such offers were accepted by landowners who

---

45 *St Martins* at [33].

46 See, for example, *On Tower UK Limited v AP Wireless II (UK) Limited* [2022] UKUT 152 (LC) at [261] per Judge Cooke.

47 see *Cornerstone Telecommunications Infrastructure Limited v The Mayor and Burgesses of the London Borough of Hackney* [2022] UKUT 210 (LC) at [94].

48 *On Tower UK Ltd v JH & FW Green Ltd* [2020] UKUT 348 (LC) at [148].

49 These comments surely apply in the same way to valuers' fees as they do to solicitors' fees.

50 In *On Tower Ltd v AP Wireless (II) (New Zealand Farm)* [2022] EW Misc 6 (CC), Martin Rodger QC, sitting as a county court judge, referred at [86] to 'the derisory rents offered by operators to unrepresented site providers in the earliest days of the Code', and it is fair to comment that in those days, the offers of contributions in respect of transactional costs often followed a similar theme.

did not wish to argue over small sums before a judge, consensually-agreed figures may have undervalued what might have been reasonable in a given case. Furthermore, if a matter is before a tribunal, one might expect there to have been more difficulty, and hence more time spent, in negotiating terms. Tough and lengthy negotiations are not necessarily evidence of any unreasonableness.

14.74 It is to be remembered that evidence of what fees were agreed in another case is not a 'comparable' which enables the tribunal to set some notional market rate to which the parties would agree by way of professional fees. The task of the tribunal is to compensate the site provider for the professional fees actually expended, insofar as that expenditure is reasonable.

14.75 It seems reasonably clear[51] that para 84(2) is not intended to be an exhaustive list of items that might be recoverable as compensation. Further, the 'reasonable legal and valuation expenses' within para 84(2)(a) are not said to be an exhaustive treatment of all categories of 'expenses' that might be claimed under para 84(2)(a).

14.76 There will be cases where surveyors or agents conduct negotiations as to the terms of a Code agreement on behalf of a client, potentially both as to consideration and other matters. Under the Old Code, aided by the market value assumptions for valuation purposes, agents had a good track record of reaching agreement on behalf of their clients without the need to trouble the courts. Even under the New Code, much can be achieved through discussions between professional persons with a practical understanding of a building and potentially a technical understanding of the installation of ECA. There seems no reason why negotiation of agreement terms should not be carried out through agents, and if reasonable costs are incurred in that process, there seems no reason why those costs should be any less recoverable than the costs of solicitors debating the same terms.

14.77 In an appropriate case, there is no reason in principle why surveyor and solicitor fees would not both be recoverable where such costs are reasonably incurred and reasonable in amount. It is not uncommon on sensitive sites, or sites where the financial stakes are substantial, for surveyors to begin negotiations and for lawyers to come in at a later stage. This can be to seek to resolve a stalemate, to discuss more detailed drafting points following Heads of Terms, or because tribunal proceedings have now been actively threatened. The recovery of any sums will be fact-specific, and tribunals will be alive to the need not to allow unnecessary costs for duplicative work, but there seems no reason why sums cannot be recovered in respect of two types of professional.

Evidence as to professional expenses

14.78 Although the sums claimed are not litigation costs, they are often made up of time spent by a number of legal professionals with hourly rates and are typically recorded by reference to units of such professionals' time. Accordingly, it is perfectly reasonable to communicate the quantum and particularisation of such a claim by

51 The tribunal having expressed a reasoned preliminary view to this effect, despite leaving the question formally open in *Islington*.

reference to a Statement of Costs, or similar document. Ideally, such a document will be verified with a statement of truth.

14.79 The tribunal ordered the £8,000-odd in the Dale Park case on the basis of a costs schedule.[52] The total amount claimed was awarded on the basis that solicitors' time was particularised on relevant matters such as reviewing and updating the draft lease and communicating with other parties. There was no mention of 'activities specific to the litigation'.

14.80 The Tribunal is not likely to consider it proportionate in most cases to produce long witness statements explaining the transactional costs that have been incurred, by whom, at what stage, and dealing with what points of dispute. Common sense should be used as regards such proportionality. However, where there is a particularly contentious point that consumed an unexpected amount of time or where there is anything else out of the ordinary that might need explaining, witness statements from those involved might be justified.

Transactional claims in the different tribunals

14.81 In principle, the FTT and the UT should address quantum in the same way. A compensation claim is a claim for which an operator is said to be liable under the Code. If it is established that the operator is indeed liable in principle, the fact that any matters of dispute are ultimately being dealt with in the FTT rather than the UT should not affect the question of what sums were reasonable to expend on negotiating or seeking advice.

Agreeing transactional costs consensually

14.82 There is of course nothing to prevent the parties from agreeing the quantum of compensation for professional fees consensually, either in cases where the parties enter into a Code agreement with no need to resort to the tribunal or in cases where they are seeking to narrow the issues within a Tribunal Reference. As the Deputy President said in *HSBC*,[53] transactional costs, as distinct from the costs of participating in the Reference, are to be agreed or determined by the tribunal.

Diminution in value

14.83 By para 84(3)(a), rules (2) to (4) of section 5 of the Land Compensation Act 1961 apply (with any necessary modifications) to a claim in respect of diminution in value. These include an open market valuation on the basis that the seller is willing.

14.84 There has been at least one substantial claim for compensation in respect of a penthouse apartment whose value was said to have been affected by the exercise of Code rights. However, this case settled without going to trial. Thus, there has been no detailed judicial consideration of the principles that will apply. Valuers who advise

52 See the *Dale Park* case: *On Tower UK Ltd v JH & FW Green Ltd* [2020] UKUT 348 (LC) at [147].
53 *EE Ltd and Hutchison 3G UK Ltd v HSBC Bank Plc* [2022] UKUT 174 (LC) at [7].

landowners are overwhelmingly of the view that the presence of ECA on buildings causes a substantial diminution in value in most cases, and one can expect further claims of this nature to come forward in the future. There will doubtless be numerous points taken in respect of matters such as causation, the distinction between the grant of Code rights and their 'exercise', and whether any alleged loss has already been accounted for in consideration.

Para 44(5): Compensation for loss incurred while the landowner has a right to require removal

14.85 Part 6 of the Code creates a regime whereby a landowner can secure the removal of ECA once it has a right to require that removal. That regime is discussed in Chapter 18. Where a landowner seeks a removal Order and has suffered loss as a result of the presence of ECA whilst it had the right to require its removal, there is a special power to order compensation. This is contained at para 44(5).

14.86 Paragraph 44(5) provides as follows:

> '(5) An order under this paragraph on an application under paragraph 40 may require the operator to pay compensation to the landowner for any loss or damage suffered by the landowner as a result of the presence of the apparatus on the land during the period when the landowner had the right to require the removal of the apparatus from the land but was not able to exercise that right.'

14.87 By para 84(1)(b), para 84 applies to para 44(5) cases, so the (presumably non-exhaustive) heads of loss at para 84(2) are relevant.

14.88 It is worth noting that, similarly to the para 25(2)(a) power to order compensation at the point of imposing a para 20 agreement, the para 44(5) power is not expressly contingent on an application for compensation having been made. One would, however, imagine that in reality this power will most often be exercised upon receipt of an application from the landowner.

14.89 The para 44(5) power does however *appear* to arise only where there has been an 'application under' para 40, on the literal wording of the provision. One would imagine that an 'application under' para 40 would cover the following species of applications:

- a para 40(6)(a) application for an Order requiring removal;
- a para 40(6)(b) application for an Order enabling a landowner to remove the ECA;
- a para 40(7) application for an Order enabling a landowner to remove the ECA.

14.90 It is perhaps notable that although the para 44(5) power is contingent on there being a para 40 application, it is not expressly contingent on that application resulting in a removal Order, or any other Order, being made.

14.91 Thus, where there is a para 40(6)(a) application seeking an Order for removal that also seeks para 44(5) compensation and the operator removes the ECA before the application can be determined, one would think that the tribunal retains jurisdiction to order compensation in respect of the period whilst the ECA remained present. In this way, the operator cannot avoid paying compensation during a period when its ECA was present despite no Code right nor contractual right existing, simply by removing the ECA before the hearing.

14.92 One lacuna, however, might be said to be a situation in which the presence of ECA (without any Code right or contractual right) is causing loss to a landowner, and so it enters into correspondence with the operator asking for the ECA to be removed so that it can proceed with its plans for the land. If the operator removes the ECA before an application is made under para 40 (perhaps because the landowner is seeking to exercise good practice as regards pre-action correspondence), it may be that para 44(5) is not available to the landowner. After all, it is not able to make a para 40 application as there is no ECA in respect of which such an application could be made. In such a situation, a landowner may be left to a common law claim for trespass.

14.93 In many cases, whether the presence of ECA without a Code right or contractual rights constitutes a trespass might be a purely academic question. But not here. If the ECA is not trespassing, it is hard to see how the landowner has a money claim. It is sometimes said that in remaining on land, an operator can rely on its 'Part 6 rights'. But the function of Part 6 is not to confer rights on operators. As is made clear both from its contents and from its introductory paragraph at para 36, Part 6 informs us when a person has a right to require removal of ECA or restoration of land, how it might discover whether ECA is present under a Code right, and the means by which its right to require removal or restoration can be enforced.

14.94 In requiring a landowner to go through Part 6, the Code is placing a procedural hurdle in front of a landowner, in a similar way to that in which Part 55 of the Civil Procedure Rules 1998 imposes certain procedural requirements on a landowner who is seeking possession of its land, including from trespassers. Certainly in *Crawley*,[54] the tribunal held that there is no discretion on the part of the tribunal as to whether the landowner is entitled to an Order for removal, where it has a 'right' to require removal as described at para 37. Further, para 40(8) merely regulates the order in which an operator's para 20 application and a landowner's para 40 application are to be determined; it does not confer any right on the operator (even to make a para 20 application).[55]

14.95 If an operator has no Code right, and no agreement whether imposed under the Code or agreed consensually, it is hard to see how it is not trespassing. But this is not a point that has yet been determined.

Compensation under para 85: injurious affection

The right to such compensation

14.96 By para 85(1), para 85 applies where a right conferred by or in accordance with any provision of Parts 2 to 9 of the Code is exercised by an operator. In the vast majority of cases, this will entail the exercise of a 'Code right'. However, it is

54 *Crawley Borough Council v EE Ltd and another* [2022] UKUT 158 (LC), and as described in *Gravesham BC v On Tower UK Limited* [2024] UKUT 151 (LC) at [24].

55 See the *Gravesham* case on appeal in the Upper Tribunal.

worth noting that para 85(1) is broad enough to encompass the exercise of any right conferred by a consensual or imposed Code agreement and not merely the exercise of a right listed within the menu of Code rights at para 3.

14.97 Where para 85 applies, para 85(2) creates a right to compensation for injurious affection in the following terms:

> '...compensation is payable by the operator under section 10 of the Compulsory Purchase Act 1965 (compensation for injurious affection to neighbouring land) as if that section applied in relation to injury caused by the exercise of such a right as it applies in relation to injury caused by the execution of works on land that has been compulsorily acquired'.

14.98 A person claiming compensation under para 85 need not have any interest in the land in relation to which the right referred to in para 85(1) is exercised.[56]

Legal and valuation expenses

14.99 By para 85(9), compensation under para 85 may include reasonable legal and valuation expenses, subject to the powers of the court or tribunal by whom an order for compensation is made to award costs.

No de minimis claims

14.100 Finally, by para 85(7), compensation is payable on a claim for compensation under para 85 only if the amount of the compensation exceeds £50.

Para 86: The exclusion of additional compensation

14.101 Under the heading '*No other compensation available*', para 86 provides as follows:

> 'Except as provided by any provision of Parts 2 to 13 of this code or this Part,[57] an operator is not liable to compensate any person for, and is not subject to any other liability in respect of, any loss or damage caused by the lawful exercise of any right conferred by or in accordance with any provision of those Parts.'

14.102 Paragraph 86 falls right at the end of Part 14, which deals with compensation. Although the full extent of the provision has not yet been clarified, it makes clear that the compensation provisions of the Code are exhaustive.[58] One consequence of this is that there is no right to compensation under para 25 save where the necessary criterion of an agreement having been imposed under the Code is not met. Thus one cannot ask for compensation from the court under the 1954 Act where a lease that grants Code rights is renewed or from the tribunal where a Code agreement has been entered into consensually. A right to compensation is created in respect of injurious

56 Para 85(8).

57 Para 86 is within Part 14 of the Code, which deals with Compensation under the Code, and includes paras 84 and 85.

58 This is a different question than the question whether the list of possible heads of loss are set out exhaustively by the Code.

affection under section 10 of the Compulsory Purchase Act 1965, but this right is conferred expressly by para 85 of the Code. Absent such express statements in the Code, it will not be possible to imply compensation rights into the Code which apply under other statutory regimes.

Para 86 and damages claims

14.103 Paragraph 86 does not, of course, limit liability for unlawful activity, presumably including the purported exercise of a Code right in an unlawful manner. One would think it uncontroversial that a site provider can in principle bring a damages claim against an operator in respect of a breach of terms of an agreement that causes loss or damage. This would surely not be prevented by para 86, and it may be that the reason for this is that such a breach would not constitute 'the lawful exercise' of a right conferred by the agreement. An alternative or additional answer may lie in para 100, which is considered further below.

A bespoke contractual compensation mechanism?

14.104 Further, it would appear that para 86 does not prevent parties from agreeing a contractual compensation mechanism within agreements, for example, a clause that allows arbitration or expert determination of claims that mirror para 25 compensation rights. This would allow parties to enter into an agreement consensually and without troubling the tribunal, whilst preserving the right to compensation that is available to those who have agreements imposed.

14.105 Indeed, in *London & Quadrant* at [102], the tribunal envisaged that it would be possible to make consensual contractual provision for a compensation claim, and did not raise any issue as to para 86 preventing this. It referred to the impossibility of applying for compensation under para 25 where a Code agreement had been agreed consensually rather than imposed by the tribunal, before saying:

> 'The parties to a consensual Code agreement must therefore either make contractual provision for compensation or must reflect the risk of loss and damage caused by the exercise of the code rights in the consideration they agree.'[59]

The interplay between para 86 and para 100

14.106 If para 86 prevents compensation otherwise than as prescribed by certain specified provisions of the Code, how are parties able to provide for compensation in a different way? It is respectfully suggested that the answer lies in para 100.

14.107 Paragraph 100(1) provides that:

> 'This code does not affect any rights or liabilities arising under an agreement to which an operator is a party'.

---

59 [2020] UKUT 282 (LC) at [102].

14.108 Paragraph 100(2) disapplies para 100(1) 'in relation to' certain parts of the Code, as follows:

> 'Sub-paragraph (1) does not apply in relation to paragraph 99 or Parts 3 to 6 of this code.'

14.109 Thus, para 100(2) renders para 100(1) inapplicable 'to' Part 4 of the Code (which includes para 25), but it does not render it inapplicable to Part 14 of the Code (which includes para 86 and indeed para 84).

14.110 It thus seems perfectly arguable that by para 100(1), nothing in para 86 affects contractual rights and liabilities, but that because of para 100(2), para 25 does affect contractual rights and liabilities. In other words, one can expressly or impliedly 'contract out' of the effect of para 86 by providing for additional or different compensation mechanisms or rights than are provided for in the Code, but one can never disapply para 25 or cut it down.

14.111 Thus, seemingly the parties cannot have an agreement imposed and then later agree to amend it so as to *remove* a person's para 25(2)(b) right to make a later application to the tribunal for compensation.

14.112 It is fair to note however that there is not yet clarity as to the extent to which parties to a consensual agreement can put a site provider in a better position as regards compensation than para 25 does.

14.113 In *Audley House*, the tribunal cited para 86, before saying:

> 'Accordingly it is not open to the parties to improve upon the site provider's position by providing contractual liabilities in its favour in addition to paragraph 25 in respect of loss or damage caused by the exercise of the operator's Code rights. The parties have agreed a number of additional provisions for [the site provider's] protection, which must be read in the light of paragraph 86.'[60]

14.114 It is not clear that the above was a determination of a dispute that was subject to argument, rather than a passing observation. It does not appear that any potential effect of para 100 was considered. One might as why parties' agreed terms need to be read subject to para 86 if para 100(1) allowed them to contract however they liked?

14.115 Paragraph 86 provides that an operator is not liable to compensate 'except as provided for' by certain provisions of the Code. If para 100(1) for some reason does not allow the parties to override para 86 consensually, then even a contractual mechanism that seeks to *replicate* para 25-style entitlements through an arbitration process could be said to fall foul of para 86, as such an entitlement is not one that is 'provided for' by para 25. Paragraph 25 relates only to imposed agreements.

14.116 If para 86 were to prevent *consensual* provisions as to the future payment of compensation, difficulties and absurdities may result:

---

60 The tribunal also commented at [195] that 'any nuisance caused by the exercise of the Code rights is amply provided for in paragraph 25 of the Code and cannot be extended because of the provision of paragraph 86 of the Code'. Again, whether para 100 makes any difference to this analysis does not appear to have been considered.

(i) The parties would be able to provide in a consensual agreement for whatever level of consideration they wished, even though the Code aimed at limiting unearned rewards to landowners for value generated by networks, but would not be similarly free in relation to merely providing for a compensatory mechanism to negate losses which a landowner genuinely suffers. That would seem a strange consequence as a matter of policy.

(ii) Parties could end up in disputes as to whether an agreed contractual provision is ineffective, by reference to whether it provides for compensation, consideration, or some other species of payment. This may well be impractical and lead to arbitrary distinctions.

(iii) It would necessitate applications to the tribunal for the imposition of an agreement even where parties would have been happy to agree a bespoke compensation provision, thus increasing costs and consuming tribunal resources.

(iv) It may prevent the agreement of even a modest specified payment in respect of the attendance of a member of staff of the site provider where an operator wishes to gain access to a sensitive or difficult location. The site provider would have no right to seek such payment under para 25 in the case of a consensual agreement.

15

Third parties: who is bound, registration and assignment

Who is bound by a Code right?

15.01 The first part of this chapter considers agreements coming into being after the coming into force of the Code. Subsisting agreements will be considered later in this chapter, from **15.76** onwards.

Introduction

15.02 As the Deputy President said in *Gencomp*:[1]

> 'The basic principle reflected in Parts 2 and 4 is that only occupiers of land can *confer* code rights, while others with an interest in land, or rights over it, may only be *bound* by code rights.'

15.03 The Code makes provision as to who is 'bound' by a Code right. Although the Code does not spell it out in this language, it is obvious that a person who confers a Code right on an operator is bound by that Code right,[2] in the sense that it is enforceable against that person.

15.04 A Code right can only be conferred by an agreement between an operator and an occupier.[3] An agreement conferring a Code right can of course be imposed by a tribunal, and such an agreement is treated as[4] an agreement under Part 2 (ie, as a consensual agreement between operator and occupier). Perhaps the most obvious power by which such an imposition occurs is that in para 20. Paragraph 20 applies where an operator requires a person to agree either to confer a Code right, or 'to be *otherwise* bound by' a Code right (emphasis added). Thus it is clear that a person who confers a Code right is considered 'bound by' a Code right, whilst the relevant agreement continues between the original parties. A person who is rendered bound by an Order of the tribunal is, of course, also bound by a Code right.

---

1 [2022] UKUT 223 (LC) at [12]. The UT's conclusion was overturned by the Court of Appeal on appeal, but this observation remains undisturbed, as the appeal related to the effect of para 10(3) specifically.

2 [2022] UKUT 223 (LC) at [100]. The UT's conclusion was overturned by the Court of Appeal on appeal, but the first sentence of [100] is uncontroversial.

3 This is by para 9(1) and is subject to the narrow point made at para 9(2) in respect of sharing the use of ECA (namely that an agreement can allow an operator who has the right to share the use of ECA with a second operator to permit that second operator to exercise a Code right conferred on the first operator, in connection with that sharing).

4 Para 22.

15.05 Paragraph 10 of the Code is headed 'Who else is bound by code rights?' and deals with persons who find themselves bound for reasons other than those mentioned above.

Para 10 of the Code

15.06 Paragraph 10 applies where, pursuant to an agreement under Part 2 (or Part 4A[5]):

> 'a code right is conferred on an operator in respect of land by a person ('O') who is the occupier of the land when the code right is conferred'.[6]

Successors to 'O' (and persons with subordinate rights and interests)

15.07 Paragraph 10(2) then makes provision for certain successors to the original conferring occupier ('O'), and persons with rights and interests which are subordinate to O to be bound.

15.08 It provides as follows:

> '(2) If O has an interest in the land when the code right is conferred, the code right also binds—
>
> (a) the successors in title to that interest,
>
> (b) a person with an interest in the land that is created after the right is conferred and is derived (directly or indirectly) out of—
>
> (i) O's interest, or
>
> (ii) the interest of a successor in title to O's interest, and
>
> (c) any other person at any time in occupation of the land whose right to occupation was granted by—
>
> (i) O, at a time when O was bound by the code right, or
>
> (ii) a person within paragraph (a) or (b).'

15.09 It will be observed that although para 10(2) binds those with interests derived out of O's right, it does not bind those with interests out of which O's right was derived. Thus O's tenant will be bound,[7] but O's landlord will not be.

15.10 Paragraph 10(2)(c) ensures that an occupier with no interest in land is bound if they were granted a right to occupy either by O (O having an interest in the land) or by someone else with an interest who is bound under para 10(2)(a) or (b). Where a person who is bound because of para 10(2)(c) has a contractual right to allow others to occupy, the others who are allowed to occupy have no interest in the land, and neither do they appear to be bound by para 10(2)(c), at least on the literal words of the provision.

5 Part 4A relates to unresponsive occupiers in certain leasehold situations, and is seldom used.

6 Para 10(1).

7 Assuming O's tenant's interest was created after the Code right was conferred.

15.11 More fundamentally, if O confers Code rights on an operator despite having no interest in the land, para 10(2) does not operate so as to render any other person bound by the Code right. For example, where O grants contractual rights to others to occupy the land, those other persons are seemingly not bound by the Code rights previously conferred by O on an operator.

15.12 As the Deputy President put the point in *Gencomp*:[8] 'a licensee cannot grant code rights which will bind others'.

15.13 Where an occupier is not bound by extant Code rights for whatever reason, and the operator finds that it is practically or legally necessary or desirable for that person to be bound, the operator can serve notices and apply to the tribunal for Code rights under para 20, or under para 26. It will only be possible to do the same under para 27 where (inter alia) the intended respondent has a right to require removal under para 37,[9] and thus this option will not be available where that intended respondent has no interest in the land.[10]

Persons who agree to be bound

15.14 Paragraph 10(4) provides that a Code right 'also binds any other person with an interest in the land' provided that that person has 'agreed to be bound by it'. As originally enacted, this provision did not clarify what form such an agreement had to take.[11] However, amendments made by the Telecommunications Infrastructure (Leasehold Property) Act 2021[12] to give effect to the unresponsive occupiers provisions of Part 4A have also clarified that a person is only bound under para 10(4) where it has agreed to be bound 'pursuant to an agreement under this Part' (ie, Part 2), or under Part 4A.

15.15 One consequence of this is that where a person seeks to enter into a consensual agreement to be bound by Code rights, as envisaged under para 10(4), it must seemingly comply with each[13] of the formality and mandatory content requirements of para 11(1). On the face of it, this would include the requirement at para 11(1)(c) that the agreement must state for how long the Code right is exercisable. This might seem an odd requirement in respect of an agreement that merely renders someone bound by a Code right that may have already been brought into existence

8 [2022] UKUT 223 (LC) at [12]. The UT's conclusion was overturned by the Court of Appeal on appeal, but this observation remains undisturbed, as the appeal related to the effect of para 10(3), and not para 10(2).

9 See para 27(1)(c).

10 Because only a 'landowner' (ie, someone with an interest in the land) can ever have a right to require removal under para 37: see para 37(1).

11 Although it was a provision within Part 2, and hence it may have been thought that an agreement under para 10(4) was an agreement under Part 2 and hence had to comply with para 11.

12 Section 3(3)(b)(4), Sch para 4(2)(b), together with SI 2022/1308, reg 3(c).

13 It seems strange that an agreement merely to be bound by a Code right must rehearse the period for which the Code right is exercisable and the period of notice to terminate it, but that seems to be the effect of the literal words para 11(1) in tandem with the confirmation at para 10(4) that such an agreement is an agreement under Part 2. Any conclusion which rests on literal words is always amenable to overturning on the basis of a purposive construction, in this sphere at least as much as any other, and in any event the failure to include statutorily mandatory content in a document does not necessarily affect that document's validity or effect.

and described with total precision in a different Code agreement. However, this is not a point that has been the subject of a judicial decision thus far.

15.16 In *Edelwind*,[14] Judge Cooke referred to an agreement by which a person becomes bound by a Code agreement as a 'secondary code agreement' (as opposed to a 'primary' agreement by which the Code rights were conferred). In *Gencomp*,[15] the Deputy President observed that an alternative classification would consist of 'conferring agreements' and 'binding agreements'.

15.17 It is important to note that para 10(4) will not render someone bound by a Code right where that person has no interest in the land. The extent to which someone in that position will be bound will therefore be a matter of contract law. Even if that person is indeed bound to some extent by the operator's rights, that contractual binding would not be capable of being transmitted to others by operation of the Code.

Successors to 'P' (and persons with subordinate rights and interests)

15.18 Paragraph 10(5) refers to a person who has agreed, as per para 10(4), to be bound by a Code right, as 'P'. It does for 'P' something very similar to that which para 10(2) does in respect of 'O'. That is, it makes provision for certain successors to P, and persons with rights and interests which are subordinate to P, to be bound.

15.19 Paragraph 10(5) provides as follows:

> '(5) If such a person ('P') agrees to be bound by the code right, the code right also binds—
>
> (a) the successors in title to P's interest,
>
> (b) a person with an interest in the land that is created after P agrees to be bound and is derived (directly or indirectly) out of—
>
> (i) P's interest, or
>
> (ii) the interest of a successor in title to P's interest, and
>
> (c) any other person at any time in occupation of the land whose right to occupation was granted by—
>
> (i) P, at a time when P was bound by the code right, or
>
> (ii) a person within paragraph (a) or (b).'

Persons 'treated as a party to the agreement'

15.20 Only a site provider who is 'a party to a code agreement' can bring a Code agreement to an end by the service of a para 31 notice.[16] Further, only a person who

14 *EE and H3G v Edelwind* [2020] UKUT 272 (LC) at [7].

15 [2022] UKUT 223 (LC) at [12]. The UT's conclusion was overturned by the Court of Appeal on appeal, but this observation was not disturbed.

16 Para 31(1).

is 'a party to a code agreement' can seek to renew or modify a Code agreement by the service of a para 33 notice.[17]

15.21 Certain persons are to be treated as parties to a Code agreement by virtue of the Code despite not having been original contracting parties. It is thus important not merely to understand who is *bound* by a Code right but who is to be *treated as a party* to the agreement by which the Code right was conferred in order to understand who has the power to seek to terminate or modify a Code agreement.

15.22 It is not all persons who are 'bound' by a Code right who are to be treated as a party to the agreement by which that right was conferred; otherwise, all persons who are bound could terminate such an agreement. Paragraph 10(3) provides that a successor who is bound by virtue of para 10(2)(a) 'is to be treated as a party to the agreement by which O conferred the right'. This, of course, makes sense. A successor should be the one who has the right to terminate or modify an agreement, and not the original contracting party who retains no interest. Given that Code agreements need not be leases, some statutory intervention or at least clarification in respect of this point was necessary, and para 10(3) provides it.

15.23 Similarly, by para 10(6), a successor who is bound by a Code right by virtue of para 10(5)(a) 'is to be treated as a party to the agreement by which P agreed to be bound by the right'.

Para 10(3) is not exhaustive

15.24 However, although para 10 is a careful and relatively detailed provision that has been the subject of some thought, it has been held that para 10(3) is not an exhaustive description of who is to be treated as a party to the agreement. The extent to which additional categories of person are to be treated as a party to an agreement is perhaps not certain, but one additional category has been identified by the Court of Appeal in *Gencomp* in order to make sense of the scheme of the Code. That case related to the position of a concurrent lessee, and is considered below.

The position of concurrent lessees – *Gencomp*

15.25 Where a site provider grants a concurrent lease to a third party after it has conferred Code rights on an operator, the concurrent lessee is to be treated as a party to the agreement by which the Code rights were conferred.

15.26 This proposition is not apparent from the plain words of para 10(3), but was established in the Court of Appeal in *Gencomp*.[18] In that case, the freeholder granted a lease to a mobile network operator ('MNO') in respect of the tower of an old fire station. Whilst the lease was still current, after the New Code came into force,

17 Para 31(1).

18 *Vodafone Ltd v Potting Shed Bar and Gardens Ltd & Anor* [2023] EWCA Civ 825 at [15], in which the freeholder had at first instance been known as Gencomp (No 7) Ltd. The case became known as '*Gencomp*' for that reason, and the Court of Appeal referred to the freeholder as 'Gencomp' in its judgment out of convenience (judgment, at [4]).

the freeholder granted a concurrent lease to an infrastructure provider, such that the infrastructure provider became the MNO's immediate landlord. As the Deputy President had explained at first instance,[19] a 'concurrent or overriding lease is one granted subject to and with the benefit of a lease which is already in existence.'

15.27 There was no dispute that the MNO should be granted a renewal of its rights under the Code.[20] However, there was disagreement as to what the proper mechanism was in order for the MNO to achieve such a renewal. If its immediate landlord was to be treated as a party to the agreement that had conferred the Code rights, then it would be proper to serve notices on that immediate landlord in order to seek the renewal agreement under Part 5. If, however, the immediate landlord was not to be treated as a party, then no notice under para 33 could be served on it.

15.28 Where an operator wishes to start the renewal process under Part 5, para 33(1) states that it must 'by notice in accordance with this paragraph, require the other party to the agreement to agree'. Thus, if the immediate landlord is not to be treated as the other 'party to the agreement', then no notice can be served on it, and it can never be required to grant the relevant rights. By contrast, the superior landlord (the concurrent lessee's immediate landlord) was properly to be treated as a party to the agreement but was not the occupier (ignoring, as one must, under *Compton Beauchamp*,[21] the presence of the operator itself) and hence could not confer new Code rights under para 9(1). In any event, the superior landlord could not grant rights that it no longer had following the grant of the concurrent lease.

15.29 At first instance, the Deputy President rejected the submission that para 10(3) is not intended comprehensively to define all those who are to be treated as parties to a code agreement. Furthermore, the concurrent lessee could not be considered to be a 'successor in title' to the interests of the person who granted the Code rights.

15.30 In doing so, he concluded that there was a 'small but potentially important structural defect'[22] in the Code. Although the case related to the renewal of Code rights, if the tribunal's conclusion had stood, it would have left a concurrent lessee 'with no obvious means'[23] of bringing Code rights to an end. It could not serve a para 31 notice unless it was to be treated as a party to the Code agreement.

15.31 However, the Court of Appeal reversed the UT's decision. It accepted that the concurrent lessee was not a 'successor in title'[24] and hence did not fall under the express words of para 10(3). However, it reached the conclusion that it should be treated as a party nonetheless.

---

19 [2022] UKUT 223 (LC) at [57]. There is a useful discussion of the law relating to such leases at [57] and [58] of the Upper Tribunal's decision, which the Court of Appeal described as 'an impeccable summary' ([2023] EWCA Civ 825 at [12]).

20 The MNO's lease was a subsisting agreement, but had been 'contracted out' of the security of tenure provisions of the 1954 Act, and accordingly by para 7(1) of the Transitional Provisions, Part 5 of the Code applied to it, albeit subject to the modifications made by para 7 of the Transitional Provisions.

21 [2022] UKSC 18.

22 [2022] UKUT 223 (LC) at [120].

23 [2022] UKUT 223 (LC) at [121].

24 [2023] EWCA Civ 825 at [44]–[50].

15.32 Nugee LJ (with whom the remainder of the court agreed) cited Lady Rose's guidance, given in the Supreme Court in the *Compton Beauchamp*[25] case, as to how to interpret the Code, given in a case where the meaning of 'occupier' was in dispute:

> 'The correct approach is to work out how the regime is intended to work and then consider what meaning should be given to the word 'occupier' so as best to achieve that goal.'

15.33 Applying that approach, Nugee LJ considered that:

> 'the regime is intended to work in such a way that the person currently entitled to the benefit and burden of the agreement as operator, and the person currently entitled to the benefit and burden of the agreement as site provider, are parties to the agreement and can exercise the rights conferred by Part 5 of the Code.'[26]

15.34 This result was achieved by construing para 10(3) as not defining exhaustively who was to be treated as a party to the agreement.

15.35 Nugee LJ noted that following an assignment of a Code agreement by an operator to another operator (as is facilitated by para 16), it is the assignee operator on whom a site provider must serve a para 31 notice, and not the assignor operator. This was not only common ground but was 'the only sensible interpretation'. And yet there is no provision making matters similarly clear in respect of site providers. If an assignee operator can be a party to the agreement without express provision, 'it would seem odd if the same was not also true of the site provider'.

Imposed agreements rendering a person bound

15.36 The tribunal has powers to impose agreements which provide for a Code right to bind a person, under the following provisions:

(i) Under para 20(4)(b), following the usual para 20 procedure.

(ii) Under para 26(1)(a), following the usual para 26 procedure. Such agreement is imposed 'on an interim basis' (as that phrase is defined at para 26(2)), meaning that it comes to an end after the period specified by the tribunal, or upon the occurrence of an event specified by the tribunal.

(iii) Under para 27(2), following the usual para 27 procedure. Such agreement renders a person bound by 'temporary code rights'.

15.37 Where any such agreement is imposed, it is deemed by para 22[27] to take effect as an agreement under Part 2. It will be noted that para 10(4) now makes clear that a consensual agreement to be bound is indeed capable of being an 'agreement under Part 2'.

25 [2022] UKSC 18 at [106].
26 [2023] EWCA Civ 825 at [75].
27 Para 22 applies to para 26 cases by virtue of para 26(4)(b) and to para 27 cases by virtue of para 27(4)(b).

Statutory continuation of agreements to be bound

15.38 The statutory continuation caused by para 30(2) applies not just to agreements that confer Code rights, but also to agreements by which a person is bound by a Code right. This seems clear from para 30(1)(a):

> '(1) Sub-paragraph (2) applies if—
>
> (a) a code right is conferred by, or is otherwise binding on, a person (the 'site provider') as the result of a code agreement…'

15.39 Note that the expression used is 'code agreement' rather than 'agreement'. A 'code agreement', by para 29(5), is an agreement to which Part 5 of the Code applies. By para 29(1), Part 5 of the Code applies to 'an agreement under Part 2 of this code',[28] and we know from para 10(4) (post-amendment) that an agreement to be bound can be an agreement under Part 2.

15.40 It surely follows that an agreement that merely binds a person (but does not itself confer Code rights) is capable of being a 'code agreement', ie, an agreement to which Part 5 applies. It would therefore be capable of attracting the statutory continuation under para 30(2).

15.41 That being the case, a person entering into such an agreement should be wary of paras 26 and 27 in just the same way as a person entering into an agreement conferring Code rights. Under para 26(1)(b), an agreement can be imposed 'on an interim basis' (as that term is used in para 26(2)), which renders a person bound by Code rights. Similarly, under para 27(2), an agreement can be imposed that renders a person bound by temporary Code rights. These types of agreement will not attract statutory continuation under para 30(2) because of para 30(3). However, in order to avoid that statutory continuation, these agreements must be *imposed*. A *consensual* agreement is definitionally incapable of falling under paras 26 or 27. Just as with an agreement that *confers* Code rights, any agreement to be *bound* that the parties wish to be a para 26 or para 27 agreement must be the subject of the notice procedure in those respective paragraphs and the subject of an application to the tribunal for an Order that it be imposed.

Is it necessary to obtain an agreement binding all landowners?

15.42 Where an operator has Code rights over land, there is not an automatic need for it to ensure that all persons with an interest in that land are bound by the Code right.

15.43 In *St Martins*,[29] the First Respondent was the occupier of a building under a lease that still had over 100 years left to run. The Deputy President noted that the freeholder's immediate interest was remote, and that the operator did not need its permission in order to carry out the proposed MSV surveys. The First Respondent's lease included a covenant not to interfere with the structure of the building or to carry out modifications to it. The stated concern was that the First Respondent might be put in breach of covenant if it entered into an agreement with the operator that

---

28 Subject to para 29(2) to (4), which sub-paras only relate to some types of leases. Where a lease's primary purpose is to grant Code rights, para 29(2) to (4) have no effect.

29 [2021] UKUT 262 (LC) at [6]–[10].

investigative work could be carried out to the structure. The operator thus sought an Order under para 26(1)(b)[30] that the freeholder be bound by the Code rights.

15.44 The Deputy President considered it to be 'entirely unnecessary' for the freeholder to be party to the proceedings. An Order under para 26 imposes an agreement on the parties (without them even needing to execute any documents themselves[31]). A leaseholder would not be in breach of covenant prohibiting it to carry out work, or from 'permitting or suffering' a third party to carry out work, when the works are carried out 'by a third party whom the leaseholder had no power to resist because it acted under rights imposed by the tribunal'.

15.45 There was no need for the freeholder to be made a party given that:

- it did not intend to complain if the rights are exercised, and
- there is no realistic prospect of the lease being terminated during the short period while the Code rights will be exercisable.

15.46 The claim against the freeholder was therefore dismissed (with costs), as it ought not to have been included as a party. The Deputy President gave the guidance that:

> 'Nor should it be necessary for other freeholders in the same position be made parties to references under paragraph 26 (at least where the only rights sought are to carry out an MSV).'

15.47 It is fair to observe that the *St Martins* matter was an application for interim rights to undertake MSVs, and as such, the Order conferred more short-term and less extensive rights than a 'full' Code agreement under para 20. Nonetheless, parties should carefully consider who really needs to be bound by Code rights and therefore who should be served with notices and be named as a party to proceedings. Early communication with interested parties is surely to be encouraged.

15.48 In *Audley House*,[32] the operator sought a new right to park on an access, and the site provider was not the freehold owner of the land. The tribunal noted that unless it conferred on the site provider the right to control what the operator was doing on an access, it could have no liability in respect of anything done. It therefore imposed an agreement in which the operator was granted the right to park on the access insofar as the site provider was able to grant that right. It noted that if any superior landlord takes the view that the site provider is not able to grant the right, the operator 'will have to negotiate with, and if necessary issue a reference against, the superior landlord'.

Registration of agreements concerning Code rights

15.49 Under section 27(2)(b)(i) of the Land Registration Act 2002, a lease of more than seven years' duration is required to be completed by registration. That provision states:

30 This is the interim rights equivalent of para 20(4)(b).

31 Similarly to an Order under para 20, as explained in *Islington* [2019] UKUT 53 (LC) at [150] and referenced in *St Martins* at [9].

32 [2022] UKUT 152 (LC).

'(2) In the case of a registered estate, the following are the dispositions which are required to be completed by registration—

...

(b) where the registered estate is an estate in land, the grant of a term of years absolute—

(i) for a term of more than seven years from the date of the grant,

...'

15.50 Many agreements which confer Code rights are leases. Thus, if they are granted for a term of more than seven years, as many are, it would seem that they are required to be registered.

15.51 However, para 14 of the Code provides as follows:

'Where an enactment requires interests, charges or other obligations affecting land to be registered, the provisions of this code about who is bound by a code right have effect whether or not that right is registered.'

15.52 Although the above provision does not expressly mention leasehold estates, obviously such estates are interests in land. The effect of para 14 is therefore that the provisions of para 10 (which govern who is bound by a Code right) have effect regardless of whether the agreement conferring the Code right is registered.

15.53 It is nonetheless inherent in para 14 of the Code that enactments may require interests to be registered, and para 14 does not seek to disapply any such statutory requirements. Despite this, many Code agreements are not registered. This is perhaps consistent with the fact that many older agreements appear to hedge their bets as to whether they are leases or licences by including ambiguous features and terminology. An operator may take the view that if it were to register a Code agreement as a lease at HM Land Registry, it would be more difficult thereafter for it to argue that it is a licence, if that suited its case in proceedings. Further, the administrative cost of registering thousands of leases surely adds up, and if the agreement is going to be binding in any event, it may not be thought financially worthwhile.

Assignment: para 16

15.54 Although para 16 is headed 'Assignment of code rights', it is clear that it allows and regulates the assignment of agreements[33] under Part 2, and not merely the assignment of the Code rights in isolation. The Code seeks to ensure that assignment of new agreements between operators can always occur and at no cost to the operator, and clarifies the effect of such assignments. The same policy does not apply to subsisting agreements, and hence the law is modified in relation to them.

33 See paras 15(a), 16(1) and 16(4).

Voiding of restrictions on assignment to operators

15.55 Paragraph 16(1) renders certain contractual provisions which restrict assignment between operators void:

'(1) Any agreement under Part 2 of this code is void to the extent that—

(a) it prevents or limits assignment of the agreement to another operator, or

(b) it makes assignment of the agreement to another operator subject to conditions (including a condition requiring the payment of money).'

15.56 Where para 16(1) applies to an agreement, its effect is absolute and clear. It will render void any contractual provision to the extent to which it attempts to do any of those things specified at sub-paras (a) and (b), without voiding the remainder of the agreement.

15.57 However, it is worth noting that para 16(1) says nothing in relation to restrictions on assignments to non-operators. In principle, a clause preventing such an assignment is permissible, as is one that permits such assignments subject to conditions, including one that requires the payment of money.

15.58 NB: para 16, and hence the para 16(1) voiding provision, does not apply in the case of subsisting agreements, as discussed below.

Permissibility of requirement for guarantee agreements

15.59 Paragraph 16(2) provides that the voiding provision at para 16(1) does not apply to a term that requires the assignor to enter into a guarantee agreement.

15.60 Paragraph 16(7) defines a 'guarantee agreement' thus:

'(7) A "guarantee agreement' is an agreement, in connection with the assignment of an agreement under Part 2 of this code, under which the assignor guarantees to any extent the performance by the assignee of the obligations that become binding on the assignee under sub-paragraph (4) (the 'relevant obligations').'

15.61 Para graph16(8) gives more detail as to requirements, liabilities or restrictions which a 'guarantee agreement' cannot impose:

'(8) An agreement is not a guarantee agreement to the extent that it purports—

(a) to impose on the assignor a requirement to guarantee in any way the performance of the relevant obligations by a person other than the assignee, or

(b) to impose on the assignor any liability, restriction or other requirement of any kind in relation to a time after the relevant obligations cease to be binding on the assignee.'

15.62 Thus, a term in a Part 2 agreement *would* be void to the extent that it *requires* an operator to enter into an annexed purported guarantee agreement (which included terms that imposed any of the requirements, liabilities, or restrictions specified in para 16(8)(a) or (b)) as a condition of being allowed to assign the Part 2 agreement.

15.63 The term creating the condition might be argued to be entirely void because it creates a requirement that something be entered into, which is not a 'guarantee agreement'. Alternatively, the term creating the condition might be argued to be effective so as to require a guarantee agreement in the annexed form, but with the removal of the provisions that offended para 16(8)(a) or (b).

15.64 Note that para 16(8) itself is not worded as a voiding provision in the same way as para 16(1). Thus, if an operator *were* to enter into a purported guarantee agreement that included terms that imposed any of the requirements, liabilities, or restrictions specified in para 16(8)(a) or (b), there does not seem to be any express provision in the Code that would override or negate such terms.

15.65 Subject to para 16(8), para 16(9) sets out three things that a 'guarantee agreement' may do, as follows:

> '(a) impose on the assignor any liability as sole or principal debtor in respect of the relevant obligations;
>
> (b) impose on the assignor liabilities as guarantor in respect of the assignee's performance of the relevant obligations which are no more onerous than those to which the assignor would be subject in the event of the assignor being liable as sole or principal debtor in respect of any relevant obligation;
>
> (c) make provision incidental or supplementary to any provision within paragraph (a) or (b).'

Effect of assignment

15.66 Paragraph 16(4) provides that:

> '(4) From the time when the assignment of an agreement under Part 2 of this code takes effect, the assignee is bound by the terms of the agreement.'

15.67 The absolute proposition in para 16(4) that the assignee is bound by the 'terms of the agreement' applies equally to agreements under Part 2 regardless of whether they the form of a lease or a licence.

15.68 Where an agreement is agreed as a lease or is imposed by the tribunal in the form of a lease, the usual rules as to the assignment of leases will apply. It is of course perfectly possible to assign a lease such that the assignee of the lessee's leasehold estate takes on the lessee's benefits and burdens thereunder.

15.69 However, in the case of a contractual licence, under the general law, the same is not true. As Nugee LJ said in Court of Appeal in *Gencomp*:[34]

> 'Under the general law the assignment of a contract is effective to confer the benefit of the contract on an assignee but not normally the burden of the

34 *Vodafone Ltd v Potting Shed Bar and Gardens Ltd & Anor* [2023] EWCA Civ 825 (aka '*Gencomp*') at [60].

contract. But paragraph 16(4) provides that from the time when the assignment of an agreement under Part 2 takes effect, the assignee is bound by the terms of the agreement. In this way the assignee takes both the benefit and the burden of the agreement.'

15.70 Paragraph 16(4) thus provides welcome clarity as regards agreements entered into after the New Code came into force. It makes no distinction between benefits and burdens, making clear that the *whole* agreement can be assigned.

This is in contrast to the position in respect of non-lease agreements made under the Old Code. In the *Burlington Gardens* case,[35] Edwin Johnson J (sitting as the President of the Lands Chamber) held that the burden of the obligations of an operator in a contractual agreement under the Old Code was not capable of assignment to a third party operator, either by the common law or by statute or under the terms of the agreement.

Assignor's liability for post-assignment breaches

15.71 Paragraph 16(5) creates a mechanism by which an assignor will not be liable for post-assignment breaches. This provision is, however, subject to the terms of any guarantee agreement.[36]

15.72 By para 16(5), an assignor 'is not liable for any breach of a term of the agreement that occurs after the assignment if (and only if), before the breach took place, the assignor or the assignee gave a notice in writing to the other party to the agreement…'. OFCOM has published[37] two versions of a template form for this species of notice, one which can be given by the assignor, and one which can be given by the assignee. In order for the notice to have the effect provided for at para 16(5), it must have done two things[38]:

(a) identified the assignee; and

(b) provided an address for service for the assignee, for the purposes of para 91(2)(a).

Application of para 16(1) to imposed agreements

15.73 Paragraph 16(1) relates to any 'agreement under Part 2', and para 16(4) provides for the consequences of an assignment of an 'agreement under Part 2'.

15.74 It is unlikely that an agreement would be *imposed* with the inclusion of a term that offends para 16(1)(a) or (b), given that consistency with the Code has been treated as an important principle when considering what terms are 'appropriate' under para 23(2). However, in the unlikely event that such a term were to find its way

35 *AP Wireless II (UK) Ltd v On Tower UK Ltd* [2024] UKUT 263 (LC) at [227].

36 See para 16(6) and (7).

37 Although para 16(5) notices are not referred to in para 89(1), and hence the requirement at para 89(2) to use the prescribed form does not appear to apply, it is surely good practice and common sense to use the published form.

38 By para 16(5).

into an agreement imposed under the New Code, para 16 would surely apply, such that the offensive term is voided. Similarly, the effect of validly assigning an imposed Code agreement would surely be the same as if that agreement had been consensually entered into, namely the effect provided for at para 16(4).

15.75 These conclusions result because an agreement imposed under the New Code 'takes effect for all purposes of this code as an agreement under Part 2'.[39] It is not difficult to see the legislative intent that agreements under the New Code should not contain terms that constrain assignment in the ways set out at para 16(1)(a) and (b) and should be assignable with the clear and practical result set out at para 16(4).

Subsisting agreements

Who is bound?

15.76 Subsisting agreements are discussed in Chapter 16. They have effect as an agreement under Part 2 of the New Code, subject to the modifications made by the Transitional Provisions.[40] The Transitional Provisions include rules governing who is bound by a subsisting agreement.

Disapplication of Code para 16

15.77 Paragraph 5(1) of the Transitional Provisions disapplies para 16 of the Code in relation to subsisting agreements.[41]

15.78 Similarly, para 5(2) of the Transitional Provisions[42] disapplies para 16 'in relation to a code right conferred under the new code if, at the time when it is conferred, the exercise of the right depends on a right that has effect under a subsisting agreement'.

15.79 The principal consequences of para 16 being disapplied in these cases are considered below.

(i) Restrictions on assignment are not voided

Where para 16 is disapplied, contractual provisions within a subsisting agreement which prevent or limit assignment of the agreement to an operator, or which make such assignment subject to conditions such as the payment of money, will be valid.

Where a subsisting agreement is a 1954 Act tenancy that is renewed, one would expect any provisions that fall foul of para 16(1) to be deleted upon renewal. If they are not, one would expect that any such provisions would be

---

39 Para 22.

40 Para 2(1) of the Transitional Provisions, ie, Sch 2 to the Digital Economy Act 2017.

41 This remains the case following the 2023 changes to the Transitional Provisions made by the PSTIA 2022. The Transitional Provisions originally disapplied the whole of Part 3 in the case of subsisting agreements. Now, the only provision of Part 3 which remains entirely disapplied is para 16. See ss 58(3) and 79(2) PSTIA 2022, and reg 3(a) of the Product Security and Telecommunications Infrastructure Act 2022 (Commencement No. 1) Regulations 2023.

42 Sch 2 to the Digital Economy Act 2017.

considered void in any renewal tenancy. It is established that such a renewal tenancy will be an agreement to which Part 5 of the Code applies. As Part 5 is said to apply to an agreement under Part 2 (see para 29(1)), one would imagine that the renewal tenancy will be treated as an agreement under Part 2, with the effect that para 16(1) would render certain provisions void.

Where a subsisting agreement is one that is renewed under Part 5, any Order under para 34(6) would terminate it, and the new agreement is treated as if it were a Part 2 agreement (see para 34(8)). Thus any provisions that offended para 16(1) but somehow remained in the 'new agreement' would be voided by para 16(1). If a type of Order within para 34 is chosen that does *not* terminate the existing agreement, one would imagine that the modified or extended agreement will continue to be a 'subsisting agreement', and hence para 16 would continue not to apply. This may very well be a reason cited by an operator when arguing that a para 34(6) Order is the appropriate form of Order in a 'renewal' case.

(ii) Effect of purported assignment potentially unclear

Paragraph 16(4) makes clear that an 'agreement under Part 2' of the New Code can be assigned, and that the assignee is immediately bound by the 'terms of the agreement', making no distinction between benefits and burdens.

However, as para 16(4) does not apply to subsisting agreements, this welcome clarity is absent in respect of the assignment of a subsisting agreement. Where the subsisting agreement is a lease, there is no difficulty, as the usual rules as to the assignment of leases will apply. It is perfectly commonplace to assign a lease such that the assignee of the lessee's leasehold estate takes on the lessee's benefits and burdens thereunder.

However, in respect of a subsisting agreement that is not a lease, the effect of any purported assignment is perhaps not entirely clear. This is because of the point mentioned above that the assignment of a contract is effective to confer the benefit of the contract on an assignee but not normally the burden of the contract.[43] Furthermore, the assignment of purely contractual rights in breach of covenant is not effective.44

---

43 As to which, see the discussion of this point in the *Burlington Gardens* case.

44 see *Edelwind* [2020] UKUT 272 (LC), at [52].

16

Termination and renewal of agreements

16.01 How an agreement is terminated or renewed will depend upon which statutory regime (if any) applies to it. In situations where Code rights were first granted before the New Code came into force, it is not always entirely straightforward to ascertain which termination and/or renewal mechanisms apply. The various different situations in respect of such 'subsisting agreements' are considered later in this chapter. Section A of this chapter (from **16.05** onwards) considers the termination of agreements, and Section B (from **16.195** onwards) considers renewal.

Part 5 of the Code

16.02 As Part 5 of the Code deals with both termination and renewal, it is worth setting out the basic structure of Part 5 at the outset.

16.03 Part 5 is the part of the Code that deals with the termination and renewal of agreements. The agreements to which Part 5 applies are those referred to as 'Code agreements'.[1] These will include all Part 2 agreements entered into after the coming into force of the Code whose primary purpose is to grant Code rights.[2]

16.04 A summary of the structure of Part 5 is as follows:

(i) Paragraph 30(2) statutorily continues a Code agreement beyond its contractual term. This statutory continuation is discussed further below.

(ii) If a site provider who is a party to a Code agreement wishes to terminate it, it can serve a notice under para 31. The notice must normally be at least 18 months[3] in duration (ending after the contractual end date of the agreement) and must state a para 31(4) statutory ground for termination.

(iii) The Code agreement will come to an end in accordance with the para 31 notice unless the operator gives a counter-notice under para 32(1)(a) and applies under para 32(1)(b) for an Order under para 34.

(iv) Upon an operator's para 32(1)(b) application, if the site provider proves a ground in its para 31 notice, the tribunal must order that the Code agreement comes to an end.[4]

(v) If the site provider does not prove such a ground, the tribunal must[5] make an Order under para 34.

1 Para 29(5).
2 Paras 29(1) and (2).
3 See para 31(3).
4 See para 32(4).
5 See para 32(5).

(vi) If an operator or a site provider who is a party to a Code agreement wishes to renew or modify the Code agreement, it may serve a notice under para 33. At least six months'[6] notice (ending after the contractual end date of the agreement), must be given of the date on which it is proposed that the renewal or modification would take effect.

(vii) If the parties do not reach agreement during the period of six months after the notice is given, the operator or the site provider may make a para 33(5) application to the tribunal for an Order under para 34.

(viii) There are various Orders which may be made under para 34. The two broad categories into which these fall are:

(a) Orders which modify some element of the current agreement going forward; and

(b) Orders which terminate the existing agreement and order the parties to enter into a new agreement.

Section A
The termination of an agreement

16.05 The first part of this chapter considers the termination of agreements that confer Code rights or which render a person bound by Code rights. A 'flow chart' is included in Chapter 19, which attempts to provide a streamlined process for ascertaining the method of termination by a landowner of the rights that an operator holds and the achievement of vacant possession.

16.06 It is important to note that even once an agreement has been brought to an end such that the operator no longer has any Code rights, Part 6 of the Code places constraints on how the landowner vindicates its right to require the removal of ECA. Part 6 is considered in Chapter 18

Termination of an agreement by a landowner[7]

16.07 The method by which an agreement can be terminated is dependent upon the characteristics of the agreement. The Code makes detailed provision for the termination of agreements, under Part 5. However, the Part 5 termination process does not apply to all agreements which confer Code rights. The 1954 Act still provides the procedural mechanism under which certain leases are terminated by a landlord, as will be explained below.

16.08 The following are examples of different categories of agreement which are worthy of consideration:

(1) An agreement conferring Code rights which was created following the coming into force[8] of the New Code, either:

6 See para 33(3).

7 The word 'landowner' in this context is simply intended as short-hand for a non-operator party to an agreement.

8 The New Code came into force on 18 December 2017.

(a) by the parties contracting consensually; or

(b) by the tribunal making an Order imposing it.

(2) An agreement which was entered into under the Old Code and whose contractual term was continuing when the New Code came into force. Such an agreement is called a 'subsisting agreement'.[9]

(3) An agreement which was entered into under the Old Code and whose contractual term expired before the coming into force of the New Code.

16.09 Each of these categories of case will be considered below.

(1) Consensual or imposed agreements under the New Code

16.10 This section is considering only agreements consensually entered into, and agreements imposed, following the coming into force[10] of the New Code.

16.11 Code rights can only be conferred by an agreement between an occupier and an operator (see para 9(1) of the Code). Para 11 sets out formalities and content requirements for such an agreement. Both para 9 and para 11 are within Part 2 of the Code. A consensual agreement that satisfies the description in para 9 and the requirements in para 11 is therefore 'an agreement under Part 2'[11] of the Code.

16.12 An agreement under para 10(4) by which a person agrees to be bound by a Code right is also an agreement under Part 2.[12]

16.13 The following imposed agreements take effect as 'an agreement under Part 2' of the Code:

(i) an agreement imposed under para 20;[13]

(ii) a new agreement imposed (as what one might call a renewal) under para 34(6);[14]

(iii) an agreement imposed 'on an interim basis' under para 26;[15]

(iv) an agreement imposed in relation to 'temporary' Code rights under para 27.[16]

9 See para 1(4) of the Transitional Provisions.

10 Which occurred on 28 December 2017.

11 This is an important expression within the Code and appears at para 29(1) and elsewhere.

12 The expression used by para 10(4), which is within Part 2, is in fact 'an agreement under this Part'. Also, a Part 4A agreement can constitute an agreement by which a person agrees to be bound as per para 10(4), but these agreements only relate to unresponsive occupiers and leasehold land and are vanishingly rare.

13 By para 22.

14 By para 34(8). In actual fact, whereas para 22 says that an agreement to which it relates takes effect 'as an agreement under Part 2', para 34(8) says that the Code applies to an agreement imposed under para 34(6) 'as if it were an agreement under Part 2'. These different formulations are surely to the same effect. It is of course possible for a tribunal to make a different Order under para 34 than a para 34(6) Order for a termination and new agreement. However, where it does so, the existing agreement will in effect continue, and Part 5 will apply to it in the same way as it applied to the agreement before the tribunal's Order.

15 It seems unlikely that a para 26 agreement will need to be terminated under the Part 5 procedure as such agreements typically have a shorter duration, and are not subject to any statutory continuation under para 30(2) (due to para 30(3))..

16 It seems most unlikely that a para 27 agreement will ever need to be terminated under the Part 5 procedure, as they are only imposed pending the trial in respect of the parallel para 20 application, and also have no statutory continuation under para 30(2) (due to para 30(3)).

16.14 Accordingly, the same set of rules as to termination (and indeed renewal) applies to agreements consensually entered into following the coming into force of the New Code, and to the above species of imposed agreements. These rules are to be found in Part 5 of the Code, and are discussed below.

Application of Part 5 of the Code

16.15 By para 29(1), Part 5 applies to:

> 'an agreement under Part 2 of this code, subject to sub-paragraphs (2) to (4)'.[17]

16.16 'Sub-paragraphs (2) to (4)' of para 29 remove very particular types of leases from Part 5. For the purposes of England and Wales, only sub-paras (2) to (3) are of relevance.

16.17 Paragraph 29(2) provides that Part 5 does not apply to a lease of land in England and Wales if:

> '(a) its primary purpose is not to grant code rights, and
>
> (b) it is a lease to which Part 2 of the Landlord and Tenant Act 1954 (security of tenure for business, professional and other tenants) applies.'

16.18 Paragraph 29(3) adds this qualification:

> '(3) In determining whether a lease is one to which Part 2 of the Landlord and Tenant Act 1954 applies, any agreement under section 38A (agreements to exclude provisions of Part 2) of that Act is to be disregarded.'

16.19 By section 43(4) of the 1954 Act, any lease whose 'primary purpose' is to grant Code rights, and which is entered into *after* the coming into force of the New Code, is not capable of being a lease to which Part 2 of the 1954 Act applies, and hence is not terminable under the 1954 Act machinery.

16.20 Thus, where the 'primary purpose' of an agreement is to grant Code rights, and it comes into being consensually or by imposition after the coming into force of the New Code, its status as a lease or otherwise will not affect its mode of termination or renewal. The route to terminate or renew it is through Part 5 of the Code.

16.21 NB: at present, the only agreements that are being considered are those that came into being following the coming into force of the New Code. For an explanation of which pre-New Code agreements Part 5 applies to and with what modifications, see the section on 'subsisting agreements' below.

'Primary purpose'

16.22 The question of 'primary purpose' (an expression found within para 29(2) as set out above) is not one that has yet exercised the tribunals to a great extent. However,

17 As agreements imposed under paras 20, 26, and 27 take effect 'as' Part 2 agreements, and the Code applies to agreements imposed under para 34(6) 'as if' they were Part 2 agreements, it is clear that all of these species of imposed agreements in principle fall within the ambit of those agreements which para 29(1) renders subject to Part 5 of the Code.

in the Upper Tribunal in *Ashloch*,[18] the Deputy President gave the following example of a tenancy that might be a 'primary purpose' tenancy:

> 'An example of such a tenancy might be a lease of an office building or shop which, incidentally, conferred Code rights on the tenant to install electronic communications apparatus on the demised premises.'

16.23 It is evident from leases which grant Code rights that they typically envisage that the demise will be occupied only by ECA for the vast majority of the time, and not by people. Most such leases relate to sites such as the upper parts of a building or structure, the corner of a field, or open land such as car parks. These are not sites that will be occupied by the presence of people. Clearly, on days when no people visit a site, ECA being 'kept installed' under para 3(b) for the statutory purposes mentioned at para 4 is simply the exercise of an archetypal Code right.

16.24 In respect of sites such as those mentioned, people (such as operators' employees and contractors) are likely to be present only for purposes that constitute the exercise of a Code right, or are incidental and ancillary to the exercise of a Code right. One thinks of installation, inspection, repair, maintenance, alteration, upgrading, and the gaining of access for those purposes. All of these activities are referred to expressly in para 3 within the definition of the Code rights. Decommissioning of ECA is another obvious activity, and whilst this is not expressly referred to in para 3, to decommission and remove may be to 'alter' or 'adjust',[19] which are referred to in para 3. If not, decommissioning and removal by operators are plainly functionally incidental to the exercise of Code rights, and logically contingent thereon.

16.25 In cases where the right to install ECA is clearly ancillary to the primary use of premises (for example, a shop or office), it will not normally be difficult to see that the grant of the Code rights is not the primary purpose of the lease.

16.26 There may, in theory, be some cases where the rights granted by the lease are both in respect of the occupation of land for a purpose other than exercising Code rights and where the Code rights granted are not functionally ancillary or incidental to the other purpose. Particularly where the area of the demise dedicated to the 'Code rights' purpose and the other purpose are similar in size, one might not be able to discern with ease whether the grant of Code rights was the primary purpose of the lease. But it is difficult to think of what such a use of land would look like in practice, and such cases will surely be extremely rare. The question of 'primary purpose' is therefore unlikely to arise frequently.

The para 29(3) qualification

16.27 The effect of this provision appears to be that Part 5 will not apply to a lease to which Part 2 of the 1954 Act applies (because of para 29(2)), regardless of whether there is a 'contracting out' of the security of tenure provisions under the 1954 Act. This is consistent with section 43(4) of the 1954 Act, which makes clear that Part 2 of the

18 [2019] UKUT 338 (LC) at [44].

19 At para 3(c) in respect of adjusting and altering, para 3(e) in respect of carrying out any works for adjustment and alteration, and para 3(f) in respect of entering the land to adjust or alter.

1954 Act *cannot* apply to any tenancy whose primary purpose is to grant Code rights, and which is granted after the Code comes into force.

The statutory continuation under para 30

16.28 It is convenient to discuss at this point the statutory continuation of agreements which are effected by the Code. Those familiar with commercial leases will be aware of the statutory continuation of business tenancies that is effected by section 24 of the 1954 Act. Paragraph 30 of the Code achieves something similar, but not identical, in respect of agreements to which Part 5 apply.

16.29 As with the 1954 Act, where an agreement is continued by the Code, a statutory procedure exists by which the agreement can be terminated, in reliance upon a notice stating a statutory ground for termination. An operator can accept the effect of the notice or can take the matter to the tribunal for a determination of the question of whether that ground is made out.

16.30 Paragraph 30 provides as follows:

'(1) Sub-paragraph (2) applies if—

(a) a code right is conferred by, or is otherwise binding on, a person (the 'site provider') as the result of a code agreement, and

(b) under the terms of the agreement—

(i) the right ceases to be exercisable or the site provider ceases to be bound by it, or

(ii) the site provider may bring the code agreement to an end so far as it relates to that right.

(2) Where this sub-paragraph applies the code agreement continues so that—

(a) the operator may continue to exercise that right, and

(b) the site provider continues to be bound by the right.

(3) Sub-paragraph (2) does not apply to a code right which is conferred by, or is otherwise binding on, a person by virtue of an order under paragraph 26 (interim code rights) or 27 (temporary code rights).

(4) Sub-paragraph (2) is subject to the following provisions of this Part of this code.'

16.31 By para 29(5), a 'code agreement' is an agreement to which Part 5 applies. So where Part 5 applies, and either a Code right is conferred by an agreement, or a person is otherwise bound by that agreement, the agreement is continued by para 30(2) in the two circumstances mentioned at para 30(1)(b).

16.32 The first of these circumstances is the cessation of the right being exercisable, or binding the person, 'under the terms of the agreement'. The most obvious case to which this refers is where the express agreement term has expired. In that case, para 30(2) will continue the agreement, until it is terminated lawfully in accordance with Part 5 (or by some other means under the general law that is not precluded by the Code).

16.33 The second of these circumstances is where the site provider (the person who conferred the Code right or is bound) 'may bring the Code agreement to an end' (so far as it relates to the Code right). The most obvious[20] case to which this refers is where the site provider 'may' trigger a break right that is contained in the agreement. To be properly understood, this provision is to be read in conjunction with para 31(3)(b), which stipulates the period of notice for terminating agreements under Part 5. When one reads these two provisions together, the proper conclusion is that para 30(1)(b)(ii) applies such that para 30(2) will continue an agreement where a site provider *could have* terminated that agreement under, for example, a break right. It is not necessary for the site provider *actually* to have terminated, or purported, to terminate the agreement by serving a contractual notice separately from a statutory Code notice.[21] This point is discussed further below.

Nature of the statutory continuation

16.34 Paragraph 30(2) does not merely provide that the Code right can continue to be exercised, but that the agreement continues. Thus one would imagine that insofar as the agreement conferred an estate in land, that estate in land continues in a similar way to a tenancy continued by section 24 of the 1954 Act.

16.35 However, the Code does not expressly state that a Code agreement can only be brought to an end in accordance with the statutory method, nor does it state what other termination mechanisms remain open. The 1954 Act, by contrast, states that a tenancy 'shall not come to an end unless terminated in accordance with the provisions of this Part of this Act'.[22] That Part of the 1954 Act then expressly keeps open the possibility of terminating a tenancy by tenant's notice to quit, surrender, or forfeiture.[23] The lack of any similar provision in the Code is curious, as it leaves a potential lack of clarity as to how an operator, or both parties by agreement, can bring an end to a Code agreement. This question is considered further below.

Cases where the statutory continuation does not apply

16.36 It is important to note that the para 30(2) continuation does not apply to a Code right that is conferred, or made binding, by an Order under para 26 or 27.[24] Paragraph 26 and 27 agreements can only come into existence by being imposed by Order, and cannot be agreed consensually. The manner in which they come to an end is considered further below.

20 Another method by which contractual terms might allow a landlord to terminate an agreement which is a lease is a forfeiture clause giving a right of re-entry. An attempt to forfeit a Code lease would be very unusual, and it does not appear that there has been any reported case on this issue, but in any event this possibility is considered further below.

21 This was decided in the *BT (Kenton Road)* case ([2024] UKUT 51 (LC) at [66]–[90]).

22 Section 24(1).

23 Section 24(2).

24 This is because of para 30(3).

Termination of a Code agreement: the para 31 notice

16.37 A site provider who is a party[25] to a Code agreement may bring the agreement to an end by giving a notice in accordance with para 31 to an operator who is a party to the agreement.[26]

16.38 Para 31(2) provides that the notice must comply with para 89, must specify a termination date, and must state a termination ground (sub-paras (a), (b), and (c) respectively).

16.39 More details of what is necessary to be included in this notice and how it is to be served are considered in Chapter 20. However, the termination date and termination grounds are considered below.

Termination date (period of notice)

16.40 The period of notice is governed by para 31(3), which provides that the date (for termination of an agreement) specified in a para 31 notice must fall:

'(a) after the end of the period of 18 months beginning with the day on which the notice is given, and

(b) after the time at which, apart from paragraph 30, the code right to which the agreement relates would have ceased to be exercisable or to bind the site provider or at a time when, apart from that paragraph, the code agreement could have been brought to an end by the site provider.'

16.41 The 18-month period at para 31(3)(a) is a considerable one and longer than that required under the 1954 Act. This restraint on landowners' ability to recover the use of their land is one reason why they are often less than enthusiastic to sign up to Code agreements.

16.42 Clearly the two requirements at paras 31(3)(a) and (b) are not alternatives and must both be satisfied. The requirement at para 31(3)(b) means that, where there is more than 18 months left to run on a fixed term with no exercisable break clause, any para 31 notice must give not merely 18 months' plus one day, but must expire after the end of the fixed term, however long that may be. Technically, a site provider could give such a para 31 notice on day one of a Code agreement.[27]

16.43 Where the contractual fixed term of an agreement has less than 18 months to run, or has already expired, or where there is a contractual break right stated to be exercisable on notice of less than 18 months, clearly the para 31 notice will still have to give more than 18 months' notice because of para 31(3)(a).

25 Or treated as a party: see para 10(3), the Court of Appeal's decision in *Gencomp*, and the discussion of this concept in Chapter 15.

26 By para 31(1).

27 This was confirmed in the *BT (Kenton Road)* case at [2024] UKUT 51 (LC), at [89]. The possibility calls to mind a similar approach formerly taken by many residential landlords, who used to serve s 21 notices under the Housing Act 1988 at the outset of residential tenancies, asking for possession of the dwelling-house. An unusual greeting card.

Is a contractual termination notice necessary?

16.44 Paragraph 30(1)(b)(ii) clearly envisages a situation where, as a matter of contract, a site provider would be able to terminate the agreement, for example, by serving a break notice. Thus, para 30(2) does not merely continue a Code agreement that has reached its contractual fixed term end date; it also continues an agreement where the site provider would otherwise have been able to bring it to an end with a break notice.

16.45 The second limb of para 31(3)(b) deals with the requirement for the period of notice in such a case. Just as the first limb requires the period of notice to end after the contractual fixed term end date, the second limb requires the period of notice to end after the date on which the agreement would have ended by virtue of the exercise of a break right.

16.46 Where Part 5 applies to an agreement, the question arises whether a site provider must actually serve its contractual break notice, in addition to its para 31 notice, or whether a para 31(3)(b)-compliant notice under para 31 is sufficient on its own.

16.47 In the *BT (Kenton Road)*[28] case, the Upper Tribunal held that service of a break notice is not required[29] for the validity of a para 31 notice in such a case. Referring to the wording of para 31(3)(b), the tribunal said:

> 'The key word is 'could'. It refers not to something that would actually happen absent paragraph 30, but to something that could have been made to happen absent paragraph 30.'[30]

16.48 It thus concluded as follows:

> 'On the date notice is given the recipient has to look at the proposed termination date and ask itself: does that date fall after a date on which the landlord could have brought the lease to an end? In other words, could the landlord, hypothetically, absent paragraph 30, have brought the lease to an end before the proposed termination date. It does not have to ask whether that date falls after a date on which the lease would in fact have come to an end, owing to the service of an actual break notice, but for paragraph 30.'[31]

16.49 As regards the practicalities of giving the para 31 notice where the landlord relies on a contractual break right, the tribunal further held[32] that:

- where the lease prescribes certain formalities for the giving of a notice (for example the use of pink paper), these do not have to be complied with in order to make the para 31 notice valid; and

28 *On Tower UK Ltd v British Telecommunications Plc* [2024] UKUT 51 (LC).
29 This decision is of potential interest in respect of the meaning of the similar wording in the 1954 Act, and in considering the similarities with the 1954 Act regime at [76]–[81], the tribunal noted that there are authorities which appear to contradict the proposition that a contractual break notice ever needs to be served in addition to a statutory notice under s 25 of that Act.
30 [2024] UKUT 51 (LC) at [75].
31 [2024] UKUT 51 (LC) at [90].
32 [2024] UKUT 51 (LC) at [84] and [85].

- where the lease allows termination only where certain grounds are met (for example if the landlord obtains planning permission for redevelopment, or intends to use the premises itself), the tenant has to be told on what ground the landlord relies. However, the site provider can choose whether to provide that information in the form of an actual break notice, or it might simply tell the tenant on what ground it could have brought the lease to an end absent para 30.

16.50 At trial, the landlord would need to demonstrate that the contractual ground for termination relied upon under the lease was available to it. It will also need to prove whichever ground is stated in its para 31 notice. Where redevelopment is intended, it may be that these two matters will be similarly or identically worded. As can be seen in Chapter 11, where the tribunal imposes a landlord's redevelopment break right in a Code agreement, it tends to adopt the wording of para 31(4)(c) in the agreement for consistency.

16.51 Where an agreement does not have to be terminated in accordance with some statutory termination procedure (such as that under the Code or under the 1954 Act), it will come to an end in accordance with its own contractual terms. These may allow for a landowner to serve a break notice in order to bring the agreement to an end before the expiration of its full contractual term. Thus, where there is any doubt about whether a statutory regime applies at all (perhaps because of formalities requirements, or the status of the person on whom the rights were conferred, or because the 1954 Act has ceased to apply because the tenant is no longer in occupation), a landowner may wish to serve a contractual break notice together with any other notices that may apply, in order that all possible bases are covered. Such multiple notices should, as a matter of good practice, be expressly stated to be served without prejudice to each other.

Termination grounds (for inclusion within a para 31 notice)

16.52 Paragraph 31(4) provides that the 'ground' stated under para 31(2)(c) must be 'one of the following':

'(a) that the code agreement ought to come to an end as a result of substantial breaches by the operator of its obligations under the agreement;

(b) that the code agreement ought to come to an end because of persistent delays by the operator in making payments to the site provider under the agreement;

(c) that the site provider intends to redevelop all or part of the land to which the code agreement relates, or any neighbouring land, and could not reasonably do so unless the code agreement comes to an end;

(d) that the operator is not entitled to the code agreement because the test under paragraph 21 for the imposition of the agreement on the site provider is not met.'

16.53 The first three of these grounds are similar to grounds of opposition available under section 30(1) of the 1954 Act.

Grounds (a) and (b)

16.54 Although under para 32(4) the tribunal 'must' order the termination of the Code agreement if it 'decides that the site provider has established any of the grounds', the first two grounds entail the tribunal deciding whether the agreement 'ought' to come to an end. This presumably connotes a degree of discretion.

16.55 Where standard commercial leases are subject to forfeiture due to a breach, a Court retains a discretion as to whether to grant relief from forfeiture. It is therefore perhaps unsurprising that a Tribunal appears to have such a discretion in respect of an attempt to terminate a Code agreement due to breaches thereof.

16.56 Unlike under the 1954 Act, a person with the benefit of a Code right will necessarily be an operator. It will therefore have been approved as such, will be regulated by OFCOM, and will typically be a well-funded commercial entity. In that context, and given the express acknowledgement by the Code that there is a 'public interest in access to a choice of high quality electronic communications services',[33] one would imagine that it would take something rather serious to satisfy grounds (a) or (b) of para 31(4).

Ground (c)

16.57 The redevelopment ground at para 31(4)(c) is the ground that is most frequently invoked. It is largely the same ground as that under para 21(5), on which a person can rely in seeking to resist the initial imposition of an agreement because of intended redevelopment, although the factual circumstances of the argument are different because necessarily the operator is already in situ in the para 31 context.[34] The redevelopment ground also shares similarities with ground (f) under section 30(1)(c) of the 1954 Act, but is not worded identically. Given its importance, the redevelopment ground is addressed separately in more detail in Chapter 17

Ground (d)

16.58 The ground at para 31(4)(d) allows a reapplication of the para 21 test that applies on the initial imposition of an agreement. This involves the tests at para 21(2) and (3), which are dealt with in more detail in Chapter 8. It may be that a site provider can also argue under para 31(4)(d) that the para 21 test is not satisfied because para 21(5) is not satisfied. However, this is the subject of its own ground (ground (c), as mentioned above). Relying on the para 21(5) redevelopment test under ground (d) rather than under ground (c) would in reality only make any sense if a site provider erred by neglecting to state the para 31(4)(c) redevelopment ground in its para 31 notice.

Multiple grounds under para 31(4)

16.59 One might wonder whether it is permissible to state more than one termination ground, given that it is said to be mandatory to state 'one' of those listed

33 Para 21(4).

34 For more details of the subtle distinctions between paras 21(5) and 31(4)(c) see the discussion of the redevelopment grounds within Chapter 17.

at para 31(4). The OFCOM prescribed form for a para 31(1) notice gives all of the possible grounds, each in square brackets, and the relevant note at the end of the notice states:

> 'Please delete as appropriate to state the ground on which you propose to end the Agreement.'

16.60 Under the 1954 Act, the 'grounds' on which a landlord may rely in its section 25 notice in order to oppose the grant of a new tenancy are said to be 'such of the following grounds as may be stated in the landlord's notice'.[35] It is perhaps unfortunate that the Code does not similarly make clear that multiple grounds are permissible. However, it is not uncommon to see two grounds stated in a para 31 notice (sometimes grounds (c) and (d) as a 'belt and braces' strategy where redevelopment is envisaged). Indeed, para 32(4) refers to the mandatory termination of the current agreement where the tribunal 'decides that the site provider has established *any of the grounds* stated in the site provider›s notice' (emphasis added). This appears to indicate that multiple grounds are permitted.

16.61 There does not appear to be any policy reason why more than one ground should not be relied on, and one would imagine that if the point were taken, the tribunal would conclude that the possibility of multiple grounds in the alternative would be more consistent with the proper functioning of the Code.

16.62 If support is needed from other property-related statutes, section 146 of the Law of Property Act 1925 requires a landlord as a pre-requisite to forfeiture for a non-rent breach to specify 'the particular breach complained of' (note the use of the singular). It is commonplace for multiple breaches to be relied on and stated in one notice, and if only one breach is successfully proven, that does not render the notice invalid. Conversely, under the Landlord and Tenant Act 1988, where a landlord has a qualified duty to approve consent under a lease but does indeed refuse consent, section 3(2)(b)(ii) requires a landlord to give 'the reasons for withholding' consent (note the use of the plural). It is clear that a landlord may simply have one good reason, and thus the stated reasons need not be plural.[36]

Effect of a para 31 notice

16.63 By para 32(1), the Code agreement will come to an end in accordance with the para 31 notice, unless:

> '(a) within the period of three months beginning with the day on which the notice is given, the operator gives the site provider a counter-notice in accordance with sub-paragraph (3), and
>
> (b) within the period of three months beginning with the day on which the counter-notice is given, the operator applies to the court for an order under paragraph 34.'

35 Section 30(1) of the Landlord and Tenant Act 1954.

36 Where one good reason is stated among other "bad" (unreasonable, impermissible) reasons, the notice will normally be valid (*No.1 West India Quay (Residential) Ltd v East Tower Apartments Ltd* [2018] EWCA Civ 250 at [24], [31], [40]). It would be absurd to expect a landlord with one good reason to state additional bad reasons in order that the reasons given are plural.

16.64 By para 32(2), the parties can agree to the continuation of the Code agreement, and in that event the para 31 notice will not terminate the Code agreement.

The operator's counter-notice

16.65 The operator's counter-notice must state one of the following options, essentially communicating to the site provider what the operator is seeking to achieve:

'(a) that the operator does not want the existing code agreement to come to an end,

(b) that the operator wants the site provider to agree to confer or be otherwise bound by the existing code right on new terms, or

(c) that the operator wants the site provider to agree to confer or be otherwise bound by a new code right in place of the existing code right.'[37]

16.66 The counter-notice must also give certain information about alternative dispute resolution.[38]

The operator's application under para 32(1)(b)

16.67 As indicated above, a para 32(1)(b) application for an Order under para 34 must be made by an operator within the period of three months beginning with the day on which its counter-notice is given.

16.68 Before applying under para 32(1)(b), the operator 'must, if it is reasonably practicable to do so, consider the use of one or more alternative dispute resolution procedures to reach agreement with the site provider',[39] and either party may at any time give a notice to the other party stating that it wishes to engage in alternative dispute resolution.[40]

16.69 There are potential costs consequences if a party unreasonably refuses to engage in alternative dispute resolution (under para 96(2)(b), discussed further in **Chapter 23**.

16.70 Where a para 32(1)(b) application is made, if the tribunal decides that the site provider has established any of the grounds stated in its para 31 notice, it 'must order that the code agreement comes to an end in accordance with the order'.[41]

16.71 In any other case, the tribunal must make one of the orders specified in para 34.[42]

37 Para 32(3).
38 Para 32(3A).
39 Para 32(6).
40 Para 32(7).
41 See the discussion in Chapter 17 regarding whether there is a discretion as to timing.
42 Para 32(5).

16.72 Para 34 is considered in Section B of this chapter (from **16.195** onwards), in the context of an application by either party for a renewal of modification of a Code agreement under para 33(5), following service of a para 33 notice. However, it applies in the same way in a case where there has been a para 32(1)(b) application and the site provider's ground is not made out. Accordingly, readers are directed to the relevant passage below within Section B for an explanation of the para 34 options open to a Tribunal.

16.73 Similarly, para 35 applies in respect of interim consideration following an application under para 32(1)(b) as it does where there is an application under para 33(5). This issue is also addressed below within Section B of this chapter (from **16.195** onwards).

(2) Subsisting agreements

16.74 Subsisting agreements are principally agreements in writing for the purposes of paras 2 and 3 of the Old Code, which are treated differently in some respects by virtue of the Transitional Provisions.[43] Broadly, the effect of the Transitional Provisions is that subsisting agreements have effect as if they were agreements under Part 2 of the New Code, subject to some modifications,[44] but that some subsisting agreements are terminated or renewed under the 1954 Act and not under Part 5 of the Code. Subsisting agreements and the effect of the Transitional Provisions are considered in more detail below.

The rationale and the legislation

16.75 There were, of course, a substantial number of agreements entered into when the Old Code was in force, by which rights to install ECA (and other rights now referred to as 'Code rights') were granted. A substantial number of these agreements continued in force at the time at which the New Code came into force.

16.76 The Transitional Provisions at Schedule 2 to the Digital Economy Act 2017 contain important provisions as to these agreements, including as to their termination. These provisions have been referred to by the Supreme Court as 'complex'.[45]

16.77 The rationale for the Transitional Provisions insofar as they relate to subsisting agreements is the desire to give effect to the policy decision that the Code would not have entirely retrospective effect on agreements that had been entered into within the ecosystem of the Old Code, and especially on those agreements that were tenancies to which Part 2 of the 1954 Act applied. The 1954 Act has its own termination and renewal mechanism, its own valuation methodology[46] (which is in theory more generous to a landlord than that under the Code), and different provisions guiding the ascertainment of the other terms of the new tenancy than those under the Code

---

43 Sch 2 to the Digital Economy Act 2017, brought into force on 28 December 2017 by reg 2 of the Digital Economy Act 2017 (Commencement No. 3) Regulations 2017.

44 As the Deputy President commented in *Gencomp* [2022] UKUT 223 (LC) at [23]. The UT's decision was overturned by the Court of Appeal on appeal, but this comment was uncontroversial.

45 See *Compton Beauchamp* [2022] UKSC 18 at [61].

46 Albeit soon to be amended by the PSTIA 2022 to bring it into line with the Code, assuming the relevant provisions of that Act are brought into force.

(which are more likely to give pre-eminence to the terms of the existing tenancy and hence might be thought to be less operator-friendly than the Code).

16.78 Given that the parties' previous bargain was struck against this backdrop, in the expectation that the agreement would be renewed under the 1954 Act, applying the full force of the Code to those agreements might be thought to be meddling in pre-existing commercial bargains in a way that English law typically attempts to avoid.

16.79 Under the clear heading 'The revised Code should not be retrospective', the Law Commission[47] said as follows:

> '1.43 We are conscious that the introduction of the revised Code will need to be managed with care and considerable thought given to transitional provisions. We do not think that it would be practicable or appropriate simply to apply the revised Code to existing arrangements. This would result in retrospective application, affecting rights which had already arisen. In some cases, there would be disruption to carefully-negotiated agreements by which the parties have sought to strike a balance within the context of the existing Code.'

16.80 Whilst not all of the Law Commission's careful and considered conclusions were taken forward by the Government when the New Code was brought before Parliament, the principle of no retrospectivity was (at least initially[48]) respected and enacted. It is true that an old 1954 Act tenancy would have been expected to be renewed under the 1954 Act repeatedly, and this is not something that the Transitional Provisions allow to occur. However, the Law Commission envisages that eventually the Old Code would become obsolete through the expiration and renewal of agreements. Any transitional legislation surely aims at a transition from one regime (or set of regimes) to another, without the unfairness, arbitrariness, uncertainty or chaos that might have resulted if no transitional provisions had been enacted.

16.81 What was the problem confronting the Law Commission? Paragraph 3 of the Executive Summary[49] of its ultimate report concisely described both the pathology and the intended remedy:

> 'The current Code is complex and confusing, it is inconsistent with other legislation, and it is not up-to-date with modern technology. Our Report recommends a revised Code which sets out the legal position in clear terms and provides an efficient forum for dispute resolution.'

16.82 This particular project of the Law Commission was inherently looking to bring legislation up-to-date with modern technology and provide the certainty and flexibility that the future would surely demand. Given this, and that the Law Commission would rightly be confident that its solution would create an improved statutory scheme, it surely made sense that renewals of old agreements which were

---

47 At Law Com 336, para 1.43.

48 Aspects of the PSTIA 2022 have now applied some provisions of the Code to subsisting agreements which were initially excluded by the Transitional Provisions, for example para 17 of the Code in relation to sharing and upgrading. Further, assuming they are brought into force, there are provisions of the PSTIA 2022 which would affect the basis on which 1954 Act tenancies whose primary purpose is to grant Code rights are renewed, including by bringing the valuation of rent in line with the Code.

49 Law Com 336 (Summary), published 28 February 2013. This report can currently be downloaded at: https://lawcom.gov.uk/project/electronic-communications-code/.

previously governed by a different statutory scheme would eventually be governed by the new statutory scheme. This will eventually yield a degree of consistency and homogeneity of approach to agreements across the network (or across the land, depending on one's frame of reference).

16.83 Thus, the Transitional Provisions, together with the insertion of section 43(4) into the 1954 Act, have been interpreted as providing for a single renewal under the 1954 Act, with the resulting agreement being a true Code agreement to which Part 5 of the Code will apply. Accordingly, where one has a subsisting agreement that is a 1954 Act tenancy that has not been 'contracted out' of the security of tenure provisions of the 1954 Act, and whose primary purpose is to confer Code rights, there is one renewal under the 1954 Act, but subsequent renewals will occur under the Code.

16.84 The detail of the legislative process by which the Old Code was repealed, and the New Code and Transitional Provisions were brought into force, is dealt with in Chapter 3.

Definition of 'subsisting agreement'

16.85 Certain paragraphs of the Transitional Provisions[50] mention 'the time the new code comes into force'.[51] The date on which the New Code came into force was 28 December 2017.

16.86 Paragraph 1(4) of the Transitional Provisions defines a 'subsisting agreement' as follows:

> '(4) A 'subsisting agreement' means—
>
> (a) an agreement for the purposes of paragraph 2 or 3 of the existing code, or
>
> (b) an order under paragraph 5 of the existing code,
>
> which is in force, as between an operator and any person, at the time the new code comes into force (and whose terms do not provide for it to cease to have effect at that time).'

16.87 In the Transitional Provisions, the 'existing code'[52] is the Old Code, and the 'new code'[53] is of course the New Code.

16.88 What constitutes an Order under para 5 of the Old Code should not be a difficult question. One might conceivably face evidential issues in the event that the Order was made a long time ago and can no longer be found, or if the Order can be found, but is arguably ambiguous as to the paragraph of the Old Code under which it was made. However, these will simply be a question of evidence and argument, and the law is straightforward.

50 Sch 2 to the Digital Economy Act 2017.

51 For example, para 4 of the Transitional Provisions.

52 By the definition at para 1(2) of the Transitional Provisions. The old code is Sch 2 to the Telecommunications Act 1984.

53 The new code is of course Sch 3A to the Communications Act 2003.

16.89 The substantial majority of subsisting agreements will be those which fall under para 1(4)(a) of the Transitional Provisions, ie, 'an agreement for the purposes of paragraph 2 or 3' of the Old Code. Those two types of agreements will now be addressed.

Old Code para 2 agreements

16.90 An agreement for the purposes of para 2 of the Old Code will include an agreement under para 2(1) of the Old Code, which provides/provided[54] as follows:

> 'The agreement in writing of the occupier for the time being of any land shall be required for conferring on the operator a right for the statutory purposes—
>
> (a) to execute any works on that land for or in connection with the installation, maintenance, adjustment, repair or alteration of telecommunication apparatus; or
>
> (b) to keep telecommunication apparatus installed on, under or over that land; or
>
> (c) to enter that land to inspect any apparatus kept installed (whether on, under or over that land or elsewhere) for the purposes of the operator's system.'

16.91 Note that para 2(1) does not speak of 'an agreement', but 'The agreement in writing of the occupier.' The Old Code does not contain the same formalities requirements as exist in para 11 of the New Code, and 'required only the written permission of the occupier of the land and says nothing about a signature'.[55]

16.92 In addition to the agreement of a person under para 2(1), there is a further type of agreement provided for by para 2 of the Old Code. Paragraph 2(4) of the Old Code provided for a person owning an interest in land to agree in writing that his interest should be bound by an Old Code para 2(1) right, and set out the consequences of such agreement as regards who was to be bound by the rights. Given that such an agreement is 'an agreement for the purposes of paragraph 2', it would seem that it is capable of being a 'subsisting agreement'. Paragraph 1(4)(a) of the Transitional Provisions does not refer exclusively to para 2(1) of the Old Code, but para 2 of the Old Code more broadly.

16.93 Where an agreement was entered into whilst the Old Code was in force, is clearly a written agreement satisfying the formalities requirements of the Old Code, and grants rights to install apparatus,[56] there should not be a difficulty in concluding that such an agreement was 'an agreement for the purposes of paragraph 2 or 3 of the existing code', and accordingly if it remained in force on 28 December 2017, such an agreement is a subsisting agreement.

---

54 Despite the Old Code having been repealed, the Transitional Provisions keep it alive to a certain extent and in respect of certain specified situations.

55 Per Judge Cooke in the *Arqiva* case [2020] UKUT 195 (LC). This case went to the Supreme Court together with *Compton Beauchamp*, but this description of the limited formality requirements of the Old Code is uncontroversial.

56 Referred to at para 2(1) of the Old Code as 'telecommunication apparatus'.

Old Code para 3 agreements

16.94 The reference in para 1(4)(a) of the Transitional Provisions to an agreement for the purposes of para 3 of the Old Code is a reference to an agreement by which an occupier conferred on an occupier the right to interfere with or obstruct an access.

16.95 Under para 3(1) of the Old Code, where an operator had a right the exercise of which would mean that it would 'interfere with or obstruct any means of entering or leaving any other land', it would need the occupier of that other land to confer the right to interfere or obstruct, or be otherwise bound by such a right.

16.96 Paragraph 3(2) of the Old Code provided that the 'agreement in writing of the occupier for the time being of the other land shall be required for conferring' such a right on the occupier.

16.97 These agreements will have been substantially rarer than agreements under para 2 of the Old Code, and will not frequently be encountered in the context of 'subsisting agreements' following the coming into force of the New Code.

Effect of status as a 'subsisting agreement'

16.98 Paragraph 2(1) of the Transitional Provisions provides that a subsisting agreement has effect 'as an agreement under Part 2' of the New Code, but subject to the modifications made by the Transitional Provisions.

16.99 There are a number of different modifications made by the Transitional Provisions, and in certain respects, these vary by reference to the characteristics of the particular agreement. As regards termination, the relevant provisions are examined below by reference to different agreement types.

16.100 Where an agreement whose primary purpose was to grant Code rights was entered into *after* the New Code came into force, it will be terminable and renewable under Part 5 regardless of whether it is a lease or not.[57] However, in respect of subsisting agreements, this is not the case.

16.101 Paragraph 6(1) of the Transitional Provisions provides that, in relation to a subsisting agreement, para 6 of the Transitional Provisions applies in place of para 29(2) to (4) of the New Code. Paragraph 6 of the Transitional Provisions relates to the termination and modification of agreements. The effect of these provisions is to alter the way in which certain Old Code leases are terminated or renewed.

16.102 For completeness, a person bound by para 2(4) of the Old Code in consequence of a subsisting agreement is now treated as a person bound pursuant to Part 2 of the New Code.[58]

---

57 Because section 43(4) of the 1954 Act prevents the 1954 Act from applying to such agreements, and the Transitional Provisions do not apply to an agreement which comes into being after the New Code came into force.

58 By para 2(2) of the Transitional Provisions.

Different categories of subsisting agreement

16.103

(i) Certain Old Code leases to which Part 5 will not apply

Part 5 of the Code does not apply[59] to a subsisting agreement that is a lease, where either:

(a) Part 2 of the 1954 Act applies to it, and it is *not* 'contracted out'[60] (see para 6(2) of the Transitional Provisions); or

(b) The primary purpose of the lease is not to grant Code rights,[61] and it *is* 'contracted out' (see para 6(3) of the Transitional Provisions).

In the former case, the termination and renewal mechanism of Part 2 of the 1954 Act will apply to the lease. This is considered further below.

In the latter case, the 1954 Act process will not apply because the lease is 'contracted out', but neither will the Code apply, because of para 6(3) of the Transitional Provisions.

(ii) Old Code leases to which Part 5 applies (with modifications)

It will be apparent that the Transitional Provisions do not disapply Part 5 from all Old Code leases. Where a subsisting agreement is a lease that was entered into under the Old Code, with the primary purpose of conferring Code rights, but it was 'contracted out' under section 38A of the 1954 Act, Part 5 will apply. However, by para 7 of the Transitional Provisions, Part 5 will apply with certain modifications described below.

(iii) Other Old Code agreements to which Part 5 applies (with modifications)

Paragraph 7 of the Transitional Provisions provides that Part 5 applies with modifications to all subsisting agreements, save for those in whose case para 6 of the Transitional Provisions disapplies Part 5.

Thus, where a subsisting agreement is not a lease at all, Part 5 will also apply with the modifications set out in para 7 of the Transitional Provisions, which are described immediately below.

The para 7 (Transitional Provisions) modifications to Part 5

16.104 Where para 6 of the Transitional Provisions has not disapplied Part 5 from a subsisting agreement, Part 5 applies to that agreement whether it is a lease or not, but subject to the following modifications:[62]

59 By virtue of para 6(2) of the Transitional Provisions.

60 Ie, there is no agreement under s 38A of the 1954 Act disapplying the security of tenure provisions of ss 24 to 28 of the 1954 Act.

61 In this situation, the definition of 'code rights' is altered by para 3 of the Transitional Provisions, such that it refers to the equivalent rights under the Old Code. In the case of an agreement under para 2 of the Old Code, the relevant rights are those at para 2(1)(a) to (c) of the Old Code. In the case of an agreement under para 3 of the Old Code, the relevant rights are those mentioned in that paragraph.

62 At para 7(2) to (4) of the Transitional Provisions.

'(2) The 'site provider' (see paragraph 30(1)(a) of the new code) does not include a person who was under the existing code bound by the agreement only by virtue of paragraph 2(2)(c) of that code.

(3) Where the unexpired term of the subsisting agreement at the coming into force of the new code is less than 18 months, paragraph 31 applies (with necessary modification) as if for the period of 18 months referred to in sub-paragraph (3)(a) there were substituted a period equal to the unexpired term or 3 months, whichever is greater.

(4) Paragraph 34 applies with the omission of sub-paragraph (13)(d).'

16.105 It will be seen that para 7(3) of the Transitional Provisions reduces the termination notice period, that needs to be given under para 31 in certain cases. The effect of para 7(4) of the Transitional Provisions is that when a tribunal is considering what Order to make under para 34, on a renewal of a subsisting agreement under Part 5, the amount of consideration payable is not a matter to which the tribunal has to have regard.

(3) Agreements which expired before the New Code came into force

16.106 Where an agreement was entered into under the Old Code and its contractual end date fell before the New Code came into force on 28 December 2017, it would not have been statutorily continued by either Code. Thus, unless it was a lease that was statutorily continued by section 24 of the 1954 Act,[63] it will have come to an end before the New Code came into force.

16.107 Such an agreement may have been a lease that was contracted out of the security of tenure provisions of the 1954 Act, or it may have been a contractual licence.

16.108 If that were the end of the story, once the Code came into force, the landlord/grantor under the expired agreement would now have a right to require removal of the relevant ECA under para 37(2) as no Code rights would have bound it since the coming into force of the New Code. The operator, however, would in principle be able to serve a new para 20 notice and seek new Code rights.

16.109 However, one must consider the possibility that an implied agreement may be deemed to have arisen by the conduct of the parties after the contractual expiry of the written agreement. If that is the case, the implied agreement itself will need to be terminated in order for the landowner to recover its land, and the extent of the ability on the part of the operator to seek new Code rights may depend on what species of implied agreement has arisen.

Implied agreements following pre-New Code expiry

16.110 Whether such an implied agreement has arisen is a question that arises in all manner of non-telecoms contexts in the world of commercial leases and will be familiar to most property lawyers. It is a matter that will be determined by an analysis

63 Such a lease will of course be a 'subsisting agreement' as explained above.

of all the circumstances in order to discern the objectively-inferred intentions of the parties. The acceptance of rent or an occupational payment for a considerable period with a long cessation of negotiations for a new written agreement may, in an appropriate case, give rise to the inference of a new tenancy or of a new contractual licence. In other cases, particularly where negotiations are (or were until recently) ongoing as regards the grant of a new agreement, the tribunal may infer that a tenancy at will has arisen.

16.111 If a new implied tenancy is considered to have arisen before the New Code came into force, that tenancy would be overwhelmingly likely to be a periodic tenancy and hence cannot be 'contracted out' of the security of tenure provisions of the 1954 Act. In order to terminate that tenancy, the landlord would have to follow the procedure set out in Part 2 of the 1954 Act. Having a ground for termination that would satisfy para 31(4) of the Code would not assist the landlord if it did not have a ground for termination under section 30(1) of the 1954 Act. If the original written agreement ended before the New Code came into force, but the new implied periodic tenancy is considered to have arisen only *after* the Code came into force, such a tenancy cannot be one to which Part 2 of the 1954 Act applies,[64] assuming its 'primary purpose' is to grant Code rights; it must therefore be terminated contractually in accordance with the common law and its own terms.

16.112 If an implied agreement arose before the coming into force of the Code, the conventional analysis is that this is not an agreement 'in writing',[65] for the purposes of the Old Code or the New Code, and hence such an agreement does not constitute a subsisting agreement for the purposes of the Transitional Provisions.

16.113 This was the conclusion arrived at by Judge Cooke in the *Arqiva*[66] case in the Upper Tribunal. We know following *Compton Beauchamp*[67] that *if* the operator has no Code rights following their expiration with no statutory right of renewal, the operator is free to apply for Code rights under para 20 despite physically being the occupier of the land. In the meantime, the landowner has the right to require removal[68] under Part 6. Paragraph 40(8) has the result that the landowner will not be able to achieve a removal Order under Part 6 until any application by the operator for new Code rights under para 20 has been determined.

16.114 An alternative possibility to this orthodox position arose from the observations of Lady Rose in *Compton Beauchamp*.[69] An implied agreement might constitute an agreement 'for the purposes of' para 2 of the Old Code, because that cited expression[70] does not mean 'under' or 'complying with' but rather refers to the 'statutory purposes'

64 By section 43(4) of the 1954 Act.

65 Both paras 2 and 3 of the Old Code, and para 11 of the New Code require the formality of writing in order to create a valid agreement under each respective Code, but each provision is worded slightly differently.

66 At [67]–[84]. This case was known as *Arqiva Services Ltd v AP Wireless II (UK) Ltd* [2020] UKUT 195 (LC). By the time the matter reached the Supreme Court as an appeal heard with the *Compton Beauchamp* case, Arqiva Services Ltd was known as On Tower UK Ltd, and in the Supreme Court the case was renamed accordingly.

67 [2022] UKSC 18.

68 That right deriving from para 37(2). The right would need to be enforced by the service of a para 40 notice and following the Part 6 procedure.

69 See *Compton Beauchamp* [2022] UKSC 18 at [90]–[93].

70 Contained within para 1(4)(a) of the Transitional Provisions (Sch 2 to the Digital Economy Act 2017).

which are listed in para 2 of the Old Code (to execute works in connection with installation, to keep apparatus installed, to enter land to inspect apparatus, etc). It must be emphasised that there was no appeal in respect of this point, this was no throwaway line in the Supreme Court's decision. The court was considering three different cases which each raised three slightly different but related questions as to how the Code was supposed to work. The thinking of the Supreme Court in this context might be expected to have some influence. Having said that, the Upper Tribunal's conclusion on the point would be thought by most to be part of the *ratio* of its decision, and hence would constitute a precedent at FTT level.

16.115 Indeed, in the *Patricroft*[71] case, Judge Jackson in the FTT followed the reasoning of Judge Cooke in *Arqiva*, describing Lady Rose's observations in *Compton Beauchamp* as 'clearly obiter'.[72] It was further held that rent remands and receipts, without more, did not constitute the 'agreement in writing of the occupier' for the purposes of para 2 of the Old Code and so it did not elevate an unwritten implied agreement into a subsisting agreement.

16.116 There is no longer quite so much hinging on the question whether the orthodox view above is correct as had appeared the case in *Arqiva*. This is because, post-*Compton Beauchamp*, we now know that an operator in situ is not prevented from applying for Code rights under para 20 by the mere fact that it is already in occupation of the land to which those rights would relate.

16.117 In such a situation, an operator may then argue that, as it has no Code rights, it is entitled to seek them by serving a new notice. Assuming the landowner accepts there is a right to seek such rights, it may seek to argue that the para 21(3) balance is not satisfied in the operator's favour because the operator has a contractual right to keep its ECA installed and provide its network services, and that it can seek Code rights when its agreement expires or is terminated.

Alternatively, the landowner may seek to argue that the operator is not entitled to seek new Code rights. Whether it is so entitled may depend on what kind of implied rights it has. For example, in *Patricroft* (see **16.211**)it was held that an operator which is a tenant under an implied periodic tenancy is not entitled to serve a notice seeking Code rights.

Expiration of the term of a 1954 Act lease prior to the Code

16.118 It should be underlined that an implied agreement arising after the expiration of a fixed term agreement *without* statutory protection is a different creature from a statutory continuation tenancy arising under section 24 of the 1954 Act following the expiration of the contractual term of a tenancy to which Part 2 of the 1954 Act applies.

16.119 Where Part 2 of the 1954 Act applies to a tenancy, and there is no 'contracting out', section 24(1) of that Act provides that that tenancy 'shall not come to an end' unless terminated in accordance with the 1954 Act. Accordingly, as long as the original

71 *On Tower UK Limited v AP Wireless II (UK) Limited* LC-2023-000852 (re *Patricroft* and five other properties), decision dated 2 September 2024.

72 The *Patricroft* case at [19].

1954 Act tenancy is in writing, the statutory continuation of it does not lack writing. Thus, where a statutory fixed term of a 1954 Act tenancy expires before the coming into force of the Code, the statutory continuation is similarly an agreement for the purposes of para 2 of the Old Code, and accordingly will be a subsisting agreement for the purposes of para 1(4) of the Transitional Provisions. Following the coming into force of the New Code, it therefore has effect[73] as an agreement under Part 2 of the New Code, subject to the modifications made by the Transitional Provisions. It would need to be terminated under the 1954 Act.

How might forfeiture of a lease interact with Code rights?

16.120 Code agreements do not exist in a vacuum as regards the general law, and in the absence of a provision of the Code that expressly or impliedly disapplies a concept from the law of landlord and tenant, one might expect such concepts to apply with full force to a lease whose primary purpose is to confer Code rights. However, there is nothing in the Code that states that a lease which grants Code rights may be subject to forfeiture. This constitutes a difference from the statutory scheme of the 1954 Act, which expressly allows for forfeiture[74] as an exception to the general position that leases must be terminated in accordance with the procedure under the 1954 Act.

16.121 Part 5 of the Code will apply to a lease whose primary purpose is to grant Code rights, if it was either: (a) granted after the coming into force of the Code, or (b) granted before the coming into force of the Code, and there was a 'contracting out' of the security of tenure provisions of the 1954 Act under section 38A of that Act.

16.122 Where Part 5 applies, the difficulty with forfeiture is that a valid act of forfeiture renders a lease at an end, and we know that para 30(2) continues an agreement where under the terms of the agreement a site provider may bring it to an end. The answer might be that where a right to forfeit arises, a similar situation to a landlord's break right arises. In the case of a contractual break right, a purported exercise by a landlord will not terminate the tenancy, but the opportunity to break means that the landlord can serve a para 31 notice terminating immediately after the potential break date, rather than immediately after the expiry date of the full contractual term.

16.123 As per *BT (Kenton Road)*[75] (see **16.47**), a landlord seeking to take advantage of the fact that it could have broken the lease but for para 30, can simply serve a para 31 notice, and need not serve a separate contractual break notice. Assuming in theory a right to forfeit a lease is preserved, must the landlord carry out an act of forfeiture, or can it simply rely on the fact that it *could have* forfeit, and serve a para 31 notice? If it is determined in para 31 proceedings that an operator would have obtained relief from forfeiture, does this prevent the landlord from arguing that the Code agreement 'could have been brought to an end' for para 31(3)(b) purposes at all? These are not questions that have come before the tribunal. In any event, if a landlord is tempted to try to forfeit in order to engage in these arguments, 'peaceable re-entry' (as opposed to the service of forfeiture proceedings) may be inconsistent with the requirements of Part 6 as to how one achieves the removal of ECA.

73 By para 2(1) of the Transitional Provisions.
74 See section 24(2) of the 1954 Act.
75 *On Tower UK Ltd v British Telecommunications Plc* [2024] UKUT 51 (LC).

16.124 In the case of a subsisting agreement which is a lease that is susceptible to termination under the 1954 Act, slightly different considerations apply. By para 6(2) of the Transitional Provisions, Part 5 does not apply to such a lease. Accordingly, para 30 cannot continue it, and no para 31 notice is relevant to its termination. That being the case, forfeiture would not come into collision with para 30, and appears to be allowed by section 24(2) of the 1954 Act. The option of forfeiture may therefore remain open to a landlord in this situation. Again it must be emphasised that this has not been the subject of any reported decision.

16.125 However, if forfeiture is theoretically possible, the tenant will have a right to seek relief from forfeiture. One would imagine that in exercising any discretion the court will have in mind the desirability of maintaining connectivity, even if the provisions of the Code are not of direct relevance.

16.126 Further, even where a lease is terminated, a landlord would have to respect Part 6 as regards seeking removal of ECA. The operator may attempt to serve a fresh para 20 notice, and an argument as to whether the operator is entitled to seek new rights in the circumstances may ensue. If it is indeed permitted to seek new rights, timescales may be such that para 40(8) would stop the landowner from obtaining a removal Order before the para 20 application is heard.

Lease vs licence

16.127 It is well-established that an agreement granting code rights may be a lease or a licence. In *EE Ltd & Anor v London Borough Of Islington*[76] Martin Rodger QC (Deputy President of the Upper Tribunal (Lands Chamber) held that the tribunal could impose a lease upon the parties under Part 4 of the Code. It of course follows that a lease[77] can grant Code rights, and that a document granting Code rights can be a lease.

16.128 However, the judge acknowledged that a document granting code rights need not necessarily be a lease, stating as follows at [45] and [46]:

> '45. On the other hand, the right to keep equipment installed on land does not necessarily involve a grant of exclusive possession. For example, the land on which an automated teller machine is located in a supermarket is capable of being concurrently in the occupation of the bank which owns the machine and the store which hosts it and to involve no grant of exclusive possession: see *Cardtronics Europe Ltd v Sykes (VO)* [2018] EWCA Civ 2472 at [81].
>
> 46. The starting point of our analysis is the absence of any express restriction in Part 4 on the type of agreement by which Code rights may be imposed. Because of the variety of circumstances in which rights may be required we do not consider it significant that the Code lacks any specific reference in Part 4 to rights being conferred by the grant or imposition of a lease.'

76 [2019] UKUT 53 (LC).

77 Although in *Islington*, the site provider was seeking to argue that the tribunal could not impose a lease, it is now evident that there is at least one advantage to a site provider where a Code agreement takes the form of a lease. Where an operator is given exclusive possession of an area of land, a site provider can more safely conclude that it will be the operator which is liable for any health and safety breaches than where a site provider retains possession of the areas in which operators have their ECA installed. There may be other reasons making it preferable for a Code agreement to be a lease or licence in any given case.

16.129 The Code is fairly indifferent to whether a new agreement, consensual or imposed, is a lease or a licence. Because of section 43(4) of the 1954 Act, a lease whose primary purpose is to grant Code rights that is entered into after the coming into force of the New Code cannot be a tenancy to which Part 2 of the 1954 Act applies. Accordingly, the termination and renewal mechanism in that Act cannot apply to it. Thus, whether it is a lease or licence, an agreement entered into after the Code came into force and whose primary purpose is to grant Code rights, is to be terminated or renewed under Part 5 of the Code.

16.130 However, in respect of agreements entered into before the New Code came into force, the question whether it is a lease or not is capable of making a substantial difference to how an operator's rights are to be terminated (or renewed). This will be particularly so where there is no hint of a 'contracting out' agreement[78] under section 38A of the 1954 Act.

16.131 One of the effects of the New Code in legal terms has thus been to revive the age-old chestnut, the 'lease-licence distinction', the consideration of which has been a rite of passage for property law students for generations. Indeed, some Old Code agreements could easily have been written as undergraduate questions or mooting problems, such is their remarkable capacity to include features that push and pull in different directions.

16.132 Before the New Code was enacted, there was not total clarity as to the interaction[79] between the Old Code and the 1954 Act. Perhaps for this reason, and perhaps for the purposes of maintaining tactical agility, many agreements entered into under the Old Code do not make it clear whether they are intended to be leases or licences.

16.133 The general law in respect of what constitutes a tenancy is well-known to most property lawyers, not least the House of Lords decision in *Street v Mountford*.[80] That being the case, this section will concentrate on decisions in the Code context, which have applied the law to the particular circumstance of agreements conferring Code rights.

The Burlington Gardens case

16.134 The most thorough treatment by the Upper Tribunal of the lease/licence question, and so far the only appellate decision on the point, is the recent *Burlington*

78 The presence of such a purported agreement is not necessarily determinative that the document in question is a lease. For example, on particular facts there might be insufficient certainty of term for a tenancy to be created, or on a proper interpretation the document may not confer exclusive possession. Moreover, a s 38A 'contracting out' agreement was sometimes included in agreements entered into under the Old Code on the express basis that the parties do not intend the relationship of landlord and tenant to arise, but that if it were deemed to have arisen, the parties agree under s 38A to exclude ss 24 to 28 of the 1954 Act in respect of the tenancy.

79 The Law Commission (Law Com 336), at para 6.54 onwards, discussed this relationship. It noted the problem of dual protection, and of the endless circularity of logic that, on one reading of the two statutory codes, would have rendered it impossible to achieve removal of apparatus (see para 6.57 of the report).

80 [1985] AC 809.

Gardens[81] case. The parties were in dispute as to whether two agreements that granted Code rights were leases or licences. The Chamber President, Mr Justice Edwin Johnson, considered the proper approach to take in such a case by reference to the established case law. The following propositions arise:

(i) The starting point is *Street v Mountford*. The question whether a contractual agreement for the occupation of land creates a lease or licence depends on whether it grants exclusive possession of the relevant land for a term at a rent [74]. The principles in *Street v Mountford* (a residential case) apply equally to business premises[82] [77].

(ii) The label attached by the parties to the relevant agreement may be indicative, and thus is not totally irrelevant. However, it is not determinative [79].

(iii) It is necessary to look at the whole of the agreement and analyse the substance and effect of the rights granted and the obligations undertaken [80].

(iv) Ordinary principles of construction apply [83].

(v) Where an agreement is entered into by a commercial entity,[83] the idea of 'business common sense' has a role to play in the construction process [84].

(vi) Construction of a contract involves ascertaining what a reasonable person would have understood the parties to have meant. Such a person has all the background knowledge available to the parties, and so an examination of the circumstances in which the agreement was made is required [85].

(vii) The Code does not exist in a vacuum, but is subject to the ordinary law of landlord and tenant, where relevant.[84] The same is true when considering agreements entered into under the Old Code [89].

(viii) While documents forming part of the same transaction may be used to construe a document in that transaction, documents outside that transaction cannot be used in the same way [91]. Further, conduct of the parties subsequent to entering into the agreement cannot as a general rule be relied upon in construing the agreement[85] [92].

16.135 Leaving aside the point relating to whether one of the agreements had a sufficiently certain term, the Judge stated that the principal question was whether each agreement 'took effect as the grant of exclusive possession of land'.

---

81 *AP Wireless II (UK) Limited v On Tower UK Limited* [2024] UKUT 263 (LC).

82 Citing the *Clear Channel* case, mentioned again below.

83 As is the case for the vast majority of operators.

84 Reference is made to the *Gencomp* case in the Court of Appeal, at [78] of that judgment.

85 So where a later document is entered into between the same party, it is unlikely to be admissible to elucidate whether the initial agreement granted a lease or licence. However, one might think that where a later document is capable of giving rise to a contractual estoppel or estoppel by convention, by including an express recital or declaration that the document was a lease, this could constitute a different point (not relevant before the judge). Similarly, where a later document amends the initial agreement, and in so doing might be argued to have converted it from a licence to a lease, again, one might think this is a different point. How likely the parties would have intended such a change will depend on all the relevant circumstances, and one might think that a tribunal would start from a position of scepticism.

Exclusive possession of land: the various categories of terms

16.136 In determining whether each agreement granted exclusive possession, the judge divided his analysis of the provisions of each agreement into a number of thematic sections, before 'standing back' and considering the terms of each agreement in their entirety.

16.137 There are numerous different types of terms that might be capable of having an impact on whether exclusive possession is granted. The consideration of the different categories of term in *Burlington Gardens* is summarised below. It is likely that the FTT in future cases will follow a similar approach. As to the conclusion on the substance, each case will be fact-specific, and even old agreements based on the same standard template relating to similar land may not necessarily yield the same conclusion, because of the addition of a particular term, particular wording, or the absence of a plan, or a line from a plan. However, where the judge considers the presence or absence of a particular term to be more indicative of a lease or a licence, one can expect that conclusion to be at least persuasive in future cases in the FTT.

16.138

(i) The operative words of grant or demise, and the plans

The absence of specific words of demise was not considered by the judge to be decisive; what matters is the overall substance and effect of the agreement. The wording chosen, which granted a bundle of rights rather than being expressed as a 'demise', was neutral in its effect, and could not be read in isolation.

The rights were tied to an identifiable area of land. There was a plan showing the site with red edging, and the site was intended to be a fenced compound. The plans pointed in favour of a lease. The extent of control given to the operator pointed strongly against a licence.

An agreement conferring rights over a rooftop is a different beast than one that grants rights over a defined area of open land that is intended to be fenced, and the judge readily distinguished the case of *Edelwind*,[86] in which the Upper Tribunal had held that a rooftop agreement was a licence.

(ii) Fencing obligations

The obligation to fence off an area of land is not to be deemed irrelevant merely on the basis that the reason for the fencing was to keep equipment secure, rather than fencing off the land itself. Although there are many different reasons in different cases as to why fencing is desired, these reasons do not negate that enclosure is the result, as a matter of fact. Whether such enclosure supports an argument that there is exclusive possession will depend on the circumstances of the case.

(iii) Rights of access

The owner's rights of access were limited to reasonable access by prior appointment for inspection only. This was held to be strongly suggestive of a lease.

86 As to which see below.

(iv) Sharing rights

The owner was allowed install or grant consent to third parties to install equipment on its wider land, but this right expressly excluded 'the Site', which was the area. This provision was held to be more consistent with a grant of exclusive possession of 'the Site'. It also contrasted sharply with the operator's wide rights to share the use of the Site with others.

(v) Chattels

The terms of the agreement provided that the operator would vacate the Site at the agreement's end and remove its chattels, which were to be treated as tenant's fixtures. It was held that the effect of chattels being stationed on land may be such as to exclude use of the land by the landowner, and that this would depend on all the circumstances.

The judge held that the operator had been granted what might reasonably be described as an exclusive right to keep and operate equipment, and that this might be thought to support exclusive possession.

(vi) Right of relocation and redevelopment

The agreement contained a break clause that was consistent with either a lease or licence. In addition, there was a provision allowing the landlord to terminate the agreement in the event of redevelopment, but with an obligation to seek to agree a suitable relocation of the equipment. It was held that this was not inconsistent with exclusive possession: there was no general right to require relocation of the equipment, but rather a limited right in the case of redevelopment. It was held that the parties can be taken to have the Old Code in mind when entering into the agreement, and the above provision should be seen as a version of the right of alteration contained at para 20 of the Old Code. The relocation provision was therefore seen as equally consistent with a lease or licence.

(vii) Successors in title

The agreement contained a clause which is not uncommon in old agreements conferring Code rights, stating that the parties intended that the agreement 'shall continue to bind their respective successors in title'.

The judge referred to the principle that the burden of a mere contract cannot be assigned. He concluded that an Old Code agreement that was not a lease was also subject to this principle. Although paras 2(3) and (4) of the Old Code provided a mechanism by which landowners' successors would be bound by a grantor's obligations, there was nothing in the Old Code[87] which gave rise to the conclusion that the operator's burden in an Old Code agreement could be assigned if it were not a lease. Neither could the doctrine of 'mutual benefit and burden' be relied upon to transfer the operator's burden. It was considered appropriate to assume that the parties would have been aware of the legal position at the time when the agreement was entered into.

87 This is different from the position under the New Code, under which the benefit and burden can both be assigned, by virtue of the provisions of para 16. Para 16(4) in particular makes clear that the assignee is bound by the obligations in the agreement. Para 16 is disapplied in respect of subsisting agreements, by para 5(1) of the Transitional Provisions.

If an agreement was not able to be assigned in full unless it was a lease, the parties' reference to successors being bound is indicative of an intention that the agreement was a lease. Furthermore, the expression 'successors in title' would be inapt on the operator's side if there was no lease. In that event, the operator would have no title, and hence could have no successor in title. This clause was therefore considered strongly indicative of a lease, although the Judge did not accept that the clause was decisive on its own.

(viii) Agreement not made by deed

The judge noted that a lease which should have been made by deed could still take effect in equity if not at law. However, the absence of a deed was an indication against the intention to create a lease.

(ix) Absence of reference to the 1954 Act

The document did not refer to the 1954 Act. The judge at first instance had thought that the parties would have referred to that Act if the operator was to have the benefit of it. On appeal, the Upper Tribunal disagreed. Parties generally do not record that a lease is subject to the 1954 Act, and as such, the absence of such reference was a neutral factor.

(x) Other provisions

Other provisions were considered, none of which were considered to point in one direction or the other. These were as follows:

- No clause for quiet enjoyment: considered a neutral factor.
- No obligation to keep the *Site* in repair, as distinct from the *equipment*: this was not considered to have any particular effect, as there was nothing to repair on this bare land apart from the equipment.
- Warranties of title by the owner: considered a neutral factor.
- Owner's right to terminate in the event of a breach: considered a neutral factor. It could be considered a forfeiture clause if the agreement is a lease, or as a contractual termination provision if not.
- Operator's obligation to pay rates: considered a neutral factor.

16.139 Taking all of the terms of the agreements together, each agreement *was* considered to grant exclusive possession. The enclosure of the land by the operator, the enclosed land being occupied solely by the operator's equipment, the operator having rights to share its (effectively exclusive) rights of use, and the owner having no such rights, appear to have been the key features[88] that, taken together, demonstrated and constituted the grant of exclusive possession.

Certainty of term

16.140 It is trite law that a lease must have a sufficiently certain term. One of the agreements in the *Burlington Gardens* case granted rights for a defined 'minimum term', with the agreement then expressly continuing, terminable on 12 months'

88 This inference is drawn from the judge's summary at [256].

notice, expiring at any time. This sounds like an unusual provision, but it is commonly encountered in older agreements entered into by the particular operator in this case.

16.141 The judge referred to a number of authorities on this question before concluding that the term was not sufficiently certain and that therefore the agreement could not constitute a lease. Leaving aside special cases such as a tenancy for life, he held that the requirement for certainty of term was satisfied in three different categories of case:

(i) tenancies granted for a fixed term;

(ii) tenancies granted as periodic tenancies; and

(iii) tenancies granted for an initial fixed term, and then continuing as periodic tenancies.

16.142 The judge was doubtful that there was a fourth category of tenancy in which a tenancy continued after an initial specified term, when either could serve notice terminating the tenancy at any time, with no contractual fetter on when such notice could be served. Neither did this agreement fall within the third category mentioned above, as a periodic tenancy must be terminated by a notice that coincides with a period. If in a given case it were possible to construe an agreement as requiring a termination notice to coincide with the anniversary of the end of the fixed term, the position would be different.

16.143 Finally, an alternative submission was made that although the agreement had not taken effect as a lease because the term was uncertain, a periodic tenancy arose by virtue of exclusive possession and the periodical payment of rent. This argument was rejected. To conclude thus would be to impute intentions to the parties of a nature that would be quite inconsistent with the express written terms that they clearly intended would govern their relationship.

Previous Code cases

16.144 Although each case will turn on its own facts, it may be thought following *Burlington Gardens* that the tribunal will be more ready to find that an agreement grants exclusive possession than had previously been thought the case, at least in a case involving open land rather than an urban roof.

16.145 For a time, in the absence of much Upper Tribunal authority in this area, the FTT decision in *Allison*[89] was sometimes cited in argument or debate. The tribunal had held that the agreement in question was a licence. The agreement contained a number of features that were present in *Burlington Gardens*, including the same 'minimum term' problem. The FTT reached the same conclusion that there was no certainty of term, and the case was therefore correctly decided.

16.146 However, the FTT had also considered that a reference to the apparatus belonging to the operator 'as if it were a tenant's fixture' was indicative of the apparatus not being the tenant's fixture because the agreement is not a lease. Further, the reference

89 *On Tower UK Limited v Robert Graeme Allison and others* LC-2022-000322.

to the parties intending the agreement to bind successors was considered consistent with either a lease or a licence, because under para 2 of the Old Code either could be made binding upon successors in title. Each of these latter dicta appear at odds with *Burlington Gardens*.

16.147 In *Edelwind*,[90] the Upper Tribunal concluded that an agreement conferring Code rights was a licence. In *Keast*[91] at [48] Judge Cooke had used the phrase 'exclusive licence', and presumably this refers to a licence under which equipment was installed such as to have the effect of excluding others.

16.148 In *Edelwind*, Judge Cooke noted that many rooftop Code agreements are accompanied by a plan with a red line around one or more areas reserved to the operator, but that the agreement did not have such a structure in the present case. Rather, the agreement stated that the operator was to have the rights set out in a schedule. It was held that there was no indication that the operator was to have the use of a particular area shown on a plan, and there was no designated area of the roof reserved for the operator's exclusive use. It was therefore held that there was no grant of exclusive possession.

16.149 Although Judge Cooke did consider a number of terms of the agreement, it would appear that: (a) whether exclusive possession was granted was considered the key question, and that (b) the fact that there was no red line area reserved for exclusive use was a highly material factor in answering that question.

16.150 It is notable that in *Burlington Gardens*, the Chamber President referred to *Edelwind*, expressing that he had no quarrel with the decision.[92] He expressly distinguished that case on the basis of differences in the agreement,[93] and the differing natures of the land in each case was clearly a factor.[94] The absence of a red line on a plan in *Edelwind*, given substantial weight by Judge Cooke, can also be seen to constitute a clear and material difference.

Effect of clauses which assert that no tenancy is created

16.151 In *Clear Channel*,[95] the Court of Appeal had to consider the nature of an agreement conferring rights to use land for stationing advertising hoardings. The case was therefore not decided in the Code context. However, as noted in *Burlington Gardens*,[96] the general law in respect of the lease/licence distinction applies to Code cases, albeit carrying with it the need to construe agreements against their relevant factual and statutory background. Further, as in most Code cases, the principal occupation was to be by the presence of an object affixed to land, with more occasional visits by personnel.

90 *EE Ltd v Edelwind Ltd* [2020] UKUT 272 (LC).
91 *Cornerstone Telecommunications Infrastructure Ltd v Keast* [2019] UKUT 116 (LC).
92 At [158].
93 At [146].
94 The judge expressly noted at [151] that the land in question was not urban, and made repeated reference to the fact that *Edelwind* concerned the grant of rights over a rooftop site.
95 *Clear Channel UK Limited v Manchester City Council* [2005] EWCA 1304. This case was referred to in *Burlington Gardens*, but not in respect of the point being considered here.
96 At [121].

16.152 The agreement contained a clause that provided that the agreement was a licence, conferred no tenancy, and that possession of the land would be retained by the landowning Council. Expressly casting no doubt on *Street v Mountford*, Jonathan Parker LJ observed[97] that this provision was not a mere label but rather a clause that set out in unequivocal terms the parties' intention as to its legal effect. The agreement had been negotiated between two substantial parties of equal bargaining power and with the benefit of full legal advice. In that context he considered it unedifying that a reputable commercial organisation would seek to invite the court to conclude that an agreement expressly stated not to constitute a lease nonetheless was just that. The Court of Appeal held that the agreement was a licence, on the totality of its terms. However, Jonathan Parker LJ said that he would in any event have 'taken some persuading' that the true effect of the agreement was 'directly contrary to that expressed intention' contained in the clause mentioned above.

16.153 In some older agreements conferring Code rights, one does sometimes find clauses of this nature. The tribunals have not yet had to grapple with the interaction between such a clause and any combination of other terms that may point one way or another. However, one would think that a powerful argument could be made against a tenancy being created, in reliance on the dictum in *Clear Channel*. The less such a clause resembles a mere label and the more it represents the parties' active efforts to make clear that no tenancy is to be created or no exclusive possession is to be conferred, the stronger such an argument may be.

A potential third category?

16.154 Some commentators have raised the possibility that a Code agreement which is not a lease may be capable of being a sui generis form of agreement which is not entirely consistent with either a licence either.

16.155 In *University of London*,[98] the Court of Appeal noted that the Code was 'designed to be, so far as possible, a self-contained Code'.

16.156 However, the fact that Code rights are sui generis does not mean that there is anything magical about a Code agreement, which can take many forms. Those forms essentially boil down to those which grant proprietary rights, and those which are essentially contractual.

16.157 In *Gencomp*,[99] Nugee LJ commented that:

> 'It is to be noted that code agreements may take the form of the grant of property rights (either in the form of a lease or an easement), but may take the form of merely contractual arrangements.'

16.158 Having said that, the Code constitutes a statutory overlay that applies (to differing degrees, given the Transitional Provisions) to all agreements that confer Code rights. Thus, a person with no interest in land can be bound by a Code agreement that

97 At [28] and [29].
98 *Cornerstone Telecommunications Infrastructure Ltd v University of London* [2019] EWCA 2075 at [34].
99 [2023] EWCA Civ 825 at [75].

itself grants no proprietary interest in land, merely by virtue of the provisions of the Code (see para 10).

16.159 In *Compton Beauchamp,* Lady Rose referred to the Code as creating a 'sui generis form of statutory rights which use contractual agreement as their foundation' [117].

16.160 However, in *Burlington Gardens,*[100] Mr Justice Edwin Johnson concluded that Code agreements themselves are not in a special category of their own, in terms of identifying what rights of use and/or occupation of land they may grant.

16.161 Thus, Code rights are a unique statutory concept, and there are unique statutory rights and burdens created by the Code, but the agreement itself is essentially either a mere contract or a contract that also happens to grant exclusive possession and thereby create a legal estate in land.

16.162 In *Gencomp,*[101] Nugee LJ commented that:

> 'The Code has to be applied both to contractual arrangements such as licences or wayleaves and to the grants of property rights such as leases. But I do not accept that this means that one jettisons the ordinary law of landlord and tenant, or, as Lewison LJ put it in argument, that the Code exists in a legal vacuum.'

16.163 There are a good many types of tenancies that have a statutory overlay governing aspects such as security of tenure, how they can be terminated or renewed, terms that apply during any continuation, the review of rent, and how and when the tenancy comes to an end once terminated following litigation.

16.164 Two well-known examples are the 1954 Act, which statutorily continues a business tenancy, and the Housing Act 1988, which statutorily continues certain types of residential tenancies. The fact that these statutes govern these tenancies in this way does not stop the tenancies from being tenancies. Although there may be legitimate academic discussion as to the true nature of a tenancy whilst it is being continued, there is no doubt that the landlord and the tenant retain their roles as such.

16.165 A business lease continues statutorily at the end of its term (unless the relevant provisions are consensually disapplied), whereas a licence would not, but for the fact that para 30 does this job in the case of a licence, that is a Code agreement.

16.166 A business lease can be renewed statutorily, whereas a licence would not be able to be, but for the fact that Part 5 provides for a renewal procedure for licences that are Code agreements.

16.167 Leases and licences differ in their capacity to bind third parties. Para 10, once properly understood, provides a statutory overlay that ensures that certain persons are bound regardless of what species of agreement is used. Similarly, leases and licences differ in their capacity to be assigned. Paragraph 16 provides a statutory overlay that ensures that Code can be assigned and that both benefits and burdens are transmitted.

100 At [121].
101 [2023] EWCA Civ 825 at [78].

16.168 Thus, considering certain Code agreements to be licences, or wayleaves, causes no real difficulties where the provisions of the Code apply. One potential area of difficulty concerns the purported assignment of agreements that confer Code rights, but were entered into before the Code came into force. In respect of these, para 16 is disapplied. Thus, where such agreements are not leases, there is a question as to how and to what extent benefits and burdens can be assigned together.

Interplay between terminating an agreement and requiring removal of ECA

16.169 One can envisage certain, probably rare, situations in which a landowner appears to have a 'right to require the removal' of ECA under para 37 despite a contractual agreement remaining between the parties under which the operator has a right to keep its ECA at the site.

16.170 Examples might include the following situations where the non-operator party is a landowner:[102]

(i) An agreement under which an operator is granted a right to keep ECA on land might be entirely open-ended and hence specify no period during which that right is exercisable. It would then fall foul of para 11(1)(c) and therefore presumably[103] could not confer Code rights. That being the case, the landowner[104] has a right to require the removal of the ECA under para 37(2).

(ii) The same logic would apply to a consensual[105] agreement which falls foul of para 11(1)(a) by not being in writing, or one which contravenes para 11(1)(b) by not being signed by on behalf of the parties.

(iii) An operator might have apparatus installed on land under an agreement, but the apparatus might no longer be used for the purposes of its network. That being the case, the landowner might have a right to require the removal of the ECA under para 37(6).

16.171 The language of para 37 is fairly absolute: there is said to be a right to require removal in the stated cases. There is not the right to apply to the tribunal, with a test that balances the rights of the parties or even the interests of the landowner against the public interest. Accordingly, as confirmed in *Crawley*, there is no discretion on the part of the tribunal in the event that a landowner establishes one of the conditions at para 37. That being the case, in theory a landowner could seek an Order from the tribunal requiring the removal of the ECA despite an agreement continuing contractually, which allows it to be present.

16.172 It may be that the tribunal does not have the discretion to refuse such an application. The answer may well have been found in para 100(1), which provides

102 A 'landowner' under para 37(1) is a 'person with an interest in land'.

103 The Code does not in terms spell out the consequences of a failure to comply with the mandatory ('must...') requirements of para 11. See the discussion on para 11 in Chapter 6.

104 Assuming the non-operator party to the agreement is a 'landowner' under para 37(1), ie, is a 'person with an interest in land'.

105 An agreement imposed under Part 4 by the tribunal seemingly need not comply with the requirements of para 11, including the requirement for a signature at para 11(1)(b). See the discussion on this point, and on whether the same is the case for renewal agreements resulting from para 34(6) at Chapter 6.

that the Code does not affect rights and liabilities under an agreement to which an operator is a party. However, para 100(2) provides that para 100(1) does not apply to Part 6 of the Code, which includes paras 37 and 40.

16.173 There is scope for a potential argument that the landowner would be derogating from its grant by either seeking or enforcing such an Order, and it may be that by a purposive interpretation the tribunal considers that it is inherent in para 37 that a person cannot have a right to require removal under the Code if they do not under the general law. Alternatively, an operator may have a damages claim against the landowner. There is a certain lack of clarity here, and it is not easy to ascertain how the provision would be interpreted, given the range of contextual factors which are often in play when the interpretation of the Code is subject to judicial consideration.

16.174 In any event, if the operator wished to remain, in many cases it would be entitled to make an application under para 20 for any Code rights that it lacked. Paragraph 40(8) would prevent any Order for removal being granted before the para 20 application is determined, and if the Code rights were granted, it may be that they would sit in an agreement alongside the existing contractual non-Code agreement.

Para 26 and para 27 agreements

16.175 These agreements share the common feature that they are excluded by para 30(3) from the security of tenure provisions of para 30(2). Nonetheless, it is worth addressing how they come to an end, and how a landowner might thereafter seek removal of ECA.

Para 26 agreements

16.176 By para 26(2), a para 26 agreement will come to an end in accordance with the terms of the Order imposing it. In practice, the agreement itself is also likely to state either its duration, or the event that will cause it to come to an end.[106] Indeed, para 23(7) appears to require that a term be included that deals with such information.[107] Thus the Order presumably may simply impose the agreement that contains this information rather going into more detail on its face. When the para 26 agreement comes to an end (because the period specified under para 26(2)(a) has expired or the event specified under para 26(2)(b) has occurred), the non-operator party has the right to require removal of the ECA placed on the land under that agreement.[108] That right is enforceable under the Part 6 procedure, which is dealt with in **Chapter 18**.

16.177 It seems unlikely that a para 26 agreement will need to be terminated under the Part 5 procedure, as this type of agreement will typically be of a shorter duration

106 By para 26(2), a para 26 agreement can be imposed either for a specified period or until the occurrence of a specified event.

107 Para 23(7) is applied to a para 26 case by para 26(4)(c).

108 See para 26(7) and (8) and para 37(3)(a). Query whether such a right is contingent on the person asserting the right being a "landowner" under para 37(1), as per para 37(3)(a). That is necessary for all of the conditions set out at para 37 but is not mentioned in paras 26(7) or (8).

and has no security of tenure under para 30(2). Further, the Part 5 timetable entails an 18-month notice for termination under para 31(3)(a). However, by para 26(4)(b) and para 22, such an agreement strictly takes effect as an agreement under Part 2, and hence by para 29(1), Part 5 seems to apply to it.

Para 27 agreements

16.178 Similarly, a para 27 agreement will come to an end in accordance with the Order imposing it under para 27(2). The objective for which the para 27 agreement will have been imposed is essentially that service be maintained until para 20 proceedings (and any para 40 proceedings) are determined. Accordingly, one would expect the Order imposing the para 27 agreement ordinarily to impose it until the determination of those other proceedings, or further Order. As with para 26, strictly, it would seem that para 23(7) requires that a term be included in a para 27 agreement, that deals with how long Code rights are exercisable thereunder.[109]

16.179 Perhaps surprisingly, para 37 makes no provision in respect of a right to require removal arising following the expiration of a para 27 agreement, as it does in respect of a para 27 agreement.[110] Further, there is no equivalent in para 27 to the provisions at paras 26(7) and (8), which make clear that a right to removal arises once a para 26 agreement is at an end.

16.180 The resulting questions might be: 'why should this be?' and 'how does a landowner achieve the removal of the ECA which remained under the para 27 agreement?'

16.181 The first of these questions might possibly be answered by reference to para 27(1)(c). This provides that a necessary pre-requisite of a para 27 agreement being imposed is that the non-operator party has a right to require the removal of the ECA already. As it is already established that this person has a right to require removal, perhaps the intention is that if and when the temporary para 27 agreement comes to an end without any para 20 agreement being imposed, that right to require removal simply remains. However, if the landowner's original right to require removal arose under para 37(2) (ie, that it has *never* been bound by a Code right), it might seem strange if it could assert that right under a Part 6 removal application even though in the intervening period there was indeed a para 27 agreement conferring Code rights which bound the landowner.

16.182 This might be explained away by interpreting 'code right' at para 37(2) so as not to include the concept of a 'temporary code right', which is referred to at para 27(2). After all, it seems clear from the scheme of the Code that once a temporary agreement has come to an end, there should be no continuing Code rights (see para 30(3)). If there is no agreement any longer, and no continuing Code right (temporary or otherwise), it would be entirely anomalous if the operator enjoyed a permanent ability to resist the removal of its ECA. From the landowner's point of view, it would surely be absurd if it is put in a worse position as a result of the operator being granted a

109 Para 23(7) is applied to a para 27 case by para 27(4)(c).
110 At para 37(3)(a).

temporary para 27 agreement and then failing to achieve a para 20 agreement at trial than it was before the para 27 agreement was imposed.

16.183 A landowner cannot obtain a removal Order whilst a temporary agreement is ongoing, because a para 27 agreement can only be granted where there is a para 20 application on foot, and a removal Order cannot be made until that para 20 application has been determined.[111]

16.184 It seems most unlikely that a para 27 agreement will need to be terminated under the Part 5 procedure, as this type of agreement only continues until a pending para 20 agreement is determined, and it also has no security of tenure. Further, the Part 5 timetable entails an 18-month notice for termination under para 31(3)(a), which is surely longer than para 27 agreements are likely to last. However, by para 27(4)(b) and para 22, such an agreement strictly takes effect as an agreement under Part 2, and hence by para 29(1), Part 5 seems to apply to it.

How can an operator, or the parties together, terminate a Code agreement?

16.185 As explored in Section B of this chapter (from **16.195** onwards) either an operator or a site provider which is a party to a Code agreement can seek to renew or modify such an agreement under Part 5 by serving a para 33 notice. However, the Code does not detail how an operator may bring an *end* to a Code agreement, either by its own act, or by agreement with the other party.

Mutually agreed termination or surrender

16.186 Given that voluntary agreements between parties for the conferral of rights is the 'optimal way for the regime to operate',[112] it would seem consent.

16.187 In *Gencomp,*[113] Nugee LJ commented that:

> 'The Code has to be applied both to contractual arrangements such as licences or wayleaves and to the grants of property rights such as leases. But I do not accept that this means that one jettisons the ordinary law of landlord and tenant, or, as Lewison LJ put it in argument, that the Code exists in a legal vacuum.'

16.188 Although the Upper Tribunal's decision was overturned on appeal in *Gencomp*, the Deputy President had made a similar point at first instance in saying:

> 'Orthodoxy requires that a statute be interpreted with the same awareness of the relevant pre-existing law as Parliament must be presumed to have had.'[114]

111 See para 40(8).
112 Per Lady Rose in *Compton Beauchamp* at [117].
113 [2023] EWCA Civ 825 at [78].
114 [2022] UKUT 223 (LC) at [66], citing *R v G* [2004] 1 AC 1034 at [46] per Lord Steyn, and *Attorney General v Prince Ernest Augustus of Hanover* [1957] AC 436, at [461] per Lord Simmonds.

16.189 One would therefore think that the starting point is that the parties can mutually agree the termination of an agreement, without para 30(2) of the Code continuing the agreement.

16.190 Although the Code does not expressly say that an operator can surrender[115] a lease which is a Code agreement, or mutually agree a termination with a landowner, it makes obvious practical sense for this to be permitted.

16.191 First, it allows parties relatively easily to settle or compromise disputes, including proceedings under the Code. Second, it avoids an absurd situation where the parties have to concoct a contrived solution to terminate the agreement early. For example, the ECA to which the agreement relates could be switched off such that it is no longer being used for the purposes of the operator's network, giving rise to a right on the part of the site provider to require removal under para 37(6). As the Code is habitually interpreted so as to give effect to how it is supposed to function, one would imagine that a court would not find it difficult to recognise the obvious merit in allowing an agreed surrender of a Code agreement.

Termination by an operator

16.192 It is clear that both the 1954 Act and the Code contain their continuation and termination mechanisms for the benefit and protection of the tenant/licensee. There is therefore something of an intentional asymmetry in both regimes. Under the 1954 Act, the possibility of a tenant bringing the tenancy to an end by notice to quit is maintained by section 24(2), without any ground for termination having to be given by the tenant. Absent a power to bring an end to a tenancy, a tenant may find itself stuck in a tenancy forever, which would not only be absurd but would not constitute a protection for the tenant so much as a prison. By contrast, the landlord cannot terminate a 1954 Act tenancy without having grounds to do so. It must give sufficient notice under section 25 and prove its stated termination ground.

16.193 There is also an asymmetry in the wording of the Code, but it is a different asymmetry. Para 31 provides a mechanism by which a site provider party may terminate a Code agreement, but there is no express mechanism by which an operator can do so. The Code agreement is continued either where its fixed term expires, or where a site provider could have brought it to an end, with no mention being made of an operator doing so. Then, by para 30(2), the agreement continues so that 'the operator may continue to exercise that right', and the site provider continues to be bound. Although an agreement may be mutually beneficial, the language very much indicates a protection for an operator and a constraint on a site provider. The fact that an operator 'may' continue to exercise its Code rights may indicate that it goes without saying that an operator does not have to, but may terminate an agreement that is continuing under para 30(2), by notice to quit (or notice to terminate).

16.194 Indeed, tribunals have included operator's break clauses in agreements. Where a landlord exercises a break clause in a Code agreement, that does not prevent it from having to terminate the agreement under para 31 and give the requisite 18-month

---

115 Unlike the 1954 Act, which creates a bespoke procedure for terminating business tenancies, but which preserves the ability to terminate such tenancies by surrender (see s. 24(2) thereof).

notice. However, as there is no procedure in the Code that an operator can follow to terminate the agreement, an operator break notice would either terminate an agreement with no further action necessary, or it is completely ineffective. The tribunal is clearly proceeding on the basis that such break rights are indeed effective. If there is nothing in para 30(2) that renders an operator break notice ineffective, then surely the same could be said of an operator notice to quit (or termination notice) during a para 30(2) continuation following the expiration of a fixed term. It may be that this is not a question that will arise frequently, as a landowner is ordinarily not keen to keep an operator on its land for longer than it wishes to be there.

Section B
Renewals and modifications of agreements

16.195 As mentioned in Chapter 6, the parties to a Code agreement are in principle entitled to amend it consensually, as long as the formalities and content requirements of para 11 are met.[116]

16.196 This section of this chapter considers the availability of a statutory procedure whereby the parties might seek to have an agreement renewed, or seek the modification of its terms, as it approaches the end of its contractual term, or during a period after its contractual end date has passed and it is being continued statutorily.[117]

16.197 The possibility of an operator seeking to modify the terms of an agreement, or to augment its rights under an agreement, *during the term of that agreement* and before any specific statutory 'renewal' rights have arisen, is addressed below.[118]

16.198 Just as a landowner seeking to terminate a Code agreement must consider whether such termination must proceed under the Part 5 Code machinery or the 1954 Act machinery, a party that wishes to renew or modify a Code agreement must consider whether the correct route is Part 5 of the Code or Part 2 of the 1954 Act.

No election as to which statutory regime is followed

16.199 As has been seen above, there is more than one statutory procedure for the termination of an agreement.

16.200 The clear indication given by the various statutes (including the Code, Transitional Provisions and 1954 Act as recently amended) is that the termination and renewal of an agreement may be governed by the Code or the 1954 Act, but not both. This is supported by the Law Commission's discussion[119] of the undesirability of possible 'dual protection', as may have been the case under the Old Code:

116 Para 11(2) requires variations to comply with the para 11(1)(a) and (b) formalities requirements. Para 11(3) requires the agreement as varied to comply with the content requirements at para 11(1)(c) and (d).

117 Either under para 30(2) of the Code, or s 24 of the 1954 Act, depending on which statutory regime applies.

118 Under the heading: 'The modification of an agreement before renewal rights arise'.

119 At paras 6.56 and 6.57 et seq of Law Com No 336.

> '6.56 At present, where Code Rights are conferred by the grant of a lease, that lease will be protected by the 1954 Act unless the parties have contracted out; and the apparatus itself will be protected by paragraph 21 of the 2003 Code.
>
> 6.57 It is not clear that having this dual protection is necessary or helpful to either party. Indeed, it has been argued that the two regimes interact to make it impossible, in theory, for the Site Provider to regain vacant possession. It is argued that a landowner whose tenant is protected by the 1954 Act cannot remove apparatus under paragraph 21 before he has obtained the right to require removal by bringing the tenancy to an end; yet under the 1954 Act the landowner cannot oppose a renewal on the ground that he intends to demolish or reconstruct the premises unless he is entitled to do so – and paragraph 21 prevents him from doing so.'

16.201 The Law Commission therefore stated that it was 'attracted to the idea of adapting, and incorporating within the revised Code, the regime found in the 1954 Act, while eliminating the current dual protection'.[120] The provisions of Part 5, by which Code agreements can be terminated and renewed, are best understood in that context.

16.202 The dichotomy between those cases where an agreement is terminable/renewable under Code machinery and those in respect of which the 1954 Act must be used is also made clear in the case law interpreting the New Code. In *Ashloch,* it was held by the Upper Tribunal, Court of Appeal, and Supreme Court that there was no right of election on the part of an operator to utilise the Part 4 procedure to seek Code rights as a means of renewing a lease to which Part 2 of the 1954 Act applies and whose primary purpose is to grant Code rights.

16.203 In the Supreme Court, Lady Rose noted that the Upper Tribunal had rejected the numerous arguments put forward as to why the operator should be considered to have a choice of procedure, saying:

> 'It pointed out at para 96 that such a choice would go against the Law Commission's recommendation that operators should not obtain the benefits of the new Code retrospectively and that operators with the benefit of the protection of Part 2 of the 1954 Act should be required to use that route even though it had serious disadvantages compared with Part 4 of the new Code.'

16.204 Accordingly, just as there is always a 'correct answer' as to what statute applies (if any) to the termination of an agreement, there is no choice of statutory regime for renewing a Code agreement. If there is a right to seek renewal, that right derives either from the Code or from the 1954 Act, and not both.

Which renewal procedure applies in which cases?

16.205 Where an operator is in situ but with no Code rights, it may in many cases seek to obtain Code rights under Part 4, by serving a para 20 notice and making an application to the tribunal. This may sometimes be seen as a quasi-renewal, as the operator may well have had a previous agreement under the Old Code that expired before the New Code came into force.

120 Law Com No 336 at 6.80.

16.206 However, in a true 'renewal', where an agreement dealing with Code rights already exists and a party seeks to renew that agreement, the only routes that can be pursued are either: (i) Part 5 of the Code, or (ii) the 1954 Act procedure.

16.207 Taking the same three categories of cases set out in Section A above in respect of terminations, the position as to which regime to follow for renewals and modifications of Code agreements is as follows.

(1) Consensual or imposed agreements under the New Code

In Section A of this chapter (from **16.05** onwards) it is discussed which agreements within this category are subject to Part 5 of the Code. If Part 5 applies to an agreement for the purposes of its termination, then Part 5 also applies for the purposes of renewal. Where an agreement is entered into, or imposed, after the coming into force of the Code, and its primary purpose is to grant Code rights, then Part 5 applies to it. The Part 5 renewal procedure is discussed below.

(2) Subsisting Agreements

In Section A of this chapter (from **16.05** onwards) 'subsisting agreements' are defined, and it is explained which are subject to the 1954 Act renewal termination and renewal procedure, and which are subject to Part 5 of the Code. The modifications made to Part 5 in respect of certain such agreements by the Transitional Provisions are also set out. That part of this chapter is of equal application for renewal as it is for termination.

(3) Agreements which expired before the New Code came into force

Where a written agreement came to an end before the coming into force of the Code, was not continued statutorily, and no further agreement has arisen by implication, the operator will have no Code rights. We know from *Compton Beauchamp* that it is entitled to use Part 4 of the Code to seek new Code rights.

16.208 Also in Section A of this chapter, the possibility of a new agreement having arisen by implication, due to the conduct of the parties, is considered (from **16.09** onwards). This part of the chapter proceeds on the basis that such an implied agreement is not capable of being a subsisting agreement as it is not in writing.[121] If it cannot be a subsisting agreement, then it will not be treated as though it were an agreement under Part 2 of the Code. No Part 5 renewal is therefore possible.

16.209 The question whether an operator can seek new Code rights, and how, will depend on what sort of implied agreement has arisen. Different possibilities are considered below.

Implied periodic tenancy

16.210 Where an implied periodic tenancy is held to have arisen, it is likely that the tenant will be in occupation for the purposes of its business, and therefore that Part 2 of the 1954 Act will in principle apply to that tenancy. Further, a periodic tenancy

121 As held by Judge Cooke in *Arqiva*, and as discussed in Section A of this chapter, from **16.112** onwards.

cannot be the subject of a section 38A agreement 'contracting out' of the security of tenure provisions of Part 2 of the 1954 Act.

16.211 In the *Patricroft*[122] case, the FTT held that an operator that continues to occupy under an implied periodic tenancy that is protected by the 1954 Act cannot seek new Code rights under Part 4. This is so even though the operator does not currently have Code rights because the periodic tenancy is not in writing. *Ashloch* was considered to be the starting point, and the reasoning in that case and others[123] emphasises that an operator occupying under a 1954 Act tenancy should receive no retrospective benefit from the Code, and that dual regimes should not co-exist.

16.212 Neither can the tenant operator force its way into a 1954 Act lease renewal process. A landlord may serve notice under section 25 of the 1954 Act and thereby seek to terminate the periodic tenancy. In those circumstances, the tenant operator can apply to court for a new tenancy by virtue of section 24(1)(a) of the 1954 Act. However, if the landlord chooses not to serve a section 25 notice, the tenant operator cannot itself obtain access to the 1954 Act renewal process by serving a request under section 26 of the 1954 Act, because such a request can only be served where the existing tenancy has a fixed term exceeding one year, or was granted for a fixed term and 'thereafter from year to year'.[124] A periodic tenancy does not fall into either of those categories.

16.213 Whether it is open to a tenant operator wishing to force the amendment of the current terms of its implied periodic tenancy by terminating that tenancy with a notice to quit and *then* seeking new rights under para 20 is perhaps not entirely clear.[125]

Implied licence or tenancy at will

16.214 It has been held at FTT level in the *Patricroft*[126] case that an operator under an implied periodic[127] licence *can* serve a para 20 notice and seek new Code rights without first terminating its licence. There is no policy imperative preventing such a course, in contrast to the policy that operators who had the protection of the 1954 Act should not receive the retrospective protection of a different statute.

16.215 The logic in *Patricroft* is that the imposition of a new agreement by the tribunal will operate as a surrender and re-grant of the previous licence. The landowner has no

122 *On Tower UK Limited v AP Wireless II (UK) Limited* LC-2023-000852 (re *Patricroft* and five other properties), decision dated 2 September 2024.

123 Including the then recent UT appeal decision in *Gravesham BC v On Tower* [2024] UKUT 151 (LC).

124 Section 26(1) of the 1954 Act.

125 One might say that the availability of this option is the implication in *Patricroft* at [31] from the conclusion that Part 4 is not available without first having terminated the tenancy. However, that is not the clear conclusion given the context of the rest of the judgment. In any event, the point was acknowledged as obiter. One could envisage a landowner in future arguing that an operator intentionally terminating a 1954 Act protected tenancy in order to use Part 4 would either: (i) have the same effect as the final determination of the 1954 Act proceedings in *Gravesham*, or (ii) constitute a freestanding abuse of process. Such arguments would not have been relevant in the circumstances of the preliminary issues in *Patricroft*.

126 *On Tower UK Limited v AP Wireless II (UK) Limited* LC-2023-000852 (re *Patricroft* and five other properties), decision dated 2 September 2024.

127 Presumably this refers to a licence which has been inferred from payments made from time to time which are referable to periods of occupation.

option but to comply with the Order and hence cannot act inconsistently with having accepted the surrender.[128] One would think that a tenancy at will would be subject to the same logic, as Part 2 of the 1954 Act does not apply to tenancies at will.

Renewal or modification under Part 5 of the Code

16.216 The Code does not talk of renewals. Instead, Part 5 is headed 'Termination and modification of agreements'. Para 28, which tells us the scope of Part 5, uses the expression 'changing an agreement relating to code rights'. Para 33, which allows a notice to be served that kicks off the 'renewal' procedure, is headed 'How may a party to a code agreement require a change to the terms of an agreement which has expired?'

16.217 However, as long as one realises that there are numerous options open to the tribunal as to the Order it makes within the 'renewal' procedure, the word 'renewal' is a convenient and readily understood shorthand, and it is used in very many of the cases.

16.218 A 'renewal' under Part 5 can be reached by two different routes:

(1) as a result of an attempt by a site provider to terminate a Code agreement which is resisted by an operator; and

(2) as a result of one or other party actively seeking to bring about such a 'renewal'.

16.219 Section A of this chapter (from **16.05** onwards) sets out how the parties arrive at the tribunal under the first of those routes. This part of the chapter will detail the procedure for the second of those routes, and will then consider the options open to the tribunal under para 34 regardless of which route led to consideration of the "renewal".

Seeking a renewal or modification: the para 33 notice

16.220 Under para 33(1), an operator or a site provider who is a party to a Code agreement[129] may require the other party to the Code agreement to agree certain modifications to the Code agreement, or that it be replaced by a new agreement, by serving a notice on that other party. The requirements as to the form and contents of a para 33(1) notice are also discussed in Chapter 20.

Server/recipient

16.221 It is worth noting that a para 33(1) notice can only be served by a party to a Code agreement on 'the other party' thereto. A person is a party to an agreement if it was an original contracting party, or if it is to be treated as a party by virtue of para 10(3) or 10(6), or the Court of Appeal decision in *Gencomp*.[130]

---

128 *Patricroft* at [32]–[35].

129 Being a Code agreement by which a Code right is conferred by or otherwise binds the site provider.

130 That case is discussed within Chapter 15. In short it is necessary to understand that para 10(3) was held not to be exhaustive in describing who is to be treated as a party.

16.222 As multi-party agreements are possible, it is considered prudent to serve a para 33(1) notice on all persons who are parties (or who are to be treated as parties). Who is to be treated as a party to a Code agreement is considered in more detail in Chapter 15

The options for changing the agreement

16.223 The options as to what a person may require the other party to agree in its para 33(1) notice are set out at para 33(1)(a) to (d). A summary of those options is as follows:

(a) *Modification of agreement*: that the Code agreement should have effect with modified terms.

(b) *Code right deletion*: that one of the (plural) Code rights dealt with in the current agreement should no longer be conferred or bind the site provider.

(c) *Code right addition*: that an additional Code right should be conferred or bind the site provider, in the agreement.

(d) *New agreement*: that the agreement should be terminated and a new agreement should have effect (which confers a Code right, or provides for a Code right to bind the site provider).

16.224 The details required to be specified

16.225 Paragraph 33(2)(c) requires 'the details' to be specified, of (in short):

(i) the proposed modified terms;

(ii) the Code right proposed for deletion;

(iii) the Code right proposed for addition; 'or'

(iv) the proposed terms of the new agreement.

16.226 These are required to be specified 'as the case may be', and it is apparent which required details relate to which para 33(1) option.

The period of notice

16.227 Paragraph 33(2)(b) requires the giver of the notice to specify the day from which the change proposed in the notice should take effect (ie, either the modification, the deletion, the addition, or the termination and re-grant, depending on which sub-paragraph of para 33(1) is proposed).

16.228 Paragraph 33(3) sets out when that date 'must fall', namely:

'(a) after the end of the period of 6 months beginning with the day on which the notice is given, and

(b) after the time at which, apart from paragraph 30, the code right to which the existing code agreement relates would have ceased to be exercisable or to bind the site provider or at a time when, apart from that paragraph, the code agreement could have been brought to an end by the site provider.'

16.229 Paragraph 33(3)(a) guarantees a minimum six-month notice period.

16.230 Paragraph 33(3)(b) creates an additional requirement as to the period of notice, and it is in the same terms as para 31(3)(b), creating the same requirement for a site provider's para 31 termination notice (considered above in Section A). The basic point of para 33(3)(b) is to stop a party from abandoning its bargain and renewing an agreement during its term. The para 33 notice must include a proposed date, that is either after the contractual end date of the existing agreement, or after a date when a site provider could have brought the agreement to an end (most obviously by a break clause).

16.231 In the case of para 31, it is obvious why this last alternative is included. If a site provider has the benefit of a break clause, the site provider should not be prevented from taking advantage of the break clause by the Code, albeit that para 31 ordinarily requires a long notice period of 18 months. Where a site provider wishes to take advantage of a break right in order to terminate with a para 31 notice, it does not actually have to serve a contractual break notice.[131]

16.232 In the case of para 33, similarly, if a site provider can bring an end to an agreement contractually, the Code allows it to use that right to trigger a right to seek 'renewal'. Again, for the same reasons as in the case of para 31, it seems that the site provider does not need to serve a contractual break notice. However, where an operator wishes to renew by serving a para 33(1) notice (and it is usually an operator who serves such a notice), is it able to take advantage of a site provider-only break clause, in order to satisfy para 33(3)(b) and renew sooner than the contractual end of the term? That is not something that has yet been explored by the tribunals. On the literal wording of para 33, it could be argued that there is nothing stopping an operator from doing so. However, on a purposive reading, one can readily see the argument that it would be surprising if a break right given only to a site provider should give rise to a right to renew on the part of an operator.

The application to the tribunal

16.233 In *Stephenson*, Fancourt J (sitting as the Chamber President) described the purpose of the para 33(1) notice as follows:

> 'The purpose of the notice is so that the parties can spend up to 6 months trying to reach agreement on what has been proposed.'[132]

16.234 Of course it is possible that a notice gives more than six months for this purpose, but the point remains that the notice allows time for negotiation before any application is made to the tribunal for the renewal that is sought.

16.235 If the notice served is valid and the proposed change is not agreed, the giver of the notice has the right to apply[133] to the tribunal for an Order under para 34,

131 See the *BT (Kenton Road)* case, as discussed at **16.47** above.

132 *EE Ltd and Hutchison 3G UK Ltd v Stephenson and AP Wireless II (UK) Ltd* [2021] UKUT 167 (LC) at [63].

133 The right to apply arises from para 33(4) and (5).

after the end of the period of six months[134] from when the notice was served. An application in reliance on the para 33(1) notice is an application under para 33(5).

16.236 The tribunal 'must then decide which order to make, if any, and specify the terms of any new code rights or new agreement to the extent that the parties have not agreed them'.[135] The Orders open to a tribunal are set out at para 34, and these are considered below.

16.237 The relationship between a party's para 33 notice and its case is considered in the Chapter on Notices in Chapter 20.

Para 33(5) applications: obligations in respect of ADR

16.238 Before either party makes an application under para 33(5), that party must, if it is reasonably practicable to do so, 'consider the use of one or more alternative dispute resolution procedures to reach agreement with the other party' (para 33(6)[136]). By para 33(7), either party may at any time give the other a notice in writing stating that it wishes to engage in alternative dispute resolution in relation to the para 33(1) notice.

16.239 There are potential cost consequences if a party unreasonably refuses to engage in alternative dispute resolution (under para 96(2)(b), discussed in Chapter 23).

The Order for renewal or modification: para 34

16.240 Paragraph 34 makes provision for the different Orders that may be made in 'renewal' cases. As previously indicated, the tribunal proceeds under para 34 in each of two scenarios,[137] namely where:

- (i) an operator has applied under para 32(1)(b), the tribunal has concluded that the site provider has not established any of the termination grounds set out in its para 31 notice, and is therefore mandated by para 32(5) to make an Order under para 32(4); or
- (ii) either party has applied under para 33(5) for an Order under para 34.

16.241 In either of those scenarios, the tribunal has the following options:

- Para 34(2): it may order the existing agreement to continue for a specified period.

134 NB, the right to apply arises after a fixed period of six months has elapsed from when the para 33(1) notice was given. It is not the arrival of the date specified under para 33(2)(b) which gives rise to the right to apply to the Tribunal, and nor does the applicant have to apply to the Tribunal *before* the para 33(2)(b) date.

135 *Stephenson* at [62].

136 This provision, together with para 33(7), was inserted on 7 November 2023 by s 69(4)(b) of the Product Security and Telecommunications Infrastructure 2022. Accordingly, the para 33(6) obligation to consider ADR did not apply to applications made before 7 November 2023.

137 See para 34(1).

- Para 34(3): it may order 'the modification of the terms' of the agreement. This power is not limited to the precisely worded modifications sought (see para 34(11), para 23(2) to (8), and see below).
- Para 34(4): it may modify the agreement by deleting a Code right (providing that it is no longer conferred or no longer binds the site provider).
- Para 34(5): it may modify the agreement by adding a Code right (providing that it is additionally to be conferred or bind the site provider).
- Para 34(6): it may order the termination of the Code agreement and order the parties to enter into a new agreement which confers a Code right or renders the site provider bound by a Code right.

The tribunal's two decisions

16.242 When contemplating an Order under para 34, the tribunal has to decide two matters:

(i) what order to make, from the menu of possible Orders at para 34(2) to (6); and

(ii) if applicable, what terms to order.[138]

What Order to make?

16.243 Paragraph 34(13) requires the tribunal, in determining what kind of Order to make (out of the menu of options at para 34(2) to (6), to have regard to all the circumstances of the case, and 'in particular' to:

(a) the operator's business and technical needs;

(b) the use that the site provider is making of the land to which the existing Code agreement relates;

(c) any duties imposed on the site provider by an enactment; and

(d) the amount of consideration payable by the operator to the site provider under the existing Code agreement.[139]

16.244 A preliminary issue arose in *Stephenson*[140] as to whether an operator was entitled to ask the tribunal for a different form of Order than that specified in its notice. Fancourt J[141] held that it was not.

16.245 The purpose of the notice is for the parties to spend up to six months trying to reach agreement on what has been proposed, and this purpose would be undermined, causing unfairness to the respondent if the applicant could apply for an

138 Per Fancourt J in *EE v Stephenson* [2021] UKUT 167 (LC) at [50].

139 This last point is not a consideration in the case of the renewal of a subsisting agreement (see the Transitional Provisions (Sch 2 to the Digital Economy Act 2017) at para 7(4)).

140 *EE Ltd and Hutchison 3G UK Ltd v Stephenson and AP Wireless II (UK) Ltd* [2021] UKUT 167 (LC) at [60]–[66].

141 Sitting as the President of the Upper Tribunal.

order that had not been previously identified. However, it is open to a respondent to waive any such non-compliance if it is content to meet the application as made. He concluded:

> 'In my judgment, it is not permissible for an applicant to plead an alternative case for a different change to the existing agreement unless it has served a notice that identifies the relief sought. That is so whether the alternative relief sought is specific or 'such other relief as the Tribunal thinks fit to grant'. The issue of whether a different order is more appropriate will be determined if raised by the respondent to the application, in which case an applicant is entitled to respond to the case that it faces, both in principle and as to the terms of the order proposed. But an applicant may not in the guise of reply to the respondent's case seek another different type of order.'[142]

16.246 However, it was held that the tribunal nonetheless has *jurisdiction* to make 'any of the orders on the menu, whether the applicant has applied for them or not'. The respondent is entitled to plead that a different order is more appropriate, and the applicant will engage with that argument in its points of reply. Finally, it was confirmed that each of the five types of Order identified in para 34(2) to (6) is available in the case of an application under para 33(5), regardless of whether the application is made by an operator or by a site provider.[143]

What terms to order?

16.247 If the court decides to make an Order conferring additional Code rights (para 34(5)) or terminating the existing agreement and requiring a new agreement (para 34(6)), the terms are such as are agreed between the parties.[144]

16.248 If the parties are unable to agree the terms, the tribunal must on an application by either party make an Order under specifying the terms (by para 34(10)).

16.249 Paragraph 34(11) applies a number of provisions from elsewhere in the Code, such that:

(i) As regards deciding terms:

- para 23(2) to (8) apply to an Order under para 34(3), (4), or (5), insofar as it modifies or specifies the terms of the agreement.
- para 23(2) to (8) also apply to an Order under para 34(10). In addition, in such a case, the Tribunal "must" also have regard to the terms of the existing Code agreement. As to the latter obligation, see the discussion in Chapter 11.

(The provisions of para 23 are discussed in Chapter 11.)

(ii) As regards consideration, para 24 applies to an Order under para 34(3), (4), (5) or (10);

(The provisions of para 24 are discussed in Chapter 13.)

142 At [66].
143 *Stephenson* at [60].
144 Para 34(9).

(iii) As regards compensation, paras 25 and 84 apply to an Order under para 34(3), (4), (5) or (10);

(The provisions of paras 25 and 84 are discussed in Chapter 14.)

16.250 Three observations arising from the above are as follows:

(a) As paras 25 and 84 apply to an Order under para 34(3), (4), (5) or (10), one would imagine that this means that a site provider can thenceforth make an application for compensation under para 25(1) where an agreement has been amended under these paragraphs, even though it could not have done so under the pre-existing agreement.

(b) Paragraphs 25 and 84 are not said to apply to an Order under para 34(6) that does not entail para 34(10) (ie, where the agreement is terminated and a new one ordered, and the parties themselves agree terms). Thus, if the parties agree terms, it may be that the site provider cannot in the future make an application for compensation under para 25. Para 34(8) provides that the new agreement is treated as an agreement under Part 2, but that alone is not sufficient to allow the site provider to make an application under para 25. This slightly odd wrinkle could be said to mirror the fact that a party to a consensual agreement following a para 20 notice has no ability to make a compensation application unless the parties agree express terms to that effect (see the discussions of this point in Chapters 6 and 14).

(c) It makes sense that para 34(11) does not render an Order under para 34(2) subject to additional provisions of the Code as to how terms are to be determined because the pre-existing agreement is only *extended* by a para 34(2) Order, and none of its other terms changes. Again, paras 25 and 84 are not applied to an Order under para 34(2), such that, presumably, a site provider who has had an agreement extended has no access to the statutory right to apply for compensation under para 25(2)(b). This might be justified by the fact that it is likely still to be receiving a higher Old Code rent.

16.251 Chapter 11 refers to a number of renewal decisions in which disputed terms were determined by the tribunal.

Additional consideration for para 30(2) continuation period

16.252 Where a para 34 Order is made, the tribunal 'may' also order the operator to pay to the site provider a particular additional sum by way of consideration in respect of the 'relevant period',[145] as follows:

- The additional sum is: the amount (if any, and there may very well be none) by which A exceeds B, where A is the consideration that would have been payable for the relevant period if that amount had been assessed on the same basis as the consideration payable as the result of the Order, and B is the consideration payable for the relevant period.
- The 'relevant period' is essentially the period for which para 30(2) has continued the agreement, until the date of the Order.

145 By paras 34(14) and (15).

Para 35: interim modification of terms

16.253 Where an application has been made under para 33(5) (just as under para 32(1)(b)), para 35(2A) makes provision for either party to apply for an Order in respect of interim consideration to be payable until the application is finally determined, or for an Order otherwise modifying the terms of the agreement until that time. The typical practice of the tribunals has been to quantify such consideration at the final hearing.

16.254 More detail is given within Chapter 11 relating to the terms of agreements.

Status of amended or new agreement

16.255 The existing agreement is, by definition, one to which Part 5 applies. It retains this status following any Order made by the Tribunal amending it under paras 34(2) to (5). Thus, assuming it is not a para 26 or 27 agreement, it will be subject to the statutory continuation under para 30(2). Similarly, if it was a 'subsisting agreement', one would think that it would remain a subsisting agreement once amended or extended.

16.256 In the case of an Order under para 34(6), the existing agreement continues until the new agreement has effect,[146] and the new agreement takes effect as if it were a Part 2 agreement.[147] The new agreement will not be a 'subsisting agreement', even if it replaces a subsisting agreement, as it will not have been in force when the Code came into force.[148]

The modification of an agreement before renewal rights arise

16.257 There is no statutory procedure under the 1954 Act that allows a tenant to apply to court to modify the terms of a telecoms lease (for example, to add a Code rights or to reduce the rent), before the right arises under Part 2 of the 1954 Act to seek a renewal of its tenancy. The parties are in effect "stuck with their bargain" until renewal rights arise, or unless one can persuade the other to modify the terms of the bargain consensually through negotiation.

16.258 However, under the Code, the position is not quite that straightforward. Following the *Compton Beauchamp* decision in the Supreme Court, an operator that is in occupation of land by the siting of ECA under an agreement conferring Code rights can in certain circumstances seek additional Code rights.

16.259 In the Court of Appeal, it had been held that an operator that is already in occupation of a site could never apply to the tribunal for Code rights under Part 4 of the Code in respect of that site. This conclusion relied on the proposition in para 9 of the Code that Code rights could only be conferred by an agreement between an operator and an occupier. If an operator was itself the occupier, nobody could confer Code rights on it.

---

146 Para 34(7).

147 Para 34(8).

148 See the Transitional Provisions (Sch 2 to the Digital Economy Act 2017) at para 1(4).

16.260 The Supreme Court overturned this decision by reference to the inferred intention as to how the Code as a whole was supposed to work, rather than by seeking to ascertain the meaning of the particular word 'occupier'. It held that it was necessary in certain circumstances to disregard the occupation of the operator in order to ensure that the Code operated as intended. Where an operator was in situ under an agreement that gave it the benefit of Code rights, it was entitled to seek additional Code rights from which it did not yet benefit. However, it was not able to seek to modify the Code rights already granted. In respect of those Code rights, it was stuck with the bargain that had already been struck until Part 5 renewal rights arose, at which point the Part 5 process would determine the extent to which there should be modifications to existing terms.

16.261 Lady Rose said as follows at [130]–[131]:

> '130. I would hold therefore that para 20 can only be used to impose additional code rights and not to impose a modification of the rights already conferred in an existing Part 2 agreement or in a code agreement to which Part 5 applies. The parties should generally be kept to their bargains and just because, for example, an operator has second thoughts about the consideration it has agreed to pay for the grant of code rights, that does not entitle it to ask the tribunal to vary the agreement before the Part 5 rights become available (of course, it always has the option of negotiating a consensual variation under para 11).
>
> 131. But if the operator needs additional code rights in respect of the land on which its ECA is already installed during the term of an existing agreement in order, for example, to facilitate the roll out of a new network, it can seek an order imposing a new agreement for the grant of such rights if the landowner is not willing to confer them.'

16.262 In the majority of cases, this determination solves the difficulty of the operator in situ that is stuck with no Code rights at all. Further, it avoids, or at least drastically reduces the frequency of, the need for an operator to make an application for Code rights in respect of land "slightly to one side" of the land in respect of which it currently has Code rights, solely in order to avoid the previously understood prohibition on seeking Code rights whilst in occupation of land.

16.263 However, it does give rise to more than one question as to how the resulting system should work where an operator in situ under a Code agreement seeks *additional* rights a 'new agreement' (to use the Supreme Court's words). First, how would such a new agreement sit alongside the existing agreement? Care should be taken to ensure that the two agreements dove-tailed successfully, without any contradiction or excessive room for dispute as to the interaction between the two agreements. But as the operator's application would be a standalone application in reliance on a standalone para 20 notice, the tribunal would at least have jurisdiction to impose wholly different terms, and even a longer term. Although this might be thought to be unlikely, it perhaps remains unclear as to how the terms of an existing agreement will influence those of the additional agreement.

16.264 Second, how and where might the tribunals draw the dividing line between a *permissible* application for 'additional' Code rights, and an *impermissible* application for 'modification of the rights already conferred'?

16.265 This difficulty was considered in *Compton Beauchamp*. The Court of Appeal referred to examples given in the Explanatory Notes.[149] At note 499 of those Notes it had been asserted that where an operator had an existing right to site access upon 72 hours' notice, and wished to be able to enter upon 48 hours' notice, the latter would constitute a 'new right, more onerous for the landowner', for which the operator could apply to the tribunal in default of agreement, and the para 21 test would be applied. At note 497, however, it was stated that 'Agreements for code rights are final so that once agreed (see Part 2), it is not possible for either party to re-open the agreement.' The example was then given of the permissibility of a party applying to the court 'to get a better price or improve the accompanying terms that relate to the code right that has been agreed'. The Court of Appeal considered that it was 'very difficult (if not impossible) to reconcile' notes 499 and 497.

16.266 However, in the Supreme Court Lady Rose felt that these notes were:

> '...attempting to capture the distinction I have drawn above between requiring the existing agreement to run on undisturbed until Part 5 becomes available whilst giving the operator the flexibility to add further code rights if the need for them arises during the course of the initial contractual term.'

16.267 Her Ladyship did recognise that there might be difficulty in some cases in ascertaining where this distinction falls, but did not feel that it would be an insurmountable problem for the tribunals. Referring to the 48-hour notice example from the Explanatory Notes, she said:

> '134. ... I recognise that the appellants' interpretation of the new Code which I prefer may create the need in some cases for nice distinctions to be made. It may well be open to argument, for example, whether the scenario described in the Explanatory Notes of a change from a 72 to a 48 hour notice period really would constitute a new code right rather than a variation of the existing code right. But the parties to the existing agreement should be able to agree that variation if they so wish. If the landowner is faced with an unwelcome application under para 20 by an operator who is party to an existing agreement under Part 2 in respect of the same land, he may submit to the tribunal that the operator is illegitimately dressing up a modification of the existing agreement as a request for new rights. That would be an illegitimate attempt to bypass the fact that the existing agreement has not yet reached the end of its contractual term and Part 5 is not available.
>
> 135. In most circumstances the tribunal will be able without much difficulty to determine whether the application is really for new code rights or whether it is a disguised attempt to improve on the bargain struck as to the price or duration of the existing rights.'

16.268 There surely remains uncertainty following the Supreme Court's decision in respect of how the 48-hour notice example from the Explanatory Notes would be determined. Operators would doubtless rely on the conclusion in the Explanatory Notes themselves, in submitting that what is being sought is a different right of access

149 Ie, the Explanatory Notes to the Digital Economy Act 2017, whose Sch 1 inserted the Code into the Communications Act 2003 as Sch 3A thereto. The Explanatory Notes to the Digital Economy Act 2017 can be found within the legislation.gov.uk website, and are currently at the following URL: https://www.legislation.gov.uk/ukpga/2017/30/notes

which is thus a wholly new Code right (under para 3(f)), and hence it is permissible to apply for it before a Part 5 renewal right arises.

16.269 Landowners, for their part, could well argue that:

(i) there is an established distinction between a 'code right' and 'the other terms of the agreement', as is made clear within para 20(2)(a);

(ii) the operator already has a Code right of access under para 3(f) on the facts of the case;

(iii) that Code right would have had to be specified using the words of para 3(f) in any prescribed form para 20 notice that was served before the original agreement was entered into;

(iv) the 'other terms of the agreement that the operator seeks' would also have had to be specified in the para 20 notice, and those terms would have included a provision as to a notice period. In this case, they required 72 hours' notice;

(v) an attempt to apply for a Code right of access is an attempt to apply for the same Code right which already exists, but subject to a different term as to notice;

(vi) that constitutes an impermissible attempt to modify the existing bargain.

16.270 Whichever way that particular question would be resolved, it is clear that the Supreme Court has established only that there is a dividing line between a permissible mid-term Part 4 application and an impermissible one. It has not established what falls on either side of that line, with the exception of making clear that the duration of an agreement and the consideration payable thereunder are not to be disturbed under the Part 4 process. This should certainly not be read as establishing that those are the only two terms of an agreement that are 'off limits' when an operator makes a mid-term Part 4 application. After all, the Supreme Court was careful to recognise that the 48-hour notice example was subject to argument, and that it was only in 'most' and not all circumstances that the tribunal would be able to determine the legitimacy of a Part 4 application without much difficulty.

16.271 Given that it was established in *Keast* that as a matter of jurisdiction the tribunal is unencumbered as to what terms are capable of being imposed, there is at least a theoretical possibility of substantial changes being sought to bargains through Part 4.

Termination and renewal under the 1954 Act

16.272 The only statutory route for the termination or renewal of some agreements is under the 1954 Act. 1954 Act lease renewal proceedings will be well-known to those whose practice includes the law of landlord and tenant, and a detailed treatment of the law in this area is beyond the scope of this book.

16.273 Following the New Code coming into force, a new tenancy that results from 1954 Act lease renewal proceedings, whose primary purpose is to grant Code rights, will be a Code agreement and will be renewable and terminable under Part 5 of the Code. So too will a consensual renewal lease or agreement that is entered into in the context of potential 1954 Act lease renewal proceedings. Accordingly, as more and more subsisting agreements which were granted as leases and not contracted out of the security of tenure provisions of the 1954 Act come up for renewal, fewer and fewer agreements conferring Code rights will be within the 1954 Act regime.

16.274 For those who require a very basic overview of the 1954 Act process:

(i) Where a tenant occupies premises for the purposes of its business, Part 2 of the 1954 Act is capable of applying to its tenancy.

(ii) Part 2 of the 1954 Act confers security of tenure on the tenant in those circumstances, although the parties can 'contract out' of that protection under section 38A. It is not possible to 'contract out' in this way when the tenancy is periodic.

(iii) The security of tenure provisions ensure that the tenancy continues unless terminated in accordance with Part 2 of the 1954 Act (section 24(1)), although the Act preserves certain modes of termination outside of the 1954 Act notice procedure (surrender, forfeiture, and certain tenants' notices to quit) (section 24(2)).

(iv) A landlord can seek to terminate a tenancy to which Part 2 of the 1954 Act applies by serving a section 25 notice.

(v) The section 25 notice must be given not more than 12 months and not less than six months before the date specified in the notice at which the tenancy is to end.[150]

(vi) A section 25 notice which seeks to terminate the tenancy must state a ground on which the landlord would oppose the grant of a new tenancy. The relevant potential grounds are those at section 30(1).

(vii) Those grounds include ground (f), which is the most likely to be pertinent to a tenancy granting Code rights. That ground is sometimes referred to as the 'redevelopment' ground. It is considered by contrast with the Code redevelopment grounds in Chapter 17.

(viii) Similarly, a tenant may seek to terminate a current tenancy by serving a section 26 request for a new tenancy (but only if its tenancy is for a term of years certain exceeding one year, or for a term of years certain and thereafter from year to year).

(ix) A section 26 request must specify the proposed date for the start of the new tenancy (not more than 12 nor less than 6 months after the making of the request), and the tenant's proposals for the property to be comprised in the new tenancy, the rent, and the other terms.

(x) If a landlord wishes to oppose any application for the grant of a new tenancy, it gives a counter-notice under section 26(6) within two months of the tenant's request. The counter-notice must state the section 30 ground(s) on which the landlord will oppose the new tenancy.

(xi) If either a section 25 notice or section 26 request has been served, either party may apply to court for an Order for the grant of a new tenancy (section 24(1)).

150 There are further rules to be observed as to the period of notice that must be given – see s 25.

(xii) If a landlord opposes a tenant's section 24(1) application for a new tenancy on a section 30 ground, the court shall not make an Order for the grant of a new tenancy (section 31(1)). In this event, the pre-existing tenancy shall end in accordance with section 64.

(xiii) If either the landlord has served a section 25 notice or it has served a counter-notice under section 26(6) in response to a tenant's section 26 request, the landlord may apply to court under section 29(2) for an Order terminating the tenancy.

(xiv) On a landlord's section 29(2) application, if the landlord establishes a ground of opposition, the court must order the termination of the tenancy, and it shall end in accordance with section 64. If the landlord fails to establish a ground, the court must make an Order for a new tenancy.

(xv) Where a new tenancy is granted:

- (a) the property to be comprised in the tenancy, and the duration of the tenancy, are determined in accordance with sections 32 and 33 respectively;
- (b) the rent under the tenancy is determined in accordance with section 34;
- (c) the other terms of the tenancy are determined in accordance with section 35.

17

Redevelopment

17.01 Under the 1954 Act, a landlord may oppose the grant of a new tenancy on the grounds that it intends to carry out works that may be conveniently referred to as 'redevelopment'. Drawing inspiration from that statutory ground, the architects of the Code have allowed an intention to carry out redevelopment to constitute:

- a ground for termination of a Code agreement (under para 31(4)(c)); and
- a defence (under para 21(5)) to the imposition of a Code agreement under para 20.

17.02 As is discussed further below, the Law Commission's proposal for the para 21(5) redevelopment defence was modelled on 'ground (f)' (ie, section 30(1)(f)) of the 1954 Act). The para 31(4)(c) termination ground is in very similar terms to the para 21(5) defence.

17.03 However, the wording of ground (f) is materially different, and accordingly one must acknowledge the possibility that a landowner intending a particular scheme of development may satisfy ground (f) and not the Code redevelopment test, or vice versa.

The wording of Ground (f) under the 1954 Act

17.04 Because ground (f) was the inspiration for the Code redevelopment test, and also because some tenancies[1] granting Code rights must still be terminated under the 1954 Act, it is worth considering ground (f) at least in brief.

17.05 Section 30(1) of the 1954 Act sets out the grounds on which a landlord may rely in seeking to oppose the grant of a new business tenancy. If it succeeds in establishing a ground for opposition, there will be no new tenancy and the current tenancy will come to an end in accordance with section 64 of the 1954 Act.[2]

17.06 Ground (f) of section 30(1) is worded as follows:

> '(f) that on the termination of the current tenancy the landlord intends to demolish or reconstruct the premises comprised in the holding or a substantial part of those premises or to carry out substantial work of construction on the holding or part thereof and that he could not reasonably do so without obtaining possession of the holding;'.

1 Ie, those to which the 1954 Act applied (and in respect of which there is no 'contracting out' s 38A agreement), which were granted before the coming into force of the Code, and which remained in force at the date of the Code coming into force.

2 Section 29(4)(a) and s 31(1) of the 1954 Act.

The wording of the para 31(4)(c) redevelopment ground

17.07 When serving a para 31 notice to seek the termination of an agreement, a site provider who is a party to that agreement must state at least one ground for termination that falls within para 31(4). The third of those grounds, the para 31(4)(c) redevelopment ground, is surely the most commonly used of these grounds. It states:

> '(c) that the site provider intends to redevelop all or part of the land to which the code agreement relates, or any neighbouring land, and could not reasonably do so unless the code agreement comes to an end'.

The wording of the para 21(5) redevelopment defence

17.08 When faced with a para 20 application, the respondent to such an application (the 'relevant person') has a complete defence in the event that it can satisfy para 21(5), which is in the following terms:

> '(5) The court may not make an order under paragraph 20 if it thinks that the relevant person intends to redevelop all or part of the land to which the code right would relate, or any neighbouring land, and could not reasonably do so if the order were made.'

Ground (f) vs the Code tests

17.09 As is apparent, the two Code redevelopment tests are in similar terms. There are some minor differences between these, mainly arising from their different factual contexts (these are discussed further below). However, the contrasts between ground (f) and the Code tests are of more substance.

Similarities between the 1954 Act and the Code

17.10 There are some obvious similarities between the component parts of the ground (f) rubric and the Code tests:

- both require the person relying on the ground to show an intention;
- it is the person relying on the ground who must have that intention;
- that intention must be to carry out some act which might loosely be thought of as 'redevelopment' (the difference in wording is considered below);
- the 'redevelopment' must be of such a character that it could not reasonably be carried out if the operator 'got its way' (either by keeping landlord out of possession, by preventing the Code agreement from coming to an end, or by obtaining an Order for a Code agreement).

17.11 To date, the *Meyrick*[3] case has been the only fully contested 'redevelopment' case heard by the Upper Tribunal. In that case, the tribunal gave useful guidance on the extent of the similarities between ground (f) and the Code redevelopment tests.

---

3 *EE Limited and Hutchison 3G UK v Meyrick 1968 Combined Trust of Meyrick Estate Management* [2019] UKUT 164 (LC).

17.12 The tribunal noted that para 21(5) was 'explicitly modelled, by the Law Commission' on ground (f), stating that the 'core idea is the same'. It described the difference in wording as 'trivial' and 'dictated by its context'. This difference was to allow for the fact that Code rights need not necessarily be conferred in a lease and may relate to a temporary matter such as lopping trees. It was for this reason that 'wider language is used' in para 21(5). The tribunal also noted that the connection with ground (f) was 'apparent from the terms of the Law Commission's recommendation' of a redevelopment ground.

17.13 As discussed in Chapter 7, the Law Commission report[4] is a potential 'legitimate external aid' and 'useful tool' in interpreting the Code, especially when considering discrete matters on which the report's recommendations were accepted, such as the 'redevelopment' ground.

17.14 The report said as follows at 6.109:

> 'Crucial to the regime is the list of grounds on which Code Rights, or the lease that confers them, can be brought to an end. *The grounds we have recommended will be readily recognised from section 30(1) of the 1954 Act*, with the omission of three provisions that are not suitable. [Footnote: Section 30(1)(d), (e) and (g).] It will be seen that the grounds encapsulate both *the possibility of redevelopment* and the cases where the Code Operator's conduct has been such that it ought not to be allowed to remain on the land….' [emphasis added]

17.15 The relevant ground for termination was proposed at para 6.110:

> '(3) that the Site Provider intends to redevelop all or part of the land on which the apparatus is sited, or neighbouring land, and could not reasonably do so unless the Code Rights are brought to an end;[5]

Applicability of ground (f) case law

17.16 In *Meyrick*, the tribunal noted that ground (f) case law is not binding authority in the context of the Code, saying:

> 'Clearly the Code, new as it is, must be looked at with a clean slate and as a fresh start. The principles applicable to the 1954 Act should be adopted where they are relevant, although we are mindful of the need to be aware of the different context in Code cases. Not all principles will be relevant and the factual background will have an effect on this; issues of timing, for example, need to be carefully considered.'

17.17 However, it accepted that the following propositions from the following cases should be adopted in relation to the Code:

(i) It is the intention at the date of the hearing that is relevant: *Betty's Cafes Ltd v Phillips Furnishing Stores Ltd*[6].

4 The relevant report is LAW COM No 336 'THE ELECTRONIC COMMUNICATIONS CODE', published on 27 February 2013.

5 Compare section 30(1)(f) of the Landlord and Tenant Act 1954.

6 [1959] AC 20.

(ii) The well-known two-stage test for intention established in *Cunliffe v Goodman*,[7] comprising subjective and objective elements, applies. Asquith LJ (at p 253) said as follows:

> 'An 'intention' to my mind connotes a state of affairs which the party 'intending' … does more than merely contemplate: it connotes a state of affairs which, on the contrary, he decides, so far as in him lies, to bring about, and which, in point of possibility, he has a reasonable prospect of being able to bring about, by his own act of volition.'

(iii) Lord Sumption's acid test in *Franses*,[8] applicable to root out a conditional intention that would not exist if the tenant were to leave voluntarily, was also to apply. That test was expressed as follows:

> 'The landlord's intention to carry out the works cannot therefore be conditional on whether the tenant chooses to assert his claim to a new tenancy and to persist in that claim. The acid test is whether the landlord would intend to do the same works if the tenant left voluntarily.'

17.18 In *Meyrick* that test was approved because if the respondent's intention was only to prevent the acquisition of Code rights, 'then that is an intention to frustrate a central policy of the Code'.

Differences between the 1954 Act and the Code

17.19 Although the tribunal in *Meyrick* described the differences in language between ground (f) and para 21(5) as 'trivial', one might argue that that was in the context of deciding whether the 1954 Act case law could be applied to the Code as a matter of principle. There are clearly some differences in wording, and one can conceive of situations in which these are capable of making a difference to the outcome of a case. Some differences are considered below.

(i) When the 'redevelopment' is intended to occur

A 'reasonable time' requirement?

17.20 Under the 1954 Act, ground (f) expressly provides that the landlord's works must be intended to occur 'on the termination of the current tenancy'. This does not mean that they must be instantaneous. Rather, it is sufficient if they are intended to occur within a reasonable time of the end of the tenancy.[9]

17.21 By contrast, under the Code there is no mention of when the redevelopment must be intended to occur. One would imagine that the law would similarly imply

7 [1950] 2 KB 237.

8 *S Franses Ltd v Cavendish Hotel (London) Ltd* [2018] UKSC 62.

9 As discussed in the High Court decision in *Franses v Cavendish* [2017] EWHC 1670 (QB) at [47] and [75]–[77]. That judgment was appealed up to the Supreme Court of course, but the paragraphs mentioned above refer to the fact that the courts have held that a 'reasonable time' test applies, and digests some of the cases which give rise to this position. The discussion of that discrete point is not affected by the further appeal.

that the intention must be to carry out (or commence?) redevelopment within some timescale. It is not the policy of the Code to thwart redevelopment, but neither is it the policy of the Code to prevent or curtail an operator's plans immediately where no redevelopment is intended for a very considerable period.

17.22 It would make sense for a 'reasonable time' yardstick to be chosen, in the absence of any other obvious solution, and for consistency with the familiar 1954 Act approach. That reasonable time might be expected to run from when the respondent can be expected to recover possession following a termination, or from the date of the tribunal's decision in a Part 4 case.

Might a 'reasonable time' be different under the Code?

17.23 It is of note that in *Meyrick* the tribunal thought that 'issues of timing' would need to be carefully considered.

17.24 There are a number of differences in the timetables and structure of the different statutes and of the factual circumstances that may exist under the two different regimes, which might cause tribunals to allow longer periods when considering what is 'reasonable' under the Code.

17.25 First, in the 1954 Act context, the legislation already makes clear that the works must be intended '*on* the termination…', [emphasis added] and the reasonable time requirement is implied to make that stipulation have real-world sense. A landlord carrying out a modern development cannot reasonably be expected to commence its works forthwith, and the policy of the Act is not such that that level of alacrity is necessary. Accordingly, the implication of the reasonable time requirement is a slight loosening of the words of the statute, which loosening cannot be expected to be taken too far.

17.26 By contrast, under the Code, there is no statement that the redevelopment must be intended to occur 'on' the tribunal making its decision, despite the Law Commission being meticulously versed in the wording, history, and function of the 1954 Act scheme. Any imposition of a reasonable time requirement in the Code context would be to ensure there is *some* temporal limit, rather than to give the landlord a little respite from the apparent immediacy of a legislative requirement of the kind found in ground (f). In other words, it makes the ground more strict than its plain words. Again, that likely judicial gloss should not go too far.

17.27 A second, and more concrete, reason why a site provider might be accorded more time under the Code is that the site provider might genuinely have an intention to carry out redevelopment as soon as possible, but it might be prevented from acting quickly by the structure of the Code itself. It is common for buildings to host a number of different operators, and it is not uncommon for at least some of those operators to have separate agreements. If a landowner is intending to commence redevelopment in, say, two years' time, and already has one or more operators on its building, it may well not yet have served a para 31 notice. Indeed, it may not yet be entitled to. If at that point it is served with a para 20 notice by an additional operator and wishes to rely on para 21(5) in order to resist an agreement, it would need to show (under the objective limb of intention, as to which see below) that it would be able to remove the other operator(s) in order to carry out its redevelopment. The timescales for so doing may not be such as to constitute a reasonable time for the purposes of the 1954 Act.

But under the 1954 Act, notice under section 25 need not be anywhere near as long in duration as the 18 months required by para 31.

17.28 Further, under the 1954 Act, there is no possibility of a brand new tenancy popping up unexpectedly – new tenancies arise only as renewals of existing tenancies. Thus, a landlord can be expected to know how many tenants it needs to evict under the 1954 Act, and what the timescales for such evictions might be.

17.29 As it is no policy of the Code to prevent redevelopment, one must surely take these difficulties that are inherent in the Code into account when considering what constitutes a reasonable time. Whether they make a telling difference may depend upon the facts of the case. It is worth noting that under para 21(3) and also para 31(4) (d), a landowner can always argue that the prejudice from which it would suffer would outweigh the public benefit of the Code rights. In a case where the tribunal considered that the redevelopment was too far off, it may conceivably be persuaded that this alternative argument would succeed, especially if the new agreement sought is of considerable length. Alternative options would be a landlord redevelopment break clause in a new agreement (of the kind that is now granted frequently by the tribunals) or a short-term extension agreement in a Part 5 case. It is unlikely that a new agreement would be imposed under para 20 with a very short term (of say two years) on any normal set of facts.

(ii) The land on which the works are to occur

17.30 Because the 1954 Act uses the language of the 'holding',[10] and Code agreements may not be leases, different language is used in the Code, as observed by the tribunal in *Meyrick*.

17.31 It is well established that in order for works to satisfy ground (f), they do not need to be works to load-bearing elements of the structure of a building. *Pumperninks of Piccadilly Ltd v Land Securities Plc*[11] was a noted case in which only the internal 'skin' of the relevant part of a building was demised, and relatively limited works were held to be sufficient in that case because of the restricted nature of what fabric was actually demised.

17.32 In the telecoms context, it may be that works are intended to land that is not demised under a lease. In some cases, such works may satisfy the tests under the Code, because those works may nonetheless be works to land to which the Code agreement would relate, or to which the Code right currently relates. Or indeed, to neighbouring land.

(iii) The works which are to occur

17.33 Under the 1954 Act, there are a number of different types of works that are capable of qualifying, namely demolition or reconstruction (of the holding or a

10 Essentially the demise under the tenancy, less an area occupied neither by the tenant nor by a person employed by the tenant (s 23(3), 1954 Act).

11 [2002] EWCA Civ 621.

substantial part thereof), and/or a substantial work of construction (on the holding or part thereof).

17.34 Under the Code, what must be intended is 'to redevelop' all or part of the land to which the code agreement relates (or to which the Code right *would* relate), or any neighbouring land.

17.35 There is a question as to what 'redevelop' means in para 31(4)(c) of the Code, and in particular whether it requires active construction (and/or a new use), rather than merely demolition that may only later allow new construction works to occur.

17.36 There has certainly been at least one Case Management Hearing under the Code at which it has been assumed that the intended demolition of the building on which the ECA sat would make it a very clear case in which the landowner would succeed. However, there has not yet been a case that has considered and finally determined this question on the basis of argument.

17.37 One might begin by considering the ordinary English meaning of the word 'redevelop'. Below are definitions from four popular online dictionary sites:

https://www.dictionary.com/browse/redevelop

'1. to rebuild or replan (a building, area, etc)'.

https://dictionary.cambridge.org/dictionary/english/redevelop

'to change an area of a town by replacing old buildings, roads, etc. with new ones'.

https://www.collinsdictionary.com/dictionary/english/redevelop

'When an area is redeveloped, existing buildings and roads are removed and new ones are built in their place.'

https://www.ldoceonline.com/dictionary/redevelop

'to make an area more modern by putting in new buildings or changing or repairing the old ones'.

17.38 As will readily be seen, each of the above definitions includes the notion of new buildings, or rebuilding.

17.39 The definition of 'development' under the Town and Country Planning Act 1990 ('TCPA 1990') (for which one needs planning permission by virtue of section 57 of that Act) is of possible interest. By TCPA 1990, s 55(1) it includes, inter alia, 'building operations', which in turn includes, at section 55(1A)(a), 'demolition of buildings'. This is a different statute with a different purpose, but it is at least clear that demolition constituting development is not alien to the statute book.

17.40 If there is a building present it is evident that the relevant land has already been 'developed', and if that is the case, then a *further* act of development (potentially consisting of demolition) might therefore be said to constitute *re*development.

17.41 However, in the context of the Code, the approach to interpretation that has been favoured at the higher levels has not been one that relies too heavily on textual analysis (see Chapter 7). Rather, it has been to consider the overall working of the scheme of the Code and whether a particular meaning of a word would be conducive to how the Code is supposed to function.

17.42 The redevelopment ground was intended by the Law Commission to be 'readily recognised' from within section 30(1) of the 1954 Act, ie, ground (f). Further, in *Meyrick*, the Upper Tribunal indicated that the difference in wording between ground (f) and the Code largely came from the fact that under the Code an agreement is not always a lease. There does not seem to be any obvious policy reason why demolition should not be sufficient under the Code, when it clearly is under the 1954 Act.

17.43 The Law Commission Report cites consultation responses talking of 'redevelopment', and one suspects that this is a convenient shorthand word for a consultee to include in a consultation response rather than using phrases like 'substantial work of reconstruction', or 'demolition of all or a substantial part of the holding'. This shorthand may simply have been carried over to the recommendation, and of course the Law Commission was never invited to set out the precise wording of the potential legislation in a draft Bill.

Consequences of a para 31(4) ground being 'established' or not

17.44 Following the service by a site provider of a notice under para 31 seeking to terminate a Code agreement, if an operator makes an application to the tribunal under para 32(1)(b) for an Order under para 34, the tribunal will consider whether the site provider has established one of the para 31(4) grounds stated in its para 31 notice.

17.45 If the tribunal decides that the site provider has established one of its grounds, it 'must order that the code agreement comes to an end in accordance with the order'.[12]

17.46 No automatic or default time at which the Code agreement will come to an end is stated in the Code. This is in contradistinction to the position under the 1954 Act, where a tenancy terminates at the expiration of three months beginning with the date on which the application to court is 'finally disposed of'.[13]

17.47 Operators would argue that this gives the tribunal a discretion as to the period of time within which the Code agreement is to come to an end. A counter-argument is that a site provider cannot obtain possession of its land until it has been through the procedure set out in Part 6. An Order requiring an operator to remove ECA under para 44 must specify the period during which it must do so, and the tribunal has confirmed in *EE v Crawley* that it has discretion as to how long it gives an operator to do so. Thus, the operator is already given an element of procedural protection from immediate eviction.

17.48 Given this safeguard, and in the absence of any similar mention in para 32(4) of the period after which the agreement will come to an end, it may be argued that a para 32(4) Order is one that terminates an agreement immediately. Certainly, if there is discretion, site providers are likely to argue that the Part 6 safeguards mean that there is no justification in a typical case for not terminating the Code agreement immediately.

12 By para 32(4) of the Code.
13 By s 64(1) of the 1954 Act.

17.49 If the site provider fails to satisfy a termination ground that was stated in its para 31 notice, the tribunal 'must make one of the orders specified in paragraph 34'.

Consequences of the para 21(5) defence being 'established' or not

17.50 If the para 21(5) ground is proven by the respondent would-be site provider, it is clear that the tribunal 'may not' impose an agreement, and the substantive Reference will be at an end.

17.51 If the respondent does not satisfy para 21(5) for whatever reason, the tribunal will proceed to consider whether the para 21(2) and (3) conditions are satisfied, and therefore whether an agreement will be imposed. If an agreement is to be imposed, it will then determine the terms of that agreement, insofar as they remain in dispute.

17.52 In 1954 Act renewal cases where ground (f) is in issue, it is common to direct a trial of a preliminary issue, namely whether the ground of opposition to the new lease is made out. In the context of para 21(5), there is often an imperative to decide the Reference within six months (see Chapter 21). Thus if a preliminary issue trial is directed at all, it will often involve determining not only whether para 21(5) is established, but also whether the para 21(2) and (3) conditions are met (in the event that para 21(5) is not established).

17.53 It could be argued that it is problematic to determine under para 21(3) what prejudice will result from the Order, when the precise terms of the agreement are not yet known. If this is genuinely thought to be an issue of substance in a given case, rather than a merely theoretical objection, the tribunal can always hear evidence on terms at the same trial, or merely deal with para 21(5) on its own, and then the remainder of the Reference at a subsequent trial if appropriate.

Differences between para 21(5) and 31(4)(c)

17.54 The redevelopment ground under para 21(5) applies where an operator is seeking new or additional Code rights, whereas the para 31(4)(c) ground applies when the site provider is seeking to bring an agreement to an end.

17.55 In the case of para 21(5), the land that must be intended to be redeveloped is 'all or part of the land to which the code right would relate' (or any neighbouring land). In the case of para 31(4)(c), the land that must be intended to be redeveloped is 'all or part of the land to which the code agreement relates' (or any neighbouring land).

17.56 Each of these grounds requires the site provider (or 'relevant person' in the case of para 21(5)) to prove that it intends to redevelop land, and that it could not reasonably do so on a particular hypothesis.

17.57 Under para 31(4)(c), the tribunal must consider whether the person could reasonably redevelop the relevant land without bringing to an end the particular Code agreement that already exists. The existing Code agreement will have one set of terms and one meaning, and having determined the meaning of that set of terms, the tribunal must come to a factual findings as to the extent to which the redevelopment could reasonably be carried out.

17.58 However, under para 21(5), the task of the tribunal is to consider whether the person could reasonably redevelop the relevant land if 'the order were made'. One may ask, 'what order?' The answer to that question seems likely to be 'an order under paragraph 20'.

17.59 The language of both para 21(1) and the opening lines of para 21(5) refers to 'an order under paragraph 20'. The question that arises is whether this means 'any order which would be open to the tribunal under para 20', or whether it is restricted to an Order to impose the particular agreement that is sought in the operator's Notice of Reference.

17.60 The para 20 process, of course, commences with the service of a notice under para 20(2) by the operator. Paragraph 20(2)(a) provides that the operator must set out all of the terms that it seeks. However, the tribunal is not bound as a matter of jurisdiction only to grant Code rights on the particular terms set out in (or attached to) the para 20(2) notice. Rather, para 23(1) expressly provides that the tribunal may make such modifications to the terms sought as it 'thinks appropriate', and para 23(2) gives the tribunal a broad discretion to impose whatever terms it 'thinks appropriate' subject to paras 23(3) to (8).

17.61 It is against this legislative backdrop that the tribunal typically orders the parties to produce an electronic 'travelling draft' in which each party seeks amendments to the terms as sought by the opposing party. This process often results in a number of iterations of various terms and can result in certain terms being agreed through iterative negotiation. Where the parties have shifted their position over time but have not arrived at agreement the operator is in practice not treated as being tied to the terms as sought in its notice, but is typically permitted to contend for wording that may have crept into its preferred version of the agreement through the travelling draft process. This is of potential importance in the case of para 21(5).

17.62 It may be, for example, that a para 20 notice proposes that ECA be installed in a location that would be quite incompatible with sincerely intended redevelopment. In that case, a landowner may consider that it has a very strong case under para 21(5). However, the site provider may seek to amend the terms which it seeks in order to incorporate a 'lift and shift' provision that would allow the landowner in certain circumstances to insist that the ECA be moved either temporarily or permanently in order to allow the redevelopment to proceed.

17.63 Indeed, para 23(8)(b) positively requires the tribunal to consider including a term enabling the relevant person to require the operator to reposition or temporarily remove the ECA to which the agreement relates, and if so, in what circumstances. As the tribunal has to consider whether such a clause should be included in an agreement imposed by its Order, it could be argued that it would be artificial to exclude such a clause from consideration under para 21(5).

17.64 The question under para 21(5) might then become whether the relevant person could reasonably carry out its intended redevelopment if an Order were to be made imposing the agreement with the specific 'lift and shift' provision within it. The answer to that question would, of course, depend on the facts of the particular case.

17.65 Thus, in a para 21(5) case, it may be that the scope of the tribunal's enquiry is not limited to the particular Code agreement that was initially proposed. On the other hand, in a para 31(4)(c) case, it would seem that the tribunal's enquiry is indeed limited to the particular agreement that remains in force.

17.66 This constitutes a potentially significant difference from the position under the redevelopment ground of the 1954 Act,[14] where the question is whether the intended scheme of works could reasonably be carried out 'without obtaining possession of the holding'.

Redevelopment: relevance to paras 26 and 27

Para 26 applications

17.67 Where an operator applies for interim rights under para 26, it must only show a 'good arguable case'[15] that the para 21 test is met. Clearly, the para 21 test cannot be met if a landowner establishes the redevelopment defence under para 21(5). How a redevelopment argument is considered in practice in a para 26 case is likely to depend on the facts of each case.

17.68 Para 26 cases do not typically involve a full trial with cross-examination of witnesses. In some cases, it may be that a Tribunal can dismiss a landowner's objection summarily, for example:

- Where there is an application for an MSV alone, although installation and operation of ECA would be inconsistent with a landowner's proposed redevelopment, the MSV itself may cause no prejudice, and accordingly in an appropriate case the application might be allowed, even assuming the landowner's factual assertions are true.
- Similarly, if there is a freestanding para 26 application for very short-term rights to install ECA, it may be that the tribunal considers that even if the landowner's factual assertions are correct, it can still 'reasonably' redevelop its land, because the evidence suggests that it will not commence works until after the para 26 agreement will have expired.
- Where a para 26 application is accompanied by a para 20 application for a full Code agreement with security of tenure, it may be that the para 26 agreement can safely be granted for a term that does not interfere with the landowner's asserted redevelopment plans, with a full para 20 trial listed to occur at a reasonable time during the currency of the para 26 agreement.

17.69 Conversely, in other cases, it may be that a tribunal would dismiss the para 26 application summarily where redevelopment is raised, particularly where para 26 rights are sought for a substantial time, and they would conflict with clear-cut redevelopment plans and timescale of a landowner. A Tribunal might reach that conclusion by different routes depending on the particular facts:

14 Section 30(1)(f) thereof.
15 Para 26(3)(b).

- Where there is *prima facie* credible evidence of an intention to redevelop (even where that evidence has not been tested), it may be that the tribunal feels that it is able to conclude that the operator has not shown a 'good arguable case' that it satisfies the para 21 test. After all, the UT has previously referred to the *Canada Trust* case, from which it appears necessary for an applicant to show 'a much better argument on the material available'. This may well not be the case if the redevelopment assertion is *prima facie* credible.
- Even if it cannot go as far as to find against the operator on the 'good arguable case' test, in some cases a tribunal may nonetheless refuse a para 26 in the exercise of its discretion. The tribunal has often reasserted that it is no policy of the Code to thwart the redevelopment intentions of landowners, for example when imposing redevelopment break clauses in favour of landlords. This factor may well weigh in the balance when considering the application of its discretion, so long as the landowner's evidence is *prima facie* credible.

17.70 If the tribunal is, on a summary basis, neither able to dismiss the landowner's objections, nor to refuse the application, one would imagine that it would have to determine the landowner's redevelopment case. It would need to be given a reasonable time to produce its evidence. This would be difficult to achieve fairly, especially in a case where the operator asserts that there is some urgency in installing its ECA on the land. It may prove difficult to balance the rights and opportunities of the parties. The difficulties inherent in this predicament may cause the tribunal either to grant a para 26 agreement with a shorter term than that sought, or to grant a para 26 agreement that terminates upon an event occurring, such as the grant of planning permission for the proposed redevelopment.

Para 27 applications

17.71 It is not immediately apparent how a landowner's redevelopment argument enters into the decision-making process under para 27. Paragraph 27(2) appears to confer a discretion on the tribunal which is unfettered by the application of a precise test. Again, policy considerations around not thwarting intended development might be thought to be relevant to the exercise of that discretion.

17.72 In any event, a para 27 agreement is only ever imposed where there is an extant application under para 20. The landowner will have the right to argue the para 21(5) redevelopment defence in the conventional way when the para 20 application comes to trial. A para 27 application would therefore only be expected to be refused on redevelopment grounds if there is a credible possibility that waiting until trial to determine the redevelopment ground would delay or jeopardise the asserted redevelopment and thereby cause prejudice to the landowner.

18

Part 6 of the Code – removal of ECA

18.01 Part 6 of the Code sets out the process for requiring and enforcing the removal of ECA from land, and associated matters such as the costs of so doing, and the restoration of the land to its former condition. In principle it will apply to all situations[1] where a person wishes to achieve such removal and/or restoration.

Right to require removal

18.02 Paragraph 37 of the Code sets out the circumstances in which a person with an interest in land has a 'right to require the removal' of ECA. Such a right exists 'if and only if'[2] one or more of the five conditions at para 37 is met. Each of these conditions shall now be considered in turn.

First condition: landowner never bound by Code right

18.03 The first condition is that the landowner has never since the coming into force of the Code been bound by a Code right entitling an operator to keep the ECA on, under, or over the land (para 37(2)). The first condition is subject to para 37(4), as to which see below.

18.04 For the purposes of the Code, a 'landowner' is a 'person with an interest in land'.[3]

18.05 Examples of situations that would fall within the first condition would include the following:

(i) Where an operator had the benefit of an agreement under the Old Code, which expired before the New Code came into force.

1 This is subject to the point that where a person has given notice under para 21(2) of the Old Code (requiring removal of apparatus) before the Old Code was repealed, the repeal does not affect the operation of para 21 of the Old Code in relation to anything done or that may be done under that paragraph following the giving of the notice (para 20(2) of the Transitional Provisions, ie, Sch 2 to the Digital Economy Act 2017). However, as the Old Code has been repealed for some years now, and given the recent recognition by the FTT in the *Patricroft* case that Code notices may become stale, it may be that this Transitional Provision has now run its course.

2 Para 37(1).

3 This definition is contained within para 37(1) and applied to the Code as a whole by para 108(1).

(ii) Where an operator has never had any written agreement[4] under which it has apparatus installed, or even any agreement of any kind.

(iii) Where an operator has the benefit of Code rights to keep ECA installed on nearby land, but has installed the ECA in the wrong place, where there exist no Code rights for any installation.

(iv) Where a different operator has the benefit of Code rights to keep ECA installed, but on a proper analysis of the facts, that operator is not the person who is keeping the ECA on the land. There has not yet been detailed consideration of what occupier is keeping ECA installed, or is occupying the land in question, in the context of any dispute about that question, but it is anticipated that such questions may come before the tribunals before long.

(v) Where an operator has a Code right to keep ECA installed, but that Code right does not bind the landowner in question, in accordance with the rules set out at para 10 of the Code.

18.06 It is considered that the reference within the first condition to 'an operator' is likely to be read as referring to the operator in question, ie, the operator against which a right to require removal is being asserted. Were it otherwise, a landowner may well enjoy no right to require removal as against an operator that has taken over ownership and operation of ECA without being assigned or granted any Code rights to keep that ECA installed.

Second condition: Code right has come to an end

18.07 The second condition is that a Code right entitling an[5] operator to keep the apparatus on, under, or over the land has either come to an end or has ceased to bind the landowner in one of the five specified circumstances set out at para 37(3). The second condition is also subject to para 37(4), as to which see below.

18.08 The five circumstances are as follows:

Paragraph 37(3)(a): 'as mentioned in paragraph 26(7) and (8)'. This is where a para 26 agreement has been imposed 'on an interim basis' and the term of that agreement has come to an end either because of the effluxion of time or the occurrence of the event that had been specified as causing its termination,[6] without a para 20 agreement having been imposed under para 20. It will be

---

4 Following the decision of the Upper Tribunal in *Arqiva Services Ltd v AP Wireless II (UK) Ltd* [2020] UKUT 195 (LC), any implied or oral agreement that exists does not constitute a subsisting agreement for the purposes of para 1(4)(a) of the Transitional Provisions. For the installation of ECA, this would have required 'the agreement *in writing* of the occupier for the time being'. Further, an implied or oral agreement entered into since the coming into force of the Code cannot confer Code rights as para 11 of the Code creates formalities requirements for agreements conferring Code rights, including that they be in writing and be signed.

5 As with the first condition, it is considered that the reference within the second condition to 'an operator' is likely to be read as referring to the operator in question, ie, the operator against which a right to require removal is being asserted. Were it otherwise, a landowner would have the right to require removal as against operator B despite operator B having a perfectly good Code right in respect of it, merely on the ground that operator A's Code right in respect of the same apparatus has expired in one of the stated ways.

6 See para 26(2)(b) of the Code.

remembered that para 30(2) does not continue such an agreement beyond its stated term, by virtue of the exception stated at para 30(3).

Paragraph 37(3)(aa): 'as mentioned in paragraph 27G(1) and (4)'. This relates solely to a circumstance in which rights granted under Part 4A of the Code, which is the particular regime dealing with unresponsive occupiers in the leasehold context, cease to have effect (or cease to bind the grantor). A Part 4A Code right comes to an end[7] (or ceases to bind the grantor):

(a) where a replacement agreement comes into effect; or

(b) where the court or tribunal refuses an application for a replacement agreement; or

(c) where (a) and (b) do not apply, at the end of the period of no more than 18 months specified in regulations made by the Secretary of State.

Paragraph 37(3)(b): 'as the result of paragraph 32(1)'. By para 32(1), where a site provider gives a notice under para 31 in relation to a Code agreement comes to an end automatically in accordance with[8] that notice unless:

– the operator gives a counter-notice in accordance with para 32(3) within three months of the para 31 notice being given;[9] and

– the operator applies to the 'court' for an order under para 34, within three months of the counter-notice being given under para 32(3).[10]

Naturally when the Code agreement comes to an end, any Code rights conferred by it come to an end, thus satisfying the 'second condition'.

If the operator and the site provider agree to the continuation of the Code agreement, para 32(1) does not apply[11] (and hence does not operate so as to bring the Code agreement to an end).

Paragraph 37(3)(c): 'as the result of an order under paragraph 32(4) or 34(4) or (6)'.

An Order under para 32(4) is one made where a landowner succeeds in terminating a Code agreement pursuant to a ground stated in its para 31 notice.

An Order under para 34(4) is one type of Order that may be made in the context of a para 32 application by a site provider seeking to terminate a Code agreement,

---

7 See para 27G(1) of the Code.

8 Ie, the agreement will come to an end on the date on which the site provider proposes in the notice as the dated on which the agreement should come to an end. Such a date must satisfy the requirements in para 31(a) and (b).

9 See para 32(1)(a).

10 See para 32(1)(b).

11 This is by virtue of para 32(2). It is not expressly stated that an agreement to continue the agreement has to be in writing. Neither is it expressly stated that such an agreement has to be entered into prior to the date on which para 32(1) would bring an end to the Code agreement. However, one would imagine that this is a requirement. Otherwise, para 32(1) would have effect and terminate the agreement, and only after such a date would para 32(2) be engaged to generate the effect that para 32(1) does not apply. One might think that it has already applied. Further, if this is not a requirement, then there would seem to be no specified deadline, which is a recipe for uncertainty, and the seeming lack of a formalities requirement would mean that a Code agreement could be revived much later without even the basic requirement for writing, which has existed since the days of the Old Code in respect of the creation of Code rights.

or a party seeking to renew a Code agreement. Such an Order modifies the terms of a Code agreement such as to remove a Code right from the agreement. In order for such an Order to fall within the second condition at para 37(3)(c), surely the Code right that is being removed from the agreement by the para 34(4) Order must be a right to keep the ECA on, under or over the land, otherwise the opening criterion in para 37(3) is not satisfied.

An Order under para 34(6) is another type of Order that may be made in the context of a para 32 application by a site provider seeking to terminate a Code agreement, or a party seeking to renew a Code agreement. Such an Order is one that terminates an existing Code agreement and orders the site provider and operator to enter into a new agreement that confers a Code right or provides for a Code right to bind the site provider.

Paragraph 37(3)(d): 'where the right was granted by a lease to which Part 5 of this code does not apply.'

18.09 Part 5 of the Code deals with the termination, modification and renewal of Code agreements. It does not apply to all agreements that confer Code rights. Two examples of categories of Code agreements to which Part 5 does not apply are explained below, namely leases that fall within para 29(2), and those affected by para 6 of the Transitional Provisions.

Para 29(2) situations

18.10 By para 29(2) of the Code, Part 5 does not apply to a lease whose primary purpose is not to grant Code rights but to which Part 2 of the 1954 Act applies.[12] Such a lease is still able to be created. Section 43(4) of the 1954 Act provides that Part 2 of that Act does not apply to a tenancy granted after the coming into force of the Code whose 'primary purpose' is to grant Code rights.

18.11 Thus, one can still create a lease whose primary purpose is not to grant Code rights, but which nonetheless does grant Code rights (such as the installation of ECA). Assuming that such a lease is not 'contracted out'[13] of the security of tenure provisions of the 1954 Act, that lease will need to be terminated in accordance with the provisions of the 1954 Act. Once the lease has been terminated in accordance with the provisions of the 1954 Act,[14] the Code right is at an end, and therefore there is a right to require removal under para 37(3)(d). If such a lease is indeed 'contracted out'[15] of the security of tenure provisions of the 1954 Act, then it will come to an end in accordance with its own terms, and because of the exclusion in para 29(2) of the Code, para 30(2) of the Code does not continue it.

12 And by para 29(3), one is to ignore any 'contracting out' of the security of tenure provisions of the 1954 Act which has been agreed under s 38A of the 1954 Act.

13 Pursuant to an agreement under s 38A of the 1954 Act.

14 Whether through the statutory termination procedure, or through a means of termination of tenancies that s 24(2) of the 1954 Act expressly preserves, such as forfeiture and surrender.

15 Pursuant to an agreement under s 38A of the 1954 Act.

Para 6 Transitional Provisions situations

18.12 Paragraph 6 of the Transitional Provisions[16] applies in respect of subsisting agreements[17] in place of para 29(2) to (4) of the Code,[18] and provides that Part 5 of the Code does not apply to two categories of subsisting agreements. The two categories are as follows:

- a 1954 Act lease which is not 'contracted out'[19] (such a case is specified at para 6(2) of the Transitional Provisions). In such a case, the lease must be terminated in accordance with the 1954 Act,[20] and once such termination has taken effect, the Code right has come to an end, and there is a right to require removal of the relevant ECA; and
- a lease whose 'primary purpose' is not to grant Code rights, which is 'contracted out' of the security of tenure provisions of the 1954 Act (such a case is specified at para 6(3) of the Transitional Provisions). Such a lease will come to an end in accordance with its own terms, and because of the exclusion in para 6(3) of the Transitional Provisions, para 30(2) of the Code (which is within Part 5 of the Code) does not continue it. Thus the Code right to keep ECA installed comes to an end, and there is a right to require removal under para 37(3)(d).

Para 37(4): a disqualification from the first and second conditions

18.13 As stated above, the first condition and the second condition are each expressly subject to para 37(4).

18.14 Paragraph 37(4) provides that the landowner does not meet either the first or second condition if the land is occupied by a person who conferred a Code right entitling an operator to keep the ECA on, over, or under land (or is otherwise bound by such a Code right), and that Code right was not conferred in breach of a covenant enforceable by the landowner.

Third condition: ECA no longer used for network

18.15 The third condition[21] is that an operator *does* currently have the benefit of a Code right entitling it to keep the ECA, but:

- the ECA is not, or is no longer, used for the purposes of the operator's network; and
- there is no reasonable likelihood that the ECA will be used for that purpose.

18.16 This provision has not yet been the subject of a great deal of judicial consideration.

---

16 Sch 2 to the Digital Economy Act 2017.

17 For a discussion of 'subsisting agreements', see Chapter 17.

18 By para 6(1) of the Transitional Provisions.

19 Ie, a lease to which Part 2 of the 1954 Act applies, but in respect of which there is no agreement under s 38A of the 1954 Act to exclude the security of tenure provisions of the 1954 Act.

20 See the *Ashloch* case, in the Upper Tribunal, Court of Appeal or Supreme Court.

21 At para 37(6).

18.17 It will be a question of fact as to whether any lack of use for the purposes of the network has been of such character and sufficient duration to satisfy the first of these criteria, and similarly a question of fact as to the reasonableness of any likelihood of use arising. In this context it is worth remembering that the operator's 'network'[22] may be an electronic communications network or an infrastructure system. The latter term is defined at para 7 and includes infrastructure 'provided so as to be available for use' by providers of networks. There may be a question in respect of infrastructure providers whether a mast (for example) simply being available constitutes use for the purposes of the operator's network, where no communications use is ongoing or likely. One would imagine that such disputes would occur rarely.

Fourth condition: the Code has ceased to apply

18.18 The fourth condition[23] is that:

'(a) this code has ceased to apply to a person so that the person is no longer entitled under this code to keep the apparatus on, under or over the land,

(b) the retention of the apparatus on, under or over the land is not authorised by a scheme contained in an order under section 117, and

(c) there is no other person with a right conferred by or under this code to keep the apparatus on, under or over the land.'

18.19 The language 'entitled under this code' is perhaps not entirely clear. Although there has been no ruling on the extent of the fourth condition, it is considered that a right to require removal would only arise where the contractual agreement allowing the keeping of ECA has come to an end *and* there is no continuation under para 30(2) because the ECA-keeping party is no longer an operator.

18.20 If an operator enters into a Code agreement allowing it to install ECA, but then ceases to be an operator during the agreement term, that person would be contractually entitled to keep its ECA installed for the remainder of the agreement term (absent any contractual provision to the contrary[24]). It seems doubtful that criterion (a) of the fourth condition would be immediately satisfied where a tenant loses operator status during the contractual term of an agreement, as that would allow a landowner to require removal of ECA during a contractual term without the contract having been terminated. Rather, it seems likely that criterion (a) is targeted at situations where a contractual agreement term has expired and is not continuing under para 30(2), either because the telecoms entity loses or never gains the benefit of para 30(2) because of its loss of operator status.

18.21 Paragraph 30(2) only continues an agreement so that an 'operator' may continue to exercise a Code right. Reading para 37(7) and para 30(2) together, it may be that an originally valid para 30(2) continuation comes to an end where the tenant

22 See the definition at para 6.

23 At para 37(7).

24 A tribunal could include a break right in a new agreement which is triggered where the tenant loses operator status. As mentioned in Chapter 11, the tribunal has granted rent review clauses allowing an open market rent review when the tenant ceases to be an operator. The logic of doing so proceeds on the basis that the contractual term of the agreement *prima facie* is not disturbed by the tenant's loss of operator status.

ceases to be an operator. That would then mean that the former operator no longer has the benefit of any agreement, and of course it cannot have Code rights if it is not an operator.

Fifth condition

18.22 The fifth condition applies where the ECA was kept pursuant to a transport land right (under Part 7) or a street work right (under Part 8), the right has ceased to be exercisable in relation to the land by virtue of para 54(9), and there is no other person with a right conferred by or under the Code to keep the ECA.

Removal rights arising otherwise than under the Code

18.23 Paragraph 37 'does not affect rights to require the removal of apparatus under another enactment'.[25] Paragraph 41(1) provides that the right of a person to require the removal of ECA under a different enactment, or otherwise than under an enactment, is exercisable only in accordance with para 41. Paragraph 41 makes provision for a notice and counter-notice procedure, and for applications to be made to the tribunal for an Order that would allow the removal of the ECA.

Right to require removal: neighbouring land

18.24 Where ECA is kept over land in exercise of a Code right within para 3(1)(a) to (g) or (i), or any other right mentioned in para 13(1),[26] a landowner or occupier of other land has the right to require its removal in certain specific circumstances set out in para 38.

18.25 The land of which the person seeking removal is the landowner or occupier is referred to in para 38 as the 'neighbouring land'. The following two conditions must both[27] be satisfied for the right to require removal to arise:

> '(2) The first condition is that the apparatus interferes with or obstructs a means of access to or from the neighbouring land.
>
> (3) The second condition is that the landowner or occupier of the neighbouring land is not bound by a code right within paragraph 3(1)(h) entitling an operator to cause the interference or obstruction.'

18.26 However, a landowner of the neighbouring land who is not the occupier of the land does not meet the second condition if the occupier conferred (or is otherwise bound by) an extant Code right entitling an operator to cause the interference or obstruction, and that Code right was not conferred in breach of a covenant enforceable by the landowner.[28]

25 Para 37(9).

26 These are: a right under Part 8 (street works rights), a right under Part 9 (tidal water rights), or (d) a right under para 74 (power to fly lines).

27 Para 38(1).

28 Para 38(4).

Enforcing removal of ECA

(i) Service of the para 40 notice

18.27 The right of a landowner or occupier to require the removal of ECA (under either para 37 or para 38) is enforceable only in accordance with para 40.[29] Paragraph 40 creates a notice procedure, which is a pre-requisite for any application to the tribunal for an Order for removal.

18.28 Where a landowner or occupier[30] has a right to require removal of ECA under either para 37 or 38, it may give a notice under para 40(2) to the operator 'whose apparatus it is'. The notice is one that requires the operator to remove the apparatus and to restore the condition of the land to its prior state.

18.29 There is a prescribed form for this notice. The notice must comply with para 89,[31] and specify the period during which the operator must complete the works.[32] Such period must be a reasonable one.[33]

(ii) Application for an Order in reliance on para 40 notice

18.30 The landowner or occupier can then make an application to the tribunal under para 40(6) for an Order requiring the operator to remove the ECA (under 44(1)), or for an Order enabling the landowner to remove and sell the ECA (under para 44(3)), if within 28 days of service of the para 40 notice the landowner or occupier and operator do not reach agreement on any of the following matters[34]:

(a) that the operator will remove the apparatus;

(b) that the operator will restore the land to its condition before the apparatus was placed on, under or over the land;

(c) the time at which or period within which the apparatus will be removed;

(d) the time at which or period within which the land will be restored.

18.31 The types of Orders that a tribunal can make upon such an application, and the question of what discretion is has, are dealt with below.

Orders under para 44 (following para 40(6) application)

18.32 Paragraph 44 sets out the different types of Order which the tribunal can make. The substantive orders (ie, not as to litigation costs or compensation) available following a para 40 notice are set out at para 44(1) and 44(3), and can be summarised as follows:

---

29 Para 40(1).

30 Note the meaning of 'occupier' as provided for at para 105, and the extensive discussion of who is the 'occupier' especially when an operator is already in situ, in *Compton Beauchamp*.

31 Para 40(3)(a).

32 Para 40(3)(b).

33 Para 40(4).

34 Para 40(5).

- A para 44(1) Order: requires the operator to remove the ECA and[35] restore the land to its prior condition, within a specified period. Such an Order takes effect as an agreement between the operator and landowner.
- A para 44(3) Order: allows the person applying for the Order to remove the ECA, sell it, recover the costs of so doing, and of restoring the land, and retain proceeds of sale up to the value of those costs.

18.33 Under para 40(6) one can apply for an Order under either para 44(1) or (3) following a para 40 notice being served and the relevant time having elapsed. If an Order is made under para 44(1), but not complied with, an application for a para 44(3) Order may be made.[36]

The right to require restoration: para 43

18.34 Paragraph 43 creates a separate right to apply for an Order for restoration of land in certain circumstances. Paragraph 43 applies where the condition of land has been affected by the exercise of a Code right, and restoration of the land to its prior condition does not involve the removal of ECA.[37]

18.35 In such circumstances, an occupier, freeholder, or lessee of the land who is not for the time being bound by the Code right has the 'right to require the operator to restore the land'.[38] This occupier, freeholder, or lessee is referred to in para 43(2) as the 'relevant person'.

18.36 However, this right to require restoration does not arise if the circumstances described at para 43(3) exist, namely where:

- the land is occupied by a person who conferred (or is otherwise bound by) a Code right which is in force;
- that Code right entitles the operator to affect the condition of the land in the same way as has in fact transpired; and
- that Code right was not conferred in breach of a covenant enforceable by the 'relevant person'.[39]

Enforcing restoration

(i) Service of the para 43(5) notice

18.37 Paragraph 43 creates a notice procedure which is a pre-requisite for any application to the tribunal for an Order for restoration.

---

35 One would hope that, in an appropriate case, an Order could be made under para 44(1) for the removal of ECA without also requiring restoration of the land. For example, if ECA has to be removed because a site provider has demonstrated an intention to redevelop the site completely, including by demolishing a building on which ECA is installed, it would seem futile, costly, and generative of delay to order the operator to restore the roof of a building to its former condition.

36 By para 40(7).

37 Para 43(1).

38 Para 43(2).

39 As defined at para 43(2).

18.38 A person who has the right to require restoration under para 43 may give a notice to the operator requiring it to restore the land to its condition before the Code right was exercised.[40]

18.39 There is a prescribed form for this notice. The notice must comply with para 89,[41] and specify the period during which the operator must complete the works.[42] Such period must be a reasonable one.[43]

(ii) Application for an Order in reliance on para 43(5) notice

18.40 The 'relevant person'[44] can then make an application to the tribunal under para 43(9) for an Order requiring the operator to restore the land (under 44(2)), or for an Order enabling the landowner to recover the cost of restoring the land (under para 44(4)), if within 28 days of service of the para 40 notice the landowner and operator do not reach agreement on any of the following matters:[45]

(a) that the operator will restore the land to its condition before the Code right was exercised;

(b) the time at which or period within which the land will be restored.

18.41 The types of Orders that a tribunal can make upon such an application, and the question of what discretion is has, are dealt with below.

Orders under para 44 (following para 43(9) application)

18.42 Paragraph 44 sets out the different types of Order which the tribunal can make. The substantive orders (ie, not as to litigation costs or compensation) available following a para 43(5) notice are set out at para 44(2) and 44(4), and can be summarised as follows:

- A para 44(2) Order: requires the operator to restore the land to its prior condition, within a specified period. Such an Order takes effect as an agreement between the operator and landowner.
- A para 44(4) Order: allows the landowner to recover from the operator the costs of restoring the land to its prior condition.

18.43 Under para 43(9) one can apply for an Order under either para 44(2) or (4) following a para 43(5) notice being served and the relevant time having elapsed. If an Order is made under para 44(2), but not complied with, an application for a para 44(4) Order may be made.[46]

40 Para 43(5).
41 Para 43(6)(a).
42 Para 43(6)(b).
43 Para 43(7).
44 As defined at para 43(2).
45 Para 43(8).
46 By para 43(10).

Para 44(5) – power to award compensation

18.44 There is a power on the part of the tribunal to require the operator to pay compensation to the landowner for any loss or damage suffered by the landowner as a result of the presence of the ECA on the land during the period when the landowner had the right to require the removal of the apparatus from the land but was not able to exercise that right.

18.45 This provision is discussed in more detail in Chapter 14 (Compensation).

Lack of discretion in para 40 cases

18.46 The effect of the Tribunal's decision in *Crawley BC v EE* is that where there is a right to require removal, and the procedure set out in para 40 has been correctly followed, the Tribunal does not have the power to refuse an Order requiring removal.

18.47 As the Deputy President later said in *Gravesham*, the effect of the *Crawley* decision where the para 40 requirements are met is that an Order for removal is 'not discretionary and involves no balancing of the interests of the landowner and those of the operator or the wider public'.

18.48 It was also held in *Crawley* that, as such an Order is not discretionary, the tribunal should not delay the making of such an Order by allowing a stay of the application. It is true to say that in *Crawley*, the tribunal proceeded on the basis of the law in *Compton Beauchamp* at its Court of Appeal stage in refusing the operator a stay in order to enable it to seek new para 20 rights in the event that the Supreme Court reversed the Court of Appeal decision to allow such applications. The Supreme Court did duly reverse the Court of Appeal decision, and hence the operator had been right that there was a possibility of making a para 20 application. Paragraph 40(8) would have prevented any Order for removal being made before any live para 20 application had been determined. However, the point of principle surely remains that the making of an Order under Part 6 is not discretionary, and also that granting a stay may have the effect of depriving a landowner of what it is entitled to as of right, namely an Order under Part 6. Were the same case to come before the tribunal today, those fundamental points would surely hold good. If a para 20 application were already to have been made, para 40(8) would bite. Whether the tribunal would indulge an operator with a stay in order to allow a para 20 notice to be served is a different question.

18.49 The only live question in a para 40 application, where there is an acknowledged right to require removal, is therefore as to the terms of the Order.

18.50 Paragraph 44(1) makes clear that an Order requiring removal and restoration of the land to its prior condition will require such action to be taken 'within the period specified in the order', and the same form of words is found in para 44(2) pertaining to Orders for mere restoration of land to its former condition. It is unsurprising that a period will be specified in the Order, for without that, the Order would not be readily enforceable.

18.51 It appears that in all cases where the tribunal is being asked to consider making an Order for removal or restoration, or some combination of the two, it will have discretion as to the time period for the carrying out of the necessary works. It will surely be relevant what works need to be done in practice, how long they would reasonably take, and the consequences for the landowner of its right to possession not being vindicated within a certain timescale. One would imagine that an operator would argue that the effect on the continuity of service to consumers of the ECA being removed would also be a relevant consideration.

The effect of para 40(8)

18.52 In *Gravesham*,[47] the Deputy President noted that although an Order for removal was not discretionary, this was subject to an 'important qualification' in para 40(8). Paragraph 40(8) provides as follows:

> '(8) On an application under sub-paragraph (6) or (7) the court may not make an order in relation to apparatus if an application under paragraph 20(3) has been made in relation to the apparatus and has not been determined.'

18.53 It is inherent in para 40(8) that there are some situations in which an application under Part 4 for fresh Code rights may coincide with a removal application under Part 6. Paragraph 40(8) thus 'regulates the sequence in which the tribunal must determine the removal application and any pending application under paragraph 20 to grant new rights'.[48]

18.54 However, this does not mean that *whenever* a landowner is proceeding under Part 6, an operator will always have the ability to make an application for fresh Code rights under Part 4. Paragraph 40(8) does not create a freestanding right on the part of an operator to do so. As the Deputy President said in *Gravesham* at [36]:

> 'The direction that, on a removal application, the tribunal may not make an order in relation to apparatus if an application under paragraph 20(3) has been made in relation to the apparatus and has not been determined does not in itself authorise the making of an application under Part 4. The right to make such an application must be found elsewhere.'

18.55 Situations in which a Part 4 application for fresh Code rights might properly coincide with a landowner's Part 6 removal application include the following:[49]

- where a para 26 interim Code agreement has come to an end in accordance with its terms;
- where an operator occupies as a former tenant, its tenancy having been 'contracted out' of the security of tenure provisions of the 1954 Act under section 38A of that Act, and that tenancy having come to an end before the Code came into force;
- where an operator has installed ECA on land believing it had the right to do so when in fact it did not. In *Crawley*,[50] the Tribunal noted that one way in which the Old Code was unsatisfactory was that it was difficult for landowners

47 At [24].
48 See *Gravesham* at [40].
49 See *Gravesham* at [40] and [41].
50 Per Judge Cooke at [8].

to achieve the removal of apparatus which should never have been present, for example where was never any right for it to be installed. Part 6 of the Code ameliorates this position.

Finding out whether apparatus is on land pursuant to a Code right

18.56 A landowner or occupier may be uncertain about whether Code rights are asserted in respect of apparatus that is present, about whether an operator retains any apparatus at the land at all, or about which apparatus belongs to which operator.

18.57 Paragraph 39 contains a procedure whereby a notice can be served in order to seek to elicit such information.

Notices under para 39(1) – landowners

18.58 A notice under para 39(1) can only be served by a 'landowner'. For the purposes of the Code, a 'landowner' is a 'person with an interest in land'.[51]

18.59 Such a notice requires an operator to disclose whether the operator:

- owns ECA on, under, or over land in which the landowner has an interest (para 39(1)(a)); and/or
- uses ECA on, under, or over land in which the landowner has an interest for the purposes of the operator's network (also para 39(1)(a)); and/or
- has the benefit of a Code right entitling the operator to keep ECA on, under, or over land in which the landowner has an interest (para 39(1)(b)).

Notices under para 39(2) – neighbouring landowners/occupiers

18.60 A notice under para 39(2) can only be served by a 'landowner' or 'occupier' of neighbouring land. For the purposes of the Code, a 'landowner' is a 'person with an interest in land'.[52] The occupier is ordinarily 'the occupier of the land for the time being'.[53] However, para 105 does make particular provision for certain specific situations ,[54] some of which may well be relevant to a notice under para 39(2).

18.61 A para 39(2) notice requires an operator to disclose whether the operator:

- owns ECA on, under, or over land that forms[55] a means of access to the neighbouring land occupied by the person serving, or in which the person serving has an interest (para 39(2)(a)); and/or

51 This definition is contained within para 37(1) and applied to the Code as a whole by para 108(1).
52 This definition is contained within para 37(1) and applied to the Code as a whole by para 108(1).
53 Para 105(1).
54 For example, by virtue of para 105(2), in respect of a footpath or bridleway which crosses agricultural land, the occupier is the occupier of the agricultural land.
55 Or *would* form, if it were not for the ECA.

- uses ECA on, under, or over land that forms[56] a means of access to the neighbouring land occupied by the person serving, or in which the person serving has an interest for the purposes of the operator's network (also para 39(2)(a)); and/or
- has the benefit of a Code right entitling the operator to keep ECA on, under, or over land that forms[57] a means of access to the neighbouring land occupied by the person serving or in which the person serving has an interest (para 39(2)(b)).

18.62 If the operator responds to a para 39 notice, the content of that response may well inform the landowner's approach in seeking to achieve its objectives. Such objectives may include obtaining vacant possession of the land. For example, if no Code rights are asserted, but ECA is present, a landowner may decide to seek removal by serving a para 40 notice. However, if Code rights are asserted, the landowner may decide to serve a notice under para 31 to bring any extant agreement to an end, without prejudice to any contention it may wish to make that there are no Code rights. Although a para 39 notice may ask whether the operator has the benefit of any Code rights, a response to such a notice cannot, of course, be determinative of that question. A response merely sets out the operator's position on the point.

Mandatory use of standard form for para 39 notices

18.63 Paragraph 39(3) provides that notices served under para 39 must comply with the requirements of para 89. These requirements relate to the mandatory use of OFCOM's prescribed forms and are discussed in Chapter 20.

Costs consequences in connection with para 39

18.64 If an operator does not, within three months of service of a para 39(1) or (2) notice, give a notice to the landowner or occupier that discloses the information sought (and complies with para 88[58]), it may suffer certain prescribed costs consequences. In such a case, where the landowner or occupier takes action under para 40 to enforce the removal of the apparatus and it is established that the operator owns apparatus (or uses it for its network) and has the benefit of a Code right in respect of it, the operator must bear the costs of any action taken to enforce the removal.59

56 Or *would* form, if it were not for the ECA.

57 Or *would* form, if it were not for the ECA.

58 Para 88 contains a number of requirements which an operator must satisfy when giving a notice under the Code. These pertain to the content of the notice, and the use of prescribed forms. By para 88(3), the failure to comply with para 88 renders a notice invalid.

59 By para 39(4) and (5) of the Code.

19

Obtaining vacant possession: the flow chart

Introduction

19.01 Below is a flow chart that attempts to show what will need to be done in order to terminate the rights of an operator to keep ECA installed and then to secure removal of the ECA in a wide variety of situations. The idea is to start at '1.' below and follow the instructions as you go.

19.02 If the answer to any question is uncertain, it may be that the more detailed commentary in other parts of this book will be of some assistance in resolving that lack of clarity. Where there are multiple potential 'right answers', depending on what facts are found, or what interpretation[1] is placed on those facts, consider serving multiple notices without prejudice to each other. In any event, the below is intended as a simple guide, rather than a substitute for full and detailed legal advice, especially where the facts are complex, unusual, or uncertain.

19.03 It is important that notices are served in the appropriate form, contain the requisite information, are served at the right time and containing the right dates, are given by and to the right persons, and are served in the correct manner. These issues are dealt with in more detail in Chapter 20.

Assumptions on which the flow chart proceeds

19.04 A number of assumptions are made. Where a written agreement is involved, it is assumed that that agreement satisfies the Old Code or New Code (depending on when it was entered into) as regards: (i) the identity[2] of the parties entering into the agreement, and (ii) the formalities and mandatory contents[3] of the agreement. It is also assumed that any agreement binds the person who wishes to obtain vacant possession. It is further assumed that where a lease is involved, the primary purpose of the lease

1 The most common uncertainties are: (i) whether an Old Code written agreement is a lease or a licence; and (ii) what type of agreement, if any, is to be inferred from the parties' conduct where no written agreement existed, or any written agreement has expired. These issues are addressed within Chapter 16.

2 Code rights can only be conferred on an 'operator'. Accordingly, if the person granted the rights in an agreement is not an operator, any agreement will still need to terminated, but nothing needs to be done *under the Code* in order to terminate it, and there can of course be no security of tenure under s 30(2) of the Code. Similarly, the rights at para 2 of the Old Code are those held by operators, and so no agreement can be a subsisting agreement for the purposes of the Transitional Provisions if there was never any operator involved.

3 See para 11 of the New Code, and para 2 of the Old Code.

was to grant Code rights. Finally, it is assumed that no special regime applies, such as those for street works rights, transport land rights, or tidal water rights.

Flow chart

19.05

1. Has there ever been any written[4] agreement for the installation of the ECA?

   If yes, go to 2.

   If no, go to 12.

2. Did the agreement term end before 28 December 2017?

   If yes, go to 3.

   If no, go to 6.

3. Was it a lease?

   If yes, go to 4.

   If no, go to 11.

4. Was it a lease to which Part II of the 1954 Act applied?[5]

   If yes, go to 5.

   If no, go to 11.

5. Was it 'contracted out'?[6]

   If yes, go to 11.

   If no, go to **Conclusion B below.**

6. Was the agreement in force before 28 December 2017?

   If yes, go to 7.

   If no, go to 16.

7. Was it a lease?

   If yes, go to 8.

   If no, go to 10.

8. Was it a lease to which Part II of the 1954 Act applied?[7]

---

4 Note that under para 2 of the Old Code what was required was 'The agreement in writing of the occupier for the time being', whereas under para 9 of the New Code what is required is 'an agreement' between occupier and operator. Under the New Code, a written permission of a landowner for ECA to be installed by an operator will not constitute a written agreement satisfying para 11(1) if it is not signed on behalf of the operator, whereas such a written document may well have constituted the valid agreement of the occupier for the purposes of para 2 of the Old Code.

5 This involves consideration of questions like whether the tenant was in occupation for the purposes of its business.

6 Ie, were the security of tenure provisions at ss 24 to 28 of the 1954 Act properly excluded, by an agreement under s 38A of the 1954 Act or under the predecessor legislation.

7 This involves consideration of questions like whether the tenant was in occupation for the purposes of its business.

If yes, go to 9.

If no, go to 10.

9. Was it 'contracted out'?[8]

If yes, go to 10.

If no, **go to Conclusion B below**.

10. Part 5 of the New Code applies to this 'subsisting agreement', with the modifications made by para 7 of the Transitional Provisions.[9] **Go to Conclusion A below**, but bear in mind that those modifications apply to Part 5 in this particular case.

11. The written agreement ended before the Code came into force and was not statutorily continued. Whether any further agreement has impliedly arisen due to the conduct of the parties, and if so what kind of agreement, will be a question to determine on the facts as found. Go to 13.

12. As there is no written agreement, it follows that there is either an express oral agreement, an agreement that has arisen impliedly by the conduct of the parties, or no agreement at all. Whether any unwritten agreement has arisen due to the conduct of the parties, and if so what kind, will be a question to determine on the facts as found. For the purposes of terminating an agreement, it will make no difference whether it was an express oral agreement, or an implied agreement: each is an unwritten agreement. Go to 13.

13. If there is an unwritten periodic tenancy, go to 14. If there is an unwritten contractual licence or tenancy at will, **go to Conclusion C2 below**. If no agreement now exists, **go to Conclusion C3 below**.

14. Did the unwritten periodic tenancy come into being before 28 December 2017?

If yes, **go to Conclusion C1 below**.

If no, go to 15.

15. It would appear that Part II of the 1954 Act cannot apply to this periodic tenancy because of s. 43(4) of the 1954 Act, despite the fact that Part 5 of the Code does not apply to it either, because no Code rights can be granted by an unwritten agreement. **Go to Conclusion C2 below**.

16. Was the agreement imposed judicially under either para 26 or 27 of the Code?

If yes, go to 17.

If no, go to **Conclusion A.**

17. Was the agreement imposed judicially under para 26 of the Code?

If yes, go to 18.

If no, go to 19.

---

8 Ie, were the security of tenure provisions at ss 24 to 28 of the 1954 Act properly excluded, by an agreement under s 38A of the 1954 Act or under the predecessor legislation.

9 Ie, Sch 2 to the Digital Economy Act 2017.

18. The agreement is an agreement imposed under para 26 of the Code. The agreement and/or the Order imposing it specifies when the agreement will end. The agreement will end at that time, and will not be continued statutorily under para 30, because of para 30(3). Once the agreement is over, the operator has no Code rights, and there is a right to require removal under para 37(3)(a).

19. The agreement is an agreement imposed under para 27 of the Code. Such an agreement is imposed for the objective of maintaining the network until a para 20 application is determined. Accordingly, the agreement or the Order imposing it will have made provision for how long it is to last. The agreement will end at that time, and will not be continued statutorily under para 30, because of para 30(3). Once the agreement is over, the operator has no Code rights. One would imagine that there is a right to require removal, whether under para 37 or para 41. However, the precise basis for the right to require removal does not appear to be spelt out in the Code.

Conclusion A:

19.06 It will be necessary to serve a notice under para 31 of the Code in order to terminate this agreement,[10] stating reliance on a ground contained in para 31(4). If the operator does not both serve a counter-notice and make an application to the tribunal under para 32(1) of the Code, the agreement will come to an end, and there will be a right to require removal under para 37(3)(b).

19.07 If the operator makes a valid application to the tribunal under para 32(1)(b), and the landlord proves a para 31(4) ground stated in its para 31 notice, the tribunal has to order the termination of the agreement under para 32(4). Once the agreement has come to an end by virtue of that Order, there will be a right to require removal under para 37(3)(c). Go to **Right to Require Removal**, below.

Conclusion B

19.08 The lease needs to be terminated under the 1954 Act. The landlord can serve a notice under section 25 of the 1954 Act in the prescribed form specifying a ground for termination of the tenancy contained in section 30(1) of the 1954 Act. If the notice expires without the tenant applying for a new tenancy, the tenancy will expire. If the tenant applies for a new tenancy, the landlord will have to prove its section 30(1) ground for termination. If it does so, the tenancy will come to an end under section 64 of the 1954 Act. Section 24(2) and (3) of the 1954 Act also preserve certain other specific means of terminating tenancies. Once the lease has been terminated, if the ECA remains in situ, the landlord has a right to require removal under para 37(3)(d) of the Code. Go to **Right to Require Removal**, below.

Conclusion C1

19.09 If a periodic tenancy arose (for example, due to the payment and acceptance of money), that tenancy cannot have been contracted out of the 1954 Act. Assuming

10 Unless this unusual situation has come about: the tribunal has modified the agreement under para 34(4) or (6) in such a way as to bring to an end the Code right under which the ECA is being kept at the land. If that is the position, there is a right to require removal of that ECA under para 37(3)(c).

it is considered not to be a subsisting agreement because it is not written,[11] then the operator has no Code rights, but the tenancy will need to be terminated in accordance with section 25 of the 1954 Act (**go to Conclusion B above**). Even if it is a subsisting agreement because it is considered to be in writing, then by para 6(2) of the Transitional Provisions,[12] Part 5 of the Code does not apply anyway, and so the tenancy will need to be terminated in accordance with section 25 of the 1954 Act (**go to Conclusion B above**).

Conclusion C2

19.10 If the agreement is not in writing, the operator has no Code rights. The agreement can be terminated in accordance with its own contractual terms under common law. Once it has been terminated, there is a right to require removal under para 37(2) because the landowner has not been bound by any Code right since the Code came into force. Go to **Right to Require Removal**, below.

Conclusion C3

19.11 If no contractual agreement can be inferred, such that the operator's right to occupy the land is entirely precarious or immediately terminable, the landlord should serve a notice terminating any possible right that may have arisen, for the avoidance of doubt. It is prudent to give reasonable notice. There is a right to require removal under para 37(2) because the landowner has not been bound by any Code right since the Code came into force. Go to **Right to Require Removal**, below.

Right to require removal

19.12 Once there is a right to require removal of the ECA, unless the operator agrees to remove the ECA, the landowner must follow the provisions of Part 6 in order to achieve vacant possession. This will mean serving a notice under para 40 and, if necessary, making an application for a para 44(1) removal Order, and potentially for other ancillary or related orders described in para 44. For more detail on Part 6, see Chapter 18 'Last chance saloon'.

19.13 It is worth bearing in mind that in some situations following a right to removal arising in favour of a landowner, an operator may be able at that stage to serve a Code notice and seek (new) Code rights. Whether it can do so in any given case will depend on a proper interpretation[13] of the Code, and also on the question of whether it would be an abuse of process in the circumstances to do so. Certainly, in a case where the operator never had any Code rights or had rights under the Old Code that expired without any right to renew having arisen, the operator will be able to serve a notice under para 20 (or para 26, and in most cases para 27) and seek Code rights by application if necessary. A landowner will then need to decide whether to oppose any such application and, if so, on what grounds. Legal advice should be sought.

---

11 See the discussion in Chapter 16 on this point.

12 Ie, Sch 2 to the Digital Economy Act 2017.

13 See the Upper Tribunal appeal decision in *Gravesham*, in which it was held that an operator whose 1954 Act lease renewal claim had been dismissed (albeit on a procedural basis rather than following trial) was not entitled to a second opportunity to renew its Code rights by making a Code application.

20

Notices under the Code

By whom and to whom must a notice be given?

20.01 This section sets out a brief description of who must serve on whom, in respect of the most common notices served under the Code.

20.02 **Paragraph 20(2) notice:** this is a notice given by an operator to a 'relevant person' seeking the conferral of Code rights (or requiring the relevant person otherwise to be bound by Code rights). A relevant person is simply a person who is required by an operator to confer the rights or otherwise be bound.

20.03 Accordingly, the notice cannot found a valid Reference if it is given to a person who cannot confer any rights which the notice seeks to be conferred. In this context, it must be remembered that para 9 provides that Code rights can only be conferred by an agreement between an operator and the occupier of land.[1]

20.04 **Paragraph 20(3)(b) notice:** this is a notice given in writing by a relevant person to an operator stating that they do not agree to confer or otherwise be bound by the Code right sought under para 20. There is no obligation to serve such a notice – the only consequence is that the operator can apply to the tribunal as soon as this notice is given rather than having to wait for the 28 day period set out at para 20(3)(a).

20.05 **Paragraph 26(3):** Where an operator seeks an agreement 'on an interim basis',[2] it must give a notice 'which complies with paragraph 20(2)' to the person on whom it seeks for an agreement to be imposed. If the notice seeks the conferral of rights, it must be served on the 'occupier'.

20.06 **Paragraph 27(1):** Where a person has the 'right to require removal' of ECA under para 37, an operator may give that person a notice seeking temporary Code rights. Such a notice is required to be a notice under para 20(2).

20.07 **Paragraph 31(1) notice:** A site provider who is a party to a Code agreement may bring the agreement to an end by giving a notice to an operator who is a party to the Code agreement.

20.08 **Paragraph 32(1)(a) counter-notice:** Where a site provider gives a notice to an operator under para 31, the Code agreement will come to an end unless the operator gives a counter-notice under para 32(1)(a) to the site provider (and also

1 Subject to the gloss placed on the word 'occupier' by the Supreme Court in *Compton Beauchamp*, which requires the operator's actual occupation to be disregarded in certain circumstances.
2 See para 26(2) for a definition of the phrase 'on an interim basis'.

applies to the tribunal for an Order under para 34, within three months of giving the counter-notice).

20.09 Paragraph 33(1) notice: An operator or site provider who is a party to a Code agreement[3] may require the other party to the agreement to agree certain modifications to the agreement, or that it be replaced by a new agreement (see the options at para 33(1)(a) to (d)) by giving a notice under para 33(1).

20.10 Paragraph 39(1) notice: A landowner[4] may serve a notice under para 39(1) requiring an operator to disclose whether it owns or uses ECA on land in which the landowner has an interest, or whether it has the benefit of a Code right entitling it to keep ECA on such land.

20.11 Paragraph 39(2) notice: A landowner[5] of neighbouring land may serve a notice under para 39(2) requiring an operator to disclose whether it owns or uses ECA on land that forms a means of access to the neighbouring land, or whether it has the benefit of a Code right entitling it to keep ECA on such land.

20.12 Paragraph 39(4) notice: This provision provides for an operator give a notice to the landowner or occupier[6] who has sought information under either para 39(1) or (2), disclosing the information sought within three months. Failure to comply with this provision may lead to the costs consequences at para 39(5).

20.13 Paragraph 40(2) notice: Where a landowner or occupier[7] has a right to require removal of ECA under either para 37 or 38, it may give a notice under para 40(2) to the operator 'whose apparatus it is'. The notice is one which requires the operator to remove the apparatus and to restore the condition of the land to its prior state.

20.14 Paragraph 41(2) notice: Where a third party has a right to require removal of ECA under an enactment other than the Code, it may give a notice under para 41(2) to the operator whose apparatus it is. The notice is one which requires the operator to remove the apparatus and to restore the condition of the land to its prior state.

Difficulties in identifying the person on whom to serve

Which operator is in situ?

20.15 Where there is a difficulty in ascertaining whose ECA is present on land, or which operator is using ECA that is present on land, the ability to serve a notice under para 39 to seek such information may be of assistance.

3 Being a Code agreement by which a Code right is conferred by or otherwise binds the site provider.
4 By para 108, 'landowner' has the meaning provided for in para 37(1), namely 'A person with an interest in land'.
5 By para 108, 'landowner' has the meaning provided for in para 37(1), namely 'A person with an interest in land'.
6 Note the meaning of 'occupier' as provided for at para 105, and the extensive discussion of who is the 'occupier' especially when an operator is already in situ, in *Compton Beauchamp*.
7 Note the meaning of 'occupier' as provided for at para 105, and the extensive discussion of who is the 'occupier' especially when an operator is already in situ, in *Compton Beauchamp*.

Names of operators

20.16 Due to mergers, acquisitions, consolidation, and rebranding in the industry, the name of the operator that has a Code right may well have changed multiple times. Indeed, one should be wary of the possibility that more than one entity related to an operator has had the same name at different times. It is therefore highly desirable to check Companies House in order to verify whether: (i) an operator who is assumed not to have any Code or contractual rights is actually a renamed entity with such rights, or (ii) an entity that entered into an agreement a number of years ago still has the same name (and potentially also address for service).

Assignment of Code agreements

20.17 Where a Code agreement is a lease, it may well have been assigned, sometimes numerous times. It is worth considering whether a purported assignment took place validly in terms of formalities, and in terms of obtaining the landlord's consent, and what the consequences are.

20.18 Para 16 of the Code makes provision as to the assignment of Code agreements, including para 16(4) which provides that an assignee is bound by the terms of the agreement. Thus, even where a Code agreement is not a lease, it may be assigned. The validity of purported assignments of agreements under the Old Code, that took place before the New Code came into force, is a more complex question. If such agreements were leases, they could be assigned in the normal way. However, if such agreements were not leases, it would seem that the burden could not be assigned.[8]

Registration of Code agreements

20.19 Where a Code agreement is a lease and is required to be registered, para 14 provides that the provisions of the Code as to who is bound will have effect regardless of whether or not it is in fact registered. Although this provision does not create an exemption from the requirement to register, many Code agreements are not registered. This may be due to historical uncertainties as to whether a particular agreement is a lease or not. It may therefore be that the position on the face of any register is not definitive as to the extent of Code rights and the identity of the appropriate recipient of a notice.

Where the name and address of the 'occupier' or 'owner' is unknown

20.20 There are special procedures which may be followed where the name and address of the 'occupier' or the 'owner of an interest in land' cannot be found out after reasonable enquiries.[9] These are dealt with below in the section of service of notices.

8 See the *Burlington Gardens* case on this point, as referred to in Chapter 15.

9 These are set out at para 94(3) to (6).

Validity of Code notices

20.21 The content of Code notices is essentially prescribed in two different ways. First, there are general requirements set out at paras 88 and 89 for operators and non-operators respectively. These include the use of prescribed forms in certain cases. Second, the provisions of the Code that allow or require notices to be served themselves set out requirements as to the contents of particular notices. These requirements are examined in more detail below.

20.22 It is a common and instinctive reaction amongst many property lawyers to look to '*Mannai*' an unfortunately-worded notice in order to render it valid. That is, to interpret it in accordance with how a reasonable recipient would, in order to cure a literal defect on the face of the notice, such exercise given wide notoriety by the case of *Mannai Investment Co Ltd v Eagle Star Life Assurance Co Ltd*[10].

20.23 The principle of interpreting a notice how a reasonable recipient would is a sound one. However, one should remember that even in *Mannai* it was recognised that some requirements,[11] when spelled out clearly, would have to be complied with in order to produce a valid notice, even if the requirement was apparently arbitrary, and the intended meaning of the notice perfectly clear.

20.24 As will be seen in this chapter, the Code creates a number of apparently obligatory requirements as to the form and contents of notices. However, in *Central St Giles*[12] at [24], the Deputy President said that:

> 'The Tribunal is not attracted to excessively technical arguments about the form of Code notices where no question of jurisdiction is engaged.'

20.25 It is fair to say that the tribunal has been consistent in maintaining the disposition set out above. However, it is important to note that many questions as to the validity of Code notices *do* engage the question of jurisdiction, and also that where the Code makes express provision as to the automatic consequences of failure to comply with the requirements of a valid notice, it would appear that the tribunal does not have the discretion to reject those consequences.[13]

Validity of a notice: jurisdictional questions

20.26 Numerous notices under the Code have been invalid because there was no underlying right to serve the notice, and hence no jurisdiction could be conferred upon the tribunal. For example, pursuant to *Compton Beauchamp*, a notice served by an operator in situ that seeks to renew Code rights on different terms by the impermissible route of para 20, rather than seeking genuinely additional Code rights.

---

10 [1997] AC 749.

11 One thinks of Lord Hoffmann's famous example at p 776B: "If the clause had said that the notice had to be on blue paper, it would have been no good serving a notice on pink paper, however clear it might have been that the tenant wanted to terminate the lease."

12 *Cornerstone Telecommunications Infrastructure Ltd v Central Saint Giles General Partner Ltd* [2019] UKUT 183 (LC).

13 For example, paras 88(3) and 89(3) of the Code.

However, it is also worth considering notices that may be invalidated because of some defect in their contents, or in the timing of their service.

20.27 In *Gravesham*,[14] the Deputy President held that a notice under para 20 (and also seeking temporary rights under para 27) was invalid, for two reasons. The fundamental problem was that an operator was held not to be entitled to seek Code rights in order to remain on land when its claim for a 1954 Act renewal had been dismissed. Separately the notice itself was invalid because it was given at a time when the operator already had Code rights under a 1954 Act lease which had not yet expired. The lease was soon to come to an end by virtue of the effect of section 64 of the 1954 Act and the dismissal of the claim on procedural grounds. Thus, the operator was at risk of soon being required to remove its ECA via the Part 6 Code process. At first instance, the FTT held that as the operator was at risk in this way, it was entitled to serve a notice and seek Code rights under para 20.

On the first appeal to the UT from the FTT under the Code, the Deputy President held that being at risk of a Part 6 application was not sufficient to allow the operator to serve a para 20 (and para 27) notice. As regards para 27, it is spelt out in para 27(1)(c) that para 27 only applies where a person has a 'right to require removal' of ECA. Paragraph 37 sets out the specific circumstances in which one has a 'right to require removal', which are indicated by para 37(1) to be exhaustive ('if and only if…'). These circumstances include where a 1954 Act tenancy (to which Part 5 of the Code does not apply) has been terminated.[15] However, in *Gravesham*, the tenancy was still continuing when the notice was served. There was accordingly not (at that point) any right to require removal, and hence the notice could not be valid under para 27.

20.28 The Deputy President also held that the notice was invalid under para 20. The operator was barred from serving a valid para 20 notice whilst its tenancy was being continued by the 1954 Act. *Compton Beauchamp* had confirmed that an operator cannot make an application for an agreement containing Code rights that it already has (including Code rights under a subsisting agreement that is a 1954 Act tenancy). However, *Gravesham* confirms that during such a period, an operator is not even entitled to serve a notice that would be a necessary precursor to such an application.

Relationship between a party's notice and its case

Part 4 cases

20.29 A number of notices served by operators under Part 4 are required to give details of what they seek. For example, para 20(2)(a) requires the Code right and terms of the agreement sought to be set out. Paragraphs 26(3) and 27(1)(a) apply this requirement to interim and temporary rights situations.

20.30 The question arises as to the extent to which the operator serving the notice can change its case following such service.

20.31 There appears to be a distinction in the case law between 'Code rights' and 'terms', although where a notice is required to state both, the requirement in respect of

14 *Gravesham Borough Council v On Tower UK Limited* [2024] UKUT 151 (LC).
15 See para 37(3)(d).

each is not stated with a differing degree of force, or with a prescription as to differing consequences.

20.32 In *Keast*,[16] Judge Cooke considered that a Code right not stated in a notice could not be granted by a tribunal, presumably as a matter of jurisdiction:

> 'Obviously the Tribunal cannot impose upon the occupier of land any Code right that has not been sought in the paragraph 20 notice; that is perfectly clear from the terms of paragraph 20.'

20.33 No firm conclusion needed to be made as to the landowner's contention that a para 20 notice is invalidated when there is a more than *de miminis* difference between what was claimed in the tribunal, the notice was invalidated. However, it expressed a provisional view that this was doubtful.

20.34 The tribunal acknowledged that the parties' positions as to terms may change in practice:

> 'Negotiations with the occupier of the land will, almost invariably, have begun long before the paragraph 20 notice is drafted and there may well be changes of position on both sides in the course of negotiations.'

20.35 In the *Patricroft*[17] case, the FTT held that an inconsistency between proposed Heads of Terms annexed to para 20 notices and a draft agreement attached to, and sought by, a statement of case, is not a jurisdictional issue. Rather, it is a matter that is relevant at trial when considering what terms should be imposed. It was said that where sharing rights were not sought in the notice (a Code right in itself under para 3(1)(ca)), but were sought in the statement of case, that would open the way for arguments under the above principle in *Keast*, but would not invalidate the notice.[18]

20.36 Given that the tribunal is entitled to depart from the terms as sought by making 'modifications' to what was sought and must select terms that it considers appropriate (rather than being hamstrung by the precise terms sought), it would seem that whether a party can argue for drafting that differs from its notice is generally likely to be a matter of case management rather than jurisdiction.

20.37 Typically, there will be a 'travelling draft' process ordered whereby the parties can amend the terms that are sought, and of course, in a perfect world, this will yield agreement on some terms, or at least a narrowing of the dispute. It must therefore be the case as a matter of jurisdiction that there is no absolute bar on a party contending for different wording than that proposed in a notice.

20.38 However, where a party is in substance seeking to change its case markedly, the tribunal must surely be permitted to exercise case management powers so as to prevent it from doing so, if appropriate, or to apply costs consequences. For example, if a party starts by contending for one rent, and then argues for a considerably higher or lower rent, there may be consequences in respect of the evidence that the other

---

16 [2019] UKUT 116 (LC) at [27] onwards.

17 *On Tower UK Limited v AP Wireless II (UK) Limited* LC-2023-000852 (re *Patricroft* and five other properties), decision dated 2 September 2024.

18 *Patricroft* at [51]–[54].

party may wish to adduce, or even whether it wishes to oppose the Reference at all. Similarly, if a party has admitted that certain terms are appropriate, but has done so on the strength of a representation that an operator is offering an attractive rent, but then the operator seeks to argue for a lower rent, there may be scope for a submission that the respondent would suffer prejudice if the operator is allowed to revoke its pleaded rental offer.

Part 5 renewal cases

20.39 Part 5 also contains requirements for a party to a renewal to state in its notice what it is seeking. Paragraph 32(3) requires an operator's counter-notice to a site provider's para 31 termination notice to state one of three options as to what the operator wants (essentially: no termination, replacement terms, or replacement Code right). Similarly, para 33(1) allows either party seeking a renewal by notice to require the other party to agree to: (a) a modification of terms, (b) the deletion of a Code right, (c) the addition of a Code right, or (d) termination of the agreement and imposition of a new agreement. Paragraph 33(2)(c) requires details to be specified, in the notice, of the option that is selected.

20.40 A preliminary issue arose in *Stephenson*[19] as to whether an operator was entitled to ask the tribunal for a different form of renewal Order than that stated in its notice. Fancourt J[20] held that it was not, but that the tribunal nonetheless had jurisdiction to opt for any of the alternative forms of Order available under para 34.

Validity of notice: requirements as to contents

Requirements for notices served by operators

20.41 Paragraph 88(1) provides that a notice given under the Code by an operator must:

'(a) explain the effect of the notice,

(b) explain which provisions of this code are relevant to the notice, and

(c) explain the steps that may be taken by the recipient in respect of the notice.'

20.42 Paragraph 88(2) requires that where an operator gives a notice under the Code, the notice must be in the form prescribed by OFCOM, if such a form has been prescribed for the notice in question.[21] In practice, the prescribed form will be designed to take account of the above para 88(1) requirements, but strictly speaking, the requirements of paras 88(1) and (2) are discrete requirements.

20.43 The impact of a prescribed form omitting to deal with one of the matters dealt with at para 88(1), or dealing with it erroneously is not entirely clear, although this argument is one that has been raised in statements of case before the tribunals.

19 *EE Ltd and Hutchison 3G UK Ltd v Stephenson and AP Wireless II (UK) Ltd* [2021] UKUT 167 (LC).
20 Sitting as the President of the Upper Tribunal.
21 Para 88(2).

20.44 Where a statutory requirement is not complied with in the content of a notice, even if that requirement is expressed in ostensibly the most mandatory of terms, it does not follow that the notice is automatically invalid and of no effect.

20.45 In *R v Soneji and Another*,[22] the question arose as to the circumstances in which non-compliance with statutory requirements would cause invalidity. Lord Steyn at [23] said as follows:

> 'the emphasis ought to be on the consequences of non-compliance and posing the question whether parliament can fairly be taken to have intended total invalidity. That is how I would approach what is ultimately a question of statutory construction'.

20.46 There is therefore a lot of case law dealing with the consequences of non-compliance in the case of a plethora of different statutory provisions contravened in numerous different ways, both in the sphere of property notices and many others.

20.47 However, as Lord Steyn said at [15], it was 'necessary to have regard to the fact that Parliament ex hypothesi did not consider the point of the ultimate outcome'. By contrast, in the case of para 88 of the Code, Parliament *has* considered the ultimate outcome. The consequence of non-compliance is spelled out expressly. Para 88(3) states that:

> 'A notice which does not comply with this paragraph is not a valid notice for the purposes of this code.'

20.48 Thus, the case law addressing the proper consequences of various failures to comply with statutory provisions may simply be irrelevant to questions under para 88.

20.49 It is to be noted that it is any want of compliance with para 88 (and not merely the prescribed form requirement) that would render a notice invalid under para 88(3).

20.50 There are numerous examples in legislation of stipulations that require property notices to be in a prescribed form, or a form substantially to the same effect.[23] However, in paras 88 and 89, there is no such express leeway given.

20.51 In the context of what may be viewed as a draconian sanction for erring in the drafting of a notice, a tribunal may strive to find that the content of a notice did not in fact constitute a lack of compliance with para 88, especially where no prejudice was caused to the recipient. However, where it is held that a notice does not comply with para 88, there appears to be no discretion on the part of the tribunal to find that the lack of compliance can be cured or overlooked on the basis of a lack of prejudice, or on the basis of the tangential relevance of the subject matter of the error to the facts of the case.

---

22 [2006] 1 AC 340.

23 See, for example, reg 2(2) of The Landlord and Tenant Act 1954, Part 2 (Notices) Regulations 2004 in respect of notices under the 1954 Act.

20.52 Finally, it is worth noting that although para 88(3) says that a notice that does not comply with para 88 is invalid, that provision does not prevent a recipient from relying on the notice if that person chooses to do so.[24]

Requirements for notices served by non-operators

20.53 Where a person other than an operator gives a notice under the Code, there is a requirement that the notice be in the form prescribed by OFCOM, if such a form has been prescribed for the notice in question.[25] However, this requirement only applies to a notice given under paras 31(1), 33(1), 39(1) or 40(2).[26]

20.54 A notice that does not comply with the requirement to use any prescribed form in respect of the types of notice mentioned in the preceding paragraph is not a valid notice for the purposes of the Code.[27] However, the recipient operator may nonetheless rely on the notice if it chooses to do so.[28]

20.55 In respect of notices given under any provision other than those mentioned above, there are potential costs consequences for non-operators in failing to use the prescribed form. Where the following three criteria are satisfied, the non-operator's notice is valid, but it must bear the costs incurred by the operator of failing to use the prescribed form:

(i) where OFCOM has prescribed a form for a notice given by someone other than an operator;

(ii) the notice is given in response to a notice given by an operator; and

(iii) the operator has, in giving the notice, drawn the person's attention to the prescribed form.[29]

20.56 However, it is difficult to see these costs consequences arising with any great frequency.

Requirements as to the contents of particular notices

20.57 The content and form requirements for the notices most commonly served under the Code are as follows:

Paragraph 20(2) notice: There is a prescribed form for this notice. In addition, there are separate requirements set out within para 20. First, these notices are applicable where an operator requires a relevant person to confer a Code right on it or otherwise be bound by a Code right.[30] The content requirements in para 20 are as follows. The notice must:

24 Para 88(4).

25 Para 89(2).

26 Para 89(1). Where OFCOM has published a template form, it is good practice to use that form, even where it relates to a provision not mentioned in para 89(1). For example, there are published forms for notices given under para 16(5) by an assignor or assignee of a Code agreement.

27 Para 89(3).

28 Para 89(4).

29 Para 89(5) and (6).

30 Para 20(1).

(i) set out the Code right sought;[31]

(ii) set out 'the land to which it relates' (ie, to which the Code right relates);[32]

(iii) set out all other terms of the agreement that the operator seeks;[33]

(iv) state that the operator seeks the person's agreement to terms which are set out within the notice;[34] and

(v) contain information about the availability of alternative dispute resolution in the event that the operator and the relevant person are unable to reach agreement and explain the possible consequences of refusing to engage in alternative dispute resolution.

The last of the above requirements (relating to ADR) is created by para 20(2A), which was inserted on 7 November 2023 by section 69(2)(a) of the Product Security and Telecommunications Infrastructure 2022. In the *Patricroft*[35] case, notices were served before the ADR-related requirements relating to paragraph 20 came into force, but the References founded on those notices were commenced following the relevant legislative change. Judge Jackson held that the notices could properly found a Reference as they were valid when served.

Paragraph 20(3)(b) notice: There is no prescribed form for this notice. The notice must simply be in writing and convey that the giver of the notice does not agree to confer or otherwise be bound by the Code right sought under para 20.

Paragraph 26(3): There is a prescribed form for this notice. This notice must comply with para 20(2) and state that an agreement is sought on an interim basis.

Paragraph 27(1): There is a prescribed form for this notice. The Code requires the notice to be one under para 20(2), and convey that the notice requires the recipient to agree on a temporary basis in respect of a right which is to be exercisable in relation to ECA which is already installed.

Paragraph 31(1) notice: There is a prescribed form for this notice. The notice must:[36]

(i) comply with para 89 (including the requirement as to a prescribed form);

(ii) specify the date on which the site provider proposes the Code agreement should come to an end. The date must satisfy the requirements of para 31(3); and

(iii) state the ground on which the site provider proposes to bring the Code agreement to an end. The ground must be one of those stated at para 31(4).

---

31 Para 20(2)(a).

32 This requirement was inserted into para 20(2)(a) by s 3(3)(b)(4) of the Telecommunications Infrastructure (Leasehold Property) Act 2021 on 15 March 2021 for specified purposes and on 26 December 2022 for England and Wales insofar as not already in force. It would be a rare notice that failed to specify to some degree the land over which the Code right is sought. In any event, the OFCOM prescribed form of notice under para 20(2) includes a definition of the 'Land' over which Code rights are to be sought, and para 88(2) requires an operator to use a prescribed form where one has been published by OFCOM.

33 Para 20(2)(a).

34 Para 20(2)(b). In practice, the terms are usually set out in the form of an attached draft agreement.

35 *On Tower UK Limited v AP Wireless II (UK) Limited* LC-2023-000852 (re *Patricroft* and five other properties), decision dated 2 September 2024 at [66].

36 Para 31(2) to (4).

Paragraph 32(1)(a) counter-notice: There does not appear to be a prescribed form for this notice. The counter-notice must state[37] either:

(i) that the operator does not want the existing code agreement to come to an end;

(ii) that the operator wants the site provider to agree to confer or be otherwise bound by the existing Code right on new terms; or

(iii) that the operator wants the site provider to agree to confer or be otherwise bound by a new Code right in place of the existing Code right.

In addition, para 32(3A)[38] requires a para 32(1)(a) counter-notice to contain information about the availability of alternative dispute resolution in the event that the operator and the relevant person are unable to reach agreement, and explain the possible consequences of refusing to engage in alternative dispute resolution.

Paragraph 33(1) notice: There is a prescribed form for this notice. The notice must require the other party to agree to a change to the terms of an agreement whose contractual term has expired. The different types of change are set out at para 33(1)(a) to (d) and are in summary: (a) modified terms, (b) removal of a Code right, (c) additional Code right, or (d) termination and new agreement. The notice must:[39]

(i) comply with para 88 or 89 (depending on whether given by an operator or another person);

(ii) specify the day of the proposed change to the terms of the agreement (para 33(3) creates requirements as to when that day shall be); and

(iii) set out the details of the change that is proposed.

In addition, para 33(3A)[40] requires any para 33(1) notice that is given by an operator to contain information about the availability of alternative dispute resolution in the event that the operator and the relevant person are unable to reach agreement, and explain the possible consequences of refusing to engage in alternative dispute resolution.

Paragraph 39(1) notice: There is a prescribed form for this notice. The notice must comply with para 89.[41]

Paragraph 39(2) notice: There is a prescribed form for this notice. The notice must comply with para 89.[42]

37 Para 32(3).

38 This provision was inserted on 7 November 2023 by s 69(3)(a) of the Product Security and Telecommunications Infrastructure 2022. Accordingly, it would seem that this requirement would not render invalid a notice served prior to that date. See the reference to the *Patricroft* case above in respect of the same point under para 20 notices.

39 Para 33(2).

40 This provision was inserted on 7 November 2023 by s 69(4)(a) of the Product Security and Telecommunications Infrastructure 2022. Accordingly, it would seem that this requirement would not render invalid a notice served prior to that date. See the reference to the *Patricroft* case above in respect of the same point under para 20 notices.

41 Para 39(3).

42 Para 39(3).

Paragraph 39(4) notice: There is no prescribed form for this notice. The notice must comply with para 88,[43] and disclose the information sought in the preceding para 39(1) or 39(2) notice.

Paragraph 40(2) notice: There is a prescribed form for this notice. The notice must comply with para 89,[44] and specify the period during which the operator must complete the works.[45] Such period must be a reasonable one.[46]

Paragraph 41(2) notice: There is a prescribed form for this notice. The notice must comply with para 89,[47] and specify the period during which the operator must complete the works.[48] Such period must be a reasonable one.[49]

The prescribed forms

20.58 The principal requirements of paras 88 and 89 of the Code are those requiring the use of prescribed forms. Paragraph 90 requires OFCOM to prescribe the form of a notice to be given under each provision of the Code that 'requires' a notice to be given. It may be that where the service of a counter-notice is optional, OFCOM has concluded that it is not required to create a standard form. That would explain the lack of a prescribed form for a counter-notice under para 32 and for a response under para 39(4) for example.

20.59 OFCOM's website states that for the purpose of the prescribed form requirements in the Code it has prescribed 'template notices' which are set out on its website.[50] The template notices currently published on the OFCOM website are those which relate to the following provisions of the Code:

Paras 16(5), 17(6), 17A(6), 20(2), 26(3), 27(1), 27(C), 31(1), 33(1), 39(1), 39(2), 40(2), 41(2), 41(5), 43(5), 49(1), 50(2), 50(3), 51(2), 51(4), 51(7), 53(1), 53(2), 54(7), 67(1), 68(2), 71(2), 75(2), 78(1), 82(3), and 82(4).

20.60 The prescribed forms are published online in Word format and contain yellow highlighting where there are deletions that must or may be made, where there are insertions that may be made, or where there are alternatives from which one can choose. It might be wise to strike through some optional items rather than deleting them, as the latter approach may alter the numbering or lettering of a list.

20.61 Care should be taken over deleting parts of a prescribed notice, as that would run the risk that the notice would be found not to 'be in' the 'form' of the prescribed form.

43 Para 39(4)(a)(i).
44 Para 40(3)(a).
45 Para 40(3)(b).
46 Para 40(4).
47 Para 41(3)(a).
48 Para 41(3)(b).
49 Para 41(4).
50 https://www.ofcom.org.uk/phones-telecoms-and-internet/information-for-industry/policy/electronic-comm-code/notices.

Service of notices

20.62 It should be remembered that the Code is contained in Schedule 3A to the Communications Act 2003, and accordingly the service of notices under the Code is governed by section 394 of that Act, but subject to the provisions of para 91.[51]

20.63 Section 394(3) provides that notices may be given to the person in question:

> '(a) by delivering it to him;
>
> (b) by leaving it at his proper address; or
>
> (c) by sending it by post to him at that address.'

20.64 The above provision appears to be worded in a permissive rather than exhaustively prescriptive manner, and therefore may be thought not to exclude actual service by all other means.

20.65 In *Goulandris v Knight*[52], a similarly-structured provision at section 15(1) of the Party Wall etc. Act 1996 was held to be permissive and thus did not exclude service by email. In determining whether such a provision was intended merely to be permissive, it was noted that it was necessary to have regard to the totality of the relevant provisions and to construe them by reference to the regime which they were intended to facilitate, taking into account any contra-indications in the language of the section itself.

20.66 In the case of the Code, the suggestion that section 394(3) may well merely be permissive is subject to consideration of other express provisions placing constraints on service. Paragraph 91 places particular constraints on service by post (again, see below). Further, it may be that there is no carte blanche given to actual service by email, as section 395 (discussed below) makes express provision for situations where service may be effected by email.

Service by post

20.67 It is important to note that para 91(1) of the Code contains a further requirement as to the use of post:

> 'A notice given under this code must not be sent by post unless it is sent by a registered post service or by recorded delivery.'

20.68 The consequence of ignoring this restriction is not specified. As has been said elsewhere in this section as regards the content of a notice, where the consequences of contravening the requirement of a statute are not specified, the question is whether parliament can fairly be taken to have intended total invalidity, having regard to the consequences of non-compliance.[53]

51 Section 394(11) Communications Act 2003.
52 [2018] 1 WLR 3345.
53 *R v Soneji and Another* [2006] 1 AC 340 at [23].

20.69 It might be argued that as section 394(3) allows an agent to deliver a notice perfectly validly, it would seem unfortunate if proven and uncontroversial actual delivery by the postal service were to be deemed invalid. Having said that, plainly it is desirable to comply with the stipulation in para 91(1) and use the registered post service or recorded delivery where service by post is attempted.

Address for service

20.70 If a person has given the notice-giver an address for service under the Code, then that person's 'proper address' for service is that address.[54] Otherwise, the 'proper address' is the address given by section 394.[55] These rules apply for the purposes of both section 394 of the 2003 Act and section 7 of the Interpretation Act 1978 (as to which, see below in respect of deemed service).

20.71 The address given by section 394 is as follows:[56]

'(a) in the case of body corporate, the address of the registered or principal office of the body;

(b) in the case of a firm, unincorporated body or association, the address of the principal office of the partnership, body or association;

(c) in the case of a person to whom the notification or other document is given or sent in reliance on any of subsections (4) to (6), the proper address of the body corporate, firm or (as the case may be) other body or association in question; and

(d) in any other case, the last known address of the person in question.'

20.72 Section 394(4) provides that a notice may be given or sent to a body corporate by being given or sent to the secretary or clerk of that body. Section 394(5) provides that a notice may be given or sent to a firm by being given or sent to a partner in the firm, or a person having the control or management of the partnership business. Section 394(6) provides that a notice may be given or sent to an unincorporated body or association by being given or sent to a member of the governing body of the body or association.

20.73 Where a company is registered outside the UK, a firm carries on business outside the UK, or an unincorporated body or association has offices outside the UK, the term 'principal office' at section 394(7) includes references to its principal office within the UK (if any).[57]

Service by email

20.74 Where service is effected electronically (including by email), it has effect for the purposes of the Code, but only if the requirements of section 395 of the 2003 Act

54 Para 91(2).
55 Para 91(2).
56 Specifically, s 394(7).
57 Section 394(8).

are met.[58] Those include (where the recipient is a person other than OFCOM) that the recipient or person on whose behalf the recipient receives the notice has indicated to the notice-giver the recipient's willingness to receive notice 'in the form and manner used'.[59] Further requirements as to exactly how an indication of such willingness is given are set out at section 394(6).

Deemed service

20.75 Section 7 of the Interpretation Act 1978 makes provision as to deemed service in respect of posting a notice:

> 'Where an Act authorises or requires any document to be served by post (whether the expression 'serve' or the expression 'give' or 'send' or any other expression is used) then, unless the contrary intention appears, the service is deemed to be effected by properly addressing, pre-paying and posting a letter containing the document and, unless the contrary is proved, to have been effected at the time at which the letter would be delivered in the ordinary course of post.'

20.76 The above deeming provision only applies where service by post is authorised by statute. One would therefore think that, in relation to the Code, the deeming provision only applies in respect of posting where the method used is a registered post service or recorded delivery, as no other method of posting is authorised.[60]

Unknown occupier

20.77 Where it is not practicable to find out, after reasonable enquiries, the name and address of a person who is the occupier of land, a notice may be given to the occupier:[61]

(i) by addressing it to a person by the description of 'occupier' of the land, and describing the land; and

(ii) by delivering it to a person who is on the land, or if there is no person on the land to whom it can be delivered, by affixing it (or a copy of it) to a conspicuous object on the land.

Unknown owner of an interest in land

20.78 Where it is not practicable to find out, after reasonable enquiries, the name and address of a person who is the owner of an interest in land, a notice may be given to the owner:[62]

(i) by addressing it to a person by the description of 'owner' of the interest, and describing the interest and the land; and

58 Section 394(2).
59 Section 394(5).
60 See para 91(1).
61 See paras 91(3) and (4).
62 See paras 91(5) and (6).

(ii) by delivering it to a person who is on the land, or if there is no person on the land to whom it can be delivered, by affixing it (or a copy of it) to a conspicuous object on the land.

Power to abridge notice period

20.79 Where an operator seeks an Order under para 26 (interim rights cases), or para 27 (temporary rights cases), it may abridge the time for service of the relevant notice in certain specific circumstances.

20.80 Paragraphs 26(5) and 27(5), in relation to interim rights cases and temporary rights cases respectively, both state as follows:

> 'The court may make an order under this paragraph even though the period mentioned in paragraph 20(3)(a) has not elapsed (and paragraph 20(3)(b) does not apply) if the court thinks that the order should be made as a matter of urgency.'

20.81 For completeness, para 20(3)(b) applies where the recipient of the notice gives notice in writing to the operator that it does not agree to confer the right (or otherwise be bound by it, as the case may be).

20.82 Strictly speaking, para 20(3)(a) creates a 28-day notice period, which, at least on a literal reading, appears to prevent an *application* to the tribunal for an Order. However, the para 26(5)/para 27(5) abridgement of time provision is not couched in terms of enabling the tribunal to allow an *application* to be made early. Rather, it allows the tribunal to make an *Order* during the 28-day period. Necessarily the application will have been made within the 28-day period. But consider a situation where the notice is given, and the application is made *within* the 28-day period in contravention of para 20(3)(a), but the hearing is *after* the 28-day period has expired. In such a case, a tribunal that might wish to make an Order pursuant to the application would not fall within the literal words of para 26(5) or para 27(5) – it would not be making an Order at a time when the 28-day period has not elapsed. Yet there was still a defect in the notice.

20.83 One would imagine that one of two solutions may be adopted:

(i) The tribunal may choose to interpret paras 26(5) and 27(5) as conferring on the tribunal to make an order notwithstanding that the para 20(3)(a) period has not elapsed or had not elapsed when the application was made. After all, the clear purpose of the provision is to allow an Order to be made on shorter notice than stipulated at para 20(3)(a), and the respondent surely suffers less prejudice if the hearing is after the 28-day period rather than during it; or

(ii) Alternatively, the tribunal may instead prefer to interpret para 20(3)(a) such that a premature application is not automatically outside of its jurisdiction. After all, although para 20(3) does purport to set out the circumstances in which an operator is permitted to make an application, it does not spell out the consequences of a want of compliance with all of the features of those circumstances. This latter solution might not be considered ideal for two reasons:

(a) paras 26(5) and 27(5) allow abridgement only in cases of urgency. If there is a general discretion on the part of the tribunal to allow short notice, this may be seen as rendering paras 26(5) and 27(5) futile. It might also be seen as extending the discretion beyond the circumstances in which Parliament has indicated there should be one; and

(b) paras 26(5) and 27(5) allow abridgment of time in para 26 and 27 cases only, and not under para 20. A general discretion on the part of the tribunal to allow short notice under para 20 would apply to a broader array of cases, including those which (unlike paras 26 and 27) confer automatic security of tenure. This might seem odd where Parliament has chosen not to include a similar provision to paras 26(5) and 27(5) within para 20 itself.

When might a tribunal allow short service under para 26(5) or 27(5)?

20.84 The reference in paras 26(5) and 27(5) to the notice period not having elapsed surely implies that the notice period has started. Thus, it is pre-supposed that a notice has been served. This provision presumably does not give the tribunal the power to waive the requirement for a notice altogether. This conclusion would certainly chime with the absolutist 'if (and only if)' formulation in para 26(3), which appears to preclude the tribunal from making an Order where no notice has been served.

20.85 The notice requirement is clearly intended for the benefit of the recipient. This is made clear by the provision at para 20(3)(b), which allows a recipient to give notice refusing to grant Code rights, thus allowing an *immediate* application to the tribunal by the operator.

20.86 In all cases where the tribunal agrees to shorten the time for service, it can be expected to have careful regard to whether any real prejudice has been caused to the respondent. This is in effect a compulsory acquisition power, and although there is no security of tenure[63] under para 26 or para 27, there is a shortened time for a respondent to produce evidence, and a reduced burden of proof[64] on the operator when compared with a para 20 case. Although 'urgency' is a necessary criterion for proceeding under para 26(5) or 27(5), the use of the word 'may', coupled with the fact that the tribunal would be granting an indulgence to a party, appears to indicate that there remains a discretion even where there is urgency. Or, to put it another way, there may be some 'urgency' but in view of prejudice to the landowner, it might not think that an Order 'should be made' (see paras 26(5) and 27(5)).

20.87 There have not been many occasions on which the tribunals have had to determine a request to abridge time for service. However, in *EE v Aviva Investors (and others)*,[65] the operators had sought an abridgement of time in seeking a further interim Code agreement, asserting urgency arising from the expiration of an initial interim Code agreement. Submissions were made as to costs which criticised the operators as to their conduct, including their application for the abridgement of time. In giving an oral judgment as to costs, Judge Cooke found that it had not been urgent to bring the Reference before the ordinary notice period had expired. This was because it was clear that nobody was seeking removal of the ECA at the end of the first interim Code agreement, as no para 40 notice had been served.

63 Because of para 30(3).
64 Under para 26(3)(b).
65 Case No. LC-2023-89, heard in the Upper Tribunal.

20.88 Possible examples of situations where an operator might seek an abridgement under para 26(5) might include the following:

(i) Where there is a particular event that is about to occur, for which it is important that communications services are provided, and the operator needs to get onto the land quickly in order to provide those services.

(ii) Where an operator is already on the land but is in danger of having its ECA removed from the land pursuant to the Part 6 process. If a hearing has been listed to deal with an application by a landowner for a removal Order, no removal Order can be made under para 40(8) until any para 20 application has been determined. A tribunal may consider that it should, on the facts, abridge time for service of a para 20 notice in order to allow the application to be heard. Such a proposed course of action would in many cases draw forceful submissions from a landowner as to the vindication of its 'right' to require removal. It may be submitted that para 40(8), which applies where a para 20(3) application 'has been made', only applies where an application has been validly made, having given the notice as required in the Code.

(iii) Where an operator is already on the land, but it is urgent for some reason that an agreement is imposed to regularise the relationship between the parties (perhaps because of a particular term that an operator is seeking to have imposed, such as granting rights of access where access has been denied).

(iv) Query whether a tribunal might be prepared to find that an Order should be made 'as a matter of urgency' where it is preferable to make the Order rather than requiring a new application, so as to save time and costs. Whilst it might be tempting to take this course, the mere fact that no prejudice is caused to the landowner by an application having been made slightly early does not mean that there is any 'urgency', as distinct from convenience or proportionality of costs.

Service of multiple notices

20.89 Where there is uncertainty as to whether a Code agreement is a lease or not, and/or whether it is governed by the 1954 Act or not, it is open to a landowner to serve multiple notices on different hypothetical premises as to the status of the agreement. Such notices should be served with a covering letter making clear that the notice in question is served without prejudice to any other notices that may have been served in respect of the land/the ECA.

Stale notices?

20.90 The Code creates various different minimum periods after the service of a notice, which must expire before the serving party may make an application to the tribunal. However, there is no *maximum* period stated. The question that arises is whether a notice can ever become 'stale' such that the serving party can no longer rely on it.

20.91 The only substantive consideration of an argument that a notice is 'stale' has come in the *Patricroft*[66] case. Judge Jackson in the FTT noted that para 20(3) requires

66 *On Tower UK Limited v AP Wireless II (UK) Limited* LC-2023-000852 (re *Patricroft* and five other properties), decision dated 2 September 2024, at [45]–[50].

a claimant to wait for only 28 days before making a tribunal application and referred to the six-month time limit[67] for determining some Code References. He considered that 'a delay of nearly 4 years in issuing a reference would, absent special circumstances, inexorably lead to a strike out', for abuse of process. However, on the particular facts of the case, and having regard to the special relationship between the parties (who have litigated numerous recent matters under the Code), it was considered that exceptional circumstances did exist. He was persuaded that the context in the particular case was 'lengthy, difficult and ongoing commercial negotiations across a large number of sites between business competitors'. The notices were therefore held to be valid. However, following this decision, it seems that the FTT will be prepared to accept that, in an appropriate case, reliance on an excessively 'stale' notice constitutes an abuse of process.

---

67 Under reg 3(2) of the Electronic Communications and Wireless Telegraphy Regulations 2011.

21

Procedure and practice

Commencing a reference: jurisdiction

21.01 The functions conferred by the Code on 'the court' are exercisable not only by the county court, but also by the FTT and the UT,[1] and any provision of the Code that confers a function on the court is to be read as if the reference to the court included reference to those tribunals.[2]

21.02 For the first few years of litigation under the Code, there was a requirement for 'Relevant proceedings' to be commenced in the UT.[3] Such proceedings included those under Parts 4, 5, 6, 12, or 13 of the Code, or under para 53 of the Code,[4] ie, the large majority of References under the Code.

21.03 Accordingly, the jurisdiction of the FTT which was created in respect of 'relevant proceedings' in practice could only be exercised in connection with relevant proceedings that had been transferred to the FTT by the UT.[5]

21.04 By contrast, 'Part 4A proceedings' had to (and still have to) be commenced in the FTT.[6] These are proceedings under Part 4A of the Code, and relate to Code rights in respect of land connected to leased premises, where there are unresponsive occupiers. Such proceedings are expected to be vanishingly rare.

21.05 However, from 6 April 2024, the requirement to bring relevant proceedings in the UT was removed,[7] with the expectation now very much that Code matters will be commenced in the FTT. However, for reasons that are not entirely clear, the former requirement to issue in the UT was not replaced with any requirement to commence in the FTT. As a consequence, it would seem that bringing code applications in the county court would be procedurally regular, whether by accident or design.

21.06 Within the Tribunal system, however, References should now be commenced within the Property Chamber of the FTT, and not in the UT. With effect from 6 April 2024, the First-tier Tribunal and Upper Tribunal (Chambers) Order 2010, which sets out the 'functions' of the different tribunals and their chambers, was amended. As from

1 Reg 3(1)(aa) of the Electronic Communications Code (Jurisdiction) Regulations 2017.
2 Reg 3(3) of the Electronic Communications Code (Jurisdiction) Regulations 2017.
3 By reg 4(1)(a) of the Electronic Communications Code (Jurisdiction) Regulations 2017 as it then stood.
4 By reg 2(1) of the Electronic Communications Code (Jurisdiction) Regulations 2017.
5 By reg 3(2)(a) of the Electronic Communications Code (Jurisdiction) Regulations 2017.
6 By reg 4(2) of the Electronic Communications Code (Jurisdiction) Regulations 2017, with effect from 26 December 2022.
7 By reg 2(3)(a) of the Electronic Communications Code (Jurisdiction) (Amendment) Regulations 2023, amending reg 4 of the Electronic Communications Code (Jurisdiction) Regulations 2017.

that date, proceedings under the Code became a 'function' of the Property Chamber of the FTT.[8] At the same time, legislative amendments were made which had the effect that first-instance Code matters only constitute a 'function' of the Lands Chamber of the UT where they have been transferred from the FTT.[9]

21.07 Accordingly, Code applications will be brought as References in the Property Chamber of the FTT. The UT has communicated this clearly to stakeholders, and in view of the April 2024 amendments to the 2010 Order, it was not considered necessary to proceed with a potential Practice Direction setting out the intended future practice.

Transfer to the FTT (previous practice)

21.08 From 1 June 2021, during the period when Code references had to be commenced in the UT, suitable cases started to be transferred from the UT to the FTT for case management and hearing. The first cases considered appropriate for such transfer were redevelopment cases and smaller cases affecting individual householders, but this subsequently increased to include a far greater range of References. In 2022, 36 of 171 References (ie 21%) were transferred to the FTT. In 2023 that figure rose to 105 of 222 (ie 47%), and in 2023 that figure had reached a majority.

21.09 The latest iteration of the Upper Tribunal (Lands Chamber) Practice Directions is that dated 2 January 2024. Paragraph 15.2 of the Practice Directions provides that:

> 'Code references commenced in the Tribunal will usually be transferred for case management and hearing to the First-tier Tribunal (Property Chamber), which has concurrent jurisdiction.'[10]

21.10 Such transfer typically occurred at the point at which a Reference was issued. As the majority of References are issued by operators rather than site providers, this often meant that the matter was transferred to the FTT before the site provider was aware that a reference had been issued. The UT then sent its transfer Order to the respondent, typically setting a deadline for the filing of a statement of case by the respondent. A case management hearing in the FTT typically followed, with the parties encouraged and/or ordered to seek to agree directions in advance.

21.11 Where the parties to a Reference agreed that a new or important point of principle was likely to be raised, a request could be made for the UT to retain the Reference rather than transferring it to the FTT.

8 Art. 2(2) of the First-tier Tribunal and Upper Tribunal (Chambers) (Amendment) Order 2024 inserted art. 5A(j) into the First-tier Tribunal and Upper Tribunal (Chambers) Order 2010, such that Code matters became a function of the Property Chamber of the FTT.

9 Art. 2(4) of the First-tier Tribunal and Upper Tribunal (Chambers) (Amendment) Order 2024 caused art. 12(a)(v) to be omitted from the First-tier Tribunal and Upper Tribunal (Chambers) Order 2010, and amended art. 12(cc) of the 2010 Order. The effect of this was to remove Code matters from the list of functions of the UTLC, but to include in that list certain matters transferred to the UT by the FTT, including Code matters.

10 Following the April 2024 legislative changes described above, one should not now expect the UT to issue a Reference which is filed with it. Such Reference may be rejected, given that first instance Code References are no longer a function of the UT, save for where they have been transferred from the FTT.

Proceedings now issued in the FTT: initial directions

21.12 Now that References are commenced in the First-tier Tribunal, directions are sent out by the First-tier Tribunal upon receipt of a Reference, and the procedure will then continue much as before. In most cases, respondents will be directed to file a statement of case. In some types of case, the initial directions Order will go further and require the parties to send an electronic travelling draft backwards and forwards, setting out their rival contentions as to the appropriate terms of the agreement sought. In other cases, the tribunal will consider what further directions are able to be given once the content of the respondent's statement of case has been considered.

Transfer from the First-tier Tribunal to the Upper Tribunal

21.13 It will still be possible for a party to request that the Reference be transferred to the UT where a point of principle arises.

21.14 Under rule 25 of the FTT Rules, the tribunal may refer a case to the President of the Property Chamber with a request that the case be considered for transfer to the UT. If that is done, the President of the Property Chamber may direct that the case be transferred to the UT, but only with the concurrence of the President of the Lands Chamber (rule 25(2)). By rule 25(3), the President of the Property Chamber may only make such a direction if they consider that the issues in dispute are 'likely to be further appealed to the Upper Tribunal', and furthermore will require lengthy or complex evidence at a lengthy hearing, involve a complex or important principle or issue, or involve a large financial sum.

21.15 The process is thus cumbersome, and the tests which are required to be surmounted appear high.

21.16 There is an alternative route open to the tribunal under rule 6(3)(n)(ii) of the FTT Rules, which allows it to transfer proceedings to another court or tribunal with jurisdiction if it considers that the other court or tribunal 'is a more appropriate forum for the determination of the case'. This provision, on the face of it, grants broader discretion and entails a less cumbersome procedure.

21.17 A case will not be heard by the UT at first instance simply because the point that arises is academically interesting. Requests to the UT to retain a Reference were relatively rare, but there has been at least one example of a case[11] where the UT has refused to retain a case, on the ground that the facts were relatively niche. Thus it is likely that it must be shown that the determination of the point of principle in question will be of some broader import.

21.18 Applications for transfer to the UT are to be made to the FTT. It is thought that in deciding whether to send a matter to the UT, the FTT will apply similar criteria to those applied formerly by the UT in deciding whether to refrain from transferring a matter to the FTT. One might expect it to become more difficult to have a matter proceed in the UT now that the norm has been well-established that

---

11 The *Gravesham Borough Council* 'Hive' case, which did eventually return to the UT on appeal (LC-2023-810).

cases are commenced in the FTT, and now that the UT has heard its first appeals from the FTT in Code matters.

21.19 However, where important points of law arise in parts of the Code that the UT has yet to consider, the FTT may be open to persuasion. Also, where there is a challenge to a valuation principle or practice that has been laid down by the UT, it might be thought that the expense of a long FTT trial with expert evidence might be undesirable if there is a high prospect that an appeal to the UT will result in any event.

21.20 Another reason why the matter may be transferred to the UT is that it might be practically or logically sensible for a Code Reference to be managed alongside, and heard together with, a lease renewal under the 1954 Act. Certain judges are empowered to sit as county court judges, and these include the Deputy President of the Lands Chamber. Accordingly, he can sit as a county court judge for the purposes of the 1954 Act lease renewal (which at time of writing must occur in the county court[12]), whilst simultaneously sitting as an Upper tribunal judge in the related Code matter. This approach was endorsed by the FTT in the circumstances of the *Knowsley MBC*[13] case, which otherwise the FTT would not have been minded to (re-)transfer.

Specialist judges hearing 1954 Act matters in the county court

21.21 Whilst 1954 Act lease renewals in telecoms matters are still proceeding in the county court,[14] there may be self-contained lease renewal cases under the 1954 Act that one or more parties consider would be appropriately heard by the Deputy President or another specialist judge of the Upper Tribunal. The privilege of asking for such a matter to be allocated to such a specialist judge should be exercised sparingly, but some cases may raise sufficiently important points to justify this approach.[15] The object of this process is largely to have sufficient cases determined by judges with Code experience to provide guidance to parties in other cases.

21.22 Such an allocation is not a transfer from the county court to the tribunal system, but merely an allocation of the case to a particular judge. A decision to make such an allocation is made by the Designated Civil judge for the relevant county court. As such, a request for a particular judge to hear a case should not be made by an application in the case, but by letter to the Designated Civil judge,[16] explaining the reasons for the request. The suggested practice is to copy in the Deputy President of the Lands Chamber of the UT, who would liaise with the relevant Designated Civil judge. If such an allocation is made, the case would then usually, as a matter of practice, be managed from the UT.[17]

12 The PSTIA 2022 contains amendments which will alter this position, and are expected to come into force soon.

13 *Telefonica UK Ltd v Knowsley Metropolitan Borough Council* LC-2023-715.

14 The PSTIA 2022 contains amendments which will alter this position, and are expected to come into force in due course.

15 The Deputy President has heard the *Hanover, Morriss* and *New Zealand Farm* cases sitting as a county court judge.

16 UT Telecoms User Group minutes, 25 May 2021, para 8.1.

17 UT Telecoms User Group minutes, 2 February 2021, para 5.2.

Volume of Code References

21.23 On 12 October 2023, it was reported to the telecoms user group that the UT had received 785 Code References since the inception of the Code. In 2018 and 2019, there were 49 and 59 References respectively, rising to 101 in 2020. Taking a year end of 30 March for each year, 106 References were received in 2021, rising to 171 in 2022, and again to 222 in 2023. The consensus of the user group was that the number of References received in the year to March 2024 would likely exceed 300. Accordingly, there has been a continued growth rather than a decline in the number of Code References being made.

21.24 Further, when[18] renewals of telecoms leases under the 1954 Act are heard in the tribunals rather than in the county court, the number of cases heard by the tribunals entailing the conferral of Code rights will grow yet further. The view of the telecoms user group was that it may even double. Although the number of judges who have substantively dealt with Code cases remains relatively small, it has been reported that there are a considerable number of FTT judges who are interested in hearing such cases and who have already participated in relevant training.

Time taken to hear Code matters

Cases which must be determined within six months

21.25 Certain categories of case must be determined within six months. This has an inevitable impact on the conduct of the litigation by the parties. For example, where a landowner wishes to redevelop its premises (and hence rely on para 21(5) of the Code to prevent a Code agreement from being granted), the six-month time limit would shorten the period during which it would be able to assemble its evidence to prove its case. Unlike under the 1954 Act, where one is aware of the date at which a lease is due to end, a Code application can catch a landowner by surprise. Accordingly, a landowner may not have started the process of seeking planning permission for a major scheme, even though the commencement of a redevelopment in the next year or two may be genuinely intended. On the other hand, operators fairly point to the legislative purpose of seeking to enable the rollout of telecommunications networks without delay. The six-month time limit itselfthus has the power to give rise to yet more disagreement between the parties.

21.26 Paragraph 97 of the Code makes quite clear that those enacting the Code considered the six-month time limit to apply to certain applications under the Code:

> 'Regulation 3 of the Electronic Communications and Wireless Telegraphy Regulations 2011 (SI 2011/1210) makes provision about the time within which certain applications to the court under this code must be determined.'

21.27 Regulation 3(2) of the Electronic Communications and Wireless Telegraphy Regulations 2011 sets out the six-month requirement as follows:

> '6 month period for deciding application to install facilities

18 Following the amendments made to the 1954 Act by the Product Security and Telecommunications Infrastructure Act 2022.

3.—

(1) This regulation applies where—

(a) a person authorised to provide public electronic communications networks applies to a competent authority for the granting of rights to install facilities on, over or under public or private property for the purposes of such a network,

(b) a person authorised to provide electronic communications networks other than to the public applies to a competent authority for the granting of rights to install facilities on, over or under public property for the purposes of such a network, or

(c) a person applies to OFCOM for a direction applying the electronic communications code in the person's case.

(2) Except in cases of expropriation, the competent authority must make its decision within 6 months of receiving the completed application.'

21.28 It is thus notable that on its face, the requirement is only engaged where there is an application to install ECA. It is also not restricted to court or tribunal decisions, but includes certain decisions by OFCOM.

21.29 In *Islington*,[19] the Deputy Chamber President explained the tribunal's view that the six-month limit arises in respect of new sites.

21.30 The relevant passage at [10] was as follows:

> '10. One important feature of the Code is the obligation it places on the Tribunal to resolve dispute without delay. Regulation 3(2) of the Electronic Communications and Wireless Telegraphy Regulations 2011, referred to in paragraph 97 of the Code, requires the Tribunal to determine applications for the grant of rights to install apparatus to provide electronic communication networks within 6 months of receiving the application. That obligation is imposed in the public interest, rather than for the convenience of operators, and it is not one which the parties are free to dispense with. Nevertheless, having regard to the relevant EU Directives which are the source of the domestic regulation (the Framework Directive 2002/21/EC and the Better Regulation Directive 2009/140/EC), *the view taken by the Tribunal has been that the obligation arises in the case of applications concerning new sites*, rather than sites over which rights already exist which an operator seeks to renew and which will continue pending the determination of the application. The application in this case relates to a new site on which no apparatus has yet been installed, and the duty to determine the application within 6 months is therefore engaged.' [emphasis added]

21.31 In *Knowsley*, the FTT was faced with the question whether an application for Code rights was subject to the six-month time limit where the operator's primary case was that it already had rights to keep ECA installed, which was already present on a site. The operator also sought certain additional rights, including the right to station a crane for upgrade works. The FTT held that the six-month time limit did not apply.

19 *EE Ltd & Hutchison 3G UK Ltd v London Borough Of Islington* [2018] UKUT 0361 (LC).

The point was then appealed to the UT, but the appeal itself was not determined within the six-month period, and was settled.

21.32 In *EE Limited v MacDonald*[20], the Lands Tribunal for Scotland briefly considered the meaning of 'expropriation' in regulation 3(2).[21] The rights sought in that case were merely access rights over the Respondent's land, and no rights to install any ECA on that land were sought. In that context, the tribunal did not recognise anything within the proceedingsas 'expropriation', as 'no right of the respondent's is being taken away, certainly no right of property'.[22]

21.33 There may be scope for argument that the grant of a full Code agreement for the installation of ECA constitutes 'expropriation', and accordingly that the six-month time limit should not be considered to apply. This would not necessarily rob para 97 of its force, as it would leave open the possibility that other species of application under the Code do not entail expropriation and hence that they fall within the six-month rule.

Cases not treated as subject to the six-month rule

21.34 Part 5 renewals have not been treated as subject to the six-month time limit by the UT. All contested renewals have been heard within 12 months of the Reference being commenced (other than where they have been appealed or stayed pending an appeal in another case). Certain applications under paragraph 20 that in effect constitute 'renewal' case because the operator is already on the site, have been comparatively few in number; this is in part because they were not thought possible until the Supreme Court's decision in *Compton Beauchamp*[23] in June 2022. However, there is no reason to think that these have not proceeded reasonably quickly, and it would seem likely that their timetables in general would be similar to renewals under Part 5.

The telecoms user group

21.35 There is a telecoms user group that meets periodically to discuss issues relating to the conduct of Code matters within the tribunal system. For a number of years, this was a user group under the auspices of the Upper Tribunal. However, now that the vast majority of cases proceed in the FTT, it is intended that this specific group will be an FTT user group.

21.36 The minutes of the user group have to date been published online and can provide a useful indication of the tribunal's thinking on practical and administrative matters. Such discussions do not have the force of a judgment or formal practice direction, but nonetheless, it is self-evidently a good idea to be aware of the preferences and exhortations of the judges who will be dealing with cases. The fact that there

20 LTS/ECC/2019/009.
21 Ie, reg 3(2) of the Electronic Communications and Wireless Telegraphy Regulations 2011.
22 At [40] of the Judgment.
23 [2022] UKSC 18.

have been comparatively few judges deciding the vast majority of the cases perhaps increases the value to practitioners of insights of this kind.

Upper Tribunal (Lands Chamber) Practice Directions

21.37 As mentioned above, the latest iteration of the Upper Tribunal (Lands Chamber) Practice Directions is that dated 2 January 2024 ('the 2024 PD').

21.38 The 2024 PD contains the first changes since the previous review in October 2020. Perhaps the principal changes from the point of view of Code cases are as follows:

- A new section 3 explains how best to communicate with the tribunal. The use of CE-File (the online system for filing documents electronically) is now mandatory for professional users throughout the Upper Tribunal.
- Section 15, dealing with References under the Code has been substantially reduced to reflect the transition to first-instance Code cases being heard in the FTT.
- Paragraph 20.3 deals with the form of hearing bundles. A hybrid approach involving a full electronic bundle and a paper core bundle is often most helpful, where the parties are represented.

Striking out a reference

21.39 Both the UT and the FTT have power to strike out proceedings. Indeed, each tribunal must strike out proceedings before it if it does not have jurisdiction in relation to those proceedings and does not exercise its power to transfer the proceedings to another court or tribunal.[24]

21.40 There are a number of other circumstances in which the tribunals may strike out proceedings.[25] For example, the tribunal may strike out the whole or a part of the proceedings if it considers there is no reasonable prospect of a party's case, or part of it, succeeding.[26] Accordingly, it is clear that in an appropriate case, proceedings may be struck out on the merits.

21.41 A case can be struck out can be made for jurisdictional reasons, for example because:

(i) there is some technical invalidity in the content or attempted service of the notice on which the Reference is sought to be based, such as to deprive the tribunal of jurisdiction in the matter; or

(ii) the claim proceeds on the basis that an agreement between the parties is amenable to being renewed under the Code, when in fact it is a subsisting agreement that is a lease enjoying statutory protection under Part II of the

24 This is the effect of rule 8(2) of the UT Rules, and rule 9(2) of the FTT Rules respectively.
25 These are set out at rule 8(3) of the UT Rules, and rule 9(3) of the FTT Rules respectively.
26 Rule 8(3)(c) of the UT Rules, and rule 9(3)(e) of the FTT Rules respectively.

1954 Act, and hence cannot be renewed under the Code but only under the 1954 Act following the appropriate 1954 Act notice;

(iii) on a proper interpretation of the operator's case, it is seeking Code rights when it has no right to seek Code rights (for example because its attempted 1954 Act lease renewal has already failed (see the *Gravesham* case); or

(iv) on a proper interpretation of the operator's case, it is seeking to modify the Code rights that already exist under a written agreement during its term, rather than seeking additional Code rights that it currently lacks (such a claim being impermissible pursuant to the Supreme Court's decision in *Compton Beauchamp*[27]).

21.42 Equally, a Reference may be struck out for merits-based reasons, where appropriate.

21.43 In each tribunal there are rules as to allowing representations to be made before the making of an Order for strike out.[28]

The conduct of the parties

21.44 Code cases have at times been conducted in a manner which might be described as robust, or alternatively hostile. There are numerous factors that have surely contributed to this. The following might be thought to be merely some of the more obvious:

- brand new legislation allowing a 'gold rush' on the part of those interested in establishing positive early precedents;
- a dearth of decisions under the Old Code which has created a vacuum into which such litigants have rushed;
- the relatively deep pockets of some of the commercial actors in Code cases;
- the likely substantial change in consideration payable under the New Code compared with the Old Code;[29] and
- sincerely-held but polarised views on the part of expert valuers.

21.45 The tribunal has on numerous occasions thought it necessary to give guidance, warnings, and even admonition when it comes to the conduct of the parties and their representatives. Those advising and acting for parties would do well to heed those sentiments, not least because of the potential impact on Orders for Costs that the tribunal may make.

21.46 In *UAL*, the tribunal warned the parties as to the level of conduct that is expected in terms that are likely to have a wider useful application:

27 [2022] UKSC 18 at [130] thereof.

28 Rule 8(4) of the UT Rules, and rule 9(4) of the FTT Rules respectively.

29 This factor is a 'double whammy': (i) it is valuable to operators and to site providers with numerous sites to establish a principle in their favour; and (ii) the worse the outcome of consideration decisions for site providers, the greater the disincentive to encourage ECA onto their land, thus promoting resistance on the part of landowners, rather than conciliation.

> '66. The level of hostility that we have observed between the parties to this reference has been unseemly and unnecessary, and has inflated costs on both sides. As the Tribunal observed at the first case management hearing, the parties have behaved as if they are enemies. We understand the caution of the respondent about matters of operational safety and convenience, and we understand the frustration of the claimant in the face of what it perceives as unnecessary caution. But the caution, and the frustration, have been taken too far, despite the fact that each party is providing a public service and endeavouring to do so safely and efficiently and neither is seeking to wrong the other or to do anything illegal.

...

> 68. The respondent accepts that the claimant is entitled to put equipment on the roof-top site, albeit on an interim basis not a secure one, and it is therefore in the interests of both parties to build a relationship that will work well in the coming years. The parties to a reference under the Code will be served well by lawyers who seek to build consensus and to help their clients see the other party's point of view; an approach that assumes the worst in all circumstances and requires provision in the agreement for duplicated safeguards and excessive bureaucracy will generate pointless costs, is likely to lead (as we shall see) to contradictory obligations, and will sour the atmosphere for the future. Sadly that is what has happened here.'[30]

Applying for case management directions in the FTT

21.47 The FTT (Property Chamber) has an application form[31] for case management orders or other interim orders. A request for directions or any other decision by a judge should be made using that form, and not in the body of an email. It should be 'copied' to the opposing party.

21.48 On 12 October 2023, it was confirmed at the telecoms user group meeting that no fees were payable for such applications in Code cases. The Fees Order[32] applicable to the FTT had not been amended so as to include Code cases. Until such amendment takes place, or any comparable new legislation comes forward, no fee is payable.

The approval of agreed directions in renewal cases

21.49 The FTT does not routinely approve directions agreed between the parties in renewal cases, because experience suggests many will not need to be listed for hearing. Listing will generally not take place until evidence is complete in order to avoid over-filling the tribunal's diary with cases that are likely to settle. The benefit of this is typically an earlier hearing date for cases which require a hearing, often within one to two months of the close of evidence.

30 [2020] UKUT 248 (LC) at [66] and [68]. The intervening [67] concerned the conduct of the parties as regards disclosure, and the giving of expert evidence, and is referred to at **21.52** below.

31 https://www.gov.uk/government/publications/ask-the-first-tier-tribunal-property-chamber-for-case-management-or-other-interim-orders

32 The First-tier Tribunal (Property Chamber) Fees Order 2013.

Statements of case

21.50 Statements of case should be relatively economical, with annexes ideally limited to a plan and the agreement sought.

21.51 The tribunals have in particular expressed a desire for statements of case in MSV applications to be concise. However, they can additionally have copies of any relevant correspondence annexed, since such matters are frequently determined at the first hearing.

Co-operation as to disclosure

21.52 In *UAL*, there was a plea from the tribunal to the parties to engage cooperatively in disclosure exercises,[33] which was later referred to in *L&Q* as follows:

> 'The Tribunal does not order disclosure as a matter of course, and leans against indiscriminate disclosure. But parties should not lose sight of the Tribunal's power to direct disclosure where it is necessary to do so, as it was in this case. It is part of the duty of solicitors to consider and agree what directions for the exchange of information and disclosure of documents should be sought from the Tribunal at the case management hearing. Expert witnesses should also consider between themselves before they prepare their reports what information they reasonably require to enable them to provide their evidence. Where that information is held by one of the parties the experts should request it, and it should be provided. If it is not provided an application should be made to the Tribunal, but compulsion ought not to be necessary. The Tribunal stated in *Cornerstone Telecommunications Infrastructure Limited v University of the Arts London* [2020] UKUT 248 at [67]:
>
> 'Disputes would be avoided if material can be shared, as a matter of courtesy and helpfulness even where there is no obligation to do so.'
>
> It is disappointing that the reluctance to share information continues, creating unnecessary mistrust between the parties, and delays which frustrate the work of the Tribunal.'

21.53 One category of document that has been the subject of a number of disclosure applications is documentation evidencing transactions, which might then be used as comparable evidence in assessing rent. The tribunal has concluded in Code matters that telecoms-related comparables are not useful evidence. However, in 1954 Act lease renewals, there is more scope for a disclosure Order to be made, which requires a site provider to disclose details of transactions to which it was a party. A landowner may argue that the operator has information relating to a considerable number of transactions to which the landowner does not have access.

21.54 In *Morriss*, HHJ Mills made a disclosure Order requiring such information to be given over. At trial, the Deputy President (sitting as a county court judge) made reference to 'capital incentive payments' which did not form part of the stated rent under the leases, but which sat alongside them as a capital incentive to the site provider. At least in the 1954 Act context, this is market information that is relevant to the

33 *UAL* at [67].

determination of rent, and it was held that the hypothetical landlord would have regard to such payments in negotiations, as it would be aware that they are commonplace in the market when a landowner seeks them. But for the disclosure Order, it may be that that evidence would not have come to light. Any request or application made by a landowner would need to be sufficiently targeted not to require the operator to undertake work that is disproportionate to the matters in issue. It will be wise to make an application supported by evidence[34] if such an Order is sought.

21.55 Once the 1954 Act is amended by the PSTIA 2022 such that the valuation formula follows that of the Code, the prospect of such a disclosure Order is likely to be greatly reduced.

Witness evidence

21.56 Witness evidence is given by witness statement, and witnesses are called to give sworn evidence at a contested hearing.

21.57 In summary matters (such as para 26 applications), it is typical for the tribunal to proceed solely on the basis of witness statements without witnesses being called to give live evidence. There is no specific limit on the number of witnesses a party can call. However, in summary matters, one would expect most cases can proceed on the basis of written evidence from one witness per side. The tribunal is well aware of many common issues that arise in Code cases, and in a summary matter it will adopt a practical approach in accepting evidence from a professional witness that has a technical component, without that witness formally being called as an expert.

Permission for expert valuation evidence in Code cases

21.58 The tribunal has expressed a marked and growing frustration with expert evidence in Code matters. Complaints have included that the comparables used are too historical or offend the no-network assumption, that a proposed alternative use is clearly not feasible in the subject location, that the report is too lengthy, that experts have not understood or taken account of previous guidance of the tribunal, or that the evidence as a whole is just not helpful.

21.59 Given these complaints, given that the values likely to be awarded are relatively low, and given that there is said to be a pattern emerging from the cases, one can see why expert evidence may not be required in every case.

21.60 Although the standard Draft Directions[35] in Code cases contain permission for each party to adduce expert evidence on valuation, following the recent scepticism of the tribunal as to the need for, or helpfulness of, valuation evidence in a typical case, there is no guarantee that permission will always be given for expert evidence. The

34 In *Vodafone Ltd v Gravesham BC* (Claim No. K00BS429) a Deputy District judge declined to make a direction for disclosure of such material at a directions hearing where no application had been made with evidence in support.

35 These were published on 1 March 2021. At time of writing, these can be found here: https://www.gov.uk/government/publications/ecc1-draft-directions-for-an-electronic-communications-code-reference.

minutes of the Telecoms User Group from October 2022 indicate the UT's disposition in relation to the matter at that time:

> 'Permission to rely even on one expert will not be given in routine cases until the parties have clearly identified that there is an issue which requires expert evidence, but where there is a need permission will be given.[36]'

21.61 It is worth noting that valuation experts have been appearing in the First-tier Tribunal in the very recent past, and the decisions that emerge from such cases may well be instructive as to the likely future role that valuation experts will have in Code litigation.

Form of Order settling a Reference

21.62 A Consent Order format should be used when settling Code References, but not usually a Tomlin Order. See the discussion of this point in Chapter 22 including as to the differing requirements of the UT and FTT.

Virtual hearings

21.63 The Upper Tribunal was particularly responsive to the desirability of conducting hearings by a remote video platform during the Covid-19 pandemic lockdowns, and this responsiveness has ensured that it has been well placed to continue to hold hearings remotely where that is appropriate. In principle, all hearings are conducted in public, and access to virtual hearings is available to the public.

21.64 The practice established in the UT was that case management hearings and cases of a summary nature where a decision is made on written evidence only (such as MSV cases) would generally be held remotely, while other substantive hearings would generally be in person.

21.65 In the FTT, the majority of cases have been noted as being held remotely,[37] but with facilities available for in-person hearings if either party prefers.

Summary assessment of costs

21.66 The tribunal's preference is to conduct a summary assessment of costs in cases lasting one day or less, but it does not insist on doing so if the parties prefer a detailed assessment. It is not necessary for parties to provide a statement of costs before a final hearing. Parties can make submissions on costs and other consequential matters in writing after a decision is handed down, at which point a statement of costs can be filed.

21.67 Parties do sometimes agree that costs submissions will follow in writing, after a summary hearing determining a para 26 matter. This can be a sensible practical

---

36 Upper Tribunal Lands Chamber Telecommunications Users Group meeting minutes – 13 October 2022. This meeting was held around 9 months after the *Affinity Water* decision was given.

37 As at 12 October 2023: see the relevant telecoms user group meeting minutes.

measure, especially where the parties' resources have been dedicated to seeking to negotiate down to the wire, and therefore arguments in respect of costs have not been uppermost in the parties' minds. However, unless there is a good reason for this approach to be taken, the FTT does prefer to be able to deal with costs on the day of such a hearing.

Reporting of judgments in cases relating to the Code

Decisions above FTT level in general

21.68 The principal paid-for case law services have a good archive of Code cases, both in the UT and also on appeal to the higher courts.

21.69 Further, BAILII[38] is a good free online resource for Code cases in the UT (and the higher courts).

Decisions of the Upper Tribunal (Lands Chamber)

21.70 UT decisions are published on the gov.uk website. The Lands Chamber section of that website has a searchable archive of decisions available at the following URL: https://landschamber.decisions.tribunals.gov.uk/.

21.71 There is not a thorough search facility by bespoke keyword, but one can search by party name, or filter to just Code cases by selecting '26 ELECTRONIC COMMUNICATIONS CODE' from the 'Category' drop-down menu and clicking 'Search >>'. Similarly, one can filter to specific types of Code cases by using the 'SubCategory' drop-down menu, but there are only a few dozen UT Code cases in total that have been the subject of a written final decision and published in this way.

Decisions of the First-tier Tribunal (Property Chamber)

21.72 The conduct of litigation in Code cases is often hard-fought, involves only a handful of commercial parties on the operator side (who are therefore more sophisticated and clued-up than most litigants), and there is much communication between those who habitually act for parties on one 'side of the fence' or the other. For reasons that include these, any decision that is considered to be advantageous to one set of parties is invariably seized upon and relied upon in correspondence and in litigation.

21.73 It should be remembered that although any detailed reasoning in FTT decisions might be persuasive, such decisions do not carry any particular precedent value. Care should be taken not to elevate a conclusion of the FTT into an established and immutable rule of law. It is fair to say though that FTT decisions may very well be illustrative of the manner in which that tribunal can be expected to approach a case. Now that the FTT is dealing with the majority of Code cases, that is valuable in itself.

38 British and Irish Legal Information Institute: bailii.org.

21.74 It is therefore pleasing that FTT decisions have started to be made available online, albeit perhaps not in the most obvious of places.

21.75 In order to find them, first visit the residential property decisions section (sic) of the FTT Property Chamber website at the following URL: https://www.gov.uk/residential-property-tribunal-decisions.

21.76 Then check the box 'Electronic Communications Code', which filters the listed decisions down to those that have been logged as pertaining to the Code. The judgments started being listed from December 2023, as the FTT was taking on more of the Code caseload from the UT. It is not known if there are plans to make available the earlier FTT Code decisions on this website, but it is in any event worth bearing in mind that this resource may not constitute a comprehensive archive.

21.77 Naturally, the way in which these decisions are made available online, and the particular URL of the relevant webpage may well change in the future. If that is the case, it is worth remembering that the initial decision was taken to list Code cases under 'residential property', and this may aid in retrieving the relevant decisions. For the avoidance of doubt, not all of the Code cases made available in this way pertain to residential property, or to buildings containing a residential element.[39]

21.78 At the time of writing, BAILII[40] does not appear to publish FTT decisions in Code cases.

21.79 The paid-for case law services do not currently appear to have an exhaustive archive of FTT decisions under the Code, but some decisions have been published on such services. The cases that might be expected to be selected for inclusion are those which are subject to appeal[41] to the UT and sometimes beyond.

The tribunals and precedent

21.80 The Tribunals, Courts and Enforcement Act 2007 ('TCEA 2007') created a new tribunal system. The former Lands Tribunal was abolished and replaced by the Upper Tribunal (Lands Chamber) ('UTLC'). The UTLC[42] hears appeals from the Property Chamber of the FTT.

21.81 The TCEA 2007 implemented many of the recommendations of the committee chaired by Sir Andrew Leggatt, whose report was entitled: *Tribunals for users—One System, One Service (2001).* The report recommended the creation of a unified tribunals service with a two-tier structure.

---

39 For example, the case of *Cornerstone Telecommunications Infrastructure Limited v (1) The Mayor and Burgesses of the London Borough of Merton (2) Centrica Combined Common Investment Fund Limited*: LC-2023-000668 involved a multi-storey car park.

40 British and Irish Legal Information Institute: bailii.org.

41 By way of example, the FTT decision in *On Tower UK Ltd v Gravesham BC* has been reported by Westlaw under their case reference [2023] 10 WLUK 699. The UT appeal decision overturning that decision has reference [2024] UKUT 151 (LC).

42 It can also act as a first-instance tribunal, but in Code cases it does so much more rarely following the legislative amendments made in April 2024.

21.82 The report recommended that the tribunals should be organised by subject area into Divisions, each with a first-tier tribunal and a related second-tier appellate Division.

21.83 The report at para 6.32 stated that:

> 'The aim for the new appellate Division will be to develop, by its general expertise and the selective identification of binding precedents, a coherent approach to the law. In this… it will be comparable in authority to the High Court so far as Tribunals are concerned.'

21.84 By section 3(5) of the TCEA 2007, the UT is a 'superior court of record'. As such, it is 'empowered to make precedent'.[43]

21.85 The FTT is thus bound by decisions of the UT.[44] The UT is not strictly bound by a decision of the High Court,[45] but it will normally follow High Court decisions as a matter of comity unless the UT is convinced that the decision is wrong.[46]

21.86 Where a decision of the UT conflicts with a decision of the High Court the FTT is bound to follow the UT precedent, rather than that of the High Court.[47]

Decisions given 'on the papers'

21.87 The Deputy President has expressed doubt as to whether a decision 'on the papers' would necessarily be cheaper or quicker than a decision following an oral hearing. Even in MSV cases, there is no intention to depart from the tribunal's current practice of fixing an early hearing at which the parties could usually expect a final determination.

21.88 Judge Jackson (the Regional judge of the Property Chamber with responsibility for supervising Code cases) has expressed a willingness to deal with cases on paper where it is suitable, but that in this field there will typically be an issue that needs to be considered at a hearing.

21.89 Where all parties agree that a discrete issue, such as a preliminary issue, can be efficiently dealt with in writing, it is worth suggesting that at an early stage. It would even be open to the parties to agree on such an approach in principle prior to a Reference being issued, such that the parties can make reference to such a suggestion before any directions are given.

Part 4A of the Code: Unresponsive Occupiers

21.90 Part 4A of the Code is found at paras 27A to 27I. It creates a procedure by which an Order may be made imposing an agreement which provides that Code

---

43 *R (Cart) v The Upper Tribunal* [2011] UKSC 28; [2012] 1 AC 663 at [43] per Lady Hale.

44 As noted for example, by the Administrative Appeals Chamber of the UT in *Kirkham v Information Commissioner (Record of Proceedings)* [2020] UKUT 336 (AAC) at [19] as part of a broader discussion as to the UT and *stare decisis*.

45 *Gilchrist v Revenue and Customs Commissioners* [2015] Ch 183 at [85].

46 *Kirkham v Information Commissioner (Record of Proceedings)* [2020] UKUT 336 (AAC) at [16].

47 *Kirkham v Information Commissioner (Record of Proceedings)* [2020] UKUT 336 (AAC) at [19].

rights are exercisable by an operator for the purpose of providing an electronic communications service to leased premises where:

(a) the rights are required in respect of land that is connected to the leased premises, and

(b) the occupier or another person with an interest in the land has not responded to repeated notices given by the operator seeking agreement to confer or otherwise be bound by the rights.[48]

21.91 The procedure entails the service of repeated notices, and an application to the tribunal.

21.92 Para 2 of the relevant FTT Practice Direction[49] notes that Form ECC1 is prescribed for the purposes of making an application under para 27D of Part 4A.

21.93 At the user group meeting of 12 October 2023, nobody was aware of any use having been made of this regime. Applications under Part 4A can be expected to be extremely rare. For that reason, Part 4A is not dealt with in further detail in this book, and there is no case law to elucidate the bare provisions of the Code in any event.

Appeals

Appeals from the FTT

21.94 Where a Code case is determined by the FTT, the proper route of appeal is to the UT. This is so even if the case was originally commenced in the UT and was transferred to the FTT.[50]

21.95 By section 11(1) and (2) of the Tribunals, Courts and Enforcement Act 2007, any party to a case has a right of appeal to the UT on a point of law. By section 11(3) and (4), that right may only be exercised with permission, which may be given by the FTT or the UT on an application of the party.

21.96 This general right of appeal does not apply to 'excluded decisions'. In telecoms cases, excluded decisions do not include what one might describe as substantive decisions. By section 11(5)(d) they include decisions to review or not to review an earlier decision, to take no action in light of a review of an earlier decision, to set aside an earlier decision, or to refer (or not to refer) a matter to the UT. Further, by section 11(5)(e), there is no right to appeal a decision that has been set aside.

21.97 A person seeking permission to appeal a decision must make a written application to the FTT,[51] which must be received within 28 days of the FTT sending to the person the written reasons for the decision (or of sending notification of amended

48 Para 27A.

49 FTT Practice Direction: 'Cases in the Property Chamber under Part 4A of the Electronic Communications Code' (9 May 2023).

50 User group minutes, 4 November 2021, para 2.1.

51 Rule 52(1) of the FTT Rules.

reasons for the decision, correction of the decision, or of an application to set aside having been unsuccessful).[52] There is a procedure for seeking an extension of time.[53]

21.98 An application to the FTT for permission to appeal must identify the decision to which it relates, state the grounds of appeal, and state the result that the applicant is seeking.[54]

21.99 The FTT must first consider, taking into account the overriding objective,[55] whether to review the decision in accordance with rule 55 of the FTT Rules. It may only undertake a review if it is satisfied that a ground of appeal is likely to be successful.[56]

21.100 If it decides not to review, or to review but take no action in relation to the decision, it must consider whether to give permission to appeal.[57] The FTT must send a record of its decision to the parties as soon as practicable and must give reasons if it refuses permission.[58]

21.101 A party seeking a stay of implementation of a decision pending the outcome of an appeal must make an application for such a stay to the FTT at the same time as seeking permission to appeal.[59] Before a decision is made on the stay application, the FTT must allow the parties to make representations.[60]

21.102 If the FTT refuses an application for permission to appeal, the proposed appellant would need to obtain permission from the UT in order to proceed with its appeal.

21.103 The proposed appellant may apply to the UT for permission to appeal against an FTT decision only if it has first made an application to the FTT for permission to appeal[61] which has not resulted in permission being granted.

21.104 The application to the UT must be made in writing and received by the UT no later than 14 days after the date on which the FTT sent notice of refusal of permission to appeal (or refusal to admit the application for permission to appeal, or notice of grant of permission on limited grounds).[62]

21.105 There are requirements as to the contents of the permission to appeal application, and what documents must be provided with it.[63] There is a procedure for seeking an extension of time.[64]

---

52 Rule 52(2) of the FTT Rules.
53 See rule 52(4) of the FTT Rules.
54 Rule 52(5) of the FTT Rules.
55 Under rule 3 of the FTT Rules.
56 Rule 55(1)(b) of the FTT Rules.
57 Rule 53(2) of the FTT Rules.
58 Rule 53(3) and (4) of the FTT Rules.
59 Rule 54(1) of the FTT Rules.
60 Rule 54(3) of the FTT Rules.
61 Rule 21(1) of the UT Rules.
62 Rule 21(2) of the UT Rules.
63 See rule 21(3), (4) and (7) of the UT Rules.
64 See rule 21(5) of the UT Rules.

Appeals from the UT to the Court of Appeal

21.106 By section 13(1) and (2) of the Tribunals, Courts and Enforcement Act 2007, any party to a case has a right of appeal to the Court of Appeal[65] on a point of law. By section 13(3) and (4), that right may only be exercised with permission, which may be given by the UT or the Court of Appeal on an application of the party.

21.107 This general right of appeal does not apply to 'excluded decisions'. In telecoms cases, excluded decisions do not include what one might describe as substantive decisions. By section 15(8)(c) they include a decision of the UT regarding permission to appeal. By section 15(8)(d) they also include decisions to review or not to review an earlier decision, to take no action in light of a review of an earlier decision, or to set aside an earlier decision. Further, by section 13(8)(e), there is no right to appeal a decision that has been set aside.

21.108 A person seeking permission to appeal a decision must make a written application to the UT.[66] Provisions as to the timing and content of a permission to appeal application are set out at rule 55 of the UT Rules.

Second appeals to the Court of Appeal

21.109 Where a party seeks permission to appeal from any decision of the Upper Tribunal that was itself made on an appeal under section 11 of the Tribunals, Courts and Enforcement Act 2007 (an appeal from the FTT on a point of law), there is a more stringent second appeal test. Under this test, permission shall not be granted unless the Upper Tribunal (or, where the Upper Tribunal refuses permission, the Court of Appeal) considers that:[67]

> '(a) the proposed appeal would raise some important point of principle or practice; or
>
> (b) there is some other compelling reason for the relevant appellate court to hear the appeal.'

21.110 The CPR[68] contains a very similar second appeal test for appeals to the Court of Appeal, which adds a 'real prospect of success' requirement to limb (a) of the above test.

21.111 Parties applying to the Court of Appeal should consult Practice Direction 52C (headed 'appeals to the court of appeal'), which supplements CPR Part 52.

'Leapfrog' appeals from the UT to the Supreme Court

21.112 The UT has the power to grant a 'leapfrog' certificate allowing an application to be made directly to the Supreme Court seeking permission to appeal. The UT may grant a certificate only where it is satisfied that:

---

65 The route of appeal from the UT in England and Wales is to the Court of Appeal: s 13(12) of the Tribunals, Courts and Enforcement Act 2007.

66 Rule 55(1) of the UT Rules.

67 This test is set out at Art 2 of the Appeals from the Upper Tribunal to the Court of Appeal Order 2008, made under s 13(6) of the Tribunals, Courts and Enforcement Act 2007.

68 Rule 52.7(2) of the Civil Procedure Rules 1998.

(i) the conditions in s 14A(4) or (5) of the 2007 Act are satisfied;[69] and

(ii) a 'sufficient case' has been made out to justify an application to the Supreme Court seeking permission to appeal under s 14B of the 2007 Act.[70]

The section 14A(4) and (5) conditions

21.113 Either s 14A(4) or s 14A(5) must be satisfied in order for there to be a power to grant a leapfrog certificate.

21.114 Section 14A(4) is satisfied where a point of law of general public importance is involved which either:

(i) relates wholly or mainly to the construction of an earlier enactment or statutory instrument, *and* was fully argued in the proceedings and fully considered in the judgment;[71] or

(ii) is one in respect of which the UT is bound by a decision of the relevant appellate court or the Supreme Court in previous proceedings, *and* which was fully considered in the binding judgment.[72]

21.115 Section 14A(5) is satisfied where a point of law of general public importance is involved and either:

(i) a matter of national importance is involved;[73] or

(ii) the result of the proceedings is so significant as to justify a hearing by the Supreme Court;[74] or

(iii) the UT is satisfied that the benefits of earlier consideration by the Supreme Court outweigh the benefits of consideration by the Court of Appeal.[75]

21.116 It is fair to note that 'leapfrog' certificates can be expected to be granted only very rarely. The UT granted one in the *Arqiva* case.[76] However, there were two exceptionally unusual circumstances referred to by the applicant in its application for a leapfrog certificate, namely:

(i) Judge Cooke in her judgment made clear that although she thought that the law may have taken a 'wrong turn'[77] in *Compton Beauchamp*, she was bound by the decision of the Court of Appeal in that case. That being the case, she indicated of her own motion that she would grant the operator permission

69 Section 14A(1)(a) of the 2007 Act.
70 Section 14A(1)(b) of the 2007 Act.
71 Section 14A(4)(a) of the 2007 Act.
72 Section 14A(4)(b) of the 2007 Act.
73 Section 14A(5)(a) of the 2007 Act.
74 Section 14A(5)(b) of the 2007 Act.
75 Section 14A(5)(c) of the 2007 Act.
76 *Arqiva Services Ltd v AP Wireless II (UK) Ltd* [2020] UKUT 195. This case was considered by the Supreme Court together with two other cases under the citation [2022] UKSC 18, by which point the operator had changed its name to On Tower UK Limited. The case is also sometimes referred to as 'Queens Oak' because the matter concerned land at Queens Oak Farm in Towcester, Northants.
77 See [177] of the UT judgment in the *Arqiva* case.

to appeal to the Court of Appeal, and that the Court of Appeal may wish to consider hearing the *Arqiva* case together with the *Ashloch* case;[78] and

(ii) After that indication had been given in the judgment, permission to appeal had been given by the Supreme Court for an appeal to proceed in *Compton Beauchamp*, the case whose judgment in the Court of Appeal had bound Judge Cooke in *Arqiva*, and which was followed in *Ashloch*.

21.117 Accordingly, there was a rare opportunity for the Supreme Court to hear matters together which raised related issues on different sets of facts. Ultimately the Supreme Court heard *Compton Beauchamp*, *Ashloch* and *Arqiva* together and Judge Cooke's observation that the law may have taken a wrong turn was vindicated.

21.118 When an application is made to the Supreme Court for permission to appeal under section 14B following the grant of a 'leapfrog' certificate, the Supreme Court may grant permission to appeal if it appears to it to be 'expedient to do so'.[79]

Appeals from the county court

21.119 Where a 1954 Act lease renewal case is determined by a District judge, the destination for an appeal is a Circuit judge sitting in the county court. Where such a case is determined by a Circuit judge in the county court, the destination for an appeal is a single judge of the High Court.[80]

21.120 The procedure to be followed in initiating such an appeal is governed by the usual rules under Part 52 of the CPR. In short:

(i) Permission to appeal is required (CPR r. 52.3(1)(a)).

(ii) An application for permission to appeal may be made to the lower court (r. 52.3(2)(a) at the hearing at which the decision to be appealed was made, or any adjournment of that hearing, or to the appeal court in an appeal notice (r. 52.3(2)(b)).

(iii) Where the lower court refuses an application for permission to appeal, a further application may be made to the appeal court (r. 52.3(3)(a)).

(iv) The appeal court will determine any such application on paper without an oral hearing unless the court otherwise directs (r. 52.4(1)).

(v) The appellant may request a refusal of permission to be reconsidered at an oral hearing (r. 52.4(2)).

(vi) In respect of any consideration of the application for permission to appeal, permission may only be given where the court considers that the appeal would have a real prospect of success, or there is some other compelling reason for the appeal to be heard (r. 52.6(1)).

---

78 See [181] of the UT judgment in the *Arqiva* case.

79 See s 14B(3) of the 2007 Act.

80 See Table 1 within para 3.5 of CPR Practice Direction 52A.

(vii) Unless a different time limit is directed by the lower court, an appellant's notice must be filed at the appeal court within 21 days of the decision which the appellant wishes to appeal (r. 52.12(2)(b)).

(viii) Paragraph 4.2 of PD52A sets out the documents which must be filed with an appellant's notice.

(ix) An application to vary the time limit for filing an appeal notice must be made to the appeal court (r. 52.15(1)), and the court may grant such an extension even where the application for an extension of time is made after the time for filing the appellant's notice has expired (r. 3.1(2)(a)). The parties may not agree such an extension between themselves (r. 52.15(2)).

22

Settling Code Disputes

Reaching agreement before a Reference is issued

22.01 As with any potential dispute, a resolution without reference to a court or tribunal has much to recommend it. In respect of Code-related matters, consensual agreements, rather than agreements imposed by a tribunal, should be considered to be the optimal[1] outcome and default setting. Relatively recent changes to the Code have reinforced this notion by requiring consideration of ADR.

22.02 In most cases, there is no problem with the parties entering into a consensual agreement conferring Code rights (or rendering a person bound by Code rights) on mutually acceptable terms. However, as mentioned elsewhere, there are two potential difficulties for site providers in particular, which should be kept in mind:

(i) *Compensation*: A site provider has no right to seek compensation under para 25 where an agreement is consensual rather than imposed (as already discussed in Chapters 6 and 14). In short, a contractual compensation mechanism should be considered, or alternatively, an application can be made to the tribunal in order to have an agreement imposed that has been agreed in principle between the parties. Thought will need to be given to what notices will need to be served in order to be able to give the tribunal jurisdiction; and

(ii) *Paragraphs 26 and 27 agreements can never be consensual*: Agreements under paras 26 and 27 are, by definition, imposed by tribunal.[2] Where agreements are imposed by the tribunal under paras 26 and 27, the effect of para 30(2) is excluded,[3] and the agreement comes to an end in accordance with its contractual terms. If an agreement is consensual and grants Code rights, there is no way of excluding para 30(2).[4] A compromise should therefore be effected by means of an application to the tribunal for the imposition of an agreement that has been agreed in principle between the parties, with the requisite Code notices having been served and the requisite period having expired.

Heads of Terms are not usually binding

22.03 A negotiation between the parties to a potential property transaction often commences with a set of Heads of Terms passing back and forth between the parties'

1 In *Compton Beauchamp* ([2022] UKSC 18 at [117]), Lady Rose described the negotiation of voluntary agreements as being the optimal way for the regime to operate.

2 See paras 26(1) and (3), and 27(2) respectively.

3 Para 30(3).

4 Any attempt to do so will be ineffective by virtue of para 100(2).

representatives, often with tracked changes and/or comments made in the margins of electronic copies of such documents. Sometimes operators will attach Heads of Terms to notices in an attempt to comply with the para 20(2)(a) requirement to set out all of the terms of the agreement that is sought.

22.04 Heads of Terms often pass between representatives of parties. These are often lawyers, but equally can be land agents or surveyors. It is good practice to head such a document as 'Subject to contract' to indicate clearly that the parties' intention is to embody any concluded agreement in a formal contract. Whether a binding contract has been reached will always be a question of applying the relevant law to the facts. However, as a general proposition, a recognisable Heads of Terms document is unlikely to be taken to be an agreement that the parties intended as binding.[5]

22.05 One might think that this conclusion would be reached more readily in a Code case than in the general landlord and tenant context. Operators can be readily taken to want Code rights rather than merely contractual rights to which the Code does not apply. The parties' representatives will typically understand that para 9 requires an agreement under Part 2 of the Code to be signed by the parties to it, and Heads of Terms are seldom signed.

Without prejudice communications

22.06 The classic statement of the law relating to 'without prejudice' communications is to be found in Lord Griffiths' speech in *Rush & Tomkins v GLC*:[6]

> 'The 'without prejudice' rule is a rule governing the admissibility of evidence and is founded upon the public policy of encouraging litigants to settle their differences rather than litigate them to a finish … The rule applies to exclude all negotiations genuinely aimed at settlement whether oral or in writing from being given in evidence. A competent solicitor will always head any negotiating correspondence 'without prejudice' to make clear beyond doubt that in the event of the negotiations being unsuccessful they are not to be referred to at the subsequent trial. However, the application of the rule is not dependent upon the use of the phrase 'without prejudice' and if it is clear from the surrounding circumstances that the parties were seeking to compromise the action, evidence of the content of those negotiations will, as a general rule, not be admissible at the trial and cannot be used to establish an admission or partial admission'.

22.07 Thus, it is not safe to assume that a communication will be admissible in proceedings merely because it was not marked 'without prejudice'.

22.08 It is a common feature of Code disputes that parties will be negotiating the terms of a proposed agreement on an ongoing basis, sometimes from the very first communication between the parties until after directions are given within a Tribunal Reference. Standard directions typically ask the parties to engage in a 'travelling draft' process whereby they seek to narrow the issues of drafting that exist between the

5 *Pretoria Energy Company (Chittering) Ltd v Blankney Estates Ltd* [2023] EWCA Civ 482 is a recent example of such a case. The Court of Appeal upheld a finding that a Heads of Terms document in respect of a proposed agreement for lease was not a binding contract, for a variety of reasons.

6 [1989] 1 AC 1280, at pp 1299–1300.

parties by making tracked changes to an electronic draft agreement. This is a process that has often begun long before directions are given, as the parties try to agree on the terms of an agreement. However, it can lead to a 'rough and ready' approach to whether negotiations are genuinely without prejudice, or whether they are 'fair game' to be referred to in statements of case, witness statements, cross examination, and submissions.

22.09 Once a travelling draft process is ordered, and the parties send their communications back and forth in accordance with it, one would think that the draft becomes akin to a 'Scott Schedule'. This is a document now used in numerous fields of law, including property disputes, to set out the parties' respective positions on a number of points that are in dispute, for example numerous alleged defects in a building project. Thus, the travelling draft can become an iterative pleading of the parties' cases on certain terms. As such, it may be unrealistic for a party to consider that this 'back and forth' is subject to without prejudice privilege. However, parties should exercise proper care as to what prior negotiations are referred to before the tribunal.

22.10 Under para 20(3)(a), an operator may apply to the tribunal for a Code agreement where a person has not agreed to confer the requested Code right. It is therefore perfectly proper for an operator to make reference in its Statement of Case to the fact that a notice was served on a particular date, and that no agreement has been reached between the parties as to the grant of a Code right. However, how much further it is proper to go in making reference to prior negotiations is a more difficult question. Once the Respondent's statement of case has confirmed that (for example) the principle of a Code agreement is not in dispute but that terms relating to X, Y, and Z are not agreed, one has an openly pleaded position. However, at the prior stage of the Claimant's statement of case, it may be that reference to the Respondent being agreeable to a Code agreement in principle would be a breach of without prejudice privilege. Similarly, if term X is in dispute, a later reference in evidence by one party to the other party's prior negotiating position in respect of that term may similarly be a breach of without prejudice privilege.

Settlement of References: practice and procedure

22.11 As at 12 October 2023, 351 of 785 References (ie, 45%) had been recorded by the UT as having settled by consent, without being transferred to the FTT.

22.12 A Consent Order format should be used when settling Code References, but not usually a Tomlin Order.

22.13 A Tomlin Order typically stays a case upon terms of settlement (set out in an attached Schedule) having been reached by the parties, and grants permission to the parties to apply in order to enforce the agreed settlement terms without the need to bring a fresh claim.

22.14 The FTT does not make Tomlin orders because it does not have enforcement powers. Agreements between parties should therefore be in (non-Tomlin) Consent Order format.

22.15 The UT has also repeatedly discouraged the attempted use of Orders in 'Tomlin' form. Although it theoretically does have enforcement powers, it is rare that it is asked to use them. Accordingly, it will typically not order stays of proceedings after an agreement has been reached, unless there is some very good reason.

22.16 In both tribunals, then, Consent Orders whose object is to settle proceedings should provide for full and final settlement. These should either be signed, or some other explicit confirmation of consent by both sides should always be provided to the tribunal.

22.17 There are differing requirements in the FTT and UT as follows:

- *In the FTT*: when filing a Consent Order for approval, a Word version of the Order should be attached, and a separate pdf version of any agreement which is to be annexed to the Order;
- *In the UT*: the preference of the UT is to include an imposed agreement as part of a single electronic document comprising the Order and the agreement. This is to avoid the risk of any uncertainty about what has been imposed. Therefore, in the UT a single document should be supplied, with both the Order and the agreement in Word format.

Will agreeing certain terms affect decisions in future References?

22.18 In the *Hackney* (Tradescant House)[7] case, the tribunal commented that parties to a consensual agreement might agree to include particular terms for a wide variety of reasons, and that agreement in a previous case does did not affect the tribunal's decision on terms in a later Code Reference. It went on to confirm that the same proposition applied to Consent Orders which are approved by the tribunal. The tribunal's assent to a particular deal that has been reached does not create a precedent that must be followed. Judge Cooke said as follows:

> 'The fact that the Tribunal has on a previous occasion by consent imposed an agreement that contained, or did not contain, an approval condition does not mean that its hands are tied, still less that the Tribunal's hands are tied, on a future occasion when that term is in dispute. Where the term is in dispute the decision will be taken on the basis of what the Code provides, without regard to what these parties or other parties have agreed on previous occasions.'[8]

Costs in settled matters

22.19 As there is considerable encouragement by both the statutory scheme and the judiciary to settle matters where possible, and as the costs of full litigation are frequently disproportionate, many matters under the Code do settle. On occasion, the parties settle their substantive dispute, but do not reach an agreement on costs. What Order will the tribunal make in respect of costs where this occurs?

22.20 There are very often many 'moving parts' to a Code reference, often involving parties shifting their position on terms, and sometimes at very late stages. The potential for disagreement as to whose fault the costs are, and who has obtained most from the

7 [2022] UKUT 210 (LC) at [43]–[49].
8 [2022] UKUT 210 (LC) at [49].

newly-agreed terms, is considerable. Further, the first few years of the Code have seen numerous jurisdictional points argued, often going to the heart of how the Code is supposed to function. That being the case, it has been inevitable that those making applications have taken approaches that were never permissible, and a change of position in litigation has therefore resulted.

22.21 An example of such a case was the case that began life as *Ashloch*, and which went up to the Supreme Court within the *Compton Beauchamp* litigation. The Supreme Court held that an operator that is a tenant under a subsisting agreement cannot seek to renew that agreement under Part 4 of the Code (the Transitional Provisions already ruling out a renewal under Part 5), and the only option for a renewal was to proceed under the 1954 Act. However, the Supreme Court did say that although it is not open to an operator to seek to improve on the bargain embodied by its tenancy during the term of that tenancy, and hence it could not modify the terms on which Code rights were already subsisting, it *could* apply under Part 4 for additional Code rights. It was not clear to the Supreme Court on the material before it to what extent the operator was seeking additional Code rights, and to what extent it was impermissibly seeking to improve its bargain. The matter came back before the Upper Tribunal as *Gateway Properties*.[9] The tribunal directed the operator to 'amend its pleading, or serve a new pleading, clearly identifying which terms of its agreement were said to be new Code rights which it was entitled to apply for, and which it acknowledged were not in that category',[10] Having previously maintained that it was entitled to an entirely new agreement, the operator changed tack and identified four additional rights that it intended to seek. The site provider proposed an amendment to the existing lease to give effect to the four additional terms, and the parties reached an agreement.

22.22 The tribunal then had to decide what was to be done about costs. Submissions were made as to 'the approach which should be taken where the parties have settled their dispute but have not managed to agree what should happen about costs'.[11] The tribunal adopted the following summary of four principles that emerge from the authorities:

> 'First, where the parties have settled their dispute, save as to the question of costs, it is not right that the likely order is no order for costs.
>
> Secondly, in such a case the Tribunal will consider whether it can fairly and sensibly make an order for costs in favour of one party without a disproportionate expenditure of judicial time.
>
> Thirdly, if the Tribunal considers that it can make such an order, then it will take into account relevant factors, including, in particular, the result of the settlement, the conduct of the parties in the course of the litigation, and any reasonable offers of settlement that had been made.
>
> Fourthly, and finally, the Tribunal will only consider which party would have succeeded at trial where this is tolerably clear or obvious and that should not involve giving a fully reasoned judgment on the points, nor in deciding an important issue in dispute which no longer exists.'

---

9 *Cornerstone Telecommunications Infrastructure Ltd v Gateway Properties Ltd & Anor* [2023] UKUT 188 (LC).
10 At [17].
11 At [22].

22.23 Before it could apply those principles, the tribunal first had to decide on the terms of the Order for the substantive disposal of the References. It decided that it was appropriate to dismiss the References rather than to make no substantive Order on them. The reasons for this were that: (i) this was the final hearing, and there was no evidence on which relief could be granted, (ii) it is unsatisfactory to leave References in abeyance without being brought definitely to an end, and (iii) due to an earlier costs Order, a portion of the site provider's costs were its 'costs in the Reference', and this was not an insignificant sum. A disposal which gives effect to that costs Order was appropriate.

22.24 The tribunal then considered, 'in accordance with the usual principle', who had been the successful party. It decided that the site provider had been. The operator had sought a new 10-year agreement under the Code at a consideration of £50 a year on its standard terms. It had been granted no new lease and occupies under the original 1954 Act tenancy at a rent exceeding £5,000 per annum, with only modest variations. It had failed to establish the 'strategic principles for which it contended', namely that agreements originally granted to one operator could be renewed by a different operator under the Code. The additional terms that had been achieved were 'modest rights' that were 'hardly worth the candle' and were in any event not the reason for the commencement of the References. It was necessary to look at the References as a whole and not merely what had occurred since the Supreme Court's judgment.[12]

12 It should be added that the Tribunal was dealing with all of the costs of the References save for the costs of the preliminary issues which went for determination in the Supreme Court; the Supreme Court was to deal with those costs, but had not yet made a determination at the date of the Tribunal's costs decision.

23

Costs

23.01 This chapter relates solely to litigation costs. It does not deal with 'transactional costs' (ie, the costs of negotiating the terms of an agreement, or of professional advice on the consequences of an agreement or its terms). Such 'transactional costs' are dealt with in Chapter 14, relating to Compensation under the Code.

23.02 As a matter of jurisdiction, both the UT and the FTT are able to make an award of costs in a Code case, as explained below.

The FTT's power to award costs

23.03 The FTT has the power to make an Order for costs in proceedings under the Code, including those that have been transferred from the UT.[1]

23.04 The above power is separate from the general power of the FTT to make an Order for costs where a person has 'acted unreasonably in bringing, defending or conducting proceedings'.[2] Thus, there is no need for any tribunal to have concluded that a party has behaved unreasonably in order for it to have jurisdiction to award costs.

23.05 Where the FTT awards costs in respect of a matter that has been transferred from the UT, it may make an Order in respect of the costs of the proceedings in the FTT and also the proceedings occurring in the UT prior to the transfer (unless the UT has made an Order to the contrary).[3]

The UT's power to award costs

23.06 The tribunal may make an order for costs in proceedings 'under Schedule 3A to the Communications Act 2003',[4] ie, the Code. Clearly, this includes References under the Code that were commenced in the UT and are determined by the UT. As set out above, the FTT may make a costs Order in respect of a Reference commenced in the UT and transferred to the FTT by the UT, both in respect of the period before and after the transfer (subject to any Order previously made by the UT to the contrary).

1 Rule 13(i)(d) of the FTT Rules. Prior to 6 April 2024, when Code references were required to be commenced in the UT, the FTT's Rule 13 power to award costs in Code cases only applied to Part 4A cases, and cases which had been transferred to it by the UT. However the position was changed from 6 April 2024 by an amendment made to Rule 13 by The Tribunal Procedure (Amendment) Rules 2024.

2 This power is derived from rule 13(i)(b) of the FTT Rules and applies in all cases except for those within the categories mentioned in para 13(1ZA).

3 Rule 13(1A) of the FTT Rules.

4 Rule 10(6)(e) of the UTLC Rules.

23.07 What is not expressly stated is the UT's power to award costs in an appeal from the FTT relating to a Code matter. In the UTLC an Order for costs 'may only be made in accordance with the conditions or in the circumstances referred to in paragraphs (3) to (6)' (of rule 10 of the UTLC Rules).

23.08 Rule 10(3) gives powers to the UT in any proceedings to make a wasted costs Order,[5] an Order for costs where a party or representative has behaved unreasonably,[6] and an Order for a party to pay to another party a tribunal fee that has been paid.[7] Rule 10(5) gives the power to award costs in judicial review proceedings.

23.09 Rule 10(6) sets out a number of categories of cases in which the UT may make a costs Order. As stated above, these include proceedings under the Code.[8] Also included are appeals from a Valuation Tribunal,[9] and appeals 'relating to' a Reference by the Chief Land Registrar, or 'relating to… any other application, matter or appeal under the Land Registration Act 2002'.[10] As these are the only appeals provided for in rule 10(6), a textual argument could conceivably be made that no other appeals fall within rule 10(6). Further, rule 10(6)(g) concerns appeals 'relating to' references and other matters under the Land Registration Act 2002. It would therefore seem to catch both appeals made from the FTT under the Land Registration Act 2002,[11] and appeals made under the Tribunals, Courts and Enforcement Act 2007, on a point of law, relating to proceedings which had occurred at first instance under the Land Registration Act 2002. The language used in this part of rule 10 is not the same as the language used in respect of Code matters at rule 10(6)(e).

23.10 Appeals from the FTT in Code matters would seem to be caught by Rule 10(6) only if an appeal against a decision made by the FTT in a Code matter itself constitutes 'proceedings under' the Code. When one commences a Reference, one is clearly commencing proceedings under the Code. Although an appeal against a decision made under the Code is not itself instituted or carried on 'under' the Code, one would think that it does constitute 'proceedings under' the Code.

23.11 It is doubtful that there is any justification for an appeal to be some sort of no-costs jurisdiction when the first instance proceedings had entailed full costs powers. Although it would have been easy for the legislation simply to provide that costs may be awarded in any appeal from a decision in proceedings in which the FTT had full discretionary costs powers, that was not the drafting that was chosen. When the reference to proceedings under the Code was included in the procedure rules, it would have been widely expected that most Code cases would have been dealt with at first instance by the UT. That being the case, appeals to the UT under the Code were perhaps not considered. Indeed, it was nearly six years between the first Code cases being heard in 2018, and the first appeal[12] to the UT relating to a Code matter in 2024.

5 Rule 10(3)(a) of the UTLC Rules.
6 Rule 10(3)(b) of the UTLC Rules.
7 Rules 10(3)(c) and 10(14) of the UTLC Rules.
8 Rule 10(6)(e) of the UTLC Rules.
9 Rule 10(6)(d) of the UTLC Rules.
10 Rule 10(6)(g) of the UTLC Rules.
11 See s 111(1) and (2) of the Land Registration Act 2002 which make clear that an appeal may proceed to the UT under the Land Registration Act 2002 otherwise than on a point of law, or under s 11 of the Tribunals, Courts and Enforcement Act 2007 on a point of law.
12 Ie, the *Gravesham* case.

23.12 It is worth noting that para 96(1) of the Code (concerning costs) only relates to proceedings in which a tribunal exercises functions by virtue of regulations under para 95(1), and that para 95(1) only allows regulations to be made that provide for a function conferred by the Code on 'the court' to be exercised by a tribunal. The Code does not confer an appellate function on 'the court', and as such, it would appear that para 96(1) does not itself give the UT the power to award costs in an appeal. One would think that it derives that power from rule 10 of the UTLC Rules, on a proper interpretation of that rule.

23.13 Where costs are not awardable under rule 10(5) or (6), the tribunal may, with the consent of the parties, or where there is a disparity of interest or resources between the parties, direct that an order for costs may be made in the proceedings in respect of the costs incurred after such a direction.[13]

The Upper Tribunal (Lands Chamber) Practice Direction

23.14 The Upper Tribunal (Lands Chamber) Practice Direction, dated 2 January 2024, includes a paragraph relating to the exercise of its power to award costs, at para 25.10:

> 'The Tribunal's power to award costs is discretionary, and it will usually be exercised in accordance with the principles applied in the High Court. The general rule is that the successful party ought to receive their costs from the unsuccessful party. (A different general rule applies to applications to discharge or modify a restrictive covenant – see paragraph 16.10 above). The Tribunal will have regard to all the circumstances of the case, including the conduct of the parties; whether a party has succeeded on part of their case, even if they have not been wholly successful; and admissible offers to settle. The conduct which may be taken into account will include conduct during and before the proceedings; whether a party has acted reasonably in pursuing or contesting an issue; the manner in which they have conducted their case; whether or not they have exaggerated their claim; and whether they have unreasonably refused to engage in ADR or comply with a relevant pre-reference protocol.'

23.15 Given that the Code itself includes provisions relating to costs, the above general practice has to be considered in the light of those provisions.

The Code power to award costs and its exercise

23.16 Paragraph 96(1) of the Code provides that:

> '(1) Where in any proceedings a tribunal exercises functions by virtue of regulations under para 95(1) it may make such order as it thinks fit as to costs, or, in Scotland, expenses.
>
> (2) The matters a tribunal must have regard to in making such an order include in particular–
>
> (a) the extent to which any party is successful in the proceedings, and
>
> (b) any unreasonable refusal by a party to engage in alternative dispute resolution.'

13 Rule 10(4) of the UTLC Rules.

23.17 It is surely the case that para 96(1) confers a broad discretion on a tribunal that is making a decision on costs under the Code. In respect of this discretion, a tribunal must surely take into account all relevant matters that are drawn to its attention or that are self-evident. One of these matters, by para 96(2), is the extent to which a party is successful in proceedings, and one relates to the unreasonable refusal of ADR.

23.18 In the case of court proceedings to which the rules in the CPR apply, CPR rule 44.2(2) creates a well-known 'general rule' that 'the unsuccessful party will be ordered to pay the costs of the successful party',[14] but 'the court may make a different order'.[15] It is perhaps notable that the Code does not use the same language.

23.19 Paragraph 96(2) uses the expression 'in particular' in respect of the two specified matters. Where no issues of ADR arise, it is still considered that this phrase does not quite create a 'general rule' in respect of the 'successful' party receiving its costs in all types of Code cases. It might be thought to create a 'starting point', in the sense that it is the only particular factor which the tribunal is specifically mandated to consider (where no ADR issues arise). If one party has succeeded in a fully contested Reference, and all other things are equal, the successful party might expect to obtain an Order for costs.

23.20 However, the tribunals have recognised the particular nature of proceedings under the Code, and a number of decisions have either accepted or rejected analogies with other areas of land-related litigation with particular practices as to costs.

23.21 In the very early Code case of *EE v Islington*, for the reasons given in its Costs Order, the UT rejected a submission that the discretion as to costs should be exercised in a similar manner to applications to modify or discharge restrictive covenants under section 84(1) of the Law of Property Act 1925 ('LPA 1925').

23.22 Under section 84(1), the established practice of the UT is that a party who has sought to defend the benefit of a covenant but has ultimately been unsuccessful will not be ordered to pay the costs of the successful applicant but will have to bear its own costs. The exception to this is where the respondent has acted unreasonably in seeking to defend the benefit of the covenant, in which case it can expect to be ordered to pay the applicant's costs. This established practice is reflected at para 16.10 of the UTLC's Practice Directions (published on 2 January 2024).

23.23 The submission was made in *Islington* that an applicant for Code rights is similarly seeking the indulgence of the tribunal in order to override the property rights of a respondent to allow physical works and a new use of land to be instituted in a manner that is argued to be consistent with the public interest. The comparison between the Code and restrictive covenant regimes was rejected in the circumstances of the case.

23.24 It is fair to acknowledge the circumstances of *Islington*, namely that the matters in dispute were: (a) the terms of a Code agreement, and (b) the monies payable for consideration and compensation under the Code agreement. The respondent was debarred from disputing the terms that had been proposed by the operator because

14 CPR r. 44.2(2)(a).
15 CPR r. 44.2(2)(b).

its solicitors had not engaged in the 'travelling draft' process that had been ordered by the UT, and therefore the operator obtained the terms that it had sought. Further, the consideration that was offered by the operator and which formed part of the resulting agreement was actually higher than that determined by the UT. As regards compensation, there were numerous heads sought by the respondent, which were rejected. Such a case might be said to be more similar to an unopposed lease renewal under the 1954 Act, in which a court would be highly likely to award the landlord its costs where it succeeds on all of its terms and substantially succeeds on rent.

23.25 However, more recently, the UT has accepted certain parallels between the Code and the compulsory purchase regime in the context of considering costs.

23.26 In *HSBC*,[16] the Deputy President noted that most para 26 References relating to surveys (often called 'MSVs'[17]) are resolved by consensus without the need for a hearing. In such cases, it is often agreed that there be no order as to costs. However, where there was no such agreement on costs, the usual order was that the operator should pay the site provider's costs, which would then usually be summarily assessed.

23.27 The rationale for this usual Order was then set out as follows:[18]

> '10. The Tribunal's usual order reflects the principle that the costs of a reference are necessary because interim Code rights cannot be conferred by agreement but may only be imposed by order of the Tribunal. Statutory rights of compensation may also only be conferred by order of the Tribunal. The costs incurred by a site provider in a reference made necessary because an operator wishes to have a Code right to undertake a survey ought not in principle to fall on the site provider.
>
> 11. The Tribunal's usual order also reflects its practice in other circumstances where, in the public interest, powers of compulsory acquisition are exercisable on terms to be determined by the Tribunal. The costs incurred by claimants in establishing the amount of compensation to which they are entitled following the compulsory acquisition of their land are part of the expense that has been imposed on them by the acquisition. For that reason, the Tribunal will normally make an order that the costs incurred by a claimant who is awarded compensation should be paid by the acquiring authority (see paragraph 24.2 of the Tribunal's Practice Directions[19]).'

23.28 Accordingly, one reason for the usual Order for costs in para 26 cases relates to the fact that such rights cannot be conferred by agreement without the need for the tribunal's involvement. It makes sense for a cooperative site provider to have its reasonable litigation costs reimbursed in such circumstances.

23.29 However, the second reason for the usual Order reflects the fact that the Code is in essence a vehicle for the compulsory acquisition of land rights. The cost of establishing the quantum of compensation to which a site provider is entitled is itself a cost forced on the site provider by the acquisition process. Naturally, if an operator

16 *EE Ltd and Hutchison 3G UK Ltd v HSBC Bank Plc* [2022] UKUT 174 (LC) at [8]–[11].

17 Multi-skilled visits.

18 *HSBC*, [10] and [11].

19 This proposition is now contained at para 23.10 of the latest version of the UTLC Practice Directions, published on 2 January 2024.

has already made a fulsome offer of compensation that exceeds that to which the site provider is ultimately entitled, such an offer will be taken into account in respect of costs. This is the position under the compulsory purchase regime, as described at para 23.11 sub para 2 of the UTLC Practice Direction (2 January 2024).

23.30 Of course, the compulsory purchase proceedings (which are taken as an analogue for Code proceedings determining compensation) are not necessarily interim proceedings. Accordingly, it would appear that there is no reason why the second limb of the justification given in *HSBC* for the usual Order on costs should only apply in para 26 cases. One might think thatthe same logic applies in any case where the site provider is agreeable in principle to the making of a Code agreement, but wishes to have its compensation determined.

The first limb of the justification given in *HSBC*, that para 26 agreements must always be imposed by the tribunal, might at first glance not appear to be of relevance in cases where a consensual agreement is possible. However, in the FTT in *On Tower UK Limited v IX Limited*,[20] Judge Jackson recognised that a respondent is 'fully entitled to insist on the imposition of a new agreement by the tribunal' in order to protect their position as to compensation under para 25, describing that stance as a 'thoroughly principled position to take'.[21]

23.31 How far this principle extends remains an open question. The financial package payable under the Code includes both consideration and compensation. Consideration is an amount payable in respect of the acquisition and exercise of rights, according to a statutorily defined formula. In principle, it has much in common with compensation under the compulsory purchase regime. One might ask rhetorically whether a site provider is prima facie entitled to its reasonable costs of any Reference whose sole or principal function is to determine the consideration payable by an operator (together with para 25 compensation or on its own).

23.32 Indeed, para 11 of the *HSBC* judgment refers to situations where, in the public interest, rights are compulsorily acquired 'on terms to be determined by the tribunal'. One might even rhetorically ask why financial terms should be held to constitute a special case. There are frequently other terms in dispute in a Code reference, and it could be argued that the cost of ascertainment of these other terms is just as necessary as the cost of ascertainment of financial terms. On the other hand, it could equally be said that non-financial terms form part of that which is being acquired, rather than what is given to a site provider in recompense. In reality, there will be some terms that exist principally to protect a site provider and some terms that enlarge the rights of an operator. In any event, where an operator has succeeded in achieving all of the terms which it sought, in the face of resistance from a site provider, one might view the originally proposed Code agreement as a species of open offer. That being the case, if the operator succeeds in obtaining exactly what it sought, there can be expected to be negative costs consequences for a site provider.

23.33 Further, in FTT proceedings in *IX Limited*,[22] it was argued by the site provider that the principle in *HSBC* was logically of similar application to Part 5 Code renewal

20 Case number LC-2022-000361.
21 *IX Limited* at [15].
22 Case number LC-2022-000361.

proceedings, ie, where a new agreement was sought that was not interim in any way. After all, para 26 proceedings are not by necessity interim in the traditional sense of being determined pending the resolution of a final merits-based decision.

23.34 In *IX Limited*, the site provider's pleaded case agreed to the agreement sought by the operator in its entirety. In addition, it sought an Order under para 25 for the payment of its transactional costs, and an Order for (litigation) costs. Slightly unusual facts then developed, in that the operator then sought to pay consideration of £850 rather than the £1,500 which it had pleaded. The site provider then ultimately agreed to that amended rental figure.

23.35 The relevance of the proposition in *HSBC* as to the usual Order was not disputed in *IX Limited* by the operator, although the operator did seek to resist a costs order on the facts. The site provider was awarded its costs, although the FTT did not include any treatment of the submissions as to the relevance of the general rule in *HSBC* in its judgment, that question not having been the subject of dispute between the parties.

23.36 Judge Jackson took the opportunity to reiterate a costs proportionality warning previously given in *St Martins* in respect of MSVs (discussed below), indicating that the Deputy President's observations resonated even more strongly in unopposed renewal proceedings.[23] The judge also appeared to indicate that parties should seek to conduct cases in the FTT in a manner which is more economical than in the UT or the High Court.[24] However, it should be borne in mind that fewer cases at that time were being sent to the FTT by the UT, such that the FTT had not yet become the commonplace destination for Code cases. Indeed, the judge made reference to the case having been transferred to the FTT because no point of principle was engaged and there was no other compelling reason for it to continue it the UT. Where cases are litigated in the FTT which previously would have been litigated in the UT, and the parties are using specialist solicitors and counsel, it might be argued that what is a proportionate level of costs in the FTT would be similar to that in the UT.

The effect of an offer to settle

23.37 As in most litigation, where a party makes a timely offer to settle which is refused, and then it substantially beats that offer at trial, this can be expected to be relevant to the question of costs. However, it may often be unclear whether a party has clearly beaten its offer, and even if it has done so, this will not always be automatically determinative.

23.38 In *Green*,[25] the Upper Tribunal did not consider that settlement offers made by the claimant before the trial should determine the outcome on costs. Even where it beat its offer on consideration, the offer related to different terms, and so it was not possible to say that the claimant made an offer that the respondent failed to beat.

23 *IX Limited* costs decision at [54].
24 See *IX Limited* at [55].
25 [2020] UKUT 348 (LC), at [172].

The effect of one party looking for a precedent

23.39 In *Green*, it was argued that the tribunal should reduce the costs to which the operator was entitled, on the basis that it was said to be seeking a precedent on certain issues for its own wider commercial purposes. The tribunal rejected this argument,[26] holding that the operator succeeded on the relevant issues and should be entitled to its costs.

23.40 Naturally, when such costs are assessed, arguments may still be made as to reasonableness and proportionality to the issues in the Reference in question. One might expect that when a large commercial undertaking is litigating a point that it considers to be of wider importance to its own business, it may be prepared to spend sums that would be considered unreasonable and/or disproportionate when subject to assessment in the context of one Reference.

The unreasonable refusal of ADR

23.41 On the question of costs, one of the factors to which the tribunal is required to have regard 'in particular' is 'any unreasonable refusal by a party to engage in alternative dispute resolution'.[27] This provision applies in all cases regardless of whether there was a Code-imposed obligation to consider ADR.

Quantum of costs in MSV cases

23.42 The UT has been clear and firm in respect of its treatment of costs in MSV cases. One driver of this robust approach has been the purpose of the Code, and the need to discourage conduct that defeats or frustrates that purpose.

23.43 As early as 2021 in *St Martins*,[28] the Deputy President was moved to make reference to 'the Tribunal's repeated insistence that references seeking access rights under paragraph 26 should be conducted as economically as possible'.

23.44 One such insistence, which the Deputy President surely had in mind, was *Cornerstone Telecommunications Infrastructure Ltd v Central Saint Giles General Partner Ltd*[29]. In that case, three parties incurred more than £100,000 in aggregate[30] in a dispute over access to the roof of a residential building. It is fair to say that that is not an isolated occurrence. In that case, the tribunal said as follows:

> 'The new Code regime is intended to facilitate the provision of telecommunications services without delay and at limited cost. The preparatory stages of the installation of new equipment (at least if the site itself is a new one) will almost always require a survey, conducted over a period of a few weeks and involving a small number of visits by a limited group of individuals, before a decision can be taken about the suitability of the site. If those preparatory stages are allowed to become the

26 [2020] UKUT 348 (LC), at [169].
27 See para 96(2)(b).
28 At [20].
29 [2019] UKUT 183 (LC).
30 This figure was quoted by the Deputy President in the *St Martins* case at [42].

occasion for preliminary trials of strength involving legal firepower on the scale deployed in this reference there is a serious risk of the objectives of the Code being frustrated.'[31]

23.45 The tribunal awarded the two respondents £5,000 each in costs (they had been substantially successful on the substance of the dispute). It is fair to note that the respondents had raised points that 'were completely unnecessary, and which have not been pursued',[32] and this was taken into account in respect of costs. However, a substantial reason for the low level of costs recovery was proportionality. It was held that the sum awarded was a proportionate sum for the resolution of the issues on which the respondents could be considered to have been successful, and that they need not have incurred nearly as much as they did.

23.46 The tribunal then issued a warning of general application at [30]:

> 'The Tribunal wishes it to be known by other parties who refuse access to their land or buildings for surveys that, whatever the outcome, they cannot expect to recover costs on the scale incurred by the parties in these proceedings. Equally, the Tribunal wishes to make it clear to operators, as it has done in the past, that they cannot simply demand unquestioning cooperation from property owners. The claimant's wooing of potential site providers has become a little less rough, but its technique still has a long way to go.'

23.47 This particular warning was referred to and reiterated in *St Martins*.[33] In that case, despite allowing the Respondent to recover its transactional costs in full as compensation, the tribunal substantially cut down the recoverable litigation costs. The Deputy President referred to another MSV case that had come before the tribunal the same day, in which the site provider's solicitors had incurred some £6,500. It was noted that this did not set a benchmark for MSV cases because each case will involve a particular building and particular issues, for example the 'important dispute' over intrusive works in *St Martins*. However, the £6,500 bill of costs showed that MSV proceedings could be conducted at quite modest expense. The operator in *St Martins* had incurred some £30,500, and the site provider had incurred more than twice as much, including surveyor's fees. The tribunal awarded the site provider £12,500, to reflect both the extent of the site provider's success, 'and the proportionate cost of achieving it'.[34]

Assessment of the quantum of Costs

23.48 The FTT has the power to carry out a summary assessment of costs,[35] or the quantum of costs can be determined by detailed assessment either on the standard or

31 At [4].

32 See *Cornerstone Telecommunications Infrastructure Ltd v Central Saint Giles General Partner Ltd* [2019] UKUT 183 (LC) at [29].

33 At [42] and [43].

34 The Tribunal's reasoning and conclusion on costs in *St Martins* is set out at [39]–[46] thereof. It is worth noting that in the *IX Limited* case (discussed above at **23.33** onwards), Judge Jackson in the FTT assessed quantum by asking a question which closely followed the Deputy President's words, by asking at [57]: 'What sum reflects both the extent of the respondent's success and the proportionate cost of achieving it?'

35 Rule 13(7)(a) of the FTT Rules.

indemnity basis, depending on the Order of the FTT.[36] Alternatively, the paying person and receiving person may determine the quantum of costs by agreement.[37]

23.49 The FTT may order an amount to be paid on account before the assessment of costs has occurred.[38]

Settlement of a Reference: who pays the costs?

23.50 It is of course open to the parties to make provision as to costs where a Reference is settled by consent, and this frequently happens. Sometimes a site provider has resisted a Code agreement but made sufficient mileage on consideration and terms that it is content to settle a Reference with no Order as to costs. Sometimes a preliminary issue has been determined, which makes the remainder of the Reference eminently settleable, and the appropriate Costs consequences are often obvious to the parties. However, there are occasions where the parties ultimately reach substantive settlement but their positions on costs remain rather more entrenched. The tribunal may have to determine the appropriate Order as to costs in such a situation. There is no presumption that there will be no Order as to costs in such circumstances. This situation arose in *Gateway Properties*,[39] in which the relevant principles that arise from the authorities were summarised by the Deputy President at [23]. This summary is reproduced in Chapter 22 at **22.19** onwards above within a discussion of the decision on costs in that case.

36 Rule 13(7)(c) of the FTT Rules. Rule 13(8) also has the effect of applying various standard provisions to a detailed assessment under rule 13(7)(c) as though the proceedings had been in a court to which the Civil Procedure Rules 1998 apply.

37 Rule 13(7)(b) of the FTT Rules.

38 Rule 13(9) of the FTT Rules.

39 *Cornerstone Telecommunications Infrastructure Ltd v Gateway Properties Ltd & Anor* [2023] UKUT 188 (LC).

Appendix

The Electronic Communications Code

Communications Act 2003, Sch 3A

Section 106

Part 1
Key concepts

INTRODUCTORY

1

(1) This Part defines some key concepts used in this code.

(2) For definitions of other terms used in this code, see—

(a) paragraph 94 (meaning of 'the court').

(b) paragraph 105 (meaning of 'occupier'),

(c) paragraph 108 (general interpretation),

(d) section 32 (meaning of electronic communications networks and services), and

(e) section 405 (general interpretation).][1]

AMENDMENTS

1 Schedule inserted by the Digital Economy Act 2017, s 4(2), Sch 1.

[THE OPERATOR

2

In this code 'operator' means—

(a) where this code is applied in any person's case by a direction under section 106, that person, and

(b) where this code applies by virtue of section 106(3)(b), the Secretary of State or (as the case may be) the Northern Ireland department in question.][1]

AMENDMENTS

1 Schedule inserted by the Digital Economy Act 2017, s 4(2), Sch 1.

[THE CODE RIGHTS

3

[(1)][1] For the purposes of this code a 'code right', in relation to an operator and any land, is a right for the statutory purposes—

(a) to install electronic communications apparatus on, under or over the land,

(b) to keep installed electronic communications apparatus which is on, under or over the land,

(c) to inspect, maintain, adjust, alter, repair, upgrade or operate electronic communications apparatus which is on, under or over the land,

[(ca) to share with another operator the use of electronic communications apparatus which the first operator keeps installed on, under or over the land,][2]

(d) to carry out any works on the land for or in connection with the installation of electronic communications apparatus on, under or over the land or elsewhere,

(e) to carry out any works on the land for or in connection with the maintenance, adjustment, alteration, repair, upgrading or operation of electronic communications apparatus which is on, under or over the land or elsewhere,

[(ea) to carry out any works on the land for the purposes of, or in connection with, sharing with another operator the use of electronic communications apparatus which the first operator keeps installed on, under or over the land or elsewhere,][2]

(f) to enter the land to inspect, maintain, adjust, alter, repair, upgrade or operate any electronic communications apparatus which is on, under or over the land or elsewhere,

[(fa) to enter the land for the purposes of, or in connection with, sharing with another operator the use of electronic communications apparatus which the first operator keeps installed on, under or over the land or elsewhere,][2]

(g) to connect to a power supply,

(h) to interfere with or obstruct a means of access to or from the land (whether or not any electronic communications apparatus is on, under or over the land), or

(i) to lop or cut back, or require another person to lop or cut back, any tree or other vegetation that interferes or will or may interfere with electronic communications apparatus.

[(2) In sub-paragraph (1), references to 'the first operator' are to the operator mentioned in the opening words of that sub-paragraph.][2]][3]

AMENDMENTS

1 Renumbered by the Product Security and Telecommunications Infrastructure Act 2022, s 57(1), (2)(a).

2 Inserted by the Product Security and Telecommunications Infrastructure Act 2022, s 57(1), (2)(b), (c).

3 Schedule inserted by the Digital Economy Act 2017, s 4(2), Sch 1.

[THE STATUTORY PURPOSES

[4

(1) In this code 'the statutory purposes', in relation to an operator, means—

(a) in relation to sharing rights, the purposes of enabling the provision by other operators of their networks, and

(b) in relation to rights other than sharing rights—

(i) the purposes of providing the operator's network, or

(ii) the purposes of providing an infrastructure system.

(2) In sub-paragraph (1), 'sharing right' means a right within paragraph 3(1)(ca), (ea) or (fa).][1]][2]

AMENDMENTS

1 Substituted by the Product Security and Telecommunications Infrastructure Act 2022, s 57(1), (3).

2 Schedule inserted by the Digital Economy Act 2017, s 4(2), Sch 1.

[ELECTRONIC COMMUNICATIONS APPARATUS, LINES AND STRUCTURES

5

(1) In this code 'electronic communications apparatus' means—

(a) apparatus designed or adapted for use in connection with the provision of an electronic communications network,

(b) apparatus designed or adapted for a use which consists of or includes the sending or receiving of communications or other signals that are transmitted by means of an electronic communications network,

(c) lines, and

(d) other structures or things designed or adapted for use in connection with the provision of an electronic communications network.

(2) References to the installation of electronic communications apparatus are to be construed accordingly.

(3) In this code—

'line' means any wire, cable, tube, pipe or similar thing (including its casing or coating) which is designed or adapted for use in connection with the provision of any electronic communications network or electronic communications service;

'structure' includes a building only if the sole purpose of that building is to enclose other electronic communications apparatus.][1]

AMENDMENTS

1 Schedule inserted by the Digital Economy Act 2017, s 4(2), Sch 1.

[THE OPERATOR'S NETWORK

6

In this code 'network' in relation to an operator means—

(a) if the operator falls within paragraph 2(a), so much of any electronic communications network or infrastructure system provided by the operator as is not excluded from the application of the code under section 106(5), and

(b) if the operator falls within paragraph 2(b), the electronic communications network which the Secretary of State or the Northern Ireland department is providing or proposing to provide.][1]

AMENDMENTS

1 Schedule inserted by the Digital Economy Act 2017, s 4(2), Sch 1.

[INFRASTRUCTURE SYSTEM

7

(1) In this code 'infrastructure system' means a system of infrastructure provided so as to be available for use by providers of electronic communications networks for the purposes of the provision by them of their networks.

(2) References in this code to provision of an infrastructure system include references to establishing or maintaining such a system.][1]

AMENDMENTS

1 Schedule inserted by the Digital Economy Act 2017, s 4(2), Sch 1.

[Part 2
Conferral of code rights and their exercise

INTRODUCTORY

8

This Part of this code makes provision about—

(a) the conferral of code rights,

(b) the persons who are bound by code rights, and

(c) the exercise of code rights.][1]

AMENDMENTS

1 Schedule inserted by the Digital Economy Act 2017, s 4(2), Sch 1.

[WHO MAY CONFER CODE RIGHTS?

9

[(1)][1] A code right in respect of land may only be conferred on an operator by an agreement between the occupier of the land and the operator.

[(2) But in a case where an operator ('the first operator') has the right to share the use of electronic communications apparatus with another operator ('the second operator') under or by virtue of an agreement under this Part, sub-paragraph (1) does not prevent the agreement from providing for the first operator to permit the second operator to exercise, in connection with the sharing, a code right conferred on the first operator by the agreement.][2]][3]

AMENDMENTS

1 Renumbered by the Product Security and Telecommunications Infrastructure Act 2022, s 57(1), (4)(a).

2 Inserted by the Product Security and Telecommunications Infrastructure Act 2022, s 57(1), (4)(b).

3 Schedule inserted by the Digital Economy Act 2017, s 4(2), Sch 1.

[WHO ELSE IS BOUND BY CODE RIGHTS?

10

(1) This paragraph applies if, [pursuant to an agreement under this Part or Part 4A][1], a code right is conferred on an operator in respect of land by a person ('O') who is the occupier of the land when the code right is conferred.

(2) If O has an interest in the land when the code right is conferred, the code right also binds—

(a) the successors in title to that interest,

(b) a person with an interest in the land that is created after the right is conferred and is derived (directly or indirectly) out of—

(i) O's interest, or

(ii) the interest of a successor in title to O's interest, and

(c) any other person at any time in occupation of the land whose right to occupation was granted by—

(i) O, at a time when O was bound by the code right, or

(ii) a person within paragraph (a) or (b).

(3) A successor in title who is bound by a code right by virtue of sub-paragraph (2)(a) is to be treated as a party to the agreement by which O conferred the right.

(4) The code right also binds any other person with an interest in the land who has[, pursuant to an agreement under this Part or Part 4A,][2] agreed to be bound by it.

(5) If such a person ('P') agrees to be bound by the code right, the code right also binds—

(a) the successors in title to P's interest,

(b) a person with an interest in the land that is created after P agrees to be bound and is derived (directly or indirectly) out of—

(i) P's interest, or

(ii) the interest of a successor in title to P's interest, and

(c) any other person at any time in occupation of the land whose right to occupation was granted by—

(i) P, at a time when P was bound by the code right, or

(ii) a person within paragraph (a) or (b).

(6) A successor in title who is bound by a code right by virtue of sub-paragraph (5)(a) is to be treated as a party to the agreement by which P agreed to be bound by the right.][3]

AMENDMENTS

1 Substituted by the Telecommunications Infrastructure (Leasehold Property) Act 2021, s 2, Schedule, paras 1, 4(1), (2)(a).

2 Inserted by the Telecommunications Infrastructure (Leasehold Property) Act 2021, s 2, Schedule, paras 1, 4(1), (2)(b).

3 Schedule inserted by the Digital Economy Act 2017, s 4(2), Sch 1.

[REQUIREMENTS FOR AGREEMENTS

11

(1) An agreement under this Part—

(a) must be in writing,

(b) must be signed by or on behalf of the parties to it,

(c) must state for how long the code right is exercisable, and

(d) must state the period of notice (if any) required to terminate the agreement.

(2) Sub-paragraph (1)(a) and (b) also applies to the variation of an agreement under this Part.

(3) The agreement as varied must still comply with sub-paragraph (1)(c) and (d).][1]

AMENDMENTS

1 Schedule inserted by the Digital Economy Act 2017, s 4(2), Sch 1.

[EXERCISE OF CODE RIGHTS

12

(1) A code right is exercisable only in accordance with the terms subject to which it is conferred.

(2) Anything done by an operator in the exercise of a code right conferred under this Part [or Part 4A][1] in relation to any land is to be treated as done in the exercise of a statutory power.

(3) Sub-paragraph (2) does not apply against a person who—

(a) is the owner of the freehold estate in the land or the lessee of the land, and

(b) is not for the time being bound by the code right.

(4) Sub-paragraph (2) does not apply against a person who has the benefit of a covenant or agreement entered into as respects the land, if—

(a) the covenant or agreement was entered into under a enactment, and

(b) by virtue of the enactment, it binds or will bind persons who derive title or otherwise claim—

(i) under the covenantor, or

(ii) under a party to the agreement.

(5) In the application of sub-paragraph (3) to Scotland the reference to a person who is the owner of the freehold estate in the land is to be read as a reference to a person who is the owner of the land.][2]

AMENDMENTS

1 Inserted by the Telecommunications Infrastructure (Leasehold Property) Act 2021, s 2, Schedule, paras 1, 4(1), (3).

2 Schedule inserted by the Digital Economy Act 2017, s 4(2), Sch 1.

[ACCESS TO LAND

13

(1) This paragraph applies to an operator by whom any of the following rights is exercisable in relation to land—

(a) a code right within paragraph (a) to (g) or (i) of [paragraph 3(1)][1];

(b) a right under Part 8 (street works rights);

(c) a right under Part 9 (tidal water rights);

(d) a right under paragraph 74 (power to fly lines).

(2) The operator may not exercise the right so as to interfere with or obstruct any means of access to or from any other land unless, in accordance with this code, the occupier of the other land has conferred or is otherwise bound by a code right within paragraph (h) of [paragraph 3(1)][1].

(3) A reference in this code to a means of access to or from land includes a means of access to or from land that is provided for use in emergencies.

(4) This paragraph does not require a person to whom sub-paragraph (5) applies to agree to the exercise of any code right on land other than the land mentioned in that sub-paragraph.

(5) This sub-paragraph applies to a person who is the occupier of, or owns an interest in, land which is—

(a) a street in England and Wales or Northern Ireland,

(b) a road in Scotland, or

(c) tidal water or lands within the meaning of Part 9 of this code.][2]

AMENDMENTS

1 Substituted by the Product Security and Telecommunications Infrastructure Act 2022, s 57(1), (5).

2 Schedule inserted by the Digital Economy Act 2017, s 4(2), Sch 1.

[CODE RIGHTS AND LAND REGISTRATION

14

Where an enactment requires interests, charges or other obligations affecting land to be registered, the provisions of this code about who is bound by a code right have effect whether or not that right is registered.][1]

AMENDMENTS

1 Schedule inserted by the Digital Economy Act 2017, s 4(2), Sch 1.

[Part 3
Assignment of code rights, and upgrading and sharing of apparatus

INTRODUCTORY

15

This Part of this code makes provision for—

(a) operators to assign agreements under Part 2,

(b) operators to upgrade electronic communications apparatus [which—

(i) is electronic communications apparatus to which such an agreement relates, or

(ii) is electronic communications apparatus installed before 29 December 2003][1], and

(c) operators to share the use of any such electronic communications apparatus.][2]

AMENDMENTS

1 Substituted by the Product Security and Telecommunications Infrastructure Act 2022, s 59(1), (2).

2 Schedule inserted by the Digital Economy Act 2017, s 4(2), Sch 1.

[ASSIGNMENT OF CODE RIGHTS

16

(1) Any agreement under Part 2 of this code is void to the extent that—

(a) it prevents or limits assignment of the agreement to another operator, or

(b) it makes assignment of the agreement to another operator subject to conditions (including a condition requiring the payment of money).

(2) Sub-paragraph (1) does not apply to a term that requires the assignor to enter into a guarantee agreement (see sub-paragraph (7)).

(3) In this paragraph references to 'the assignor' or 'the assignee' are to the operator by whom or to whom an agreement under Part 2 of this code is assigned or proposed to be assigned.

(4) From the time when the assignment of an agreement under Part 2 of this code takes effect, the assignee is bound by the terms of the agreement.

(5) The assignor is not liable for any breach of a term of the agreement that occurs after the assignment if (and only if), before the breach took place, the assignor or the assignee gave a notice in writing to the other party to the agreement which—

(a) identified the assignee, and

(b) provided an address for service (for the purposes of paragraph 91(2)(a)) for the assignee.

(6) Sub-paragraph (5) is subject to the terms of any guarantee agreement.

(7) A 'guarantee agreement' is an agreement, in connection with the assignment of an agreement under Part 2 of this code, under which the assignor guarantees to any extent the performance by the assignee of the obligations that become binding on the assignee under sub-paragraph (4) (the 'relevant obligations').

(8) An agreement is not a guarantee agreement to the extent that it purports—

(a) to impose on the assignor a requirement to guarantee in any way the performance of the relevant obligations by a person other than the assignee, or

(b) to impose on the assignor any liability, restriction or other requirement of any kind in relation to a time after the relevant obligations cease to be binding on the assignee.

(9) Subject to sub-paragraph (8), a guarantee agreement may—

(a) impose on the assignor any liability as sole or principal debtor in respect of the relevant obligations;

(b) impose on the assignor liabilities as guarantor in respect of the assignee's performance of the relevant obligations which are no more onerous than those to which the assignor would be subject in the event of the assignor being liable as sole or principal debtor in respect of any relevant obligation;

(c) make provision incidental or supplementary to any provision within paragraph (a) or (b).

(10) In the application of this paragraph to Scotland references to assignment of an agreement are to be read as references to assignation of an agreement.

(11) Nothing in the Landlord and Tenant Amendment (Ireland) Act 1860 applies in relation to an agreement under Part 2 of this code so as to—

(a) prevent or limit assignment of the agreement to another operator, or

(b) relieve the assignor from liability for any breach of a term of the agreement that occurs after the assignment.][1]

AMENDMENTS

1 Schedule inserted by the Digital Economy Act 2017, s 4(2), Sch 1.

[POWER FOR OPERATOR TO UPGRADE OR SHARE APPARATUS

17

(1) An operator ('the main operator') who has entered into an agreement under Part 2 of this code may, if the conditions in sub-paragraphs (2) and (3) are met—

(a) upgrade the electronic communications apparatus to which the agreement relates, or

(b) share the use of such electronic communications apparatus with another operator.

(2) The first condition is that any changes as a result of the upgrading or sharing to the electronic communications apparatus to which the agreement relates have no adverse impact, or no more than a minimal adverse impact, on its appearance.

(3) The second condition is that the upgrading or sharing imposes no additional burden on the other party to the agreement.

(4) For the purposes of sub-paragraph (3) an additional burden includes anything that—

(a) has an additional adverse effect on the other party's enjoyment of the land, or

(b) causes additional loss, damage or expense to that party.

(5) Any agreement under Part 2 of this code is void to the extent that—

(a) it prevents or limits the upgrading or sharing, in a case where the conditions in sub-paragraphs (2) and (3) are met, of the electronic communications apparatus to which the agreement relates, or

(b) it makes upgrading or sharing of such apparatus subject to conditions to be met by the operator (including a condition requiring the payment of money).

(6) References in this paragraph to sharing electronic communications apparatus include carrying out works to the apparatus to enable such sharing to take place.][1]

AMENDMENTS

1 Schedule inserted by the Digital Economy Act 2017, s 4(2), Sch 1.

[17A

(1) This paragraph applies where—

(a) an operator ('the main operator') keeps electronic communications apparatus installed under land,

(b) the main operator is not a party to an agreement under Part 2 of this code in relation to the electronic communications apparatus, and

(c) the electronic communications apparatus was installed before 29 December 2003.

(2) If the conditions in sub-paragraphs (3), (4) and (6) are met, the main operator may—

(a) upgrade the electronic communications apparatus, or

(b) share the use of the electronic communications apparatus with another operator.

(3) The first condition is that the upgrading or sharing has no adverse impact on the land.

(4) The second condition is that the upgrading or sharing imposes no burden on any person with an interest in the land.

(5) For the purposes of sub-paragraph (4) a burden includes anything that—

(a) has an adverse effect on the person's enjoyment of the land, or

(b) causes loss, damage or expense to the person.

(6) The third condition is that, before the beginning of the period of 21 days ending with the day on which the main operator begins to upgrade the electronic communications apparatus or (as the case may be) share its use, the main operator attaches a notice, in a secure and durable manner, to a conspicuous object on the relevant land.

(7) A notice attached for the purposes of sub-paragraph (6) must—

(a) be attached in a position where it is reasonably legible,

(b) state that the main operator intends to upgrade the electronic communications apparatus or (as the case may be) share its use with another operator,

(c) state the date on which the main operator intends to begin to upgrade the electronic communications apparatus or (as the case may be) share its use with another operator,

(d) state, in a case where the main operator intends to share the use of the electronic communications apparatus with another operator, the name of the other operator, and

(e) give the name of the main operator and an address in the United Kingdom at which the main operator may be contacted about the upgrading or sharing.

(8) Any person giving a notice at that address in respect of that electronic communications apparatus is to be treated as having been given that address for the purposes of paragraph 91(2).

(9) Nothing in this paragraph is to be read as conferring a right on the main operator to enter the land for the purpose of upgrading or sharing the use of the electronic communications apparatus.

(10) References in this paragraph to sharing electronic communications apparatus include carrying out works to the electronic communications apparatus to enable such sharing to take place.

(11) In this paragraph 'the relevant land' means—

(a) in a case where the main operator has a right to enter the land under which the electronic communications apparatus is installed, that land;

(b) in any other case, the land on which works will be carried out to enable the upgrading or sharing to take place or, where there is more than one set of works, the land on which each set of works will be carried out.][1]

AMENDMENTS

1 Inserted by the Product Security and Telecommunications Infrastructure Act 2022, s 59(1), (3).

[EFFECT OF AGREEMENTS ENABLING SHARING BETWEEN OPERATORS AND OTHERS

18

(1) This paragraph applies where—

(a) this code has been applied by a direction under section 106 in a person's case,

(b) this code expressly or impliedly imposes a limitation on the use to which electronic communications apparatus installed by that person may be put or on the purposes for which it may be used, and

(c) that person is a party to a relevant agreement or becomes a party to an agreement which (after the person has become a party to it) is a relevant agreement.

(2) The limitation does not preclude—

(a) the doing of anything in relation to that apparatus, or

(b) its use for particular purposes,

to the extent that the doing of that thing, or the use of the apparatus for those purposes, is in pursuance of the relevant agreement.

(3) This paragraph is not to be construed, in relation to a person who is entitled or authorised by or under a relevant agreement to share the use of apparatus installed by another party to the agreement, as affecting any consent requirement imposed (whether by an agreement, an enactment or otherwise) on that person.

(4) In this paragraph—

'consent requirement', in relation to a person, means a requirement for the person to obtain consent or permission to or in connection with—

(a) the installation by the person of apparatus, or

(b) the doing by the person of any other thing in relation to apparatus the use of which the person is entitled or authorised to share;

'relevant agreement' means an agreement in relation to electronic communications apparatus which—

(a) relates to the sharing by different parties to the agreement of the use of that apparatus, and

(b) is an agreement that satisfies the requirements of sub-paragraph (5).

(5) An agreement satisfies the requirements of this sub-paragraph if—

(a) every party to the agreement is a person in whose case this code applies by virtue of a direction under section 106, or

(b) one or more of the parties to the agreement is a person in whose case this code so applies and every other party to the agreement is a qualifying person.

(6) A person is a qualifying person for the purposes of sub-paragraph (5) if the person is either—

(a) a person who provides an electronic communications network without being a person in whose case this code applies, or

(b) a designated provider of an electronic communications service consisting in the distribution of a programme service by means of an electronic communications network.

(7) In sub-paragraph (6)—

'designated' means designated by regulations made by the Secretary of State;

'programme service' has the same meaning as in the Broadcasting Act 1990.][1]

AMENDMENTS

1 Schedule inserted by the Digital Economy Act 2017, s 4(2), Sch 1.

[Part 4
Power of court to impose agreement

INTRODUCTORY

19

This Part of this code makes provision about—

(a) [certain circumstances][1] in which the court can impose an agreement on a person by which the person confers or is otherwise bound by a code right [(see also Part 4A)][2],

(b) the test to be applied by the court in deciding whether to impose such an agreement,

(c) the effect of such an agreement and its terms,

(d) the imposition of an agreement on a person on an interim or temporary basis.][3]

AMENDMENTS

1 Substituted by the Telecommunications Infrastructure (Leasehold Property) Act 2021, s 2, Schedule, paras 1, 4(1), (4)(a).

2 Inserted by the Telecommunications Infrastructure (Leasehold Property) Act 2021, s 2, Schedule, paras 1, 4(1), (4)(b).

3 Schedule inserted by the Digital Economy Act 2017, s 4(2), Sch 1.

[WHEN CAN THE COURT IMPOSE AN AGREEMENT?

20

(1) This paragraph applies where the operator requires a person (a 'relevant person') to agree—

(a) to confer a code right on the operator, or

(b) to be otherwise bound by a code right which is exercisable by the operator.

(2) The operator may give the relevant person a notice in writing—

(a) setting out the code right, [the land to which it relates][1] and all of the other terms of the agreement that the operator seeks, and

(b) stating that the operator seeks the person's agreement to those terms.

[(2A) The notice must also—

(a) contain information about the availability of alternative dispute resolution in the event that the operator and the relevant person are unable to reach agreement, and

(b) explain the possible consequences of refusing to engage in alternative dispute resolution.][2]

(3) The operator may apply to the court for an order under this paragraph if—

(a) the relevant person does not, before the end of 28 days beginning with the day on which the notice is given, agree to confer or be otherwise bound by the code right, or

(b) at any time after the notice is given, the relevant person gives notice in writing to the operator that the person does not agree to confer or be otherwise bound by the code right.

(4) An order under this paragraph is one which imposes on the operator and the relevant person an agreement between them which—

(a) confers the code right on the operator, or

(b) provides for the code right to bind the relevant person.

[(5) Before applying for an order under this paragraph, the operator must, if it is reasonably practicable to do so, consider the use of one or more alternative dispute resolution procedures to reach agreement with the relevant person.

(6) The operator or the relevant person may at any time give the other a notice in writing stating that the operator or the relevant person (as the case may be) wishes to engage in alternative dispute resolution with the other in relation to the agreement sought by the operator.][2]][3]

AMENDMENTS

1 Inserted by the Telecommunications Infrastructure (Leasehold Property) Act 2021, s 2, Schedule, paras 1, 4(1), (5).

2 Inserted by the Product Security and Telecommunications Infrastructure Act 2022, s 69(1), (2).

3 Schedule inserted by the Digital Economy Act 2017, s 4(2), Sch 1.

[WHAT IS THE TEST TO BE APPLIED BY THE COURT?

21

(1) Subject to sub-paragraph (5) [and paragraph 27ZA][1], the court may make an order under paragraph 20 if (and only if) the court thinks that both of the following conditions are met.

(2) The first condition is that the prejudice caused to the relevant person by the order is capable of being adequately compensated by money.

(3) The second condition is that the public benefit likely to result from the making of the order outweighs the prejudice to the relevant person.

(4) In deciding whether the second condition is met, the court must have regard to the public interest in access to a choice of high quality electronic communications services.

(5) The court may not make an order under paragraph 20 if it thinks that the relevant person intends to redevelop all or part of the land to which the code right would relate, or any neighbouring land, and could not reasonably do so if the order were made.][2]

AMENDMENTS

1 Inserted by the Product Security and Telecommunications Infrastructure Act 2022, s 66(1), (3).

2 Schedule inserted by the Digital Economy Act 2017, s 4(2), Sch 1.

[WHAT IS THE EFFECT OF AN AGREEMENT IMPOSED UNDER PARAGRAPH 20?

22

An agreement imposed by an order under paragraph 20 takes effect for all purposes of this code as an agreement under Part 2 of this code between the operator and the relevant person.][1]

AMENDMENTS

1 Schedule inserted by the Digital Economy Act 2017, s 4(2), Sch 1.

[WHAT ARE THE TERMS OF AN AGREEMENT IMPOSED UNDER PARAGRAPH 20?

23

(1) An order under paragraph 20 may impose an agreement which gives effect to the code right sought by the operator with such modifications as the court thinks appropriate.

(2) An order under paragraph 20 must require the agreement to contain such terms as the court thinks appropriate, subject to sub-paragraphs (3) to (8).

[(2A) In determining the terms of the agreement the court may take into account, among other things, any breach by the operator of an agreement between the operator and the relevant person which was imposed by an order under Part 4A (whether or not in force).][1]

(3) The terms of the agreement must include terms as to the payment of consideration by the operator to the relevant person for the relevant person's agreement to confer or be bound by the code right (as the case may be).

(4) Paragraph 24 makes provision about the determination of consideration under sub-paragraph (3).

(5) The terms of the agreement must include the terms the court thinks appropriate for ensuring that the least possible loss and damage is caused by the exercise of the code right to persons who—

(a) occupy the land in question,

(b) own interests in that land, or

(c) are from time to time on that land.

(6) Sub-paragraph (5) applies in relation to a person regardless of whether the person is a party to the agreement.

(7) The terms of the agreement must include terms specifying for how long the code right conferred by the agreement is exercisable.

(8) The court must determine whether the terms of the agreement should include a term—

(a) permitting termination of the agreement (and, if so, in what circumstances);

(b) enabling the relevant person to require the operator to reposition or temporarily to remove the electronic communications equipment to which the agreement relates (and, if so, in what circumstances).][2]

AMENDMENTS

1 Inserted by the Telecommunications Infrastructure (Leasehold Property) Act 2021, s 2, Schedule, paras 1, 4(1), (6).

2 Schedule inserted by the Digital Economy Act 2017, s 4(2), Sch 1.

[HOW IS CONSIDERATION TO BE DETERMINED UNDER PARAGRAPH 23?

24

(1) The amount of consideration payable by an operator to a relevant person under an agreement imposed by an order under paragraph 20 must be an amount or amounts representing the market value of the relevant person's agreement to confer or be bound by the code right (as the case may be).

(2) For this purpose the market value of a person's agreement to confer or be bound by a code right is, subject to sub-paragraph (3), the amount that, at the date the market value is assessed, a willing buyer would pay a willing seller for the agreement—

(a) in a transaction at arm's length,

(b) on the basis that the buyer and seller were acting prudently and with full knowledge of the transaction, and

(c) on the basis that the transaction was subject to the other provisions of the agreement imposed by the order under paragraph 20.

(3) The market value must be assessed on these assumptions—

(a) that the right that the transaction relates to does not relate to the provision or use of an electronic communications network;

(b) that paragraphs 16[, 17 and 17A][1] (assignment, and upgrading and sharing) do not apply to the right or any apparatus to which it could apply;

(c) that the right in all other respects corresponds to the code right;

(d) that there is more than one site which the buyer could use for the purpose for which the buyer seeks the right.

(4) The terms of the agreement may provide for consideration to be payable—

(a) as a lump sum or periodically,

(b) on the occurrence of a specified event or events, or

(c) in such other form or at such other time or times as the court may direct.][2]

AMENDMENTS

1 Substituted by the Product Security and Telecommunications Infrastructure Act 2022, s 59(1), (4).

2 Schedule inserted by the Digital Economy Act 2017, s 4(2), Sch 1.

[WHAT RIGHTS TO THE PAYMENT OF COMPENSATION ARE THERE?

25

(1) If the court makes an order under paragraph 20 the court may also order the operator to pay compensation to the relevant person for any loss or damage that has been sustained or will be sustained by that person as a result of the exercise of the code right to which the order relates.

(2) An order under sub-paragraph (1) may be made—

(a) at the time the court makes an order under paragraph 20, or

(b) at any time afterwards, on the application of the relevant person.

(3) An order under sub-paragraph (1) may—

(a) specify the amount of compensation to be paid by the operator, or

(b) give directions for the determination of any such amount.

(4) Directions under sub-paragraph (3)(b) may provide—

(a) for the amount of compensation to be agreed between the operator and the relevant person;

(b) for any dispute about that amount to be determined by arbitration.

(5) An order under this paragraph may provide for the operator—

(a) to make a lump sum payment,

(b) to make periodical payments,

(c) to make a payment or payments on the occurrence of an event or events, or

(d) to make a payment or payments in such other form or at such other time or times as the court may direct.

(6) Paragraph 84 makes further provision about compensation in the case of an order under paragraph 20.][1]

AMENDMENTS

1 Schedule inserted by the Digital Economy Act 2017, s 4(2), Sch 1.

[INTERIM CODE RIGHTS

26

(1) An operator may apply to the court for an order which imposes on the operator and a person, on an interim basis, an agreement between them which—

(a) confers a code right on the operator, or

(b) provides for a code right to bind that person.

[(1A) But an operator may not make an application under this paragraph if there is a relevant Part 4A agreement in effect between the operator and the person.

(1B) In sub-paragraph (1A) 'relevant Part 4A agreement' means an agreement imposed by an order under Part 4A by which the person—

(a) confers a Part 4A code right on the operator, or

(b) otherwise agrees to be bound by a Part 4A code right which is exercisable by the operator,

where the Part 4A code right is in respect of the same land as the code right mentioned in sub-paragraph (1).][1]

(2) An order under this paragraph imposes an agreement on the operator and a person on an interim basis if it provides for them to be bound by the agreement—

(a) for the period specified in the order, or

(b) until the occurrence of an event specified in the order.

(3) [Subject to paragraph 27ZA,][2] the court may make an order under this paragraph if (and only if) the operator has given the person mentioned in sub-paragraph (1) a notice which complies with paragraph 20(2) stating that an agreement is sought on an interim basis and—

(a) the operator and that person have agreed to the making of the order and the terms of the agreement imposed by it, or

(b) the court thinks that there is a good arguable case that the test in paragraph 21 for the making of an order under paragraph 20 is met.

(4) Subject to sub-paragraphs (5) and (6), the following provisions apply in relation to an order under this paragraph and an agreement imposed by it as they apply in relation to an order under paragraph 20 and an agreement imposed by it—

(a) paragraph 20(3) (time at which operator may apply for agreement to be imposed);

(b) paragraph 22 (effect of agreement imposed under paragraph 20);

(c) paragraph 23 (terms of agreement imposed under paragraph 20);

(d) paragraph 24 (payment of consideration);

(e) paragraph 25 (payment of compensation);

(f) paragraph 84 (compensation where agreement imposed).

(5) The court may make an order under this paragraph even though the period mentioned in paragraph 20(3)(a) has not elapsed (and paragraph 20(3)(b) does not apply) if the court thinks that the order should be made as a matter of urgency.

(6) Paragraphs [20(3), 22,][1] 23, 24 and 25 apply by virtue of sub-paragraph (4) as if—

(a) references to the relevant person were to the person mentioned in sub-paragraph (1) of this paragraph, and

(b) the duty in paragraph 23 to include terms as to the payment of consideration to that person in an agreement were a power to do so.

(7) Sub-paragraph (8) applies if—

(a) an order has been made under this paragraph imposing an agreement relating to a code right on an operator and a person in respect of any land, and

(b) the period specified under sub-paragraph (2)(a) has expired or, as the case may be, the event specified under sub-paragraph (2)(b) has occurred without (in either case) an agreement relating to the code right having been imposed on the person by order under paragraph 20.

(8) From the time when the period expires or the event occurs, that person has the right, subject to and in accordance with Part 6 of this code, to require the operator to remove any electronic communications apparatus placed on the land under the agreement imposed under this paragraph.][3]

AMENDMENTS

1 Inserted by the Telecommunications Infrastructure (Leasehold Property) Act 2021, s 2, Schedule, paras 1, 4(1), (7).

2 Inserted by the Product Security and Telecommunications Infrastructure Act 2022, s 66(1), (4).

3 Schedule inserted by the Digital Economy Act 2017, s 4(2), Sch 1.

[TEMPORARY CODE RIGHTS

27

(1) This paragraph applies where—

(a) an operator gives a notice under paragraph 20(2) to a person in respect of any land,

(b) the notice also requires that person's agreement on a temporary basis in respect of a right which is to be exercisable (in whole or in part) in relation to electronic communications apparatus which is already installed on, under or over the land, and

(c) the person has the right to require the removal of the apparatus in accordance with paragraph 37 or as mentioned in paragraph 40(1) but the operator is not for the time being required to remove the apparatus.

(2) [Subject to paragraph 27ZA,][1] the court may, on the application of the operator, impose on the operator and the person an agreement between them which confers on the operator, or provides for the person to be bound by, such temporary code rights as appear to the court reasonably necessary for securing the objective in sub-paragraph (3).

(3) That objective is that, until the proceedings under paragraph 20 and any proceedings under paragraph 40 are determined, the service provided by the operator's network is maintained and the apparatus is properly adjusted and kept in repair.

(4) Subject to sub-paragraphs (5) and (6), the following provisions apply in relation to an order under this paragraph and an agreement imposed by it as they apply in relation to an order under paragraph 20 and an agreement imposed by it—

(a) paragraph 20(3) (time at which operator may apply for agreement to be imposed);

(b) paragraph 22 (effect of agreement imposed under paragraph 20);

(c) paragraph 23 (terms of agreement imposed under paragraph 20);

(d) paragraph 24 (payment of consideration);

(e) paragraph 25 (payment of compensation);

(f) paragraph 84 (compensation where agreement imposed).

(5) The court may make an order under this paragraph even though the period mentioned in paragraph 20(3)(a) has not elapsed (and paragraph 20(3)(b) does not apply) if the court thinks that the order should be made as a matter of urgency.

(6) Paragraphs [20(3), 22,][2] 23, 24 and 25 apply by virtue of sub-paragraph (4) as if—

(a) references to the relevant person were to the person mentioned in sub-paragraph (1) of this paragraph, and

(b) the duty in paragraph 23 to include terms as to the payment of consideration to that person in an agreement were a power to do so.

(7) Sub-paragraph (8) applies where, in the course of the proceedings under paragraph 20, it is shown that a person with an interest in the land was entitled to require the removal of the apparatus immediately after it was installed.

(8) The court must, in determining for the purposes of paragraph 20 whether the apparatus should continue to be kept on, under or over the land, disregard the fact that the apparatus has already been installed there.][3]

AMENDMENTS

1 Inserted by the Product Security and Telecommunications Infrastructure Act 2022, s 66(1), (5).

2 Inserted by the Telecommunications Infrastructure (Leasehold Property) Act 2021, s 2, Schedule, paras 1, 4(1), (8).

3 Schedule inserted by the Digital Economy Act 2017, s 4(2), Sch 1.

[REFUSAL OF APPLICATION ON GROUNDS OF NATIONAL SECURITY ETC

27ZA

(1) This paragraph applies where an operator applies to the court for an order under paragraph 20, 26 or 27 which would impose an agreement between the operator and another person.

(2) The court must refuse the application if the Secretary of State gives a certificate to the court certifying that the condition in sub-paragraph (3) is met.

(3) The condition is that the Secretary of State is satisfied that the order applied for by the operator would be likely to prejudice national security, defence or law enforcement.

(4) If the Secretary of State gives a certificate to the court under sub-paragraph (2) the Secretary of State must give a copy of it to the operator and the other person.

(5) In this paragraph, 'law enforcement' means the prevention, investigation, detection or prosecution of criminal offences including the safeguarding against and the prevention of threats to public security.][1]

AMENDMENTS

1 Inserted by the Product Security and Telecommunications Infrastructure Act 2022, s 66(1), (2).

[Part 4A
Code rights in respect of land connected to leased premises: unresponsive occupiers

INTRODUCTORY

27A

This Part of this code makes provision for the court to make an order imposing an agreement which provides that code rights are exercisable by an operator for the purpose of providing an electronic communications service to leased premises where—

(a) the rights are required in respect of land which is connected to the leased premises, and

(b) the occupier or another person with an interest in the land has not responded to repeated notices given by the operator seeking agreement to confer or otherwise be bound by the rights.][1]

AMENDMENTS

1 Part inserted by the Telecommunications Infrastructure (Leasehold Property) Act 2021, s 1.

[CIRCUMSTANCES IN WHICH AN APPLICATION FOR AN ORDER UNDER THIS PART CAN BE MADE

27B

(1) Paragraphs 27C and 27D apply where—

(a) premises within the scope of this Part are occupied under a lease (the 'target premises'),

(b) the lessee in occupation requests an operator to provide an electronic communications service to the target premises,

(c) in order to fulfil that request, the operator requires a person (the 'required grantor') to agree—

(i) to confer on the operator a code right in respect of connected land, or

(ii) otherwise to be bound by such a code right exercisable by the operator,

(d) the operator has, on or after the day on which section 1 of the Telecommunications Infrastructure (Leasehold Property) Act 2021 comes fully into force, given the required grantor a notice in accordance with paragraph 20(2) of this code seeking that agreement (the 'request notice'), and

(e) the required grantor has not responded to the operator.

(2) Premises are within the scope of this Part if they—

(a) form part of a multiple dwelling building (see paragraph 27I(1)), or

(b) are other premises of a description specified in regulations made by the Secretary of State.

(3) In this Part 'connected land', in relation to the target premises, means land which—

(a) is in common ownership with the target premises (see paragraph 27I(2)), and

(b) is held or used for access to, or otherwise in connection with, the target premises.

(4) For the purposes of this paragraph, the required grantor responds to the operator if the required grantor—

(a) agrees or refuses, in writing, to confer or otherwise be bound by the code right specified in the request notice on the terms that the operator seeks, or

(b) otherwise acknowledges the request notice in writing.][1]

AMENDMENTS

1 Part inserted by the Telecommunications Infrastructure (Leasehold Property) Act 2021, s 1.

[REQUIREMENTS TO BE MET BEFORE APPLYING FOR AN ORDER UNDER THIS PART

27C

(1) Before applying to the court for an order under this Part (a 'Part 4A order') (see paragraph 27E(2)) the operator must, in accordance with this paragraph, give the required grantor—

(a) two warning notices, and

(b) a final notice.

(2) A 'warning notice' is a notice in writing which—

(a) includes a copy of the request notice,

(b) states that it is the first or (as the case may be) second of three notices that, unless the required grantor responds to the operator, will allow the operator to apply for a Part 4A order, and

(c) explains the effect of a Part 4A order.

(3) The first warning notice may only be given after the end of the period of seven days beginning with the day on which the request notice was given.

(4) The second warning notice may only be given after the end of the period of seven days beginning with the day on which the first one was given.

(5) A 'final notice' is a notice in writing which—

(a) includes a copy of the request notice,

(b) states that unless the required grantor responds to the operator before the end of the period of 14 days beginning with the day on which the final notice is given, the operator intends to apply for a Part 4A order, and

(c) explains the effect of a Part 4A order.

(6) A final notice may only be given within the permitted period.

(7) The 'permitted period' means the period which—

(a) begins immediately after the end of whichever of the following ends last—

(i) the period of seven days beginning with the day on which the second warning notice was given;

(ii) the period of 28 days beginning with the day on which the request notice was given, and

(b) ends at the end of the period of 28 days beginning with the day on which the second warning notice was given.

(8) The Secretary of State may by regulations specify other conditions that the operator must satisfy before giving the required grantor a final notice.][1]

AMENDMENTS

1 Part inserted by the Telecommunications Infrastructure (Leasehold Property) Act 2021, s 1.

[27D

(1) The operator may apply to the court for a Part 4A order in relation to the code right specified in the request notice if—

(a) the operator has satisfied the notice requirements set out in paragraph 27C,

(b) the period of 14 days beginning with the day on which the final notice was given has ended,

(c) the required grantor has not responded to the operator, and

(d) the operator has satisfied any other specified conditions.

(2) An application for a Part 4A order may not be made after the end of the specified period beginning with the day on which the final notice is given.

(3) The operator must give the required grantor notice of an application for a Part 4A order.

(4) For the purposes of this paragraph, the required grantor responds to the operator if the required grantor—

(a) agrees or refuses, in writing, to confer or otherwise be bound by the code right specified in the request notice on the terms that the operator seeks, or

(b) otherwise acknowledges, in writing, the request notice, a warning notice or the final notice.

(5) In this paragraph 'specified' means specified in regulations made by the Secretary of State.][1]

AMENDMENTS

1 Part inserted by the Telecommunications Infrastructure (Leasehold Property) Act 2021, s 1.

[WHEN A PART 4A ORDER CAN BE MADE AND ITS EFFECT

27E

(1) The court may make a Part 4A order if (and only if)—

(a) it is satisfied that the requirements for applying for the order have been met, and

(b) the required grantor has not objected to the making of the order.

(2) A Part 4A order is an order which imposes on the operator and the required grantor an agreement between them—

(a) by which the required grantor confers on the operator the code right identified in the request notice in respect of the connected land so identified, or

(b) which provides for the code right identified in that notice, which is exercisable by the operator in respect of the connected land so identified, otherwise to bind the required grantor.

(3) In this code, a 'Part 4A code right' means a code right which is conferred by or otherwise binds the required grantor pursuant to an agreement imposed by a Part 4A order.

(4) The terms of an agreement imposed by a Part 4A order are to be those specified in regulations made by the Secretary of State.

(5) Regulations under sub-paragraph (4) must, in particular, provide for an agreement to include terms—

(a) relating to the provision by the operator to the required grantor of details of the works to be carried out in the exercise of the Part 4A code right ('the works');

(b) relating to the obtaining by the operator of any consent, permit, licence, permission, authorisation or approval which is necessary for the works to be carried out;

(c) relating to the giving of notice by the operator to the required grantor or other specified persons before entering on the connected land in the exercise of the Part 4A code right or carrying out the works;

(d) restricting the operator's right to enter on the connected land to specified times, except in cases of emergency;

(e) as to the manner in which the works are to be carried out by the operator;

(f) relating to the restoration by the operator of the connected land at the end of the works, to the reasonable satisfaction of the required grantor;

(g) relating to the need for insurance cover or indemnification of the required grantor;

(h) relating to the maintenance or upgrading by the operator of apparatus installed on, under or over the connected land in the exercise of the Part 4A code right ('the apparatus');

(i) imposing requirements or restrictions on the required grantor for the purposes of—

(i) preventing damage to the apparatus,

(ii) facilitating access to the apparatus for the operator, or

(iii) otherwise preventing or minimising disruption to the operation of the apparatus;

(j) relating to assignment of the agreement;

(k) aimed at ensuring that nothing done by the operator in the exercise of the Part 4A code right unnecessarily prevents or inhibits the provision of an electronic communications service by any other operator.

(6) Before making regulations under sub-paragraph (4), the Secretary of State must consult—

(a) operators,

(b) persons appearing to the Secretary of State to represent owners of interests in land who are likely to be affected by the regulations, and

(c) any other persons the Secretary of State thinks appropriate.

(7) In sub-paragraph (5), 'specified' mean specified, or of a description specified, in the regulations.][1]

AMENDMENTS

1 Part inserted by the Telecommunications Infrastructure (Leasehold Property) Act 2021, s 1.

[EXERCISE OF PART 4A CODE RIGHTS

27F

(1) A Part 4A code right may be exercised by the operator in respect of the connected land for the provision of an electronic communications service to—

(a) the target premises, and

(b) other premises, but only if the provision of the service to the other premises in addition to the target premises imposes no additional burden on the required grantor.

(2) For the purposes of sub-paragraph (1)(b), an additional burden includes anything that—

(a) has an additional adverse effect on the required grantor's enjoyment of the connected land, or

(b) causes additional loss, damage or expense to the required grantor.][1]

AMENDMENTS

1 Part inserted by the Telecommunications Infrastructure (Leasehold Property) Act 2021, s 1.

[EXPIRY OF PART 4A CODE RIGHTS

27G

(1) A Part 4A code right ceases to be conferred on the operator by, or otherwise to bind, the required grantor—

(a) if a replacement agreement comes into effect, in accordance with that agreement,

(b) if the court decides to refuse an application by the operator for the imposition of a replacement agreement, in accordance with that decision, or

(c) if the right has not ceased to have that effect as mentioned in paragraph (a) or (b) before the end of the specified period beginning with the day on which the agreement imposed by the Part 4A order comes into effect, at the end of that period.

(2) In sub-paragraph (1) a 'replacement agreement', in relation to a Part 4A code right, means an agreement under Part 2 by which the required grantor confers a code right on the operator, or otherwise agrees to be bound by a code right which is exercisable by the operator, where that right is in respect of the same land as the Part 4A code right.

(3) In sub-paragraph (1)(c) 'specified period' means the period, of no more than 18 months, specified in regulations made by the Secretary of State.

(4) The required grantor has the right, subject to and in accordance with Part 6 of this code, to require the operator to remove any electronic communications apparatus placed on the connected land in the exercise of a Part 4A code right which has ceased to have effect, or otherwise to bind, the required grantor.][1]

AMENDMENTS

1 Part inserted by the Telecommunications Infrastructure (Leasehold Property) Act 2021, s 1.

[COMPENSATION

27H

(1) This paragraph applies where the court has made a Part 4A order.

(2) The court may, on the application of the required grantor, order the operator to pay compensation to the required grantor for any loss or damage that has been sustained or will be sustained by the required grantor as a result of the exercise by the operator of the Part 4A code right.

(3) An application for an order under this paragraph may be made at any time after the Part 4A order is made (including at a time when the Part 4A code right has ceased to be conferred on the operator by, or otherwise to bind, the required grantor).

(4) An order under this paragraph may—

(a) specify the amount of compensation to be paid by the operator, or

(b) give directions for the determination of any such amount.

(5) Directions under sub-paragraph (4)(b) may provide—

(a) for the amount of compensation to be agreed between the operator and the required grantor;

(b) for any dispute about that amount to be determined by arbitration.

(6) An order under this paragraph may provide for the operator—

(a) to make a lump sum payment,

(b) to make periodical payments,

(c) to make a payment or payments on the occurrence of an event or events, or

(d) to make a payment or payments in such other form or at such other time or times as the court may direct.

(7) Paragraph 84 makes further provision about compensation in the case of a Part 4A order.][1]

AMENDMENTS

1 Part inserted by the Telecommunications Infrastructure (Leasehold Property) Act 2021, s 1.

[INTERPRETATION OF THIS PART

27I

(1) In this Part—

'connected land' has the meaning given by paragraph 27B(3);

'multiple dwelling building' means a building which contains two or more sets of premises which are used as, or intended to be used as, a separate dwelling;

'Part 4A order' has the meaning given by paragraph 27C(1);

'premises' includes a part of premises;

'request notice' has the meaning given by paragraph 27B(1)(d);

'required grantor' has the meaning given by paragraph 27B(1)(c);

'target premises' has the meaning given by paragraph 27B(1)(a).

(2) For the purposes of this Part, land is in 'common ownership' with the target premises if a person with a relevant interest in the land also has a relevant interest (whether or not of the same sort) in the target premises.

(3) For the purposes of sub-paragraph (2), a person has a 'relevant interest' in land if—

(a) the person owns the freehold estate in the land (or, in relation to Scotland, is the owner of the land), or

(b) the person is the lessee of the land.][1]

AMENDMENTS

1 Part inserted by the Telecommunications Infrastructure (Leasehold Property) Act 2021, s 1.

[Part 5
Termination and modification of agreements

INTRODUCTORY

28

This Part of this code makes provision about—

(a) the continuation of code rights after the time at which they cease to be exercisable under an agreement,

(b) the procedure for bringing an agreement to an end,

(c) the procedure for changing an agreement relating to code rights, and

(d) the arrangements for the making of payments under an agreement whilst disputes under this Part are resolved.][1]

AMENDMENTS

1 Schedule inserted by the Digital Economy Act 2017, s 4(2), Sch 1.

[APPLICATION OF THIS PART

29

(1) This Part of this code applies to an agreement under Part 2 of this code, subject to sub-paragraphs (2) to (4).

(2) This Part of this code does not apply to a lease of land in England and Wales if—

(a) its primary purpose is not to grant code rights, and

(b) it is a lease to which Part 2 of the Landlord and Tenant Act 1954 (security of tenure for business, professional and other tenants) applies.

(3) In determining whether a lease is one to which Part 2 of the Landlord and Tenant Act 1954 applies, any agreement under section 38A (agreements to exclude provisions of Part 2) of that Act is to be disregarded.

(4) This Part of this code does not apply to a lease of land in Northern Ireland if—

(a) its primary purpose is not to grant code rights, and

(b) it is a lease to which the Business Tenancies (Northern Ireland) Order 1996 (SI 1996/725 (NI 5)) applies.

(5) An agreement to which this Part of this code applies is referred to in this code as a 'code agreement'.][1]

AMENDMENTS

1 Schedule inserted by the Digital Economy Act 2017, s 4(2), Sch 1.

[CONTINUATION OF CODE RIGHTS

30

(1) Sub-paragraph (2) applies if—

(a) a code right is conferred by, or is otherwise binding on, a person (the 'site provider') as the result of a code agreement, and

(b) under the terms of the agreement—

(i) the right ceases to be exercisable or the site provider ceases to be bound by it, or

(ii) the site provider may bring the code agreement to an end so far as it relates to that right.

(2) Where this sub-paragraph applies the code agreement continues so that—

(a) the operator may continue to exercise that right, and

(b) the site provider continues to be bound by the right.

(3) Sub-paragraph (2) does not apply to a code right which is conferred by, or is otherwise binding on, a person by virtue of an order under paragraph 26 (interim code rights) or 27 (temporary code rights).

(4) Sub-paragraph (2) is subject to the following provisions of this Part of this code.][1]

AMENDMENTS

1 Schedule inserted by the Digital Economy Act 2017, s 4(2), Sch 1.

[HOW MAY A PERSON BRING A CODE AGREEMENT TO AN END?

31

(1) A site provider who is a party to a code agreement may bring the agreement to an end by giving a notice in accordance with this paragraph to the operator who is a party to the agreement.

(2) The notice must—

(a) comply with paragraph 89 (notices given by persons other than operators),

(b) specify the date on which the site provider proposes the code agreement should come to an end, and

(c) state the ground on which the site provider proposes to bring the code agreement to an end.

(3) The date specified under sub-paragraph (2)(b) must fall—

(a) after the end of the period of 18 months beginning with the day on which the notice is given, and

(b) after the time at which, apart from paragraph 30, the code right to which the agreement relates would have ceased to be exercisable or to bind the site provider or at a time when, apart from that paragraph, the code agreement could have been brought to an end by the site provider.

(4) The ground stated under sub-paragraph (2)(c) must be one of the following—

(a) that the code agreement ought to come to an end as a result of substantial breaches by the operator of its obligations under the agreement;

(b) that the code agreement ought to come to an end because of persistent delays by the operator in making payments to the site provider under the agreement;

(c) that the site provider intends to redevelop all or part of the land to which the code agreement relates, or any neighbouring land, and could not reasonably do so unless the code agreement comes to an end;

(d) that the operator is not entitled to the code agreement because the test under paragraph 21 for the imposition of the agreement on the site provider is not met.][1]

AMENDMENTS

1 Schedule inserted by the Digital Economy Act 2017, s 4(2), Sch 1.

[WHAT IS THE EFFECT OF A NOTICE UNDER PARAGRAPH 31?

32

(1) Where a site provider gives a notice under paragraph 31, the code agreement to which it relates comes to an end in accordance with the notice unless—

(a) within the period of three months beginning with the day on which the notice is given, the operator gives the site provider a counter-notice in accordance with sub-paragraph (3), and

(b) within the period of three months beginning with the day on which the counter-notice is given, the operator applies to the court for an order under paragraph 34.

(2) Sub-paragraph (1) does not apply if the operator and the site provider agree to the continuation of the code agreement.

(3) The counter-notice must state—

(a) that the operator does not want the existing code agreement to come to an end,

(b) that the operator wants the site provider to agree to confer or be otherwise bound by the existing code right on new terms, or

(c) that the operator wants the site provider to agree to confer or be otherwise bound by a new code right in place of the existing code right.

[(3A) The counter-notice must also—

(a) contain information about the availability of alternative dispute resolution in the event that the operator and the site provider are unable to reach agreement, and

(b) explain the possible consequences of refusing to engage in alternative dispute resolution.][1]

(4) If, on an application under sub-paragraph (1)(b), the court decides that the site provider has established any of the grounds stated in the site provider's notice under paragraph 31, the court must order that the code agreement comes to an end in accordance with the order.

(5) Otherwise the court must make one of the orders specified in paragraph 34.

[(6) Before applying under sub-paragraph (1)(b) for an order under paragraph 34 the operator must, if it is reasonably practicable to do so, consider the use of one or more alternative dispute resolution procedures to reach agreement with the site provider.

(7) The operator or the site provider may at any time give the other party to the agreement a notice in writing stating that the operator or the site provider (as the case may be) wishes to engage in alternative dispute resolution with the other party to the agreement in relation to the site provider's notice under paragraph 31.][1]][2]

AMENDMENTS

1 Inserted by the Product Security and Telecommunications Infrastructure Act 2022, s 69(1), (3).

2 Schedule inserted by the Digital Economy Act 2017, s 4(2), Sch 1.

[HOW MAY A PARTY TO A CODE AGREEMENT REQUIRE A CHANGE TO THE TERMS OF AN AGREEMENT WHICH HAS EXPIRED?

33

(1) An operator or site provider who is a party to a code agreement by which a code right is conferred by or otherwise binds the site provider may, by notice in accordance with this paragraph, require the other party to the agreement to agree that—

(a) the code agreement should have effect with modified terms,

(b) where under the code agreement more than one code right is conferred by or otherwise binds the site provider, that the agreement should no longer provide for an existing code right to be conferred by or otherwise bind the site provider,

(c) the code agreement should—

(i) confer an additional code right on the operator, or

(ii) provide that the site provider is otherwise bound by an additional code right, or

(d) the existing code agreement should be terminated and a new agreement should have effect between the parties which—

(i) confers a code right on the operator, or

(ii) provides for a code right to bind the site provider.

(2) The notice must—

(a) comply with paragraph 88 or 89, according to whether the notice is given by an operator or a site provider,

(b) specify—

(i) the day from which it is proposed that the modified terms should have effect,

(ii) the day from which the agreement should no longer provide for the code right to be conferred by or otherwise bind the site provider,

(iii) the day from which it is proposed that the additional code right should be conferred by or otherwise bind the site provider, or

(iv) the day on which it is proposed the existing code agreement should be terminated and from which a new agreement should have effect,

(as the case may be), and

(c) set out details of—

(i) the proposed modified terms,

(ii) the code right it is proposed should no longer be conferred by or otherwise bind the site provider,

(iii) the proposed additional code right, or

(iv) the proposed terms of the new agreement,

(as the case may be).

(3) The day specified under sub-paragraph (2)(b) must fall—

(a) after the end of the period of 6 months beginning with the day on which the notice is given, and

(b) after the time at which, apart from paragraph 30, the code right to which the existing code agreement relates would have ceased to be exercisable or to bind the site provider or at a time when, apart from that paragraph, the code agreement could have been brought to an end by the site provider.

[(3A) Where the notice is given by an operator, it must also—

(a) contain information about the availability of alternative dispute resolution in the event that the operator and the site provider are unable to reach agreement, and

(b) explain the possible consequences of refusing to engage in alternative dispute resolution.][1]

(4) Sub-paragraph (5) applies if, after the end of the period of 6 months beginning with the day on which the notice is given, the operator and the site provider have not reached agreement on the proposals in the notice.

(5) Where this paragraph applies, the operator or the site provider may apply to the court for the court to make an order under paragraph 34.

[(6) Before applying under sub-paragraph (5) for an order under paragraph 34 the operator or the site provider (as the case may be) must, if it is reasonably practicable to do so, consider the use of one or more alternative dispute resolution procedures to reach agreement with the other party.

(7) The operator or the site provider may at any time give the other party to the agreement a notice in writing stating that the operator or the site provider (as the case may be) wishes to engage in alternative dispute resolution with the other party to the agreement in relation to the notice mentioned in sub-paragraph (1).][1]][2]

AMENDMENTS

1 Inserted by the Product Security and Telecommunications Infrastructure Act 2022, s 69(1), (4).

2 Schedule inserted by the Digital Economy Act 2017, s 4(2), Sch 1.

[WHAT ORDERS MAY A COURT MAKE ON AN APPLICATION UNDER PARAGRAPH 32 OR 33?

34

(1) This paragraph sets out the orders that the court may make on an application under paragraph 32(1)(b) or 33(5).

(2) The court may order that the operator may continue to exercise the existing code right in accordance with the existing code agreement for such period as may be specified in the order (so that the code agreement has effect accordingly).

(3) The court may order the modification of the terms of the code agreement relating to the existing code right.

(4) Where under the code agreement more than one code right is conferred by or otherwise binds the site provider, the court may order the modification of the terms of the code agreement so that it no longer provides for an existing code right to be conferred by or otherwise bind the site provider.

(5) The court may order the terms of the code agreement relating to the existing code right to be modified so that—

(a) it confers an additional code right on the operator, or

(b) it provides that the site provider is otherwise bound by an additional code right.

(6) The court may order the termination of the code agreement relating to the existing code right and order the operator and the site provider to enter into a new agreement which—

(a) confers a code right on the operator, or

(b) provides for a code right to bind the site provider.

(7) The existing code agreement continues until the new agreement takes effect.

(8) This code applies to the new agreement as if it were an agreement under Part 2 of this code.

(9) The terms conferring or providing for an additional code right under sub-paragraph (5), and the terms of a new agreement under sub-paragraph (6), are to be such as are agreed between the operator and the site provider.

(10) If the operator and the site provider are unable to agree on the terms, the court must on an application by either party make an order specifying those terms.

(11) Paragraphs 23(2) to (8), 24, 25 and 84 apply—

(a) to an order under sub-paragraph (3), (4) or (5), so far as it modifies or specifies the terms of the agreement, and

(b) to an order under sub-paragraph (10)

as they apply to an order under paragraph 20.

(12) In the case of an order under sub-paragraph (10) the court must also have regard to the terms of the existing code agreement.

(13) In determining which order to make under this paragraph, the court must have regard to all the circumstances of the case, and in particular to—

(a) the operator's business and technical needs,

(b) the use that the site provider is making of the land to which the existing code agreement relates,

(c) any duties imposed on the site provider by an enactment, and

(d) the amount of consideration payable by the operator to the site provider under the existing code agreement.

(14) Where the court makes an order under this paragraph, it may also order the operator to pay the site provider the amount (if any) by which A exceeds B, where—

(a) A is the amount of consideration that would have been payable by the operator to the site provider for the relevant period if that amount had been assessed on the same basis as the consideration payable as the result of the order, and

(b) B is the amount of consideration payable by the operator to the site provider for the relevant period.

(15) In sub-paragraph (14) the relevant period is the period (if any) that—

(a) begins on the date on which, apart from the operation of paragraph 30, the code right to which the existing code agreement relates would have ceased to be exercisable or to bind the site provider or from which, apart from that paragraph, the code agreement could have been brought to an end by the site provider, and

(b) ends on the date on which the order is made.][1]

AMENDMENTS

1 Schedule inserted by the Digital Economy Act 2017, s 4(2), Sch 1.

[WHAT ARRANGEMENTS ...[1] CAN BE MADE PENDING DETERMINATION OF THE APPLICATION?

35

(1) This paragraph applies where—

(a) a code right continues to be exercisable under paragraph 30 after the time at which, apart from the operation of that paragraph, the code right would have ceased to be exercisable or to bind the site provider or from which, apart from that paragraph, the code agreement relating to the right could have been brought to an end by the site provider, and

(b) the operator or the site provider has applied to the court for an order under paragraph 32(1)(b) or 33(5).

(2) The site provider may—

(a) agree with the operator that, until the application has been finally determined, the site provider will continue to receive the payments of consideration from the operator to which the site provider is entitled under the agreement relating to the existing code right, [or][2]

(b) agree with the operator that, until that time, the site provider will receive different payments of consideration under that agreement, ...[1]

(c) ...[1]

[(2A) The operator or the site provider may apply to the court for—

(a) an order specifying the payments of consideration to be made by the operator to the site provider under the agreement relating to the existing code right until the application for an order under paragraph 32(1)(b) or 33(5) has been finally determined;

(b) an order otherwise modifying the terms of that agreement until that time.

(2B) An order under sub-paragraph (2A)(a) may provide for the order to have effect from the date of the application for the order.][2]

(3) The court must determine the payments [referred to in sub-paragraph (2A)(a)][3] on the basis set out in paragraph 24 (calculation of consideration).

[(4) In determining whether to make an order under sub-paragraph (2A)(b), the court must have regard to all the circumstances of the case, and in particular to—

(a) the terms of the agreement relating to the existing code right,

(b) the operator's business and technical needs,

(c) the use that the site provider is making of the land to which the agreement relates,

(d) any duties imposed on the site provider by an enactment, and

(e) the amount of consideration payable by the operator to the site provider under the agreement.][2]][4]

AMENDMENTS

1 Repealed by the Product Security and Telecommunications Infrastructure Act 2022, s 68(1), (2)(b), (6).

2 Inserted by the Product Security and Telecommunications Infrastructure Act 2022, s 68(1), (2)(a), (3), (5).

3 Substituted by the Product Security and Telecommunications Infrastructure Act 2022, s 68(1), (4).

4 Schedule inserted by the Digital Economy Act 2017, s 4(2), Sch 1.

[Part 6
Rights to require removal of electronic communications apparatus

INTRODUCTORY

36

This Part of this code makes provision about—

(a) the cases in which a person has the right to require the removal of electronic communications apparatus or the restoration of land,

(b) the means by which a person can discover whether apparatus is on land pursuant to a code right, and

(c) the means by which a right to require removal of apparatus or restoration of land can be enforced.][1]

AMENDMENTS

1 Schedule inserted by the Digital Economy Act 2017, s 4(2), Sch 1.

[WHEN DOES A LANDOWNER HAVE THE RIGHT TO REQUIRE REMOVAL OF ELECTRONIC COMMUNICATIONS APPARATUS?

37

(1) A person with an interest in land (a 'landowner') has the right to require the removal of electronic communications apparatus on, under or over the land if (and only if) one or more of the following conditions are met.

(2) The first condition is that the landowner has never since the coming into force of this code been bound by a code right entitling an operator to keep the apparatus on, under or over the land.

(3) The second condition is that a code right entitling an operator to keep the apparatus on, under or over the land has come to an end or has ceased to bind the landowner—

(a) as mentioned in paragraph 26(7) and (8),

[(aa) as mentioned in paragraph 27G(1) and (4);][1]

(b) as the result of paragraph 32(1), or

(c) as the result of an order under paragraph 32(4) or 34(4) or (6), or

(d) where the right was granted by a lease to which Part 5 of this code does not apply.

This is subject to sub-paragraph (4).

(4) The landowner does not meet the first or second condition if—

(a) the land is occupied by a person who—

(i) conferred a code right (which is in force) entitling an operator to keep the apparatus on, under or over the land, or

(ii) is otherwise bound by such a right, and

(b) that code right was not conferred in breach of a covenant enforceable by the landowner.

(5) In the application of sub-paragraph (4)(b) to Scotland the reference to a covenant enforceable by the landowner is to be read as a reference to a contractual term which is so enforceable.

(6) The third condition is that—

(a) an operator has the benefit of a code right entitling the operator to keep the apparatus on, under or over the land, but

(b) the apparatus is not, or is no longer, used for the purposes of the operator's network, and

(c) there is no reasonable likelihood that the apparatus will be used for that purpose.

(7) The fourth condition is that—

(a) this code has ceased to apply to a person so that the person is no longer entitled under this code to keep the apparatus on, under or over the land,

(b) the retention of the apparatus on, under or over the land is not authorised by a scheme contained in an order under section 117, and

(c) there is no other person with a right conferred by or under this code to keep the apparatus on, under or over the land.

(8) The fifth condition is that—

(a) the apparatus was kept on, under or over the land pursuant to—

(i) a transport land right (see Part 7), or

(ii) a street work right (see Part 8),

(b) that right has ceased to be exercisable in relation to the land by virtue of paragraph 54(9), and

(c) there is no other person with a right conferred by or under this code to keep the apparatus on, under or over the land.

(9) This paragraph does not affect rights to require the removal of apparatus under another enactment (see paragraph 41).][2]

AMENDMENTS

1 Inserted by the Telecommunications Infrastructure (Leasehold Property) Act 2021, s 2, Schedule, paras 1, 4(1), (9).

2 Schedule inserted by the Digital Economy Act 2017, s 4(2), Sch 1.

[WHEN DOES A LANDOWNER OR OCCUPIER OF NEIGHBOURING LAND HAVE THE RIGHT TO REQUIRE REMOVAL OF ELECTRONIC COMMUNICATIONS APPARATUS?

38

(1) A landowner or occupier of any land ('neighbouring land') has the right to require the removal of electronic communications apparatus kept on, under or over other land in exercise of a right mentioned in paragraph 13(1), if both of the following conditions are met.

(2) The first condition is that the apparatus interferes with or obstructs a means of access to or from the neighbouring land.

(3) The second condition is that the landowner or occupier of the neighbouring land is not bound by a code right within [paragraph 3(1)(h)][1] entitling an operator to cause the interference or obstruction.

(4) A landowner of neighbouring land who is not the occupier of the land does not meet the second condition if—

(a) the land is occupied by a person who—

(i) conferred a code right (which is in force) entitling an operator to cause the interference or obstruction, or

(ii) is otherwise bound by such a right, and

(b) that code right was not conferred in breach of a covenant enforceable by the landowner.

(5) In the application of sub-paragraph (4)(b) to Scotland the reference to a covenant enforceable by the landowner is to be read as a reference to a contractual term which is so enforceable.][2]

AMENDMENTS

1 Substituted by the Product Security and Telecommunications Infrastructure Act 2022, s 57(1), (6).

2 Schedule inserted by the Digital Economy Act 2017, s 4(2), Sch 1.

[HOW DOES A LANDOWNER OR OCCUPIER FIND OUT WHETHER APPARATUS IS ON LAND PURSUANT TO A CODE RIGHT?

39

(1) A landowner may by notice require an operator to disclose whether—

(a) the operator owns electronic communications apparatus on, under or over land in which the landowner has an interest or uses such apparatus for the purposes of the operator's network, or

(b) the operator has the benefit of a code right entitling the operator to keep electronic communications apparatus on, under or over land in which the landowner has an interest.

(2) A landowner or occupier of neighbouring land may by notice require an operator to disclose whether—

(a) the operator owns electronic communications apparatus on, under or over land that forms (or, but for the apparatus, would form) a means of access to the neighbouring land, or uses such apparatus for the purposes of the operator's network, or

(b) the operator has the benefit of a code right entitling the operator to keep electronic communications apparatus on, under or over land that forms (or, but for the apparatus, would form) a means of access to the neighbouring land.

(3) The notice must comply with paragraph 89 (notices given by persons other than operators).

(4) Sub-paragraph (5) applies if—

(a) the operator does not, before the end of the period of three months beginning with the date on which the notice under sub-paragraph (1) or (2) was given, give a notice to the landowner or occupier that—

(i) complies with paragraph 88 (notices given by operators), and

(ii) discloses the information sought by the landowner or occupier,

(b) the landowner or occupier takes action under paragraph 40 to enforce the removal of the apparatus, and

(c) it is subsequently established that—

(i) the operator owns the apparatus or uses it for the purposes of the operator's network, and

(ii) the operator has the benefit of a code right entitling the operator to keep the apparatus on, under or over the land.

(5) The operator must nevertheless bear the costs of any action taken by the landowner or occupier under paragraph 40 to enforce the removal of the apparatus.][1]

AMENDMENTS

1 Schedule inserted by the Digital Economy Act 2017, s 4(2), Sch 1.

[HOW DOES A LANDOWNER OR OCCUPIER ENFORCE REMOVAL OF APPARATUS?

40

(1) The right of a landowner or occupier to require the removal of electronic communications apparatus on, under or over land, under paragraph 37 or 38, is exercisable only in accordance with this paragraph.

(2) The landowner or occupier may give a notice to the operator whose apparatus it is requiring the operator—

(a) to remove the apparatus, and

(b) to restore the land to its condition before the apparatus was placed on, under or over the land.

(3) The notice must—

(a) comply with paragraph 89 (notices given by persons other than operators), and

(b) specify the period within which the operator must complete the works.

(4) The period specified under sub-paragraph (3) must be a reasonable one.

(5) Sub-paragraph (6) applies if, within the period of 28 days beginning with the day on which the notice was given, the landowner or occupier and the operator do not reach agreement on any of the following matters—

(a) that the operator will remove the apparatus;

(b) that the operator will restore the land to its condition before the apparatus was placed on, under or over the land;

(c) the time at which or period within which the apparatus will be removed;

(d) the time at which or period within which the land will be restored.

(6) The landowner or occupier may make an application to the court for—

(a) an order under paragraph 44(1) (order requiring operator to remove apparatus etc), or

(b) an order under paragraph 44(3) (order enabling landowner to sell apparatus etc).

(7) If the court makes an order under paragraph 44(1), but the operator does not comply with the agreement imposed on the operator and the landowner or occupier by virtue of paragraph 44(7), the landowner or occupier may make an application to the court for an order under paragraph 44(3).

(8) On an application under sub-paragraph (6) or (7) the court may not make an order in relation to apparatus if an application under paragraph 20(3) has been made in relation to the apparatus and has not been determined.][1]

AMENDMENTS

1 Schedule inserted by the Digital Economy Act 2017, s 4(2), Sch 1.

[HOW ARE OTHER RIGHTS TO REQUIRE REMOVAL OF APPARATUS ENFORCED?

41

(1) The right of a person (a 'third party') under an enactment other than this code, or otherwise than under an enactment, to require the removal of electronic communications apparatus on, under or over land is exercisable only in accordance with this paragraph.

(2) The third party may give a notice to the operator whose apparatus it is, requiring the operator—

(a) to remove the apparatus, and

(b) to restore the land to its condition before the apparatus was placed on, under or over the land.

(3) The notice must—

(a) comply with paragraph 89 (notices given by persons other than operators), and

(b) specify the period within which the operator must complete the works.

(4) The period specified under sub-paragraph (3) must be a reasonable one.

(5) Within the period of 28 days beginning with the day on which notice under sub-paragraph (2) is given, the operator may give the third party notice ('counter-notice')—

(a) stating that the third party is not entitled to require the removal of the apparatus, or

(b) specifying the steps which the operator proposes to take for the purpose of securing a right as against the third party to keep the apparatus on the land.

(6) If the operator does not give counter-notice within that period, the third party is entitled to enforce the removal of the apparatus.

(7) If the operator gives the third party counter-notice within that period, the third party may enforce the removal of the apparatus only in pursuance of an

order of the court that the third party is entitled to enforce the removal of the apparatus.

(8) If the counter-notice specifies steps under paragraph (5)(b), the court may make an order under sub-paragraph (7) only if it is satisfied—

(a) that the operator is not intending to take those steps or is being unreasonably dilatory in taking them; or

(b) that taking those steps has not secured, or will not secure, for the operator as against the third party any right to keep the apparatus installed on, under or over the land or to re-install it if it is removed.

(9) Where the third party is entitled to enforce the removal of the apparatus, under sub-paragraph (6) or under an order under sub-paragraph (7), the third party may make an application to the court for—

(a) an order under paragraph 44(1) (order requiring operator to remove apparatus etc), or

(b) an order under paragraph 44(3) (order enabling third party to sell apparatus etc).

(10) If the court makes an order under paragraph 44(1), but the operator does not comply with the agreement imposed on the operator and the third party by virtue of paragraph 44(7), the third party may make an application to the court for an order under paragraph 44(3).

(11) An order made on an application under this paragraph need not include provision within paragraph 44(1)(b) or (3)(d) unless the court thinks it appropriate.

(12) Sub-paragraph (9) is without prejudice to any other method available to the third party for enforcing the removal of the apparatus.][1]

AMENDMENTS

1 Schedule inserted by the Digital Economy Act 2017, s 4(2), Sch 1.

[HOW DOES PARAGRAPH 40 APPLY IF A PERSON IS ENTITLED TO REQUIRE APPARATUS TO BE ALTERED IN CONSEQUENCE OF STREET WORKS?

42

(1) This paragraph applies where the third party's right in relation to which paragraph 41 applies is a right to require the alteration of the apparatus in consequence of the stopping up, closure, change or diversion of a street or road or the extinguishment or alteration of a public right of way.

(2) The removal of the apparatus in pursuance of paragraph 41 constitutes compliance with a requirement to make any other alteration.

(3) A counter-notice under paragraph 41(5) may state (in addition to, or instead of, any of the matters mentioned in paragraph 41(5)(b)) that the operator requires the third party to reimburse the operator in respect of any expenses incurred by the operator in or in connection with the making of any alteration in compliance with the requirements of the third party.

(4) An order made under paragraph 41 on an application by the third party in respect of a counter-notice containing a statement under sub-paragraph (3) must, unless the court otherwise thinks fit, require the third party to reimburse the operator in respect of the expenses referred to in the statement.

(5) Paragraph 44(3)(b) to (e) do not apply.

(6) In this paragraph—

'road' means a road in Scotland;

'street' means a street in England and Wales or Northern Ireland.][1]

AMENDMENTS

1 Schedule inserted by the Digital Economy Act 2017, s 4(2), Sch 1.

[WHEN CAN A SEPARATE APPLICATION FOR RESTORATION OF LAND BE MADE?

43

(1) This paragraph applies if—

(a) the condition of the land has been affected by the exercise of a code right, and

(b) restoration of the land to its condition before the code right was exercised does not involve the removal of electronic communications apparatus from any land.

(2) The occupier of the land, the owner of the freehold estate in the land or the lessee of the land ('the relevant person') has the right to require the operator to restore the land if the relevant person is not for the time being bound by the code right.

(3) The relevant person does not have that right if—

(a) the land is occupied by a person who—

(i) conferred a code right (which is in force) entitling the operator to affect the condition of the land in the same way as the right mentioned in sub-paragraph (1), or

(ii) is otherwise bound by such a right, and

(b) that code right was not conferred in breach of a covenant enforceable by the relevant person.

(4) In the application of sub-paragraph (3)(b) to Scotland the reference to a covenant enforceable by the relevant person is to be read as a reference to a contractual term which is so enforceable.

(5) A person who has the right conferred by this paragraph may give a notice to the operator requiring the operator to restore the land to its condition before the code right was exercised.

(6) The notice must—

(a) comply with paragraph 89 (notices given by persons other than operators), and

(b) specify the period within which the operator must complete the works.

(7) The period specified under sub-paragraph (6) must be a reasonable one.

(8) Sub-paragraph (9) applies if, within the period of 28 days beginning with the day on which the notice was given, the landowner and the operator do not reach agreement on any of the following matters—

(a) that the operator will restore the land to its condition before the code right was exercised;

(b) the time at which or period within which the land will be restored.

(9) The landowner may make an application to the court for—

(a) an order under paragraph 44(2) (order requiring operator to restore land), or

(b) an order under paragraph 44(4) (order enabling landowner to recover cost of restoring land).

(10) If the court makes an order under paragraph 44(2), but the operator does not comply with the agreement imposed on the operator and the landowner by virtue of paragraph 44(7), the landowner may make an application to the court for an order under paragraph 44(4).

(11) In the application of sub-paragraph (2) to Scotland the reference to a person who is the owner of the freehold estate in the land is to be read as a reference to a person who is the owner of the land.][1]

AMENDMENTS

1 Schedule inserted by the Digital Economy Act 2017, s 4(2), Sch 1.

[WHAT ORDERS MAY THE COURT MAKE ON AN APPLICATION UNDER PARAGRAPHS 40 TO 43?

44

(1) An order under this sub-paragraph is an order that the operator must, within the period specified in the order—

(a) remove the electronic communications apparatus, and

(b) restore the land to its condition before the apparatus was placed on, under or over the land.

(2) An order under this sub-paragraph is an order that the operator must, within the period specified in the order, restore the land to its condition before the code right was exercised.

(3) An order under this sub-paragraph is an order that the landowner, occupier or third party may do any of the following—

(a) remove or arrange the removal of the electronic communications apparatus;

(b) sell any apparatus so removed;

(c) recover the costs of any action under paragraph (a) or (b) from the operator;

(d) recover from the operator the costs of restoring the land to its condition before the apparatus was placed on, under or over the land;

(e) retain the proceeds of sale of the apparatus to the extent that these do not exceed the costs incurred by the landowner, occupier or third party as mentioned in paragraph (c) or (d).

(4) An order under this sub-paragraph is an order that the landowner may recover from the operator the costs of restoring the land to its condition before the code right was exercised.

(5) An order under this paragraph on an application under paragraph 40 may require the operator to pay compensation to the landowner for any loss or damage suffered by the landowner as a result of the presence of the apparatus on the land during the period when the landowner had the right to require the removal of the apparatus from the land but was not able to exercise that right.

(6) Paragraph 84 makes further provision about compensation under sub-paragraph (5).

(7) An order under sub-paragraph (1) or (2) takes effect as an agreement between the operator and the landowner, occupier or third party that—

(a) requires the operator to take the steps specified in the order, and

(b) otherwise contains such terms as the court may so specify.][1]

AMENDMENTS

1 Schedule inserted by the Digital Economy Act 2017, s 4(2), Sch 1.

[Part 7
Conferral of transport land rights and their exercise

INTRODUCTORY

45

This Part of this code makes provision about—

(a) the conferral of transport land rights, and

(b) the exercise of transport land rights.][1]

AMENDMENTS

1 Schedule inserted by the Digital Economy Act 2017, s 4(2), Sch 1.

[TRANSPORT LAND AND TRANSPORT UNDERTAKERS

46

In this Part of this code—

'transport land' means land which is used wholly or mainly—

(a) as a railway, canal or tramway, or

(b) in connection with a railway, canal or tramway on the land;

'transport undertaker', in relation to transport land, means the person carrying on the railway, canal or tramway undertaking.][1]

AMENDMENTS

1 Schedule inserted by the Digital Economy Act 2017, s 4(2), Sch 1.

[CONFERRAL OF TRANSPORT LAND RIGHTS

47

(1) An operator may exercise a transport land right for the statutory purposes.

(2) But that is subject to the following provisions of this Part of this code.][1]

AMENDMENTS

1 Schedule inserted by the Digital Economy Act 2017, s 4(2), Sch 1.

[THE TRANSPORT LAND RIGHTS

48

(1) For the purposes of this code a 'transport land right', in relation to an operator, is—

(a) a right to cross any transport land with a line;

(b) a right, for the purposes of crossing any transport land with a line—

(i) to install and keep the line and any other electronic communications apparatus on, under or over the transport land;

(ii) to inspect, maintain, adjust, alter, repair, upgrade or operate electronic communications apparatus on, under or over the transport land;

(iii) a right to carry out any works on the transport land for or in connection with the exercise of a right under sub-paragraph (i) or (ii);

(iv) a right to enter the transport land to inspect, maintain, adjust, alter, repair, upgrade or operate the line or other electronic communications apparatus.

(2) A line installed in the exercise of a transport land right need not cross the transport land in question by a direct route or the shortest route from the point at which the line enters the transport land.

(3) But the line must not cross the transport land by any route which, in the horizontal plane, exceeds that shortest route by more than 400 metres.

(4) The transport land rights do not authorise an operator to install a line or other electronic communications apparatus in any position on transport land in which the line or other apparatus would interfere with traffic on the railway, canal or tramway.][1]

AMENDMENTS

1 Schedule inserted by the Digital Economy Act 2017, s 4(2), Sch 1.

[NON-EMERGENCY WORKS: WHEN CAN AN OPERATOR EXERCISE THE TRANSPORT LAND RIGHTS?

49

(1) Before exercising a transport land right in order to carry out non-emergency works, the operator must give the transport undertaker notice of the intention to carry out the works ('notice of proposed works').

(2) Notice of proposed works must contain a plan and section of the works; but, if the transport undertaker agrees, the notice may instead contain a description of the works (whether or not in the form of a diagram).

(3) The operator must not begin the proposed works until the notice period has ended.

(4) But the operator's power to carry out the proposed works is subject to paragraph 50.

(5) In this paragraph—

'non-emergency works' means any works which are not emergency works under paragraph 51;

'notice period' means the period of 28 days beginning with the day on which notice of proposed works is given.][1]

AMENDMENTS

1 Schedule inserted by the Digital Economy Act 2017, s 4(2), Sch 1.

[WHAT IS THE EFFECT OF THE TRANSPORT UNDERTAKER GIVING NOTICE OF OBJECTION TO THE OPERATOR?

50

(1) This paragraph applies if an operator gives a transport undertaker notice of proposed works under paragraph 49.

(2) The transport undertaker may, within the notice period, give the operator notice objecting to the proposed works ('notice of objection').

(3) If notice of objection is given, the operator or the transport undertaker may, within the arbitration notice period, give the other notice that the objection is to be referred to arbitration under paragraph 52 ('arbitration notice').

(4) In a case where notice of objection is given, the operator may exercise a transport land right in order to carry out the proposed works only if they are permitted under sub-paragraph (5) or (6).

(5) Works are permitted in a case where—

(a) the arbitration notice period has ended, and

(b) no arbitration notice has been given.

(6) In a case where arbitration notice has been given, works are permitted in accordance with an award made on the arbitration.

(7) In this paragraph—

(a) 'arbitration notice period' means the period of 28 days beginning with the day on which objection notice is given;

(b) expressions defined in paragraph 49 have the same meanings as in that paragraph.][1]

AMENDMENTS

1 Schedule inserted by the Digital Economy Act 2017, s 4(2), Sch 1.

[EMERGENCY WORKS: WHEN CAN AN OPERATOR EXERCISE THE TRANSPORT LAND RIGHTS?

51

(1) An operator may exercise a transport land right in order to carry out emergency works.

(2) If the operator exercises a transport land right to carry out emergency works, the operator must give the transport undertaker an emergency works notice as soon as reasonably practicable after starting the works.

(3) An 'emergency works notice' is a notice which—

(a) identifies the emergency works;

(b) contains a statement of the reason why the works are emergency works; and

(c) contains either—

(i) the matters which would be included in a notice of proposed works (if one were given in relation to the works), or

(ii) a reference to a notice of proposed works which relates to the works that are emergency works (if one has been given).

(4) A transport undertaker may, within the compensation notice period, give the operator notice which requires the operator to pay compensation for loss or damage sustained in consequence of the carrying out of emergency works ('compensation notice').

(5) The operator must pay the transport undertaker any compensation which is required by a compensation notice (if given within the compensation notice period).

(6) The amount of compensation payable under sub-paragraph (5) is to be agreed between the operator and the transport undertaker.

(7) But if—

(a) the compensation agreement period has ended, and

(b) the operator and the transport undertaker have not agreed the amount of compensation payable under sub-paragraph (6),

the operator or the transport undertaker may give the other notice that the disagreement is to be referred to arbitration under paragraph 52.

(8) A reference in this paragraph to emergency works includes a reference to any works which are included in a notice of proposed works but become emergency works before the operator is authorised by paragraph 50 or 51 to carry them out.

(9) In this paragraph—

'compensation agreement period' means the period of 28 days beginning with the day on which a compensation notice is given;

'compensation notice period' means the period of 28 days beginning with the day on which an emergency works notice is given;

'emergency works' means works carried out in order to stop anything already occurring, or to prevent anything imminent from occurring, which is likely to cause—

(a) danger to persons or property,

(b) the interruption of any service provided by the operator's network, or

(c) substantial loss to the operator,

and any other works which it is reasonable (in all the circumstances) to carry out with those works;

'notice of proposed works' means such notice given under paragraph 49.][1]

AMENDMENTS

1 Schedule inserted by the Digital Economy Act 2017, s 4(2), Sch 1.

[WHAT HAPPENS IF A DISPUTE ABOUT THE TRANSPORT LAND RIGHTS IS REFERRED TO ARBITRATION?

52

(1) This paragraph applies if notice is given under paragraph 50(3) or 51(7) that the following matter (the 'matter in dispute') is to be referred to arbitration—

(a) an objection to proposed works;

(b) a disagreement about an amount of compensation.

(2) The matter in dispute is to be referred to the arbitration of a single arbitrator appointed—

(a) by agreement between the parties, or

(b) in the absence of such agreement, by the President of the Institution of Civil Engineers.

(3) If the matter in dispute is an objection to proposed works, the arbitrator has the following powers—

(a) power to require the operator to give the arbitrator a plan and section in such form as the arbitrator thinks appropriate;

(b) power to require the transport undertaker to give the arbitrator any observations on such a plan or section in such form as the arbitrator thinks appropriate;

(c) power to impose on either party any other requirements which the arbitrator thinks appropriate (including a requirement to provide information in such form as the arbitrator thinks appropriate);

(d) power to make an award—

(i) requiring modifications to the proposed works, and

(ii) specifying the terms on which, and the conditions subject to which, the proposed works may be carried out;

(e) power to award one or both of the following, payable to the transport undertaker—

(i) compensation for loss or damage sustained by that person in consequence of the carrying out of the works;

(ii) consideration for the right to carry out the works.

(4) If the matter in dispute is a disagreement about an amount of compensation, the arbitrator has the following powers—

(a) power to impose on either party any requirements which the arbitrator thinks appropriate (including a requirement to provide information in such form as the arbitrator thinks appropriate);

(b) power to award compensation, payable to the transport undertaker, for loss or damage sustained by that person in consequence of the carrying out of the emergency works.

(5) The arbitrator may make an award conditional upon a party complying with a requirement imposed under sub-paragraph (3)(a), (b) or (c) or (4)(a).

(6) In determining what award to make, the matters to which the arbitrator must have regard include the public interest in there being access to a choice of high quality electronic communications services.

(7) The arbitrator's power under sub-paragraph (3) or (4) to award compensation for loss includes power to award compensation for any increase in the expenses incurred by the transport undertaker in carrying on its railway, canal or tramway undertaking.

(8) An award of consideration under sub-paragraph (3)(e)(ii) must be determined on the basis of what would have been fair and reasonable if the transport undertaker had willingly given authority for the works to be carried out on the same terms, and subject to the same conditions (if any), as are contained in the award.

(9) In this paragraph 'party' means—

(a) the operator, or

(b) the transport undertaker.][1]

AMENDMENTS

1 Schedule inserted by the Digital Economy Act 2017, s 4(2), Sch 1.

[WHEN CAN A TRANSPORT UNDERTAKER REQUIRE AN OPERATOR TO ALTER COMMUNICATIONS APPARATUS?

53

(1) A transport undertaker may give an operator notice which requires the operator to alter a line or other electronic communications apparatus specified in the notice ('notice requiring alterations') on the ground that keeping the apparatus on, under or over transport land interferes with, or is likely to interfere with—

(a) the carrying on of the transport undertaker's railway, canal or tramway undertaking, or

(b) anything done or to be done for the purposes of its railway, canal or tramway undertaking.

(2) The operator may, within the notice period, give the transport undertaker notice ('counter-notice') specifying the respects in which the operator is not prepared to comply with the notice requiring alterations.

(3) The operator must comply with the notice requiring alterations, within a reasonable time and to the reasonable satisfaction of the transport undertaker, if—

(a) the notice period has ended, and

(b) no counter-notice has been given.

(4) If counter-notice has been given (within the notice period), the transport undertaker may apply to the court for an order requiring the operator to alter any of the specified apparatus.

(5) The court must not make an order unless it is satisfied that the order is necessary on one of the grounds mentioned in sub-paragraph (1).

(6) In determining whether to make an order, the matters to which the court must also have regard include the public interest in there being access to a choice of high quality electronic communications services.

(7) An order under this paragraph may take such form and be on such terms as the court thinks fit.

(8) In particular, the order—

(a) may impose such conditions, and

(b) may contain such directions to the operator or the transport undertaker, as the court thinks necessary for resolving any difference between the operator and the transport undertaker and for protecting their respective interests.

(9) In this paragraph—

'notice period' means the period of 28 days beginning with the day on which notice requiring alterations is given;

'specified apparatus' means the line or other electronic communications apparatus specified in notice requiring alterations.][1]

AMENDMENTS

1 Schedule inserted by the Digital Economy Act 2017, s 4(2), Sch 1.

[WHAT HAPPENS TO THE TRANSPORT LAND RIGHTS IF LAND CEASES TO BE TRANSPORT LAND?

54

(1) This paragraph applies if an operator is exercising a transport land right in relation to land immediately before a time when it ceases to be transport land.

(2) After that time, this Part of this code — except for paragraph 53 — continues to apply to the land as if it were still transport land (and, accordingly, the operator may continue to exercise any transport land right in relation to the land as if it were still transport land).

(3) But sub-paragraph (2) is subject to sub-paragraphs (4) to (9).

(4) In the application of this Part of this code to land in accordance with sub-paragraph (2), references to the transport undertaker have effect as references to the occupier of the land.

(5) The application of this Part of this code to land in accordance with sub-paragraph (2) does not authorise the operator—

(a) to cross the land with any line that is not in place at the time when the land ceases to be transport land, or

(b) to install and keep any line or other electronic communications apparatus that is not in place at the time when the land ceases to be transport land.

(6) But sub-paragraph (5) does not affect the power of the operator to replace an existing line or other apparatus (whether in place at the time when the land ceased to be transport land or a replacement itself authorised by this sub-paragraph) with a new line or apparatus which—

(a) is not substantially different from the existing line or apparatus, and

(b) is not in a significantly different position.

(7) The occupier of the land may, at any time after the land ceases to be transport land, give the operator notice specifying a date on which this Part of this code is to cease to apply to the land in accordance with this paragraph ('notice of termination').

(8) That date specified in the notice of termination must fall after the end of the period of 12 months beginning with the day on which the notice of termination is given.

(9) On the date specified in notice of termination in accordance with sub-paragraph (8), the transport land rights cease to be exercisable in relation to the land in accordance with this paragraph.][1]

AMENDMENTS

1 Schedule inserted by the Digital Economy Act 2017, s 4(2), Sch 1.

[OFFENCE: OPERATORS WHO DO NOT COMPLY WITH THIS PART OF THIS CODE

55

(1) An operator is guilty of an offence if the operator starts any works in contravention of any provision of paragraph 49, paragraph 50 or paragraph 51.

(2) An operator guilty of an offence under this paragraph is liable on summary conviction to a fine not exceeding level 3 on the standard scale.

(3) In a case where this Part of this code applies in accordance with paragraph 54, the reference in this paragraph to paragraph 49, paragraph 50 or paragraph 51 is a reference to that paragraph as it applies in accordance with paragraph 54.][1]

AMENDMENTS

1 Schedule inserted by the Digital Economy Act 2017, s 4(2), Sch 1.

[Part 8
Conferral of street work rights and their exercise

INTRODUCTORY

56

This Part of this code makes provision about—

(a) the conferral of street work rights, and

(b) the exercise of street work rights.][1]

AMENDMENTS

1 Schedule inserted by the Digital Economy Act 2017, s 4(2), Sch 1.

[STREETS AND ROADS

57

In this Part of this code—

'road' means—

(a) a road in Scotland which is a public road;

(b) a road in Northern Ireland;

'street' means a street in England and Wales which is a maintainable highway (within the meaning of Part 3 of New Roads and Street Works Act 1991), other than one which is a footpath, bridleway or restricted byway that crosses, and forms part of, any agricultural land or any land which is being brought into use for agriculture.][1]

AMENDMENTS

1 Schedule inserted by the Digital Economy Act 2017, s 4(2), Sch 1.

[CONFERRAL OF STREET WORK RIGHTS

58

(1) An operator may exercise a street work right for the statutory purposes.

(2) But that is subject to the following provisions of this Part of this code.][1]

AMENDMENTS

1 Schedule inserted by the Digital Economy Act 2017, s 4(2), Sch 1.

[THE STREET WORK RIGHTS

59

(1) For the purposes of this code a 'street work right', in relation to an operator, is—

(a) a right to install and keep electronic communications apparatus in, on, under, over, along or across a street or a road;

(b) a right to inspect, maintain, adjust, alter, repair, upgrade or operate electronic communications apparatus which is installed or kept by the exercise of the right under paragraph (a);

(c) a right to carry out any works in, on, under, over, along or across a street or road for or in connection with the exercise of a right under paragraph (a) or (b);

(d) a right to enter any street or road to inspect, maintain, adjust, alter, repair, upgrade or operate electronic communications apparatus which is installed or kept by the exercise of the right under paragraph (a).

(2) The works that may be carried out under sub-paragraph (1)(c) include—

(a) breaking up or opening a street or a road;

(b) tunnelling or boring under a street or a road;

(c) breaking up or opening a sewer, drain or tunnel.][1]

AMENDMENTS

1 Schedule inserted by the Digital Economy Act 2017, s 4(2), Sch 1.

[Part 9
Conferral of tidal water rights and their exercise

INTRODUCTORY

60

This Part of this code makes provision about—

(a) the conferral of tidal water rights, and

(b) the exercise of tidal water rights.][1]

AMENDMENTS

1 Schedule inserted by the Digital Economy Act 2017, s 4(2), Sch 1.

[TIDAL WATER OR LANDS

61

In this Part of this code 'tidal water or lands' includes—

(a) any estuary or branch of the sea,

(b) the shore below mean high water springs, and

(c) the bed of any tidal water.][1]

AMENDMENTS

1 Schedule inserted by the Digital Economy Act 2017, s 4(2), Sch 1.

[CONFERRAL OF TIDAL WATER RIGHTS

62

(1) An operator may exercise a tidal water right for the statutory purposes.

(2) But that is subject to the following provisions of this Part of this code.][1]

AMENDMENTS

1 Schedule inserted by the Digital Economy Act 2017, s 4(2), Sch 1.

[THE TIDAL WATER RIGHTS

63

(1) For the purposes of this code a 'tidal water right', in relation to an operator, is—

(a) a right to install and keep electronic communications apparatus on, under or over tidal water or lands;

(b) a right to inspect, maintain, adjust, alter, repair, upgrade or operate electronic communications apparatus on, under or over the tidal water or lands;

(c) a right to carry out any works on, under or over any tidal water or lands for or in connection with the exercise of a right under paragraph (a) or (b);

(d) a right to enter any tidal water or lands to inspect, maintain, adjust, alter, repair, upgrade or operate electronic communications apparatus which is installed or kept by the exercise of the right under paragraph (a).

(2) The works that may be carried out under sub-paragraph (1)(c) include placing a buoy or seamark.][1]

AMENDMENTS

1 Schedule inserted by the Digital Economy Act 2017, s 4(2), Sch 1.

[EXERCISE OF TIDAL WATER RIGHT: CROWN LAND

64

(1) An operator may not exercise a tidal water right in relation to land in which a Crown interest subsists unless agreement to the exercise of the right in relation to the land has been given in respect of that interest by the appropriate authority in accordance with paragraph 104.

(2) Where, in connection with an agreement between the operator and the appropriate authority for the exercise of such a right, the operator and the appropriate authority cannot agree the consideration to be paid by the operator, the operator or the appropriate authority may apply to the appointed valuer for a determination of the market value of the right.

(3) An application under sub-paragraph (2) must be made in writing and must include—

(a) the proposed terms of the agreement, and

(b) the reasoned evidence of the operator and of the appropriate authority as to the market value of the right.

(4) As soon as reasonably practicable after receiving such an application, the appointed valuer must—

(a) determine the market value of the tidal water right; and

(b) notify the operator and the appropriate authority in writing of its determination and the reasons for it.

(5) If the agreement mentioned in sub-paragraph (2) or an agreement in substantially the same terms is concluded following a determination under

sub-paragraph (4), the consideration payable by the operator must not be more than the market value notified under sub-paragraph (4)(b).

(6) For this purpose the market value of a tidal water right is, subject to sub-paragraph (7), the amount that, at the date the market value is assessed, a willing buyer would pay a willing seller for the right—

(a) in a transaction at arm's length,

(b) on the basis that the buyer and seller were acting prudently and with full knowledge of the transaction, and

(c) on the basis that the transaction was subject to the proposed terms set out in the application.

(7) The market value must be assessed on these assumptions—

(a) that the right that the transaction relates to does not relate to the provision or use of an electronic communications network;

(b) that the right in all other respects corresponds to the tidal water right;

(c) that there is more than one site which the buyer could use for the purpose for which the buyer seeks the right.

(8) The appointed valuer may charge a fee in respect of the consideration of an application under sub-paragraph (4) and may apportion the fee between the operator and the appropriate authority as the appointed valuer considers appropriate.

(9) In this paragraph 'the appointed valuer' means—

(a) such person as the operator and the appropriate authority may agree;

(b) if no person is agreed, such person as may be nominated, on the application of the operator or the appropriate authority, by the President of the Royal Institution of Chartered Surveyors.][1]

AMENDMENTS

1 Schedule inserted by the Digital Economy Act 2017, s 4(2), Sch 1.

[Part 10
Undertaker's works affecting electronic communications apparatus

INTRODUCTORY

65

This Part of this code makes provision about the carrying out of undertaker's works by undertakers or operators.][1]

AMENDMENTS

1 Schedule inserted by the Digital Economy Act 2017, s 4(2), Sch 1.

[KEY DEFINITIONS

66

(1) In this Part of this code—

'undertaker' means a person (including a local authority) of a description set out in any of the entries in the first column of the following table;

'undertaker's works', in relation to an undertaker of a description set out in a particular entry in the first column of the table, means works of the description set out in the corresponding entry in the second column of the table.

'undertaker'	**'undertaker's works'**
A person authorised by any enactment (whether public general or local) or by any order or scheme made under or confirmed by any enactment to carry on any railway, tramway, road transport, water transport, canal, inland navigation, dock, harbour, pier or lighthouse undertaking	Works that the undertaker is authorised to carry out for the purposes of, or in connection with, the undertaking which it carries on
A person (apart from the operator) to whom this code is applied by a direction under section 106 of the Communications Act 2003	Works that the undertaker is authorised to carry out by or in accordance with any provision of this code
Any person to whom this Part of this code is applied by any enactment (whenever passed or made)	Works for the purposes of which this paragraph is applied to the undertaker

(2) In this Part of this code—

(a) a reference to undertaker's works which interfere with a network is a reference to any undertaker's works which involve, or are likely to involve, an alteration of any electronic communications apparatus kept on, under or over any land for the purposes of an operator's network;

(b) a reference to an alteration of any electronic communications apparatus is a reference to a temporary or permanent alteration of the apparatus.][1]

AMENDMENTS

1 Schedule inserted by the Digital Economy Act 2017, s 4(2), Sch 1.

[WHEN CAN AN UNDERTAKER CARRY OUT NON-EMERGENCY UNDERTAKER'S WORKS?

67

(1) Before carrying out non-emergency undertaker's works which interfere with a network, an undertaker must give the operator notice of the intention to carry out the works ('notice of proposed works').

(2) Notice of proposed works must specify—

(a) the nature of the proposed undertaker's works,

(b) the alteration of the electronic communications apparatus which the works involve or are likely to involve, and

(c) the time and place at which the works will begin.

(3) The undertaker must not begin the proposed undertaker's works (including the proposed alteration of electronic communications apparatus) until the notice period has ended.

(4) But the undertaker's power to alter electronic communications apparatus (in carrying out the proposed undertaker's works) is subject to paragraph 68.

(5) In this paragraph—

'non-emergency undertaker's works' means any undertaker's works which are not emergency works under paragraph 71;

'notice period' means the period of 10 days beginning with the day on which notice of proposed works is given.][1]

AMENDMENTS

1 Schedule inserted by the Digital Economy Act 2017, s 4(2), Sch 1.

[WHAT IS THE EFFECT OF THE OPERATOR GIVING COUNTER-NOTICE TO THE UNDERTAKER?

68

(1) This paragraph applies if an undertaker gives an operator notice of proposed works under paragraph 67.

(2) The operator may, within the notice period, give the undertaker notice ('counter-notice') stating either—

(a) that the operator requires the undertaker to make any alteration of the electronic communications apparatus that is necessary or expedient because of the proposed undertaker's works—

(i) under the supervision of the operator, and

(ii) to the satisfaction of the operator; or

(b) that the operator intends to make any alteration of the electronic communications apparatus that is necessary or expedient because of the proposed undertaker's works.

(3) In a case where counter-notice contains a statement under sub-paragraph (2)(a), the undertaker must act in accordance with the counter-notice when altering electronic communications apparatus (in carrying out the proposed undertaker's works).

(4) But, if the operator unreasonably fails to provide the required supervision, the undertaker must act in accordance with the counter-notice only insofar as it requires alterations to be made to the satisfaction of the operator.

(5) In a case where counter-notice contains a statement under sub-paragraph (2)(b) (operator intends to make alteration), the undertaker must not alter

electronic communications apparatus (in carrying out the proposed undertaker's works).

(6) But that does not prevent the undertaker from making any alteration of electronic communications apparatus which the operator fails to make within a reasonable time.

(7) Expressions defined in paragraph 67 have the same meanings in this paragraph.][1]

AMENDMENTS

1 Schedule inserted by the Digital Economy Act 2017, s 4(2), Sch 1.

[WHAT EXPENSES MUST THE UNDERTAKER PAY?

69

(1) This paragraph applies if an undertaker carries out any non-emergency undertaker's works in accordance with paragraph 67 (including in a case where counter-notice is given under paragraph 68).

(2) The undertaker must pay the operator the amount of any loss or damage sustained by the operator in consequence of any alteration being made to electronic communications apparatus (in carrying out the works).

(3) The undertaker must pay the operator any expenses incurred by the operator in, or in connection with, supervising the undertaker when altering electronic communications apparatus (in carrying out the works).

(4) Any amount which is not paid in accordance with this paragraph is to be recoverable by the operator from the undertaker in any court of competent jurisdiction.][1]

AMENDMENTS

1 Schedule inserted by the Digital Economy Act 2017, s 4(2), Sch 1.

[WHEN CAN THE OPERATOR ALTER APPARATUS IN CONNECTION WITH NON-EMERGENCY UNDERTAKER'S WORKS?

70

(1) An operator may make an alteration of electronic communications apparatus if—

(a) notice of proposed works has been given,

(b) the notice period has ended, and

(c) counter-notice has been given which states (in accordance with paragraph 68(2)(b)) that the operator intends to make the alteration.

(2) If the operator makes any alteration in accordance with this paragraph, the undertaker must pay the operator—

(a) any expenses incurred by the operator in, or in connection with, making the alteration; and

(b) the amount of any loss or damage sustained by the operator in consequence of the alteration being made.

(3) Any amount which is not paid in accordance with sub-paragraph (2) is to be recoverable by the operator from the undertaker in any court of competent jurisdiction.

(4) Expressions defined in paragraph 67 have the same meanings in this paragraph.][1]

AMENDMENTS

1 Schedule inserted by the Digital Economy Act 2017, s 4(2), Sch 1.

[WHEN CAN AN UNDERTAKER CARRY OUT EMERGENCY UNDERTAKER'S WORKS?

71

(1) An undertaker may, in carrying out emergency undertaker's works, make an alteration of any electronic communications apparatus kept on, under or over any land for the purposes of an operator's network.

(2) The undertaker must give the operator notice of the emergency undertaker's works as soon as practicable after beginning them.

(3) This paragraph does not authorise the undertaker to make an alteration of apparatus after any failure by the undertaker to give notice in accordance with sub-paragraph (2).

(4) The undertaker must make the alteration to the satisfaction of the operator.

(5) If the undertaker makes any alteration in accordance with this paragraph, the undertaker must pay the operator—

(a) any expenses incurred by the operator in, or in connection with, supervising the undertaker when making the alteration; and

(b) the amount of any loss or damage sustained by the operator in consequence of the alteration being made.

(6) Any amount which is not paid in accordance with sub-paragraph (5) is to be recoverable by the operator from the undertaker in any court of competent jurisdiction.

(7) In this paragraph 'emergency undertaker's works' means undertaker's works carried out in order to stop anything already occurring, or to prevent anything imminent from occurring, which is likely to cause—

(a) danger to persons or property,

(b) interference with the exercise of any functions conferred or imposed on the undertaker by or under any enactment, or

(c) substantial loss to the undertaker,

and any other works which it is reasonable (in all the circumstances) to carry out with those works.][1]

AMENDMENTS

1 Schedule inserted by the Digital Economy Act 2017, s 4(2), Sch 1.

[OFFENCE: UNDERTAKERS WHO DO NOT COMPLY WITH THIS PART OF THIS CODE

72

(1) An undertaker, or an agent of an undertaker, is guilty of an offence if that person—

(a) makes an alteration of electronic communications apparatus in carrying out non-emergency undertaker's works, and

(b) does so—

(i) without notice of proposed works having been given in accordance with paragraph 67, or

(ii) (in a case where such notice is given) before the end of the notice period under paragraph 67.

(2) An undertaker, or an agent of an undertaker, is guilty of an offence if that person—

(a) makes an alteration of electronic communications apparatus in carrying out non-emergency undertaker's works, and

(b) unreasonably fails to comply with any reasonable requirement of the operator under this Part of this code when doing so.

(3) An undertaker, or an agent of an undertaker, is guilty of an offence if that person—

(a) makes an alteration of electronic communications apparatus in carrying out emergency undertaker's works, and

(b) does so without notice of emergency undertaker's works having been given in accordance with paragraph 71.

(4) A person guilty of an offence under this paragraph is liable on summary conviction to—

(a) a fine not exceeding level 4 on the standard scale, if the service provided by the operator's network is interrupted by the works or failure, or

(b) a fine not exceeding level 3 on the standard scale, if that service is not interrupted.

(5) This paragraph does not apply to a Northern Ireland department.][1]

AMENDMENTS

1 Schedule inserted by the Digital Economy Act 2017, s 4(2), Sch 1.

[Part 11
Overhead apparatus

INTRODUCTORY

73

This Part of this code—

(a) confers a power on operators to install and keep certain overhead apparatus, and

(b) imposes a duty on operators to affix notices to certain overhead apparatus.][1]

AMENDMENTS

1 Schedule inserted by the Digital Economy Act 2017, s 4(2), Sch 1.

[POWER TO FLY LINES

74

[(1) This paragraph applies where an operator ('the main operator') keeps electronic communications apparatus on or over any land for the purposes of the main operator's network.]

(2) The [main][2] operator has the right, for the statutory purposes, to install and keep lines which—

(a) pass over other land adjacent to, or in the vicinity of, the land on or over which the apparatus [mentioned in sub-paragraph (1)][2] is kept,

(b) are connected to that apparatus, and

(c) are not, at any point where they pass over the other land, less than three metres above the ground or within two metres of any building over which they pass.

[(2A) With the agreement of the main operator, another operator has the right, for the statutory purposes, to install and keep lines which—

(a) pass over other land adjacent to, or in the vicinity of, the land on or over which the apparatus mentioned in sub-paragraph (1) is kept,

(b) are connected to that apparatus, and

(c) are not, at any point where they pass over the other land, less than three metres above the ground or within two metres of any building over which they pass.][2]

(3) [Sub-paragraphs (2) and (2A) do][1] not authorise the installation or keeping on or over any land of—

(a) any electronic communications apparatus used to support, carry or suspend a line installed under [either of those sub-paragraphs][1], or

(b) any line which, as a result of its position, interferes with the carrying on of any business carried on on that land.

[(3A) The main operator has the right to upgrade, or carry out works to, the apparatus mentioned in sub-paragraph (1) for the purposes of, or in connection with—

(a) the exercise by the main operator of the right conferred by sub-paragraph (2), or

(b) the exercise by another operator of the right conferred by sub-paragraph (2A).

(3B) With the agreement of the main operator, another operator has the right to upgrade, or carry out works to, the apparatus mentioned in sub-paragraph (1) for the purposes of, or in connection with, the exercise by the other operator of the right conferred by sub-paragraph (2A).

(3C) Sub-paragraphs (3A) and (3B) do not authorise an operator to upgrade, or carry out works to, the apparatus mentioned in sub-paragraph (1) if the upgrade or works would—

(a) have more than a minimal adverse impact on the appearance of the apparatus,

(b) have more than a minimal adverse impact on the land on or over which the apparatus is kept, or

(c) cause loss, damage or expense to any person with an interest in the land on or over which the apparatus is kept.

(3D) An operator may not enter the land on or over which the apparatus mentioned in sub-paragraph (1) is kept for the purpose of exercising a right conferred by this paragraph without the agreement of the occupier of the land.][2]

(4) In this paragraph 'business' includes a trade, profession or employment and includes any activity carried on by a body of persons (whether corporate or unincorporate).][3]

AMENDMENTS

1 Substituted by the Product Security and Telecommunications Infrastructure Act 2022, s 60(1), (2), (5).

2 Inserted by the Product Security and Telecommunications Infrastructure Act 2022, s 60(1), (3), (4), (6).

3 Schedule inserted by the Digital Economy Act 2017, s 4(2), Sch 1.

[DUTY TO ATTACH NOTICES TO OVERHEAD APPARATUS

75

(1) This paragraph applies where—

(a) an operator has, for the purposes of the operator's network, installed any electronic communications apparatus, and

(b) the whole or part of the apparatus is at a height of three metres or more above the ground.

(2) The operator must, before the end of the period of three days beginning with the day after that on which the installation is completed, in a secure and durable manner attach a notice—

(a) to every major item of apparatus installed, or

(b) if no major item of apparatus is installed, to the nearest major item of electronic communications apparatus to which the apparatus that is installed is directly or indirectly connected.

(3) A notice attached under sub-paragraph (2)—

(a) must be attached in a position where it is reasonably legible, and

(b) must give the name of the operator and an address in the United Kingdom at which any notice of objection may be given under paragraph 77(5) in respect of the apparatus in question.

(4) Any person giving such a notice at that address in respect of that apparatus is to be treated as having given that address for the purposes of paragraph 91(2).

(5) An operator who breaches the requirements of this paragraph is guilty of an offence and liable on summary conviction to a fine not exceeding level 2 on the standard scale.

(6) In any proceedings for an offence under this paragraph it is a defence for the person charged to prove that the person took all reasonable steps and exercised all due diligence to avoid committing the offence.][1]

AMENDMENTS

1 Schedule inserted by the Digital Economy Act 2017, s 4(2), Sch 1.

[Part 12
Rights to object to certain apparatus

INTRODUCTORY

76

This Part of this code makes provision conferring rights to object to certain kinds of apparatus, and makes provision about—

(a) the cases in which and persons by whom a right can be exercised, and

(b) the power and procedures of the court if an objection is made.][1]

AMENDMENTS

1 Schedule inserted by the Digital Economy Act 2017, s 4(2), Sch 1.

[WHEN AND BY WHOM CAN A RIGHT TO OBJECT BE EXERCISED?

77

(1) A right to object under this Part of this code is available where, pursuant to the right in paragraph 62, an operator keeps electronic communications

apparatus installed on, under or over tidal water or lands within the meaning of Part 9 of this code.

(2) In that case a person has a right to object under this Part of this code if the person—

(a) is an occupier of, or has an interest in, the tidal water or lands,

(b) is not bound by a code right enabling the operator to keep the apparatus installed on, under or over the tidal water or lands, and

(c) is not a person with the benefit of a Crown interest in the tidal water or lands.

(3) A right to object under this Part of this code is available where an operator keeps a line installed over land pursuant to the right in [paragraph 74(2) or (2A)][1].

(4) In that case a person has a right to object under this Part of this code if the person—

(a) is an occupier of, or has an interest in, the land, and

(b) is not bound by a code right enabling the operator to keep the apparatus installed over the land.

(5) A right to object under this Part of this code is available where—

(a) electronic communications apparatus is kept on or over land for the purposes of an operator's network, and

(b) the whole or any part of that apparatus is at a height of three metres or more above the ground.

(6) In that case a person has a right to object under this Part of this code if—

(a) the person is an occupier of, or has an interest in, any neighbouring land, and

(b) because of the nearness of the neighbouring land to the land on or over which the apparatus is kept—

(i) the enjoyment of the neighbouring land is capable of being prejudiced by the apparatus, or

(ii) any interest in that land is capable of being prejudiced by the apparatus.

(7) There is no right to object under this Part of this code in respect of electronic communications apparatus if the apparatus—

(a) replaces any electronic communications apparatus which is not substantially different from the new apparatus, and

(b) is not in a significantly different position.][2]

AMENDMENTS

1 Substituted by the Product Security and Telecommunications Infrastructure Act 2022, s 60(7).

2 Schedule inserted by the Digital Economy Act 2017, s 4(2), Sch 1.

[HOW MAY A RIGHT TO OBJECT BE EXERCISED?

78

(1) A person with a right to object under this Part ('the objector') may exercise the right by giving a notice to the operator.

(2) The right to object that the person has, and the procedure that applies to that right, depends on whether—

(a) the notice is given before the end of the period of 12 months beginning with the date on which installation of the apparatus was completed (see paragraph 79), or

(b) the notice is given after the end of that period (see paragraph 80).][1]

AMENDMENTS

1 Schedule inserted by the Digital Economy Act 2017, s 4(2), Sch 1.

[WHAT IS THE PROCEDURE IF THE OBJECTION IS MADE WITHIN 12 MONTHS OF INSTALLATION?

79

(1) This paragraph applies if the notice is given before the end of the period of 12 months beginning with the date on which installation of the apparatus was completed.

(2) At any time after the end of the period of two months beginning with the date on which the notice is given, but before the end of the period of four months beginning with that date, the objector may apply to the court to have the objection upheld.

(3) The court must uphold the objection if the following conditions are met.

(4) The first condition is that the apparatus appears materially to prejudice the objector's enjoyment of, or interest in, the land by reference to which the objection is made.

(5) The second condition is that the court is not satisfied that the only possible alterations of the apparatus will—

(a) substantially increase the cost or diminish the quality of the service provided by the operator's network to persons who have, or may in future have, access to it,

(b) involve the operator in substantial additional expenditure (disregarding any expenditure caused solely by the fact that any proposed alteration was not adopted originally or, as the case may be, that the apparatus has been unnecessarily installed), or

(c) give to any person a case at least as good as the objector has to have an objection under this paragraph upheld.

(6) If the court upholds an objection under this paragraph it may by order do any of the following—

(a) direct the alteration of the apparatus to which the objection relates;

(b) authorise the installation (instead of the apparatus to which the objection relates), in a manner and position specified in the order, of any apparatus specified in the order;

(c) direct that no objection may be made under this paragraph in respect of any apparatus the installation of which is authorised by the court.

(7) Where an objector has both given a notice under paragraph 78 and applied for compensation under any of the other provisions of this code—

(a) the court may give such directions as it thinks fit for ensuring that no compensation is paid until any proceedings under this paragraph have been disposed of,and

(b) if the court makes an order under this paragraph, it may provide in that order for some or all of the compensation otherwise payable under this code to the objector not to be so payable, or, if the case so requires, for some or all of any compensation paid under this code to the objector to be repaid to the operator.

(8) For the purposes of sub-paragraph (5)(c), the court has the power on an application under this paragraph to give the objector directions for bringing the application to the notice of such other interested persons as it thinks fit.

(9) This paragraph is subject to paragraph 81.][1]

AMENDMENTS

1 Schedule inserted by the Digital Economy Act 2017, s 4(2), Sch 1.

[WHAT IS THE PROCEDURE IF THE OBJECTION IS MADE LATER THAN 12 MONTHS AFTER INSTALLATION?

80

(1) This paragraph applies if the notice is given after the end of the period of 12 months beginning with the date on which installation of the apparatus was completed.

(2) At any time after the end of the period of two months beginning with the date on which the notice is given, but before the end of the period of four months beginning with that date, the objector may apply to the court to have the objection upheld.

(3) The court may uphold the objection only if it is satisfied that—

(a) the alteration is necessary to enable the objector to carry out a proposed improvement of the land by reference to which the objection is made, and

(b) the alteration will not substantially interfere with any service which is or is likely to be provided using the operator's network.

(4) If the court upholds an objection under this paragraph it may by order direct the alteration of the apparatus to which the objection relates.

(5) An order under this paragraph may provide for the alteration to be carried out with such modifications, on such terms and subject to such conditions as the court thinks fit.

(6) But the court must not include any such modifications, terms or conditions in its order without the consent of the objector, and if such consent is not given may refuse to make an order under this paragraph.

(7) An order made under this paragraph must, unless the court otherwise thinks fit, require the objector to reimburse the operator in respect of any expenses which the operator incurs in or in connection with the execution of any works in compliance with the order.

(8) This paragraph is subject to paragraph 81.

(9) In this paragraph 'improvement' includes development and change of use.][1]

AMENDMENTS

1 Schedule inserted by the Digital Economy Act 2017, s 4(2), Sch 1.

[WHAT LIMITATIONS ARE THERE ON THE COURT'S POWERS UNDER PARAGRAPH 79 OR 80?

81

(1) This paragraph applies where the court is considering making—

(a) an order under paragraph 79 directing the alteration of any apparatus or authorising the installation of any apparatus, or

(b) an order under paragraph 80 directing the alteration of any apparatus.

(2) The court must not make the order unless it is satisfied—

(a) that the operator has all such rights as it appears to the court appropriate that the operator should have for the purpose of making the alteration or, as the case may be, installing the apparatus, or

(b) that—

(i) the operator would have all those rights if the court, on an application under paragraph 20, imposed an agreement on the operator and another person, and

(ii) it would be appropriate for the court, on such an application, to impose such an agreement.

(3) For the purposes of avoiding the need for the agreement of any person to the alteration or installation of any apparatus, the court has the same powers as it would have if an application had been duly made under paragraph 20 for an order imposing such an agreement.

(4) For the purposes of this paragraph, the court has the power on an application under paragraph 79 or 80 to give the objector directions for bringing the application to the notice of such other interested persons as it thinks fit.][1]

AMENDMENTS

1 Schedule inserted by the Digital Economy Act 2017, s 4(2), Sch 1.

[Part 13
Rights to lop trees

RIGHTS TO LOP TREES

82

(1) This paragraph applies where—

(a) a tree or other vegetation overhangs a street in England and Wales or Northern Ireland or a road in Scotland, and

(b) the tree or vegetation—

(i) obstructs, or will or may obstruct, relevant electronic communications apparatus, or

(ii) interferes with, or will or may interfere with, such apparatus.

(2) In sub-paragraph (1) 'relevant electronic communications apparatus' means electronic communications apparatus which—

(a) is installed, or about to be installed, on land, and

(b) is used, or to be used, for the purposes of an operator's network.

(3) The operator may, by notice to the occupier of the land on which the tree or vegetation is growing, require the tree to be lopped or the vegetation to be cut back to prevent the obstruction or interference.

(4) If, within the period of 28 days beginning with the day on which the notice is given, the occupier gives the operator a counter-notice objecting to the lopping of the tree or cutting back of the vegetation, the notice has effect only if confirmed by an order of the court.

(5) Sub-paragraph (6) applies if at any time a notice under sub-paragraph (3) has not been complied with and—

(a) the period of 28 days beginning with the day on which the notice was given has expired without a counter-notice having been given, or

(b) an order of the court confirming the notice has come into force.

(6) The operator may cause the tree to be lopped or the vegetation to be cut back.

(7) Where the operator lops a tree or cuts back vegetation in exercise of the power in sub-paragraph (6) the operator must do so in a husband-like manner and in such a way as to cause the minimum damage to the tree or vegetation.

(8) Sub-paragraph (9) applies where—

(a) a notice under sub-paragraph (3) is complied with (either without a counter-notice having been given or after the notice has been confirmed), or

(b) the operator exercises the power in sub-paragraph (6).

(9) The court must, on an application made by a person who has sustained loss or damage in consequence of the lopping of the tree or cutting back of the vegetation or who has incurred expenses in complying with the notice, order the operator to pay that person such compensation in respect of the loss or damage as it thinks fit.][1]

AMENDMENTS

1 Schedule inserted by the Digital Economy Act 2017, s 4(2), Sch 1.

[Part 14
Compensation under the code

INTRODUCTORY

83

This Part of this code makes provision about compensation under this code.][1]

AMENDMENTS

1 Schedule inserted by the Digital Economy Act 2017, s 4(2), Sch 1.

[COMPENSATION WHERE AGREEMENT IMPOSED OR APPARATUS REMOVED

84

(1) This paragraph applies to the following powers of the court to order an operator to pay compensation to a person—

(a) the power in paragraph 25(1) (compensation where order made imposing agreement on person);

[(aa) the power in paragraph 27H(2) (compensation where Part 4A order made);][1]

(b) the power in paragraph 44(5) (compensation in relation to removal of the apparatus from the land).

(2) Depending on the circumstances, the power of the court to order the payment of compensation for loss or damage includes power to order payment for—

(a) expenses (including reasonable legal and valuation expenses, subject to the provisions of any enactment about the powers of the court by whom the order for compensation is made to award costs or, in Scotland, expenses),

(b) diminution in the value of the land, and

(c) costs of reinstatement.

(3) For the purposes of assessing such compensation for diminution in the value of land, the following provisions apply with any necessary modifications as they apply for the purposes of assessing compensation for the compulsory purchase of any interest in land—

(a) in relation to England and Wales, rules (2) to (4) set out in section 5 of the Land Compensation Act 1961;

(b) in relation to Scotland, rules (2) to (4) set out in section 12 of the Land Compensation (Scotland) Act 1963;

(c) in relation to Northern Ireland, rules (2) to (4) set out in Article 6(1) of the Land Compensation (Northern Ireland) Order 1982 (SI 1982/712 (NI 9)).

(4) In the application of this paragraph to England and Wales, section 10(1) to (3) of the Land Compensation Act 1973 (compensation in respect of mortgages, trusts of land and settled land) applies in relation to such compensation for diminution in the value of land as it applies in relation to compensation under Part 1 of that Act.

(5) In the application of this paragraph to Scotland, section 10(1) and (2) of the Land Compensation (Scotland) Act 1973 (compensation in respect of restricted interests in land) applies in relation to such compensation for diminution in the value of land as it applies in relation to compensation under Part 1 of that Act.

(6) In the application of this paragraph to Northern Ireland, Article 13(1) to (3) of the Land Acquisition and Compensation (Northern Ireland) Order 1973 (SI 1973/1896 (NI 21)) (compensation in respect of mortgages, trusts for sale and settlements) applies in relation to such compensation for diminution in the value of land as it applies in relation to compensation under Part II of that Order.

(7) Where a person has a claim for compensation to which this paragraph applies and a claim for compensation under any other provision of this code in respect of the same loss, the compensation payable to that person must not exceed the amount of that person's loss.][2]

AMENDMENTS

1 Inserted by the Telecommunications Infrastructure (Leasehold Property) Act 2021, s 2, Schedule, paras 1, 4(1), (10).

2 Schedule inserted by the Digital Economy Act 2017, s 4(2), Sch 1.

[COMPENSATION FOR INJURIOUS AFFECTION TO NEIGHBOURING LAND ETC

85

(1) This paragraph applies where a right conferred by or in accordance with any provision of Parts 2 to 9 of this code is exercised by an operator.

(2) In the application of this paragraph to England and Wales, compensation is payable by the operator under section 10 of the Compulsory Purchase Act 1965 (compensation for injurious affection to neighbouring land) as if that section applied in relation to injury caused by the exercise of such a right as it applies in relation to injury caused by the execution of works on land that has been compulsorily acquired.

(3) In the application of this paragraph to Scotland, compensation is payable by the operator under section 6 of the Railway Clauses Consolidation (Scotland) Act 1845 as if that section applied in relation to injury caused by the exercise of such a right as it applies in relation to injury caused by the execution of works on land that has been taken or used for the purpose of a railway.

(4) Any question as to a person's entitlement to compensation by virtue of sub-paragraph (3), or as to the amount of that compensation, is, in default of agreement, to be determined by the Lands Tribunal for Scotland.

(5) In the application of this paragraph to Northern Ireland, compensation is payable by the operator under Article 18 of the Land Compensation (Northern Ireland) Order 1982 (SI 1982/712 (NI 9)) as if that section applied in relation to injury caused by the exercise of such a right as it applies in relation to injury caused by the execution of works on land that has been compulsorily acquired.

(6) Any question as to a person's entitlement to compensation by virtue of sub-paragraph (5), or as to the amount of that compensation, is, in default of agreement, to be determined by the Lands Tribunal for Northern Ireland.

(7) Compensation is payable on a claim for compensation under this paragraph only if the amount of the compensation exceeds £50.

(8) Compensation is payable to a person under this paragraph irrespective of whether the person claiming the compensation has any interest in the land in relation to which the right referred to in sub-paragraph (1) is exercised.

(9) Compensation under this paragraph may include reasonable legal and valuation expenses, subject to the provisions of any enactment about the powers of the court or tribunal by whom an order for compensation is made to award costs or, in Scotland, expenses.][1]

AMENDMENTS

1 Schedule inserted by the Digital Economy Act 2017, s 4(2), Sch 1.

[NO OTHER COMPENSATION AVAILABLE

86

Except as provided by any provision of Parts 2 to 13 of this code or this Part, an operator is not liable to compensate any person for, and is not subject to any other liability in respect of, any loss or damage caused by the lawful exercise of any right conferred by or in accordance with any provision of those Parts.][1]

AMENDMENTS

1 Schedule inserted by the Digital Economy Act 2017, s 4(2), Sch 1.

[Part 15
Notices under the code

INTRODUCTORY

87

This Part makes provision—

(a) about requirements for the form of notices given under this code by operators,

(b) about requirements for the form of notices given under this code by persons other than operators, and

(c) about procedures for giving notices.][1]

AMENDMENTS

1 Schedule inserted by the Digital Economy Act 2017, s 4(2), Sch 1.

[NOTICES GIVEN BY OPERATORS

88

(1) A notice given under this code by an operator must—

(a) explain the effect of the notice,

(b) explain which provisions of this code are relevant to the notice, and

(c) explain the steps that may be taken by the recipient in respect of the notice.

(2) If OFCOM have prescribed the form of a notice which may or must be given by an operator under a provision of this code, a notice given by an operator under that provision must be in that form.

(3) A notice which does not comply with this paragraph is not a valid notice for the purposes of this code.

(4) Sub-paragraph (3) does not prevent the person to whom the notice is given from relying on the notice if the person chooses to do so.

(5) In any proceedings under this code a certificate issued by OFCOM stating that a particular form of notice has been prescribed by them as mentioned in this paragraph is conclusive evidence of that fact.][1]

AMENDMENTS

1 Schedule inserted by the Digital Economy Act 2017, s 4(2), Sch 1.

[NOTICES GIVEN BY OTHERS

89

(1) Sub-paragraph (2) applies to a notice given under paragraph 31(1), 33(1), 39(1) or 40(2) by a person other than an operator.

(2) If OFCOM have prescribed the form of a notice given under the provision in question by a person other than an operator, the notice must be in that form.

(3) A notice which does not comply with sub-paragraph (2) is not a valid notice for the purposes of this code.

(4) Sub-paragraph (3) does not prevent the operator to whom the notice is given from relying on the notice if the operator chooses to do so.

(5) Sub-paragraph (6) applies to a notice given under any other provision of this code by a person other than an operator if—

(a) OFCOM have prescribed the form of a notice given under that provision by a person other than an operator,

(b) the notice is given in response to a notice given by an operator, and

(c) the operator has, in giving the notice, drawn the person's attention to the form prescribed by OFCOM.

(6) The notice is a valid notice for the purposes of this code, but the person giving the notice must bear any costs incurred by the operator as a result of the notice not being in that form.

(7) In any proceedings under this code a certificate issued by OFCOM stating that a particular form of notice has been prescribed by them as mentioned in this paragraph is conclusive evidence of that fact.][1]

AMENDMENTS

1 Schedule inserted by the Digital Economy Act 2017, s 4(2), Sch 1.

[PRESCRIPTION OF NOTICES BY OFCOM

90

(1) OFCOM must prescribe the form of a notice to be given under each provision of this code that requires a notice to be given.

(2) OFCOM may from time to time amend or replace a form prescribed under sub-paragraph (1).

(3) Before prescribing a form for the purposes of this code, OFCOM must consult operators and such other persons as OFCOM think appropriate.

(4) Sub-paragraph (3) does not apply to the amendment or replacement of a form prescribed under sub-paragraph (1).][1]

AMENDMENTS

1 Schedule inserted by the Digital Economy Act 2017, s 4(2), Sch 1.

[PROCEDURES FOR GIVING NOTICE

91

(1) A notice given under this code must not be sent by post unless it is sent by a registered post service or by recorded delivery.

(2) For the purposes, in the case of a notice under this code, of section 394 of this Act (service of notifications and other documents) and section 7 of the Interpretation Act 1978 (references to service by post), the proper address of a person ('P') is—

(a) if P has given the person giving the notice an address for service under this code, that address, and

(b) otherwise, the address given by section 394.

(3) Sub-paragraph (4) applies if it is not practicable, for the purposes of giving a notice under this code, to find out after reasonable enquiries the name and address of a person who is the occupier of land for the purposes of this code.

(4) A notice may be given under this code to the occupier —

(a) by addressing it to a person by the description of 'occupier' of the land (and describing the land), and

(b) by delivering it to a person who is on the land or, if there is no person on the land to whom it can be delivered, by affixing it, or a copy of it, to a conspicuous object on the land.

(5) Sub-paragraph (6) applies if it is not practicable, for the purposes of giving a notice under this code, to find out after reasonable enquiries the name and address of the owner of an interest in land.

(6) A notice may be given under this code to the owner—

(a) by addressing it to a person by the description of 'owner' of the interest (and describing the interest and the land), and

(b) by delivering it to a person who is on the land or, if there is no person on the land to whom it can be delivered, by affixing it, or a copy of it, to a conspicuous object on the land.][1]

AMENDMENTS

1 Schedule inserted by the Digital Economy Act 2017, s 4(2), Sch 1.

[Part 16
Enforcement and dispute resolution

INTRODUCTORY

92

This Part of this code makes provision about—

(a) the court or tribunal by which agreements and rights under this code may be enforced,

(b) the meaning of references to 'the court' in this code, and

(c) the power of the Secretary of State by regulations to confer jurisdiction under this code on other tribunals.][1]

AMENDMENTS

1 Schedule inserted by the Digital Economy Act 2017, s 4(2), Sch 1.

[ENFORCEMENT OF AGREEMENTS AND RIGHTS

93

An agreement under this code, and any right conferred by this code, may be enforced—

(a) in the case of an agreement imposed by a court or tribunal, by the court or tribunal which imposed the agreement,

(b) in the case of any agreement or right, by any court or tribunal which for the time being has the power to impose an agreement under this code, or

(c) in the case of any agreement or right, by any court of competent jurisdiction.][1]

AMENDMENTS

1 Schedule inserted by the Digital Economy Act 2017, s 4(2), Sch 1.

[MEANING OF 'THE COURT'

94

(1) In this code 'the court' means—

(a) in relation to England and Wales, the county court,

(b) in relation to Scotland, the sheriff court, and

(c) in relation to Northern Ireland, a county court.

(2) Sub-paragraph (1) is subject to provision made by regulations under paragraph 95.][1]

AMENDMENTS

1 Schedule inserted by the Digital Economy Act 2017, s 4(2), Sch 1.

[POWER TO CONFER JURISDICTION ON OTHER TRIBUNALS

95

(1) The Secretary of State may by regulations provide for a function conferred by this code on the court to be exercisable by any of the following—

(a) in relation to England, the First-tier Tribunal;

[(aa) in relation to Wales, the First-tier Tribunal, but only in connection with proceedings under Part 4A;][1]

(b) in relation to England and Wales, the Upper Tribunal;

(c) in relation to Scotland, the Lands Tribunal for Scotland;

(d) in relation to Northern Ireland, the Lands Tribunal for Northern Ireland.

(2) Regulations under sub-paragraph (1) may make provision for the function to be exercisable by a tribunal to which the regulations apply—

(a) instead of by the court, or

(b) as well as by the court.

(3) The Secretary of State may by regulations make provision—

(a) requiring proceedings to which regulations under sub-paragraph (1) apply to be commenced in the court or in a tribunal to which the regulations apply;

(b) enabling the court or such a tribunal to transfer such proceedings to a tribunal which has jurisdiction in relation to them by virtue of such regulations or to the court.

(4) The power in section 402(3)(c) for regulations under sub-paragraph (1) or (3) to make consequential provision includes power to make provision which amends, repeals or revokes or otherwise modifies the application of any enactment.

(5) Before making regulations under sub-paragraph (1) or (3) the Secretary of State must—

(a) so far as the regulations relate to Scotland, consult the Scottish Ministers;

(b) so far as the regulations relate to Northern Ireland, consult the Department of Justice in Northern Ireland.][2]

AMENDMENTS

1 Inserted by the Telecommunications Infrastructure (Leasehold Property) Act 2021, s 2, Schedule, paras 1, 4(1), (11).

2 Schedule inserted by the Digital Economy Act 2017, s 4(2), Sch 1.

[AWARD OF COSTS BY TRIBUNAL

96

(1) Where in any proceedings a tribunal exercises functions by virtue of regulations under paragraph 95(1), it may make such order as it thinks fit as to costs, or, in Scotland, expenses.

(2) The matters a tribunal must have regard to in making such an order include in particular—

[(a)][1] the extent to which any party is successful in the proceedings[, and

(b) any unreasonable refusal by a party to engage in alternative dispute resolution.][2]][3]

AMENDMENTS

1 Renumbered by the Product Security and Telecommunications Infrastructure Act 2022, s 69(1), (5)(a).

2 Inserted by the Product Security and Telecommunications Infrastructure Act 2022, s 69(1), (5)(b).

3 Schedule inserted by the Digital Economy Act 2017, s 4(2), Sch 1.

[APPLICATIONS TO THE COURT

97

Regulation 3 of the Electronic Communications and Wireless Telegraphy Regulations 2011 (SI 2011/1210) makes provision about the time within which certain applications to the court under this code must be determined.][1]

AMENDMENTS

1 Schedule inserted by the Digital Economy Act 2017, s 4(2), Sch 1.

[APPEALS IN NORTHERN IRELAND

98

Article 60 of the County Courts (Northern Ireland) Order 1980 (ordinary appeals from the county court in civil cases) is to apply in relation to any determination of the court in Northern Ireland under this code in the same manner as it applies in relation to any decree of the court made in the exercise of the jurisdiction conferred by Part 3 of that Order.][1]

AMENDMENTS

1 Schedule inserted by the Digital Economy Act 2017, s 4(2), Sch 1.

[Part 17
Supplementary provisions

RELATIONSHIP BETWEEN THIS CODE AND EXISTING LAW

99

(1) This code does not authorise the contravention of any provision of an enactment passed or made before the coming into force of this code.

(2) Sub-paragraph (1) does not apply if and to the extent that an enactment makes provision to the contrary.][1]

AMENDMENTS

1 Schedule inserted by the Digital Economy Act 2017, s 4(2), Sch 1.

[RELATIONSHIP BETWEEN THIS CODE AND AGREEMENTS WITH OPERATORS

100

(1) This code does not affect any rights or liabilities arising under an agreement to which an operator is a party.

(2) Sub-paragraph (1) does not apply in relation to paragraph 99 or Parts 3 to 6 of this code.][1]

AMENDMENTS

1 Schedule inserted by the Digital Economy Act 2017, s 4(2), Sch 1.

[OWNERSHIP OF PROPERTY

101

The ownership of property does not change merely because the property is installed on or under, or affixed to, any land by any person in exercise of a right conferred by or in accordance with this code.][1]

AMENDMENTS

1 Schedule inserted by the Digital Economy Act 2017, s 4(2), Sch 1.

[CONDUITS

102

(1) This code does not authorise an operator to do anything inside a relevant conduit without the agreement of the authority with control of the conduit.

(2) The agreement of the authority with control of a public sewer is sufficient in all cases to authorise an operator to exercise any of the rights under this code in order to do anything wholly inside that sewer.

(3) In this paragraph the following expressions have the same meanings as in section 98 of the Telecommunications Act 1984—

(a) 'public sewer' and 'relevant conduit';

(b) references to the authority with control of a relevant conduit.][1]

AMENDMENTS

1 Schedule inserted by the Digital Economy Act 2017, s 4(2), Sch 1.

[DUTIES FOR OFCOM TO PREPARE CODES OF PRACTICE

103

(1) OFCOM must prepare and publish a code of practice dealing with—

(a) the provision of information for the purposes of this code by operators to persons who occupy or have an interest in land;

(b) the conduct of negotiations for the purposes of this code between operators and such persons;

(c) the conduct of operators in relation to persons who occupy or have an interest in land adjoining land on, under or over which electronic communications apparatus is installed;

(d) such other matters relating to the operation of this code as OFCOM think appropriate.

(2) OFCOM must prepare and publish standard terms which may (but need not) be used in agreements under this code.

(3) OFCOM may from time to time—

(a) amend or replace a code of practice or standard terms published under this paragraph;

(b) publish the code or terms as amended or (as the case may be) the replacement code or terms.

(4) Before publishing a code of practice or standard terms under this paragraph, OFCOM must consult operators and such other persons as OFCOM think appropriate.

(5) Sub-paragraph (4) does not apply to—

(a) the publication of amendments to a code of practice or standard terms, or

(b) the publication of a replacement code or replacement terms.][1]

AMENDMENTS

1 Schedule inserted by the Digital Economy Act 2017, s 4(2), Sch 1.

[APPLICATION OF THIS CODE TO THE CROWN

104

(1) This code applies in relation to land in which there subsists, or at any material time subsisted, a Crown interest as it applies in relation to land in which no such interest subsists.

(2) In this code 'Crown interest' means—

(a) an interest which belongs to Her Majesty in right of the Crown,

(b) an interest which belongs to Her Majesty in right of the Duchy of Lancaster,

(c) an interest which belongs to the Duchy of Cornwall,

(d) an interest which belongs to a government department or which is held in trust for Her Majesty for the purposes of a government department, or

(e) an interest which belongs to an office-holder in the Scottish Administration or which is held in trust for Her Majesty for the purposes of the Scottish Administration by such an office-holder.

(3) This includes, in particular—

(a) an interest which belongs to Her Majesty in right of Her Majesty's Government in Northern Ireland, and

(b) an interest which belongs to a Northern Ireland department or which is held in trust for Her Majesty for the purposes of a Northern Ireland department.

(4) Where an agreement is required by this code to be given in respect of any Crown interest subsisting in any land, the agreement must be given by the appropriate authority.

(5) Where a notice under this code is required to be given in relation to land in which a Crown interest subsists, the notice must be given by or to the appropriate authority (as the case may require).

(6) In this paragraph 'the appropriate authority' means—

(a) in the case of land belonging to Her Majesty in right of the Crown, the Crown Estate Commissioners or the relevant person or, as the case may be, the government department or office-holder in the Scottish Administration having the management of the land in question;

(b) in the case of land belonging to Her Majesty in right of the Duchy of Lancaster, the Chancellor of the Duchy of Lancaster;

(c) in the case of land belonging to the Duchy of Cornwall, such person as the Duke of Cornwall, or the possessor for the time being of the Duchy of Cornwall, appoints;

(d) in the case of land belonging to an office-holder in the Scottish Administration or held in trust for Her Majesty by such an office-holder for the purposes of the Scottish Administration, the office-holder;

(e) in the case of land belonging to Her Majesty in right of Her Majesty's Government in Northern Ireland, the Northern Ireland department having the management of the land in question;

(f) in the case of land belonging to a government department or a Northern Ireland department or held in trust for Her Majesty for the purposes of a government department or a Northern Ireland department, that department.

(7) In sub-paragraph (6)(a) 'relevant person', in relation to land to which section 90B(5) of the Scotland Act 1998 applies, means the person having the management of that land.

(8) Any question as to the authority that is the appropriate authority in relation to any land is to be referred to the Treasury, whose decision is final.

(9) Paragraphs 55 (offence in relation to transport land rights) and 75(5) (offence in relation to notices on overhead apparatus) do not apply where this code applies in the case of the Secretary of State or a Northern Ireland department by virtue of section 106(3)(b).

(10) References in this paragraph to an office-holder in the Scottish Administration are to be construed in accordance with section 126(7) of the Scotland Act 1998.][1]

AMENDMENTS

1 Schedule inserted by the Digital Economy Act 2017, s 4(2), Sch 1.

[MEANING OF 'OCCUPIER'

105

(1) References in this code to an occupier of land are to the occupier of the land for the time being.

(2) References in this code to an occupier of land, in relation to a footpath or bridleway that crosses and forms part of agricultural land, are to the occupier of that agricultural land.

(3) Sub-paragraph (4) applies in relation to land which is—

(a) a street in England and Wales or Northern Ireland, other than a footpath or bridleway within sub-paragraph (2), or

(b) a road in Scotland, other than such a footpath or bridleway.

(4) References in this code to an occupier of land—

(a) in relation to such a street in England and Wales, are to the street managers within the meaning of Part 3 of the New Roads and Street Works Act 1991,

(b) in relation to such a street in Northern Ireland, are to the street managers within the meaning of the Street Works (Northern Ireland) Order 1995 (SI 1995/3210 (NI 19)), and

(c) in relation to such a road in Scotland, are to the road managers within the meaning of Part 4 of the New Roads and Street Works Act 1991.

(5) Sub-paragraph (6) applies in relation to land which—

(a) is unoccupied, and

(b) is not a street in England and Wales or Northern Ireland or a road in Scotland.

(6) References in this code to an occupier of land, in relation to land within sub-paragraph (5), are to—

(a) the person (if any) who for the time being exercises powers of management or control over the land, or

(b) if there is no person within paragraph (a), to every person whose interest in the land would be prejudicially affected by the exercise of a code right in relation to the land.

(7) In this paragraph—

(a) 'agricultural land' includes land which is being brought into use for agriculture, and

(b) references in relation to England and Wales to a footpath or bridleway include a restricted byway.][1]

AMENDMENTS

1 Schedule inserted by the Digital Economy Act 2017, s 4(2), Sch 1.

[LANDS TRIBUNAL FOR SCOTLAND PROCEDURE RULES

106

The power to make rules under section 3(6) of the Lands Tribunal Act 1949 (Lands Tribunal for Scotland procedure rules) for the purposes of this code or regulations made under it is exercisable by the Scottish Ministers instead of by the Secretary of State (and any reference there to the approval of the Treasury does not apply).][1]

AMENDMENTS

1 Schedule inserted by the Digital Economy Act 2017, s 4(2), Sch 1.

[ARBITRATIONS IN SCOTLAND

107

Until the Arbitration (Scotland) Act 2010 is in force in relation to any arbitrations carried out under or by virtue of this code, that Act applies as if it were in force in relation to those arbitrations.][1]

AMENDMENTS

1 Schedule inserted by the Digital Economy Act 2017, s 4(2), Sch 1.

[GENERAL INTERPRETATION

108

(1) In this code—

'agriculture' and 'agricultural'—

(a) in relation to England and Wales, have the same meanings as in the Highways Act 1980,

(b) in relation to Scotland, have the same meanings as in the Town and Country Planning (Scotland) Act 1997, and

(c) in relation to Northern Ireland, have the same meanings as in the Agriculture Act (Northern Ireland) 1949;

'bridleway' and 'footpath'—

(a) in relation to England and Wales, have the same meanings as in the Highways Act 1980,

(b) in relation to Scotland, have the same meanings as Part 3 of the Countryside (Scotland) Act 1967, and

(c) in relation to Northern Ireland, mean a way over which the public have, by virtue of the Access to the Countryside (Northern Ireland) Order 1983 (SI 1983/1895 (NI 18)), a right of way (respectively) on horseback and on foot;

'code agreement' has the meaning given by paragraph 29(5);

'Crown interest' has the meaning given by paragraph 104(2) and (3);

'enactment' includes—

(a) an enactment comprised in subordinate legislation within the meaning of the Interpretation Act 1978,

(b) an enactment comprised in, or in an instrument made under, a Measure or Act of the National Assembly for Wales,

(c) an enactment comprised in, or in an instrument made under, an Act of the Scottish Parliament, and

(d) an enactment comprised in, or in an instrument made under, Northern Ireland legislation;

'land' does not include electronic communications apparatus;

'landowner' has the meaning given by paragraph 37(1);

['lease'—

(a) in relation to England and Wales and Northern Ireland, includes—

(i) any head lease, sub-lease or underlease,

(ii) any tenancy (including a sub-tenancy), and

(iii) any agreement to grant any such lease or tenancy,

but does not include a mortgage by demise or sub-demise;

(b) in relation to Scotland, includes any sub-lease and any agreement to grant a sub-lease,

and 'leased premises' and 'lessee' are to be read accordingly;][1]

['Part 4A code right' has the meaning given by paragraph 27E(3);][2]

'relevant person' has the meaning given by paragraph 20(1);

'restricted byway' has the same meaning as in Part 2 of the Countryside and Rights of Way Act 2000;

'road'—

(a) in relation to Scotland, has the same meaning as in Part 4 of the New Roads and Street Works Act 1991;

(b) in relation to Northern Ireland, has the same meaning as in the Roads (Northern Ireland) Order 1993 (SI 1993/3160 (NI 15));

'site provider' has the meaning given by paragraph 30(1);

'street'—

(a) in relation to England and Wales, has the same meaning as in Part 3 of the New Roads and Street Works Act 1991, and

(b) in relation to Northern Ireland, has the same meaning as in the Street Works (Northern Ireland) Order 1995 (SI 1995/3210 (NI 19)).

(2) In this code, references to the alteration of any apparatus include references to the moving, removal or replacement of the apparatus.][3]

AMENDMENTS

1 Substituted by the Telecommunications Infrastructure (Leasehold Property) Act 2021, s 2, Schedule, paras 1, 4(1), (12)(a).

2 Inserted by the Telecommunications Infrastructure (Leasehold Property) Act 2021, s 2, Schedule, paras 1, 4(1), (12)(b).

3 Schedule inserted by the Digital Economy Act 2017, s 4(2), Sch 1.

The Electronic Communications Code: transitional provisions

Digital Economy Act 2017, Sch 2

Section 4

INTERPRETATION

1

(1) This paragraph has effect for the purposes of this Schedule.

(2) The 'existing code' means Schedule 2 to the Telecommunications Act 1984.

(3) The 'new code' means Schedule 3A to the Communications Act 2003.

(4) A 'subsisting agreement' means—

(a) an agreement for the purposes of paragraph 2 or 3 of the existing code, or

(b) an order under paragraph 5 of the existing code,

which is in force, as between an operator and any person, at the time the new code comes into force (and whose terms do not provide for it to cease to have effect at that time).

(5) Expressions used in this Schedule and in the new code have the same meaning as in the new code, subject to any modification made by this Schedule.

EFFECT OF SUBSISTING AGREEMENT

2

(1) A subsisting agreement has effect after the new code comes into force as an agreement under Part 2 of the new code between the same parties, subject to the modifications made by this Schedule.

(2) A person who is bound by a right by virtue of paragraph 2(4) of the existing code in consequence of a subsisting agreement is, after the new code comes into force, treated as bound pursuant to Part 2 of the new code.

LIMITATION OF CODE RIGHTS

3

In relation to a subsisting agreement, references in the new code to a code right are—

(a) in relation to the operator and the land to which an agreement for the purposes of paragraph 2 of the existing code relates, references to a right for the statutory purposes to do the things listed in paragraph 2(1)(a) to (c) of the existing code;

(b) in relation to land to which an agreement for the purposes of paragraph 3 of the existing code relates, a right to do the things mentioned in that paragraph.

LIMITATION OF PERSONS BOUND

4

(1) A person bound by a code right by virtue only of paragraph 2(3) of the existing code continues to be bound by it so long as they would be bound if paragraph 2(3) of the existing code continued to have effect.

(2) In relation to such a person, paragraph 4(4) to (12) of the existing code continue to have effect, but as if in paragraph 4(4)(b) the reference to paragraph 21 of the existing code were a reference to Part 6 of the new code.

EXCLUSION OF ASSIGNMENT ...[1] PROVISIONS

5

(1) [Paragraph 16 of the new code (assignment of code rights)][2] does not apply in relation to a subsisting agreement.

(2) [Paragraph 16][2] of the new code does not apply in relation to a code right conferred under the new code if, at the time when it is conferred, the exercise of the right depends on a right that has effect under a subsisting agreement.

AMENDMENTS

1 Repealed by the Product Security and Telecommunications Infrastructure Act 2022, s 58(1), (2).

2 Substituted by the Product Security and Telecommunications Infrastructure Act 2022, s 58(1), (3).

[UPGRADING AND SHARING PROVISIONS

5A

Paragraph 17 of the new code (power for operator to upgrade or share apparatus) applies in relation to an operator who is a party to a subsisting agreement, but as if for sub-paragraphs (1) to (6) there were substituted—

'(1) This paragraph applies where—

(a) an operator ('the main operator') keeps electronic communications apparatus installed under land, and

(b) the main operator is a party to a subsisting agreement in relation to the electronic communications apparatus.

(2) If the conditions in sub-paragraphs (3), (4) and (6) are met, the main operator may—

(a) upgrade the electronic communications apparatus, or

(b) share the use of the electronic communications apparatus with another operator.

(3) The first condition is that the upgrading or sharing has no adverse impact on the land.

(4) The second condition is that the upgrading or sharing imposes no burden on any person with an interest in the land.

(5) For the purposes of sub-paragraph (4) a burden includes anything that—

(a) has an adverse effect on the person's enjoyment of the land, or

(b) causes loss, damage or expense to the person.

(6) The third condition is that, before the beginning of the period of 21 days ending with the day on which the main operator begins to upgrade the electronic communications apparatus or (as the case may be) share its use, the main operator attaches a notice, in a secure and durable manner, to a conspicuous object on the relevant land.

(7) A notice attached for the purposes of sub-paragraph (6) must—

(a) be attached in a position where it is reasonably legible,

(b) state that the main operator intends to upgrade the electronic communications apparatus or (as the case may be) share its use with another operator,

(c) state the date on which the main operator intends to begin to upgrade the electronic communications apparatus or (as the case may be) share its use with another operator,

(d) state, in a case where the main operator intends to share the use of the electronic communications apparatus with another operator, the name of the other operator, and

(e) give the name of the main operator and an address in the United Kingdom at which the main operator may be contacted about the upgrading or sharing.

(8) Any person giving a notice at that address in respect of that electronic communications apparatus is to be treated as having been given that address for the purposes of paragraph 91(2).

(9) Any agreement under Part 2 of this code is void to the extent that—

(a) it prevents or limits the upgrading or sharing, in a case where the conditions mentioned in sub-paragraphs (3), (4) and (6) are met, of any electronic communications apparatus to which the agreement relates that is installed under land, or

(b) it makes upgrading or sharing of such electronic communications apparatus subject to conditions to be met by the operator (including a condition requiring the payment of money).

(10) Nothing in this paragraph is to be read as conferring a right on the main operator to enter the land for the purpose of upgrading or sharing the use of the electronic communications apparatus.

(11) References in this paragraph to sharing electronic communications apparatus include carrying out works to the electronic communications apparatus to enable such sharing to take place.

(12) In this paragraph—

'the relevant land' means—

(a) in a case where the main operator has a right to enter the land under which the electronic communications apparatus is installed, that land;

(b) in any other case, the land on which works will be carried out to enable the upgrading or sharing to take place or, where there is more than one set of works, the land on which each set of works will be carried out;

'subsisting agreement' has the meaning given by paragraph 1(4) of Schedule 2 to the Digital Economy Act 2017.'][1]

AMENDMENTS

1 Inserted by the Product Security and Telecommunications Infrastructure Act 2022, s 58(1), (4).

TERMINATION AND MODIFICATION OF AGREEMENTS

6

(1) This paragraph applies in relation to a subsisting agreement, in place of paragraph 29(2) to (4) of the new code.

(2) Part 5 of the new code (termination and modification of agreements) does not apply to a subsisting agreement that is a lease of land in England and Wales, if—

(a) it is a lease to which Part 2 of the Landlord and Tenant Act 1954 applies, and

(b) there is no agreement under section 38A of that Act (agreements to exclude provisions of Part 2) in relation the tenancy.

(3) Part 5 of the new code does not apply to a subsisting agreement that is a lease of land in England and Wales, if—

(a) the primary purpose of the lease is not to grant code rights (the rights referred to in paragraph 3 of this Schedule), and

(b) there is an agreement under section 38A of the 1954 Act in relation the tenancy.

(4) Part 5 of the new code does not apply to a subsisting agreement that is a lease of land in Northern Ireland, if it is a lease to which the Business Tenancies (Northern Ireland) Order 1996 (SI 1996/725 (NI 5)) applies.

7

(1) Subject to paragraph 6, Part 5 of the new code applies to a subsisting agreement with the following modifications.

(2) The 'site provider' (see paragraph 30(1)(a) of the new code) does not include a person who was under the existing code bound by the agreement only by virtue of paragraph 2(2)(c) of that code.

(3) Where the unexpired term of the subsisting agreement at the coming into force of the new code is less than 18 months, paragraph 31 applies (with necessary modification) as if for the period of 18 months referred to in sub-paragraph (3)(a) there were substituted a period equal to the unexpired term or 3 months, whichever is greater.

(4) Paragraph 34 applies with the omission of sub-paragraph (13)(d).

APPARATUS, WORKS ETC

8

(1) Paragraphs 9 to 14 of the existing code (rights in relation to street works, flying lines, tidal waters, linear obstacles) continue to apply in relation to anything in the process of being done when the new code comes into force.

(2) Apparatus lawfully installed under any of those provisions (before or after the time when the new code comes into force) is to be treated as installed under the corresponding provision of the new code if it could have been installed under that provision if the provision had been in force or applied to its installation.

(3) The corresponding provisions are—

(a) Part 7 (transport land rights), in relation to paragraph 12 of the existing code;

(b) Part 8 (street work rights), in relation to paragraph 9 of the existing code;

(c) Part 9 (tidal water rights), in relation to paragraph 11 of the existing code;

(d) paragraph 74 (power to fly lines), in relation to paragraph 10 of the existing code.

9

Any agreement given in accordance with paragraph 26(3) of the existing code for the purposes of paragraph 11(2) of that code has effect for the purposes of paragraph 64 of the new code as if given in accordance with paragraph 104 of that code.

10

Any agreement that has effect under paragraph 15 of the existing code and that would be sufficient for the purpose of doing anything wholly inside a sewer if that paragraph continued in force is sufficient for that purpose under paragraph 102(2) of the new code.

COURT APPLICATIONS FOR REQUIRED RIGHTS ETC

11

(1) This paragraph applies where—

(a) before the time when the new code comes into force, a notice has been given under paragraph 5(1) of the existing code, and

(b) at that time no application has been made to the court in relation to the notice.

(2) The notice has effect as if given under paragraph 20(2) of the new code.

12

(1) This paragraph applies where before the time when the new code comes into force—

(a) a notice has been given under paragraph 5(1) of the existing code, and

(b) an application has been made to the court in relation to the notice.

(2) Subject to sub-paragraph (3), the existing code continues to apply in relation to the application.

(3) An order made under the existing code by virtue of sub-paragraph (2) has effect as an order under paragraph 20 of the new code.

TEMPORARY CODE RIGHTS

13

The coming into force of the new code does not affect any application or order made under paragraph 6 of the existing code.

COMPENSATION

14

The repeal of the existing code does not affect paragraph 16 of that code, or any other right to compensation, as it applies in relation to the exercise of a right before the new code comes into force.

OBJECTIONS IN RELATION TO APPARATUS

15

The repeal of the existing code does not affect paragraphs 17 and 18 of that code as they apply in relation to anything whose installation was completed before the repeal comes into force.

16

(1) Subject to the following provisions of this paragraph, the repeal of the existing code does not affect paragraph 20 of that code as it applies in relation to anything whose installation was completed before the repeal comes into force.

(2) A right under paragraph 20 is not by virtue of sub-paragraph (1) exercisable in relation to any apparatus by a person who is a party to, or is bound by, an agreement under the new code in relation to the apparatus.

(3) A subsisting agreement is not an agreement under the new code for the purposes of sub-paragraph (2).

17

Part 12 of the new code does not apply in relation to apparatus whose installation was completed before the new code came into force.

TREE LOPPING

18

(1) This paragraph applies where—

(a) before the time when the new code comes into force, a notice has been given under paragraph 19 of the existing code, and

(b) at that time no application has been made to the court in relation to the notice.

(2) The notice and any counter-notice under that paragraph have effect as if given under paragraph 82 of the new code.

19

(1) This paragraph applies where before the time when the new code comes into force—

(a) a notice has been given under paragraph 19 of the existing code, and

(b) an application has been made to the court in relation to the notice.

(2) The existing code continues to apply in relation to the application.

RIGHT TO REQUIRE REMOVAL OF APPARATUS

20

(1) This paragraph applies where before the repeal of the existing code comes into force a person has given notice under paragraph 21(2) of that code requiring the removal of apparatus.

(2) The repeal does not affect the operation of paragraph 21 in relation to anything done or that may be done under that paragraph following the giving of the notice.

(3) For the purposes of applying that paragraph after the repeal comes into force, steps specified in a counter-notice under sub-paragraph (4)(b) of that paragraph as steps which the operator proposes to take under the existing code are to be read as including any corresponding steps that the operator could take under the new code or by virtue of this Schedule.

UNDERTAKER'S WORKS

21

The repeal of the existing code does not affect the operation of paragraph 23 of that code in relation to works—

(a) in relation to which a notice has been given under that paragraph before the time when that repeal comes into force, or

(b) which have otherwise been commenced before that time.

SUPPLEMENTARY

22

Any agreement which, immediately before the repeal of the existing code, is a relevant agreement for the purposes of paragraph 29 of that code is to be treated in relation to times after the coming into force of that repeal as a relevant agreement for the purposes of paragraph 18 of the new code.

23

Part 15 of the new code applies in relation to notices under this Schedule as it applies in relation to notices under that code.

24

Paragraphs 24 to 27 of the existing code continue to have effect in relation to any provision of that code so far as the provision has effect by virtue of this Schedule.

25

A person entitled to compensation by virtue of this Schedule is not entitled to compensation in respect of the same matter under any provision of the new code.

Index

References are to paragraph number.

0–9
1954 Act cases
compensation
generally, 14.08
interaction with consideration, 13.199–13.230, 14.36
post-PSTIA 2022 amendments, 14.10–14.13
pre-PSTIA 2022 amendments, 14.09
consideration/compensation interaction
generally, 13.199–13.200, 14.36
rent, 13.201–13.204
valuation (post-PSTIA 2022 amendments), 13.224–13.230
valuation (pre-PSTIA 2022 amendments), 13.205–13.223
court determinations on terms
access, 11.258
break clause, 11.263–11.280
contractual compensation provisions, 11.251–11.257
equipment rights (including upgrading), 11.247–11.250
generally, 11.246
indemnity, 11.259
non-interference by landlord, 11.260–11.262
rent, 11.283–11.284
rent review, 11.281–11.282
imposed terms
all other terms, 11.234–11.245
court determinations on terms, 11.246–11.284
duration of tenancy, 11.228–11.233
generally, 11.226
property comprised in tenancy, 11.227
judges hearing 1954 Act matters in county court, 21.21–21.22
lease vs licence
Burlington Gardens case, 16.134–16.135
certainty of term, 16.140–16.143
effect of clause asserting that no tenancy is created, 16.151–16.153
exclusive possession of land, 16.136–16.139
generally, 16.127–16.133
1954 Act cases – *contd*
lease vs licence – *contd*
potential third category, 16.154–16.168
previous Code cases, 16.144–16.150
modification of agreements, 16.272–16.274
redevelopment
applicability of ground (f) case law, 17.16–17.18
definition, 17.33–17.43
differences from Code tests, 17.19–17.43
generally, 17.01–17.03
land on which works are to occur, 17.30–17.32
'reasonable time', 17.20–17.29
similarities of ground (f) to Code tests, 17.10–17.15
wording, 17.04–17.06
works which are to occur, 17.33–17.43
termination or renewal of agreements, 16.272–16.274

A
Access
1954 Act cases, 11.258
access requirements, 11.56–11.65
costs of access, 11.100–11.101
Agreements conferring Code rights
see also **Terms of agreement conferring Code rights**
conflict between agreement and Code
'contracting in', 6.32
contractual obligations are effective, 6.22–6.29
voiding provisions, 6.30–6.31
consensual agreements
disadvantage for site providers, 6.35–6.37
formalities and content requirements, 6.07–6.11
generally, 6.05–6.06
prejudicing later Code References, 6.38
when consensual agreement cannot be used, 6.33–6.34
definition of'Code agreement', 5.50

Agreements conferring Code rights – *contd*
generally, 6.01–6.04
imposed agreements
generally, 6.12
Order is operative instrument under para 20, 6.13–6.16
position under para 34(6), 6.19–6.21
position under paras 26 and 27, 6.17–6.18
later consensual amendment, 6.39–6.41
Alteration of agreements
see **Modification of agreements**
Alteration of apparatus
definition, 5.56
Alternative agreements at proposed site
application for imposed agreement, 8.35
Alternative dispute resolution
application for imposed agreement, 8.07–8.09
costs consequences of refusal, 23.41
interim Code rights, 9.88–9.90
renewal or modification of agreements, 16.238–16.239
Alternative sites
application for imposed agreement, 8.35
Amendment of agreements
see **Modification of agreements**
Amendments to Code
generally, 3.18–3.22
Apparatus
see also **Removal of ECA**
1954 Act cases, 11.247–11.250
generally, 11.66–11.73
Appeals
appeals from county court, 21.119–21.120
appeals from FTT to UT, 21.94–21.105
appeals from UT to Court of Appeal, 21.106–21.108
'leapfrog' appeals from UT to Supreme Court, 21.112–21.118
second appeals to Court of Appeal, 21.109–21.111
Application for imposed agreement
ADR obligations, 8.07–8.09
discretion of tribunal, 8.36–8.39
factors to be taken into account
alternative agreements at proposed site, 8.35
alternative sites, 8.35
high quality communications services, 8.26–8.31
irrelevant factors, 8.35
other factors, 8.32–8.34
public 'disbenefit', 8.35
generally, 8.05–8.06
national security bar, 8.52
para 20 notice, 8.03–8.04
Application for imposed agreement – *contd*
Part 4, 8.01–8.02
redevelopment defence
generally, 8.40–8.43
operator not yet on land, 8.44–8.46
terms of agreement not yet known, 8.47–8.51
test for making Order
generally, 8.10–8.11
para 21(2) condition, 8.12–8.19
para 21(3) condition, 8.12–8.13, 8.20–8.25
Assignment
assignor's liability for post-assignment breaches, 15.71–15.72
effect, 15.66–15.70
generally, 15.54
guarantee agreements, 15.59–15.65
imposed agreements, 15.73–15.75
service of notices, 20.17–20.18
voiding of restrictions on assignment, 15.55–15.58
Assumptions
disapplication of paras 16 and 17, 13.82–13.93
generally, 13.59–13.62
'no-network' assumption
generally, 13.63–13.66
impact on assumed agreement terms, 13.73–13.81
rejection of use of Old Code comparables, 13.67–13.72
plurality of sites (no ransom), 13.94–13.96
Authorised guarantee agreements
terms of agreement, 11.154–11.158

B

Background to Code
amendments to Code, 3.18–3.22
generally, 3.01–3.13
machinery bringing Code into force, 3.14–3.17
Breach by operator
termination of agreements, 16.54–16.56
Break clauses
1954 Act cases, 11.263–11.280
landlord
conditions other than redevelopment, 11.24–11.27
redevelopment purposes, 11.14–11.23
wording of redevelopment break clause, 11.21–11.23
tenant, 11.28
Business tenancies
see **1954 Act cases**

C

Case management directions
  applications, 21.47–21.48
  approval of agreed directions in renewal cases, 21.49
Code agreement
  see also **Agreements conferring Code rights**
  definition, 5.50
Code rights
  definition, 5.18
  effects of a right being a Code right, 5.21–5.23
  requirement to specify in notice, 5.19–5.20
Coming into force of Code
  generally, 3.14–3.17
Compensation
  1954 Act cases
    generally, 14.08
    post-PSTIA 2022 amendments, 14.10–14.13
    pre-PSTIA 2022 amendments, 14.09
  consideration, interaction with
    generally, 13.199–13.200, 14.36
    rent in 1954 Act cases, 13.201–13.204
    valuation under 1954 Act (post-PSTIA 2022 amendments), 13.224–13.230
    valuation under 1954 Act (pre-PSTIA 2022 amendments), 13.205–13.223
  diminution in value, 14.83–14.84
  directions under para 25(3)(b), 14.43–14.48
  discretion, 14.30–14.31
  exclusion of additional compensation
    bespoke contractual compensation scheme, 14.104–14.105
    damages claims, 14.103
    generally, 14.101–14.102
    interaction between paras 86 and 100, 14.106–14.116
  expenses, 14.52–14.55
  generally, 14.01–14.02
  heads of loss
    diminution in value, 14.83–14.84
    expenses, 14.52–14.55
    generally, 14.49–14.51
    transactional costs, 14.56–14.82
  injurious affection
    de minimis claims, 14.100
    legal and valuation expenses, 14.99
    right to compensation, 14.96–14.98
  loss incurred while landowner has right to require removal, 14.85–14.95
  Order imposing an agreement, 14.05–14.07
Compensation – *contd*
  para 20 cases, 14.15
  para 25, 14.03–14.48
  para 26 cases, 14.16
  para 27 cases, 14.17
  para 34 cases, 14.18–14.22
  person to whom payable, 14.14
  pre-requisite, 14.05–14.07
  procedural options open to tribunal
    determining compensation at the outset, 14.38–14.42
    directions under para 25(3)(b), 14.43–14.48
    generally, 14.37
  removal of ECA, 18.44–18.45
  requirements to be satisfied, 14.32–14.35
  right under para 25, 14.01–14.04
  terms of agreement, 11.53–11.54
  transactional costs
    claims in the different tribunals, 14.81
    consensual agreement, 14.82
    evidence as to professional expenses, 14.78–14.80
    generally, 14.56–14.61
    non-lawyer costs, 14.72–14.77
    quantum, 14.62–14.71
  when compensation may be ordered
    generally, 14.23
    pursuant to a subsequent application, 14.26–14.29
    upon imposition of agreement, 14.24–14.25
Concurrent lessees
  generally, 15.25–15.35
Conduct of parties
  negotiating terms, 11.216–11.220
  tribunal proceedings, 21.44–21.46
Conduits
  right to lay on superior landlord's land, 11.202–11.203
Conferral of Code rights
  see **Agreements conferring Code rights**
Conflict between agreement and Code
  'contracting in', 6.32
  contractual obligations are effective, 6.22–6.29
  voiding provisions, 6.30–6.31
Consent orders
  generally, 21.62, 22.11–22.17
Consideration
  Affinity Water
    generally, 13.123–13.134
    impact of *Vache Farm*, 13.171–13.174
    subsequent developments, 13.135–13.137

Consideration – *contd*
  assumptions
    disapplication of paras 16 and 17, 13.82–13.93
    generally, 13.59–13.62
    'no-network' assumption, 13.63–13.81
    plurality of sites (no ransom), 13.94–13.96
  compensation, interaction with
    generally, 13.199–13.200, 14.36
    rent in 1954 Act cases, 13.201–13.204
    valuation under 1954 Act (post-PSTIA 2022 amendments), 13.224–13.230
    valuation under 1954 Act (pre-PSTIA 2022 amendments), 13.205–13.223
  consensual consideration, 13.25–13.32
  delay in payment, 16.54–16.56
  determination of terms of agreement, 11.08–11.10
  form of payments, 13.37–13.38
  generally, 13.01–13.05
  hypothetical transaction
    assumptions, 13.59–13.96
    characteristics of seller, 13.52
    consequence of lack of bidders, 13.53–13.55
    conventional hypothetical exercise, 13.44–13.47
    para 24(2) description, 13.40–13.41
    presumption of reality, 13.48–13.51
    prudent and informed parties, 13.56
    unusual statutory wording, 13.42–13.43
    valuation hypothesis, 13.39
    what agreement terms are being valued, 13.57–13.58
  imposed consideration (para 20 cases)
    assumptions, 13.59–13.96
    form and timing of payments, 13.37–13.38
    generally, 13.33–13.36
    hypothetical transaction, 13.39–13.96
  imposed consideration (para 26 cases), 13.183–13.186
  imposed consideration (para 27 cases), 13.187–13.189
  imposed consideration (renewal cases)
    generally, 13.190–13.195
    market value rent review, 13.196–13.198
  interim consideration (para 35), 13.177–13.182
  Islington valuation, 13.97–13.101
  Law Commission recommendations, 13.15–13.20
  ministerial statement regarding New Code, 13.21–13.24

Consideration – *contd*
  'no-network' assumption
    generally, 13.63–13.66
    impact on assumed agreement terms, 13.73–13.81
    rejection of use of Old Code comparables, 13.67–13.72
  Old Code, 13.06–13.14
  plurality of sites (no ransom), 13.94–13.96
  rent in 1954 Act cases, 11.283–11.284, 13.201–13.204
  staged approach, 13.102–13.122
  timing of payments, 13.37–13.38
  tribunal's approach
    Affinity Water, 13.123–13.134
    Islington valuation, 13.97–13.101
    post-*Affinity Water*, 13.135–13.137,13.135–13.137
    staged approach, 13.102–13.122
    Vache Farm, 13.138–13.182
  Vache Farm
    Affinity Water table, 13.171–13.174
    comparables in para 24 valuations, 13.140–13.150
    generally, 13.138–13.139
    impact on urban cases, 13.177–13.182
    reassessment, 13.151–13.170
Costs
  assessment, 21.66–21.67, 23.48–23.49
  Code power to award, 23.16–23.36
  FTT's power to award, 23.03–23.05
  generally, 23.01–23.02
  party seeking a precedent, 23.39–23.40
  Practice Direction, 23.14–23.15
  quantum in MSV cases, 23.42–23.47
  refusal of ADR, 23.41
  refusal of offer to settle, 23.37–23.38
  settlement of Reference, 22.19–22.24, 23.50
  UT's power to award, 23.06–23.13
Court
  definition, 5.02
  terminology, 1.07–1.09

D

Damage
  minimising loss and damage, 11.164–11.176
  use of site not to cause damage, 11.113
Definitions
  alteration, 5.56
  Code agreement, 5.50
  Code rights
    effects of a right being a Code right, 5.21–5.23
    generally, 5.18

Definitions – *contd*
Code rights – *contd*
requirement to specify in notice, 5.19–5.20
court, 5.02
electronic communications apparatus, 5.26–5.38
electronic communications network, 5.42–5.44
infrastructure system, 5.48–5.49
land
chattels attached to land, 5.39–5.41
generally, 5.26–5.38
landowner, 5.54–5.55
network, 5.45–5.47
occupier
generally, 5.06–5.10
identity and evidence under Old Code, 5.15–5.17
land unoccupied, 5.13
no operator in occupation, 5.11–5.12
streets, 5.14
operator, 5.03–5.05
site provider, 5.52–5.53
statutory purposes, 5.24–5.25
subsisting agreement, 5.51
Delay in payment
termination of agreements, 16.54–16.56
Determination of agreement terms
see **Terms of agreement conferring Code rights**
Diminution in value
compensation, 14.83–14.84
Disclosure
generally, 21.52–21.55
Dispute resolution clauses
terms of agreement, 11.153
Drop zone warranty
terms of agreement, 11.135
Duplication
terms of agreement, 11.224–11.225
Duration of agreement
generally, 11.08, 11.11

E
Easements
implication in renewal agreements, 11.201
Electricity
generators, 11.103–11.108
right to install electricity supply, 11.102
Electronic communications apparatus
definition, 5.26–5.38
Electronic communications network
definition, 5.42–5.44
Evidence
co-operation as to disclosure, 21.52–21.55
expert valuation evidence, 21.58–21.61
Evidence – *contd*
terms of agreement, 11.221–11.223
witness evidence, 21.56–21.57
Expenses
reimbursement, 11.89–11.99

F
Forfeiture of lease
termination of agreements, 16.120–16.126

G
Guarantee agreements
assignment, 15.59–15.65

H
Health and safety
terms of agreement, 11.114–11.129
High quality communications services
application for imposed agreement, 8.26–8.31

I
ICNIRP exclusion zones
terms of agreement, 11.130–11.134
Indemnities
1954 Act cases, 11.259
generally, 11.136–11.152
Infrastructure system
definition, 5.48–5.49
Injurious affection
de minimis claims, 14.100
legal and valuation expenses, 14.99
right to compensation, 14.96–14.98
Interim Code rights
ADR obligations, 9.88–9.90
applications, 9.40
burdens and risks on landowners, 9.66
circumstances in which Order can be made, 9.41–9.46
discretionary remedy, 9.53–9.55
duration of agreement, 9.59
evidence, 9.52
generally, 9.01–9.04
length and complexity of agreement, 9.64–9.65
MSV agreements
agreeing terms, 9.84–9.87
generally, 9.67
intrusive works, 9.68–9.78
term, 9.79–9.83
multi-skilled visits, 9.09–9.16
national security bar, 9.47
nature of agreements
can be sought on a freestanding basis, 9.22–9.35
can only be imposed by tribunal, 9.17–9.21

Interim Code rights – *contd*
nature of agreements – *contd*
generally, 9.05–9.08
multi-skilled visits, 9.09–9.16
notice of application
generally, 9.37–9.39
pre-condition for jurisdiction, 9.48
previous negotiations, relevance of, 9.56
procedure for obtaining para 26 Order
application, 9.40
conditions to be satisfied for Order to be made, 9.41–9.46
generally, 9.36
notice, 9.37–9.39
renewal agreements, 11.285–11.287
terms
judicial guidance as to content, 9.63–9.66
MSV agreements, 9.67–9.87
relevant provisions, 9.60–9.62
urgency, 9.57–9.58
when application is determined, 9.49–9.51
Interpretation of Code
external aids to construction, 7.19–7.24
introduction, 7.01–7.05
purposive approach, 7.10–7.18
strict approach in appropriation statutes, 7.06–7.09

J
Jurisdiction
commencement of a Reference, 21.01–21.07

L
Land
chattels attached to land, 5.39–5.41
definition, 5.26–5.38
Landlord and Tenant Act 1954
see **1954 Act cases**
Landowner
definition, 5.54–5.55
identity unknown, 20.20, 20.78
termination of agreements, 16.07–16.09
Leases
forfeiture, 16.120–16.126
lease vs licence
Burlington Gardens case, 16.134–16.135
certainty of term, 16.140–16.143
effect of clause asserting that no tenancy is created, 16.151–16.153
exclusive possession of land, 16.136–16.139
generally, 16.127–16.133
potential third category, 16.154–16.168
previous Code cases, 16.144–16.150

M
Modification of agreements
1954 Act cases, 16.272–16.274
generally, 16.195–16.198
interim modification of terms, 16.253–16.254
introduction, 16.01
modification before renewal rights arise, 16.257–16.271
no election as to statutory regime, 16.199–16.204
Order for modification
decisions for tribunal, 16.242
generally, 16.240–16.241
what Order to make, 16.243–16.246
what terms to order, 16.247–16.251
para 33 notice
ADR obligations, 16.238–16.239
generally, 16.220
options for changing the agreement, 16.223–16.226
period of notice, 16.227–16.232
server/recipient, 16.221–16.222
tribunal application, 16.233–16.239
Part 5, 16.216–16.219
status of amended agreement, 16.254
Multi-skilled visits
generally, 9.09–9.16
MSV agreements
agreeing terms, 9.84–9.87
generally, 9.67
intrusive works, 9.68–9.78
term, 9.79–9.83

N
National security bar
application for imposed agreement, 8.52
interim Code rights, 9.47
temporary Code rights, 10.17
Network
definition, 5.45–5.47
'No-network' assumption
generally, 13.63–13.66
impact on assumed agreement terms, 13.73–13.81
rejection of use of Old Code comparables, 13.67–13.72
Notices
by and to whom notice must be given, 20.01–20.14
contents
notices served by non-operators, 20.53–20.56
notices served by operators, 20.41–20.52
particular notices, 20.57

Notices – *contd*
identifying person on whom to serve
assignment of Code agreements, 20.17–20.18
name and address of 'occupier' or 'owner' unknown, 20.20
names of operators, 20.16
registration of Code agreements, 20.19
which operator is in situ, 20.15
multiple notices, 20.89
prescribed forms, 20.58–20.61
relationship between a party's notice and its case
Part 4 cases, 20.29–20.38
Part 5 renewal cases, 20.39–20.40
service
address for service, 20.70–20.73
deemed service, 20.75–20.76
email, 20.74
generally, 20.62–20.66
post, 20.67–20.69
unknown occupier, 20.77
unknown owner of an interest in land, 20.78
short service
power to abridge notice period, 20.79–20.83
when tribunal might allow short service, 20.84–20.88
stale notices, 20.90–20.91
validity
contents of notices, 20.41–20.56
generally, 20.21–20.25
jurisdictional questions, 20.26–20.28
relationship between a party's notice and its case, 20.29–20.40

O

Occupier
definition, 5.06–5.10
identity and evidence under Old Code, 5.15–5.17
identity unknown, 20.20, 20.77
land unoccupied, 5.13
no operator in occupation, 5.11–5.12
streets, 5.14
OFCOM standard terms
generally, 11.04
Old Code
background, 3.01–3.13
consideration, 13.06–13.14
continuing effect
compensation, 2.11–2.13
generally, 2.01, 3.17
notices, 2.07
overhead apparatus, 2.14
parts that continue to apply, 2.06–2.17

Old Code – *contd*
continuing effect – *contd*
pending applications made under Old Code, 2.09–2.10
pending notices served under Old Code, 2.08
power to require alteration of apparatus, 2.15–2.16
right to require removal of apparatus, 2.17
subsisting agreements and who is bound, 2.02–2.05
replacement by New Code, 3.14–3.17
subsisting agreements
definition, 5.51, 16.85–16.89
persons who are bound, 15.76–15.79
termination, 16.74–16.105
upgrading and sharing, 12.40–12.42
Operator
definition, 5.03–5.05
standard terms, 11.05
Overview of Code
generally, 4.01–4.14
Owner
definition, 5.54–5.55
identity unknown, 20.20, 20.78
termination of agreements, 16.07–16.09

P

Para 26 agreements/Orders
see **Interim Code rights**
Para 27 agreements/Orders
see **Temporary Code rights**
Persons bound by Code rights
agreement binding all landowners, 15.42–15.48
assignment
assignor's liability for post-assignment breaches, 15.71–15.72
effect, 15.66–15.70
generally, 15.54
guarantee agreements, 15.59–15.65
imposed agreements, 15.73–15.75
voiding of restrictions on assignment, 15.55–15.58
concurrent lessees, 15.25–15.35
imposed agreements rendering a person bound, 15.36–15.37
introduction, 15.02–15.05
para 10, 15.06
para 10(3) not exhaustive, 15.23
persons 'treated as a party to the agreement', 15.20–15.23
persons who agree to be bound, 15.14–15.17
registration of agreements concerning Code rights, 15.49–15.53

Persons bound by Code rights – *contd*
statutory continuation of agreements to be bound, 15.38–15.41
subsisting agreements
disapplication of para 16, 15.77–15.79
persons who are bound, 15.76
successors to 'O', 15.07–15.13
successors to 'P', 15.18–15.19
Planning applications
notification, 11.204–11.205
objections, 11.206
Practice Direction
costs, 23.14–23.15
generally, 21.37–21.38
Precedent
costs where one party seeks a precedent, 23.39–23.40
tribunals, 21.80–21.86
Procedure and practice
appeals
appeals from county court, 21.119–21.120
appeals from FTT to UT, 21.94–21.105
appeals from UT to Court of Appeal, 21.106–21.108
'leapfrog' appeals from UT to Supreme Court, 21.112–21.118
second appeals to Court of Appeal, 21.109–21.111
case management directions in FTT
applications, 21.47–21.48
approval of agreed directions in renewal cases, 21.49
conduct of parties, 21.44–21.46
consent orders, 21.62
co-operation as to disclosure, 21.52–21.55
costs
assessment, 21.66–21.67, 23.48–23.49
Code power to award, 23.16–23.36
FTT's power to award, 23.03–23.05
generally, 23.01–23.02
party seeking a precedent, 23.39–23.40
Practice Direction, 23.14–23.15
quantum in MSV cases, 23.42–23.47
refusal of ADR, 23.41
refusal of offer to settle, 23.37–23.38
settlement of Reference, 22.19–22.24, 23.50
UT's power to award, 23.06–23.13
decisions 'on the papers', 21.87–21.89
evidence
co-operation as to disclosure, 21.52–21.55
expert valuation evidence, 21.58–21.61
witness evidence, 21.56–21.57
initial directions, 21.12

Procedure and practice – *contd*
judges hearing 1954 Act matters in county court, 21.21–21.22
jurisdiction, 21.01–21.07
Order settling a Reference, 21.62
Practice Direction, 21.37–21.38
precedent, 21.80–21.86
reporting of judgments
decisions above FTT level in general, 21.68–21.69
decisions of FTT (Property Chamber), 21.72–21.79
decisions of UT (Lands Chamber), 21.70–21.71
statements of case, 21.50–21.51
striking out, 21.39–21.43
summary assessment of costs, 21.66–21.67
telecoms user group, 21.35–21.36
time limit
cases not subject to six-month rule, 21.34
cases which must be determined within six months, 21.25–21.33
transfer from FTT to UT, 21.13–21.20
transfer to FTT (previous practice), 21.08–21.11
unresponsive occupiers, 21.90–21.93
virtual hearings, 21.63–21.65
volume of Code References, 21.23–21.24

R

Redevelopment
application for imposed agreement
generally, 8.40–8.43
operator not yet on land, 8.44–8.46
terms of agreement not yet known, 8.47–8.51
definition, 17.33–17.43
generally, 17.01–17.03
ground (f) under 1954 Act
applicability of ground (f) case law, 17.16–17.18
differences from Code tests, 17.19–17.43
generally, 17.09
similarities to Code tests, 17.10–17.15
wording, 17.04–17.06
land on which works are to occur, 17.30–17.32
para 26 applications, 17.67–17.70
para 27 applications, 17.71–17.72
redevelopment defence (para 21(5))
application for imposed agreement, 8.40–8.51
consequences of defence being 'established' or not, 17.50–17.53
para 31(4)(c) distinguished, 17.54–17.66
wording, 17.08

Redevelopment – *contd*
redevelopment ground (para 31(4)(c))
consequences of ground being 'established' or not, 17.44–17.49
para 21(5) distinguished, 17.54–17.66
wording, 17.07
termination of agreements, 16.57
when 'redevelopment' is intended to occur
'reasonable time' under 1954 Act, 17.20–17.29
'reasonable time' under Code, 17.23–17.29
works which are to occur, 17.33–17.43
References
see **Procedure and practice**
Registration of agreements
generally, 15.49–15.53
service of notices, 20.19
Removal of ECA
application for fresh Code rights not determined, 18.52–18.55
compensation, 18.44–18.45
discretion, 18.46–18.51
enforcing removal
application for Order, 18.30–18.31
service of para 40 notice, 18.27–18.29
finding out whether apparatus is on land pursuant to Code right
costs consequences, 18.64
generally, 18.56–18.57
para 39(1) notices (landowners), 18.58–18.59
para 39(2) notices (neighbouring landowners/occupiers), 18.60–18.62
standard form for para 39 notices, 18.63
generally, 18.01
neighbouring land, 18.24–18.26
obtaining vacant possession (flow chart)
assumptions, 19.04
flow chart, 19.05–19.11
introduction, 19.01–19.03
right to require removal, 19.12–19.13
Orders under para 44, 18.32–18.33
para 40(8), 18.52–18.55
restoration
application for Order, 18.40–18.41
Orders under para 44, 18.42–18.43
power to award compensation, 18.44–18.45
right to require restoration, 18.34–18.36
service of para 43(5) notice, 18.37–18.39
right to require removal
Code has ceased to apply, 18.18–18.21
Code right has ended, 18.07–18.09
Removal of ECA – *contd*
right to require removal – *contd*
ECA no longer used for network, 18.15–18.17
generally, 18.02
landowner never bound by Code right, 18.03–18.06
neighbouring land, 18.24–18.26
para 6 transitional provisions situations, 18.12
para 29(2) situations, 18.10–18.11
para 37(4) disqualification, 18.13–18.14
rights arising otherwise than under Code, 18.23
street work rights, 18.22
transport land rights, 18.22
termination of agreements, 16.169–16.174
terms of agreement, 11.30–11.33
Renewal of agreements
1954 Act cases, 16.272–16.274
additional consideration for continuation period, 16.252
applicable renewal procedure
generally, 16.205–16.209
implied licence or tenancy at will, 16.214–16.215
implied periodic tenancy, 16.210–16.213
generally, 16.195–16.198
imposed terms in renewal agreements
conduct in negotiating terms, 11.216–11.220
duplication, 11.224–11.225
evidence relating to terms of agreement, 11.221–11.223
exclusion of LPA 1925, s 62, 11.201
generally, 11.177–11.179
implication of easements, 11.201
landlord's right to enter and carry out repairs, 11.207
new agreements compared, 11.180–11.191
non-interference by operator, 11.208
payment of compensation as a contractual debt, 11.209–11.215
planning applications, notification of, 11.204–11.205
planning applications, objections to, 11.206
right to lay conduits on superior landlord's land, 11.202–11.203
upgrading and sharing, 11.192–11.200
interim terms in renewal agreements, 11.285–11.287
introduction, 16.01
modification of agreement before renewal rights arise, 16.257–16.271

Renewal of agreements – *contd*
no election as to statutory regime, 16.199–16.204
Order for renewal
decisions for tribunal, 16.242
generally, 16.240–16.241
what Order to make, 16.243–16.246
what terms to order, 16.247–16.251
para 33 notice
ADR obligations, 16.238–16.239
generally, 16.220
options for changing the agreement, 16.223–16.226
period of notice, 16.227–16.232
server/recipient, 16.221–16.222
tribunal application, 16.233–16.239
Part 5, 16.216–16.219
status of new agreement, 16.254
Rent
see also **Consideration**
1954 Act cases, 11.283–11.284, 13.201–13.204
Rent review
1954 Act cases, 11.281–11.282
rent review clauses, 11.159–11.162
Reporting of judgments
decisions above FTT level in general, 21.68–21.69
decisions of FTT (Property Chamber), 21.72–21.79
decisions of UT (Lands Chamber), 21.70–21.71
Repositioning and removal
terms of agreement, 11.30–11.33
Restoration
enforcing restoration
application for Order, 18.40–18.41
service of para 43(5) notice, 18.37–18.39
Orders under para 44, 18.42–18.43
power to award compensation, 18.44–18.45
right to require restoration, 18.34–18.36

S

Service of notices
address for service, 20.70–20.73
deemed service, 20.75–20.76
email, 20.74
generally, 20.62–20.66
post, 20.67–20.69
unknown occupier, 20.77
unknown owner of an interest in land, 20.78
Set-down area
terms of agreement, 11.55
Settlement of Code disputes
costs, 22.19–22.24
costs consequences of refusal of offer to settle, 23.37–23.38
effect on decisions in future References, 22.18
generally, 22.01–22.02
heads of terms not usually binding, 22.03–22.05
practice and procedure, 22.11–22.17
without prejudice communications, 22.06–22.10
Sharing and upgrading
automatic rights (para 17)
conditions limiting rights, 12.21
generally, 12.18–12.21
voiding of restrictions on sharing and upgrading, 12.29–12.32
express terms
consensual agreements, 12.33
imposed agreements, 12.34–12.39
generally, 12.01–12.03
how rights are obtained, 12.13–12.17
right to share
ancillary Code rights, 12.10
generally, 12.08–12.09
right relates to ECA only, 12.11
sharing only with another operator, 12.12
right to upgrade
ancillary Code rights, 12.05
generally, 12.03
right relates to ECA only, 12.06–12.07
subsisting agreements, 12.40–12.42
terms of agreement
1954 Act cases, 11.247–11.250
generally, 11.74–11.88
renewal agreements, 11.192–11.200
Site payment
terms of agreement, 11.53–11.54
Site provider
definition, 5.52–5.53
Standard terms
generally, 11.04–11.05
Statements of case
generally, 21.50–21.51
Statutory purposes
definition, 5.24–5.25
Striking out a Reference
generally, 21.39–21.43
Structural surveys
terms of agreement, 11.112
Stylistic conventions
citation of cases, 1.03–1.06
'court' and 'tribunal', 1.07–1.09
quotation of legislation, 1.02
references to paragraphs within Code, 1.01

Subsisting agreements
definition, 5.51, 16.85–16.89
persons who are bound
disapplication of para 16, 15.77–15.79
generally, 15.76
termination
categories of subsisting agreement, 16.103
definition of subsisting agreement, 16.85–16.89
effect of status as a 'subsisting agreement', 16.98–16.102
generally, 16.74
Old Code para 2 agreements, 16.90–16.93
Old Code para 3 agreements, 16.94–16.97
rationale and the legislation, 16.75–16.84
transitional provisions modifications to Part 5, 16.104–16.105
upgrading and sharing, 12.40–12.42
Successors
successors to 'O', 15.07–15.13
successors to 'P', 15.18–15.19
Surrender
termination of agreements, 16.186–16.191

T

Telecoms user group
generally, 21.35–21.36
Temporary Code rights
generally, 10.01
national security bar, 10.17
nature and effect of agreement, 10.18–10.19
operator's application and its timing, 10.09–10.11
para 27 Order, 10.12–10.16
pre-conditions for para 27 Order, 10.02–10.08
terms of agreement, 10.20–10.22
Termination of agreements
1954 Act cases, 16.272–16.274
agreements expiring before New Code in force
1954 Act leases, 16.118–16.119
generally, 16.106–16.109
implied agreements following expiry, 16.110–16.117
breach by operator, 16.54–16.56
break clause (1954 Act cases), 11.263–11.280
break clause (landlord)
conditions other than redevelopment, 11.24–11.27
redevelopment purposes, 11.14–11.23
Termination of agreements – *contd*
break clause (landlord) – *contd*
wording of redevelopment break clause, 11.21–11.23
break clause (tenant), 11.28
consensual or imposed agreements under New Code
application of Part 5, 16.15–16.27
contractual termination notice, 16.44–16.51
generally, 16.10–16.14
operator's application under para 32(1)(b), 16.66
operator's counter-notice, 16.64
para 31 notice, 16.37–16.66
statutory continuation under para 30, 16.28–16.36
consensual termination, 16.186–16.191
contractual termination notice, 16.44–16.51
forfeiture of lease, 16.120–16.126
generally, 16.05–16.06
grounds for termination
breach by operator, 16.54–16.56
generally, 16.52–16.53
multiple grounds, 16.59–16.62
no entitlement to Code agreement, 16.58
persistent delay in payment, 16.54–16.56
redevelopment, 16.57
introduction, 16.01
landowner, by, 16.07–16.09
lease vs licence
Burlington Gardens case, 16.134–16.135
certainty of term, 16.140–16.143
effect of clause asserting that no tenancy is created, 16.151–16.153
exclusive possession of land, 16.136–16.139
generally, 16.127–16.133
potential third category, 16.154–16.168
previous Code cases, 16.144–16.150
multiple grounds, 16.59–16.62
mutually agreed termination, 16.186–16.191
no election as to statutory regime to follow, 16.199–16.204
no entitlement to Code agreement, 16.58
operator, by, 16.192–16.194
operator's application under para 32(1)(b), 16.66
operator's counter-notice, 16.64
para 26 agreements, 16.175–16.177
para 27 agreements, 16.175, 16.178–16.184

Termination of agreements – *contd*
para 31 notice
effect, 16.63–16.64
generally, 16.37–16.39
period of notice, 16.40–16.43
termination grounds, 16.52–16.62
Part 5, 16.02–16.04
period of notice, 16.40–16.43
persistent delay in payment, 16.54–16.56
primary purpose of agreement is to grant Code rights
application of Part 5, 16.15–16.21
para 29(3) qualification, 16.27
'primary purpose', 16.22–16.26
redevelopment, 16.57
requiring removal of ECA, interplay with, 16.169–16.174
statutory continuation
cases where inapplicable, 16.36
generally, 16.28–16.33
nature, 16.34–16.35
subsisting agreements
categories of subsisting agreement, 16.103
definition, 16.85–16.89
effect of status as a 'subsisting agreement', 16.98–16.102
generally, 16.74
Old Code para 2 agreements, 16.90–16.93
Old Code para 3 agreements, 16.94–16.97
rationale and the legislation, 16.75–16.84
transitional provisions modifications to Part 5, 16.104–16.105
surrender, 16.186–16.191
termination date, 16.40–16.43
terms of agreement
effect of para 23(8)(a), 11.29
generally, 11.12–11.13
landlord's break clause, 11.14–11.27
tenant's break clause, 11.28
Terms of agreement conferring Code rights
see also **Compensation; Consideration; Upgrading and sharing**
break clause (1954 Act cases), 11.263–11.280
break clause (landlord)
conditions other than redevelopment, 11.24–11.27
redevelopment purposes, 11.14–11.23
wording of redevelopment break clause, 11.21–11.23
break clause (tenant), 11.28
conduct in negotiating terms, 11.216–11.220
Terms of agreement conferring Code rights – *contd*
consideration, 11.08–11.10
court determinations on terms (1954 Act cases)
access, 11.258
break clause, 11.263–11.280
contractual compensation provisions, 11.251–11.257
equipment rights (including upgrading), 11.247–11.250
generally, 11.246
indemnity, 11.259
non-interference by landlord, 11.260–11.262
rent, 11.283–11.284
rent review, 11.281–11.282
discretionary terms
breadth of tribunal's discretion, 11.35–11.38
exercise of tribunal's discretion, 11.39–11.40
generally, 11.34
relevance of previously negotiated terms, 11.45–11.46
starting point and burden, 11.41–11.44
duplication, 11.224–11.225
duration of agreement, 11.08, 11.11
evidence relating to terms of agreement, 11.221–11.223
imposed terms (1954 Act cases)
all other terms, 11.234–11.245
court determinations on terms, 11.246–11.284
duration of tenancy, 11.228–11.233
generally, 11.226
property comprised in tenancy, 11.227
imposed terms (new agreements)
discretionary terms, 11.34–11.46
minimising loss and damage, 11.164–11.176
relevant provisions of Code, 11.06–11.07
repositioning and removal, 11.30–11.33
termination of agreement, 11.12–11.29
terms which must be considered, 11.12–11.33
terms which must be included, 11.08–11.11
tribunal determinations on terms, 11.47–11.163
imposed terms (renewal agreements)
conduct in negotiating terms, 11.216–11.220
duplication, 11.224–11.225
evidence relating to terms of agreement, 11.221–11.223

Terms of agreement conferring Code rights – *contd*
imposed terms (renewal agreements) – *contd*
exclusion of LPA 1925, s 62, 11.201
generally, 11.177–11.179
implication of easements, 11.201
landlord's right to enter and carry out repairs, 11.207
new agreements compared, 11.180–11.191
non-interference by operator, 11.208
payment of compensation as a contractual debt, 11.209–11.215
planning applications, notification of, 11.204–11.205
planning applications, objections to, 11.206
right to lay conduits on superior landlord's land, 11.202–11.203
upgrading and sharing, 11.192–11.200
interim terms (renewal agreements), 11.285–11.287
introduction, 11.01–11.05
minimising loss and damage, 11.164–11.176
OFCOM standard terms, 11.04
operators' standard terms, 11.05
para 23(5), impact of, 11.164–11.176
repositioning and removal, 11.30–11.33
standard terms, 11.04–11.05
termination of agreement
effect of para 23(8)(a), 11.29
generally, 11.12–11.13
landlord's break clause, 11.14–11.27
tenant's break clause, 11.28
terms which must be considered
relevant provisions of Code, 11.06–11.07
repositioning and removal, 11.30–11.33
termination of agreement, 11.12–11.29
terms which must be included, 11.07, 11.08–11.11
tribunal determinations on terms
access requirements, 11.56–11.65
apparatus (definition and caps), 11.66–11.73
authorised guarantee agreements, 11.154–11.158
compensation, 11.53–11.54
costs of access/supervision, 11.100–11.101
dispute resolution clauses, 11.153
drop zone warranty, 11.135
electricity generator, 11.103–11.108
electricity supply, right to install, 11.102
future structural surveys, 11.112

Terms of agreement conferring Code rights – *contd*
tribunal determinations on terms – *contd*
generally, 11.47–11.52
health and safety matters, 11.114–11.129
ICNIRP exclusion zones, 11.130–11.134
indemnities, 11.136–11.152
reimbursement of costs and expenses, 11.89–11.99
rent review clauses, 11.159–11.162
set-down area, 11.55
site payment, 11.53–11.54
upgrading and sharing, 11.74–11.88
use of site not to cause damage, 11.113
vacant possession, 11.163
works (method statement), 11.109–11.111
Third parties
agreement binding all landowners, 15.42–15.48
assignment
assignor's liability for post-assignment breaches, 15.71–15.72
effect, 15.66–15.70
generally, 15.54
guarantee agreements, 15.59–15.65
imposed agreements, 15.73–15.75
voiding of restrictions on assignment, 15.55–15.58
concurrent lessees, 15.25–15.35
imposed agreements rendering a person bound, 15.36–15.37
introduction, 15.02–15.05
para 10, 15.06
para 10(3) not exhaustive, 15.23
persons 'treated as a party to the agreement', 15.20–15.23
persons who agree to be bound, 15.14–15.17
registration of agreements concerning Code rights, 15.49–15.53
statutory continuation of agreements to be bound, 15.38–15.41
subsisting agreements
disapplication of para 16, 15.77–15.79
persons who are bound, 15.76
successors to 'O', 15.07–15.13
successors to 'P', 15.18–15.19
Time limit for References
cases not subject to six-month rule, 21.34
cases which must be determined within six months, 21.25–21.33
Tribunal
see also **Procedure and practice; Terms of agreement conferring Code rights**

Tribunal – *contd*
agreements imposed by tribunal
generally, 6.12
Order is operative instrument under para 20, 6.13–6.16
position under para 34(6), 6.19–6.21
position under paras 26 and 27, 6.17–6.18
application for imposed agreement
ADR obligations, 8.07–8.09
discretion of tribunal, 8.36–8.39
factors to be taken into account, 8.26–8.35
generally, 8.05–8.06
national security bar, 8.52
para 20 notice, 8.03–8.04
Part 4, 8.01–8.02
redevelopment defence, 8.40–8.51
test for making Order, 8.10–8.25
definition of 'the court', 5.02
jurisdiction, 21.01–21.07
precedent, 21.80–21.86
reporting of judgments
decisions above FTT level in general, 21.68–21.69
decisions of FTT (Property Chamber), 21.72–21.79
decisions of UT (Lands Chamber), 21.70–21.71
terminology, 1.07–1.09
volume of Code References, 21.23–21.24

U
Upgrading and sharing
automatic rights (para 17)
conditions limiting rights, 12.21
generally, 12.18–12.21
voiding of restrictions on sharing and upgrading, 12.29–12.32

Upgrading and sharing – *contd*
express terms
consensual agreements, 12.33
imposed agreements, 12.34–12.39
generally, 12.01–12.03
how rights are obtained, 12.13–12.17
right to share
ancillary Code rights, 12.10
generally, 12.08–12.09
right relates to ECA only, 12.11
sharing only with another operator, 12.12
right to upgrade
ancillary Code rights, 12.05
generally, 12.03
right relates to ECA only, 12.06–12.07
subsisting agreements, 12.40–12.42
terms of agreement
1954 Act cases, 11.247–11.250
generally, 11.74–11.88
renewal agreements, 11.192–11.200

V
Vacant possession
obligation to give, 11.163
removal of ECA
assumptions, 19.04
flow chart, 19.05–19.11
introduction, 19.01–19.03
right to require removal, 19.12–19.13
Virtual hearings
generally, 21.63–21.65

W
Without prejudice communications
settlement of Code disputes, 22.06–22.10
Works
method statement, 11.109–11.111